ABUSE OF PROCE

The University of L
Braboeuf Manor
Portsmouth Road, Guildford
Surrey GU3 1HA

The University of Law, Braboeuf Manor, Portsmouth Road, Guildford GU3 1HA
Telephone: 01483 216788   Email: library-guildford@law.ac.uk

This book must be returned on or before the last date stamped below.
Failure to do so will result in a fine.

Birmingham I Bristol I Chester I Guildford I Leeds I London I Manchester

Erratum

Abuse of Process
Third Edition
By Colin Wells
9780198786047

At chp.1.50: for "Mr Justice Simon France" read "Simon France J";
At chp. 1.52: for "Mr Justice Collins" read "Collins J";
At chp.1.54 and 1.55: for "Mr Chief Justice Elias" read "Elias CJ";
At chp. 1.59: for Mr Justice Corboy, read "Corboy J".

The Authors and Publishers apologise for these errors.

ABUSE
OF PROCESS

THIRD EDITION

COLIN WELLS

Barrister, 25 Bedford Row, London

Braboeuf Manor
Portsmouth Road
Guildford
Surrey GU3 1HA

OXFORD
UNIVERSITY PRESS

OXFORD
UNIVERSITY PRESS

Great Clarendon Street, Oxford, OX2 6DP,
United Kingdom

Oxford University Press is a department of the University of Oxford.
It furthers the University's objective of excellence in research, scholarship,
and education by publishing worldwide. Oxford is a registered trade mark of
Oxford University Press in the UK and in certain other countries

© Oxford University Press 2017

The moral rights of the authors have been asserted

Second Edition published in 2011
Third Edition published in 2017
Impression: 1

Crown copyright material is reproduced under Class Licence
Number C01P0000148 with the permission of OPSI
and the Queen's Printer for Scotland

Published in the United States of America by Oxford University Press
198 Madison Avenue, New York, NY 10016, United States of America

British Library Cataloguing in Publication Data
Data available

Library of Congress Control Number: 2017930525

ISBN 978–0–19–878604–7

Printed in Great Britain by Ashford Colour Press Ltd, Gosport, Hampshire

Links to third party websites are provided by Oxford in good faith and
for information only. Oxford disclaims any responsibility for the materials
contained in any third party website referenced in this work.

FOREWORD

This new third edition, deservedly now published by the Oxford University Press, is much to be welcomed. The subject of 'abuse of process' has been an ever-present facet of criminal litigation for decades and, as is said at the end of Chapter 1, there is no sign yet that the flow of complaints based on an alleged 'abuse of process' will soon abate. Judges at all levels and those who appear in front of them or advise either the prosecution or potential or actual defendants will find this excellent book of great assistance. Its first chapter cogently and in a scholarly fashion sets out the principles of law derived from all relevant sources, not least, recent appellate decisions, whilst successive chapters drill down into the different contexts in which arguments relating to alleged 'abuse of process' arise.

As a Judge of the Crown Court, who has had to adjudicate upon such arguments (and as a periodically appearing junior member of appellate constitutions who has heard them on appeal) for many years, I believe that the contributions to this book have provided us all with a work of both learning and practical application. The strands have been drawn together in a way which both distills the legal principles and provides a comprehensive reference guide to the specific situations in which those principles have to be applied.

I welcome too the help the reader receives through the clear expression of its content and, of particular assistance, the incorporation on each page of useful notes and citations for further reference.

I am sure too that law students and practitioners will find this book as invaluable as I suggest it will be to the judiciary.

HHJ David Radford
Honorary Recorder of Redbridge
Snaresbrook Crown Court
St. David's Day—2016

PREFACE

The abuse of process principle is still alive and kicking in criminal proceedings. The ever expanding case law is evidence of this, with a large number of decisions being made, since the second edition of this book in a number of areas: state misconduct (*Warren,*[1] *Downey*[2]); post-trial abuse (*Tague*[3]); illegally obtained evidence (*Public Prosecution Service of Northern Ireland v Elliott*[4]); linked civil proceedings *(Clayton*[5]*);* disclosure (*Austin,*[6] *R,*[7]*(S)D and S(T)*[8]); entrapment (*Moore,*[9] *Palmer*[10]*);* delay and serious specific prejudice to a fair trial (*R*[11], *F*[12]); delay and loss of records (*TBF,*[13] *RD*[14]); destruction and retention of evidence (*McCauley,*[15] *Clay,*[16] *Petrie,*[17] *Spalluto*[18]); caution disposal (*DPP v Alexander*[19]); human trafficking (*L,*[20] *NR, and Le*[21]); penalty notice (*Gavigan*[22]); misconceived charges (*Dwyer,*[23] *Antoine*[24]); local authority prosecutions (*Barons,*[25] *Clayton*[26]); special measures (*Cox,*[27] *OP*[28]); legal representation (*Crawley*[29]); confiscation (*Waya*[30]).

Although the application to stay proceedings as an abuse of process is still rarely successful, the grounds for such applications are ever evolving, with state misconduct and financial cost-cutting within the criminal justice system creating fertile ground for new arguments to develop. In addition, the ever-continuing growth of new statutory provisions,[31] regulations,

---

[1] [2012] 1 AC 22.
[2] First instance, Central Criminal Court; 21 February 2014, unreported.
[3] [2015] EWHC 3576 (Admin).
[4] [2013] UKSC 32; [2013] 1 WLR 1611.
[5] [2014] 2 Cr App R 20.
[6] *Herbert Austin* [2013] EWCA Crim 1028; [2013] 2 Cr App R 33; [2013] Crim LR 914.
[7] [2015] EWCA Crim 1941; Archbold Review [2015] 1 pp 1–2.
[8] [2015] 2 Cr App R 27.
[9] [2013] EWCA Crim 85; [2014] Crim L R 364.
[10] [2015] Crim LR 153.
[11] [2015] EWCA Crim 1941.
[12] [2011] EWCA Crim 1844; [2012] 1 All ER 565.
[13] [2011] EWCA Crim 726.
[14] [2013] EWCA Crim 1592.
[15] [2014] NICA 60.
[16] [2014] EWHC 321 (Admin); [2015] RTR1.
[17] [2015] EWHC 48 (Admin).
[18] [2015] EWHC 2211 (Admin).
[19] [2011] 1 WLR 653.
[20] [2013] EWCA Crim 991, [2014] 1 All ER 113, [2013] 2 Cr App R 23, [2014] Crim LR 150, discussed in Cambridge Law Journal 2014, 73(1), [11]–[14].
[21] [2012] EWCA Crim 189, [2012] 1 Cr App R 35, [2013] QB 379; case comment in Crim LR (2012), 958–64; Archbold Review (2012) 3, 3.
[22] [2013] EWHC 2805 (Admin), (2013) 177 JP 609.
[23] [2013] EWCA Crim 10.
[24] [2014] EWCA Crim 1971, [2015] 1 Cr App R 8.
[25] [2013] EWHC 898 (Admin).
[26] [2014] EWCA Crim 1030, [2014] 2 Cr App R 20.
[27] [2012] EWCA Crim 549, [2012] 2 Cr App R 6, (summarized at Criminal Law Review (2012) 8, pp 621–23).
[28] [2014] EWHC 1944 (Admin), [2015] Mental Health Law Reports 421.
[29] [2014] EWCA Crim 1028.
[30] [2012] UKSC 51; [2013] 2 Cr App R (S) 20; [2013] 1 AC 294.
[31] Legal Aid, Sentencing and Punishment of Offenders Act 2012, Crime and Courts Act 2013, Offender Rehabilitation Act 2014, Serious Crime Act 2015, Modern Slavery Act 2015, and Psychoactive Substances Act 2016.

practice directions, Criminal Procedure Rules, as well as the Leveson Review 2015,[32] and court emphasis on case management,[33] all provide new areas in which abuse of process applications may arise.

As Professor Rudi Fortson QC notes in Chapter 1: 'there is no sign yet that the flow of complaints based on an alleged abuse of process will soon abate'.

Case-law decisions and statutory changes have been included in the main text, with commentary attached, resulting in one new chapter on confiscation, Chapter 12, following the decision in *Waya*[34] and amendment to section 6 of the Proceeds of Crime Act 2002, which now requires any confiscation order to be 'proportionate'.

This edition continues the practice of citing important recent decisions from appellant courts in other common law jurisdictions, notably in the area of entrapment and category two abuse of state misconduct (*Wilson*,[35] *Babos*,[36] *Moti*,[37] *Culverwell v Ginbey*[38]).

This third edition would not have been possible without the assistance of a great many people.

I acknowledge Fiona Sinclair at Oxford University, who encouraged and lead commission of the text, and all those responsible for the physical publication of the book.

I thank the Recorder of Redbridge, HHJ David Radford QC for the Foreword.

I thank the practitioner contributors, who gave up their valuable time from busy practices, to add their considerable and valuable practical legal experience and knowledge to their given chapters: Professor Rudi Fortson QC, of 25 Bedford Row and Queens Mary College, London (Chapter 1 'Introduction' and for discussing many ideas, particular the 'balancing exercise' developing in category two cases); Mark Jones, solicitor at Morgan Rose (Chapter 2 'Pre-charge and investigation'); Emma Stuart Smith, barrister at 25 Bedford Row (Chapter 3 'Forums'); Tom Price QC of 25 Bedford Row (Chapter 4 'Disclosure'); Kris Gledhill, barrister and Associate Professor at AUT, Auckland (Chapter 10 'Ability to Participate'); Rebecca Niblock, solicitor at Kingsley Napley (Chapter 11 'Extradition'); Nathaniel Rudolf (Chapter 12 'Confiscation').

In addition valuable research work was undertaken by Natasha Lloyd-Owen, Nicholas Murphy, and Kerrie Rowan, all at 25 Bedford Row.

Proof reading was greatly assisted by Louise Wells.

The book contains many ideas which are the product of discussions with many practitioners, of whom I thank, in particular, Paul Hynes QC, Jeremy Dein QC, Peter Doyle QC, Simon Pentol, Arlette Piercy, Nicola Howard, Geoff Payne, Edward Henry, Michael Glesson, Andrew Keogh, Jon Black, Gary Rubin, James Quinn, Simon Rose, Scott Ewing, Nick Brett, Anthony Harris, and Richard Cornthwaite.

The clerking and administrative staff at 25 Bedford Row, headed by Guy Williams with Emma Makepeace, Alfie Lee, Nicola Harrison, Chris Jones, Charlie Gardner, Daiyaan

---

[32] Review of Efficiency in Criminal Proceedings 2015.
[33] *Boardman* [2015] 1 Cr App R 33.
[34] [2012] UKSC 51; [2013] 2 Cr App R (S) 20; [2013] 1 AC 294.
[35] [2015] NZSC 189.
[36] [2014] 1 SCR 309.
[37] [2011] HCA 50.
[38] [2016] WASC 3, at [47].

Rashid, David Kirton, Loretta Kenny, and Jacky Chase, have all assisted in the the production of this text.

This book is dedicated to Ann, Katie, Jess, Louise, Annie, and Isabella.

Colin Wells
25 Bedford Row
London
May 2016

CONTENTS

TABLE OF CASES

EUROPEAN COURT OF HUMAN RIGHTS

HONG KONG

IRELAND

JAMAICA

JERSEY

MAURITIUS

NEW ZEALAND

PITCAIRN ISLAND

SOUTH AFRICA

TRINIDAD AND TOBAGO

UNITED KINGDOM

UNITED STATES

TABLE OF LEGISLATION

STATUTORY INSTRUMENTS

INTERNATIONAL AND
REGIONAL INSTRUMENTS

EUROPEAN UNION

CANADA

UNITED STATES

1

INTRODUCTION

A. Principles and History of Staying Proceedings

Given that much has been written by scholars concerning the jurisdiction to stay proceedings **1.1** for abuse of process,[1,2] one might reasonably enquire whether a further contextualization of the principles can usefully add much to their careful analysis. However, the purpose of this chapter is not to compete or to challenge that analysis, but to give a senior practitioner's perspective on the current law in the light of recent landmark decisions such as *Maxwell*[3] and *Warren v A-G for Jersey*,[4] and to consider (among other issues) whether the tendency of the

---

[1] By Rudi Fortson QC, Barrister, 25 Bedford Row, London. Visiting Professor of Law, Queen Mary University, London. Any views of the author that are expressed in this chapter are not to be taken as being those of any other contributor to this work or as being the views of the editor.

[2] A Choo, *Abuse of Process and Judicial Stays of Criminal Proceedings* (2nd edn, Oxford University Press 2008; A Ashworth and M Redmayne, *The Criminal Process*' (4th edn, Oxford University Press 2010); C Wells, *Abuse of Process*' (2nd edn, Jordan Publishing 2011); D Young, M Summers QC, and D Corker, *Abuse of Process in Criminal Proceedings* (4th edn, Bloomsbury Publishing 2014); His Honour Judge Bray, 'Beckford and Beyond: Some Developments in the Doctrine of Abuse of Process', Denning Law Journal, 2007, Vol.11; P O'Connor QC, 'Abuse of Process after Warren and Maxwell' [2012] Crim LR 672; FG Davies, 'Abuse of Process—an Expanding Doctrine', Journal of Criminal Law, August 1991, 55; R Pattenden, 'The Power of the Criminal Courts to Stay a Criminal Prosecution' [1985] Crim LR 175; R Pattenden, 'Abuse of Process in Criminal Litigation' (1989) 53 J Crim L 341; F Lowery, 'Abuse of Process: The Need for Structure', Vol 20 (2014) Auckland University Law Review, 223 (which needs to be read in the light of *Wilson v the Queen* [2015] NZSC 189); C Warbrick, 'Judicial Jurisdiction and Abuse of Process', Current Developments: International Law, April 2000, vol 49, p 489–96.

[3] [2010] UKSC 48; [2011] 1 WLR 1837.

[4] [2012] 1 AC 22.

courts to describe the exercise of the power to stay proceedings as 'discretionary' is warranted. If the exercise is one of *judgement* (as this commentator suggests that it is) then it is necessary to consider the considerations and the approach by which a given case is to be judged in order to achieve an acceptable degree of consistent determinations. Rationalizing the outcomes of decided cases is not straightforward in respect of actions and misconduct that sometimes appear to be of similar magnitude and gravity.

Kinds of conduct giving rise to a stay for abuse of process

1.2 Not every case in which a stay is granted concerns acts performed in bad faith by state agencies or investigators (whether in or outside the UK). In 2003, a trial judge stayed a criminal trial (*Bossino*) on facts that he styled 'state created crime'.[5] The case attracted much publicity. The police had formed a 'company' as a 'front' that purported to launder £15 m, and then gave the money back to the suspects 'so that the police could continue gathering evidence'.[6] The judge said that it was a case of incompetence and not bad faith.[7]

1.3 In contrast to *Bossino*, the facts in *Maxwell*[8] were shocking. M was convicted on two counts of robbery and one of murder. The main witness against M was C, a criminal who had once served a sentence of imprisonment with M. At M's trial, C testified that by giving evidence for the Crown he had received no benefits of any kind. It subsequently transpired that this was untrue. As a result of securing and maintaining his cooperation with the police, C (and his family) received valuable benefits that were concealed from the Crown Prosecution Service and prosecuting counsel. C was permitted to visit a brothel, to engage in a sexual relationship with a woman police constable (whom C later assaulted), to visit public houses, to consume alcohol as well as cannabis and heroin. Criminal proceedings were not taken against C for acts of violence allegedly committed by him, including an allegation of the rape of a cell-mate. Police officers forged a custody record that would have revealed certain truths.[9] The intention of the police to reward C with £10,000 was communicated to him, but senior officers told the Court of Appeal (Criminal Division) that this had not occurred.[10] Thus, information had been deliberately concealed from the trial court and at a hearing before the Court of Appeal. The police had colluded in C's perjury at the original trial, and they had perjured themselves during the hearing before the Court of Appeal.[11] None of the police officers had been prosecuted or disciplined for their part in those events[12]—perhaps for permissible procedural reasons.[13] The facts were such that Lord Browne JSC said, in *Maxwell*, that 'to describe police misconduct on this scale merely as shocking and disgraceful is to understate the gravity of its impact upon the integrity of the prosecution process'.[14] As Lord Mance JSC put it, 'the egregious and persistent nature of the police misconduct' invited 'a forceful response'.[15] Unsurprisingly, the Court of Appeal quashed M's convictions, but it

[5] *Bossino and others*, 2003, unreported.
[6] <http://news.bbc.co.uk/1/hi/uk/3103199.stm>
[7] <http://news.bbc.co.uk/1/hi/uk/3103199.stm>
[8] [2010] UKSC 48; [2011] 1 WLR 1837.
[9] Judgment, para 114.
[10] See judgment, paras 8, 74, 80. Contrast the position in *Maxwell* with the position in *Moti v The Queen* [2011] HCA 50 where it was held that the payments to the complainant and her family ' … "were not designed to, and did not, procure evidence from the prosecution witnesses". Further, contrary to the appellant's submissions in this Court, the payments were not shown to be unlawful' [16, 69].
[11] Judgment, para 9.
[12] Judgment, para 41.
[13] Judgment, para 42.
[14] Judgment, para 83.
[15] Judgment, para 53.

ordered a retrial. The order was the subject of an unsuccessful appeal to the Supreme Court (discussed below).

Maxwell—abuse of process, or a discrete 'interests of justice' test?

In *Maxwell*,[16] the Supreme Court stressed[17] that the focus of the appeal was the power to order **1.4** a retrial under section 7(1) of the Criminal Appeal Act 1968, noting the crucial words: 'it appears to the Court that the interests of justice so require'.[18] The majority held[19] that the words of section 7(1) enacted a broad and uncomplicated test to be applied when a specialist criminal court decided whether the interests of justice required a retrial or not.[20] Lord Rodger JSC said that he would not gloss the words of that test.[21] Accordingly, notwithstanding the Court's extensive discussion of the principles to be applied in respect of a court's jurisdiction to stay proceedings for abuse of process, it was collateral to its construction and application of s 7(1) of the 1968 Act.

The discussion was relevant because the Court of Appeal accepted that had evidence of the **1.5** police misconduct been known at the time of the original trial, the proceedings might have been stayed as an abuse of the process of the Court, or the prosecution would have been terminated in the event that C's evidence was excluded under section 78 of the Police and Criminal Evidence Act 1984. However, M had made several admissions of guilt (after his conviction) to different persons in respect of both the murder and robberies. Those admissions had not been tainted by the earlier police misconduct. The Court of Appeal held that, in all the circumstances of the case, it was in the interests of justice for M to face a retrial. In dismissing M's appeal to the Supreme Court against that decision, Lord Dyson JSC (whose judgment represents the opinion of the majority) said that 'the question whether the interests of justice require a retrial is broader than the question whether it is an abuse of process to allow a prosecution to proceed (whether or not by retrial)'.[22] He did not agree with Lord Brown JSC[23] that in each case the question is the same, namely, 'what do the interests of justice require?' But can there be a greater consideration than the integrity of the rule of law and the criminal justice process? It is submitted that the answer is in the negative. Accordingly, regardless of whether the application is for a retrial, or for a stay of the original proceedings, the considerations that bear upon the 'interests of justice' are—as Lord Brown JSC stated in *Maxwell*[24]—surely the same.[25]

B. Categories of Abuse and the Rationale for Staying Proceedings

The Supreme Court stated in *Maxwell* that it was 'well-established' that the court has the **1.6** power to stay proceedings in two categories of cases namely, (i) where it will be impossible to

---

[16] [2010] UKSC 48; [2011] 1 WLR 1837. The facts in this case have been summarized above at para 1.3.
[17] Judgment, paras 17, 62, 111.
[18] Section 7(1) of the Criminal Appeal Act 1968 provides (as amended), 'Where the Court of Appeal allow an appeal against conviction and it appears to the Court that the interests of justice so require, they may order the appellant to be retried.'
[19] Lord Brown of Eaton-under-Heywood and Lord Collins of Mapesbury JJSC dissenting.
[20] It follows that the issue was not whether M's admissions constituted 'new and compelling evidence' for the purposes of part 10 of the Criminal Justice Act 2003 ('Retrial for Serious Offences').
[21] Judgment, para 44.
[22] Judgment, para 21.
[23] [2010] UKSC 48; [2011] 1 WLR 1837, at [98].
[24] Lord Brown JSC at [98].
[25] Contrast the judgment of Lord Dyson JSC at [21].

give the accused a fair trial, and (ii) where it offends the court's sense of justice and propriety to be asked to try the accused in the particular circumstances of the case.[26]

1.7 The above is a refinement[27] of the categories of cases as they were stated in *Ebrahim, R (on the application of) v Feltham Magistrates' Court*[28] (which the Administrative Court had derived from the decision of the Court of Appeal in *Beckford*[29]), namely:

(i) Cases where the court concludes that the defendant cannot receive a fair trial;

(ii) Cases where the court concludes that it would be unfair for the defendant to be tried.

1.8 *Beckford* was itself a refinement of the summary of the law as stated by the Divisional Court in *Derby Crown Court, ex p Brooks*,[30] in which Sir Roger Ormrod said that a stay for abuse of process arises if either:

(a) the prosecution have manipulated or misused the process of the court so as to deprive the defendant of a protection provided by the law or to take unfair advantage of a technicality, or;

(b) on the balance of probability the defendant has been, or will be, prejudiced in the preparation or conduct of his defence by delay on the part of the prosecution which is unjustifiable ... The ultimate objective of this discretionary power is to ensure that there should be a fair trial according to law, which involves fairness both to the defendant and the prosecution ...

1.9 The Court observed (in *Beckford*) that the effect of the decision of the House of Lords in *R v Horseferry Road Magistrates Court, ex p Bennett*[31] was that the power to ensure that there should be a fair trial according to law did not exhaust the jurisdiction, but it 'can be exercised in many different circumstances', and that '[in] some cases ... the two categories may overlap'.

1.10 It is submitted that this holds true in respect of the dual-classification stated in *Maxwell*. The two categories are likely to overlap in many cases. If, for example, an investigator lost a video recording that was crucial supporting evidence of the identity of the person alleged to be the culprit, the defence might seek to apply for a stay of criminal proceedings under 'category (i)'.[32] If the investigator had deliberately destroyed the video because he thought that it

---

[26] [2010] UKSC 48; [2011] 1 WLR 1837, at [13], per Lord Dyson JSC.

[27] A point that had been noted by the Court of Appeal in *Antoine (Jordan)* [2015] 1 Cr App R 8 (see the judgment of Mrs Justice Thirlwall, at [19]).

[28] [2001] EWHC Admin 130. '[18] The two categories of cases in which the power to stay proceedings for abuse of process may be invoked in this area of the court's jurisdiction are (i) cases where the court concludes that the defendant cannot receive a fair trial, and (ii) cases where it concludes that it would be unfair for the defendant to be tried. We derive these two categories from the judgment of Neill LJ in *Beckford* (1996) 1 Cr App R 94 at p 101 ... There may ... be other situations in which a court is entitled to protect its own process from abuse, for example where it considers that proceedings brought by a private prosecutor are vexatious (see *R v Belmarsh Magistrates' Court ex p Watts* [1999] 2 Cr App R 188), but we are not here attempting to carry out an exhaustive review of this jurisdiction. [19] We are not at present concerned with the second of these two categories ... in which a court is not prepared to allow a prosecution to proceed because it is not being pursued in good faith, or because the prosecutors have been guilty of such serious misbehaviour that they should not be allowed to benefit from it to the defendant's detriment. In some of these cases it is this court, rather than any lower court, which possesses the requisite jurisdiction (see *ex p Watts* per Buxton LJ at p 195).' Per Brooke LJ.

[29] (1996) 1 Cr App R 94 at p 101.

[30] (1985) 80 Cr App R 164, 168, 169.

[31] (1994) 98 Cr App R 114, [1994] AC 42.

[32] Whether a stay for abuse will be granted in this situation would obviously depend heavily on its facts: see, for example, *Medway* [2000] Crim LR 415; *Dobson* [2001] EWCA Crim 1606; *R (Ebrahim) v Feltham Magistrates Court* [2001] 2 Cr App R 23; and *Ali v Crown Prosecution Service* [2007] EWCA Crim 691.

would be a 'gift in the hands of the defence', the application might be under 'category (i)' and 'category (ii)'. There is, however, a marked difference between the two *Maxwell* categories in that whereas fairness is at the heart of 'category (i)', it is not an essential component of 'category (ii)'. Thus, in *Mullen*,[33] M conceded that he had been properly convicted in England of a conspiracy to cause explosions, but his conviction was quashed on appeal because the security services in Zimbabwe and in England had colluded to procure M's deportation from Zimbabwe in violation of Zimbabwean law and internationally recognized human rights.

Stages in the justice process when a stay may be granted

Most applications for a stay of criminal proceedings for abuse of process relate to pre-trial conduct (e.g. at the investigative stage) or in connection with a trial that is under way (e.g. disclosure, delay, or destruction of evidence). **1.11**

The power is also available *post-conviction* in connection with confiscation proceedings initiated under one of the statutory confiscation regimes (for example, the Proceeds of Crime Act 2002).[34] However, following the decision of the Supreme Court in *Waya*,[35] recourse to this power is less necessary than hitherto (most confiscation orders being considered in terms of whether the 'recoverable amount' is 'proportionate'). **1.12**

The question of whether the power to stay for abuse can be invoked *post-trial* was raised (but not decided) in *Tague v the Governor of HMP Full Sutton and the National Crime Agency*.[36] The Divisional Court was prepared to assume—in the light of a concession made by the NCA, and without the benefit of adversarial argument—that the second *Maxwell* category was wide enough to cover misconduct post-trial.[37] The facts of that case usefully illustrate a number of linked issues when a court is considering whether or not to grant a stay, including whether the *Maxwell* categories are closed, the relevance of errors or misconduct committed overseas, and the 'balancing exercise'. **1.13**

In *Tague*, T absconded during his trial in 2000 for drugs and firearms offences. The trial judge issued a bench warrant for his arrest. While T remained absent,[38] he was convicted and sentenced to a total of twenty-three years' imprisonment. In 2006, a European Arrest Warrant (EAW) was issued. T was arrested in Spain in 2013, and his case transferred to the Spanish High Court (the Audiencia Nacional), which ruled that there was no basis for refusing extradition. The Court ordered T's extradition under the EAW but it extended to T 'a guarantee that once he has surrendered, a new trial must be held should it be requested [by T]'. Between that date and February 2014, the Court had the power (and it may have been required by Spanish law) to give such a guarantee, but it acted in breach of EU law. The Court of Justice of the European Union had held in *Melloni v Ministerio Fiscal*[39] that the EAW Framework Decision precluded judicial authorities in the 'executing state' from making the execution of an EAW conditional upon the conviction being open to review in the issuing Member **1.14**

---

[33] [2000] QB 520.
[34] Consider, for example, *Shabir* [2008] EWCA Crim 1809, [2009] 1 Cr App R (S) 84.
[35] [2012] UKSC 51.
[36] [2015] EWHC 3576 (Admin).
[37] [2015] EWHC 3576 (Admin), at [34], and [42], i.e. that the challenge was 'not in response to some other proceedings that the state wishes to initiate', per Sir Brian Leveson P Counsel for T relied on *Secretary of State for the Home Department v CC and CF* [2012] EWHC 2837 (Admin) in respect of 'control orders'.
[38] The Divisional Court did not accept that T had (on the facts of this case) been tried in his absence: 'The first fact is that although verdicts of guilty were returned against the applicant in his entirely self-induced absence, the trial was most certainly not conducted in his absence and his lawyers played a full part in it from first to last. He gave evidence and called witnesses; his lawyers remained in the case after he absconded and made submissions to the jury.' Per Sir Brian Leveson P, at [60].
[39] CJEU Case C-399/11.

State, 'even when it is to avoid an adverse effect on the right to a fair trial and the rights of defence guaranteed in the Constitution of the executing Member State'.[40] The UK was not in a position to grant a re-trial had T requested one; and, having exhausted his appeal rights, T did not, as a matter of English law, have the right to apply for a re-trial when he was surrendered. Having voluntarily absconded from his trial, the trial judge was entitled to proceed in his absence (*Jones*[41]); and a foreign 'guarantee' did not give rise to any enforceable right to a re-trial in the UK: see *Davidson*,[42] and *R (on the application of the Director of Revenue and Customs Prosecutions) v Birmingham Magistrates' Court*.[43] T was returned to the UK and detained at HMP Full Sutton to serve his sentence. Proceedings against T for the offence of breaching bail (Bail Act 2006) had to be discontinued because the offence had not been the subject of the EAW, and its prosecution was precluded by s 146 of the Extradition Act 2003. Given the guarantee made by the Spanish High Court, T applied for a writ of habeas corpus on the basis (among other grounds) that his continued detention was an abuse of process. The bench warrant, issued by the trial judge in 2000, remained valid,[44] but T contended that the warrant should not be enforced in the UK, and thus T was entitled to be released from the requirement to serve his sentence.

1.15 T submitted that bad faith on the part of the Serious Organised Crime Agency[45] could be inferred because it had developed a deliberate policy not to read the full orders which have led to extradition and, in so doing, deliberately and wilfully shut its eyes to what had happened in relation to conditions placed on EAW extraditions by executing Member States.[46] The Divisional Court rejected those submissions, and the application was refused.

1.16 It is tentatively submitted that the concession made by the respondent NCA that a stay for abuse can arise post-trial, was correct. Although the categories stated in *Maxwell* relate to a *trial* of an accused, it has been said that the categories are 'never closed' (*Martin*[47]). It is doubtful that the Supreme Court in *Maxwell* considered that it was being prescriptive as to the number of categories that might exist. *Tague's* case, before the Divisional Court, was part of the history of the trial process (including sentencing) notwithstanding that continuity had been disturbed when T's absconded and remained at large for many years.

The jurisdiction to stay for abuse and the ECtHR

1.17 The European Court of Human Rights (ECtHR) has not yet suggested that the rules articulated in *Ex p Bennett*,[48] *Maxwell* or in *Warren*, are structurally unsound or deficient for the purpose of affording an accused a remedy where the action of the state is oppressive or otherwise improper. There have been several cases heard before the ECtHR (for example, *S.C. v the United Kingdom*[49]) where it had the opportunity to comment, adversely or otherwise, on the abuse of process jurisdiction. In *S.C. v the United Kingdom*, counsel for SC argued at a pre-trial hearing (relying on Articles 3 and 6 of the Convention) that the trial should be stayed as an abuse of process due to the applicant's low attention span and his cognitive abilities, which were limited to a person with an age ranging between 6 and 8 years. The trial

---

[40] *Tague v the Governor of HMP Full Sutton and the NCA* [2015] EWHC 3576 (Admin) at [11].
[41] [2003] 1 AC 1.
[42] (1977) 64 Cr App R 209, 212.
[43] [2010] EWHC 12 (Admin), [33]–[36]. See the *Tague case* [2015] EWHC 3576 (Admin), at [15].
[44] There was no suggestion that the warrant ought not to have been issued.
[45] The forerunner to the NCA.
[46] [2015] EWHC 3576 (Admin), at [50].
[47] *Martin (Alan)* [1998] 2 WLR 1 at 6.
[48] *R v Horseferry Road Magistrates' Court, Ex p Bennett* [1994] 1 AC 42.
[49] (2005) 40 EHRR 10.

judge rejected the application. He ruled that placing SC on trial in the Crown Court did not amount to inhuman or degrading treatment or would be unfair.

The Court of Appeal dismissed SC's appeal and it refused leave to argue the abuse of process/ **1.18** unfair trial ground, holding that it was clear that the first-instance judge, in exercising his discretion to allow the trial to proceed, had taken account of the applicant's age, level of maturity, and intellectual and emotional capacities. Steps had been taken to promote the applicant's ability to understand and to participate in the proceedings. During the domestic proceedings, SC did not contend that he was unfit to plead (which involves a high test).

The ECtHR held that there was a violation of Article 6.1 of the ECHR. SC had been una- **1.19** ble to fully understand and to participate in the trial to the extent required by Article 6.1 of the Convention. However, the ECtHR did not criticize the rules pertaining to the jurisdiction to stay proceedings for 'abuse of process', nor was it said that the trial judge had erred in his approach in relation to the criteria to be considered (or the weight to be given to them) on an application to stay the proceedings. The decision of the ECtHR was not that the Crown Court proceedings should have been stayed in respect of SC, but that—given SC's disabilities—the Crown Court was not the appropriate forum in which to try him.[50]

By way of contrast, in *Paulet v UK*,[51] the ECtHR held that the abuse of process jurisdiction **1.20** did not afford P protection under Article 1 of the First Protocol to the European Convention on Human Rights (A1P1). A confiscation order (following conviction[52]) was made against P under Part 2 of the Proceeds of Crime Act 2002,[53] P sought to argue before the Court of Appeal that 'oppression' should be interpreted in line with the proportionality test required by A1P1. This submission was not adopted by that court (the case pre-dated the decision of the Supreme Court in *Waya*[54]). The ECtHR noted that the Court of Appeal *did* ask whether the making of a confiscation order in P's case was in the public interest, but having decided that it was, it did not go further by exercising their power of review so as to determine 'whether the requisite balance was maintained in a manner consonant with the applicant's right to "the peaceful enjoyment of his possessions", within the meaning of the first sentence of Article 1.'[55] The Court of Appeal had declined to invoke the abuse of process jurisdiction in P's case because (among other reasons) the jurisdiction to stay for abuse had to be exercised 'sparingly'.[56]

---

[50] Judgment, at [35].

[51] [2014] Lloyd's Rep FC 484; [2014] Crim LR 750. A1P1 provides: 'Every natural or legal person is entitled to the peaceful enjoyment of his possessions. No one shall be deprived of his possessions except in the public interest and subject to the conditions provided for by law and by the general principles of international law … The preceding provisions shall not, however, in any way impair the right of a State to enforce such laws as it deems necessary to control the use of property in accordance with the general interest or to secure the payment of taxes or other contributions or penalties.'

[52] Paulet pleaded guilty in the Crown Court to three counts of dishonestly obtaining a pecuniary advantage by deception (obtaining employment by deception). He also pleaded guilty to one count of having a false identity document with intent, one count of driving whilst disqualified, and one count of driving a motor vehicle without insurance.

[53] That is to say, a money-value order (a 'confiscation order') that represents an offender's proceeds of crime ('benefit') obtained as a result of, or in connection with, his or her 'criminal conduct'.

[54] [2012] UKSC 51.

[55] *Paulet v UK* [2014] Lloyd's Rep FC 484; [2014] Crim LR 750, at [67].

[56] The power to stay is often said to be 'residual' and 'discretionary', which ought only to be employed in 'exceptional circumstances' (see *Ebrahim, R v Feltham Magistrates' Court and Anor* [2001] EWHC Admin 130, citing *A-G Ref (No 1 of 1990)* [1992] QB 630, 643G), and 'exercised carefully and sparingly and only for compelling reasons' (see *R v Horseferry Road Magistrates' Court, ex p Bennett* [1994] 1 AC 42, HL, per Lord Lowry at p 74F).

1.21 There is a 'footnote' that should be added to the decision in *Paulet*. It is correct to say that prior to the decision of the Supreme Court in *Waya*,[57] applications to stay confiscation proceedings regularly failed,[58] and, in three cases, a prosecutor's appeal was allowed against the decision of the trial judge to stay the proceedings.[59] A notable exception was *Shabir*.[60] However, following the decision in *Waya*, the issue is now one of proportionality in terms of the 'amount to be recovered' under a confiscation order,[61] albeit that the jurisdiction to stay confiscation proceedings remains available if the need arises: see *Mahmood*.[62]

C. Rationales for Staying Proceedings for Abuse of Process

1.22 Professor Andrew L-T Choo has identified three rationales for granting a stay for abuse of process, namely, remedial, deterrence, and moral integrity.[63]

1.23 Although English courts have occasionally spoken of a stay as a 'remedy',[64] the usual justification for a stay (at least in *Bennett* type cases) is to protect judicial processes and the 'rule of law'. Thus, the courts have spoken of maintaining the 'integrity of the judicial process',[65] 'fairness', 'vindication of the rule of law',[66] guarding against 'the degradation of the lawful administration of justice',[67] protecting the 'rule of law',[68] and 'upholding the rule of law'.[69] Other judicial 'tests' for a stay of proceedings in respect of the second category of cases (*Bennett* type), include:

- that a trial would offend the court's sense of justice and propriety;[70]
- that to allow the trial to proceed would undermine public confidence in the criminal justice system and bring it into disrepute;[71]
- that to refuse a stay would lead to the degradation of the lawful administration of justice.[72]

---

[57] [2012] UKSC 51. The Supreme Court held that the 'better analysis' is to refuse to make confiscation orders where to do so would be wholly disproportionate and a breach of A1P1: '[t]here is no need to invoke the concept of abuse of process' (at [18]).

[58] *Nield* [2007] EWCA Crim 993; *Farquhar* [2008] EWCA Crim 806, [2008] 2 Cr App R (S) 104; *Bhanji* [2011] EWCA Crim 1198; and *Ali* [2014] EWCA Crim 1658.

[59] *Hockey* [2007] EWCA Crim 1577; *Nelson, and Pathak* [2009] EWCA Crim 1573.

[60] [2008] EWCA Crim 1809.

[61] Pursuant to s 6(5) and s 7 of the Proceeds of Crime Act 2002. Note that since *R v Waya* was decided by the Supreme Court, Parliament gave statutory effect to its decision by amending s 6, POCA such that the duty to make a confiscation order requiring the defendant to pay the 'recoverable amount' applies 'only if, or to the extent that, it would not be disproportionate to require the defendant to pay the recoverable amount': amendment made by the Serious Crime Act 2015, s 85(1), Sch 4, para 19; in force from 1 June 2015 (see SI 2015/820).

[62] [2006] 1 Cr App R (S) 96.

[63] Andrew Choo, 'Abuse of Process and Judicial Stays of Criminal Proceedings' (2nd edn, Oxford University Press (2008)).

[64] *Nelson, R v Pathak and R v Paulet* [2009] EWCA Crim 1573.

[65] *Regan*, [2002] 1 SCR 297, 2002 SCC 12 (CanLII) at [49].

[66] *Maxwell* per Lord Brown of Eaton-under-Heywood JSC, at [61]. He had spoken in those terms in *Panday v Virgil* [2008] 1 AC 1386, at [28] (cited by Lord Brown in *Maxwell*, at [100]); and note Sharp J who spoke of the 'vindication of the court's integrity': *Att-Gen of Canada on behalf of the United States of America v Khadr* (2011) 157 ILR 700.

[67] Per Rose LJ, *Mullen* [2000] QB 520, 534.

[68] See, for example, *Ahmed (Rangzieb)* [2011] EWCA Crim 184, at [24].

[69] *Reg. v. Guildford Magistrates' Court, Ex parte Healy* [1983] 1 W.L.R. 108, cited by Lord Griffiths in *Reg. v. Horseferry Rd. Ct., Ex p Bennett* [1994] 1 AC 42 at p 64D.

[70] *R v Horseferry Road Magistrates Court, Ex p Bennett* [1994] 1 AC 42, 74G, per Lord Lowry.

[71] *Latif* [1996] 1 WLR 104, Lord Steyn, at p 112F.

[72] See *Mullen* [2000] QB 520, at p 534 per Rose LJ, and *Warren v AG for Jersey* [2012] 1 AC 22, at [83] per Lord Kerr.

In *Warren*, Lord Kerr agreed with Lord Dyson's statement in *Maxwell* that '[i]n the second **1.24** category of case, the court is *concerned to protect the integrity of the criminal justice system*' [emphasis added].[73] Lord Kerr added that 'there is much to be said for discarding the notion of fairness when considering the second category of cases'.[74]

As for the rationale of deterrence, English judicial decisions disavow the notion that **1.25** the jurisdiction to order a stay is, or should be, disciplinary in character to punish or to mark the court's disapproval of police misconduct.[75] Lowery suggests that without judicial direction, the police are unable to draw the line correctly between proper and improper investigatory conduct, and Crown Prosecutors similarly need to identify the boundary between 'proper and improper trial strategy'.[76] That said, regardless of whether a stay is granted or not, a degree of deterrence (and direction) may be achieved by way of robust observations expressed in judgments handed down by the courts: see, for example, *Regina v Horseferry Road Magistrates Court, ex parte Bennett*,[77] *Loosely*,[78] and *Warren v A-G for Jersey*.[79]

Notwithstanding the decisions in *Maxwell* and *Warren*, it is submitted that there is force **1.26** in the criticism made by Patrick O'Connor QC that the precise rationale for granting a stay remains unclear.[80] He suggests that Lord Kerr has provided 'perhaps the clearest and most apt [formulation] for the 'integrity principle'', namely, that '[t]he focus should always be on whether the stay is required in order to safeguard the integrity of the criminal justice system'.[81] However, it is submitted that even that formulation (similarly Lord Dyson's in *Maxwell*) has two significant shortcomings. First, there may be cases where the 'integrity of the criminal justice process' cuts across both categories of abuse, and this is so notwithstanding the observations of the Board in *Warren v the Att-Gen for Jersey*[82] that the two categories 'are distinct and should be considered separately'.[83] There may be cases of incompetence or misconduct—whether falling within the first or second category (or both)—that threaten, undermine, or harm, the integrity of the justice system. Secondly, Lord Kerr's formulation does not attempt to indicate the *degree* of threat or harm done to the 'integrity of justice' that justifies a stay of proceedings for abuse.

Nebulous tests: 'public confidence', 'sense of justice', 'rule of law'

Many expressions that have been used to describe the test for staying proceedings are **1.27** vague and imprecise. Apart from what may gleaned from judicial *dicta*, how is a 'court's sense of justice' to be recognized and gauged by practitioners or even by the judges? A 'sense of justice' cannot be defined: it is a matter of perception, anticipation, or hope.

---

[73] *Warren v AG for Jersey* [2012] 1 AC 22, at [83]; and *Maxwell* [2011] 1 WLR 1837, per Lord Dyson JSC at [13].

[74] [2012] 1 AC 22, at [84].

[75] *Warren v Attorney General for Jersey* [2012] 1 AC 22, at [22]–[26], [28]–[30], [36]–[37], [59], [60], [69], [72], [80], [83]–[86].

[76] Finn Lowery, 'Abuse of Process: The Need for Structure', Vol 20 (2014) Auckland University Law Review, 223, which needs to be read in the light of *Wilson v the Queen* [2015] NZSC 189.

[77] [1994] 1 AC 42.

[78] [2001] UKHL 53; [2001] 1 WLR 2060; [2001] 4 All ER 897, HL(E).

[79] [2012] 1 AC 22.

[80] P O'Connor, 'Abuse of Process after Warren and Maxwell', [2012] Crim LR 672.

[81] P O'Connor, 'Abuse of Process after Warren and Maxwell', [2012] Crim LR 672; see *Warren v AG for Jersey* [2012] 1 AC 22, p 47A [83].

[82] [2012] 1 AC 22.

[83] Judgment, para 35.

Legal practitioners often speak about 'public confidence in the rule of law',[84] but there is little agreement as to what the 'rule of law' actually is, or how best to define it.[85]

1.28 Mr. Justice Heydon, in his dissenting judgment in *Moti v The Queen* (High Court of Australia)[86] strongly criticized the use of the expression 'public confidence':[87]

> The expression is tending to become an automatic reflex, to be used in almost any context in which an attempt is made to stimulate a vague feeling of goodwill, just as restaurant owners cannot answer any question about their restaurants without referring to 'fresh ingredients'. The expression is beginning to lack meaning. It usually postpones or evades problems. It does not face them or solve them. At least that is so in this particular field. What does 'public confidence' mean? What does 'disrepute' mean? Among which members of the public is disrepute, or a rise or fall in confidence, to be searched for or avoided? Might it not be better for courts not to keep looking over their shoulders by worrying about their reputation or any perceived level of confidence in them? Should they not rather simply concentrate on doing their job diligently, carefully, honestly, and independently, whatever the public or the community think?

1.29 Mr. Justice Heydon, was also critical of the 'difficulties in perceiving the relevant test' to be applied in order to determine whether or not a stay of proceedings ought to be granted:[88]

> Thus there are references to the 'principles of the rule of law' without explanation as to how a stay order which ensures that there will be a failure to enforce the law against the accused vindicates the rule of law.[89] There are references to 'international law', 'the limits of territorial jurisdiction' and the need for 'the sovereignty of states to be respected', even though the substantive laws of international law are increasingly difficult to discern,[90] and even though the assumed rule[91] appears to apply as much to conduct in which the foreign jurisdiction acquiesces (as here) as it does to conduct against its wishes (as when Israeli agents seized Eichmann in violation of Argentinean sovereignty). There are references to 'the comity of nations'.[92] How these were reconcilable with the international rule of comity that the courts of one country will not sit in judgment on the acts of the government of another done within its own territory was not explained. There are references to 'acts which offend the court's conscience',[93] to an act which is 'an affront to the public conscience',[94] to what 'offends the court's sense of justice and propriety',[95] and to acts which 'by providing

---

[84] *R (McCann and others) v Crown Court at Manchester* [2002] UKHL 39; [2003] 1 AC 787.

[85] See, for example, Waldron, Jeremy, 'The Rule of Law and the Importance of Procedure' (2010), New York University Public Law and Legal Theory Working Papers. Paper 234; and T Bingham, 'The Rule of Law', Penguin Books.

[86] [2011] HCA 50. This was a seven judge Court. The jurisdiction of that Court is essentially federal for the whole of Australia. The judgment deserves to be read in full, not least in respect of so-called 'disguised extradition'.

[87] [2011] HCA 50, Heydon J, at [102].

[88] [2011] HCA 50, Heydon J, at [87]. The footnotes in the extract are those that appear in the judgment.

[89] For example, *Hartley* [1978] 2 NZLR 199 at 217 per Richmond P, Woodhouse, and Cooke JJ; *Bennett's* case [1994] 1 AC 42 at 55, 59, 62 and 64 per Lord Griffiths, 67 per Lord Bridge of Harwich, and 76–77 per Lord Lowry.

[90] For example, *Bennett* [1994] 1 AC 42 at 60 per Lord Griffiths, 64–65 per Lord Bridge of Harwich and 76 per Lord Lowry.

[91] Heydon J was speaking in the context of that case, in which M was brought to Australia from the Solomon Island without his consent. Officials of those Islands deported M by putting him on an aircraft bound for Brisbane without power to do so. The 'assumed rule' was coined by Heydon J [70] as being 'where an accused person is removed from one country and brought into another country in which a criminal prosecution is to take place, even though the removal does not create any risk of an unfair trial, and even though the court retains jurisdiction to try the accused person, the court has a discretionary power, or perhaps a duty, to order a permanent stay of the prosecution in certain circumstances.'

[92] For example, *Bennett's* case [1994] 1 AC 42 at 76 per Lord Lowry.

[93] For example, *Bennett's* case [1994] 1 AC 42 at 76 per Lord Lowry.

[94] *Latif* [1996] 1 WLR 104 at 112; [1996] 1 All ER 353 at 361.

[95] For example, *Bennett's* case [1994] 1 AC 42 at 74 per Lord Lowry.

a morally unacceptable foundation for the exercise of jurisdiction over the suspect taint the proposed trial'.[96] There are references to 'basic human rights'.[97] There are references to 'unworthy conduct'.[98] It has been said that the 'issues ... are basic to the whole concept of freedom in society'.[99] There are references to 'the dignity and integrity of the judicial system' and to the need for the prosecution to 'come to court with clean hands'.[100] There are references to 'the public interest in the integrity of the criminal justice system'.[101]

For Mr. Justice Heydon, those 'exercises in rhetoric do not assist in defining the relevant **1.30** test. Indeed they cast doubt on whether there is any relevant test'. As for the last remark, he is probably right. A workable test, that is defined with precision, and stripped of vague value-judgments, is probably an unrealistic goal. However, one ought not to be unduly critical of the use of expressions such as 'public confidence' or even 'the rule of law'. Although, commentators will rightly debate the meaning and value of such expressions, they do reflect sentiments that are understood by most people. Mr. Justice Caulfield was not being entirely flippant when, in a case that required the Divisional Court to decide whether or not the facts constituted an unlawful 'lottery', he said:[102]

> I would not like to define a donkey; I would not like to define a lottery. But the fact that I do not define does not prevent me from recognising a donkey or a lottery when I see it.

D. Historical Sketch of the Jurisdiction to Stay for Abuse of Process

The starting point in the development of the power to stay for abuse of process is sometimes **1.31** said to be *Connelly v Director of Public Prosecutions* (1964),[103] but the history is a great deal longer.[104] In the civil case of *Metropolitan Bank v Pooley*[105] (cited by Lord Scarman and Lord Pearce in *Connelly*),[106] Lord Blackburn said:

> But from early times ... the Court had inherently in its power the right to see that its process was not abused by a proceeding without reasonable grounds, so as to be vexatious and harassing—the Court had the right to protect itself against such an abuse; but that was not done upon demurrer, or upon the record, or upon the verdict of a jury or evidence taken in that way, but it was done by the Court informing its conscience upon affidavits, and by a summary order to stay the action which was brought under such circumstances as to be an abuse of the process of the Court; and in a proper case they did stay the action

Similarly, Lord Selbourne LC recognized that the power to stay 'seemed to be inherent in the **1.32** jurisdiction of every Court of Justice to protect itself from the abuse of its own procedure'.[107]

---

[96] For example, *Bennett's* case [1994] 1 AC 42 at 76 per Lord Lowry.

[97] For example, *Bennett's* case [1994] 1 AC 42 at 62 per Lord Griffiths.

[98] For example, *Bennett's* case [1994] 1 AC 42 at 77 per Lord Lowry.

[99] *Hartley* [1978] 2 NZLR 199 at 217 per Richmond P, Woodhouse and Cooke JJ quoted in *Bennett's* case [1994] 1 AC 42 at 54 per Lord Griffiths and 66 per Lord Bridge of Harwich.

[100] *Bennett's* case [1994] 1 AC 42 at 60 per Lord Griffiths and 65 per Lord Bridge of Harwich, quoting the headnote to *S v Ebrahim* 1991 (2) SA 553 at 555.

[101] *Latif* [1996] 1 WLR 104 at 113; [1996] 1 All ER 353 at 361.

[102] *Reader's Digest Association Ltd. v Williams* [1976] 1 WLR. 1109.

[103] [1964] AC 1254; [1964] 2 WLR 1145; [1964] 2 All ER 401, HL; and see His Honour Judge Bray, 'Beckford and Beyond: Some Developments in the Doctrine of Abuse of Process'; Denning Law Journal, 2007, Vol.11.

[104] See, for example, F G Davies, 'Abuse of Process—an Expanding Doctrine', Journal of Criminal Law, August 1991 55: 374–87.

[105] 10 App. Cas. 210 at 220.

[106] [1964] AC 1254 at 1361.

[107] *Metropolitan Bank v Pooley* 10 App. Cas. 210 at 220.

As Lord Pearce pointed out in *Connelly*, the observations made in *Pooley* were clearly not limited to the civil jurisdiction.

Growth in applications to stay

1.33   For many years, the power to stay criminal proceedings lay largely dormant. The observations of His Honour Judge Bray[108] coincide with the experience of this commentator that, in the 1970s, applications to stay proceedings for abuse of process were virtually unknown in the criminal courts. The criminal courts had developed a variety of procedural safeguards and protections against abusive conduct, which were then widely assumed to be adequate in number and in their effectiveness to ensure a fair trial for the accused (for example, the Judges' Rules,[109] *autrefois acquit* and *autrefois convict,* and the discretion to exclude prosecution evidence obtained unfairly or illegally).

1.34   The marked increase in the number of applications to stay proceedings for abuse has been due to reasons that include the growth in the number (and size) of state agencies and investigative bodies, expanding bureaucracy, the legislative entrenchment of a rights-based approach in the investigation and prosecution of offences, and blossoming human rights case law. There has also been a cultural shift towards being less tolerant of misconduct that was motivated by the belief that the 'ends justified the means'. That said, there remains no absolute rule in English law that evidence obtained illegally is automatically inadmissible (see, for example, *Kuruma v Queen*,[110] *Sang*,[111] *Khan*,[112] *Khan v United Kingdom*,[113] and more recently, *Public Prosecution Service of Northern Ireland v Elliott*[114]). Not every procedural irregularity or misfeasance in public office will afford the accused an advantage (e.g. that evidence is excluded) or a stay of proceedings.

'Permanent stay'

1.35   The expression 'permanent stay' is frequently uttered by judges both at first instance and in the appellate courts.[115] In *Canada (Minister of Citizenship and Immigration) v Tobiass*, a stay of criminal proceedings was described as 'that ultimate remedy'[116]—'ultimate' (said the Canadian Supreme Court in *Regan*) 'in the sense that it is final':[117]

> Charges that are stayed may never be prosecuted; an alleged victim will never get his or her day in court; society will never have the matter resolved by a trier of fact. For these reasons, a stay is reserved for only those cases of abuse where a very high threshold is met.[118]

1.36   The impression that a stay is 'permanent' or 'final' is perhaps bolstered by the existence of Part 9 of the Criminal Justice Act 2003 under which the prosecution has power to appeal a

---

[108] His Honour Judge Bray, 'Beckford and Beyond: Some Developments in the Doctrine of Abuse of Process'; Denning Law Journal, 2007, Vol.11.

[109] Judges Rules pre-dated the provisions of the Police and Criminal Evidence Act 1984 in respect of alleged confessions.

[110] [1955] AC 197.

[111] [1980] AC 402.

[112] [1996] 3 WLR 162.

[113] 2001 31 EHRR 45.

[114] [2013] UKSC 32; [2013] 1 WLR 1611.

[115] See, for example, *R and others* [2015] EWCA Crim 1941; *S* [2006] EWCA Crim 756; *Hussain* [2013] EWCA Crim 707 at [15]; *Basdeo Panday v Senior Superintendent Wellington Virgil* [2008] UKPC 24, at [24]; *'R' v Her Majesty's Advocate and Anor* [2002] UKPC D3.

[116] [1997] 3 SCR 391, 1997 CanLII 322 (SCC).

[117] *Regan* [2002] 1 SCR 297, 2002 SCC 12 (CanLII), at [53].

[118] *Regan* [2002] 1 SCR 297, 2002 SCC 12 (CanLII), at [53].

'terminating' or a '*de facto* terminating' ruling[119] made by a trial judge in relation to one or more offences included in the indictment (see section 58 CJA 2003).[120] In *OB*,[121] no jurisdictional point was taken in that case that section 58 did not apply in respect of the appeal against the decision of the trial judge to stay criminal proceedings,[122] and no point appears to have been taken that the trial judge's ruling to stay the proceedings was anything other than 'final' or 'permanent'.

If a stay of proceedings is truly 'final' or 'permanent', then (short of the stay being quashed **1.37** on appeal) one might have thought that a court is debarred from 'lifting' a stay, and yet, in *Gadd*,[123] the Court of Appeal did 'lift' a stay in respect of two counts that had formed part of a draft indictment[124] containing eight further counts alleging historic sex abuse in respect of three young girls. Objection was taken to the inclusion of the two counts on the ground that they had been stayed, many years earlier, for abuse of process[125] by a Stipendiary Magistrate at an 'old style committal hearing'. However, neither in *Gadd*, nor in *Wright* (where two applications to lift a stay were refused at first instance)[126] was there any discussion concerning whether or in what circumstances it is open to a court to lift a stay. In civil proceedings, there can be circumstances in which a stay may be lifted, but the jurisdiction to do so is managed partly by an application of the Civil Procedure Rules and Practice Direction, and partly by guidance given by the courts: see, for example, *Woodhouse v Consignia plc; Steliou v Compton*.[127] It is submitted that for the purpose of criminal proceedings, any rules pertaining to the lifting of a stay ought to be made pursuant to section 69 of the Courts Act 2003 (as amended). In the event that this comes to pass, references to a 'permanent stay' would be best avoided as being misleading.

E. Abuse of Process: Canadian, New Zealand, Australian Common-Law Jurisdictions

Canadian approach

In *Maxwell*,[128] the UK Supreme Court declined to accede to a suggestion made by the Crown **1.38** that the Court should adopt the approach taken by the majority of the Canadian Supreme

---

[119] 'Ruling' is defined by s.74(1) of the Criminal Justice Act 2003 to include '… a decision, determination, direction, finding, notice, order, refusal, rejection or requirement'. The Act does not in fact use the expressions 'terminating ruling' or 'de facto terminating ruling'—but those expressions are convenient.

[120] The power is described by the Government's Explanatory Notes [para.276] as applying to rulings that are 'formally terminating and those that are de facto terminating in the sense that they are so fatal to the prosecution case that, in the absence of a right of appeal, the prosecution would offer no, or no further evidence.'

[121] [2008] EWCA Crim 238, Court of Appeal, at [3].

[122] The appeal failed on its merits.

[123] [2014] EWHC 3307 (QB). The author takes this opportunity to thank Professor David Ormerod QC for drawing this decision to his attention.

[124] The prosecution had applied for leave to prefer a voluntary bill of indictment pursuant to section 2(2)(b) of the Administration of Justice (Miscellaneous Provisions) Act 1933.

[125] On the grounds of delay.

[126] [2014] EWCA Crim 1790.

[127] [2002] 2 All ER 737. Rule 3.9(1) of the Civil Procedure Rules (as at 2016) requires the court, on an application for relief from any sanction imposed for a failure to comply with any rule, practice direction or court order, to 'consider all the circumstances of the case, so as to enable it to deal justly with the application, including the need, (a) for litigation to be conducted efficiently and at proportionate cost; and (b) to enforce compliance with rules, practice directions and orders.' The previous version of this rule was rather more specific as to the factors to be considered. For a discussion of r 3.9, see *Mitchell MP v News Group Newspapers Ltd* [2013] EWCA Civ 1537.

[128] [2010] UKSC 48; [2011] 1 WLR 1837.

Court in *Regan*.[129] The *Regan* approach is more restrictive than that stated in *Maxwell* and in *Warren*. Under *Regan*, a stay will be granted only in the 'clearest of cases'—a principle that is easier to state than to apply given that in *Regan*[130] the Supreme Court of Canada was divided five judges to four when upholding (on the merits of that case) the decision of the Court of Appeal [Nova Scotia] to set aside a stay that had been granted by the trial judge.

1.39 As stated in *Regan*, there are two categories of abuse, namely, (i) when the abuse causes unfairness that renders the trial unfair, and (ii) a residual category in which trial unfairness is not affected by misconduct, but (having regard to sections 7 and 24 of the Canadian Charter of Rights and Freedoms[131]) the conduct undermines the fundamental justice of the system:

> Yet even in these cases, the important prospective nature of the stay as a remedy must still be satisfied: '[t]he mere fact that the state has treated an individual shabbily in the past is not enough to warrant a stay of proceedings' (*Tobiass*,[132] at para 91). When dealing with an abuse which falls into the residual category, generally speaking, a stay of proceedings is only appropriate when the abuse is likely to continue or be carried forward. Only in 'exceptional', 'relatively very rare' cases will the past misconduct be 'so egregious that the mere fact of going forward in the light of it will be offensive' (*Tobiass*, at para 91).

1.40 In respect of either category of abuse, two conditions must be met:

(i) that the prejudice caused by the abuse in question will be 'manifested, perpetuated, or aggravated through the conduct of the trial, or by its outcome', and

(ii) that no other remedy is reasonably capable of removing that prejudice.

1.41 Where, however, uncertainty persists about whether the abuse is sufficient to warrant the 'drastic remedy of a stay', a third criterion is considered:

> This is the stage where a traditional balancing of interests is done: 'it will be appropriate to balance the interests that would be served by the granting of a stay of proceedings against the interest that society has in having a final decision on the merits'. In these cases, 'an egregious act of misconduct could [never] be overtaken by some passing public concern [although] … a compelling societal interest in having a full hearing could tip the scales in favour of proceeding' (*Tobiass*, at para. 92).

1.42 Balancing interests is the exception, not the rule: see the *Khadr* case.[133]

New Zealand approach

Wilson v The Queen

1.43 The law in New Zealand broadly follows the principles stated in *Maxwell*[134] and *Warren*.[135]

1.44 In *Wilson v the Queen*,[136] the New Zealand Supreme Court explained that in relation to criminal proceedings, a stay may be granted where there is state misconduct that will:

(a) prejudice the fairness of a defendant's trial ('the first category'); or

---

[129] [2002] 1 SCR 297, 2002 SCC 12 (CanLII).

[130] [2002] 1 SCR 297, 2002 SCC 12 (CanLII).

[131] *Canadian Charter of Rights and Freedoms*: section 7, 'Everyone has the right to life, liberty and security of the person and the right not to be deprived thereof except in accordance with the principles of fundamental justice'; section 24(1) 'Anyone whose rights or freedoms, as guaranteed by this Charter, have been infringed or denied may apply to a court of competent jurisdiction to obtain such remedy as the court considers appropriate and just in the circumstances'.

[132] *Canada (Minister of Citizenship and Immigration) v. Tobiass* [1997] 3 SCR 391, 1997 CanLII 322 (SCC)

[133] *Att-Gen of Canada on behalf of the United States of America v Khadr* (2011) 157 ILR 700, at [69].

[134] [2010] UKSC 48; [2011] 1 WLR 1837.

[135] [2012] 1 AC 22.

[136] [2015] NZSC 189.

(b) undermine public confidence in the integrity of the judicial process if a trial is permitted to proceed ('the second category').

The analysis was said by the Court not to be 'backward-looking, in the sense of focussing on the misconduct, but rather forward-looking, in that it relates to the impact of the misconduct on either the fairness of the proposed criminal trial or the integrity of the justice process if the trial proceeds.'[137]   **1.45**

As in English law, the NZ Supreme Court has adopted a 'balancing approach' in relation to the second category of case.[138] For the purposes of that exercise, relevant considerations include: **1.46**

  (i) confidence in the rule of law; confidence in the independence of the judiciary and the genuineness of the court processes;
 (ii) the seriousness of the offending,
(iii) the impact of the misconduct,
 (iv) attitude of police,
  (v) urgency, and
 (vi) any alternative remedies which will be sufficient to dissociate the justice system from the impugned conduct.[139]

The Court had some sympathy with the criticisms made by Patrick O'Connor QC of the decisions in *Maxwell* and *Warren*,[140] and it remarked that: **1.47**

> … where the members of an appellate court conclude that they would have granted a stay in order to preserve the integrity of the criminal justice system, it is not clear why they should defer to the trial judge's contrary assessment on the basis that such assessment was reasonably open to him or her, at least on a defendant's appeal following conviction where the ultimate issue is whether there has been a miscarriage of justice. The values at stake are, after all, of fundamental importance.[141]

Wilson: the facts

The case concerned the alleged drug trafficking activities of a motorcycle gang. Drug offences were charged in respect of twenty-one defendants, including W. Part of the undercover police operation involved the infiltration of the gang by two officers of whom MW was one. Officers, who supervised MW, implemented a strategy to bolster his 'credibility' among gang members by executing a search warrant in respect of certain premises. For this purpose, they used a false search warrant (correct in format but signed by a police officer and not by a Deputy Registrar). The Chief District Judge had received details by letter of the police operation but it was unclear whether he had approved of the police proposals.   **1.48**

Following the search, and as part of the ruse, MW was arrested and charged with certain drug offences, albeit that he would have had a statutory defence to them. An Information that had been laid in respect of one charge, was false, and it involved the officer swearing an oath that he had just cause to suspect, and did suspect, that MW had committed the offence in question.[142] The judges, before whom MW appeared, believed that they were dealing with a genuine case. The police planned for MW to be represented by a duty solicitor, to enter a guilty plea, and to be sentenced. But the gang referred MW to a defence lawyer whom they   **1.49**

---

[137] Per Arnold J (for the majority) at [40].
[138] [2015] NZSC 189 at [55].
[139] [2015] NZSC 189 at [92].
[140] P O'Connor, 'Abuse of Process after Warren and Maxwell' [2012] Crim LR 672.
[141] Per Arnold J (for the majority), at [28].
[142] [2015] NZSC 189, at [22].

had previously engaged. Believing MW to be a real defendant, the lawyer advised him to defend the charges, which were withdrawn shortly after the police operation terminated.

1.50 The appellant, Wilson, pleaded guilty to all charges against him, but a few months later, Simon France J ruled that the police conduct constituted an abuse of process, and he stayed the prosecution in respect of the remaining defendants. Wilson sought to vacate his guilty pleas, but before his appeal was heard, the decision of Mr. Justice Simon France was reversed by the Court of Appeal (*Antonievic*[143]) and the Court set the stay aside. In respect of those remaining defendants, Mr. Justice Collins stayed certain charges that were categorized as 'serious'. The Crown did not appeal that ruling. Meanwhile, Wilson was granted leave to appeal to the New Zealand Supreme Court.

1.51 The Supreme Court was troubled by the false search warrant, the false charges, and the role of the Chief District Court judge:

> [33] The independent scrutiny by a judicial or quasi-judicial officer of the justification(s) for a proposed search that is a feature of the warrant process provides an important protection against state abuse of coercive powers ... There is no doubt that the fabrication and use of a search warrant by the police to further an investigation undermines important legal values, even when the warrant is used in the limited way that occurred in this case.

> [34] Second, the bringing of the false prosecution and the visit by the police officers to the Chief Judge are particularly concerning, for two reasons. The first reason concerns the mis-use of official documents, in particular the laying of the false information in relation to the possession of equipment charge. As we have noted, the standard form for an information requires that the informant swear to certain things. In relation to MW, the informant's oath was untrue and was known to be so, both by the informant and his superiors. As in the case of the bogus search warrant, this shows an unacceptable attitude to documents and processes which are important components of the criminal justice system.

> [35] ... the constitutional role of judges in New Zealand. As the third branch of government, the judiciary must act independently of the other branches, and must appear to be independent. The independence of judges from the executive, both in appearance and in reality, is critical both to the proper operation of the rule of law and New Zealand's constitutional arrangements, and to the maintenance of public confidence in their operation.

Wilson: decision on the merits

1.52 The Court concluded that although the misconduct was serious, it was not 'one of those rare cases where a stay should be granted'. However, given the decision reached by Mr. Justice Collins (from whose ruling the Crown did not appeal) W's convictions were quashed.[144]

1.53 The Court reviewed a number of authorities including *Maxwell* and *Warren*:

> There is no evidence of a systemic problem, there was no bad faith, there is no likelihood of a repetition of the conduct at issue, the scenario simply facilitated the continued gathering of evidence of offending which occurred independently of the police misconduct and a remedy has been granted (albeit that it is limited to the non-serious offending).

1.54 Mr. Chief Justice Elias differed from the majority, concluding that the decision of the Court of Appeal in *Antonievic*[145] was wrong, and that the ruling of Mr. Justice Simon France was correct when he stayed the proceedings:

---

[143] [2013] NZCA 483, [2013] 3 NZLR 806.
[144] [2015] NZSC 189 at [96–109].
[145] [2013] NZCA 483, [2013] 3 NZLR 806.

The appearance of impartiality in judicial function is critical for the maintenance of confidence in the administration of justice through the courts. What was implicated here was an unqualified 'strong right', the appearance of which was essential to the integrity of the system. That appearance was significantly compromised by the false warrant which was executed against a third party, by the false information and by the scenarios acted out in the court in respect of bail. Above all, the court itself was tainted by the informal approach for approval of the use of the court processes for the ends of the investigation.

For Mr. Chief Justice Elias,[146] where a stay is necessary to protect the integrity of the criminal justice system, ' … no further balancing of different objectives of the criminal justice system is appropriate. Nor is there any discretion in the matter. There is a 'duty' to stay, as Lord Diplock made clear in *Hunter v Chief Constable of the West Midlands Police*'.[147]   **1.55**

Wilson: the role of judges—a footnote

The New Zealand Supreme Court said that in the absence of explicit statutory authorization, it was 'quite wrong that judges should be asked to play an active part in investigative techniques involving the bringing and processing of bogus prosecutions'.[148] To do so gives 'the appearance of a lack of independence and so is corrosive of public confidence in the judiciary':[149]   **1.56**

> Judges, who should be aloof from the activities of the executive, are conscripted to become participants in those activities. Such involvement is not consistent with the judicial oath, which requires judges to treat all who come before them in accordance with law, equally and without favour.[150]

The above comments have relevance for judges of the United Kingdom. In *Wilson*, an informal approach had been made to a judge by a member of the police service. In other words, the involvement of the judge was not authorized by statute or as a matter of case law. However, even if such an approach had been permissible under statute, the risk that the integrity of justice might be compromised would remain.   **1.57**

There is obvious merit in judges overseeing acts that the executive wishes to perform, and for officials to seek the approval of the judges before those acts are carried out. For example, judges may be asked to grant search warrants, or to order the production of documents and electronically held data, or to permit the non-disclosure of information on the grounds that disclosure would not be in the 'public interest'. Many such functions are not undertaken voluntarily or at the behest of the judiciary, but are imposed upon it by legislation. To that extent, it is not possible for judges to be 'aloof from the activities of the executive'.[151] There are, however, risks attaching to functions of this kind in that when things go wrong (as they inevitably will from time to time) the reputation of the judiciary and the criminal justice processes may become tarnished (and public confidence undermined). The principal protection for judges is that of vigilance (consider, for example, the circumstances in the *Golfrate Case* in respect of the application to a judge for search and seizure warrants).[152]   **1.58**

---

[146] [2015] NZSC 189, at [154].
[147] *Hunter v Chief Constable of the West Midlands Police* [1982] AC 529 (HL), at 536.
[148] Per Arnold J (for the majority) at [36].
[149] Per Arnold J (for the majority) at [36].
[150] *Wilson v The Queen*, per William Young, Glazebrook, Arnold and Blanchard JJ.
[151] *Wilson v The Queen*, per William Young, Glazebrook, Arnold and Blanchard JJ.
[152] *Golfrate Property Management Limited and Another v The Crown Court at Southwark and Another* [2014] EWHC 840 (Admin).

Western Australian approach

1.59 The principles, as they apply in Western Australia (which appear to be broadly consistent across Australia), were summarized in the judgment of Mr Justice Corboy in *Culverwell v Ginbey* [as re-formatted and further distilled by the author]:[153]

(a) Two policy considerations are fundamental to the determination:

    (i) the public interest in the administration of justice requires that the court protect its ability to function as a court of law by ensuring that its processes are used fairly by State and citizen alike; and

    (ii) a failure by a court to protect its ability to function in that way will lead to an erosion of public confidence by reason of concern that the court's processes may lend themselves to oppression and injustice: *Williams v Spautz*;[154] *Moti v The Queen*.[155]

(b) Abuses of process cannot be restricted to defined and closed categories.

(c) Notions of justice and injustice, as well as other considerations that bear on public confidence in the administration of justice, must reflect contemporary values and take account of the particular circumstances of the case. That does not mean that the concept is at large or without meaning. It extends to proceedings that are instituted for an improper purpose and to proceedings that are 'seriously and unfairly burdensome, prejudicial or damaging' or 'productive of serious and unjustified trouble and harassment': *Ridgeway v The Queen*.[156]

(d) Although the jurisdiction to stay proceedings as an abuse of process is wide, it is not without limits. The discretion cannot be exercised to stop proceedings merely because the evidence against an accused person is weak or because the court disapproves of the prosecution: *R v Chairman, County of London Quarter Sessions; Ex parte Downes*;[157] *R v Petroulias (No 1)*.[158]

(e) The power to stay proceedings as an abuse of process was not confined to cases where the court was satisfied that the hearing would necessarily be unfair or that proceedings had been brought for an improper purpose. The power extended to all categories of cases in which the processes and procedures of the court may be converted into 'instruments of injustice or unfairness': *Walton v Gardiner*.[159] Examples include proceedings doomed to fail, proceedings commenced in a court that was clearly an inappropriate forum. and proceedings seeking to litigate a new case that had already been disposed of by earlier proceedings.[160]

(f) The question of whether criminal proceedings should be stayed was to be determined:

> ... by a weighing process involving a subjective balancing of a variety of factors and considerations. Among those factors and considerations are the requirements of fairness to the accused, the legitimate public interest in the disposition of charges of serious offences and in the conviction of those guilty of crime, and the need to maintain public confidence in the administration of justice.[161]

---

[153] [2016] WASC 3, at [47].
[154] *Williams v Spautz* (1992) 174 CLR 509 (Mason CJ, Dawson, Toohey, and McHugh JJ).
[155] (2011) 245 CLR 456 [57].
[156] (1995) 184 CLR 19, 75 (Gaudron J).
[157] [1954] 1 QB 1, 6.
[158] [2006] NSWSC 788; (2006) 177 A Crim R 153 [63].
[159] *Walton v Gardiner* (1993) 177 CLR 378.
[160] (1993) 177 CLR 378, 393.
[161] *Walton v Gardiner* (1993) 177 CLR 378, 396 (a majority decision).

(g) A prosecution will only be stayed in the most exceptional circumstances: *Jago v District Court of New South Wales*.[162] The onus of satisfying the court that there is an abuse of process lies upon the party making the allegation and the onus is a heavy one: *Williams v Spautz*.[163]

F. 'Discretion' and 'Balance'—Whether Appropriate

The courts are on their guard against the 'floodgates' being opened to unmeritorious applications for a stay of proceedings. As the Court stated in *James v DPP*, '[a]pplications for a stay on the ground of abuse of process must not themselves be permitted to become an abuse.'[164] And, as Lowery points out, unwarranted applications to stay for abuse are a waste of resources.[165] However, these undesirable consequences are not necessarily the fault of legal practitioners when the law lacks sufficient clarity and certainty to assist them and their clients. No convincing explanation has been offered in the decided cases to explain why the level of threat or harm to the integrity of the criminal justice system had been reached in, say, *Mullen*, but not in *Maxwell* or in *Warren*, notwithstanding that in the latter case, Lord Kerr joined with other Justices in unequivocally condemning the behaviour of the police officers.[166] **1.60**

Patrick O'Connor QC has counselled courts not to reduce intervention to 'finger wagging'.[167] He opines that the decisions in *Maxwell* and *Warren* 'have lowered the standard of vigilance against abuses of our criminal justice system', and that the UK senior judiciary 'has changed the tone and stepped aside'. Those are hard-hitting statements, but confidence in the criminal justice process is at risk if the courts are perceived as being weaker in their deeds than in their words when they uphold procedural safeguards and protections. That said, it has to be recognized that not every instance of police misconduct is equally serious, and not every instance will render the trial unfair or cause confidence in the administration of justice to be damaged, or even attract the attention of the media. Accordingly, not every instance of misconduct by the police, or by the executive, justifies proceedings being stayed. In *Tague*, the Divisional Court put the matter thus:[168] **1.61**

> On the one hand, there is gross misconduct which the criminal justice system cannot approbate (as in cases such as *Bennett* and *Mullen*). On the other hand, however, it is important that conduct or results that may merely be the result of state incompetence or negligence should not necessarily justify what might be colloquially described as a 'Get Out of Jail Free' card: in those cases, the public might conclude that the justice system was little more than a game.

There are two 'filters' that limit the scope of a stay being granted, and which limit decisions that may be reviewed on appeal. The first is the notion of 'discretion'. The second is the requirement that the court performs a 'balancing exercise' (in *Bennett* type cases). The balance is between 'the public interest in ensuring that those who are accused of serious crimes should be tried and the competing public interest in ensuring that executive misconduct does not **1.62**

---

[162] (1989) 168 CLR 23, 31.

[163] *Williams v Spautz* (1992) 174 CLR 509, 529.

[164] [2015] EWHC 3296 (Admin); per Ouseley J, at [58].

[165] Finn Lowery, 'Abuse of Process: The Need for Structure', Vol 20 (2014) Auckland University Law Review, 223, which needs to be read in the light of *Wilson v the Queen* [2015] NZSC 189).

[166] [2012] 1 AC 22, at [81].

[167] Patrick O'Connor QC, ' "Abuse of process" after Warren and Maxwell' [2012] Crim. L.R. 672.

[168] Sir Brian Leveson P in *Tague v the Governor of HMP Full Sutton and the National Crime Agency* [2015] EWHC 3576 (Admin) at [49].

undermine public confidence in the criminal justice system and bring it into disrepute'.[169] Each of these 'filters' is discussed, in turn, below.

Category Two stays: an exercise of 'discretion' or 'judgment'?

1.63 There are many occasions on which the courts have stated that the power to stay proceedings for abuse, of the category two *Bennett* kind, is 'discretionary': see, for example, *Latif*,[170] *Mullen*,[171] *Ebrahim*[172] and *Warren v AG for Jersey*.[173]

1.64 Whether a decision is one of 'discretion', or of strict legal principle, often matters. This is because there is a tendency for appellate courts not to entertain appeals in respect of an exercise of judicial discretion unless it can be demonstrated that the decision was '*Wednesbury* unreasonable' (being either unreasonable or irrational).[174]

1.65 In *Maxwell*,[175] the case was principally concerned with the power to order a retrial under section 7 of the Criminal Appeal Act 1968. The Supreme Court focussed on the words 'may order a retrial' and 'the interests of justice so require', as they appeared in s 7.[176] As to whether section 7 confers a 'discretion' or requires an exercise of 'judgment', the Supreme Court appears to have said that it is both of those things. Having said that the s 7 power was one of 'discretion',[177] it then proceeded to say that a decision as to what the interests of justice requires, 'calls for an exercise of *judgment* in which a number of relevant factors have to be taken into account and weighed in the balance' [emphasis added].[178]

1.66 As Bennion has pointed out, there can be circumstances in which a judge must reach a conclusion that involves the exercise of both judgment and discretion:[179]

> For example the decision-taker may first need to exercise judgment in determining whether required conditions are satisfied; and then, if they are, may be called on to judge whether or not to exercise a discretion, and then to decide in what way.

1.67 But this is not the position of a court that is tasked to decide whether or not a stay for abuse of process should be granted. In this instance, the purpose of the 'balancing' exercise—a process of judgment—is to determine whether the abuse is such that a stay would be warranted. If a judge answered that issue in the affirmative, he or she cannot 'elect' not to grant a stay. Maintaining the integrity of the criminal justice process is not a matter of 'choice', but a duty. If this analysis is correct, then the power to grant a stay in respect of the second category is an exercise of judgment and not discretion.

1.68 In *Maxwell*, the Supreme Court concluded that a decision under section 7 'should only be upset on appeal if it was plainly wrong in the sense that it is one which no reasonable court could have made or if the court took into account immaterial factors or failed to take into account material factors' (per Lord Dyson JSC).[180] But this is the language of '*Wednesbury*

---

[169] *Warren v AG for Jersey* [2012] 1 AC 22, per Lord Dyson JSC, at [26].

[170] [1996] 1 WLR 104, paras 112–13.

[171] [2000] QB 520, at 536.

[172] *Ebrahim, R (on the application of) v Feltham Magistrates' Court and Anor* [2001] EWHC Admin 130.

[173] [2012] 1 AC 22 at [25], per Lord Dyson JSC.

[174] *Associated Provincial Picture Houses, Limited v Wednesbury Corporation* [1948] 1 KB 223.

[175] [2010] UKSC 48; [2011] 1 WLR 1837.

[176] [2011] 1 WLR 1837, at [18].

[177] [2010] UKSC 48; [2011] 1 WLR 1837, at [18].

[178] [2011] 1 WLR 1837, at [19], per Lord Dyson JSC.

[179] F Bennion, 'Jaguars and Donkeys: Distinguishing Judgment and Discretion' (2000) 31, The University of West Los Angeles Law Review, p 2.

[180] [2011] 1 WLR 1837, at [19], per Lord Dyson JSC.

unreasonableness'. Lord Dyson did not believe his propositions to be controversial.[181] But the 'Wednesbury unreasonableness' test *is* controversial.[182]

Lord Bingham, in his discussion of the 'rule of law', argued that questions of legal right and **1.69** liability should ordinarily be resolved by application of the law and not by the exercise of discretion.[183] He cited Lord Shaw of Dunfermline in *Scott v Scott* who said:[184]

> ... to remit the maintenance of constitutional rights to the region of judicial discretion [is] to shift the foundations of freedom from the rock to the sands.

Coke's advice to politicians also provides sound guidance for lawyers: that it is 'good caveat **1.70** to parliaments to leave all causes to be measured by the golden and straight metwand of the law and not the uncertain and crooked cord of discretion'.[185]

Francis Bennion[186] has pointed out that what is judicially described as discretion often **1.71** turns out to be judgment, and that judges not infrequently blur the distinction between judgment and discretion.[187] He has sought to explain the difference between the two processes:[188]

> Broadly, discretion is subjective while judgment is objective. At one extreme, where the decision is to be taken in exercise of a fully open discretion, that is one which is completely unfettered, we have a situation akin to that of the Cadi sitting beneath a palm tree and pronouncing his own individual notions of justice.[3][189] At the other extreme, where the decision is to be taken in exercise of a duty to arrive at a judgment, there is no room for individual choice, even though different decision-takers may legitimately arrive at different outcomes.

> Discretion is free, except for limitations placed upon it (expressly or impliedly) by the defining formula under which it is conferred. Judgment is necessarily restricted, because its sole purpose is to arrive at a conclusion of fact or law which accurately reflects reality. Discretion necessarily (by its nature) offers choice; judgment registers the functionary's assessment of a situation offering no choice. Discretion analytically offers a variety of outcomes; judgment but one.

> The context may be more complex than this. For example the decision-taker may first need to exercise judgment in determining whether required conditions are satisfied; and then, if they are, may be called on to judge whether or not to exercise a discretion, and then to decide in what way.

Defining 'judicial discretion'

Professor Choo has suggested two possible interpretations of the concept of judicial discre- **1.72** tion, namely, (i) totally unfettered power, and (ii) the open texturedness of a test or standard

---

[181] [2011] 1 WLR 1837 at [19].

[182] Paul Daly, 'Wednesbury's Reason and Structure', Public Law, 2011, p 238.

[183] Tom Bingham, *The Rule of Law* (Penguin Books, 2011), pp 48–54.

[184] [1913] AC 417, 477.

[185] Coke's Institutes (iv), 41 (*c.*1669).

[186] A former Parliamentary Counsel.

[187] F Bennion, 'Jaguars and Donkeys: Distinguishing Judgment and Discretion' (2000) 31, The University of West Los Angeles Law Review 14.

[188] F Bennion, 'Jaguars and Donkeys: Distinguishing Judgment and Discretion' (2000) 31, The University of West Los Angeles Law Review 7; and see F Bennion, 'Judgment and Discretion Revisited: Pedantry or Substance?' Public Law (2005) 707.

[189] Footnote [3] reads: 'Goddard L.J. said of the Courts (Emergency Powers) Act 1939 that the court "is really put very much in the position of a Cadi under the palm tree. There are no principles on which he is directed to act. He has to do the best he can in the circumstances, having no rules of law to guide him": *Metropolitan Properties Co. Ltd. v Purdy* [1940] 1 All ER 188, at 191.'

to be applied in reaching a conclusion.[190] He persuasively suggests that the latter interpretation is to be preferred.

1.73 Judicial discretion is playing an increasingly important part in the administration of justice but it is not without risks that have to be 'managed' by a combination of legal principles, as well as by rules of practice, procedure, and guidance (such as the Crown Court 'Bench Book'). Professor Choo's invaluable discussion of the concept of judicial discretion[191] reveals the complexity of the concept, and that discretion is being re-defined to reflect the context in which it operates within the modern criminal justice process.

1.74 There will be many situations in which a judge must assess the circumstances of the case and decide between options (for example, whether to extend custody time limits, or the period of time in which to pay a fine, or honing jury directions to suit the case in hand). It is also true that different judges may reach a different conclusion on the same facts (evidenced by the history of the decisions in *Maxwell*[192] and *Regan*[193])— a state of affairs which, in relation to the exercise of true discretions, may be tolerated as falling within a 'margin of appreciation' or 'latitude'. Were the position otherwise, the appellate courts would be overburdened with fact-specific appeals and deflected from their primary task of deciding matters of principle.

1.75 However, where the outcome is to be determined by reference to a legal norm or test (such as whether executive conduct constitutes a serious affront to the rule of law) the duty of the judge is to honour the test. Even here, different judges may assess the circumstances differently and reach a different conclusion. But the decision of the judge is one of judgement—and not an exercise of discretion.

1.76 A legal norm, test, or rule, is often 'open-textured' but this to admit to its inherent weaknesses, including lack of clarity, the potential for inconsistent outcomes, and the risk that it will not be applied with appropriate rigour. It is in this connection that the outcomes of *Maxwell* and *Warren* have been criticized (as discussed above). Making references to the 'open texturedness' of rules and concepts, and the meaning and function of 'discretion', is to engage with HLA Hart's important but much debated 'open-texture theory'.[194] Although legal rules and maxims are often imprecise, the English legal tradition of *stare decisis* has been a reasonably effective means of proofing the texture of the legal fabric. Discretion has its part to play, but there are aspects of the legal process in respect of which (to adopt the words of Lord Simon of Glaisdale in *D v NSPCC*)[195] it should be 'law, not discretion, which is in command'.[196]

Discretion, stare decisis, and the judicial court structure

1.77 For the reasons given earlier, it was not unreasonable for the Supreme Court (in *Maxwell*)[197] and the Privy Council (in *Warren*)[198] to seek to limit appeals to the appellate courts. The

---

[190] Andrew Choo, 'Abuse of Process and Judicial Stays of Criminal Proceedings' (Oxford University Press), 2nd edn, pp 155–66.

[191] Andrew Choo, 'Abuse of Process and Judicial Stays of Criminal Proceedings' (Oxford University Press), 2nd edn, pp 155–66.

[192] [2011] 1 WLR 1837.

[193] [2002] 1 SCR 297, 2002 SCC 12 (CanLII).

[194] HLA Hart, *The Concept of Law* (2nd edn 1994, Oxford 1961).

[195] [1978] AC 171, 239G.

[196] Per Lord Simon of Glaisdale, *D v National Society for Prevention of Cruelty to Children* [1978] AC 171, 239G, cited by Lord Bingham in 'The Rule of Law', Chapter 4, fn 4. See also, *Regina v Croydon London Borough Council; PE (Peru) v Secretary of State for the Home Department* [2011] EWCA Civ 274. A point mooted in that case was whether a finding that deportation would be proportionate or not, was a question of fact, or mixed law and fact, or a question of judgement: 'I prefer the view that it is a question of judgment (not discretion)' (per Hooper LJ).

[197] [2011] 1 WLR 1837.

[198] [2012] 1 AC 22.

categorization of particular judicial tasks as exercises of 'discretion', and the application of the 'Wednesbury unreasonableness' type test, are devices ('escapes'[199]) by which appellate courts are able to confine themselves to deciding questions of law and principle. There are of course other techniques by which it is possible for this result to be achieved (for example, rules that require leave to appeal). When used appropriately, such devices have much to commend them in the development of legal principles and in maintaining the integrity of the criminal justice system.

Thurman Arnold, writing from a North American perspective,[200] remarked that 'our belief **1.78** that the courts are the chief guardians of the supremacy of law is the reason why we adopt such a respectful attitude towards them.'[201] According to Arnold, the supremacy of law is due in large part to the development of case law by which legal principles are developed and honed (and legislation clarified), and it is maintained and protected by the discrete functions played by the appellate courts (determining legal principles, correcting errors of law) and courts/tribunals of first instance (fact-finding).

> It is obvious that our belief that courts are the chief guardians of the supremacy of law is the reason why we adopt such a respectful attitude toward them. Yet this supremacy of law is a vague and very hotly contested phrase, on the meaning of which there is no agreement. It appears that two of its functions are: (i) to protect us from the tyranny of the majority and (2) to make results of disputes more logical and predictable.
>
> The first has something to do with the interpretation of a written constitution which is supreme in this country. However, it is not clear that this written constitution itself is the real protection from the tyranny of the majority because courts in England furnish the same kind of protection without a constitution.
>
> [...]
>
> The second feature of the supremacy of law, which is to make results of disputes more logical and predictable by the application of principles or the development of principles, is ordinarily referred to as the common law. It is a science of reconciling principles and precedents in an orderly way so that one will grow out of the other. Thus nothing absolutely new should come from a court without the aid of the legislature, and such new principles as appear should be the logical development of older ones applied to new cases.

Arnold's hypothesis appears to be that respect for the judiciary is the product, at least in part, **1.79** of a judicial structure by which decision-making on the merits of a given case (the function of courts at first instance) is separated, by means of various 'escapes', from the business of deciding matters of principle by appellate courts.[202] As Arnold pointed out, there is a danger that if the appellate courts routinely engage in reviewing cases on their merits, rather than acting solely as a court of error, important legal principles become lost in the facts that confuse them:[203]

> What has happened in England in the years following the Judicature Act is not the sudden substitution of enlightened judges for bigoted ones, but the insulation of the science of substantive law from the practical problem of litigation. Instead of rigidly applying the substantive-law doctrines through the principle of *stare decisis*, as many imagine, the English

---

[199] Using the language of Thurman Arnold: see Arnold, Thurman W, 'The Role of Substantive Law and Procedure in the Legal Process' (1932). Faculty Scholarship Series, Paper 4258.

[200] Albeit in 1932, but the observations continue to have substance (it is submitted).

[201] Arnold, Thurman W, 'The Role of Substantive Law and Procedure in the Legal Process' (1932). Faculty Scholarship Series. Paper 4258.

[202] Arnold, Thurman W, 'The Role of Substantive Law and Procedure in the Legal Process' (1932). Faculty Scholarship Series. Paper 4258, pp 630–31.

[203] Arnold, Thurman W, 'The Role of Substantive Law and Procedure in the Legal Process' (1932). Faculty Scholarship Series. Paper 4258 p 638.

have been devising practical escapes which separate principles of substantive law from the actual cases which confuse them. This has been done by transferring power to the trial courts and making it difficult for appellate courts to make a written application of doctrines to any case not fought with unusual determination and disregard of expense. Thus substantive law exists at the top of the very practical English system as an ideal exposition of a way of thought and expression.

1.80 Furthermore, the 'currency' of appellate courts is less likely to be 'devalued' (and public confidence less likely to be adversely affected) by outcomes that are disliked but which turned on their facts.

> In England' (wrote Arnold) 'substantive law performs its function as a philosophical guide divorced from actual cases. Power is transferred to trial courts, and to judges who are not dignified by that peculiar name.[204]

1.81 As a matter of English practice and procedure, the power of the Court of Appeal to hear evidence is narrowly prescribed. That Court typically reviews decisions on the facts as found at first instance, or agreed by the parties, or (occasionally)—as in *Bennett*—on assumed facts.[205] Accordingly, an appellate court will exercise care when commenting on the merits of a given case because it may, or may not, have all relevant facts before it.[206]

1.82 What then, is the relationship between 'substantive law' and 'procedure'? According to Arnold, 'substantive law remains 'law' which we enforce, procedure the practical rules by which we enforce it'.[207]

> We therefore always 'restate' substantive law in the light of its principles, and 'reform' procedure in the light of its practical problems.

> The distinction is most useful in the judicial system, once we realize that the difference is only in attitude, that any doctrine may be treated as procedure and the problem discussed, or as substantive law and the principle stated. The difference between procedure and substantive law is a movable dividing line which may be placed wherever an objective examination of our judicial institutions indicates is necessary.

1.83 Arnold added that 'there is no doctrine of *stare decisis*, as opposed to *stare dictum*, which prevents us from considering the practical utility of treating any problem from a procedural point of view.' The '[s]ubstantive law, is canonized procedure. Procedure is unfrocked substantive law.'[208]

---

[204] Arnold, Thurman W, 'The Role of Substantive Law and Procedure in the Legal Process' (1932). Faculty Scholarship Series. Paper 4258 p 638, 639.

[205] As Lord Hope of Craighead DPSC stated in *Warren v AG for Jersey*, 'The fact that the case was decided on assumed facts does not, of course, deprive the decision of the House of Lords in *R v Horseferry Road Magistrates' Court, Ex p Bennett* [1994] 1 AC 42 of any of its authority.

[206] As Lord Hope explained in *Warren v AG for Jersey*, the subsequent trial that investigated the facts revealed a different picture; and see Colin Warbrick, 'Judicial Jurisdiction and Abuse of Process, Current Developments: International Law, April 2001, vol 49, p 489, 491. See also *Bennett v H.M. Advocate*, 1995 SLT. 510; and see the judgment of Lord Bingham CJ in *Regina v Staines Magistrate's Court and Others* [1998] 1 WLR 652, 663H.

[207] Arnold, Thurman W, 'The Role of Substantive Law and Procedure in the Legal Process' (1932). Faculty Scholarship Series. Paper 4258, p 643. Note that Arnold stated at footnote 44: 'It must be apparent that the writer has used the terms 'substantive law' and 'procedure' to describe different attitudes, rather than the classification found in the law school curriculum. Many of the concepts which are ordinarily denominated 'procedural' have been treated with the attitude of 'substantive law' though this is becoming less frequent.

[208] Arnold, Thurman W, 'The Role of Substantive Law and Procedure in the Legal Process' (1932). Faculty Scholarship Series. Paper 4258, p 645.

In relation to the power to stay proceedings for abuse of process, there must be a 'filter' **1.84**
('escape') through which only deserving cases receive the attention of the appellate courts.
The question is how this is best achieved. The categorization of judicial decisions as ones
of 'discretion'—and particularly the application of the 'Wednesbury unreasonableness
test'—risks filtrating too restrictively and delaying the provision of clearer guidance by
the appellate courts on matters of principle and criteria (i.e. factors and their respective
weights). This does not mean that a set of rigid rules is necessary. There is no 'bright line'
(to borrow an expression)[209] that marks the boundary of the 'integrity of the legal system'
beyond which abuse of process will result in a stay: the courts cannot be as prescriptive
as they might wish to be in this area. Despite the metaphor used in *Tague* that a 'a broad
brush approach is likely to be necessary',[210] the value-judgments reached in that case,
and in *R v R*,[211] were reasoned having regard to the relevant factors and making a com-
parative evaluation of the seriousness of the matters complained of contrasted with other
decided cases.

The issue of 'balance'

As a matter of English law, confirmed by decisions such as *Maxwell* and *Mullen*, the second **1.85**
category of case (of the *Bennett* kind) requires the court to perform a 'balancing exercise'
between 'the public interest in ensuring that those who are accused of serious crimes should
be tried and the competing public interest in ensuring that executive misconduct does not
undermine public confidence in the criminal justice system and bring it into disrepute'.[212]
Under Canadian law, 'balancing' is the exception rather than the rule,[213] but this is in the
context of the power to stay being confined to the 'clearest of cases'.

The 'balancing metaphor'

One problem with the metaphor of 'balance' is that it is misleading from the outset. The **1.86**
burden of proving abuse is on the person who asserts it, and thus the 'scales' do not start
from a position of equilibrium. Ashworth and Redmayne[214] say that 'balancing' is a 'seductive notion that appears to exclude fairness almost to the point of incontrovertibility'. They
identify at least three problems with the 'balancing' metaphor:

> Our criticisms here are aimed at a vague and unprincipled use of the concept of 'balancing',
> a seductive notion that appears to exude fairness almost to the point of incontrovertibility.
> Yet talk of 'balancing' often assumes a kind of hydraulic relationship between human rights
> safeguards and the promotion of public safety, an assumption that should not be made in
> the absence of clear objective evidence. Another problem with the 'balancing' metaphor is
> that it may lead to restrictions on a small minority in the hope of enhancing the security of
> the majority? A further difficulty is that too frequently no account is taken of the increase
> in State power that accompanies curtailments of individual rights, whereas one of the fun-
> damental purposes of human rights is to protect individuals against arbitrary exercises of
> power by State officials.

---

[209] An expression used by Sir Brian Leveson P in *Tague v the Governor of HMP Full Sutton and the National
Crime Agency* [2015] EWHC 3576 (Admin) at [49]; and which he repeated a few days later in *R* [2015]
EWCA Crim 1941.
[210] *Tague v the Governor of HMP Full Sutton and the National Crime Agency* [2015] EWHC 3576 (Admin)
at [49].
[211] *R v R* [2015] EWCA Crim 1941.
[212] *Warren v AG for Jersey* [2012] 1 AC 22, per Lord Dyson JSC, at [26].
[213] *Khadr's* case, citing *Canada (Minister of Citizenship and Immigration) v Tobiass* [1997] 3 SCR 391, and
Regan [2002] 1 SCR 297.
[214] A Ashworth and M Redmayne, 'The Criminal Process' (4th edn, Oxford University Press 2010); and
see Patrick O'Connor, '"Abuse of Process" after Warren and Maxwell' [2012] Crim LR 672.

1.87 A further criticism of the use of the expression 'balance' is its association with the term 'discretion' to describe the function of the judge when considering an application for a stay of proceedings. Indeed, in *Mullen*, the Court used the expressed 'discretionary balance'.[215]

1.88 Powerful and attractive as the criticisms are of the balancing metaphor, the reality is most metaphors are poor substitutes for compendious explanations of situations that actually exist. The rule of law cannot be viewed from one direction only.[216] In the absence of a finite number of clearly defined categories of abuse (a 'matrix' of conditions) to meet the wide range of cases that could arise,[217] the courts have little option but to adjudicate upon applications to stay proceedings by reference to a set of criteria.[218] The use of the balancing metaphor—despite its shortcomings—does figuratively portray the task that a judge undertakes when required to make a decision with regard to factors that vary in their relevance and significance.

Countervailing factors and considerations

1.89 That there will be competing interests when a judge is considering whether or not to grant a stay cannot be seriously disputed. The facts in *Maxwell*[219] concerned two brutal acts of robbery of which one culminated in the murder of an elderly victim. The Supreme Court said that the interests of the public, and respect for the victims of a crime committed, were of a 'high order',[220] but the egregious conduct of the police was flagrant and appalling and none of the officers responsible had been disciplined in respect of it.

1.90 In *Tague v the Governor of HMP Full Sutton and the National Crime Agency*,[221] Sir Brian Leveson P[222] stated (rightly, it is submitted) that '[e]xercising that balance is far from straightforward'.[223] As he pointed out, 'the problem arises because maintaining confidence in the

---

[215] [2000] QB 520.

[216] A point also made by the Divisional Court in *Tague v the Governor of HMP Full Sutton and the National Crime Agency* [2015] EWHC 3576 (Admin), at [49].

[217] F Lowery suggests that abuses of process 'should be catalogued into a non-exhaustive taxonomy' (Finn Lowery; 'Abuse of Process: The Need for Structure', Vol 20 (2014) Auckland University Law Review 223, 243).

[218] Interestingly, F Lowery's suggested approach to abuse of process applications is not dissimilar from that taken by the Supreme Court in *Maxwell*; unfortunately, Lowery did not discuss the judgments in that case. At p 243, he states: '(c) The inherent power to stay can be invoked in two broad categories of abuse of process: first, where a fair trial has become impossible; and secondly, where it would offend the court's sense of justice and propriety to try the accused in the particular circumstances of the case. (d) When determining whether to stay a case that falls into the second category of abuse of process, the court should engage a clearly delineated two-stage analysis. (e) First, the court must identify the putative misconduct and ask whether, when viewed against objective standards, it renders the trial an abuse of process. It must identify the type of abuse alleged on the facts and proceed to identify the considerations and precedents that are germane to that category. (f) If the answer to (e) is no, then that is the end of the inquiry and the stay application must be dismissed. Conversely, if the answer is yes, the court proceeds to the second stage of the analysis, consisting of two further steps. (g) The first step is to ask whether any remedy short of a stay is available. In doing so, it will determine whether such remedy would be sufficient to dissociate the court from the executive's wrongdoing and to maintain the public's confidence in the administration of criminal justice. If so, then that remedy should be granted and the stay application must be denied. (h) If no other remedy is appropriate, the court engages the second step, asking whether, on a public policy balancing test, the facts of the case militate in favour of staying or continuing the prosecution. In doing so, the court must weigh all the relevant dimensions of the case to answer the ultimate question whether staying proceedings or continuing them will better maintain the public's confidence in the administration of justice.' (Finn Lowery; 'Abuse of Process: The Need for Structure', Vol 20 (2014) Auckland University Law Review 223. The article now needs to be read in the light of *Wilson v the Queen* [2015] NZSC 189).

[219] [2010] UKSC 48.

[220] Judgment, para 64.

[221] [2015] EWHC 3576 (Admin).

[222] The President of the Queen's Bench Division.

[223] [2015] EWHC 3576 (Admin), at [48].

criminal justice system (or, as it has been put, avoiding 'an affront to the public conscience') is an aim or aspiration which has to be perceived from different directions':

> On the one hand, there is gross misconduct which the criminal justice system cannot approbate (as in cases such as *Bennett* and *Mullen*). On the other hand, however, it is important that conduct or results that may merely be the result of state incompetence or negligence should not necessarily justify what might be colloquially described as a 'Get Out of Jail Free' card: in those cases, the public might conclude that the justice system was little more than a game. There is no bright line and a broad brush approach is likely to be necessary. In *CC and CF*,[224] Lloyd Jones LJ put the approach in this way (at [99]):
>
> > [T]he objective of maintaining the integrity of the legal system can be achieved only by a consideration of the entirety of the conduct in question and untrammelled by any rigid rules.

Patrick O'Connor QC has suggested that a sensible set of relevant factors to assess the seriousness of a typical police misconduct case could provide some calibration to the metaphorical balance expected from trial judges. These would include 'the degree of damage to confidence in the police' (and similarly to the justice system), and whether the rule of law has been 'vindicated in other ways by prosecution or discipline'. **1.91**

However, one needs to go further: factors or considerations cannot be discussed without regard to their *weight*. It is apparent from some decisions that the weight to be attached to a violation of human rights can be substantial. In *Warren*, the Board disapproved of the decision of the Court of Appeal in *Grant*,[225] concluding that the trial judge's decision not to stay criminal proceedings was correct.[226] The inference to be drawn is that the Board was saying that the Court of Appeal in *Grant* had erred by giving too much weight to the seriousness of the misconduct and insufficient weight to the lack of 'but for' linkage (this was certainly the view of the New Zealand Court of Appeal in *Antonievic*).[227] In *Tague*, the Divisional Court compared the seriousness of that case (summarized in 1.90) with other cases, and concluded that it was 'significantly less serious and sits far apart from *Mullen* and *Bennett*' and was also 'less serious than *CC and CF*'.[228, 229] Other decisions, including the examples cited below (*Downey, Mullen, Warren, Grant*), are not easily reconciled on their merits. In *Khadr* (1.93)[230]—a decision of the Ontario Court of Appeal—the Court was willing to pay a high price (for the high-principled reasons that it gave) to ensure that the rule of law, and the integrity of the criminal justice process, was maintained. The underlying offence in that case, was terrorism. **1.92**

Applying countervailing considerations: case examples

Att-Gen of Canada on behalf of the United States of America v Khadr

In the *Khadr* case,[231] it was alleged that K (a Canadian citizen who had travelled between Afghanistan and Pakistan) had, among other allegations, conspired to traffic in weapons, and possessed an explosive substance.[232] K's extradition was sought by the United States of **1.93**

---

[224] This was a reference to *Secretary of State for the Home Department v CC and CF* [2012] EWHC 2837 (Admin). The decision went to the Court of Appeal: see *Mohamed & CF v Secretary of State for the Home Department* [2014] EWCA Civ 559.

[225] [2006] QB 60, CA.

[226] [2012] 1 AC 22, at [36].

[227] [2013] NZCA 483 at [73].

[228] *Secretary of State for the Home Department v CC and CF* [2012] EWHC 2837 (Admin); heard on appeal: *Mohamed & CF v Secretary of State for the Home Department* [2014] EWCA Civ 559.

[229] *Tague v the Governor of HMP Full Sutton and the NCA* [2015] EWHC 3576 (Admin) at [57].

[230] (2011) 157 ILR 700.

[231] *Att-Gen of Canada on behalf of the United States of America v Khadr* (2011) 157 ILR 700.

[232] Judgment para 17.

America. Before being repatriated to Canada, K was abducted in Pakistan by a Pakistani intelligence agency, detained, beaten, and interrogated for intelligence purposes. He had been detained for fourteen months in a secret centre without being charged, without access to legal counsel or to a court or tribunal. The Ontario Court of Appeal dismissed an appeal by the United States of America against a stay granted by the extradition judge. The Court enquired whether a judge (in the context of extradition proceedings) is required to withhold a remedy necessary to protect the integrity of the judicial process, and effectively sanction 'serious violation of human rights, because of the competing societal interests in bringing alleged terrorists to justice?' It answered the questions in the negative.[233]

> Is a judge required by law to sacrifice important legal rights and democratic values in the name of ensuring that a proceeding against an alleged terrorist is able to go forward? In my view, the answer to those questions is 'no'. [per Sharp J]

1.94 The Court, having cited various decisions and academic texts,[234] endorsed the view that the rule of law must prevail—even in the face of the dreadful threat of terrorism.

> These eminent jurists make a fundamental point: the rule of law must prevail even in the face of the dreadful threat of terrorism. We must adhere to our democratic and legal values, even if that adherence serves in the short term to benefit those who oppose and seek to destroy those values. For if we do not, in the longer term, the enemies of democracy and the rule of law will have succeeded. They will have demonstrated that our faith in our legal order is unable to withstand their threats. (per Sharp J)

Downey

1.95 In *Downey*,[235] Mr. Justice Sweeney delivered a detailed and tightly reasoned ruling in which he stayed a criminal trial for abuse of process. D had been charged on five counts, of which four were murder and one of doing an act with intent to cause an explosion. The alleged offences arose out of the bombing by the Irish Republican Army (IRA) in Hyde Park, London in 1982. Thirty-one other people were injured (a number of them seriously) and seven horses were destroyed.

1.96 D contended that the proceedings should be stayed. He asserted (the 'second ground') that an expectation had been created by governmental statements that prosecutions would not be pursued in respect of persons such as D, who would otherwise qualify for early release under statute.[236] Furthermore (the 'third ground'), D was given, in 2007, a written assurance on behalf of the Secretary of State for Northern Ireland and the Attorney General that (among other things) there were no warrants in existence, that he was not wanted in Northern Ireland for arrest or questioning or charge by the police, and that the Police Service of Northern Ireland (PSNI) were not aware of any interest in him by any other police force in the United Kingdom. The letter was misleading because the PSNI were aware that D was wanted by the Metropolitan Police in relation to the bombing, but they did nothing to correct the situation. In reliance upon the letter, D (a proven supporter of the peace process) travelled on a number of occasions between Northern Ireland and the mainland, including the final occasion when he was arrested on the mainland and charged with the offences in question.

---

[233] Judgment, para 71.

[234] Louise Arbour, 'In Our Name and On Our Behalf' (2006), 4 Eur HRL Rev 371; Owen M Fiss, 'The War Against Terrorism and the Rule of Law' (2006), 26 Oxford J Legal Stud 235; David Dyzenhaus, 'Intimations of Legality Amid the Clash of Arms' (2004), 2 Int'l J Const L 244.

[235] First instance, Central Criminal Court; 21 February 2014, unreported.

[236] Namely, the Northern Ireland (Sentences) Act 1998 (enacted in accordance with the 'Good Friday Agreement'.

The prosecution contended (among other things) that the political process, the governmental **1.97** commitment not to pursue prosecutions, the underlying the administrative scheme, and the 2007 letter, should not impact upon an independent prosecutorial decision to prosecute. The letter was the product of error during the PSNI's operation as opposed to any act of bad faith, and it did not (and was not intended to) amount to an amnesty for the recipient.

The learned judge ruled that in respect of the 'second ground', the 'balancing exercise' came **1.98** down in favour of the continuation of the prosecution. However, the commitments and assurances were relevant to the 'third ground', which was upheld:[237]

> Given the core facts as I have found them to be, and the wider undisputed facts, I have conducted the necessary evaluation of what has occurred in the light of the competing public interests involved. Clearly, and notwithstanding a degree of tempering in this case by the operation of the 1998 Act, the public interest in ensuring that those who are accused of serious crime should be tried is a very strong one (with the plight of the victims and their families firmly in mind). However, in the very particular circumstances of this case it seems to me that it is very significantly outweighed in the balancing exercise by the overlapping public interests in ensuring that executive misconduct does not undermine public confidence in the criminal justice system and bring it into disrepute, and the public interest in holding officials of the state to promises they have made in full understanding of what is involved in the bargain. Hence I have concluded that this is one of those rare cases in which, in the particular circumstances, it offends the court's sense of justice and propriety to be asked to try the defendant.

Mullen

In *Mullen*,[238] the security services in Zimbabwe and in England colluded to procure M's **1.99** deportation from Zimbabwe. Contrary to Zimbabwean law and internationally recognized human rights, M had been denied access to a lawyer. M conceded that he had been *properly convicted* in England of a conspiracy to cause explosions and he was sentenced to thirty years' imprisonment. His conviction was quashed on appeal. The Court of Appeal held that the certainty of guilt could not displace the abuse of process in M's case, namely, the degradation of the lawful administration of justice. As for (what the Court called) 'discretionary balance' it said:[239]

> In these circumstances, we have no doubt that the discretionary balance conies down decisively against the prosecution of this offence. This trial was preceded by an abuse of process which, had it come to light at the time, as it would have done had the prosecution made proper voluntary disclosure, would properly have justified the proceedings being stayed. Inasmuch as that discretionary exercise now falls to be carried out by this court, we conclude that, by reason of this abuse of process, the prosecution and therefore the conviction of the defendant were unlawful.

Warren

In *Warren*,[240] the defendants were convicted of conspiracy to smuggle drugs into Jersey from **1.100** the Netherlands. By virtue of an audio monitoring device fitted to W's car, the investigating officers obtained recorded conversations between W and another person that provided compelling evidence of the smuggling venture. A senior prosecutor in the Jersey Law Officers Department informed the officers that he could not advise them to record conversations without the consent of the relevant foreign authorities—but that if they did so, and valuable

---

[237] Ruling, para 174.
[238] [2000] QB 520.
[239] [2000] QB 520, 536 F/G.
[240] [2012] 1 AC 22.

evidence was obtained, it was unlikely that a Jersey Court would exclude the evidence solely because it had been obtained unlawfully. He added that, 'if it was me I would go ahead and do it, but don't quote me on that'. In dismissing the appeal, the Privy Council held that, despite the seriousness of the misconduct, the factors, taken cumulatively, entitled the trial Commissioner to conclude *against* a stay of the proceedings because, (i) the offence was very serious, (ii) W was a professional drug dealer of the first order; (iii) the unwise advice of the prosecutor 'mitigated' to some extent the gravity of the misconduct of the police, (iv) there was no attempt to mislead the Jersey Court as to the circumstances in which the evidence had been obtained, and (v) the commission of the offence was a fast moving situation.[241]

1.101 The decision in *Warren* has been criticized,[242] not least because it is difficult to see why the prosecutor's advice 'mitigated' the misconduct: the aside, made by a member of the executive, was surely an aggravating factor. The countervailing incentives for not staying the proceedings (which, perhaps, were not spelt out as strongly as they might have been by the Board) were the scale of W's drug trafficking activities, the period of time over which those activities had been carried out, and the high probability that they would have continued until interrupted and disrupted.

Grant

1.102 In *Grant*,[243] G was convicted of conspiracy to murder his wife's lover (V). An unknown gunman shot V in the chest and thigh as he answered the front door of his home address. A pattern of phone calls between the defendants, as well as notes recovered from their property, were relied upon by the prosecution to show contact between them and the existence of a plan to harm V. G suggested that V might have been killed by criminal contacts of his own, possibly over drugs. V had connections with known criminals, including drug dealers.

1.103 G's case was one of three discrete cases tried by different judges. In each case, the police had placed covert listening devices in the exercise yard of a police station resulting in privileged communications between the detained suspects and their legal advisers (including in G's case) being improperly intercepted and recorded. The proceedings were stayed as abusive in the two cases that did not concern G (one was tried prior to G's case, and one tried subsequently). One judge appears to have been of the view, and another certainly was, that it was not necessary to prove prejudice to the defendant in order to conclude that the proceedings were tainted by the misconduct. However, in G's case, nothing was recovered from the illicit intercepts of any value to the prosecution. The defence had not established prejudice, and therefore the application for a stay was refused.

1.104 On appeal, Grant contended that there was an abuse of the process in his case—just as there had been in the two other cases in which it was found probable that the microphones were placed in the exercise yards deliberately, with the intention of capturing any conversation which might take place between the detained persons and their solicitors. G's convictions were quashed. The Court of Appeal concluded that the trial judge's approach had been mistaken and that the proceedings ought to have been stayed. Nothing had been gained from the interception of the solicitors' communications, but the Court was in 'no doubt' that 'in general unlawful acts of the kind done in this case, amounting to a deliberate violation of a suspected person's right to legal professional privilege, are so great an affront to the integrity of the justice system, and therefore the rule of law, that the associated prosecution is rendered abusive and ought not to be countenanced by the court'.[244]

---

[241] [2012] 1 AC 22, at [45–50].
[242] See P O'Connor, '"Abuse of Process" after Warren and Maxwell' [2012] Crim LR 672.
[243] [2005] EWCA Crim 1089, [2006] QB 60.
[244] [2005] EWCA Crim 1089; [2006] QB 60, at [54].

In *Warren*,[245] the Board disapproved of the decision in *Grant*.[246] It accepted that the conduct   **1.105**
of the police was the kind of 'serious affront to the integrity of the justice system which may
often lead to the conclusion that the proceedings should be stayed'.[247] But, G had been
charged with a most serious crime and—'*crucially the misconduct cause no prejudice to the
accused*'. Nothing of evidential value was recovered from the illicit intercepts of conversations. The Board remarked rhetorically, 'surely the trial judge was entitled to decide in the
exercise of his discretion to refuse a stay and the Court of Appeal should not have held that
his decision was wrong'.[248] It is submitted that the Court of Appeal in *Grant* did not simply
substitute its conclusion in the exercise of discretion for that of the trial judge. It held that
the trial judge had *erred in his approach*. Perhaps the real dispute between the Board and the
Court of Appeal in relation to *Grant* was in their assessment of the seriousness of the misconduct in that case and its impact on the integrity of justice. Inferentially, the Board did
not consider the conduct of the police to be 'so grave as to threaten or undermine the rule
of law' that it was necessary to stop the case. The Court of Appeal was plainly of a different
view. It said:[249]

> Where the court is faced with illegal conduct by police or State prosecutors which is so grave
> as to threaten or undermine the rule of law itself, the court may readily conclude that it will
> not tolerate, far less endorse, such a state of affairs and so hold that its duty is to stop the
> case. This is well supported by *R v Horseferry Road Magistrates' Court, Ex p Bennett* [1994] 1
> AC 42 (see, in particular, per Lord Griffiths, at pp 62, 64, and per Lord Lowry, at p 77), to
> which reference was made in *R v Latif* [1996] 1 WLR 104, 112–113 …

In their commentary on *Grant* (but without the benefit of the decisions in *Maxwell* and   **1.106**
Warren) Ashworth and Redmayne wrote that '[if] the court was to associate itself with the
wrongdoing in *Grant*, it would undermine its integrity as a forum for dispensing justice and
upholding the rule of law.'[250] In the event, the Board did not 'associate itself' with the conduct in *Grant* (on the contrary). But, the fact that four judicial tiers (Crown Court, Court of
Appeal, Supreme Court [*Maxwell*], and Privy Council [*Warren*]) reached varying conclusions
on the facts of *Grant*, is an indication that greater clarity of the principles, criteria, and values
in such cases is required.

R v Staines Magistrates' Court—a minimum threshold

In *R v Staines Magistrates' Court; Ex parte Westfallen and others*,[251] the respondents submit-   **1.107**
ted that what had taken place 'was not disguised extradition, but undisguised deportation' and they further submitted that 'there is no taint of impropriety against the British
authorities'.[252] In accepting those submissions, the Divisional Court held that neither the
police nor the prosecuting authorities acted illegally, or procured or connived at unlawful
procedures, or violated international law or the domestic law of foreign states, or abused
their powers in a way that should lead the Court to stay the proceedings against the
applicants. Hooper J (as he then was) found the observations in *Bennett v KM Advocate*[253]
helpful in terms of making an assessment for the purposes of the applications for judicial

---

245 [2012] 1 AC 22.
246 [2012] 1 AC 22, at [36].
247 [2012] 1 AC 22; per Lord Dyson JSC, para 36.
248 [2012] 1 AC 22; per Lord Dyson JSC, para 36.
249 [2005] EWCA Crim 1089; [2006] QB 60, per Laws LJ at [56].
250 A Ashworth and M Redmayne, *The Criminal Process* (4th edn, Oxford University Press 2010), p 273.
251 [1998] 1 WLR 652.
252 For an interesting discussion concerning 'disguised extradition', see *Moti v The Queen* [2011] HCA
50: a decision of the High Court of Australia.
253 1995 SLT 510.

review, 'as to the *minimum* threshold for a successful application of the kind being brought before this court'.[254] In *Bennett v. KM Advocate*, the High Court of Justiciary was called upon to assess the validity of a sheriff's warrant to arrest Mr Bennett (who had been the party to the proceedings before the House of Lords in 1993).[255] The Lord Justice General, Lord Hope, said:[256]

> In our opinion it would be unreasonable, where there has been no collusion, to insist that the police must refrain from arresting a person who is wanted for offences committed in this country when he arrives here simply because he is in transit to another country from where he could then be extradited.

'Balance' and ECtHR jurisprudence

'Fair balance'

1.108 Human rights case law is frequently couched in terms of 'striking a balance' between competing Convention rights (see, for example, *Evans v the United Kingdom*,[257] *Eweida and Others v the United Kingdom*[258]). In *Paulet v the UK*,[259] P complained that confiscation proceedings initiated against him under s 6 of the Proceeds of Crime Act 2002 (POCA) should have been stayed as an abuse of process. The trial judge accepted that P had paid all the tax and national insurance due on his earnings and that the money he had made from his employment had been truly earned. The ECtHR held that an interference with A1P1 will be disproportionate where the property owner concerned has had to bear 'an individual and excessive burden', such that 'the fair balance which should be struck between the protection of the right of property and the requirements of the general interest' is upset (see *Sporrong and Lönnroth v Sweden*[260]):[261]

> The striking of a fair balance depends on many factors (*AGOSI v. the United Kingdom*[262]). Although the second paragraph of Article 1 of Protocol No. 1 contains no explicit procedural requirements, the Court must consider whether the proceedings as a whole afforded the applicant a reasonable opportunity for putting his case to the competent authorities with a view to enabling them to establish a fair balance between the conflicting interests at stake (*AGOSI*[263]) ... and *Jokela v Finland*[264]).

1.109 In *Paulet v the UK*,[265] the ECtHR's reference to 'fair balance', needs to be seen (it is submitted) in the context of the wording of A1P1, which envisages cases where there can be competing interests.

---

[254] Three applicants sought to challenge the decisions of the police to arrest and to charge them, as well as the decision of the justices to hear the criminal proceedings, on grounds that included 'the decision directly or indirectly to cause the applicant's removal from Norway without recourse to extradition procedures, and thereby avoiding the safeguards for the applicant inherent in such procedures, caused the British authorities to act unlawfully such that the applicant's production before the justices amounted to an abuse of process'; and 'the procedures followed constituted a direct breach of the principles governing extradition and if condoned would render formal extradition arrangements otiose'.

[255] *R v Horseferry Rd Ct, Ex p Bennett* [1994] 1 A.C. 42.

[256] *Bennett v KM Advocate* 1995 SLT 510, p 518.

[257] No. 6339/05, § 77, ECHR 2007-I.

[258] [2013] ECHR 37.

[259] [2014] Lloyd's Rep FC 484; [2014] Crim LR 750.

[260] September 23, 1982, § 61, Series A no 52.

[261] Para 65 of the judgment.

[262] 24 October 1986, § 54, Series A no 108.

[263] October 26, 1986, § 54, Series A no 108.

[264] No. 28856/95, § 55, ECHR 2002-IV.

[265] [2014] Lloyd's Rep FC 484; [2014] Crim LR 750.

The courts have also spoken of 'striking the balance' between countervailing interests within, and between, other articles of the ECtHR (e.g., Articles 8 and 10): see, for example, the speeches of their Lordships in *Campbell v MGN Ltd.*,[266] in which both 'balance' and the 'weight' to be attached to relevant considerations, was considered by the Court. **1.110**

Article 6: unqualified rights for a fair trial, or a balancing exercise?

Article 6 appears to provide a set of unqualified rights for a fair trial. Although in some cases, steps can be taken to make fair a trial that would otherwise be unfair, in other cases, this may be impossible. At first sight, the judgment of the Supreme Court in *Maxwell* appears to support this interpretation of Article 6. It held that if it is impossible to give the accused a fair trial (the first category of abuse) the court 'will stay the proceedings without more. *No question of the balancing of competing interests arises.*' [Emphasis added][267] But is that a statement that accords with the reality of life in the criminal courts? Conceptually, fairness is binary: a state of affairs is either 'fair' or it is 'unfair'. However, the question of whether an accused's trial will be 'fair' (or not) is not always going to be answered merely by a consideration of the problem from the perspective of the accused. Is it 'fair' that a defendant stands trial on the basis of a witness statement (crucial to the outcome) which is to be read to the court but made by a witness who is no longer able to testify in person? Or, are wider considerations (including those of a complainant) to be taken into account? Issues of this sort are familiar to the courts. Can it really be said that 'balance' has not played a part in the formulation of principles that bear on the question of whether an accused can have a fair trial? **1.111**

In *O'Halloran and Francis v the United Kingdom*[268] the ECtHR has stated that the right to a fair trial under Article 6 'is an unqualified right', and yet, it went on to say that 'what constitutes a fair trial cannot be the subject of a single unvarying rule *but must depend on the circumstances of the particular case*'.[269] In *O'Halloran and Francis*, OH and F were the registered keepers of their respective motor vehicles which were caught on speed cameras driving in excess of the prescribed limit. A failure to provide information as to the identity of the driver was a criminal offence under section 172 of the Road Traffic Act 1988. Having been warned of this offence, OH admitted being the driver of his car, but F declined to do so and he was fined for that failure. The ECtHR found (by a majority) no violation of Article 6.1. **1.112**

The effect of section 172 of the 1988 Act had been decided by the Privy Council in *Brown v Stott*[270] and by the High Court in *Director of Public Prosecutions v Wilson*.[271] In *Brown v Stott*, the Privy Council held that the use of the admission did not infringe the requirements of Article 6 of the ECHR. Lord Bingham referred to 'the balance' between the interests of the community at large and the interests of the individual: **1.113**

> If, viewing this situation in the round, one asks whether section 172 represents a disproportionate legislative response to the problem of maintaining road safety, whether the balance between the interests of the community at large and the interests of the individual is struck in a manner unduly prejudicial to the individual, whether (in short) the leading of this evidence would infringe a basic human right of the respondent, I would feel bound to give negative answers.

In *O'Halloran and Francis*, the majority of the ECtHR endorsed the reasoning of Lord Bingham. The Court cited (among other cases) *Jalloh v Germany*,[272] which concerned the **1.114**

---

[266] [2004] UKHL 22.
[267] [2010] UKSC 48; per Lord Dyson JSC, at [13].
[268] (2008) 46 EHRR 21, [2007] ECHR 545.
[269] At para 53.
[270] [2001] 2 WLR 817.
[271] [2001] EWHC Admin 198.
[272] [2006] ECHR 721.

use of evidence in the form of drugs swallowed by the applicant, which had been obtained by the forcible administration of emetics. The Court said, in *Jalloh*, 'the weight of the public interest in the investigation and punishment of the particular offence in issue may be taken into consideration and be weighed against the individual interest that the evidence against him be gathered lawfully.'[273] However, the Court added:[274]

> ... public interest concerns cannot justify measures which extinguish the very essence of an applicant's defence rights, including the privilege against self-incrimination guaranteed by Article 6 of the Convention (see, *mutatis mutandis, Heaney and McGuinness v. Ireland*, no. 34720/97, §§ 57–58, ECHR 2000-XII).

1.115 But, it was societal interests—and the weight to be attached to them—that persuaded the Courts in *Brown v Stott* and in *O'Halloran and Francis* to conclude that there had been no violation of Article 6.1.

1.116 The decision of the majority in *O'Halloran and Francis* was strongly criticized by Judge Myjer (dissenting):

> In quoting and endorsing the views of Lord Bingham, the majority in fact also seem to play the 'public interest' card in the form of a rather tricky new criterion which was first stated in § 117 (but not in § 101) of *Jalloh v Germany* (no. 54810/00, ECHR 2006-IX) in order to determine whether the right not to incriminate oneself had been violated: 'the weight of the public interest in the investigation and punishment of the offence in issue'. This is, moreover, a new criterion, which is incompatible with the established case law that the use of incriminating statements obtained from the accused under compulsion in such a way as to extinguish the very essence of the right to remain silent cannot in principle be justified by reference to the public interest served.

1.117 Judge Pavlovschi, in his dissenting judgment, was no less critical [emphasis added]:

> In *Jalloh*, the Court adopted what appears to be a wholly new approach to self-incrimination. For the first time, it considered the following factors: (a) the nature and degree of compulsion used to obtain the evidence; (b) the weight of the public interest in the investigation and punishment of the offence in issue; (c) the existence of any relevant safeguards in the procedure; and (d) the use to which any material so obtained is put (see *Jalloh v Germany* [GC], no. 54810/00, §§ 117–21, ECHR 2006 IX).
>
> *The general requirements of fairness contained in Article 6, including the right not to incriminate oneself, apply to criminal proceedings in respect of all types of criminal offences without distinction, from the most simple to the most complex.* The public interest cannot be invoked to justify the use of answers compulsorily obtained in a non-judicial investigation to incriminate the accused during the trial proceedings (see *Saunders* ...[275]).

Agreeing to a rule socially beneficial: whether 'balancing' relevant

1.118 In *O'Halloran and Francis v the United Kingdom*,[276] Judge Borrego Borrego concurred with the majority that there was no violation of Article 6.1, but he did not agree with their approach or reasoning. For him, human rights are for the benefit of society as well as the individual. Accordingly, a person who has chosen to act in circumstances regulated by law (e.g. owning and driving a car) has agreed to comply with those laws. Put more elegantly than by the writer, the Judge said [author's emphasis added]:

---

273 [2006] ECHR 721, at [97].
274 [2006] ECHR 721, at [97].
275 *Saunders v the United Kingdom* (1996) 23 EHRR 313.
276 (2008) 46 EHRR 21, [2007] ECHR 545.

To my mind, the path chosen by the Court in the present judgment follows the individualist, sacrosanct approach which views human rights as abstract rights which are set in stone. According to this school of thought, human rights are not intended to enable the individual to live in society, but to place society at the service of the individual.

I do not share this view. Where human rights are concerned, we cannot and must not forget that, as far back as the French Revolution, the phrase used was 'rights of man and the citizen'. Humans are individuals but, as members of society, they become human citizens.

This obvious fact would have been a good reason for making the judgment shorter and clearer. *It would have been sufficient to say, in line with the approach adopted by the Privy Council [Brown v Stott] and others, that by owning and driving a motor car, the human citizen accepts the existence of the motor-vehicle regulations and undertakes to comply with them in order to be able to live as a member of society.* These regulations clearly entail certain responsibilities, which form the subject of the applications we have examined today. End of story.

1.119 The majority accepted that '[t]hose who choose to keep and drive motor cars can be taken to have accepted certain responsibilities and obligations as part of the regulatory regime relating to motor violations ...'[277] However, Judge Borrego Borrego's complaint was that attempts by the majority to contextualize earlier decisions of the ECtHR were not helpful, and only complicated matters. The issue in the case had less to do with 'balance' than requiring the citizen to honour the commitment that he or she had made to comply with the laws of the state.

1.120 But, how far does one take this approach? For example, anyone who chooses to run a company has accepted the responsibilities and obligations of doing so. If the law requires that person to answer questions under legal compulsion during a statutory investigation into corporate fraud (see s 432, s 434 of the Companies Act 1985), is it a violation of Article 6 of the ECHR for the prosecution to use at his trial the answers which he gave to investigators? The answer, according to *Saunders v the UK*,[278] appears to be in the affirmative.

G. 'Balancing': Conclusion

1.121 Perhaps the staunchest and most convincing critics of the 'balancing' metaphor are Ashworth and Redmayne in their work, 'The Criminal Process'.[279] However, their criticisms were expressed as the law stood in 2010—before the decisions of the Supreme Court in *Maxwell* and of the Board in *Warren*. That said, it is submitted that there remains force in their argument that if 'English courts and politicians are to continue to adopt the metaphor of 'balancing' ... they should at least move to a more rigorous and structured approach'.[280]

1.122 By way of a footnote to this topic, it should be noted that in cases where the issues are whether a defendant is 'unfit to plead' or (if so) whether he did the act charged, pursuant to ss 4, 4A of the Criminal Procedure (Insanity) Act 1964, the Court of Appeal held in *Kerr*[281] that 'the likelihood of an absolute discharge, and the lack of risk to the public are ... irrelevant to the question of stay for abuse', and it may not be appropriate to carry out a 'balancing exercise':

> Nor, in our judgment, is it appropriate, in relation to the sections 4 and 4A procedure, to conduct a balancing exercise ... taking account of the public interest in having serious

---

[277] (2008) 46 EHRR 21, [2007] ECHR 545, at [57].

[278] [1997] 23 EHRR 313, 1996-VI, [1998] 1 BCLC 362, [1996] ECHR 65.

[279] A Ashworth and M Redmayne, 'The Criminal Process' (4th edn, Oxford University Press 2010), pp 41–45, and pp 48–51.

[280] A Ashworth and M Redmayne, 'The Criminal Process'(4th edn, Oxford University Press 2010), p 50.

[281] [2002] 1 WLR 824 (medical practitioner charged on four counts of rape and fifteen counts of indecent assault).

allegations against medical practitioners investigated and hearing the complainant's allegations investigated in a public forum. All these factors are, no doubt, matters for the Crown Prosecution Service to consider when deciding whether to prosecute in the first place, or to pursue a prosecution, once started. The public interest in having serious allegations investigated is a factor behind the general principle that the power to order a stay should be exercised sparingly, even where there are proper, i e non-disability-related, grounds.[282]

1.123 There is no sign yet that the flow of complaints based on an abuse of process will soon abate.

---

[282] [2002] 1 WLR 824; per Rose LJ at [38].

2

PRE-CHARGE AND INVESTIGATION

A. Introduction

The power to stay criminal proceedings as an abuse of process is one of the checks and balances used by courts to remedy an abuse of executive power, which can occur during the investigative stage of a criminal case. This chapter will deal with the Police and Criminal Evidence Act 1984 (PACE), its Codes of Practice and the consequences of their breach, the role of the defence adviser, and a number of types of abuse of process that can occur at the police station. In the main, they concern the overriding of client privilege and breach of promise situations (including the use of cautions). **2.1**

PACE and the Codes of Practice

PACE and the eight Codes of Practice which the Secretary of State has issued[1] under the Act[2] regulate: **2.2**

(a) the exercise by police officers of their statutory power of stop and search of a person and vehicle (Part I of PACE and Code A);

---

[1] Codes A, B, E, F came into force in their current form on 27 October 2013 (see Police and Criminal Evidence Act 1984 (Codes of Practice) (Revisions to Code A, B, C, E, F and H) Order 2013 (SI 2013 No. 2685)); amendments necessary to transpose EU Directive 2012/13 on the right to information in criminal proceedings into UK law, resulted in revised Codes C and H which came into force on 2 June 2014 (see Police and Criminal Evidence Act 1984 (Codes of Practice) (Revisions to Codes C and H) Order (SI 2014 No.1237)); Code G on 12 November 2012 (see The Police and Criminal Evidence Act 1984 (Codes of Practice) (Revision of Codes C, G, and H) Order 2012 (SI 2012 No.1798)).

[2] Sections 66 and 67 PACE.

(b) the searching of premises by police officers and the seizure of property found on persons or premises (Part II of PACE and Code B);

(c) the detention, treatment, and questioning of persons in police custody (Parts IV and V of PACE and Code C);

(d) identification procedures available to police (Code D);

(e) interviewing suspects under caution by way of tape recorded interview (Code E);

(f) video recording of interviews (Code F);

(g) arrest powers (Part III of PACE and Code G);

(h) the detention of suspects under the Terrorism Act 2000 (Code H).

Arrest powers

2.3   The necessity criteria for lawful arrest is set out in Code G paras 2.4–2.9. Code G makes it clear that an arrest must be 'fully justified'. Arguably, if the arrest is arbitrary, unmerited or unfair, then an abuse of process application may follow. Such an application, of course, should only follow if no other remedy exists and there may be a proportionality point to be argued.[3]

2.4.   Applying the necessity criteria should require the police to justify why a person needs to be taken to a police station. It should, for example, prevent children or those requiring appropriate adults from being detained for extended periods simply to facilitate the provision of an appropriate adult. When required, the role of the police station adviser should be to remind the police of the necessity test (particularly in cases where the person attends for a voluntary interview) and challenge whether the arrest itself was justified[4] and whether any subsequent detention is necessary.[5]

2.5.   Regard should also be had to Code C of PACE[6] which allows those detained at a police station (or their legal representative) the right to access essential materials which may help them to challenge the lawfulness of their arrest or detention. Such materials are essential if they would undermine the need to keep the suspect in custody.[7] This requirement also applies where an officer proposes to extend detention without charge. Where the police intend to apply for a warrant of further detention, such documents and materials must be made available before the hearing.[8] This requirement also applies where a suspect is remanded in custody following charge.[9]

Breach of PACE codes

2.6   Any action by the police which amounts to a breach of major provisions of the Codes of Practice is arguably an abuse of executive power which taints the fairness of proceedings. However, a distinction needs to be made between minor breaches and substantial breaches. It is unlikely that a court will entertain an abuse argument for a minor breach of PACE codes.

2.7   Furthermore, in certain circumstances, misconduct or impropriety by the police may have been 'so unworthy or shameful' that it would be an affront to the public conscience to allow any

---

[3] Consider, for example, Article 5 ECHR and see Code G paras 1.2 and 1.3.

[4] Section 24 PACE. For discussion of the necessity requirement see *Richardson v The Chief Constable of West Midlands Police* [2011] EWHC 773 (QB).

[5] Section 37 PACE.

[6] Which came into force on 2 June 2014.

[7] Code C 2014, paragraphs 3.2(v), 3.4(b), 3.26, and Guidance Notes 3ZA (a) and (b).

[8] Code C 2014, paragraphs 15.0 and 15.7A(c).

[9] Code C 2014, paragraph 16.7A.

prosecution to proceed, as per *R v Horseferry Road Magistrates' Court ex p Bennett*[10] (category two abuse) and considered by the Privy Council in *Warren and others v Attorney General of Jersey*.[11]

Sections 76 and 78 PACE as a remedy

PACE sets out its own remedy for breaches of the codes, by permitting the exclusion of **2.8** any evidence obtained as a consequence of a breach, under sections 76 and 78. Although these sections are frequently used, it is nonetheless helpful to be reminded of the statutory protections provided by PACE in order to see what abuses are left to be covered by a stay of proceedings, or can overlap with an argument to exclude.

Section 76[12] provides protection against so called 'confession evidence' which has been **2.9** obtained in oppressive circumstances. Section 76(2) provides:

> If, in any proceedings where the prosecution proposes to give in evidence a confession made by an accused person, it is represented to the court that the confession was or may have been obtained –
> (a) by oppression of the person who made it; or
> (b) in consequence of anything said or done which was likely, under circumstances existing at the time, to render unreliable any confession which might be made by him in consequence thereof.

> The court shall not allow the confession to be given in evidence against him except in so far as the prosecution proves to the court beyond reasonable doubt that the confession (notwithstanding that it may be true) was not obtained as aforesaid.[13]

Similarly, section 78 provides for exclusion of 'unfair evidence': **2.10**

> In any proceedings the court may refuse to allow evidence on which the prosecution proposes to rely to be given if it appears to the court that, having regard to all the circumstances, including the circumstances in which the evidence was obtained, the admission of the evidence would have such an adverse effect on the fairness of the proceedings that the court ought not to admit it.

It is a wide protection and is commonly used to exclude evidence which has been obtained in **2.11** breach of the Codes of Practice. However, evidential exclusion is not automatic where there has been a breach of PACE or the Codes.[14] The breach should be significant and substantial before evidence is excluded.[15] It is the nature of the breach that is important.[16]

When considering whether there are 'exceptional circumstances' to stay criminal proceedings **2.12** as an abuse, it is also important to remember that the power should be exercised only if there is no alternative course. Sections 76 and 78 PACE provide an alternative remedy by allowing for the exclusion of evidence obtained improperly (by oppression or in breach of PACE) during the investigative process.

---

[10] *R v Horseferry Road Magistrates' Court ex p Bennett* [1994] 1 AC 42.
[11] *Curtis Francis Warren and others v Her Majesty's Attorney General of the Bailiwick of Jersey* [2011] UKPC 10, [2012] 1AC 22; as followed and approved by the New Zealand Supreme Court decision in *Max John Beckham v The Queen* [2015] NZSC 98.
[12] See also section 76A PACE (added by section 128 CJA 2003) which deals with the admission of co-accused confession evidence (see *Johnson* (2007) 171 JP 574) and section 77 PACE which deals with confessions by mentally handicapped persons (see *Lamont* [1989] Crim LR 813; *Moss* (1990) 91 Cr App R 371).
[13] For examples see *Doolan* [1988] Crim LR 747; *Chung* (1991) 92 Cr App R 314; *Waters* [1989] Crim LR 62; *DPP v Blake* [1989] 1 WLR 432; *Moss* (1990) 91 Cr App R 371; *Morse* [1991] Crim LR 195.
[14] *Walsh* (1990) 91 Cr App R 161.
[15] *Williams* [2012] EWCA Crim 264; *Delaney* (1989) 88 Cr App R 338; *Absalom* [1989] 88 Cr App R 332; *Quinn* [1990] Crim LR 581; *Keenan* [1990] 2 QB 54; *Coelho* [2008] EWCA Crim 627.
[16] *Sparks* [1991] Crim LR 128; *Stewart* [1995] Crim LR 499.

2.13 Where the trial judge wrongly allows such evidence to be admitted, it can be the subject of successful appeal.[17] It is clear that many abuses of process occur during the investigative stage of criminal proceedings, but the majority of these can be, and often are, remedied elsewhere in the trial procedure and do not therefore give rise to an application to stay.

B. Unfairness during Detention

2.14 Where unfairness occurs while a suspect is in detention that is sufficient to give rise to a claim for abuse of process, there is no power to remedy the abuse during the investigative stage.[18] The remedies afforded at common law and under article 6 of the ECHR are court-based. A legal representative at the police station concerned about the fairness of the investigative procedure cannot apply for a 'stay' of the investigation. However, an application for habeas corpus[19] should be considered if it is believed that the detention is unlawful. Examples of when detention becomes unlawful include where the statutory limit on detention without charge has been exceeded,[20] or where the grounds upon which detention was authorized cease to exist. A common example of the latter is where detention has been authorized solely for the purpose of conducting an interview under caution but the suspect, or his legal adviser has been informed beforehand that he either will, or 'may be prosecuted for' the offence(s) under investigation. Paragraph 16.5 of Code C states, inter alia, that:

> A detainee may not be interviewed about an offence after they have been charged with, or informed they may be prosecuted for it, unless the interview is necessary:
> • to prevent or minimise harm or loss to some other person, or the public
> • to clear up an ambiguity in a previous answer or statement
> • in the interests of justice for the detainee to have put to them, and have an opportunity to comment on, information concerning the offence which has come to light *since they were charged or informed they might be prosecuted* (emphasis added).

2.15 In any case where this occurs and the exceptions under para 16.5 above are not properly made out then the defence adviser may and, unless instructed that the person consents to an interview,[21] should raise an objection both to the interview and further detention with a custody officer. An application for habeas corpus can be made at this stage in the event that police refuse release from custody, or charge without further interview.

C. Police Misconduct during an Investigation

2.16 Police reprehensible behavior during an investigation is ordinarily dealt with within the trial process, by application to exclude evidence and/or by cross-examination. In the

---

[17] See *Samuel* [1988] QB 615, in which evidence of a confession in interview should have been excluded where the defendant was 'unfairly' deprived of his section 58 PACE right to legal advice. See also *Alladice* (1988) 87 Cr App R 380; *McGovern* (1991) 92 Cr App R 228; *Murray v UK* (1996) 22 EHRR 29; *Aspinall* [1999] 2 Cr App R 115; and *HM Advocate v G (Ambrose v Harris)* [2011] UKSC 43, where there was found to be a violation of Article 6(3)(c) of the ECHR.

[18] Only in the very rarest of cases, where there is no prospect of an eventual prosecution, will a court intervene to prevent an abuse of process before a suspect has been formally charged: see *R(C) v Chief Constable of A* [2006] EWHC 2352 (Admin).

[19] Civil Procedure Rules 1998 (as amended), Part 87—Applications for Writ of Habeas Corpus.

[20] Sections 41–43 of PACE 1984.

[21] If the detainee does consent to an interview then the caution differs from the standard one. It is, '*You do not have to say anything, but anything you do say may be given in evidence.*' Code C 16.5 (a).

case of *Heston-Francois*[22] there was an application to stay proceedings as an abuse after officers searched a defendant's home and removed files of documents prepared for his defence to charges of burglary. Some of those documents were shown to prosecution witnesses. The application for a stay was refused by the trial judge. The appeal court, in dismissing the defendant's appeal, found the police conduct to be reprehensible; however, such conduct could be dealt with in the trial itself and was not therefore a misuse of the court's process.

D. Role of the Defence Adviser

The defence adviser at the police station has an important role to play in protecting the rights **2.17** of a suspect. What happens at a police station has important consequences for any subsequent court proceedings.[23] At all times when representing suspects at the police station, the defence adviser should approach the process not in isolation but with regard to the first day of trial and use that perception to inform their dealings with police and the client. If a suspect is prosecuted, it is likely that much of what takes place will form part of the evidence at trial. It is not the purpose of this text to outline in full that role or advise on appropriate procedures and tactics;[24] however, the following points are noteworthy.

Taking instructions

The defence adviser must be alive to the need to explore the circumstances of the alleged **2.18** offence and their client's circumstances. This should be achieved by taking instructions from the client before interview and through keeping a full record of that information. This will inform not only their advice on whether to answer questions but also any representations that may need to be made by the adviser during interview under caution with a view to either avoiding a charge being brought, or laying the groundwork for a later application to stay proceedings. There may be relevant circumstances that are not immediately apparent from any disclosure provided about the offence, for example, in cases where victims of human trafficking are questioned as suspects.[25]

Making representations during a tape-recorded interview is one method of avoiding any later **2.19** dispute about what information the police were on notice of and should be considered by a prosecutor when applying the Full Code Test.[26]

Securing disclosure

The police station defence adviser should seek to obtain as much information as possi- **2.20** ble, from every available source in the police station, including the custody record, the custody sergeant and other custody staff, the police doctor if appropriate, the officer in the case, and interviewing officer, if different. All such information should be properly

---

[22] [1984] 1 QB 278.

[23] 'Most cases are won or lost at the police station rather than at court'. Ed Cape, *Defending Suspects at the Police Station* (6th edn, Legal Action Group 2011).

[24] Ed Cape, *Defending Suspects at Police Stations,* (6th edn, Legal Action Group 2011).

[25] *CL, HVN, THN, HDT* [2013] EWCA Crim 991, [2014] 1 All ER 113; *LM, MB, DG, BT, YT v The Queen* [2010] EWCA Crim 2327; *N* [2012] EWCA Crim 189; *O* [2011] EWCA Crim 2226; and Article 26 of the Council of Europe Convention on Action against Trafficking in Human Beings 2005. Note: the defence adviser must ensure that they take instructions before advising on the law and particularly any available *defence(s)*, so as to avoid influencing their clients' instructions, or tailoring them.

[26] The Director's Guidance On Charging 2013, (5th edn, May 2013), (Revised Arrangements).

recorded by the adviser. Inadequate or deliberately misleading disclosure[27] may amount to an abuse.

2.21 The general rule has hitherto been that the investigator is under no obligation to disclose the prosecution case or evidence of a prima facie case, to the suspect or their legal representative before questioning begins.[28] However, there may be scope for this to change, possibly significantly, following the implementation of EU Directive 2012/13/EU[29] into UK law on 2 June 2014, which resulted in revisions to Code C of PACE. Article 7(1) of the Directive places a duty on Member States to

> ensure that documents related to the specific case in the possession of the competent authorities which are essential to challenging effectively, in accordance with national law, the lawfulness of the arrest or detention, are made available to arrested persons or to their lawyers.

Article 7(2) places a duty on States to

> ensure that access is granted at least to all material evidence in the possession of the competent authorities, whether for or against suspects or accused persons, to those persons or their lawyers in order to safeguard the fairness of the proceedings and to prepare the defence.

2.22 The scope of disclosure will vary widely from case to case but the responsibility rests with the investigating officer to make documents available to the custody officer, having regard to the nature and volume of the documents and materials involved. Given that an arrest and subsequent detention is only lawful if there are reasonable grounds for suspecting that an offence has been committed by the suspect, the adviser should in every case check the custody record to ensure that the fact of disclosure being made has been recorded[30] and exercise the right to disclosure of the material as afforded by paragraphs 3.2 (a) and 3.4 (b) of Code C. If insufficient disclosure, or no disclosure has been made then the adviser should complain and have the matter referred to an inspector (paragraph 3.26 Code C).

2.23 Search warrants should be requested, disclosed, and considered by the adviser to ensure that any material which forms the basis for detention for interview has been seized lawfully.[31]

2.24 The search warrant application should be checked for its accuracy and the following must be clear on the application:

- The grounds on which the application is being made
- The statutory provision relied upon
- The address of the premise to be entered and searched, including the parts of any multiple premises
- So far as practicable the articles or persons sought.

---

[27] *Mason* [1988] 1 WLR 139.

[28] *Farrell* [2004] EWCA Crim 597.

[29] Council Directive 2012/13/EU of 22 May 2012 on the Right to Information in Criminal Proceedings [2012] OJ L142/1.

[30] Paragraph 3.4 (b) Code C PACE.

[31] It is important for search warrant applications to contain full and frank disclosure, with detailed information. In *Tchenguiz v Director of Serious Fraud Office and Others* [2012] EWHC 2254 (Admin), the SFO obtained search warrants 'by misrepresentation and non-disclosure' to the Judge. If the SFO had 'properly presented' the evidence then they would not have obtained the search warrants. In *Sweeney v Westminster Magistrates Court* [2014] EWHC 2068 (Admin) the search warrant unlawful as it failed to comply with ss 8 and 15 PACE 1984 and failed to identify as far as practicable the articles being sought. In *R(El-Kurd) v Winchester Crown Court* [2012] Crim LR 138 the court considered whether it could authorize retention of property seized under an unlawful warrant, Criminal Justice and Police Act 2001 s 59(6).

An applicant must provide all information so that a magistrate or a judge can make an **2.25** informed decision. Full and frank disclosure of information should be made by the applicant including representations which could be made by the defendant.[32]

The courts treat applications for, and the granting of, search warrants seriously.[33] Investigators **2.26** need to be able to rely upon statutory or common law authorization to justify the lawfulness of any search, seizure, and retention of items.

The applicant for a search warrant has a duty to ensure the information put before the issuing **2.27** tribunal is clear, comprehensive, accurate, and complete. Incomplete warrants[34] and those drawn too widely[35] may be set aside by the courts. The case for reasonable suspicion must be made out and matters that might undermine that case included.

The need for care and precision in framing warrant applications is highlighted in *R(AB, CD)* **2.28** *v Huddersfield Magistrates' Court & the Chief Constable of West Yorkshire Police*[36] in which Mr Justice Stuart-Smith observed:[37]

> Each application must be carefully and precisely formulated so as to satisfy both the statutory requirements and the duty of full and frank disclosure; and a decision to issue may only be taken after that level of critical scrutiny that is required when the court is asked to sanction a substantial invasion of fundamental rights.

Advising on disclosure

Without adequate disclosure, the job of advising the suspect whether to answer questions **2.29** or maintain the suspect's right to silence is difficult, if not impossible. Court of Appeal cases[38] on adverse inferences show that limited disclosure by the police may be a reasonable ground for the suspect to remain silent, depending on the circumstances of the case and whether the decision to remain silent was reasonable.[39] Where police provide little or no information about the case against a suspect, so that the defence adviser cannot usefully advise the client, a suspect may avoid an adverse inference at trial, following legal advice to stay silent.[40] If a defendant wishes the court not to draw an adverse inference, the defendant or solicitor may have to go further and state the basis or the reason for that advice.[41]

In cases of perceived insufficiency of disclosure the adviser may wish to state on tape at the **2.30** start of the interview what disclosure has been provided by police and whether sufficient disclosure, if any, has been made in accordance with Code C of PACE.

The ECtHR has said that the fact that an accused has been advised by his lawyer to remain **2.31** silent must be given appropriate weight by the domestic court as there may be a good reason

---

[32] See *Re Stanford International Bank Ltd* [2010] EWCA Civ 137, [2011] Ch 33.

[33] See *R(Redknapp) v Commissioner of the City of London Police* [2008] EWHC 1177 (Admin), [2009] 1 WLR 2091; *R(Golfrate Property Management Ltd) v Southwark Crown* [2014] EWHC 840 (Admin).

[34] *R(Global Cash & Carry Ltd) v Birmingham Magistrates' Court* [2013] EWHC 528 (Admin).

[35] *R(Hoque) v City of London Magistrates' Court* [2013] EWHC 725 (Admin); *Lees v Solihull Magistrates' Court* [2013] EWHC 3779 (Admin), [2014] Lloyd's Rep FC 233.

[36] [2014] EWHC 1089 (Admin).

[37] At [13].

[38] *Condron and Condron* [1997] 1 Cr App R 185; *Argent* [1997] 2 Cr App R 27; *Dervish* [2002] 2 Cr App R 6.

[39] *Beckles* [2005] 1 All ER 705.

[40] *Roble* [1997] Crim LR 449. See also *Beard* [2002] Crim LR 684.

[41] *Condron and Condron* [1997] 1 Cr App R 185.

for that advice;[42] one such reason being 'bona fide advice from his lawyer'.[43] Notwithstanding legal advice, an adverse inference may still be drawn against a defendant.

2.32 If the defence adviser advises the client not to answer police questions, because proper disclosure has not taken place, the adviser may, following consultation with the suspect, say something expressly for the record, although in doing so there may be a 'waiver of privilege' problem.[44] Where a defence adviser expressly states the reason why a suspect is going to remain silent, such a statement is admissible in evidence.[45]

Keeping records

2.33 It is important that defence advisers keep a full, contemporaneous record of their police station attendance for use in subsequent abuse of process arguments in court. Such notes can assist the defence evidentially in proving unfairness flowing from police error, omission, or misconduct. The importance of proper record keeping cannot be overstated. As noted above, 'in considering a stay application the [court] must make full inquiry into the procedural history of the case.'[46]

E. Abuse of Process in the Police Station: Overriding Client Privilege

2.34 The first type of abuse to be considered in relation to the police station is the police overriding solicitor–suspect client privilege.

2.35 A lawyer advising at the police station is subject to the rules governing client confidentiality.[47] This is a professional duty, which can be overridden only in certain specified circumstances.[48]

2.36 Legal professional privilege by contrast covers communications between an adviser and their client, made for the purpose of enabling the client to obtain, or the adviser to give, legal advice. Where communication is privileged, neither the police nor a court can force the adviser or client to divulge the communication.[49] Only the client can waive privilege. The client must be sure that what the client says to the defence lawyer is in confidence and will not be disclosed without the defendant's consent.[50]

2.37 The police cannot force disclosure of information covered by legal professional privilege. Police station advisers must never volunteer such information, or confidential information without their client's express consent. In practice, it is rare for the police to attempt directly to obtain such material, although it may happen covertly if an adviser is careless enough to leave such material in a non-secure location when at the police station. Terrorism

---

[42] *Condron v United Kingdom* (2001) 31 EHRR 1.

[43] *Averill v United Kingdom* (2001) 31 EHRR 36.

[44] *Bowden* [1999] 4 All ER 43.

[45] *Fitzgerald* [1998] 4 *Archbold News* 2, CA (97/2011/W5).

[46] *R v Crawley Justices ex p DPP The Times*, 5 April 1991.

[47] 'You [must] keep the affairs of *clients* confidential unless disclosure is required or permitted by law or the *client* consents'. Outcome 4(1), Solicitor's Regulation Authority Code of Conduct, 2011.

[48] See Chapter 4 of the Solicitor's Regulation Authority Code of Conduct.

[49] *R v Manchester Crown Court, ex p Rogers* [1999] 4 All ER 35, [1999] Crim LR 743.

[50] The importance of legal professional privilege is emphasized in *R v Derby Magistrates' Court, ex p B* [1996] AC 487, in which Lord Chief Justice Taylor states at p 507: '... The client must be sure that what he tells his lawyer in confidence will never be revealed without his consent. Legal professional privilege is thus more than an ordinary rule of evidence, limited in its application to the facts of a particular case. It is a fundamental condition on which the administration of justice as a whole rests'.

investigations could also result in potentially improper attempts to procure information from advisers.[51]

However if there are sufficient grounds for believing that a legal conference is being misused— **2.38**
for instance to perpetrate crime[52]—then surveillance by state agencies is justified.[53] This is on
the basis that the meeting was not one to which legal professional privilege applied because
the proper and lawful basis for the confidential meeting was vitiated by the illegal purpose or
objective. In those circumstances the privilege would not exist.[54]

Eavesdropping on a solicitor's consultation

The courts jealously protect legally privileged communications. One striking example is the **2.39**
Court of Appeal's treatment of eavesdropping in *Grant*,[55] where police covertly listened to
and tape recorded privileged conversations that took place between the defendant and his
solicitor in the police station exercise yard. In quashing the appellant's conviction for conspiracy to murder, the Court of Appeal observed that deliberate eavesdropping upon legally privileged communications was unlawful and capable of infecting the proceedings as an abuse of
the court's process.

Although it was the reprehensible conduct of the police, per se, that led to the conviction **2.40**
being quashed, the appeal courts finding in *Grant* was inextricably linked with the need
to protect legal professional privilege. Commenting on the decision in *Grant*, Professor
Ormerod observed:

> Acts done by the police, in the course of an investigation which led in due course to the
> institution of criminal proceedings, with a view to eavesdropping upon communications of
> suspected persons which were the subject of legal professional privilege were categorically
> unlawful and were so great an affront to the integrity of the justice system, and therefore the
> rule of law, that the associated prosecution was rendered abusive and ought not to be coun-
> tenanced by the court. In that regard, it was clear that the jurisprudence of the ECtHR[56]
> marched with the common law as to the importance attached to legal professional privilege ...
> As for prejudice in such circumstances, it was a particular vice of the police misconduct that
> the court could not know whether it had in fact yielded fruit in the form of evidence, whether
> directly or indirectly, without enquiry as to what the cover surveillance had revealed: but
> such an enquiry would force the defendant to waive privileged information, thereby further
> violating his right to legal professional privilege.[57]

In short, the deliberate interference with a detained suspect's right to the confidence of privileged **2.41**
communications with his solicitor seriously undermined the rule of law and justified a stay on

---

[51] See section 38B Terrorism Act 2000 and the Law Society's Practice Note on 'Anti-Terrorism', 24
October 2011.
[52] Communication to commit crime per *Cox and Railton* (1884) 14 QBD 153; *Barclays Bank v Eustice*
[1995] 1 WLR 1238.
[53] See Regulation of Investigatory Powers Act 2000 and decision in *McE v Prison Service of Northern
Ireland* [2009] UKHL 15.
[54] See also *Edward Brown* [2015] EWCA Crim 1328 in the context of trial courtroom legal conferences,
in which Fulford J (at [54]) cites, with approval, Recommendation (2006) 2 of the Council of Europe
Committee of Ministers to member states on the European Prison Rules: '23.5 A judicial authority may in
exceptional circumstances authorise restrictions on such confidentiality to prevent serious crime or major
breaches of prison safety and security'.
[55] [2005] EWCA Crim 1089, [2006] QB 60. See commentary by Professor David Ormerod and others
[2005] Crim LR 955. See also Nick Taylor, 'Abuse of Process: Covert Surveillance and Legal Professional
Privilege' [2006] 4 Journal of Criminal Law 2006, 282.
[56] See *Lanz v Austria* App no 24430/94 (ECtHR, 31 January 2002); *S v Switzerland* (1992) 14 EHRR
670; *Niemitz v Germany* (1992) 16 EHRR 97 [37]; *Brennan v UK* (2001) 34 EHRR 507.
[57] See Commentary by Professor Ormerod on *Grant* in [2005] Crim LR 955 at 956.

the grounds of abuse, notwithstanding the absence of prejudice to the defendant. The suspect is entitled to receive legal advice in private (as per section 58 PACE).

Eavesdropping on suspect

2.42 There is a clear distinction to be drawn between eavesdropping on a suspect, on one hand, and eavesdropping on a client/solicitor consultation on the other. The former is done using a listening device [58] or another prisoner to interrogate the suspect and is not regarded as an abuse. [59] The latter has been found to be an abuse.

2.43 In *Sutherland,* [60] the Lincolnshire Police were investigating a murder and had arrested a number of suspects. Whilst the suspects were detained in police custody, the police recorded privileged conversations between the suspects and their solicitors. They sought to withhold this covert 'eavesdropping' from the defence on the grounds of public interest immunity, but without success. The trial judge, Mr Justice Newman, found the police conduct to be 'reprehensible and unlawful', and a violation 'so serious that considerations as to whether any of the accused had been prejudiced were immaterial'. The fact that there had been a deliberate interference with the right to legal advice was sufficient to prevent a fair trial, and the prosecution of all five accused was stayed as an abuse of process.

2.44 *Sutherland* was one of a number of cases involving 'bugging' at the same police station. A second case *Grant* [61] was not stayed and the point was argued on appeal.

2.45 In *Grant*, it was held on appeal that deliberate interference with a detained suspect's right to the confidence of privileged communications with his solicitor seriously undermined the rule of law and justified a stay on grounds of an abuse of process (contrary to the trial judge's view), notwithstanding the absence of any actual prejudice to the defence.

2.46 In cases such as *Grant* the emphasis of the court is on whether the moral integrity of the criminal process is undermined. This is viewed in terms of a doctrine of 'serious fault abuse', as per Lord Steyn's approach in *Latif:* [62]

> When encountering considerations of policy and justice, it is for the judge in the exercise of his discretion to decide whether there has been an abuse of process, which amounts to an affront to the public conscience and requires the criminal proceedings to be stayed.

2.47 The exercise of discretion in this instance involves finding a balance between the competing public interests of ensuring that those charged with grave crimes are tried whilst the courts do not convey the impression that the end was justified by the means. The Court of Appeal in *Grant* emphasized in particular the covert nature of the activity and the nature of the police officer's conduct which 'infected' the investigation to such an extent that to proceed was an abuse of process.

2.48 However, *Grant* was deemed wrong by the Privy Council decision in *Curtis Warren and others v Her Majesty's Attorney General of the Bailwick of Jersey,* [63] as serious prosecutorial misconduct will not, in certain cases, tip the balance in favour of a stay. As Lord Dyson observed: [64]

---

[58] *Wood v UK* [2004] Po LR 326; *Mason* [2002] Crim LR 841; *Perry (Stephen Arthur) The Times,* 28 April 2000.

[59] *Allan* [2005] Crim LR 716.

[60] Unreported, 29 January 2002.

[61] [2006] QB 60, [2005] Crim LR 955.

[62] [1996] 1 WLR 104 [112], [1999] Crim LR 561, and see commentary on *Grant* by Professor Ormerod in [2005] Crim LR 955.

[63] [2011] UKPC 10 per Lord Dyson [27]–[37].

[64] *Warren* at [30].

The Board does not consider that the 'but for' test will always or even in most cases necessarily determine whether a stay should be granted on the grounds of abuse of process.

He continued:[65]

> ... the Board respectfully considers that the decision in Grant was wrong. The statement at paragraph 54 suggests that the deliberate invasion of a suspected person's right to legal professional privilege is to be assimilated to the abduction and entrapment cases where the balancing exercise will generally lead to a stay of the proceedings. The Board agrees that the deliberate invasion by the police of a suspect's right to legal professional privilege is a serious affront to the integrity of the justice system which may often lead to the conclusion that the proceedings should be stayed. But the particular circumstances of each case must be considered and carefully weighed in the balance. It was obviously right to hold on the facts in Grant that the gravity of the misconduct was a factor which militated in favour of a stay.

In *Warren*, police had misled the authorities of Jersey and three foreign states by placing listening and tracking devices in the defendants' vehicles. Absent the evidence acquired from these tactics, no prosecution would have taken place. Nonetheless, there were factors which, taken cumulatively, weighed heavily against a stay, including the infamy of the defendant, the seriousness of the offence, the fact that there had been no attempt to mislead the court, and the urgency of the police actions. The Privy Council later stated that however grave the case, there can be a point when the court's sense of justice and impropriety is offended. **2.49**

The Privy Council in *Warren* stressed, in the judgment of Lord Dyson, that: **2.50**

> the balance must always be struck between the public interest in ensuring that those who are accused of serious crimes should be tried and the competing public interest in ensuring that executive misconduct does not undermine public confidence in the criminal justice system and bring it into disrepute.[66]

Lord Dyson's judgment was cited with approval by Mr Justice O'Regan in the Supreme Court of New Zealand decision of *Max John Beckham v The Queen*.[67] The *Warren* approach was approved by Mr Justice O'Regan as being nuanced: **2.51**

> taking into account a number of factors such as seriousness of the violation of the defendant's rights, the presence or absence of bad faith, whether there was any emergency or necessity for the conduct, other available sanctions, the seriousness of the charges and the causal link between the conduct and the trial or proposed trial.[68]

Human rights

When considering communications within the police station it is also important to consider the human rights provisions in the European Convention on Human Rights (ECHR) and elsewhere. **2.52**

Communications between defence adviser and suspect are protected by ECHR Articles 6(3)(c) (an accused's right to legal assistance) and Article 8 (right to privacy). In general such communications should be private and confidential[69] because: **2.53**

> [A]n accused's right to communicate with his advocate out of the hearing of a third person is one of the basic requirements of a fair trial in a democratic society and follows from

---

[65] *Warren* at [36].
[66] *Warren* at [26].
[67] [2015] NZSC 98 at [142].
[68] [2015] NZSC 98 at [142].
[69] *Schonenberger and Durmaz v Switzerland* (1989) 11 EHRR 202 and *S v Switzerland* (1989) 11 EHRR 202.

article 6(3)(c) of the Convention. If a lawyer were unable to confer with his client and receive confidential instructions from him without such surveillance his assistance would lose much of its usefulness, whereas the ECHR is intended to guarantee rights that are practical and effective.[70]

Rule 22 of the UN Basic Principles on the Role of Lawyers[71] also states:

Governments shall recognise and respect that all communications and consultations between lawyers and their clients within their professional relationship are confidential.

The Strasbourg Court has, on a number of occasions, emphasized the importance that attaches to confidentiality between lawyer and client[72] and the importance of an accused being able to confer with his advocate in private.[73] It should be noted, however, that in spite of this, in *Ocalan v Turkey*, the ECtHR ruled[74] that the Turkish government had been entitled to impose 'legitimate restrictions' on prisoners convicted of terrorist activities in so far as they were strictly necessary to protect society against violence. The Court found that the authorities had been justified in recording confidential meetings between Ocalan and his lawyers.

Legal professional privilege and Regulation of Investigatory Powers Act 2000

2.54 In addition to *Warren,* the Lincolnshire cases must now also be read in conjunction with the House of Lords decision in *Re McE v Prison Service of Northern Ireland* and *C and M v Chief Constable of the Police Service of Northern Ireland*,[75] which considered two questions of general importance:

(1) What impact, if any, does the Regulation of Investigatory Powers Act 2000 ('RIPA') have on the common law right of legal professional privilege ('LPP')?
(2) What impact, if any, does RIPA have on the right accorded by a number of statutory provisions of a person detained in a police station or in prison to consult a lawyer privately?

2.55 The House of Lords decided that the covert surveillance provisions of Part II RIPA 2000 apply to electronic surveillance, carried out by the police, of conversations between lawyers and their suspect client, in police stations and prisons, which are ordinarily protected by legal professional privilege and the suspects right to consult privately with a lawyer (under section 58 PACE).[76]

2.56 Covert directed surveillance of such privileged conversations breached the suspect's Article 8 right to privacy, as it was disproportionate and because the level of authorization required for intrusive surveillance had not been put in place. Until an order was passed treating such

---

[70] *S v Switzerland* (1992) 14 EHRR 670 [48]. See also *Brennan v United Kingdom* (2002) 34 EHRR 18.

[71] The UN General Assembly included the Basic Principles in their 'Human rights in the administration of justice' resolution, adopted without a vote on 18 December 1990.

[72] See *Huvig v France* (1990) 12 EHRR 528 and *Kruslin v France* (1990) 12 EHRR 547. The ECtHR recognized the importance of the principle that telephone tapping had to be carried out in such a way that the exercise of the rights of the defence could not be jeopardized, and that the confidentiality of the relations between the suspect or the person accused and his lawyer was respected, as did the lawyer's duty of professional confidentiality. The importance of protecting this professional confidentiality was emphasized in *Kopp v Switzerland* (1999) 27 EHRR 91.

[73] *S v Switzerland* (1991) 14 EHRR 670.

[74] *Ocalan v Turkey (No.2)* App no 24069/03 (ECtHR, 18 March 2014).

[75] [2009] UKHL 15, [2009] 1 AC 908. See also Marney Requa, 'Defence rights in the shadow of RIPA: Covert surveillance of privileged consultations after Re McE', [2009] 4 Archbold News 6.

[76] *Re McE* [2009] UKHL 15 per Lord Phillips at [35]: '... that regulation of the way in which surveillance interacts with LPP fell within the ambit of RIPA and could properly be addressed by the Code'. See also per Lord Hope at [60]: 'The Secretary of State now accepts that directed surveillance of legal consultations in detention should be treated as intrusive surveillance for the purposes of prior authorisation under Part II of RIPA'.

surveillance as intrusive surveillance, any directed surveillance of legal consultations in the police station and prisons would be unlawful.[77]

The House of Lords recognized that LLP is a fundamental human right long established in **2.57** the common law, it being a necessary corollary of the right of any person to obtain skilled advice about the law. Such advice cannot be effectively obtained unless the client is able to put all the facts before the adviser without fear that they may afterwards be disclosed and used to his prejudice.[78] It is an important part of the right of privacy guaranteed by Article 8 ECHR.[79] However, consultations or communications between a lawyer and his client that are in furtherance of crime or fraud are not protected by LPP.[80] Lord Phillips observed that:[81]

[26] … the statutory right to consult a lawyer privately as one that confers on the detainee an absolute right to privacy that precludes covert surveillance in any circumstances.

The relevant Strasbourg case law does not produce an absolute prohibition on covert surveillance.

[27] … So far as article 6 is concerned, surveillance on communications between lawyer and client will not necessarily interfere with the absolute right to a fair trial. So far as article 8 is concerned, the issue is whether interference can be justified under article 8(2)[82]

On the question whether RIPA impacted on the express section 58 PACE right for a person **2.58** detained to consult a lawyer privately, Lord Phillips disagreed with the majority of the House of Lords. He observed:[83]

[36] The statutory right of a detainee to consult a lawyer privately was an important one. Just how important it was in the eyes of the courts is evident from the reaction of the Court of Appeal in R v Grant [2006] QB 60. Listening devices placed in the exercise yard resulted in the recording of conversations between Grant and his lawyers. The court held that this called for a stay of the proceedings on the ground of abuse of process even without proof of any prejudice to the defendant.

[37] I have drawn attention to the importance that the Strasbourg Court has attached to the right of a client to consult a lawyer in private.

[38] RIPA draws a distinction between directed surveillance and intrusive surveillance … Intrusive surveillance is governed by a regime that imposes stricter controls and requires a higher level of authorisation. If Parliament had intended RIPA to override the express statutory rights of those in custody to consult lawyers in private I find it hard to conceive that the surveillance in question would not have been placed within the category of intrusive surveillance.

[40] … RIPA should only be interpreted as qualifying the statutory rights of detainees to consult their lawyers privately if such an interpretation must necessarily be implied from the terms of the Act. There is no necessity for such an interpretation.

---

[77] Per Lord Phillips at [53] unless and until the Secretary of State 'took the appropriate steps she could not lawfully continue to carry out surveillance on legal consultations in prisons or police stations'. See also per Lord Carswell [93]: '… In the absence of an enhanced authorising regime such as that prescribed for intrusive surveillance, monitoring of lawyer/client or doctor/patient consultations could therefore not be justified under Article 8(2) of the Convention.'

[78] See *Derby Magistrates' Court, ex p B* [1996] AC 487.

[79] See *Campbell v United Kingdom* (1992) 15 EHRR 137; *Foxley v United Kingdom* (2000) 31 EHRR 637; *Australia Minining v Commission of European Communities* [1983] QB 878.

[80] See *Cox and Railton* (1884) 14 QBD 153.

[81] *Re McE* [2009] UKHL 15 per Lord Phillips [26].

[82] See *Klass v Germany* (1978) 2 EHRR 214.

[83] At paras 36–40 of the judgment.

2.59 The majority view on this point can be found in the judgment of Lord Hope:[84]

> [63] The more difficult question, perhaps, is whether the effect of RIPA, and of section 27(1) in particular, is to override the detainee's right to a private consultation under the statutes …
>
> [65] … It was inevitable that covert surveillance of the kind that RIPA was intended to provide for would intrude on conversations that were intended to be private. Privacy under a right given by statute is no exception. To conclude that consultations that were being conducted in private under a statutory right are immune from covert surveillance under RIPA would be wholly at variance with the obvious intention that RIPA should be general in its application, subject to the strict conditions that it lays down.
>
> [66] … I would hold that, as in the case of conversations that are ordinarily protected by legal professional privilege, conversations between a detainee and his solicitor that are taking place in private in the exercise of a statutory right may be subjected to intrusive surveillance that has been duly authorised under section 32 of RIPA so long as it is conducted strictly in accordance with the conditions which the authorisation lays down. In all other respects the statutory right to privacy must be respected.

2.60 In terms of the evidential use that could be made of the product of such covert surveillance, Lord Hope, commented:

> [66] Your Lordships have not been asked to decide in this case whether information disclosed in private by the detainee to the solicitor that has been obtained by the use of covert intelligence may be used against the detainee in evidence at his trial. All that needs to be said about this is that basic rules of fairness strongly indicate the contrary.

Practical points

2.61 Legal advisers should be aware of the real possibility that their conversations may be recorded. Taking instructions in cells or through the wicket should be avoided as these may well be fitted with audio devices.[85]

2.62 Section 58 of PACE contains a mandatory requirement that consultation between accused and adviser is private, but the legal adviser should nonetheless ask the officer in the case, the custody sergeant/jailer (or both) to confirm that the room (or cell) provided for consultation is private. The answer, together with the name and if applicable the police number of the person confirming that information should be recorded. The inquiry should be of particular concern, if the room in which the consultation is to be held has overt recording devices (some police cell consultation rooms now have as a permanent fixture a CCTV camera) to avoid the possibility that, if also equipped with audio recording facility, the device has not been 'accidentally' left on.

---

[84] At para 63–66 of the judgment. See also Baroness Hale judgment at para 67 '[67] … RIPA does permit the covert surveillance of communications between lawyers and their clients, even though these may be covered by legal professional privilege and notwithstanding the various statutory rights of people in custody to consult privately with their lawyers. This is an unpalatable conclusion, but one to which I am driven both by the plain words of the Act and by the history of legislation on this subject.' See also Lord Carswell's judgment at para 105 and Lord Neuberger's judgment at para 106.

[85] ACPO Guidance on The Safer Detention and Handling of Persons in Police Custody Second Edition (2012) states at section 11.5 'Refurbished or newly built custody suites may have a cell intercom system that allows custody staff to talk to detainees without having to go into the cell. Where justified, the listening system can be left on to provide additional, limited monitoring of detainees. Where the listening system is to be used in this way, the detainee should be made aware of this. It may be appropriate to display a sign that will alert all detainees to the presence of the system and its use. The listening system should be switched off if the cell is being used for confidential purposes, such as the provision of legal advice by the detainee's solicitor. If the cell is used for such a purpose, it is appropriate to advise the relevant person (solicitor or other) that the system exists, but will not be used'.

Any telephone conversation with the client whilst detained at the police station is particularly **2.63** easy to listened to and/or record; the client should therefore be advised of this. The lawyer should also be cautious of taking instructions about specifics of an allegation by telephone, and this should be reserved for private consultation in person. In any event clients should be warned of the possibility that any conversation they have may be recorded.[86] Given that it is common practice for custody suites to have video and audio recording of most areas, including those from where a suspect may use a telephone, the client should not be invited to provide confidential instructions when speaking to an adviser over the telephone.

F. Abuse of Process in the Police Station: Breach of Promise

The second type of abuse of process to be considered in relation to the police station concerns **2.64** promises made by officers. Breach of promise has long been recognized as a category of abuse of process. Where a defendant has been induced to believe that he will not be prosecuted, and then subsequently is prosecuted, this is capable of amounting to an abuse of process. Each case must be looked at on its merits.

A witness who is not a suspect

A useful starting point in this area is *Croydon Justices ex p Dean*.[87] Dean was interviewed by **2.65** police initially as a witness in a murder inquiry, during which he admitted helping to destroy the victim's car. He was told by police that he would not be prosecuted. However, the Crown Prosecution Service later decided he should be charged with assisting in the destruction of the car. The magistrates declined to stay proceedings as an abuse of process, and a judicial review action was heard at the High Court. Taking into account the lengthy period of time during which Dean had been helping police, relying in his mind on the promise he had been given, the court found he would suffer 'immense and irremediable prejudice', and the proceedings should be stayed. Lord Justice Staughton stated that 'the prosecution of a person who has received a promise, undertaking or representation from police that he will not be prosecuted is capable of being an abuse of process.'[88]

As a practical point, there was a dispute during the hearing, as to when specific assurances **2.66** were given by the police that there would be no prosecution, by whom, and how many. This serves as an important reminder to legal advisers of the vital necessity of taking a clear contemporaneous note of conversations in the police station and elsewhere.

The court in *Dean* also considered the prosecution's argument, that the police did not have **2.67** the requisite authority to tell Dean that he would not be prosecuted and that therefore there could not be an abuse of process. The court decided that the effect of the promise on Dean (who was only seventeen years old) was extremely important. It was implied that it would have been unrealistic for Dean to have recognized the CPS and the police as separate entities, and how executive authority was devolved between them.

Much of the commentary on *Dean* called for the police and CPS to co-operate and liaise **2.68** more closely. The decision came at a time when the decision as to charging was initially taken by the custody sergeant (see PACE—Code C Section16) and any charges would then be reviewed by the CPS. That regime has now been superseded by the current system in which the role of the police officer is largely limited to investigating offences, the custody sergeant's

---

[86] E Cape, *Defending Suspects at the Police Stations* (6th edn, 2011) para 1.23.
[87] [1993] QB 769, [1994] 98 Cr App R 76.
[88] [1994] 98 Cr App R 76 at 83.

role limited to monitoring and keeping a record of suspects whilst in police custody for investigation, and the CPS now has the role of making a decision about charging, and if so which charges to bring.

2.69 Many of the breach of promise abuse cases have, like *Dean*, been concerned with the blurring of the distinction between a potential witness and a suspect, typically with the 'witness' being converted to a suspect and later charged.

2.70 In stark contrast to *Dean* is the case of *Ismail Abdurahman and others*,[89] which concerned events surrounding the failed London bombings in July 2005. The defendant was convicted of one charge of assisting the main offender and four charges of failing to disclose information after the event, relating to other defendants. Abdurahman had met the bomber after publicity had spread in the wake of the attempted bombings, and he had allowed him to stay at his home. He also collected his passport and a video camera used to record a suicide message and delivered them to him. With some assistance from Abdurahman, the bomber later fled to Italy.

2.71 Abdurahman was approached by police as a potential witness. There was insufficient information to treat him as a suspect or arrest him. At the police station he was interviewed as a witness over a prolonged period into the early hours of the following morning. The interview took place without a caution and without the presence of a solicitor. However, early on in the interview, the interviewing officers concluded that as a result of his answers he should be cautioned. Advice was sought from a senior officer who instructed them to continue interviewing him as a witness. As soon as the witness statement was finished, the interviewing officers were then instructed to arrest Abdurahman. In a subsequent interview under caution, and when represented by a solicitor, Abdurahman handed the officers a prepared statement but declined to answer any further questions. Aside from challenging one or two matters of detail, his prepared statement essentially repeated the main thrust of his witness statement. In his final interview, he repeated that everything he knew was set out in his original witness statement.

2.72 At trial it was accepted that there had been a breach of the Code of Practice in failing to caution him, or offer him the services of a solicitor after it was considered that his answers were self-incriminating. The judge rejected applications to exclude the evidence pursuant to s 76 and s 78 PACE[90] and to stay proceedings on the basis of the statement which had been taken from Abdurahman when he believed that he was merely going to be a witness.

2.73 Abdurahman was convicted and appealed on grounds that it was unfair and an abuse of process to have prosecuted as a result of a statement provided when being treated as a witness. In rejecting the argument and upholding the conviction, the Court of Appeal said:

> On the contrary, he made the witness statement because he wanted to assist the police. In this type of case, the court is only likely to conclude there has been an abuse of process if a defendant can establish that there has been an unequivocal representation by those responsible for the conduct of the prosecution and that the defendant has acted to his detriment: see *Abu Hamza*,[91] in particular at paragraph 54. That was not the situation here.[92]

---

[89] *Abdul Sherif, Siraj Ali, Muhedin Ali, Wahbi Mohamed, Ismail Abdurahman, Fardosa Abdullahi* [2009] 2 Cr App R (S) 33.

[90] Primarily on the basis that in the subsequent interviews the appellant adopted the contents of the witness statement as his defence and as such, there was nothing to render the confession therein unreliable.

[91] [2007] 1 Cr. App. R 27.

[92] The case of *Abdurahman v. the UK (no. 40351/09)* is pending before the ECtHR and was mentioned in The Supreme Court judgment in Ambrose v Harris (supra).

Charge following legitimate expectation of caution

A second type of breach of promise case relevant at the police station concerns cautions. There **2.74** are a number of types of caution which include: Simple Cautions,[93] Conditional Cautions,[94] Reprimands and Final Warnings.[95] As a matter of general application and policy, it is not in the public interest to pursue criminal proceedings if the police, the CPS,[96] and a suspect are prepared to dispose of a case by way of a formal caution, reprimand or final warning.

A police 'simple caution' as a disposal is an alternative to charging the suspect. For a simple **2.75** caution to be administered, the following criteria have to be met:

(1) The prospect of a caution is not used as an incentive for the proferring of an admission.
(2) The person receiving the caution has admitted an offence.[97]

The Ministry of Justice guidance, 'Simple Cautions for Adult Offenders',[98] provides that **2.76** simple cautions cannot be offered to an offender who has not admitted that they are guilty of the offence or who has raised a defence, and cannot be given to an offender who does not agree to accept the caution.

In *R v Commissioner of Police of the Metropolis ex p P*,[99] the Divisional Court held that where a **2.77** caution was administered in clear breach of Home Office guidelines, the court could properly exercise its jurisdiction to review the legality of the caution. The caution was quashed as there was a clear breach of the condition that an offender had to admit the offence. Likewise in *R v Metropolitan Police Commissioner ex p Thompson*,[100] the Divisional Court quashed a caution since it was obtained by an inducement. In that case, the police officer had offered the suspect the prospect that he would not be prosecuted for the offence. Further, the Divisional Court will intervene if the police pressurize an accused into accepting a reprimand when they should not have.[101]

3. There must be sufficient evidence to provide a realistic prospect of conviction if the offender were to be prosecuted. However cautions should not be given if it is in the public interest for the offender to be brought before the court.

---

[93] Previously known as a formal or police caution.

[94] See section 22 and Part III of the Criminal Justice Act 2003.

[95] Simple cautions, reprimands and final warnings are an important aspect of criminal procedure as the numbers administered have in recent years been on the increase. Cautions continue to be an important means of disposal. According to figures cited in the Home Office Statistical Bulletin July 2010, of 1,212,009 total detected crimes for the period 2009/2010, 269,552 were disposed of by way of caution. Ministry of Justice figures for the year ending September 2012 show that a fifth of 'offences brought to justice' were dealt with by caution. See also *Conditional Cautions and Fair Trial Rights in England and Wales: Form versus Substance in the Diversionary Agenda'* - I. Brownlee—[2007] Crim LR 129 and R Ellis and S Biggs, 'Simple Cautions', Archbold Review [2013] 5, pp 6–7.

[96] See the CPS 'Legal Guidance on Cautioning and Diversion' at <http://www.cps.gov.uk/legal/a_to_c/cautioning_and_diversion/>

[97] For summary and either way offences (except those specified) the decision may be taken by police alone. In the case of an indictable offence, the decision must be taken by a senior officer *and* be referred to the CPS for its agreement. This is also true for the specified either way offences.

[98] See the Ministry of Justice guidance, 'Simple Cautions for Adult Offenders', dated 14 November 2013. <http://www.justice.gov.uk/out-of-court-disposals>

[99] (1996) 8 Admin LR 6, (1995), *The Times*, 24 May, QBD. As applied in *R (on the application of Lee) v Chief Constable of Essex* [2012] EWHC 283 (Admin).

[100] [1997] 1 WLR 1519. As applied in *W v Chief Constable of Merseyside* [2014] EWHC 1857 (Admin); *Caetano v Commissioner of Police of the Metropolis* [2013] EWHC 375 (Admin); *R (on the application of Lee) v Chief Constable of Essex* [2012] EWHC 283 (Admin); *Caetano v Commissioner of Police for the Metropolis* [2013] EWHC 375 (Admin).

[101] See *R. (on the application of U) v Commissioner of the Metropolis* [2003] 1 WLR 897.

4. The person has not previously been cautioned, unless the previous caution was over three years ago, or was for an unrelated offence, or there is some compelling reason why a further caution should be given as an alternative to a charge;

5. The caution must be made with the authorization of a senior police officer of at least the rank of Superintendent and of the CPS unless 'exceptional circumstances'[102] exist. Cautions should not be given for indictable or specific either-way offences.[103]

6. Consider the views of the victim, the extent of harm and loss to the victim.

7. Explain the consequences (future cases, employment, travel, and immigration) of the caution so that there can be informed consent to acceptance of it.

8. Ensure legal advice has been provided and provide disclosure of the evidence that is the basis for the caution.

2.78 It is important to note that a caution is not a criminal conviction.[104] Rather, it is a police record, held notionally for a period of three years (but in fact on the police national computer thereafter—in sexual cases the person's name is entered on the Sex Offenders Register as a preventive device)[105] and it acts as a warning to the person receiving the caution about their conduct and/or offending behaviour. The effect is that if the person receiving the caution is arrested in the future, a previous caution may be taken into account when deciding how the offence will be disposed of on the new occasion. If convicted, any court considering sentence can be advised of the fact that the defendant has previously been cautioned. The Ministry of Justice guidance states that,

> cautions do form part of an offender's criminal record and may be used in future proceedings and in certain circumstances, may be made available to an employer as part of a criminal record check. Offenders must be made aware of this before agreeing to accept a simple caution.

2.79 The caution is read to the suspect by an authorized police officer and a written record is made of the caution which the offender signs.

2.80 Since the implementation of Part 3 of the Criminal Justice Act 2003,[106] the non-statutory system for cautions has run parallel to the system of conditional cautions. Cautions for children[107] and young people are also replaced by a statutory system[108] of reprimands and warnings.[109]

2.81 Under the old system, the officer dealing with the case may make a recommendation for a caution, either with or without input from the custody sergeant, but in any event the final

---

[102] A non-exhaustive list is set out at paragraph 23 of the MOJ Guidance.

[103] Summarized as: possession of a bladed article, an offensive weapon, or firearm in public, including threatening with a bladed article or offensive weapon in a public place or a school; child prostitution and pornography; cruelty to a child; indecent photographs of children; and supplying Class A drugs.

[104] The caution is not a final determination. Section 24 Criminal Justice Act 2003 makes it clear that a prosecution may be brought if the person subject to a 'conditional caution' fails to comply with the conditions on which the caution has been issued.

[105] See *Ibbotson v United Kingdom* [1999] Crim LR 153.

[106] Sections 22–27 Criminal Justice Act 2003.

[107] See *R v Chief Constable of Kent ex p L* [1993] 1 All ER 756—a juvenile sought judicial review of a decision to prosecute rather than caution him, contrary to the police's general policy of cautioning instead of prosecuting juveniles. The discretion whether to prosecute was reviewable, but would only be interfered with if the decision to prosecute were clearly contrary to the settled policy of the DPP.

[108] Sections 65–66 Crime and Disorder Act 1998. The Secretary of State issued guidance under the title 'Final Warning Scheme', which contains a Gravity Factor Scheme, and a Home Office Circular 14/2006 explains the role of the CPS.

[109] See *R (on the application of R) v Durham Constabulary* [2006] Crim LR 87, [2005] UKHL 21; final warnings are considered and discussed by Lord Justice Maurice Kay in *D and B v Commissioner of Police for the Metropolis, CPS and Croydon Justices* [2008] EWHC 442 (Admin); [2008] ACD 47.

decision would rest with an Inspector. By contrast, under the new system of conditional cautions the CPS will make a final decision, again on the recommendation of an officer.[110]

Advising in relation to a caution

The adviser at the police station faces a difficult task when a caution may be offered. Situations **2.82** may arise where a police officer uses a caution in order to induce a suspect to make appropriate admissions.

The adviser has to consider whether the suspect is genuinely accepting some guilt, and not **2.83** feigning guilt in order to avoid further questioning. The adviser should carry out an assessment of the evidence prior to advising any acceptance of a caution. Where there appears to be strong evidence against a suspect, including where the suspect makes an admission, the adviser may seek to persuade the officer to deal with the matter by way of a caution in order to avoid the more serious and likely prospect of a criminal conviction. As Cape puts it, where a solicitor is acting in the client's best interests, this will include 'the expectation that the lawyer will, if relevant, seek to negotiate over relevant charges'.[111]

Promise of caution

When discussing the availability of a caution, difficulties can arise in deciding whether or not **2.84** those discussions amount to a 'promise'. A careful contemporaneous note is essential in order to later establish whether a caution was no more than a theoretical possibility or a promise subsequently breached.

The officer 'offering' a caution maybe insufficiently senior to make the decision as to whether **2.85** to caution or not. If that is the case, the adviser should seek confirmation from an officer with the appropriate authority, before giving advice to the suspect. It may be the case that the officer dealing with the case and making the offer may use words to the effect that they 'have already cleared it' with the inspector on duty or an officer of suitable status. Note that for specified either way and indictable offences, the minimum seniority required before a caution can be offered is that of a superintendent.

Disclosure

A suspect at the police station is entitled to informed legal advice, based on appropriate dis- **2.86** closure, as to whether to accept or decline a caution.

In *DPP v Ara*,[112] the suspect had previously been interviewed and returned on police bail. **2.87** The lawyer advising him on his return was told that the client 'was suitable for a caution'. In order to assess whether or not his client should accept the offer of a caution, the adviser sought disclosure of the contents of his client's previous interview (by way of his taped interview and custody record). That disclosure was refused, and the adviser felt that he could not properly advise his client to accept a caution without that disclosure, and subsequently the client was charged. On reaching court, it was apparent that a suitable admission had been made in the previous interview. The defence argued that the proceedings were only taking place because of the police's refusal to disclose the terms of the interview, 'without which informed advice and informed consent to a caution could not properly be given'. The justices stayed proceedings as an abuse of process.

Lord Justice Rose, in the Divisional Court, observed, 'I make it clear that this does not mean **2.88** that there is a general obligation on the police to disclose material prior to charge', as it would

---

[110] See Ministry of Justice guidance 'Simple Cautions for Adult Offenders' dated 14 November 2013.
[111] E Cape, 'Incompetent Police Station Advice and the Exclusion of Evidence' [2002] Crim LR 471.
[112] [2001] 4 All ER 559, [2002] 1 Cr App R 16.

often be impractical and in any event not something set out in any statute or code of practice, 'but, in the present case, the failure to disclose the terms of the interview followed by the institution in pursuit of a criminal trial in the circumstances described amply justified the justices in reaching the conclusion which they did.'[113]

Sections 76 and 78 of PACE

2.89 In a more typical case whereby a client makes an admission solely to secure a caution, but later, following charge, denies the offence, the usual remedy is to seek to have evidence of the interview excluded under sections 76 and 78 PACE.

Victim consultation

2.90 The Divisional Court in *Omar v Chief Constable of Bedfordshire Police*[114] considered whether prosecuting a person for an offence for which they had been cautioned was an abuse of process.

2.91 In *Omar*, the suspect was formally cautioned by a police sergeant for the offence of assault, having considered his previous good character and mitigating features. However, the police did not consult the victim about the case disposal. The victim judicially reviewed the Bedfordshire Police caution decision, complaining that there had not been a proper investigation into the attack, with a failure by police to take corroborative witness statements or view CCTV footage.

2.92 The Divisional Court in *Omar* observed that decisions to caution and prosecute are open to challenge by judicial review. However, the Divisional Court power is sparingly exercised, only granting a remedial relief for an unlawful decision. In *Manning and Melbourne v DPP*[115] Lord Chief Justice Bingham stated:

> The power to review is one to be sparingly exercised. The reasons for this are clear. The primary decision to prosecute or not to prosecute is entrusted by Parliament to the Director as head of an independent professional prosecuting service, answerable to the Attorney General in his role as guardian of the public interest, and to no one else.[116]

2.93 The judgment of Mr Justice Fulford in *Omar* on the grant of relief is worthy of consideration:[117]

> [41] … This (Divisional) court does not have the duty, or the entirety of the material necessary, to decide whether a prosecution should follow and that decision should be left solely to those charged with that responsibility.
>
> [42] The fact that there was an earlier caution given in circumstances such as these should not of itself act as a prohibition on a future prosecution or mean that a subsequent prosecution is necessarily an abuse. I am impressed in this regard by the following matters. Firstly, a confession should not be sought as part of the cautioning process, see R (on the application of Thomson) v Commissioner of the Metropolis.[118] Consequently, if the proper procedures are followed, the suspect will not have been induced into making admissions by the offer of a caution.
>
> [43] Secondly, a decision to discontinue proceedings against a defendant does not of itself give rise to a legitimate expectation that the prosecution will not be recommenced, see R (on the application of Burke) v DPP.[119] With discontinuance, this issue turns usually on what

---

[113] See [2001] 4 All ER 559 para 24 of the judgment.
[114] [2002] EWHC 3060 Admin, *The Independent*, 24 February 2003.
[115] [2001] QB 330.
[116] For an example see *R v Chief Constable of Kent ex p L* [1993] 1 All ER 756.
[117] Paras 41–47 of the judgment.
[118] [1997] 1 WLR 1519, [1997] 2 Cr App R 49.
[119] [1997] COD 16.

was said or written at the time and whether a legitimate expectation was created that the prosecution would not be reinstituted at all or only if certain pre-conditions were fulfilled. There are undoubted differences between discontinuance and caution, because following a caution the offender will usually believe that it is the disposal of his case. However, in the absence of an express undertaking that there will be no future prosecution even if circumstances materially changed, I do not consider that the legitimate expectation argument prevents a later and exceptional decision to charge for good reasons, particularly if this court has quashed the caution.

[44] Hayter v L[120] [was distinguished].

[45] Thirdly, in my view, it is in the public interests that a decision to caution should not prevent, in the right circumstances, a subsequent prosecution. As this case clearly demonstrates, these decisions may occasionally be made in error.

[46] Fourthly and finally, in circumstances in which this court has quashed a caution following a fully argued judicial review application, it is unlikely that there would be a finding that the prosecution had manipulated the process. In those circumstances, submissions as regards abuse are likely to be founded either on the creation of a legitimate expectation that there would never be a prosecution, or only if particular conditions were met, or on the basis that delay or changed circumstances (such as evidence no longer being available) has exceptionally led to the impossibility of a fair trial. As I have observed, it will be for others to decide if T should be charged and if so whether there are valid arguments that can be mounted on his behalf as regards an abuse of the process.

Mr Justice Fulford emphasized that,　　　　　　　　　　　　　　　　　　　　　　　**2.94**

judicial review of a decision by the relevant authority about whether or not to prosecute is a power that will be exercised sparingly and by analogy the same is true of linked decisions as to whether or not to administer a caution.[121]

However, he quashed the decision to caution. Failure to consult the victim without sufficient good cause, the lack of a sufficiently comprehensive investigation, and mistakes as to fact cumulatively lead Mr Justice Fulford to conclude that the decision making process was fatally flawed. *Omar* leaves open the possibility that a decision to prosecute after a caution is administered, in circumstances where an express promise was made that no prosecution would follow, can amount to an abuse of process.

Charge following legitimate expectation of final warning

The legitimate expectation of a final warning[122] for a youth (as opposed to criminal proceed-　**2.95** ings) was considered in *H v Guildford Youth Court*.[123] The Administrative Court quashed a refusal by the Guildford Youth Court to stay proceedings as an abuse of process. A fifteen-year-old was alleged to have kicked a fellow school pupil and fractured his jaw. Prior to being interviewed, it was intimated by the police that it was possible that the suspect would receive a final warning as a way of resolving the matter. When he was interviewed the suspect admitted the offence, but maintained that he had been bullied and that was the reason why he had kicked the victim in the jaw. He was bailed to an intervention clinic when it was indicated that the matter would be dealt with by way of a final warning. The CPS subsequently laid a charge of grievious bodily harm. Guildford Youth Court rejected defence submissions that the proceedings should be stayed as an abuse of process as the defendant had a legitimate expectation, as a consequence of what had been said to him at the police station at the time of the interview, that the matter would be dealt with by way of a final warning. Evidence

---

[120] [1998] 1 WLR 854.
[121] Para 47 of the judgment.
[122] The youth equivalent of an adult caution.
[123] [2008] EWHC 506 (Admin), [2008] 4 Archbold News 1.

called at the Youth Court demonstrated that there had been a clear promise that the matter would be dealt with by way of a final warning rather than a prosecution. Mr Justice Silber, in quashing the Youth Court decision and deciding that there had been an abuse of process warranting a stay, stated:

> [16] … The fact that a promise was made by an officer of the State, namely the police officer who was in charge at that stage deciding whether or not to prosecute, is something that there is a clear public interest in upholding.[124]

Practical points

2.96 When considering whether a promise, which is then reneged upon, will amount to an abuse of process, the following factors should be considered:

a) who made the promise;
b) whether that person had sufficient authority to make the promise, and if not whether it would be obvious or not that they did or did not have such authority;
c) what reliance was placed upon that promise by the recipient, and whether the recipient has relied upon it to their detriment;
d) how and when the decision to renege on the promise is made and how and when that decision is relayed;
e) whether the decision to renege on the promise was immediately challenged by the defence. Accordingly, there should be a challenge, by the legal adviser at the police station, to any such change of stance.

2.97 Where, due to inadequate disclosure, the client has made an admission which ought not to have been made, and unfairness has arisen, exclusion of the admission under PACE is likely to provide the appropriate remedy rather than an application to stay proceedings. If, however, police failure to make full or proper disclosure causes a prejudicial reaction by the client (whether on legal advice or not) which subsequently led to proceedings which might not have otherwise occurred, an application to stay proceedings may be allowed (see *Ara*).[125]

2.98 Defence advisers should also consider whether it may be appropriate to write a letter of representation to the CPS, referring them to the CPS guidelines and inviting them to discontinue the case, or suggesting a referral back to the police station for a caution. The prosecution has an ongoing duty to keep the case under continual review in accordance with their public interest criteria.

2.99 Police station advisers should obtain as full a disclosure as possible from the police officer, and if this is given orally ensure a full note should be taken.

2.100 Where, as is increasingly common, pre-prepared written disclosure is provided, then the adviser should nonetheless ask a series of questions to establish further facts if the pre-prepared disclosure is inadequate. This course should be pursued even if the officer is declining to provide any information other than that in the written statement.

2.101 Where the adviser has had to sign to acknowledge receipt of the pre-prepared written disclosure, the adviser may consider writing a series of disclosure questions, and handing a copy to the officer inviting the officer to sign to acknowledge receipt, and then request written answers to the disclosure sought. Thus a full written record of disclosure (or non-disclosure)

---

[124] Ibid at para 16. For a factual situation relating to final warnings which did not lead to a stay, see D B v Commissioner of Police for the Metropolis, CPS and Croydon Justices [2008] EWHC 442 (Admin).
[125] [2001] 4 All ER 559, [2002] 1 Cr App R 16.

is kept. Some forces will also require that disclosure is given to the adviser on tape in an interview room in a setting akin to an interview under caution. The adviser should ensure s/he is fully prepared prior to 'taped disclosure' which provides an invaluable opportunity to create an unimpeachable record of what disclosure was given, what was refused, and the reasons given, if any. It may be appropriate even if not offered, for an adviser to request that disclosure is provided in this way.

G. Private Prosecution

The issue of the appropriateness of a caution as opposed to a private prosecution was con- **2.102**
sidered by the House of Lords in *Jones v Whalley*.[126] The House of Lords held that to allow
a private prosecution of a man who had received a police caution (for an assault), which
explicitly informed him that he would not go before a criminal court, represented an abuse
of process. It was submitted, on behalf of Mr Whalley, that he had a legitimate expectation
that there would be no further criminal proceedings after he had accepted the caution.
The private prosecutor, by contrast, contended that as a private citizen he, as a private
prosecutor, had a legal right to prosecute which could not be taken away from him by the
unilateral act of the police in administering a caution, an act over which he had no influence
or control.

The House of Lords took the view that it was for the state, through the appropriate agencies, **2.103**
to investigate alleged crimes and to decide whether offenders should be prosecuted.[127] The
police officer's decision to offer a formal caution complied with Home Office guidance and
aimed to deal quickly and simply with a less serious offender to divert them from unnecessary appearance in the criminal courts and to reduce their chances of re-offending—all
worthwhile policy objectives. If the officer's decision to caution rather than to prosecute was
untenable it could be set aside on judicial review.[128] It would offend the courts sense of justice
and propriety to be asked to try the accused in the face of the assurance given by the police,
that he would not have to go to court in respect of the offence. To go behind that assurance
would undermine the cautioning regime.[129]

H. Abuse of Process in the Police Station: Bail Promise

The third, but rare, area in which a promise by the Police may lead to an abuse of process **2.104**
relates to bail. Police may inform a suspect, directly or through legal advisers, that, if the
suspect voluntarily surrenders to the police station, they would not oppose bail following
interview and any charge. If, however, bail is not granted, an abuse of process may result.

This point was considered by the Administrative Court in *R (on application of Mogens* **2.105**
Hauschildt) v Highbury Corner Magistrates' Court[130] on a habeas corpus application. Mogens

---

[126] [2006] UKHL 41; [2007] 1 AC 63;[2007] Crim LR 74; [2006] 8 Archbold News 4–5. See commentary on the decision in Francis Bennion, '*Jones v Whalley*: Constitutional Errors by the Appellate Committee'
170 JPN 847; Nick Taylor, 'The Growth of Private Prosecutions' (2007) Crim LR 74; *Jones v Whalley* followed in *Rollins* [2009] EWCA Crim 1941.
[127] See Lord Bingham judgment at para 16.
[128] See Lord Rodger judgment at para 22.
[129] See Lord Rodger judgment at para 25.
[130] [2007] EWHC 3494 (Admin).

Hauschildt, a French resident, was being investigated in England for offences of fraud. The police officer investigating the allegations communicated with Mr. Hauschildt's English solicitors and led him to believe, that if he voluntarily returned to England, he would be interviewed and, if charged, bailed.

2.106 Mr. Hauschildt, having been given such an assurance, returned to England, was interviewed and charged with various fraud offences. The custody officer invited representations as to whether or not he should be granted police bail. The investigating officer represented that he should not and bail was refused. The matter came before the Magistrates' Court and the investigating officer admitted, under cross-examination, (a) that he had given an assurance to the solicitors that he would not oppose bail if Mr Hauschildt returned to England and (b) that such an assurance was false, as the officer did not believe that the suspect would otherwise return and would avoid capture.

2.107 The proper method of procuring the return of Mr. Hauschildt to England was either to persuade him to come back (and if promises were made to ensure they were fulfilled), or to make an application for a European Arrest Warrant, after which extradition proceedings would follow. Mr. Justice Mitting observed:

> To make a promise and then break it, as blatantly as was done in this case, in my judgment is a clear abuse of process. There are two methods by which the abuse of process can be cured. One is the issue of a writ of habeas corpus and the second is for me to reconstitute myself as a District Judge exercising the powers of a District Judge, by virtue of section 66 of the Courts Act 2003, and to hear and determine a bail application on the footing that there has been a change in circumstances since yesterday. The change in circumstances is the acknowledgment by the Crown that there was here an abuse of process.[131]

2.108 Bail was granted putting Mr Hauschildt in precisely the position in which he should have been had the promise made by the police officer been fulfilled. In that way the abuse of process was cured.

I. Parallel Regulatory, Civil, and Cross-Border Litigation

2.109 There is potential unfairness arising out of parallel regulatory, civil, and cross-border proceedings, which could give rise to abuse of process arguments. The remedy for such unfairness may not be a stay, but instead it may be cured by the exclusion of any tainted evidence.

Compelled interviews

2.110 The Serious Fraud Office has the power to compel persons to answer questions under section 2 Criminal Justice Act 1987.[132] Similarly, the Financial Conduct Authority has the power to compel under section 171 Financial Services and Markets Act 2000. Generally, answers given in such compelled interviews are not admissible as evidence against the interviewee in criminal proceedings reflecting the privilege against self incrimination, as per *Saunders v UK*.[133] However it is important to understand that answers given in compelled interviews

---

[131] *R. (on application of Mogens Hauschildt) v Highbury Corner Magistrates' Court* [2007] EWHC 3494 (Admin) at para 8.

[132] As to the right of a suspect to have a legal representative present at a compelled SFO interview see *R. (on the application of Jason Lord, Paul Reynolds and Justin Maygar) v Director of SFO* [2015] EWHC 865 (Admin).

[133] (1997) 23 EHRR 313.

are admissible against interviewees in most non-criminal proceedings, such as regulatory proceedings brought by the FCA.

The right not to incriminate oneself and the right to a fair trial are of central importance **2.111** under Article 6. A person can be compelled to give answers but those answers cannot be relied on against him in criminal proceedings. However, answers given in a compelled interview can be passed to other law enforcement agencies, who can use the product of that interview to conduct their own enquiries.

Civil Proceedings

In relation to civil proceedings, section 14(1) Civil Evidence Act 1968 states that a person **2.112** can refuse to answer questions or produce documents if answering questions or producing documents would 'tend to expose' that person to criminal proceedings or criminal penalty (*Rio Tinto Zinc Corporation v Westinghouse Electric Corporation*).[134]

Section 13 of the Fraud Act 2006 removes the privilege against self incrimination in all **2.113** proceedings relating to property. However, the Act makes it clear that in accordance with *Saunders* the product of the compelled interview is inadmissible in criminal proceedings for an offence of fraud under Fraud Act 2006 or any related offence, which includes conspiracy to defraud. Care should be taken when advising any client in a civil action relating to property that they might be compelled to give information which may be later used by prosecution authorities for investigative purposes but not to incriminate them.

If admissions are made to a criminal offence during 'without prejudice' negotiations made in **2.114** order to try and settle a civil case, no exclusionary protection against admissibility is available to the maker of the admission if the prosecution obtain this information.

Cross-border litigation

The privilege against self incrimination is of central importance in the United States. The **2.115** US Constitution Fifth Amendment provides that a person cannot be compelled to answer questions regardless of whether it is a criminal or civil investigation. However, careful attention is needed where US authorities request the fruits of a compelled interview from the UK authorities. In essence, the UK authorities are being asked to hand over material which the US authorities could not obtain in the US, and therefore obtain potentially incriminating material against a suspect.

The SFO and FCA will need to take care to ensure that a suspect's Article 6 rights are not **2.116** breached. This is usually achieved by the UK authorities seeking 'Saunders style' undertakings from the US authorities, which uphold the privilege against self incrimination. However, although the transcripts of any compelled interview may be inadmissible in the US, they will have undoubtedly provided the US authorities will valuable lines of enquiry which they would otherwise been unaware of. A suspect may need to consider whether an abuse arises or if the investigation is tainted in these circumstances. In such circumstances, it is advisable to have both UK and US lawyers advising the suspect. Often suspects fear trial and extradition to the US far more than proceedings here in the UK.

In cross-border regulatory matters the prejudice to a suspect is potentially greater. The reason **2.117** for this is that the FCA does not need to seek any form of undertaking from the US regulator

---

[134] [1978] 1 All ER 434.

because the privilege against self incrimination only extends to criminal proceedings, not regulatory proceedings.

2.118 At the start of any compelled interview with the FCA, where there is a real likelihood of international cross-border regulation being involved, advisers need to consider stating at the outset of the interview that a suspect is only answering questions because to fail to do so would be a contempt of court, and that his answers are therefore involuntary. Taking such steps affords the suspect protection in respect of any subsequent regulatory proceedings in the US, as it is made clear he is not waiving his Fifth Amendment right.

J. Immunity and Agreements under Serious Organised Crime and Police Act 2005

2.119 A fifth area at the pre-charge stage that may lead to abuse of process arguments relates to immunity and agreements under the Serious Organised Crime and Police Act 2005.[135] Offenders who assist with the investigation and/or prosecution of others, are now able in certain circumstances to gain immunity from prosecution or reduced sentences. Abuse of process arguments may arise in relation to breach of legitimate expectation promises.

2.120 Section 71 SOCPA provides for full immunity from prosecution. If a 'specified prosecutor' agrees to this rare course of action then an Immunity Notice is produced setting out the conditions which need to be met in order to gain full immunity. If these conditions are not met by the person, a Revocation Notice will be issued and a prosecution can then be brought against the person.

2.121 Specified prosecutors may prosecute those who fail to comply with the conditions attached to their immunity notice. Disputes as to whether the conditions have been complied with, and whether there were any legitimate expectations, may give rise to an abuse argument on the part of a person who believed immunity from prosecution would be granted.[136]

2.122 Section 72 SOCPA concerns Restricted Use Undertakings. Information given by the person assisting the authorities will not be used against him except in circumstances prescribed in the undertaking. It is important to note that the undertaking does not prevent the person from being prosecuted where other evidence which justifies a prosecution is, or becomes, available. A potential abuse argument arises because other evidence may be obtained from another source directly or indirectly as a result of information given under a Restricted Use Undertaking.

---

[135] See sections 71–73. Section 73 SOCPA sets out the provisions for plea and reduction in sentence. This section covers situations where a defendant has assisted the investigation and/or prosecution of others and has entered into a written agreement regarding a reduction in sentence in return for his assistance. Guidance on s 73 has been provided by the Court of Appeal in *P, Blackburn* [2007] EWCA Crim 2290 and *H, D* and *Chaudhury* [2009] EWCA Crim 2485. See also *Dougall* [2010] EWCA Crim 1048, [2010] 6 Archbold News 3.

[136] See R Fortson, *Serious Organised Crime and Police Act 2005* (Sweet & Maxwell 2005) at pp 15–98.

3

FORUMS FOR RAISING ABUSE
OF PROCESS

A. Introduction

This chapter will examine the forums in which abuse of process arguments are raised, con- **3.1** sidered, and determined, starting with the first instance magistrates' court, Youth Court and moving onto the appellant level Crown Court, Divisional Court, Court of Appeal Criminal Division, and Supreme Court. The separate jurisprudence of the European Court of Human Rights (ECtHR) in Strasbourg is considered in later chapters on an issues-related basis.

B. The Magistrates' Court

Power

The magistrates' court has an inherent jurisdiction to control its own process, including **3.2** the ability to stay proceedings where that process has been abused. This power to stay proceedings relates to the two broad categories of abuse, namely category one cases where the court concludes that the defendant cannot receive a fair trial, and category two cases where it concludes that it would be unfair for the defendant to be tried. The justices' power to stay criminal proceedings should, according to the High Court, be 'very strictly confined' to:

a) matters which will have a direct effect on the fairness of the trial; and
b) only employed in exceptional cases if there is no alternative course.[1]

3.3 Magistrates may decline jurisdiction, and require abuse of process applications to be pursued in the High Court (by way of an application for judicial review). This course may be adopted due to the issue's complexity, novelty, or where a lengthy investigation is required.[2] The High Court[3] supports such an approach, emphasizing, particularly in category two abuse cases concerned with protecting the integrity of the criminal justice system, that the wider supervisory responsibility for upholding the rule of law is vested in the High Court rather than the magistrates court. As to how to proceed, Lord Justice Maurice Kay observed in *William Nembhard v DPP*:[4]

> … One way would be to adjourn so as to permit an application for judicial review of the decision to prosecute or to continue to prosecute. In that case, the application to this court will have to set out the evidential basis to which the prosecutor and/or the police can respond. The disadvantage of proceeding in this way is that this court is not in the best position to evaluate the evidence of controversial witnesses. It also causes delay.

> Alternatively, the summary trial can proceed to a conclusion without a ruling on the above application. If there is a conviction, there can be an appeal to this court by case stated, in which case this court will be greatly assisted by full findings of fact by the Magistrates' Court, which will have heard the evidence even though it has not been able to make a ruling.

Situations that may constitute an abuse of process

3.4 There are a vast number of factual and procedural situations that may give rise to abuse of process arguments specific to the summary jurisdiction of magistrates' courts. In addition, the principles developed in crown court case law apply equally to summary cases. Further, a large number of case authorities relating to committal proceedings, which have since been abolished, are still of relevance in terms of the principles developed.

3.5 Proceedings can be stayed in the magistrates' court, to prevent the court's process being mis-used in a wide range of factual and procedural situations including:

- The issue of an information[5]
- Situations which occur during summary proceedings[6] and

---

[1] *R v Horseferry Road Magistrates' Court ex p Bennett* [1994] 1 AC 42; *R v Oxford City JJ ex p Smith*, [1982] 75 Cr App R 200 at 204, per Lane LCJ; *Environment Agency v Stanford*, [1999] Env LR 286, 30 June 1998, DC, CD/4625/97; *R v Haringey Justices ex p DPP* [1996] QB 351; *DPP v Hussain* (1994) 158 JP 602; *DPP v Hussein Jimale* [2001] Crim LR 138; *R (Ebrahim) v Feltham Magistrates' Court* [2001] EWHC Admin 130, [2001] 2 Cr.App.R.23; *DPP v Holden* [2006] EWHC 658 (Admin) and *R (on application of the CPS) v City of London Magistrates' Court* [2006] EWHC 1153; *DPP v Gowing* [2013] EWHC 4614 (Admin); *DPP v Graham Petrie* [2015] EWHC 48 (Admin): the magistrates' power to stay a prosecution is only to be exercised in exceptional circumstances in order to prevent an unfair trial or to protect the integrity of the criminal process.

[2] See *R v Belmarsh Magistrates' Court ex p Watts* [1999] 2 Cr App R 188; *R v Bow Street Magistrates' Court ex p Christopher Finch and Bossino* 9 June 1999, DC, [1999] 10 Archbold News 1, DC (CO/2181/99); *William Nembhard v DPP* [2009] EWHC 194 Admin.

[3] See *R v Horseferry Road Magistrates' Court ex p Bennett* [1994] 1 AC 42.

[4] [2009] EWHC 194 Admin at paragraphs 22 and 23 of the judgment.

[5] See *Lloyd v Young* [1963] Crim LR 703. To be contrasted with the dismissal of an information, *R v Methry Tydfil Magistrates Court and Day ex p DPP* [1989] Crim LR 148. The question of whether an infor-mation had been laid outside the six-month time limit was an issue of jurisdiction and notions of abuse of process were not applicable: *Atkinson v DPP* [2004] EWHC 1457 (Admin).

[6] In *R v Faversham and Sittingbourne Justices, ex p Stickings* (1996) 160 JP 801, evidence was initially ruled inadmissible on the advice of the clerk, the case was then adjourned and the clerk was contacted by the prosecution regarding the admissibility of that evidence. The clerk subsequently advised that the evidence was

- Mandatory sentencing provisions.[7]

Other specific areas are set out below citing relevant case law.

The decision to prosecute

The decision to prosecute, if taken for improper reasons, can amount to an abuse of process.[8] **3.6**
Where the decision has been taken in breach of CPS policy,[9] the prosecutor's duty to be independent, the rule against double jeopardy, a promise not to prosecute,[10] or has been taken for
vexatious, frivolous or oppressive reasons, then that decision might constitute an abuse of process. Case law examples are set out below:

- Oppressive, frivolous, or vexatious prosecutions.[11]
- Breach of an assurance not to prosecute cannot, without more, amount to an abuse itself.[12]
  However, where a defendant has acted to his detriment in reliance on such a promise, a decision
  to proceed may constitute an abuse.[13] Where formal arrangements under sections 71–75 Serious
  Organised Crime and Police Act 2005, have been entered into, an attempt to renege on an agreement by the prosecution may result in those proceedings being stayed as an abuse of process.[14]
- Where the CPS decides not to prosecute, informs the suspect of this, and then decides
  to proceed for improper reasons, this may constitute an abuse. A decision to prosecute a
  suspect for careless driving taken in response to representations from a deceased person's
  family has been held to be an abuse.[15]

---

admissible. The reversal of the original decision by the justices was tainted by unfairness and it was unjust to
permit the prosecution to proceed with a second trial.

[7] As a general principle, courts are not concerned with the decision to prosecute, but rather with the
conduct of the trial. Any resulting harshness in that principle can be taken into account in mitigation during
sentencing. However, in *R v Liverpool Stipendiary Magistrate ex p Slade* [1998] 1 WLR 531, an application
to stay proceedings was allowed as, under s 4(1) of the Dangerous Dogs Act 1991, conviction carried with
it the mandatory sentence that the dog be destroyed and as such the circumstances in which the offence was
committed could have no effect by way of mitigation on the sentence passed. In the light of these considerations, proceeding with the action against the appellant would be unfair and offend against the court's sense
of justice.

[8] *R v Horseferry Road Magistrates' Court ex p Stephenson* [1989] COD 470, No CD/113/89; *R v Bingley
Magistrates Court ex p Morrow* (1994), *The Times* (28 April 1994); *R v Bow Street Metropolitan Stipendiary
Magistrates Ex p South Coast Shipping* (1993) 96 Cr App R 405; *R (on the application of Dacre) v Westminister
Magistrates' Court* [2009] 1 Cr App R 6, [2008] 8 Archbold News 2.

[9] Judicial review challenges to a CPS decision to prosecute or not proceed, including complainant reviews
under the Victim's Right to Review scheme, are unlikely to succeed, as the likelihood of success has been
described in *L v DPP* [2013] EWHC 1752 (Admin) as 'very, very small', an approach cited with approval in
R(S) v CPS, R(S) v Oxford Magistrates' Court [2015] EWHC 2863(Admin).

[10] In *Abdul v DPP* [2011] EWHC 247 (Admin), having regard to the decision in *Nembhard v DPP* [2009]
EWHC 194 (Admin), Gross LJ expressed the provisional view that the magistrates' court could exercise jurisdiction to stay proceedings in cases where the defendant had a legitimate expectation not to be prosecuted,
as a consequence of police action.

[11] Bros (1901) 66 JP 54, *R v Durham Magistrates ex p Davies* (1993) *The Times* (25 May 1993), *R v Bury JJ ex
p Anderton* [1987] Crim LR 638, *R v Clerk to the Bradford Justices ex p Sykes* (1999) 163 JP 224, *Barton v DPP*
(2001) 165 JP 779. In *R (on the application of Chief Constable of Northumbria) v Newcastle upon Tyne Magistrates'
Court* [2010] EWHC 935 (Admin) it was held to be an abuse of process to pursue a private prosecution for false
imprisonment against a chief constable who had no involvement in the person's arrest or detention.

[12] *R v Horseferry Road Magistrates' Court ex p DPP* [1999] COD 441.

[13] *R v Croydon JJ ex p Dean* 98 Cr App R 76; *H v Guildford Youth Court* [2008] EWHC 506 (Admin);
[2008] 4 Archbold News 1.

[14] See the section 73 SOCA case of *Dougall* [2010] EWCA Crim 1048; [2010] 6 Archbold News 3. See
also *R (Smith) v CPS [2010] EWHC 3593 (Admin)*.

[15] *Taylor* [2004] EWHC 1554 (Admin), [2004] 7 Archbold News 2. In *Christopher Killick* [2011] EWCA
Crim 1608, the Court of Appeal concluded that victims of crime have a right to seek a review of a CPS decision not to prosecute. Such a review will be a relevant factor when considering whether proceedings amount

- A decision taken to prosecute that is in breach of the CPS Code for Crown Prosecutors, or other prosecution policy, may be an abuse.[16] It is not sufficient simply to show a breach of prosecution policy: misconduct or oppression must also be shown to justify a stay of proceedings.[17]
- Where an information is laid in order to manipulate the court's procedure, the prosecution may constitute an abuse of process.[18] One example is the laying of an information to avoid a custody time limit.[19]
- Unless a retrial is ordered under s 77 Criminal Justice Act 2003 (where there is new and compelling evidence), a decision to mount a prosecution based on the same events as a previous prosecution is likely to constitute an abuse of process. The rule against double jeopardy has also resulted in a stay in the following circumstances:[20]
  - repeated applications for a summons[21]
  - a private prosecution following the collapse of a CPS prosecution[22] and
  - the laying of a fresh information after a finding of no case to answer.[23]
- Provision for the non-prosecution or non-application of penalties to victims who had offended under compulsion as a result of human trafficking. In *L*[24] the court gave guidance to courts on the approach to be taken towards those who were, or might be, victims of people trafficking, after criminal proceedings against them had begun. Such guidance will be important for the magistrates' court as well as the crown court.

Private prosecution

3.7 The bringing of a private prosecution can amount to an abuse of process. A private prosecutor is a minister of justice subject to the same obligations as the public prosecuting authorities.[25]

---

to an abuse of process. In July 2014, the CPS published final guidelines for the Victim's Right to Review Scheme: <http://www.cps.gov.uk/publications/docs/vrr_guidance_2014.pdf>.

[16] See *Adaway* [2004] EWCA Crim 2831: evidence insufficient to justify a prosecution. See also *A* [2012] EWCA Crim 434. See *R (on the application of Barons Pub Co Ltd) v Staines Magistrates' Court* [2013] EWHC 898 (Admin) regarding Local Authority's compliance with its own food hygiene enforcement policy before deciding to prosecute.

[17] *Moss & Son Ltd v Crown Prosecution Service* [2012] EWHC 3658 (Admin).

[18] *R v Basingstoke Justices ex p Howard*, CO 1562/84, 18 March 1985, QBD.

[19] In *R v Great Yarmouth Magistrates ex p Thomas, Davis and Darlington* [1992] Crim LR 116 the defendant was re-arrested on effectively the same charge. The court held that where the defence alleged mala fides by the prosecutor and dishonest contriving to manipulate the process to avoid the consequences of the CTL regulations, the issue had to be determined by the justices. There is a heavy burden on the defence to prove such dishonesty. However, in *R (Wardle) v Crown Court at Leeds* [2001] UKHL 12, a new charge was brought for the purpose of avoiding the effect of the expiration of a custody time limit. The court held that abuse of process is not confined to instances where there is evidence of an improper motive or other dishonesty on the part of the prosecuting authority. It is sufficient if the prosecutor is unable to justify the preferment of a fresh charge—abuse of process could potentially be found to exist.

[20] In *DPP v Alexander* [2010] EWHC 2266 (Admin) the magistrates had erred in dismissing, on the principle of autrefois convict and as an abuse of process, an information laid against a defendant for driving without due care and attention on the basis that he had accepted a caution for false imprisonment arising from the same incident. Autrefois convict had no application where a caution had been administered, and the differences between the offences meant there had been no abuse of process. See also: *R (on the application of Gavigan) v Enfield Mags* [2013 EWHC 2805 (Admin) and *R v Gore (Raymond)* [2009] EWCA Crim 1424, in which the court held that it was not an abuse to proceed where a fixed penalty notice had been issued.

[21] *Gleaves v Insall*, [1999] 2 Cr App R 466, where the Prosecutor failed to inform subsequent courts of the previous unsuccessful applications.

[22] *R v Grays Justices ex p Low* [1988] 3 All ER 834 and see commentary at [1989] Crim LR 69–70, where the private prosecutor did not inform the trial court of the previous prosecution involving a bind over.

[23] *R v Horsham Justices ex p Reeves* [1982] 75 Cr App R 236.

[24] [2013] EWCA Crim 991.

[25] See Lord Justice Buxton in *R v Belmarsh Magistrates' Court Ex p Watts* [1999] 2 Cr App R 188, at 200, as adopted in *R. (on application of Dacre) v Westminister Magistrates' Court* [2009] 1 Cr App R 6. Practical

The summons or information: failure to give particulars

At common law, summonses or informations that are vague and fail to disclose a clear case **3.8** against a defendant have been found to constitute an abuse of process.

Failure to give proper detail, or 'particulars' can lead to uncertainty and unfairness to an **3.9** accused. An example is *R v Newcastle-upon-Tyne Justices, ex p Hindle*,[26] where the prosecution's decision to lay an ambiguous charge was held to be an abuse of process on the basis that it was capable of referring to two possible offences. The prosecution had also failed to provide the requisite particulars when asked to do so. Accordingly, the High Court held that they had unfairly preserved an opportunity to advance their case on the basis of two inconsistent offences.

In addition, Article 6(3) ECHR guarantees a defendant the right to be 'informed promptly, **3.10** and in a language he understands, of the nature and cause of the accusation against him'.[27]

Duplicity

The rule against duplicity prevents a summons from referring to two or more offences in a **3.11** single charge. The charges can be laid under two different statutes, or under the same one.[28]

The case of *Carrington Carr v Leicestershire County Council* lists the five most common situa- **3.12** tions where an information may be duplicitous:[29]

(a) where two or more discrete offences are charged conjunctively in one information (for example, where a single information alleges both dangerous and careless driving);

(b) where two offences are charged disjunctively or in the alternative in one information (for example, where a single information alleges dangerous or careless driving);

(c) where an offence is capable of being committed in more ways than one (for example, driving under the influence of drink or drugs) and both ways are referred to in one information;

(d) where a single offence is charged in respect of an activity but the activity involved more than one act[30] and;

(e) where a single activity is charged but a number of particulars are relied on by the prosecution to prove the offence (for example, a single act of obtaining by deception where the deception involved several misrepresentations).

---

steps that can be taken to manage private prosecutions can be found in Richard Buxton's article 'The Private Prosecutor as a Minister of Justice' [2009] Crim LR 427 at 423. See also *R v Leominister Magistrates'Court ex p Aston Manor Brewery Co* (1997) *The Times* (8 January 1997) 94(5) LSG 32 where a prosecutor was also bringing civil proceedings. *R (on the application of Chief Constable of Northumbria) v Newcastle upon Tyne Magistrates' Court* [2010] EWHC 935 (Admin). See also, *R (on the application of Dacre) v Westminster Mags [2009] 1 CR App R 6*: 'a prosecution could be stayed as an abuse of process if state agents had lured a person into committing a crime. There was no reason in principle why, by analogy, a private prosecution should not be considered an abuse of process if the crime was one that had been encouraged by the private prosecutor or when in some other way the private prosecutor had essentially created the same mischief as that complained of'.

[26] [1984] 1 All ER 770.
[27] See also Schedule 1 Human Rights Act 1998.
[28] *R v Lincoln Magistrates' Court ex p Wickes Building Supplies Ltd, The Times* (6 August 1993), DC.
[29] [1993] Crim LR 938.
[30] In *Barton v DPP* [2001] EWHC Admin 223 a single information charging B with ninety-four offences of theft was not bad for duplicity, given that ninety-four separate informations would have been oppressive and the offences were all part of the same process, involving theft from a single cash till.

Selection of charges

3.13   The laying of charges that are more or less serious than that suggested by the conduct involved may amount to an abuse of process, where the over- or under-charging is done to manipulate the court process. Examples are:

- The improper laying of a less serious charge against the accused;[31]
- The laying of a more serious charge, with the effect of depriving the defendant of a summary trial, is permissible, provided that the more serious charge is justified on the evidence.[32]

3.14   In addition, the point at which additional charges are laid may be determinative. For example, the inclusion of more serious charges after magistrates had retired to consider their sentence was found to constitute an abuse of process.[33]

3.15   However, the inclusion of additional informations, by the prosecution, at the suggestion of a judge, to adequately reflect the criminality alleged, is not an abuse of process.[34] The adding of the new charges is to give effect to the judicial view that the interests of justice were not met by a single charge. It is the prosecution's prerogative to decline to accept a judge's indication to add charges, but where the prosecution chooses to do so, it is not an abuse of process.[35]

3.16   It can be an abuse of process for a defendant to be tried first on the least serious charge of a series of multiple charges.[36]

Improperly joining or separating issues

3.17   The concepts of 'joinder' and 'severance' do not apply directly to summonses or informations, as these are not subject to the Indictment Rules 1971. However, similar concepts operate at common law to ensure that they are not manipulated to render a defendant's trial unfair. Examples are:

- Separating issues, which could be tried together[37]
- Proceedings being instituted for an offence which could have been charged as part of previous proceedings.[38]

Delay

3.18   Undue delay in bringing a prosecution may amount to an abuse of process, if the delay has no justifiable reason,[39] or renders a defendant's trial unfair because the delay has caused prejudice to the defendant.[40]

---

[31] In *DPP v Hammerton* [2009] EWHC 921 (Admin), the CPS was not entitled to substitute a lesser charge for a more serious charge unless to do so was proper and appropriate to the facts of the case, its application had been made promptly, and considerations of the good administration of justice and the wider picture, for example the situation of any co-accused, had been properly considered. However, as held in *R v Sheffield Justices, ex p DPP* [1993] Crim LR 136, it is a matter for the prosecution's discretion which charge to prefer. Its motive is irrelevant in the absence of bad faith. See also *R v Canterbury and St Augustine Justices ex p Klisiak* [1981] 2 All ER 129 and *R v Sheffield Justices ex p DPP* [1993] Crim LR 136.

[32] *R v Redbridge Justices, ex p Whitehouse* (1992) 94 Cr App R 332.

[33] *Harlow Magistrates Court ex p Michael O'Farrell* [2000] Crim LR 589.

[34] *DPP v B* [2008] EWHC 201 (Admin).

[35] *DPP v B* [2008] EWHC 201 (Admin) at para 11 of Lord Justice Latham's judgment.

[36] See *R v Forest of Dean ex p Farley* [1990] R.T.R. 228, *Marcellin (Simon)* [2010] EWCA Crim 2733, *Dwyer* [2012] EWCA Crim 10 and *Antoine* [2014] EWCA Crim 1971.

[37] In *Intervisions Ltd and Norris* [1984] Crim LR 350 the sole question in each proceedings was whether the images were indecent. See also *Noe (Angela)* [1985] Crim LR 97.

[38] *Birch and Harrington* [1983] Crim LR 193.

[39] *Watford Justices ex p Outrim* [1983] RTR 26 (22 months to issue a summons). *R v Bishop's Stortford Justices ex p DPP* [1997] CLY 1258: where the defendant's own actions contributed to the delay, he should not be granted a stay of proceedings.

[40] *Brants v DPP* [2011] EWHC 754 (Admin).

In the case of most summary offences, the Magistrates' Courts Act 1980 provides that a magistrates' court 'shall not try an information or hear a complaint unless laid within six months of the offence'.[41] The purpose of this six-month limitation is to ensure that summary offences are charged and tried as soon as reasonably possible after their alleged commission, so that the recollection of witnesses may still be reasonably clear.[42]

Before exercising their discretion to issue a summons, justices are entitled to enquire into any delay that may have occurred in making the application, even if the statutory time limit for doing so has not expired.[43] If it is unclear whether an information has been laid within the requisite time, the defendant is entitled to the benefit of the doubt.[44]   **3.19**

Where the delay has been deliberate, and to the defendant's detriment, an abuse of process is likely to be found.[45] Equally, where there has been inordinate or unconscionable delay due to the prosecution's inefficiency, the proceedings may be stayed.[46]   **3.20**

However, where delay has not been deliberate or 'unconscionable', certain types of proceedings may nevertheless be stayed. An example is the case of *R v Chief Constable of Merseyside Police ex p Merrill*,[47] where disciplinary proceedings against a police officer were quashed by the Divisional Court where a Chief Constable had erroneously concluded that the service of a disciplinary complaint notice could be deferred until after related criminal proceedings had concluded.

Other examples of proceedings being stayed as a result of delay include: **3.21**

- delay by the prosecution in naming a complainant;[48]
- delay in informing the defendant of the possibility of prosecution;[49]
- delay in serving a summons for an indictable only offence until the accused attained the age of seventeen, when the justices ceased to have a discretion to commit the matter to the Crown Court.[50]

Section 51 of the Crime and Disorder Act 1998

Whilst the magistrates' court should only rarely stay proceedings as an abuse of process, it can do so where allegations were manifestly devoid of all merit, hopelessly misconceived, or   **3.22**

---

[41] Section 127 Magistrates' Court Act 1980. Other statutes have different time limits for specific offences (e.g., twelve months for summonses under the Trade Descriptions Act 1968 and Food Safety Act 1990) and make provision for extending the time for bringing summary proceedings (e.g., s 34 Health and Safety at Work Act 1974). Section 127 does not apply to court martial proceedings: *S* [2013] EWCA Crim 2579.

[42] As explained by Mr Justice May in *Newcastle-upon-Tyne Justices ex p John Bryce (Contractors) Ltd* [1976] 2 All ER 611. See also *R v Scunthorpe Justices ex p McPhee and Gallagher* (1998) 162 JP 635 Divisional Court (CO/1748/97) and the judgment of Dyson J as applied in *CPS v Gloucester Justices* [2008] EWHC 1488 (Admin). An information is laid and time stops on the offence when the information is received at the office of the justices' clerk: *Manchester Stipendiary Magistrate ex p Hill* [1983] 1 AC 328.

[43] *R v Clerk to Medway Justices ex p DHSS* [1986] Crim LR 686 and *Wei Hai Restaurant Ltd v Kingston upon Hull City Council* (2002) 166 JP 185.

[44] *Lloyd v Young* [1963] Crim LR 703. See also *Atkinson v DPP* [2004] 3 All ER 971.

[45] *R v Brentford Justices ex p Wong* [1981] QB 445.

[46] *Oxford City Justices ex p Smith* [1982] 75 Cr App R 200, *R v West London Stipendiary Magistrate ex p Anderson* [1985] 80 Cr App R 143, *R v Gateshead Justices ex p Smith* [1985] 149 JP 681 and *R v Bow Street Stipendiary Magistrate ex p Cherry* [1990] 91 Cr App R 283. See also *DPP v Alexander* [2010] EWHC 2266 (Admin).

[47] [1989] 1 WLR 1077.

[48] *Daventry District Council v Olins* (1990) 154 JP 478, [1990] Crim LR 414.

[49] *R v Bow Street Stipendiary Magistrate ex p DPP and Cherry* [1990] Crim LR 318, [1990] 91 Cr App R 283 and see *Chief Constable of Merseyside ex p Merrill* [1989] 1 WLR 1077.

[50] Considered in *R v Rotherham Magistrates' Court ex p Brough* [1991] Crim LR 522, but not stayed as High Court held there was no bad faith or manipulation of the court process.

vexatious. This applies to all cases, including those that are triable on indictment only and are sent 'forthwith' to the Crown Court under section 51 Crime and Disorder Act 1998. The sending provision under section 51 does not preclude a magistrates' court from exercising its jurisdiction to stay proceedings as an abuse of process in an appropriate case.[51] However, the Administrative court is reluctant to interfere with any magistrates' court refusal to stay proceedings in section 51 cases.[52]

Disclosure

3.23 Disclosure issues are discussed in Chapter 4 and apply equally to the summary jurisdiction of the magistrates' court. This section will consider matters specifically relating to the summary jurisdiction.

Case management powers

3.24 In relation to disclosure generally, regard should be had to (a) the case management principles embodied in the Criminal Procedure Rules (CPR) that all parties should comply with:

- the 'overriding objective' being to deal with criminal cases justly (r.1.1(1);
- dealing with the prosecution[53] and defence fairly (r.1.1.(2)(b);
- dealing with the case efficiently and expeditiously (r.1.1.(2)(e);
- and there is a duty on the court to further the overriding objective by 'actively managing the case' (r.3.2.(2)) which includes the early identification of the real issues in the case, achieving certainty as to what must be done, by whom and when, discouraging delay, and avoiding unnecessary hearings;

and (b) regard should be had to case law decisions such as *Boardman*[54] which emphasize the importance of adhering to the CPR and court orders, Sir Brian Leveson P, citing[55] with approval the *Review of Efficiency in Criminal Proceedings 2015*:

> [199] Whatever we do, we must encourage a reduced tolerance for failure to comply with court directions along with a recognition of the role and responsibilities of the Judge in matters of case management.[56] It cannot be right that a "culture of failure" has developed in the courts, fed by an expectation that deadlines will not be met. If a deadline (e.g. for service of a document(s) or an application) is not met, there must be good reason for it and there must be an expectation that the party which failed to comply can provided that reason.

Advance information

3.25 The prosecutor must make 'initial details of the prosecution case' available to the defendant no later than the beginning of the day of the first hearing, under paragraph 8.2 of the Criminal Procedure Rules 2015. The content of the 'initial details' provided will depend on whether the defendant was in police custody for the offence charged immediately before the first hearing in the magistrates' court.[57]

---

[51] *R (on the application of Chief Constable of Northumbria) v Newcastle upon Tyne Magistrates' Court* [2010] EWHC 935 (Admin).

[52] *R (S) v CPS; R(S) v Oxford Magistrates' Court* [2015] EWHC 2868 (Admin), [2015] Archbold Review 9 p 2–3.

[53] See *DPP v Gowing* [2013] EWHC 4614 (Admin), [2014] 178 JP181.

[54] [2015] EWCA Crim 175, [2015] 1 Cr App R 33.

[55] [2015] EWCA Crim 175 at para 2 of judgment.

[56] See *Jisl* [2004] EWCA Crim 464.

[57] Criminal Procedure Rules, para 8.3.

Rule 8.3 specifies that the initial details must include: **3.26**

(a) where, immediately before the first hearing in the magistrates' court, the defendant was in police custody for the offence charged—
   (i) a summary of the circumstances of the offence, and
   (ii) the defendant's criminal record, if any;

(b) where paragraph (a) does not apply—
   (i) a summary of the circumstances of the offence,
   (ii) any account given by the defendant in interview, whether contained in that summary or in another document,
   (iii) any written witness statement or exhibit that the prosecutor then has available and considers material to plea, or to the allocation of the case for trial, or to sentence,
   (iv) the defendant's criminal record, if any, and
   (v) any available statement of the effect of the offence on a victim, a victim's family or others.

However, providing the summons, information, or charge is clear, failure to provide adequate   **3.27**
advance information will not itself constitute an abuse of process. In an appropriate case the correct remedy is an adjournment, although the case may warrant an award of costs thrown away against the prosecution.[58]

Sentence indication

Sentencing indications in the magistrates court can give rise to arguments about legitimate   **3.28**
expectation. Where magistrates give an indication of sentence at a guilty plea hearing, and a subsequent sentencing hearing comes before a differently constituted court, the defence may cite the earlier indication in an attempt to bind the sentencing court to the earlier indicated sentence.

However, it is clear from the Divisional Court's decision in *Thornton v CPS*[59] that such argu-   **3.29**
ments to bind the subsequent court can only succeed if (a) the magistrates, when giving a sentencing indication, had proper regard to sentencing guidelines, issued by the Sentencing Guidelines Council, as per section 172 of the Criminal Justice Act 2003 and (b) the indication was not unreasonable.

Lord Justice Aikens in *Thornton*, cited with approval the Divisional Court judgment of   **3.30**
Wilkie J, in *Nicholas v Chester Magistrates' Court*:[60]

> We thoroughly deprecate the practice, if such it be, of one bench to adjourn sentencing for reports and in so doing give an indication as to the type of sentence which it would be appropriate to pass where that bench is not reserving sentence to itself. By so doing, as indicated in the authorities, and save in an exceptional case, the effect of that is to fetter the discretion of the sentencing court. In our judgment, that should only be done where the bench reserves to itself the sentence, or in a case where it is absolutely obvious that a certain type of sentence should be considered or should not be considered.[61]

Lord Justice Aikens went on to add, that:

> it is imperative that magistrates do not put themselves in a position which binds the hands of another bench on the question of sentence unless they are absolutely certain that it is the right course to take. Forms can be used, and forms of words used, to ensure that no expectation

---

[58] See *R (on the application of DPP) v Croydon Youth Court* (2001) 165 JPN 143.
[59] [2010] EWHC 346 (Admin).
[60] [2009] EWHC, 1405.
[61] Para 13.

about sentence, legitimate or otherwise, is engendered in the minds of defendants or their advisers.[62]

Civil proceedings

3.31 Where there are linked civil and criminal proceedings, abuse of process arguments may arise in summary proceedings. One such area concerns magistrates' court civil proceedings for cash forfeiture[63] concurrent to Crown Court proceedings. In *Barrington Payton*[64] a defendant in criminal proceedings had disclosed a considerable amount of material (such as names of witnesses who could verify the source of cash) in cash forfeiture civil proceedings in advance of the criminal trial. The defence applied to the magistrates' court to adjourn the cash forfeiture proceedings until the conclusion of the Crown Court trial, as there was the risk of prejudicing the defence at trial.

3.32 No complaint was made on appeal as to the conduct of the civil proceedings, but Lord Justice Pill was sufficiently concerned to make a number of observations as to the appropriate practice that should be adopted where civil proceedings in the magistrates' court run concurrently to criminal proceedings in the Crown Court:[65]

> [26] It is accepted that 'close liaison' would be expected between investigators in the civil and in the criminal proceedings. It is submitted that 'the overwhelming likelihood is that the police would lodge an application for forfeiture (and so effect the detention of the cash and preservation of the status quo) but then seek an adjournment of the application until criminal proceedings (including any appeal) are concluded'. The advantages of this course are described in the note. They include the preservation of the status quo and ensuring that the defendant is 'not embarrassed into having to rehearse what may be part of his defence to the criminal allegation'. The defendant is unlikely to be in receipt of public funding in the civil proceedings. The potential saving of expense by adjourning civil proceedings is also mentioned …
>
> [31] … It is, however, important that care is taken to ensure that the fair trial of a defendant is not prejudiced by anything arising in civil proceedings in the magistrates' court and steps should be taken accordingly.

3.33 Abuse of process arguments raised, on appeal from the magistrates' court to the crown court, in civil proceedings, may be statute barred. The remedy being a challenge by way of judicial review. In *Clayton*[66] the appellants appealed against their conviction for failing to comply with an enforcement notice under section 179 Town and Country Planning Act 1990. The Court of Appeal held that the crown court judge, hearing the matter on appeal from the magistrates' court, had been correct to refuse the application for a stay. Both section 285 Town and Country Planning Act 1990 and the decision in *Peter Edward Wicks*[67] precluded the judge from investigating the alleged unlawful act in the context of the criminal trial.

---

[62] Para 49. See also *R (on the application of C) v Stratford Magistrates' Court* [2012] EWHC 154 (Admin).
[63] See *Serious Organised Crime Agency v Agidi* [2011] EWHC 175 (QB) for an analysis of abuse of process in the context of cash forfeiture proceedings.
[64] [2006] EWCA Crim 1226.
[65] [2006] EWCA Crim 1226 at paras 26 and 31.
[66] [2014] 2 Cr App R 20.
[67] [1998] A.C. 92.

Timing of stay application

An application to stay proceedings may be considered at a preliminary hearing prior or **3.34** immediately prior to summary trial.[68] In *R v Aldershot Youth Court ex p A*, the High Court held that as a matter of principle the defendant should not be required to enter a plea before making his application for a stay. As the application to stay was an application to prevent the trial from commencing it was not appropriate to consider the issue within the trial itself.[69] However, where the application for the proceedings to be stayed is made on the grounds of delay, it will be rare for a court to be in a position to determine whether there was a realistic prospect of a defendant having a fair trial until some or, on occasion, all the evidence had been heard. In those circumstances courts should not generally entertain applications to stay prior to hearing evidence.[70]

Practical points

Prior to making an abuse of process application, consideration should be given to requesting **3.35** that it be heard by a district judge. In considering a stay application, the district judge or justices must make full inquiry into the procedural history of the case, particularly the extent and the reasons for any delay, considering any prejudice which the defence may suffer.[71] Formal evidence should be called.[72]

The inquiry should involve hearing representations from both the prosecution and defence.[73] **3.36** The justices must, in the interests of natural justice, allow the prosecution to put forward an explanation for any default and allow them to make submissions as to whether the criminal proceedings should be stayed.[74]

If a ruling on a stay application is made in the magistrates' court, the court should give its **3.37** reason, however briefly. Advocates are under a duty to take notes of any reasons provided. If an application for judicial review was made the court would anticipate seeing a note of those reasons.[75]

C. The Youth Court

Jurisdiction

The Youth Court's jurisdiction arises from section 45 Children & Young Persons Act 1933, **3.38** as amended by section 70(1) Criminal Justice Act 1991, which provides that it is a court of

---

[68] See Lord Justice Rose's observations in *R v Worcester Magistrates Court ex p Bell* (1993) 157 JP 921, at 929 as to the potential costs savings, and the decision in *R v Horseferry Road Magistrates Court ex p K* [1997] QB 23.

[69] In that case it was allegedly intimated to the appellant's legal representative that if he cooperated in the police interview he would be cautioned and not charged. However the interviewing officer denied making the offer. The appellant made admissions and was charged, following which he applied for a stay of proceedings on the grounds that they amounted to an abuse of process, and that was an issue which should be determined before A was required to enter a plea.

[70] *F* [2011] 2 Cr App R 28 reviewed the authorities regarding applications to stay proceedings on grounds of delay. Not to be confused with submission of no case: *T* [2010] EWCA Crim 630. See also *AT* [2013] EWCA Crim 1850.

[71] *R v Crawley Justices ex p DPP* [1991] COD 365, *The Times* (5 April 1991).

[72] *Burke v The Queen* [2005] EWCA Crim 29 and *The Department for Work and Pensions v Courts and Costello* (1991) [2006] EWHC Admin 1156.

[73] *R v Clerkenwell Stipendiary Magistrate ex p Bell* [1991] Crim LR 468.

[74] *DPP v Ayres* [2004] EWHC 2553, [2006] Crim LR 62.

[75] *R (on the application of Ebrahim) v Feltham Magistrates Court* [2001] EWHC Admin 130.

summary jurisdiction. As such, it is governed by the same statutory provisions as the magistrates' court and has the same powers, including the power to control its own process.[76]

3.39 No child under the age of 10 years' old can be guilty of a criminal offence in England and Wales; as such the Youth Court's jurisdiction extends to defendants aged between 10 and 17 years inclusive.[77] However, this is not an exclusive jurisdiction. The crown court may deal with young defendants for certain, more serious offences.

3.40 The principles of abuse of process in the magistrates' court, therefore, extend to the Youth Court. However, there are two particular additional considerations that should be borne in mind, given the nature of the Youth Court's jurisdiction, namely the timing of proceedings, where this is manipulated to determine trial venue, and the adoption of measures to ensure that young defendants are able to receive a fair trial.

Timing of summons

3.41 Deliberate delay in serving a summons until after the defendant attains the age at which the Youth Court ceases to have jurisdiction can amount to an abuse of process. In *R v Rotherham Justices ex p Brough*,[78] the prosecution delayed service of a summons until the accused attained the age of 17, when the justices no longer had discretion to allow the matter to remain in the Youth Court. Deliberate manipulation of the process will be required in most cases for an application for a stay to be successful.

Effective participation

3.42 In the Youth Court, failure to adhere to procedural safeguards for the benefit of young defendants can result in proceedings being stayed or a conviction quashed. In *R (on the Application of TP) v West London Youth Court*,[79] Scott Baker LJ noted that the following safeguards may ensure that the trial of a young defendant is conducted fairly:

- keeping the claimant's level of cognitive functioning in mind;
- using concise and simple language;
- having regular breaks;
- taking additional time to explain court proceedings;
- being proactive in ensuring the claimant has access to support;
- explaining and ensuring the claimant understands the ingredients of the charge;
- explaining the possible outcomes and sentences; and
- ensuring that cross-examination is carefully controlled so that questions are short and clear and frustration is minimized.[80]

3.43 Failure to follow the safeguards may render the proceedings unfair, particularly when a young defendant is involved.

3.44 When trying a child with learning difficulties, notwithstanding the absence of statutory powers to appoint an intermediary, the Youth Court had a duty to do so where the kind

---

[76] See *R v Barking Youth Court & CPS, ex p P* [2002] EWHC 734 (Admin).

[77] See *R v Aldershot Youth Court ex p A*, [1997] CLY 1257.

[78] [1991] Crim LR 522, but not stayed as the High Court held there was no bad faith or manipulation of the court process.

[79] [2005] EWHC 2583 (Admin).

[80] *R (on the Application of TP) v West London Youth Court, Crown Prosecution Service, Secretary of State for the Home Department* [2005] EWHC 2583 (Admin), at para 26. See also the Advocates' Gateway <http://www.theadvocatesgateway.org/>.

of assistance required to ensure that such a child had a fair trial could not be provided by a lawyer.[81]

There is no equivalent procedure to that in the Crown Court to deal with fitness to plead. **3.45** However, Youth Courts have two tools to deal with fitness to plead: an application for a stay and proceedings to make findings of fact rather than convicting, where appropriate.[82] The discretion as to whether to proceed to making a finding of guilt depends on the court's assessment and whether it was necessary in the circumstances. In *G v DPP*[83] the Divisional Court held that it had been appropriate for the magistrates' court to proceed with the trial of a young offender, because, despite expert evidence that he was not fit for trial, he understood and could engage with the trial process and an intermediary had been appointed to assist him.

Provided there is evidence from which the jury may properly convict, it is only in exceptional **3.46** circumstances that the prosecution may be required to justify the decision to prosecute.[84] It remains open to the prosecution in an individual case, for good reason, to disapply its own policy or guidance. Therefore even if it can be shown that in one respect or another, part or parts of the relevant guidance or policy have not been adhered to, it does not follow that there was an abuse of process.[85] However, in exceptional cases, it is not impossible to obtain judicial review of a decision to prosecute a child.[86]

D. Challenging the Magistrates' Court Decision: Crown Court

A decision made by a magistrates' court regarding an application to stay proceedings may be **3.47** challenged by the defence on appeal by way of rehearing at the Crown Court under section 108 of the Magistrates' Court Act 1980, or alternatively in the High Court by either party by way of judicial review.

If a defendant were to be convicted summarily and appealed to the Crown Court, the appro- **3.48** priate course is to invite the court to quash the conviction on the ground that the original trial was irremediably unfair. An appellant could not ask the Crown Court to stay proceedings, because a mere stay at the appeal stage leaves the original conviction standing: see *R v Feltham Magistrates' Court*.[87]

---

[81] In *R (on app of C) v Sevenoaks Youth Court* [2009] EWHC 3088 (Admin), when trying a child with learning difficulties, such as C, the Youth Court had a duty under both the procedural rules and the common law to ensure C had a fair trial, not just during the proceedings, but beforehand as he and his lawyers prepared for trial. C needed to be able to understand and follow the case as it progressed, communicate effectively with his lawyer, question the victim, understand how to approach the issue of his co-accused, and be able to give cohesive evidence should he choose to. It was unlikely that this kind of assistance could be provided by a lawyer and therefore an intermediary should have been appointed.

[82] *Crown Prosecution Service v P* [2007] EWHC 946 (Admin).

[83] *G v DPP* [2012] EWHC 3174 (Admin).

[84] Lord Judge CJ in *A* [2012] EWCA Crim 434, para 84.

[85] Lord Judge CJ in *A* [2012] EWCA Crim 434, para 84.

[86] In *R (on the application of E, S and R) v DPP* [2011] EWHC 1465 (Admin) the decision of a Crown prosecutor to prosecute a 14-year-old girl for the alleged sexual abuse of her two younger sisters had to be quashed: the decision-making process was flawed in that it was unclear whether the Crown prosecutor had properly taken into account the concern raised in a report by a multi-agency strategy group that prosecution was not in the best interests of any of the children. In *R (on the application of CM) v CPS* [2014] EWHC 4457 (Admin) a decision to prosecute a 10-year-old boy for sexual offences committed against a younger boy was not irrational, nor had there been a failure by the CPS to follow its settled policy on the prosecution of young offenders.

[87] [2001] 1 All ER 831.

3.49 Where a defendant invites the magistrates' court to 'state a case' for the opinion of the High Court under section 111 of the Magistrates' Court Act 1980, the right to appeal to the Crown Court ceases to exist.[88]

Powers of the Crown Court

3.50 The Crown Court may, in the course of hearing any appeal, correct any error or mistake in the order or judgment incorporating the decision which is the subject of appeal.[89]

3.51 On termination of the hearing of the appeal, the Crown Court may: confirm, reverse, or vary any part of the decision appealed against, including a determination not to impose a separate penalty in respect of an offence;[90] remit the matter with its opinion thereon to the authority whose decision is appealed against;[91] or may make such order in the matter as the court thinks just, and by such order exercise any power which the said authority might have exercised.[92]

Procedure

3.52 Procedure on appeal to the Crown Court is governed by Part 4 of the Criminal Procedure Rules 2015 (SI 2015/1490).

3.53 An appeal against the magistrates' decision must be lodged on notice, in writing within twenty-one days of that decision, to a court officer of the magistrates' court and to any other party to the appeal, stating the grounds of appeal. Applications for leave to appeal against conviction out of time can be made, in writing, stating the proposed grounds of appeal and the reason for applying out of time.

> Rule 34.2:
> (2) The appellant must serve the appeal notice—
>   (a) as soon after the decision appealed against as the appellant wants; but
>   (b) not more than 21 days after—
>   (i) sentence or the date sentence is deferred, whichever is earlier, if the appeal is against conviction or against a finding of guilt,
>   (ii) sentence, if the appeal is against sentence, or
>   (iii) the order or failure to make an order about which the appellant wants to appeal, in any other case.

3.54 The appeal to the Crown Court is a complete rehearing.[93] There is no obligation on the prosecution to put their case in the same way as in the lower court.[94]

E. Challenging the Magistrates' Court Decision: Application to the Administrative Court

3.55 The Administrative Courts' judicial review jurisdiction is supervisory rather than appellate.[95] It is concerned with procedure and the decision-making process and not the merits of the

---

[88] See MCA 1980 s111(4). The procedure for appeal to the High Court by way of Case Stated is governed by Part 35 of the Criminal Procedure Rules 2015 (SI 2015/1490).

[89] Senior Courts Act 1981 ('SCA') s48(1).

[90] SCA 1981 s48 (2)(a).

[91] SCA 1981 s48 (2)(b).

[92] SCA 1981 s48 (2)(c). Under section 48(4) this includes power to award a punishment, whether more or less severe than that awarded by the magistrates' court whose decision is appealed against, if that is a punishment which that magistrates' court might have awarded.

[93] SCA 1981 s79(3).

[94] *Hingley-Smith v DPP* [1998] 1 Archbold News 2, DC.

[95] The application for permission to apply for judicial review is made to a High Court judge, is governed by the Civil Procedure Rules part 54 and The Administrative Court Practice Direction [2000] 1 WLR 1654.

original case. It is not a system of appeal, and the administrative court, will not substitute its own decision for that of the body under review.[96]

Irrationality test

The Administrative Court will only intervene and quash a decision which was, in the words of Lord Justice Bingham in *R v Willesden Justices ex p Clemmings*, **3.56**

> ... so plainly irrational and untenable that no reasonable bench of justices, properly directed, could have reached it. That is, of course, a very high standard for an applicant to meet.[97]

Following the above 'irrationality' test, Lord Justice Brooke stated in *R v Barry Magistrates'* **3.57** *Court ex p Malpas*:

> Where magistrates have been discouraged from staying proceedings as an abuse and enjoined only to do so in exceptional circumstances, it would be difficult to overrule their decision as a wrong exercise of their discretion.[98]

> It must be recognised that a decision whether or not to stay a prosecution is pre-eminently a decision of fact and degree which it will always be difficult to attack in point of law, particularly where (as here) there has been very extensive oral evidence upon which the tribunal will have had to form a judgment. This [Divisional] Court is not a Court of Appeal and it will scarcely ever be possible to characterise a refusal to stay as perverse, least of all when the tribunal has had the advantage denied to this court of actually hearing live evidence.[99]

The above sentiments were embraced by Lord Justice Simon Brown in the unreported case of **3.58** *R v Court Martial Administration Officer ex p Jordan*.[100]

The Administrative Court has no jurisdiction to hear an application for judicial review where **3.59** proceedings before the magistrates have not concluded.[101] The court will expect to see a note of the magistrates' ruling on the stay application before deciding to grant permission for judicial review of the magistrates' decision, with an agreed note summarizing the effect of any relevant oral evidence.[102]

Issue of summons

The decision to issue a summons is subject to judicial review by the Administrative Court. **3.60** The High Court may (a) compel the issue of a summons unreasonably refused and (b) quash a summons issued as part of vexatious and oppressive allegations, which amount to an abuse of process.

Sending youth

The appropriate method of challenging a decision of justices to send a defendant aged under **3.61** eighteen for trial in the Crown Court under section 24(1) of the Magistrates' Courts Act 1980, is by way of application for judicial review, rather than by way of application to the Crown Court

---

To comply with the Pre-Action Protocol for Judicial Review, a letter before action should be sent to the defendant (state agency) and any interested parties prior to commencement of the claim. Thereafter, the claim form (N461) must be filed promptly and no later than three months after the date of decision complained of.

[96] See Lord Hailsham, *Chief Constable of North Wales v Evans* [1982] 1 WLR 1155 at 1160 <https://www.justice.gov.uk/courts/procedure-rules/civil/rules/part54>.

[97] [1988] 87 Cr App R 280 at para 286.

[98] See also *R v Liverpool City Justices and CPS ex p Price* (1998) 162 JP 766.

[99] [1998] COD 90 at p 91.

[100] 27 July 1999, DC, CO/2631/98, at p 14.

[101] *R (Hoar—Stevens) Richmond Magistrates'Court* [2004] Crim LR 474.

[102] *R v Magistrates' Court ex p Ebrahim, Mouat v DPP* [2001] 1 All ER 831.

for a stay on the ground of abuse of process. Although the position might be different where there was a patent lack of jurisdiction to commit.

3.62 A court should only send a youth charged with a grave crime to the Crown Court for trial if the offence is of such gravity that a sentence substantially beyond the two year maximum for a detention and training order is a realistic possibility.[103] The allocation decision for grave crimes has been the subject of extensive scrutiny by the Administrative Court.[104]

3.63 In *AH*[105] the justices had committed a 14-year-old for trial on a charge of robbery on the ground that he was not a 'persistent offender' (which ruled out the possibility of a detention and training order), but had indicated that custody ought to be an option in the event of conviction. It was held that they had erred in their approach. However, the justices' error did not render the committal a nullity, the Crown Court had been correct in taking the view that the appropriate method of challenge would have been by way of judicial review, and the subsequent proceedings in the Crown Court resulted in a lawful conviction and sentence.[106]

Appeal to Supreme Court

3.64 There is no right of appeal to the Court of Appeal against an Administrative Courts' refusal of leave or decision after hearing the appeal.[107] Instead an appeal from the Administrative Court lies direct to the Supreme Court, subject to leave on a point of general public importance.

Matter on indictment

3.65 The refusal by the Crown Court to stay proceedings on the grounds of abuse of process cannot be challenged in the Administrative Court, as it concerns a matter on indictment.[108] For example, judicial review is not available for challenges to the application for dismissal or for a stay of proceedings in cases committed under section 51 of the Crime and Disorder Act 1998.[109]

3.66 Section 29 SCA 1981 has been held to be compatible with the Article 6 ECHR right to a fair trial, as a defendant has a right to appeal a Crown Court decision to the Court of Appeal Criminal Division.[110]

---

[103] See the definitive guideline, 'Overarching Principles: Sentencing Youths' (2009) at para 12.11. See *R (on the application of M) v Waltham Forest Youth Court and DPP; R (on the application of W) v Thetford Youth Court and DPP,* [2003] 1 Cr App R (S) 67, concerned committal proceedings but is equally applicable to the sending provisions.

[104] Leveson J reviewed these authorities in *R (H) v Southampton Youth Court* [2004] EWHC 2912 (Admin).

[105] [2002] EWCA Crim 2938.,

[106] It is anticipated that this approach will apply equally to sending a case under section 24 MCA 1980.

[107] Under section 18(1)(a) Senior Courts Act 1981 No appeal shall lie to the Court of Appeal—(a) except as provided by the Administration of Justice Act 1960, from any judgment of the High Court in any criminal cause or matter. Where the cause or matter is one which, if carried to its conclusion, might result in the conviction of the person charged and in a sentence of some punishment, such as imprisonment or fine, it is a 'criminal cause or matter': *Amand v. Home Secretary* [1943] A.C. 147. See also *R v Tottenham Justices ex p Ewing, unreported* (1986) 30 July.

[108] See section 29 of the Senior Court Act 1981: Re *Smalley* [1985] AC 622, HL, *In re Sampson* [1987] 1 WLR 194, HL, *R v Manchester Crown Court ex p DPP* (Re Ashton) [1994] 1 AC 9.

[109] *R (on the application of Salubi) v Bow Street Magistrates' Court* [2002] 1 WLR 3073, [2002] 2 Cr App R 40, in which the Divisional Court dismissed a claim for judicial review of a judge's decision refusing to stay proceedings sent to the Crown Court under CDA 1998 s51, holding that the decision was caught by the exclusionary words of SCA 1981 s29(3). Also see *R (on the application of Lee Snelgrove) and Woolwich Crown Court* [2004] EWHC 2172 (Admin), [2005] 1 WLR 3223.

[110] *R (Shields) v Liverpool Crown Court* [2001] EWHC Admin 90, [2001] ACD 325, DC and *R v Canterbury Crown Court ex p Regentford Ltd* [2001] HRLR 18.

F. Court of Appeal Criminal Division

A refusal, at the Crown Court,to stay proceedings as an abuse of process can form the basis of **3.67** an appeal against conviction to the Court of Appeal Criminal Division.[111] Convictions can be quashed for procedural irregularity.[112]

In *Martin* Lord Hope stated:[113] **3.68**

I do not think that it can be doubted that the appeal court ... has power to declare a conviction to be unsafe and to quash the conviction if they find that the course of the proceedings leading to what would otherwise have been a fair trial has been such as to threaten either basic human rights or the rule of law.

In *Nicholas Mullen,* the Court of Appeal, in quashing a conviction for conspiracy to cause **3.69** explosions likely to endanger life, gave a legal meaning to the 'unsafe' test, which was broad enough to include pre-trial abuse of process.[114] Lord Justice Rose, giving judgment of the court, said that the British authorities had initiated and subsequently assisted in and procured the deportation of Mullen by unlawful means, which breached public international law.

In considering the 'safety' of a Crown Court conviction, the Court of Appeal should also have **3.70** regard to any breaches of Article 6. However, a Strasbourg finding of unfairness, does not, in itself establish an unsafe conviction.[115]

Prosecution appeal

Prosecution rights of appeal in relation to trials on indictment, which cover abuse of process **3.71** applications, exist for:

- rulings in preparatory hearings in serious fraud cases[116] and long and complex cases,[117] and;
- judges' rulings in relation to all trials on indictment, at any stage prior to the start of the judge's summing-up.[118] This wide right of appeal, does not apply to jury discharge rulings,[119] requires leave (of the first instance judge or the Court of Appeal)[120] and the prosecution have to accept that if the appeal is unsuccessful (either because the ruling is confirmed on appeal or leave is refused or the appeal is abandoned) then the accused is acquitted of the relevant offence;[121]
- Evidential rulings, which significantly weaken the prosecution case, limited to 'qualifying' offences, which apply pre- and at trial (up to the opening of the case for the defence).[122] An unsuccessful appeal against an evidential ruling does not automatically lead to an acquittal

---

[111] *Bloomfield* [1997] 1 Cr App R 135, and *Alan Martin* [1998] AC 917.
[112] See JR Spencer QC, 'Quashing Convictions for Procedural Irregularity' [2007] Crim LR 835.
[113] [1998] AC 917.
[114] [2000] QB 520 and see commentary at [1999] Crim LR 561–563.
[115] *Michael Lewis* [2005] Crim LR 797.
[116] Section 9 CJA 1987.
[117] Sections 35 and 36 CPIA 1996.
[118] Section 58 CJA 2003.
[119] Section 57(2) (a) CJA 2003.
[120] Section 57(4) CJA 2003.
[121] Sections 58(8), 58(12) and 61(3) CJA 2003. For observations on section 58 see *Clarke* [2008] 1 Cr.App.R.33, *H* [2008] EWCA Crim 483, *R* [2008] EWCA Crim 370, *CPS v C,M and H* [2009] EWCA Crim 2614, *NT* [2010] EWCA Crim 711. See also LH Leigh 'Some Points on Section 58 Appeals' [2010] Archbold News 2 pp 4–6.
[122] Sections 62 and 63 CJA 2003.

of the accused and can only do so if the prosecution indicates that it does not intend to proceed with the prosecution.[123]

3.72 The Court of Appeal may not reverse a ruling on appeal under the CJA 2003 provisions unless it is satisfied:

(a) that the ruling was wrong in law,

(b) that the ruling involved an error of law or principle, or that the ruling was a ruling that it was not reasonable for the judge to have made.[124]

3.73 On a cautionary note, the Court of Appeal Criminal Division are taking an increasingly critical view of unmeritorious appeals. In *Zantoe Davis and Mercedes Thabangu*[125] Lord Chief Justice Thomas held that where no competent lawyer could conceivably have advised that there were arguable grounds, the leave application was an abuse of process, being a frivolous and vexatious application. The appeal was dismissed with the matter being referred to the Solicitors Regulatory Authority and the Legal Aid Agency.

---

[123] Section 66(3) CJA 2003.

[124] Section 67 CJA 2003. This provision was considered in *B (Prosecution Appeal)* [2008] EWCA Crim 1144. The Court of Appeal in upholding the trial judge's decision to stay proceedings, criticized his grant of leave to appeal. Leave to appeal under section 57 of the Act would not be given unless it was seriously arguable, not that the discretionary jurisdiction might have been exercised differently, but that it was unreasonable for it to have been exercised in the way it had been. The mere fact that the judge could reasonably have reached the opposite conclusion to the one he did, and that he acknowledged that there were valid arguments that might have caused him to do so, did not begin to provide a basis for a successful appeal.

[125] [2013] EWCA Crim 2424.

4

DISCLOSURE

A. Introduction

In appropriate circumstances, a failure on the part of the prosecution to make proper disclosure may result in proceedings being stayed as an abuse of process. This chapter will examine the relationship between disclosure and abuse of process. **4.1**

The distinction between the issues of disclosure and abuse of process was considered in *Herbert Austin*.[1] Mr. Justice Irwin observed:[2] **4.2**

> Disclosure is concerned with the question of what material should be disclosed to the defence with a view to its being deployed before the tribunal of fact, whether that is the jury dealing with the issue of guilt or innocence, or the judge dealing with an issue such as whether proceedings should be stayed for abuse of process. It is everyday experience in criminal proceedings that a judge may be required to examine material which is prima facie disclosable in order to rule on whether disclosure to the defence should be withheld, for example on grounds of public interest immunity, and it may (although only exceptionally) be appropriate for this purpose for a special counsel to be appointed. If the judge does so rule, that material will play no further part in the trial, and the judge will put it out of his mind for the purpose of any subsequent rulings in the case, including any ruling on abuse of process. All this is well established.

The disclosure aspect has to be considered first. If the material does not fall to be disclosed, either because it does not come within the scope of the disclosure obligations or because the judge has permitted non-disclosure (for example because of public interest immunity) that is the end of the matter. The disclosure issue will have been determined, and proceedings **4.3**

---

[1] *Herbert Austin* [2013] EWCA Crim 1028; [2014] 1 WLR. 1045; [2013] 2 Cr App R 33; [2013] Crim L R 914.

[2] At para 47 of judgment.

cannot be regarded as an abuse of process where the application is based on non-disclosure of material that does not have to be disclosed.

B. Right to a Fair Trial

4.4 The importance of disclosure in ensuring the right to a fair trial cannot be overstated. Clear recognition of the need for proper disclosure can be found in the Attorney General's Guidelines:

> Disclosure is one of the most important issues in the criminal justice system and the application of proper and fair disclosure is a vital component of a fair criminal justice system. The 'golden rule' is that fairness requires full disclosure should be made of all material held by the prosecution that weakens its case or strengthens that of the defence.[3]

4.5 Fair disclosure of information to an accused, by the prosecution is 'an inseparable part of a fair trial' under Article 6 of the ECHR.[4]

4.6 As Lord Bingham stated in *H*:[5] when referring to unused material,

> [b]itter experience has shown that miscarriages of justice may occur where such material is withheld from disclosure. The golden rule is that full disclosure should be made.

C. Criminal Procedure and Investigations Act 1996

4.7 In relation to offences into which a criminal investigation was commenced on or after April 2005, the duties and responsibilities of the parties with regard to disclosure are now governed by Parts I and II of the Criminal Procedure and Investigations Act 1996 as amended by the Criminal Justice Act 2003. Part I (sections.1–21) has created a staged approach (initial prosecution disclosure, defence disclosure, continual review by the prosecution). Part II (sections 22–27) provides for a code of practice for regulating action the police must take in recording and retaining material obtained in the course of a criminal investigation and revealing it to the prosecution for a decision on disclosure. A revised code of practice was brought into operation on 19 March 2015. Revised guidelines on disclosure were published by the Attorney General in December 2013 in conjunction with a revised judicial guidance on the disclosure of unused material in criminal cases. These replace earlier guidelines and an earlier protocol and, in accordance with Criminal Practice Direction IV Disclosure 15 A, unreported, 29 September 29 2015. They should be read together as complementary, comprehensive guidance that should be complied with.

Primary disclosure

4.8 The statutory framework for criminal investigation and disclosure is contained in the CPIA and the CPIA Code of Practice. The CPIA aims to ensure that criminal investigations are conducted in a fair, objective, and thorough manner, and to require prosecutors to disclose material to the defence which has not previously been disclosed to the accused and which might reasonably be considered capable of undermining the case for the prosecution against the accused or of assisting the case for the accused. The CPIA requires a timely dialogue

---

[3] See foreword in 'Attorney-Generals Guidelines on Disclosure' (April 2005).
[4] See Para 1 of 'Attorney Generals Guidelines on Disclosure' (April 2005).
[5] [2004] UKHL 3 at para 14.

between the prosecution, defence, and the court to enable the prosecution to identify such material.[6]

4.9 The scheme under section 3(1)(a) CPIA 1996 provides a single test for disclosure and requires the prosecution to:

> disclose to the accused any prosecution material which has not previously been disclosed to the accused and which might reasonably be considered capable of undermining the case for the prosecution against the accused or of assisting the case for the accused.[7]

4.10 'Prosecution material' is defined in section 3(2) as material:

(a) which is in the prosecutor's possession, and came into his possession in connection with the case for the prosecution against the accused, or
(b) which, in pursuance of a code operative under Part II, he has inspected in connection with the case for the prosecution against the accused.[8]

The prosecution must of course also disclose the evidential basis of their case.

4.11 There are a number of consequences which arise out of this procedure.

(i) It is the prosecution who apply the test. This is of course meant to be objective, however, given some of the disclosure decisions that have historically led to the collapse of cases in the past (see later) there is bound to be some concern as to the approach taken.
(ii) The prosecution is absolved from time limits and it is common for the Crown to repeatedly return to court to seek further time for the service of material. It should be noted, however, that judges are increasingly using their powers of case management to keep trials within tighter parameters.

Disclosure guidance

4.12 For guidance as to the correct approach to disclosure one needs to refer to

- The Criminal Procedure Rules, in particular Rule 3.2 which imposes a duty on the Court to further the overriding objective 'by actively managing the case' which includes 'the early identification of the real issues'
- The CPIA Code of Practice 2015 under section 23 CPIA
- The Attorney General's Guidelines on Disclosure 2000, 2005, 2011, and 2013
- The Judicial Protocol on the Disclosure of Unused Material in Criminal Cases, December 2013
- Review of Disclosure in Criminal Proceedings, September 2011
- Sir Brian Leveson P in the Court of Appeal case of *R*,[9] sets out guidance on the proper approach to disclosure and abuse of process.

Court of Appeal guidance

4.13 Five key principles can be gleaned from *R*:

(1) The prosecution must be in the driving seat at the stage of initial disclosure,[10] adopting a considered and appropriately resourced approach, including an overall disclosure strategy, selection of software tools, identifying and isolating material that was subject

---

[6] See AG Guidelines para 1.
[7] CPIA 1996 s 3(1)(a).
[8] CPIA 1996 s 3(2).
[9] [2015] EWCA Crim 1941; Archbold Review [2015] 1 pp 1–2.
[10] At para 32 of judgment.

to legal professional privilege and proposing search terms. A disclosure management document should clarify the prosecution's disclosure approach and identify disputed issues. Explanation would prompt early engagement from the defence as embodied in the Better Case Management initiative.[11]

(2) The prosecution must encourage dialogue and prompt engagement with the defence, with the defence under a duty to engage with the prosecution. Initial disclosure required an analysis of the likely cases of the prosecution and defence.[12]

(3) The prosecution is not required to do the impossible.[13] The prosecution are entitled to use appropriate sampling of items and search terms and its record-keeping and scheduling obligations were modified by Court of Appeal case law.[14] The prosecution should formulate a disclosure strategy, discuss the same with the court and the defence, utilizing technology to make appropriate searches, and recording the same.

(4) The process of disclosure should be subject to robust judicial case management,[15] as is clear from case law since *Jisl*.[16]

(5) Flexibility is crucial, with the judge, after discussion with the parties, devising a tailored or bespoke approach to disclosure, subject to the CPIA.[17]

4.14   As pointed out by the Court of Appeal in the case of *R*,[18] the scene is set by the Criminal Procedure Rules, underlined by Gross LJ at para 31 of his review:

> The Rules now consolidate the courts's case management powers and furnish a guide to the underlying culture intended to govern the conduct of criminal trials. Accordingly, the rules are or should be of the first importance in the proper application of the disclosure regime.

Case management

4.15   Criminal court practitioners are aware of the increasing importance of case management and how it applies to considerations in relation to disclosure in the modern trial. Rule 3.2 of the Criminal Procedure Rules imposes a duty on the court to further the overriding objective 'by actively managing the case', which includes the 'the early identification of the real issues'. Rule 3.11(a) requires the Court to establish, with the active assistance of the parties, what disputed issues they intend to explore.

Defence statement

4.16   The primary disclosure required by section 3 CPIA is intended to be followed by the service of a defence statement setting out the nature of the accused's defence, including any particular defences on which he intends to rely, and indicating the matters on which he takes issue with the prosecution under section 6A of the CPIA 1996.[19]

4.17   Where the prosecutor has complied, or purported to comply with section 3 and the defendant has been charged with an indictable offence, the service of a defence statement is compulsory.[20]

---

[11] At para 34 of judgment.
[12] At para 35 of judgment.
[13] At para 36 of judgment.
[14] See *Brendan Pearson and Paul Cadman* [2006] EWCA Crim 3366 and the AG's 2013 Guidelines.
[15] At paras 39–41 of judgment.
[16] [2004] EWCA Crim 696. See also *Boardman* [2015] EWCA Crim 175.
[17] At paras 49–51 of judgment.
[18] [2015] EWCA Crim 1941.
[19] S 6A CPIA applicable to investigations after 4 April 4 2005.
[20] S 5(1),(5) CPIA 1996.

Section 6A does not require a defendant to incriminate himself: merely to disclose what is to **4.18** happen at trial. Where the defendant intends to put forward no positive case, and not to take issue with any matters of fact advanced by the prosecution, the defence statement must say that he does not admit the offence (or the relevant part of it), that he calls upon the prosecution to prove it, and that he advances no positive case. If the possibility is to be raised distinctly before the jury that the prosecution may be wrong as to a factual matter, that must be set out in the statement.[21] It should be noted, however, that, should a defendant fail to comply fully with section 5, 6B, or 6C in the view of a judge at pre-trial hearing, there is a possibility of comment being made or inferences being drawn.[22] This can often lead to protracted discussions at the pre-trial hearing as to what the issues are. Anecdotally, one understands that pre-trial hearings are often adjourned due to the lack of a defence statement. Whilst a judge is of course entitled to clarify matters and seek to identify the issues, he is not entitled to require counsel to reveal his instructions or force him to serve a defence statement.[23]

Further obligations are now imposed upon the defence. Section 6B of CPIA 1996 imposes **4.19** a duty to provide an updated defence statement (or a statement indicating that the original document stands) within a period to be specified by regulation.

There is no question but that current thought is that the service of defence statements should **4.20** be part of a 'dialogue' between the prosecution and the defence as part of the case management approach to identifying the issues. Certainly, a defence statement that consisted merely in a general denial of the counts in the indictment together with an assertion that the defendant took issue with any witness purporting to give evidence contrary to his denials did not meet the purpose of a defence statement and was described as woefully inadequate.[24]

Post defence statement

Once the defence statement has been served, the defence may make an application for spe- **4.21** cific disclosure of any material which it has reasonable cause to believe should have been disclosed pursuant to section 3.[25]

Any application for further disclosure will usually arise from the schedule of unused material **4.22** compiled by the prosecution, the MG6C, and served as part of their duties under section 3. It is usual for the MG6C to be updated as the process of disclosure continues even after service of the defence statement. Often at an early stage there will be requests by the defence for clarification as to items on the schedule which may be vaguely or incorrectly described. It is not unusual to see descriptions such as 'box of documents' on a schedule which are of no assistance to anyone, either to the prosecution in satisfying their duties to examine the material in their possession or to the defence in trying to identify material that may be of assistance to them.

Accurate scheduling is therefore essential to the proper implementation of the disclosure **4.23** regime. The CPIA Code of Practice 2015, paragraph 6.2, provides that 'material which may be relevant to an investigation, which has been retained in accordance with this code, and which the disclosure officer believes will not form part of the prosecution case, must be listed on a schedule'.

---

[21] *Rochford* [2011] 1 Cr App R 11, CA.
[22] S 6E CPIA 1996.
[23] *Rochford* [2011] 1 Cr App R 11 CA.
[24] *Bryant*, unreported, 28 July 2005, CA [2005] EWCA Crim 2079.
[25] S 8 CPIA 1996.

4.24 At paragraph 6.9, the disclosure officer should ensure that each item of material is listed separately on the schedule, and is numbered consecutively. The description of each item should make clear the nature of the item and should contain sufficient detail to enable the prosecutor to decide whether he needs to inspect the material before deciding whether or not it should be disclosed.

4.25 At paragraph 6.10 in some enquiries it may not be practicable to list each item of material separately. For example, there may be many items of a similar or repetitive character. These may be listed in a block and described by quantity and generic title. And at paragraph 6.11, even if some material is listed in a block, the disclosure officer must ensure that any items among that material which might satisfy the test for prosecution disclosure are listed and described individually.

Continuing disclosure duty

4.26 In addition, the prosecution has a continuing duty of disclosure which applies after the prosecution have complied or purported to comply, with section 3 and before the accused is acquitted or convicted or the prosecution decides not to proceed with the case concerned. The test is the same as that for section 3 CPIA, namely whether the material undermines the case for the prosecution against the accused or assists the case for the accused.

4.27 It should be noted that section 3 (and therefore section 7) does not require the prosecution to disclose material which is either neutral or adverse to the defendant. Indeed prosecutors have been consistently discouraged from disclosing material that they are not obliged to disclose, not least to avoid over-burdening and distracting the trial process with unnecessary materials.[26]

4.28 The legislation does not prescribe the method of disclosure, or the process to be adopted by the prosecution. Rather it is focused on the end result: disclosure which complies with section 3.[27]

4.29 The courts are now far more involved in cases than they were formerly and will certainly be firm in ensuring that any disclosure process is not abused:

> Prosecutors must not abrogate their duties under the CPIA by making wholesale disclosure in order to avoid carrying out the disclosure exercise themselves. Likewise, defence practitioners should avoid fishing expeditions and where disclosure is not provided using this as an excuse for an abuse of process application.[28]

D. Criminal Procedure Rules and Leveson Review

4.30 The modern approach to disclosure, case management, and engagement can be found in the Criminal Procedure Rules and Leveson Review.[29]

The early identification of trial issues is important, as highlighted in paragraph 24 of the Review. Sir Brian Leveson P stated:

> [24] The underlying approach to this Review has been to consider ways of encouraging better communication between the agencies involved in criminal justice, encouraging better

---

[26] *R* [2015] EWCA Crim 1941 CA para 10.

[27] *R* [2015]EWCA Crim 1941 para 11.

[28] Attorney General's Guidelines April 2005.

[29] Sir Brian Leveson President of the Queen's Bench Division, 'Review of Efficiency in Criminal Proceedings', January 2015.

communication between the parties to criminal litigation and maximizing the opportunities to improve effectiveness and efficiency with the use of modern IT. From first to last, it also focuses on improving the prospects of a fair and just trial, including identification of the issues, which will lead to the conviction of the guilty and the acquittal of the innocent[30]

The Review[31] emphasizes the need for case ownership. For each case, in the police, the CPS, and for the defence, in order to maximize the opportunities for case management, there must be one person who is, and is identified to be, responsible for the conduct of the case. **4.31**

In terms of direct engagement, the Review is clear: **4.32**

the Criminal Procedure Rules should place a duty of direct engagement between identified representatives who have case ownership responsibilities[32]

and

The Criminal Procedure Rules need to make it clear that the parties are under a duty to engage at the first available opportunity.[33]

Robust judicial case management is also identified in the Review as an important principle: **4.33**

the court must be prepared robustly to manage its work ... all parties must be required to comply with the Criminal Procedure Rules and to work to identify the issues so as to ensure that court time is deployed to maximum effectiveness and efficiency.[34]

The importance attached to adherence to court orders and effective case management, which obviously includes disclosure, is illustrated by the remarks of Sir Brian Leveson P in the Court of Appeal in *Boardman*:[35] **4.34**

[2] Whatever we do, we must encourage a reduced tolerance for failure to comply with court directions along with a recognition of the role and responsibilities of the Judge in matters of case management. It cannot be right that a 'culture of failure' has developed in courts, fed by an expectation that deadlines will not be met. If a deadline (e.g. for service of documents or an application) is not met, there must be good reason for it.

E. Summary Proceedings

Every case will produce its own unique set of features but traditionally many summary allegations have been met with a relative passive defence disclosure strategy, with no Defence Statement being served. Notable exceptions, which warrant an active defence engagement, include cases which feature vulnerable defendants, disputed identification, alibi, surveillance, civilian third parties (including experts), disputed admissibility, fabrication or manipulation of evidence, and defendants who are well known to the police. In some situations, particularly where there are unequivocal instructions for a positive defence, there is benefit in the defence making disclosure requests. This is particularly so, when it can be put before the court to make the point that the defence disclosed did not receive even the most cursory of prosecution consideration, still less investigation. **4.35**

The key to disclosure is the fullest possible disclosure of the details of the prosecution case. This should include unused material and the reason for not relying on it as this, absent cogent **4.36**

---

[30] Criminal Procedure Rule C1.1.
[31] At para 26.
[32] At para 33.
[33] At para 34.
[34] At para 38.
[35] [2015] EWCA Crim 175.

explanation, may fall into the category of information which may cause the tribunal of fact to have less confidence in the evidence that has been adduced.[36]

4.37 Advice at the police station may have an effect on the prosecution attitude to disclosure and this should be reviewed to see whether there is any advantage in serving a Defence Statement following a no comment interview. Investigative records should also be sought on the basis that the failure to enable comment by the defendant on the fact that the prosecution's lack of interest in an innocent explanation may in certain circumstances arguably amount to an abuse.

F. Crown Court Proceedings

4.38 As noted above, the defendant in the Crown Court now faces an array of administrative obligations (including disclosure of defence witnesses) and so a passive or reactive defence may be less attractive than was formerly the position.

4.39 The primary decision will be whether bare compliance or enthusiastic engagement is the order of the day and this, always assuming that one is in a position to produce anything that amounts to a defence within the relevant timeframe, is likely to be dependent upon the perceived advantages to be gained in the disclosure process.

4.40 A starting point is the assurance that the prosecution evidence served is the prosecution case and that there are no further areas under review or consideration. It is important to be certain that the indictment is in its final form and that the case for the prosecution is sufficiently clear. A prosecution case summary or opening note should be requested if there is any doubt. Pressure to muddle through before there is a clear understanding of the factual matrix that the jury will ultimately be requested to consider by the prosecution, including applications to adduce character and hearsay evidence, should be resisted on the basis that there is (a) an inherent and unfair disadvantage in responding to an incomplete and developing case, particularly in an adversarial system where there are sanctions for defence failures and (b) it breaches the over-arching Criminal Procedure Rule (1.1) objective of dealing with the case efficiently and expeditiously.

4.41 Having said that, the practice of drafting defence statements which do little more than enter a written not guilty plea is unlikely to be effective, and is likely to fail in the future.[37] There may well be cases where defendants, having received comprehensive advice as to the evidential consequences, wish to disclose nothing as a matter of principle rather than attract criticism for playing the disclosure system unsuccessfully.

G. Disclosure Failures

Factors

4.42 A failure on the part of the prosecution to make proper disclosure might result, in appropriate circumstances, in proceedings being stayed as an abuse of process. However, not all failures to disclose lead to proceedings being stayed, as a fair trial might still be possible.

---

[36] *R v Haringey Justices ex p DPP* [1996] QB 351.
[37] See Court of Appeal decision in *DS and TS* [2015] EWCA Crim 662 where a Prosecutor's section 58 CJA appeal was allowed, lifting a stay, on a number of grounds including a lack of proper compliance with the Criminal Procedure Rules by the Defence at an early stage of proceedings.

When considering an application to stay proceedings based on defence complaints of non-disclosure the following factors should be considered:[38] **4.43**

- Whether the failure to disclose was due to inadvertence, inefficiency or deliberate conduct
- Whether the prosecutor had acted in good faith
- Whether the non-disclosure could damage the prosecution case or advance that of the defence
- The extent of any prejudice to the accused in the conduct of the defence case as a result of the non-disclosure
- Whether the accused could nevertheless receive a fair trial without undue delay
- Whether remedies short of a stay could achieve a fair trial (such as an adjournment to allow disclosure and instructions to be taken on the new disclosure, and the exclusion of evidence)
- At appeal level, whether taking all the circumstances of the trial into account, there was a real possibility that the jury would have arrived at a different verdict.[39]

Case law examples

Set out below are a series of cases in which issues of non-disclosure have been raised as part of an abuse of process application at first instance or formed the basis of argument at appellate level. **4.44**

Viewing facilities

In *El-Treki*,[40] the trial judge ordered that the defence be given viewing facilities for CCTV camera video footage from the nightclub locus of an alleged assault. The defendant was not allowed to enter the premises with his legal advisers. This failure by the prosecution coupled with a series of earlier delays and prosecution disclosure failures lead to the proceedings being stayed as a category 2 abuse. **4.45**

Police notebook

In *Maame Osei-Bonsu*[41] the Court of Appeal quashed a conviction for assault, as unsafe. At trial, the defence applied at the end of the prosecution case to stay proceedings as an abuse of process. Before trial, the defence had sought disclosure from the CPS of the names and addresses of any witnesses on whom the prosecution did not intend to rely upon. No details were supplied. During the trial the prosecution failed to produce police officers notebooks (as they had been archived, but were no longer available) and computer aided dispatch messages (which could impact on the credibility of the prosecution witnesses, in particular as to who had complained to the police and had made the first contact with the police). **4.46**

As part of the appeal process, the defence made further disclosure requests of the CPS for the very evidence which they failed to produce at the lower court. The CPS chose to ignore such disclosure requests. Little or nothing was done to help the defence in their preparation of their appeal. **4.47**

Lord Justice Otton observed 'the information that was requested was an entirely proper request and ... the information was clearly disclosable'.

---

[38] See Mr Justice Randerson's list in *Attorney-General v District Court at Hamilton* [2004] 3 NZLR 777 at p 791.

[39] *McInnes v HM Advocate* [2010] UKSC 7 applying *Spiers v Ruddy* [2008] 1 AC 873; [2007] UKPC D2.

[40] 7 February 2000, Ipswich Crown Court, NoT990513, [2000] 8 Archbold News 3–4, discussed in Criminal Lawyer [2000] 107, 17.

[41] 22 June 2000, COACD, 99/6732/Z4.

4.48 In the Court of Appeal, one of the police officers who had attended the scene of the fight produced his Incident Report Book for the first time, which, in the words of Lord Justice Otton, contained material 'which was of considerable importance to the defence'. The police notebook contained details of a potential witness to the incident (including telephone number) which was not disclosed to the defence at trial. The witness might have thrown light on the situation to the advantage of the defence.

4.49 The Court of Appeal decided that the conviction was unsafe, as there had been a material non-disclosure of important documents and information amounting to abuse of process. There had been clear breaches of the CPIA Codes of Practice. The prosecution had failed to meet their disclosure obligations, so that the defendant did not have a fair trial.

Lord Justice Otton in his concluding remarks observed:

> the conduct of the Crown's case here through the CPS and the police has been quite deplorable. They did not give the defence a fair crack of the whip before the trial by not taking any or appropriate action on the civil request advanced by the defence team. That should have been done and we are very disturbed that the attitude of the prosecution seems to have been so lamentably slack on that occasion … the conduct here is so bad that we feel that it be quite wrong to allow this conviction to stand.

Refusal to deal with disclosure

4.50 In *Ballack, Carrick, Walters and Walker*,[42] HHJ Kathuda stayed trial proceedings on an indictment containing a conspiracy to import Class 'A' drugs (cocaine), because of misuse of executive authority relating to disclosure.

4.51 HHJ Kathuda found that the Customs disclosure officer's oversights, errors, omissions, and negligence amounted to a refusal to deal with disclosure. Further, the Customs solicitor took no action to give proper advice to the disclosure officer. The disclosure failures were deliberate and in bad faith:[43] HHJ Kathuda observing

> In my judgement, there has been a misuse of the executive authority by the prosecuting authority as a whole, by not disclosing the materials … having acted by omission, beginning at the very least carelessly, inefficiently and incompetently, if I might add that, which resulted in a deliberate failure. Shutting the mind to the consequences of disclosure, they did act in bad faith and therefore, arguably unlawfully, therefore depriving the defendants of the opportunity and perhaps the ability with regard to certain of the matters not disclosed; to the extent they were unable to exert a sufficient and broadsided challenge to the credibility and integrity of the main (prosecution informant) witness.

Systematic failures

4.52 The Crown Court decision in *Vocaturo, Brown, Drewery, Roden, Saunders, Edwards-Sayer, Sharma and Pathak*,[44] relating to a VAT fraud trial, is an example of a prosecution's (Revenue and Customs) systematic failure to make proper disclosure in criminal proceedings, leading to a stay.

4.53 The trial judge HHJ Teare found that 'there has been a significant and critical failure to fulfil either the orders of the court or the assurances given by counsel for the Crown'. Those failures lead to the need for an adjournment to consider the late service of relevant material (including Case Summaries, evidence, schedules, admissions, jury bundles and CD Roms) to ensure their accuracy and admissibility. The need for the trial to be adjourned was entirely the fault

---

[42] Isleworth Crown Court, Indictment No T1999059, T1999060 (unreported) 17 November 1999.
[43] At paras 27–29 of the judgment.
[44] At Nottingham Crown Court (Indictment No. T2002/7170), by HHJ Teare, on 8 October 2007. Quoted in [2007] EWCA Crim 3483 at para14. Discussed in John Cooper, 'Disclosure and Abuse of

of the prosecution, because 'the timetable and court orders have been ignored, promises have been broken, and disclosure has failed'.

In relation to disclosure HHJ Teare observed: **4.54**

> ... material which was disclosable was being withheld, even though the defence knew of its existence ... The failings of the prosecution have been described as systematic, and having listened carefully to argument on both sides in this case I believe that to be true. The prosecution have consistently been in possession of material which was disclosable and which, for poor reason or for thoroughly bad reason, they have not disclosed. I have no confidence that, given the history thus far, I would not be met with similar complaints in four weeks time if an adjournment were to be granted, or even during the course of the trial.

HHJ Teare went on to illustrate his concerns by citing the fact that a schedule of   **4.55** unused material had been in the possession of the Customs investigation team eighteen months before it was disclosed to the Customs disclosure team. The schedule contained a substantial amount of relevant documentation relating, inter alia, to freight forwarders:

> It is a dreadful situation. Even after present counsel have been in control of this case for 3 or 4 months, material has been kept from them and the disclosure officer until the date of the trial. How can I have any confidence that this is not going to happen again?

HHJ Teare stayed proceedings. There had been a systemic failure by the prosecution to dis- **4.56** close relevant material.

Creeping, piecemeal, drip-fed disclosure

In *Lindsay, Sinclair, George, Rachar and Cook*, HHJ Pontinus[45] stayed proceedings as an abuse **4.57** of process because of problems with 'creeping' disclosure. The case involved a Customs & Excise investigation into a VAT fraud, codenamed Operation Vitric.

In staying the indictment His Honour Judge Pontius expressed concern about the piecemeal   **4.58** disclosure which took place in the case, described by the defence as 'drip-fed' or 'creeping' disclosure:[46]

> Over these proceedings as a whole the ominous and ever-lengthening shadow of disclosure has fallen.

> Documents have been discovered and disclosed, in varying quantities, not only in the many weeks and months leading up to the start of these proceedings last February, but also throughout the two months and more of court time that they have occupied.

HHJ Pontinus found the Customs disclosure system had failed to produce the degree of   **4.59** efficient, exhaustive disclosure that a large and complex case demands. He concluded that it could justifiably be said that the larger and more complex the case, the greater the burden of

---

Process' [2008] 5 Archbold News 5–6 and John Binns and David Corker, 'False Economies' [2008] New Law Journal 158 (7302) 17. Cited in argument in *Colin Mileham and others*, Preston Crown Court (indictment No.T2011/7330) in which HHJ Byrne stayed proceedings because of systemic, fundamental, and continuing statutory disclosure failures caused by serial instances of nonfeasance or misfeasance by, inter alia, the investigative team including the officer in charge, the disclosure officer, the local authority lawyer primarily responsible for the management of the prosecution disclosure obligations, and prosecuting counsel.

[45] 18 May 2005, Blackfriars Crown Court, Indictment No T2004–7470.
[46] At p 30 of the judgment transcript.

responsibility upon the prosecuting authority to ensure that sufficient resources are devoted to the task of full, comprehensive disclosure.

4.60 HHJ Pontinus had lost confidence in the prosecution disclosure system, expressing the view that he was:[47]

> ... unable to share the prosecution's optimism that disclosure in this case is complete. Given the history of 'creeping disclosure' that we have seen during this hearing, together with what preceded it, I have no confidence that all relevant documents have now been disclosed.[48]

4.61 The possible public cost implications of the risk that further disclosure may lead to the trial collapsing or, in the event of a conviction, a future appeal being sought based on inadequate disclosure, was considered by the trial judge:

> I am conscious of the very real prospect of a trial proceeding with the inevitable continuing 'drip-feed' disclosure that has led to my decision; sooner or later the trial would be likely to collapse as a result, at far greater —and wholly unjustifiable—cost to the public purse. Worse still is the prospect—just as real—of a lengthy trial resulting in convictions which, many months later and after yet more relevant documents come to light, cannot be sustained on appeal. This court, like Customs & Excise, has a clear responsibility to protect the revenue and thus to keep unnecessary waste of public funds to a minimum and, further, but of equal and obviously related importance, to keep complex and large-scale trials within a manageable compass.

4.62 HHJ Pontinus stayed proceedings as the defendants could not be fairly tried and it was unfair in all the circumstances to try them.

Kept in the dark

4.63 In *Uddin*,[49] another VAT fraud (Operation Venison involving loss to the revenue of £100 million) was stayed as an abuse of process because of Customs prosecution disclosure failures. The trial judge, Mr Justice Crane, concluded that the prosecution failed to comply with their disclosure duties under sections 3 and 7 of CPIA 1996, the Attorney-General Disclosure Guidelines, or the Customs disclosure guidance document and investigation handbook. There were deficiencies in the disclosure of material relating to the reliability and credibility of prosecution freight forwarder and exporter witnesses, who had played a part in suspect trade outside of Operation Venison.

4.64 Having heard live evidence from Customs officers, Mr. Justice Carne was driven to the conclusion that the court had not been told the truth. He retained:

> ... very serious concerns about disclosure. The continuing difficulties, even during the hearing, do not inspire confidence that disclosure in relation to the trial itself is complete ... disclosure has been demonstrated to be flawed[50]

He continued:

> ... if prosecuting counsel were to be kept in the dark, there must have been a preparedness to keep the defence, the judge and ultimately the jury in the dark.[51]

---

[47] At p 59 of the judgment.

[48] Also see the decision in *Wharam and others*, indictment number T2004-0685 (Operation Carina), at Kingston Crown Court, 4 December 2006. HHJ Faber stayed proceedings, inter alia, on the basis of prosecution breaches of court orders relating to disclosure. HHJ Faber's confidence in the disclosure process had been undermined by the prosecution breaches.

[49] *Uddin, Ali, Baig, Chandoo,Golecha*, 25 May 2005, Southwark Crown Court, T2002-7012.

[50] At para 181 of the judgment.

[51] At para 184 of the judgment.

London City Bond cases

In *Early and others*,[52] the Court of Appeal quashed convictions where **4.65**

(1) prosecution witnesses lied in evidence in public interest immunity (PII) and abuse of process hearings and (2) the prosecution had failed to make proper disclosure, including a failure on its part to disclose the role of informants who were facilitating the frauds.

The appellants had been charged with offences involving fraud on the public revenue by **4.66** the improper diversion of duty-suspended alcohol from a bonded warehouse, London City Bond (LCB), intended for other countries in the European Community. Some thirty or forty separate scams were being conducted through LCB. These resulted in a loss to the revenue of £300 million.

The appellants all pleaded guilty. It subsequently transpired that there had been non- **4.67** disclosure of certain material by the prosecution, including the fact that informers had been acting in the bonded warehouse with the encouragement of Customs, in effect, a honey trap. The informer was not registered, nor did he have a handler or controller, as required by guidelines. Nor were proper records kept of his contacts with Customs.

Further, certain prosecution witnesses had lied to the judge on the voire dire in the case of **4.68** two of the appellants. The appellants appealed against conviction on the ground that they had pleaded guilty on the false assumption that a full and proper disclosure had been made by the prosecution, particularly in respect of the role of informers. In addition they had been precluded from making an effective application to stay proceedings as an abuse of process ... based on the prosecution's non disclosure of the true roles of two of the informants.

The Court of Appeal held, allowing the appeals, that: **4.69**

(1) If, in the course of a public interest immunity hearing or an abuse of process argument (whether on the voire dire or otherwise), prosecution witnesses lied in evidence to the judge, it was to be expected that if the judge knew of that, or the Court of Appeal sub-sequently learnt of it, an extremely serious view would be taken. It was likely that the prosecution would be tainted beyond redemption however strong the evidence against the defendant might be otherwise.

(2) Judges could only make decisions and counsel could only act and advise on the basis of information with which they were provided. The integrity of the English system of criminal trials depended on judges being able to rely on what they were told be counsel and on counsel being able to rely on what they were told by each other. A defendant who pleaded guilty at an early stage should not, if adequate disclosure had not been made, be in a worse position than a defendant who, as the consequence of an argument to stay proceedings as an abuse, benefited from further orders for disclosure culminating in the abandonment of the proceedings against him.

(3) In the instant case, there had been no-disclosure by the prosecution, including a failure on its part to disclose the role of the informants.[53] The pleas of guilty of all the appellants had, therefore, been entered on the erroneous assumption that full and proper disclosure had been made. Had the judge, in the case of two of the appellants, been aware that prosecution witnesses had lied while giving evidence in voire dires, he might not have

---

[52] [2003] 1 Cr App R 19.
[53] See *David Robert Barkshire* [2011] EWCA Crim 1885; [2012] Crim LR 453 in which the Court of Appeal quashed convictions for conspiracy to commit aggravated trespass as the prosecution had failed to disclose the role of an undercover police officer's active involvement in the criminality. The failure to disclose the role of the participating informant precluded potential defence arguments on abuse of process based on entrapment.

refused to stay proceedings as an abuse of process. Consequently, all the convictions were unsafe and would be quashed.

4.70 It was observed per curiam that it is a matter of crucial importance to the administration of justice that prosecuting authorities make full relevant disclosure prior to trial and that prosecuting authorities should not be encouraged to make inadequate disclosure with a view to defendants pleading guilty.

4.71 In *Gell, Smith, Jenkins, Challis, Grant, Johnston and Boparan*,[54] the Court of Appeal held that convictions for conspiracy to cheat the public revenue were unsafe. The convictions were quashed as the defendant's application for a stay for abuse of process might have succeeded if the prosecution had not given certain assurances, as a result of being misled by a Customs officer, over evidence in unrelated trials, which indicated that trade had been diverted from one bonded warehouse to another with Custom's knowledge.

4.72 During the second half of 1990, duty on spirits and cigarettes was evaded by the creation of false documentation which recorded the movement of goods from LCB, a bonded warehouse, to other bonded warehouses in the United Kingdom and Europe. In reality the goods went elsewhere. HM Customs became aware of the fraud and arranged for two managers ('B' and 'C') of LCB to become informants. Customs failed to follow Home Office guidelines and this was concealed from the trial judge (unconnected to the present appeals). It came to light following appeals in November 2001 whereby convictions were quashed and retrials ordered.

4.73 The circumstances of the present appeals arose from the setting up of Fort Patrick (FB), a bonded warehouse in Ipswich. FP was set up by Grant in order to facilitate fraud. Boparan was a trader and the rest of the defendants were haulers. Goods were received from a number of sources including some 37 per cent from LCB. It was the prosecution's case that 194 lorries loaded at FP with beers, wines, and spirits bound for a bonded warehouse in Spain never arrived and were diverted to destinations in the United Kingdom. No excise duty or VAT was paid on the goods with a loss of £22 million to the revenue. Following arrest and charge, the defence asked for disclosure of documents relating to B, C, and Customs, suggesting Customs may have been aware of the movement of goods from LCB to FP and allowed it to happen. In the absence of those documents an application was to be made for the trial to be be stayed as an abuse of process.

4.74 Before the unrelated appeals were heard, the prosecution made PII applications. The judge asked the prosecution, in PII hearings and in open court, whether it had any material showing Customs had diverted trade from LCB to FP. Customs answered in the negative. As a result the judge refused the application to stay proceedings stating it was mischievous and that the defendants were trying to import LCB problems into the unconnected case of FP.

4.75 At the attempted retrial of the unrelated cases further material emerged. A Customs officer, Bernard Small, was called and admitted he had misled prosecution counsel and judges who had dealt with matters of disclosure. Contact with B and C was greater than disclosed and no record was made of this. In Lord Justice Longmore's view: 'That lack of records cannot be remedied'. Small's evidence indicated, inter alia, that the goods were transferred from LCB to FP with his knowledge. As a result the prosecution abandoned the retrial.

4.76 The defendants in *Gell* appealed on the grounds that: (1) the convictions were unsafe because the prosecution could not maintain its assurances made at the PII hearing; and (2) if the

---

[54] [2003] EWCA Crim 123. Contrast the unsuccessful appeal against conviction decisions in *Austin* [2004] EWCA Crim 1983 and *Beardall and Lord* [2006] EWCA Crim 577.

prosecution could not have given those assurances the defence abuse application might have been successful.

The Court of Appeal agreed. If those matters had emerged before the abuse proceedings then **4.77** the defence argument for a stay could have been presented in a more forcible manner. It followed that the convictions were unsafe and should be quashed. It was, in the words of Lord Justice Longmore, a 'melancholy result'. The court was compelled to allow the appeal even in relation to the defendant who had pleaded guilty.

In *Gell*,[55] Lord Justice Longmore adopted the observations of the Vice President, Lord Justice **4.78** Rose, in the case of *Early*:

> Judges can only make decisions and counsel can only act and advise on the basis of the information with which they are provided. The integrity of our system of criminal trial depends on judges being able to rely on what they are told by counsel and on counsel being able to rely on what they are told by each other. This is particularly crucial in relation to disclosure and PII hearings.[56]

Balancing exercise: extreme failures

In *(S)D and S(T)*[57] the Court of Appeal considered a prosecutor's section 58 CJA 2003 appeal **4.79** against a first instance decision to stay rape and false imprisonment proceedings as an abuse of process: based on extreme failures of prosecution disclosure.

In the course of the two and half years of proceedings, the prosecution incrementally added **4.80** items to the schedule of unused material. On the eighth day, the trial judge, on the application of the defence, discharged the jury on the basis that the interests of justice and a fair trial demanded that disclosure be completed before the defence could cross-examine the complainants and the officer in the case. Following the discharge twenty-two further items were added to the unused material schedule including the fact that the mobile telephone of one of the complainants had been seized but no analysis of its content had been made and that the other complainant had received a caution for perverting the course of justice. The trial judge stayed proceedings concluding that there has been failure to make proper disclosure rather than failure to conduct a proper investigation but that there was no bad faith by the officer in the case or the prosecution. It remained possible fairly to try the defendants (category one abuse) but the abuse was so exceptional that the court ought to mark its wholesale condemnation of the prosecution by allowing stay (category two abuse). The trial judge describing what had happened as a charade which made a mockery of the judicial system. Public money was squandered, mainly because of the abject failure of the CPS to organize disclosure at any stage prior to trial. The prosecution had been totally incompetent and had disobeyed the principles of disclosure.

The Court of Appeal, adopting a balancing exercise approach,[58] allowed the prosecutors sec- **4.81** tion 58 CJA 2003 appeal and set aside the stay. Where it was impossible for a defendant to receive a fair trial (category one abuse) the court would stay proceedings without more.

---

[55] At para 22.

[56] [2003] 1 Cr App R at para 10.

[57] [2015] 2 Cr App R 27 the balancing exercise approach was cited with approval and followed by HHJ Edmunds QC in *Feroz Batliwala*, Isleworth Crown Court Indictment No.T20130334 17 July 2015 in staying proceedings for the importation of Class 'A' drugs (19 kilos of cocaine) based on prosecution pre-trial, first trial, and retrial disclosure failures (relating to observation logs, discs, disclosure notes, other unused material which indicated legitimate business activity), failures to review disclosure, failures to access NCA database and judicial loss of confidence in the prosecution disclosure process to the extent that HHJ Edmunds QC had no confidence that the trial would be fair.

[58] As per *Maxwell* [2011] 2 Cr App R 31.

However, where it would offend the court's sense of justice and propriety to try the defendant in the particular circumstances of the case, the court was concerned to protect the integrity of the criminal justice system (category two abuse) and had to weigh in the balance the public interest in ensuring that those charged with grave crimes should be tried and the competing public interest in not conveying the impression that the court would adopt the approach that the end justified the means.

4.82 In carrying out this balancing exercise it was necessary to consider a number of factors such as:

- the gravity of the charges;
- whether the complainants would be denied justice;
- the importance of disclosure in sexual offences;
- the necessity for proper attention to be paid to disclosure;[59]
- the nature and materiality of the failures;
- the waste of court resources;[60]
- the effect on the jury and
- the availability of other sanctions.[61]

4.83 On the facts of *(S)D and S(T)*, the Court of Appeal, Lord Chief Justice Thomas giving the lead judgment, decided that the balancing exercise should be resolved in favour of the stay being lifted:

- multiple rape allegations were involved;
- a stay would deny justice to complainants in abusive relationships;
- the failure to make earlier disclosure of telephone records and a caution against a complainant was only relevant to credibility;
- the lack of training and supervision of the disclosure officer was a serious failing of the Chief Constable.

4.84 Balancing those considerations and the very strong public interest in trying the serious charges and having the complainants determined at trial, it would not be in the interests of justice to stay proceedings on the basis that their continuation would undermine public confidence in the administration of justice.

Guilty plea

4.85 In *Manfo-Kwaku Asiedu*,[62] a defendant who pleaded guilty to conspiracy to causing explosions to endanger life was granted permission to appeal against his conviction when it subsequently emerged that a prosecution expert witness had failed to disclose some addendums to his report. The Court of Appeal decided that non-disclosure, by itself, was not an abuse of the court process. The remedy for non-disclosure would ordinarily be orders for the defendant to be provided with the necessary material, and such order as would ensure that the defendant was not unfairly damaged by its late delivery. The defendant's guilty plea, which had not been influenced by the expert evidence, amounted to an unambiguous and voluntary confession which unequivocally established his guilt. A guilty plea was not always a bar to quashing a conviction. Where the plea had been compelled as a matter of law because of the trial judge's adverse ruling, with the result that there was no arguable defence, a defendant could plead

---

[59] As per *Olu* [2010] EWCA Crim 2975; [2011] 1 Cr App R 33 and *Malook* [2011] EWCA Crim 254: [2012] 1 WLR 633.

[60] As per *Boardman* [2015] 1 Cr App R 33.

[61] Including the making of a wasted costs order against the CPS and Police: see *Applied Language Solutions* [2013] EWCA Crim 326; [2013] 2 Cr App R 16.

[62] [2015] EWCA Crim 714; [2015] 2 Cr App R 8.

guilty and then challenge the adverse ruling. Likewise, a conviction on a guilty plea might be found unsafe if the trial had involved an abuse of process or was an affront to justice.[63]

H. Third Party Disclosure

The duties of disclosure under the CPIA 1996 and the Code of Practice issued under the **4.86** Act created duties in respect of material that the prosecution or the police held and which the prosecution had inspected. The provisions were not directed to creating duties for third parties to follow.

Witness summons procedure

Where it is sought to obtain material from third parties the appropriate procedure is to **4.87** obtain a summons under the Criminal Procedure (Attendance of Witnesses) Act 1965.[64] The drawbacks to such procedure were highlighted by the Court of Appeal in *Alibhai*.[65] The appellant was convicted of a conspiracy involving dishonest dealing in counterfeit Microsoft products. On appeal, it was argued that the convictions were unsafe in the light of significant difficulties with, and delays in securing disclosure of material by third parties (principally Microsoft, and the FBI and an FBI participating informant who was the principal prosecution witness). The appeals were dismissed.

Where a complaint is made of non-disclosure of documents, it is not always necessary for an **4.88** appellant to demonstrate that the disclosure of the material would have affected the outcome of the proceedings (it will often be difficult to assess, even with hindsight, the effect of a failure to disclosure on the outcome).[66] In many cases, it would suffice for an appellant to show a prosecutor's disclosure failure so that it is reasonable to suppose such failure might have affected the outcome of the trial.

The Court of Appeal will not regard a conviction as unsafe unless the non-disclosure is sig- **4.89** nificant 'in regard to any real issue'.[67] There may be cases in which the prosecution conduct might be so disgraceful as to warrant a stay in proceedings. In *Alibhai*, it could not be fairly said that the prosecution themselves behaved dishonourably or abused their power. The real problem was with potentially relevant documents and information in the hands of the third parties.

Before it can be said that there has been a breach of the disclosure obligation it must be **4.90** shown that there was a suspicion that third parties not only had potentially relevant material but that the material was damaging to the prosecution or of assistance to the defendant. Even if there is a necessary suspicion, the prosecutor is not under an absolute obligation to secure the disclosure of the material or information. The prosecutor enjoys a 'margin of consideration' as to what steps are appropriate to the particular case.

The Court of Appeal in *Alibhai* did not rule out, however, the possibility that, in an extreme **4.91** case, it might be so unfair for a prosecution to proceed in the absence of material which a third party declines to produce that it would be proper to stay it, regardless of whether the prosecutor is in breach of the guidelines. This may occur where a third party complainant

---

[63] See *Chalkley* [1998] Q B 848; *Mullen* [2000] Q B 520; *Togher* [2001] 3 All E R 463; *Early* [2002] EWCA Crim 1904; [2003] 1 Cr App R 19.
[64] See Archbold 2016 p 1257 para 8–1.
[65] [2004] EWCA Crim 681; 5 Archbold News 1.
[66] *Ward* [1993] 96 Cr App R 1 at para 22.
[67] *Maguire* (1992) 94 Cr App R 133 at para 148.

improperly, for ulterior motives, claims commercial confidentiality in a bid to prevent relevant documents being supplied to the defence. If so an application can be made for a warrant under section 2 of the Criminal Procedure (Attendance of Witnesses) Act 1965 directing the person to attend the Crown Court with the required material for disclosure.

4.92 The section 2 procedure is fraught with difficulties:

(a) there is no provision for issuing a witness summons against a person outside of the jurisdiction;

(b) a witness summons to produce a 'document' will not elicit information;

(c) the document must itself, be capable of being evidence; and

(d) there is no provision for the prosecution or the defence, in the absence of agreement, to examine the documents before they are produced to the court pursuant to the witness summons.

Reasonable lines of enquiry

4.93 It should be noted that the Crown has a duty to pursue reasonable lines of enquiry in relation to material that may be held by third parties, and, if it appears that there is material that might reasonably be considered capable of undermining the prosecution case or of assisting the case for the accused, to take reasonable steps to obtain it.[68]

Inadequate defence statement

4.94 In *DPP v Debra Wood and Michael McGillicudy*,[69] the DPP appealed by way of case stated against decisions (1) ordering disclosure of material from a third party, concerning intoximeters used for testing alcohol on the breath, and (2) to stay proceedings against the respondents (W and M). W and M had been charged with driving whilst having consumed alcohol over the prescribed limit. In each case the specimens of breath had been analysed on an intoximeter.

4.95 In M's case the prosecution had sent him a letter pursuant to section 3 of CPIA 1996 stating that the prosecution had no material that required disclosure. W and M had served defence statements alleging that the device was of a type no longer approved as it had been changed without the prior consent of the Secretary of State. However, preliminary arguments had been raised about the adequacy of M's defence statement and whether the statement had been served out of time. The district judge held that service was not out of time as time did not run until service of the schedule of unused material by the prosecution, and that the defence statement was adequate.

4.96 W and M applied under section 8 of CPIA 1996 for disclosure of material relating to the device. In each case, the district judge ordered disclosure of this information including unedited printouts. The prosecution contacted the manufacturer who refused to provided the unedited printouts in its possession. In W's case, the prosecution unsuccessfully applied to vary the order. In each case, the district judge held that there was a contract between the manufacturer and the police for the supply of the devices and that the manufacturer was part of the investigating authority.

4.97 The proceedings were stayed on the basis that the non-disclosure of the material sought was an abuse of process and that W and M could not fairly be tried without such information.

---

[68] *Flook* [2010]1Cr App R 30 CA.

[69] [2006] EWHC 2986, [2006] All ER (D) 101. See Chris Taylor 'Third Party Disclosure' (2006) 70(5) Journal of Criminal Law (JoCL) 377.

On appeal the Administrative Court held: **4.98**

(1) the court had erred in ruling that disclosure was only effected on the date of service of the schedule of unused material as opposed to the date on the letter pursuant to section 3 of CPIA 1996. The letter was obviously a written statement that there was no relevant material, and that was all that was required for section 5 of CPIA 1996 to be triggered and for time to start running;

(2) the problems of deficiencies in a defence statement, under section 5 of CPIA 1996, used to ground an application for disclosure under section 8 could usually be resolved within the disclosure process. However, in M's case the request for disclosure did not satisfy section 8(2)(a) of CPIA 1996. Disclosure should have been refused as the defence statement raised no issue as to which reliability or type approval was relevant;

(3) it was *Wednesbury* unreasonable to hold that the manufacturer was the prosecutor for the purpose of sections 7 and 8 of CPIA 1996. The manufacturer did not become part of the prosecution because it had supplied the device to the police. The manufacturer was a third party. The provisions for disclosure under the 1996 Act and the code of practice were not directed to creating duties for third parties to follow. The disclosure duties were created in respect of material that the police had and which the prosecution had inspected. Material was not prosecution material under section 8(4) of CPIA 1996 unless it was held by the investigator or by the disclosure officer. Accordingly, the material sought was not material which the disclosure officer was obliged to allow the prosecutor to inspect. He did not have it in order to allow that obligation to arise. Therefore, much of the disclosure should not have been ordered and the orders should have been varied as sought by the prosecution;

(4) in the circumstances, the court was not entitled to rule that the material which it ordered to be disclosed could reasonably be expected to assist M. The material of which disclosure was sought, had to have some potential for bearing on the issue in respect of which was raised;

(5) the district judges were not entitled to rule that non disclosure of the material resulted in an abuse of process such that M and W were denied a fair trial. There was no abuse of process as no proper order was breached. Accordingly the stays of proceedings were unjustified.

The DPP's appeals were allowed.

Overseas third party disclosure

The Court of Appeal in *RF*[70] considered the extent of the Crown's duty to disclose mate-   **4.99**
rial held by individuals, companies, and governments in foreign countries. The CPIA 1996 makes no specific provision for material held or inspected overseas. However, para 3.5 of the CPIA Code provides that 'the investigator should pursue all reasonable lines of enquiry, whether these point towards or away from the suspect'. Although the Code has a domestic setting, read alongside the Attorney-General's Guidelines 2005, the Crown has a clear obligation to pursue reasonable lines of enquiry in the European Union and beyond. There might be relevant material outside the European Union where the power of the Crown and the courts in this country is limited to the Crime (International Co-operation) Act 2003 and relevant international conventions, such as the Drugs Convention. Letters of Request for production of documents may not be followed in a foreign court. Even if material were to be available for overseas, foreign states may not permit copies to be taken.

---

[70] [2010] Crim LR 148.

4.100   The Court of Appeal noted that there was no absolute obligation on the Crown to disclose relevant material held overseas outside of the European Union by entities not subject to the jurisdiction of the courts.[71] That being said, the Crown must still record in writing and explain the position, disclosing such information as the foreign state permits, and set out for the court the steps they have taken to obtain disclosure. If the Crown is not permitted by the foreign state to disclose everything they know, that fact must be made clear in the documentation provided to the court.

4.101   In *RF*, the appeal against conviction was dismissed on the facts of the case, there being no breach by the Crown of its disclosure obligations. All reasonable steps to obtain the overseas material were taken by the Crown.

I. Summary

4.102   The issue of proper effective disclosure in criminal proceedings is of fundamental importance to a defendant's right to a fair trial. Important guidance to the proper approach to disclosure and abuse of process is clearly set out by Sir Brian Leveson P in the Court of Appeal decision in *R*[72] which can be summarised as follows:

- **The prosecution is and must be in the driving seat at the stage of initial disclosure.** In order to lead (or drive) disclosure, it is essential that the prosecution takes a grip on the case and its disclosure requirements from the outset. To fulfil its duty under section 3, the prosecution must adopt a considered and appropriately resourced approach to giving initial disclosure and include the overall disclosure strategy and selection of software tools, identifying and isolating material that is subject to legal professional privilege and proposing search terms to be applied. The prosecution must explain what it is doing and what it will not be doing at this stage, ideally in the form of a Disclosure Management Document (para 34).
- **The prosecution must encourage dialogue and prompt engagement with the defence,** with the duty of the defence to engage with the prosecution.
- **The prosecution is not required to do the impossible** nor should the duty of giving initial disclosure be rendered incapable of fulfillment through the physical impossibility of reading (and scheduling) each and every item of material seized. The prosecution is entitled to use appropriate sampling and search items and its record keeping and scheduling obligations are modified accordingly (para 36).
- **The process of disclosure should be subject to robust case management by the judge, utilizing the full range of case management powers.**
- **Flexibility is critical, disclosure is not a box-ticking exercise** Judges can adopt and devise a tailored or bespoke approach to disclosure (para 49).
- **Prosecution failures, such as *Boardman*,**[73] **can bring a prosecution summarily to an end** but these can only be decided on a case by case basis and it is difficult to generalize as to the circumstances in which they arise (para 74).

4.103   It is clear that active case management and the engagement of all parties (prosecution, defence and first instance judiciary) is being encouraged and fostered by the appellant courts in an attempt to make disclosure work in criminal proceedings.

---

[71]   Also see *Alibhai* [2004] EWCA Crim 681, [2004] 5 *Archbold News* 1.
[72]   [2015] EWCA Crim 1941 judgment 21 December 2015, reported at Archbold Review issue 1, 22 February 2016.
[73]   [2015] EWCA Crim 175.

5

ENTRAPMENT

A. Introduction

This chapter examines the judicial discretion to stay proceedings where an offence has been **5.1** incited by another using deceptive techniques to test, as part of an entrapment operation, whether or not a person is willing to commit an offence. This abuse of process falls within the category 2 type of case identified as undermining public confidence in the integrity of the judicial process. The leading modern-day authority on entrapment is the House of Lords decision in *Looseley and Attorney General's Reference No 3 of 2000*.[1] To put *Looseley* in its historical context, this introduction examines the background case law and commentary which lead up to the decision.

Throughout the world, courts have considered upon which occasions, **5.2**

(a) evidence obtained by prosecuting authorities' tricks and provocation of unwitting, and at first unwilling offenders, should be excluded; and

(b) whether proceedings should be stayed as an abuse of process to prevent an abuse of executive power.

Historical context

Issues surrounding entrapment are not a recent phenomenon.[2] In 1881, the Home Secretary, **5.3** Sir William Harcourt, announced that police authorities had been instructed not to use entrapment without direct authorization by the Home Office. In 1929 the *Report of the Royal*

---

[1] [2001] UKHL 53, [2001] 4 All ER 897.

[2] See S Sharp, 'Covert Police Operations and the Discretionary Exclusion of Evidence' [1994] Crim LR 793; Geoffrey Robertson, 'Entrapment Evidence: Manna from Heaven or Fruit of the Poisoned Tree?' [1994] Crim LR 805; Andrew Ashworth, 'Should the Police be Allowed to use Deceptive Practices' (1998) 114 LQR 108; Andrew Ashworth, 'Re-drawing the Boundaries of Entrapment' [2002] Crim LR 161; David Ormerod and Andrew Roberts, 'The Trouble with Teixeira: Developing a Principled Approach to Entrapment' (2002) 6 E & P 41; Andrew Roberts, 'Court of Appeal: Entrapment: Abuse of Process' (2006) 70 Journal of Criminal Law Volume 194; David Ormerod, 'Recent Developments in Entrapment' Covert Policing Review 2006 pp 65–86.

Commission on Police Powers and Procedure[3] considered the use of an 'agent provocateur', defining the same as 'a person who entices another to commit an express breach of the law which he would not otherwise have committed, and then proceeds to inform against him in respect of such offence'.

5.4 The Royal Commission deplored 'the practice of initiating offences with a view to enticing or entrapping members of the public into committing breaches of the law'. It went on to say:

> we do not believe that a prosecution would ever be instituted on evidence obtained in such circumstances'. It made one exception: laying a trap might be justified in the case of a persistent wrongdoer, or where police had reliable information that the offence was being habitually committed.[4]

5.5 In *Brannan v Peek*[5] Lord Goddard condemned as 'wholly wrong' the practice of sending plainclothes police to commit crimes in order to obtain evidence of unlicensed betting in public houses: the fact that the defendant had been initially reluctant to bet with them made their conduct 'the more reprehensible'.

5.6 In *Birtles*,[6] Lord Parker drew the helpful distinction between police 'making use of information concerning an offence which is already laid on' and so acting to mitigate its consequences, and using an informer to encourage an offence, or an offence of a more serious character, which would otherwise not have been committed.

5.7 This general principle was reasserted in respect of terrorist offences by Lord Widgery in *Mealey*.[7] The Court approved Home Office guidelines to police:

(a) No member of a police force, and no police informant, should counsel, incite or procure the commission of a crime.

(b) Where an informant gives the police information about the intention of others to commit a crime in which they intend he shall play a part, his participation shall be allowed to continue only where:–
  (i) he does not actively engage in planning and committing the crime;
  (ii) he is intended to play only a minor role; and
  (iii) his participation is essential to enable the police to frustrate the principal criminals and to arrest them before injury is done to any person or serious damage to property.

The informant should always be instructed that he must on no account act as an agent provocateur, whether by suggesting to others that they should commit offences or encouraging them to do so...[8]

5.8 These statements of principle were the basis for the assumption by some trial judges that their common-law discretion to exclude evidence obtained unfairly or by trickery amounted to a general power to exclude evidence 'obtained by conduct of which they Crown ought not to take advantage ... even though tendered for the suppression of crime'.[9]

---

[3] (1929) Cmnd 3297.
[4] (1929) Cmnd 3297 [104]–[110].
[5] [1948] 1 KB 68, [1947] 2 All ER 572 DC.
[6] [1969] 1 WLR 1047, [1969] 53 Cr App R 469.
[7] (1974) 60 Cr.App.Rep 59, [1975] Crim LR 154.
[8] *Home Office Consolidated Circular to the police on crime and kindred matters*, section 1, [77]. See also [1969] *New Law Journal* 513.
[9] *King* [1969] 1 AC 391, PC. See also *Murphy* [1965] NILR 138.

The high-watermark of first instance exclusion of evidence in this period was the decision **5.9** in *Ameer*[10] after a police informer testified that he had used 'every trick in the book' to cajole and persuade the defendants to procure a large quantity of cannabis and then to supply it to an undercover officer, posing as big-time distributors and flashing large amounts of cash.

The judge, satisfied that the agent had played a vital role in drawing the defendants into a **5.10** criminal enterprise they would otherwise never have contemplated, excluded the evidence of their 'bust' and the case collapsed. Three detectives were suspended (the informer alleged that they regularly rewarded him by allowing him to recycle some of the drugs he procured in this fashion) and charges were dropped against twenty-six people awaiting trial on the evidence of the same informant and police officers. The seven relevant factors in deciding whether evidence should be excluded are:

(1) Was a crime of the same kind as that charged already afoot at the time of the intervention of the police agent?
(2) Had the defendant committed an offence of a class which he would not have committed but for the encouragement of the police agent?
(3) Had the defendant a propensity to engage in the crime charged?
(4) Did the police agent play a minor part in the criminal activity?
(5) Is the court certain, in retrospect, of the informer's reliability?
(6) Was the informer's participation approved at senior police level, as required by the Home Office's guidelines?
(7) Is the offence so grave that the public interest would justify the use of entrapment techniques?

The House of Lords in *Sang v DPP*[11] decided that there was no basis in law for the application **5.11** to exclude evidence, which had been made in *Ameer*. A trial judge, Lord Diplock decreed, 'has no discretion to refuse to admit relevant admissible evidence on the ground that it was obtained by improper or unfair means. The court is not concerned with how it was obtained … If it was obtained illegally there will be a remedy in civil law; if it was obtained legally but in breach of the rules of the conduct for the police, this is a matter for an appropriate disciplinary authority to deal with'. The House of Lords effectively removed the power at common law to exclude unfairly obtained evidence through the blandishments of an 'agent provocateur.'

Section 78 PACE

The introduction of Section 78 PACE effectively reversed the decision in *Sang* by requir- **5.12** ing the trial judge to exclude prosecution evidence if it appears from all the circumstances, including those in which it was obtained, that its admission would have such an adverse effect on the fairness of the proceedings that the court ought not to admit it.

The force of the word 'ought' shows that section 78 is concerned with a wider moral dimen- **5.13** sion: the question for the judge is whether it is fair—to the defendant and to the public—to permit a prosecution to proceed upon evidence, the presentation of which, in criminal proceedings is open to moral objection, or is for some reason contrary to the standards which the criminal justice system exists to uphold. Section 78 of PACE effectively nullified the *Sang* decision by allowing the exclusion of evidence if the result would mean unfairness to the defendant.

---

[10] 'Cornelius and the Case of the Vanishing Drugs' *Sunday Times* (London, 1 August 1976) 1.
[11] [1980] AC 402 [436G].

5.14   In addition to the PACE safeguard the provoked and entrapped were also allowed the consolation of substantial discounts in their sentence.[12]

5.15   The next major decision, *Smurthwaite & Gill*[13] established section 78 PACE as a legitimate means by which entrapment evidence could be excluded and developed the inherent power to stay a prosecution permanently as an abuse of process if its continuation would be unfair or oppressive.

5.16   The court in *Smurthwaite*[14] made a nodding concession to *Sang* by accepting that section 78 does not create per se a defence of entrapment:

> the fact that the evidence has been obtained by entrapment, or by agent provocateur or by a trick does not of itself require the judge to exclude it. If, however, he considers that in all the circumstances the obtaining of the evidence in that way would have the adverse effect described in the statute, then he will exclude it.

5.17   As a guide to this exercise of discretion, Lord Taylor in *Smurthwaite* cited a number of 'relevant factors' which are practically the same as those in *Ameer*, adding, in light of *Bryce*,[15] the further issue of whether the undercover officer 'has abused his role to ask questions which ought properly to have been asked as a police officer and in accordance with the PACE codes'.

Trickery

5.18   One of the relevant factors to consider is whether a defendant was tricked into offending or whether they allowed themselves to be tricked into offending. The point was considered in *Christou and Wright*,[16] where undercover police officers merely provided an opportunity for burglars and thieves to 'fence' stolen items. They did not provide a market which would not otherwise have been made available: the defendants were predisposed to the crime and had indeed committed it by the time they entered the shop. 'They were not tricked into doing what they would not otherwise have done, they were tricked into doing what they wanted to do in the first place ... the trick was not applied to the appellants: they voluntarily applied themselves to the trick'.

5.19   It is not simply a question, in entrapment cases, of asking whether the trick was applied to the defendants or whether they voluntarily applied themselves to the trick: the question is whether the trick was so alluring or so dirty that they should not be punished for falling for it. See the Court of Appeal decision in *Lawrence and Nash*.[17]

Incontrovertible account

5.20   In *Lawrence and Nash*, the Court of Appeal quashed convictions for conspiracy to supply cannabis to an undercover police officer posing as a customer for the drug. The Court found that 'the officer's role could hardly have been more active since he not merely offered to buy the cannabis resin but persistently and vigorously pressed the appellants to supply it'. The agent's credibility was shaken as the police had not tape-recorded his telephone calls and meetings—a failure the court found 'inexplicable and scarcely credible'. A relevant factor is whether there is 'an unassailable account of what occurred, or is it strongly corroborated'.

---

[12] See *Mackey and Shaw* [1992] Crim LR 602.
[13] [1994] 98 Cr App R 437.
[14] Ibid (n 13).
[15] [1992] 4 All ER 567, [1992] 95 Cr App R 320.
[16] [1992] 4 All ER 559, [1992] 95 Cr App R 264.
[17] *Lawrence and Nash* (CA, 14 December 1994).

The Court of Appeal used its exclusionary power to lay down guidelines for the police. Traps **5.21** will be unlikely to yield admissible evidence unless conversations are covertly recorded to produce an incontrovertible account.

Affront to public conscience

In *Latif and Shahzad*,[18] the House of Lords examined the relationship between abuse of **5.22** process and state entrapment, stating that a stay of proceedings could be made to prevent an affront to the public conscience. In *Latif*, an informer, encouraged by Customs officers, gave the appellant the opportunity to import heroin into the United Kingdom. After recognizing that there is no defence of entrapment under English law, Lord Justice Steyn acknowledged that the court has a discretion to stay proceedings and to weigh countervailing considerations of policy and justice so that it can determine whether there had been an abuse of process amounting to an affront to the public conscience.

Lord Justice Steyn stated:[19] **5.23**

> That judge must weigh in the balance the public interest in ensuring that those that are charged with grave crime should be tried and the competing public interest in not conveying the impression that the court will adopt the approach that the end justifies the means.[20]

The Canadian Supreme Court in Campbell made similar comments:[21] **5.24**

> The effect of police illegality on an application for a stay of proceedings depends very much on the facts of a particular case … illegality by the RCMP [Canadian Police] is neither part of any valid public purpose nor necessarily 'incidental' to its achievement. If some form of public interest immunity is to be extended to the police to assist in the 'war on drugs', it should be left to Parliament to delineate the nature and scope of the immunity and the circumstances in which it is available. Even if it should turn out here that the police acted contrary to the legal advice provided by the Department of Justice, there would still be no right to an automatic stay. The trial judge would still have to consider any other information or explanatory circumstances that emerge during the inquiry into whether the police or prosecutorial conduct 'shocks the conscience of the community'.

Rule of law and integrity of the court

The traditional judicial response to executive state entrapment is based on the need to uphold **5.25** the rule of law and protect the integrity of the judicial process. Defendants are excused, not because they are less culpable, although they may be, but because the police have behaved improperly. Police conduct which brings about state-created crime is unacceptable and improper. To prosecute in such circumstances would be, in the language of Lord Steyn in *Latif*,[22] 'an affront to the public conscience' and unfair.

Lord Steyn went on to say:

> An infinite variety of cases could arise. General guidance as to how the discretion should be exercised in particular circumstances will not be useful. But it is possible to say that in a case such as the present the judge must weigh in the balance the public interest in ensuring that those that are charged with grave crimes should be tried and the competing public interest in not conveying the impression that the court will adopt the approach that the end justifies the means.

---

[18] [1996] 1 WLR 104, [1996] 2 Cr App R 9.
[19] [1996] 1 WLR 104 [113B].
[20] As applied in *Walpole* (CA, No.96/2427/Y2). See also *Abdul Khan* (CA, 22 June 1999 No.98/6375/X3).
[21] (1999) 1 SCR 565 [565].
[22] [1996] 1 WLR 104 [112].

5.26 For consideration of judicial comment from other jurisdictions on adherence to the rule of law by investigating officers see *A v Hayden (No 2)*,[23] *Mack*,[24] *Conway*,[25] *Power*,[26] *Yip Chiu-Cheung v R*,[27] and *Campbell v R*.[28]

5.27 In *Mack*, Mr Justice Lamer identified[29] a number of reasons why police entrapment is objectionable. First, the 'state does not have unlimited power to intrude into our personal lives or to randomly test the virtue of individuals.' Second, 'entrapment techniques result in the commission of crimes by people who would not otherwise have become involved in criminal conduct'. Third, 'police should not themselves commit crimes or engage in unlawful activity solely for the purposes of entrapping others, as this seems to mitigate against the principle of the rule of law'.

No pressure

5.28 Where no pressure has been applied by the Police, entrapment arguments will fail. The Court of Appeal in *Junior Blackwood*[30] dismissed an appeal against convictions, inter alia, on the basis that the appellant had not been entrapped. The police officer involved had not put pressure on the appellant, nor had any incentive or enticement been put in his way to supply drugs. The appellant was willing to see the undercover police officer whenever she requested a meeting and to supply her with crack cocaine. There was a series of transactions showing that the appellant had access to and was willing to supply crack cocaine. The meetings were all purely voluntary on the appellant's part, attending for the sole purpose as a regular supplier of crack cocaine.[31]

Human Rights Act and ECHR

5.29 The statutory and common law developments have been reinforced in England and Wales by the Human Rights Act 1998 and the case law of the European Court of Human Rights (ECtHR). It is unlawful for courts in the United Kingdom, as public authorities, to act in a way which is incompatible with a Convention right.

Article 6 ECHR

5.30 Entrapment, and the use of evidence obtained by entrapment ('as a result of police incitement'), may deprive a defendant of their Article 6 right to a fair trial. The ECtHR in *Teixeira de Castro v Portugal*[32] held that a person with no previous drugs record, who was persuaded by police officers to buy heroin on their behalf, had not had a fair trial because 'the two officers did not confine themselves to investigating his criminal activity, but instead incited the commission of the offence, which would not have been committed without their intervention.'

5.31 Commenting on the *Texeira* decision, Lord Justice Buxton observed:[33]

> ... we see this as broadly the same as the tests in Smurthwaite and Gill[34] and Williams and O'Hare v DPP;[35] certainly, Texeira would not seem to call for a wider exclusion of evidence

---

[23] (1989) Crim LR 398.
[24] (1988) 2 SCR 903.
[25] (1989) 1 SCR 1659.
[26] (1994) 1 SCR 601.
[27] [1994] 2 All ER 924, (1994) 99 Cr App R 406.
[28] (1999) 1 SCR 565.
[29] [1988] 2 SCR 903.
[30] [2000] 6 Archbold News 1, (CA, 10 March 2000). See also *Elwell and Derby* (2001) EWCA Crim 1230.
[31] See also *Philip Hall* (CA, 23 February 2000, No.99/2823/Y4).
[32] (1999) 28 EHRR 101.
[33] 'The Human Rights Act and the Criminal Justice and Regulatory Process', University of Cambridge Centre for Public Law Conference 1999, [52]–[53].
[34] (1994) 98 Cr App R 437.
[35] [1993] 3 All ER 365, (1994) 98 Cr App R 209.

than is at present practiced in England. This outcome is achieved in the Strasbourg Court by concluding that under article 6 the defendant has been deprived of a 'fair' trial from the beginning: with, therefore, no occasion for the adoption of the usual balancing exercise. The English courts cannot complain of that, having themselves accepted that 'proceedings' under section 78 of PACE include, or at least requires the consideration of, the gathering of evidence pretrial.[36]

The test laid down in *Teixera* has been followed by the ECtHR in other entrapment cases. In **5.32** *Vanyan v Russia*[37] Teixeira was applied and police officers were found to have incited the supply of drugs, the police having no reason to suspect Vanyan of being a drug supplier prior to police involvement. The Teixeira test was applied in *Eurofinacom v France*[38] with the opposite result. The ECtHR rejected Eurofinacom's Article 6(1) application in relation to convictions for assisting and profiting from prostitution. Although the undercover police operation had, to a certain extent, provoked the offers of prostitution, there was evidence from prostitutes that the company's electronic messaging service was being used for the purposes of prostitution some time prior to police involvement. Further the police operation had been judicially authorized and supervised by the prosecuting authorities. Since the elements of the offences had been in existence prior to the police operation and there had been proper authorization and supervision, there was no unfairness and the complaint under Article 6(1) was dismissed.

Article 8 ECHR

Courts also need to consider compliance with Article 8 privacy rights in relation to covert **5.33** surveillance operations. The court's obligation, as a public authority, is not to act illegally in relation to evidence obtained in breach of Article 8. The court decides the admissibility of such covert surveillance evidence in terms of fairness under section 78 of PACE.[39] However, as Professor Ormerod observes:[40]

> Breaches of Article 8 will not be crucial to the success of the operation. In *Paulssen*,[41] for example, it was accepted that there had been breaches of the RIPA Codes and that there was action without authorisation, but it had been in good faith. Similarly, in *Marriner and Frain*,[42] the Court of Appeal accepted that the use of undercover devices by BBC journalists was not a breach of Article 8.

B. Categories of Entrapment

Having considered the historical background to entrapment in terms of section 78 and **5.34** domestic and ECHR case law, it is possible to identify three broad categories of modern-day entrapment: state executive; private commercial; and informant. There is no discernible difference in domestic and ECHR law on the issue of entrapment.

Executive state entrapment: *Looseley*

The leading case on executive state entrapment is the House of Lords decision in *R v Looseley* **5.35** *and Attorney General's Reference No 3 of 2000*.[43]

---

[36] See *Matto v Wolverhampton Crown Court* [1987] RTR 337.
[37] App No 53203/99, First section (15 December 2005). See also *Ramanauskas v Lithuania* [2008] Crim LR 639 and *Khudobin v Russia* (2009) 48 EHRR 22.
[38] [2005] Crim LR 134.
[39] *Button* [2005] Crim LR 571.
[40] 'Recent Developments in Entrapment' [2006] Covert Policing Review pp 65–86.
[41] [2003] EWCA Crim 2855.
[42] [2002] EWCA Crim 2855.
[43] [2001] UKHL 53, [2001] 4 All ER 897.

5.36　The House of Lords considered what conduct by undercover police officers in obtaining evidence against drugs dealers will constitute entrapment of such a nature that either a prosecution based on that evidence will be stayed as an abuse of process, or the evidence excluded under section 78 PACE.

5.37　The prosecution case against the appellant, Grant Looseley, was that he had supplied heroin to an undercover police officer on three occasions, at the telephone request of the undercover officer.

5.38　At trial, it was submitted as a preliminary issue that the indictment ought to be stayed as an abuse of the process or, alternatively, that the undercover officer's evidence should be excluded pursuant to section 78 PACE. Having heard evidence from the undercover officer and from the officer in charge of the operation on a *voir dire*, the judge rejected the defence applications. Following this ruling, the appellant pleaded guilty. The Court of Appeal dismissed the appeal and certified a point of law of general public importance for the opinion of the House of Lords.

5.39　In the second case, *Attorney General's Reference No 3*, the acquitted person faced counts of supplying heroin and being concerned in the supply of heroin. The prosecution case was that undercover police officers supplied the defendant with contraband cigarettes, and asked the defendant, 'can you sort out any brown?' Later on, the officers persuaded the defendant to provide them with heroin. The defendant said at one stage, 'I'm not really into heroin myself.' When interviewed by the police after his arrest, defendant said that he had had 'nothing at all' to do with heroin, and that he was 'not interested' in it, but that he had become involved because two men had approached him offering to sell him cheap cigarettes. He said that the two men 'were getting me cheap fags, so as far as I was concerned a favour for a favour'.

5.40　At the commencement of the trial a defence application to stay the proceedings as an abuse of process was allowed. The undercover officers had gone further than was permissible by inciting the defendant to commit an offence he would not otherwise have committed. The prosecution offered no evidence and verdicts of not guilty were entered.

5.41　Upon acquittal, the Attorney General referred the following point of law to the Court of Appeal for its opinion,

> In a case involving the commission of offences by an accused at the instigation of undercover police officers to what extent, if any, have: (i) The judicial discretion conferred by section 78 of the Police and Criminal Evidence Act 1984; and (ii) The power to stay the proceedings as an abuse of the court; have been modified by article 6 of the European Convention on Human Rights and the jurisprudence of the European Court of Human Rights?

The Court of Appeal referred the point of law to the House for its opinion.

5.42　Lord Nicholls giving the first judgment, of the House of Lords, observed:

> 1)　... It is simply not acceptable that the state through its agents should lure its citizens into committing acts forbidden by the law and then seek to prosecute them for doing so. That would be entrapment. That would be a misuse of state power, and an abuse of the process of the courts ... The role of the courts is to stand between the state and its citizens and make sure this does not happen.
>
> 2)　... The difficulty lies in identifying conduct, which is caught by such imprecise words as lure or incite or entice or instigate. If police officers acted only as detectives and passive observers, there would be little problem in identifying the boundary between permissible and impermissible police conduct. But that would not be a satisfactory place for the boundary line ... in some instances a degree of active involvement by the police in the

commission of a crime is generally regarded as acceptable … Test purchases fall easily into this category.[44]

3) …

4) Thus, there are occasions when it is necessary for the police to resort to investigatory techniques … Sometimes the particular technique adopted is acceptable. Sometimes it is not. For even when the use of these investigatory techniques is justified, there are limits to what is acceptable. Take a case where an undercover policeman repeatedly badgers a vulnerable drug addict for a supply of drugs in return for excessive and ever increasing amounts of money. Eventually the addict yields to the importunity and pressure, and supplies drugs. He is then prosecuted for doing so. Plainly, this result would be objectionable. The crime committed by the addict could readily be characterised as artificial or state-created crime. In the absence of the police operation, the addict might well never have supplied drugs to anyone.

In considering the criteria by which a trial judge is to distinguish the acceptable from the unacceptable, Lord Nicholls commented: **5.43**

A useful guide is to consider whether the police did no more than present the defendant with an unexceptional opportunity to commit a crime… whether the police conduct preceding the commission of the offence was no more than might have been expected from others in the circumstances. Police conduct of this nature is not to be regarded as inciting or instigating crime … the overall consideration is always whether the conduct of the police or other law enforcement agency was so seriously improper as to bring the administration of justice into disrepute …

He then listed some of the relevant circumstances:

(a) the nature of the offence;
(b) the reason for the particular police operation, with reasonable grounds for suspicion, possibly centred on a particular place or individual;
(c) the nature and extent of police participation/inducement in the crime, with regard to the defendant's circumstances, including his vulnerability;
(d) the defendant's criminal record and linked matters.

The appeal in *Looseley* was dismissed. Looseley was an active and current drugs dealer. The undercover police officer made contact with Looseley in the course of an undercover police operation concerning the supply of Class 'A' drugs. A senior police officer had authorized the operation and had overseen its progress. The undercover officer had presented himself as a heroin addict to Looseley as an ideal customer for a drugs deal, but did not go beyond that portrayal. Looseley supplied the undercover officer with heroin on more than one occasion. **5.44**

In the *Attorney General's Reference No 3 of 2000* Lord Hutton agreed with the trial judge's decision to stay the proceedings. The defendant had not previously dealt in heroin. He was induced to procure heroin for the undercover officers by the prospect of a profitable trade in **5.45**

---

[44] For examples of undercover and covert operations see *DPP v Marshall and Downes* [1988] 3 All ER 683 (unlicensed liquor); *London Borough of Ealing v Woolworth's PLC* (1995) Crim LR 58 (video sales to person under age); *Taunton Deane Borough Council v Brice* (1997) 31 *Licensing Review*, October 1997 24; *Nottingham City Council v Amin* [2000] 1 WLR 1071, [2000] 1 Cr App R(S) 426 (unauthorized mini-cabs); *Harrow L.B.C. v Shah and Shah* [2000] Crim LR 692 (sale of lottery tickets to child under 16 years old); *Dianna Rose Moon* [2004] EWCA Crim 2872, 70 JCL 194 (heroin); *Aylesbury Vale District Council v Basharat Khan and others* [2005] EWHC 841 (Admin) (unlicensed mini-cabbing); *Robinson v Woolworths Ltd* [2005] NSWCCA 426, [2006] Crim LR 379 (cigarette sales to under age children); *East Riding of Yorkshire Council v Dearlove* [2012] EWHC 278 (Admin), [2012] RTR 29. See also section 27 Trade Descriptions Act 1968 (which authorizes local authority trading standards officers to make test purchases) and section 31 Criminal Justice and Police Act 2001 (which authorizes the Police to use persons under 18 years old for test purchases of alcohol).

smuggled cigarettes. The judge was entitled to take the view that the police had caused the defendant to commit an offence which he would not otherwise have committed.

5.46 In relation to the ECHR, Lord Nicholls observed:[45]

> ... I do not discern any appreciable difference between the requirements of Article 6, or the Strasbourg jurisprudence,[46] and English law as it has developed in recent years.

5.47 The House of Lords concluded that it would be unfair and an abuse of process if a person had been incited or pressurized by an undercover police officer into committing a crime, which he would not otherwise have committed. It would not be objectionable if the officer, behaving as an ordinary member of the public would, gave a person an unexceptional opportunity to commit a crime and that person freely took advantage of it. Every case depends upon its own facts.

5.48 Subsequent to *Looseley*, case law has developed highlighting the fact-specific nature of the entrapment jurisprudence. A number of those cases are considered below to illustrate some of ways offenders having willingly participated in crime, as opposed to having being enticed or lured into offending.

Willing participant

5.49 An example of a willing participant is the case of *Michael Lewis*.[47] The appellant at first instance applied to have proceedings against him (for three counts of having custody of counterfeit currency notes) stayed on the grounds of entrapment. The defence argued that the activities of undercover police officers and/or a participating informant meant it was not possible for the appellant to have a fair trial and the moral integrity of the criminal proceedings had been impugned. The lower court refused the application and the appellant pleaded guilty.

5.50 The trial judge, in rejecting the abuse of process submission, found as a matter of fact that

(a) The defendant was in possession of counterfeit notes both in his car and at home. He admitted in interview that he knew the notes were counterfeit and that he had been tempted into it due to financial circumstances. Those matters were sufficient evidence to found the three counts indicted.

(b) Based on covertly tape-recorded conversations between the defendant and the undercover police officer, it was clear that the officer coaxed the defendant into selling the counterfeit notes. However, the police persuasion did not amount to pressure, nor did the defendant complain of pressure when he was interviewed. The defendant was not forced or pushed into committing offences he would not otherwise have committed. He appeared, on tape, to be willing to supply counterfeit money.

5.51 The trial judge also refused an application, made in the alternative, that the evidence relied upon by the prosecution should be excluded under section78 PACE.

5.52 The matter was referred to the European Court of Human Rights, which ruled,[48] that there had been a breach of the applicant's right to a fair trial under Article 6(1).[49] The defendant

---

[45] At [30].

[46] See *Lüdi v Switzerland* (1993) 15 EHRR 173 and *Teixeira de Castro v Portugal* (1999) 28 EHRR 101, [1998] Crim LR 751. Post *Loosely*, *Teixeira* was applied and followed in *Eurofinacom v France* [2005] Crim LR 134 and *Ramanauskas v Lithuania* [2008] Crim LR 639. In neither *Teixeira* nor *Ramanauskas* was there any evidence that the accused had committed any previous offences.

[47] [2005] Crim LR 796, see para 1.9 above.

[48] 22 July 2003 (15 BRHC 189).

[49] [57]–[59].

appealed to the Court of Appeal where the appeal was dismissed. The ECtHR finding of a Article 6(1) breach did not automatically make the conviction unsafe.

The Court of Appeal dismissed the defence entrapment arguments that had beeen advanced **5.53** before the trial judge, making reference to a number of factual features:

(a) The appellant's willingness and ability to provide large quantities of counterfeit currency.
(b) Neither on arrest nor in interview did the appellant complain that he had been set up, pressured or forced into committing the offence. He admitted that he had been tempted by reason of his financial circumstances.
(c) No evidence called from the defendant asserting that pressure had been put on him.

The Court of Appeal was in no doubt that entrapment in and of itself does not necessarily **5.54** give rise to such an abuse of process as would require a stay of proceedings.[50]

A point very much illustrated by decision in *Raymond Harmes and Gary Crane*.[51] The lack of **5.55** proper authorization during an undercover police operation, in breach of the Regulation of Investigatory Powers Act 2000 and the Covert Human Intelligence Sources Code of Practice, did not merit a stay of proceedings on a conspiracy count.

Undercover police had supplied Harmes with soft drinks in exchange for a small amount **5.56** of drugs (cocaine). Harmes subsequently revealed to another officer how drugs could be imported into Heathrow Airport with the assistance of an airport worker, Crane. Applications at trial to stay proceedings were rejected. Harmes and Crane had willingly participated in drug smuggling for their own subsequent gain, several months after the initial contact with the undercover officers. The police had failed to keep a careful record of that which was proposed and approved, which deprived the court of the opportunity of assessing whether the undercover actions of officers were necessary and proportionate. There was neither a record of who authorised the undercover tactics and when they were adopted, nor of any review of the same. However, those breaches did not merit a stay of proceedings. The undercover police officer's suggestion that they should be supplied with cocaine in exchange for soft drinks did not trap Harmes and Crane into the agreement, several months later, to import substantial quantities of drugs. The request for payment in drugs had merely been the trigger for the revelation by Harmes of a method for importing drugs that he had at his disposal. It was the prospect of financial gain, not the supply of drinks, that persuaded Harmes to become involved in the proposed importation. Although the undercover police officers' conduct was criminal and not properly authorized, it was not so seriously improper to warrant a stay of proceedings; the conduct did not stray beyond that which was permissible to investigate. The officer's activities were insignificant compared to Harmes offer to import large quantities of high value drugs.

Similarly in *Tre Palmer, Christopher Gyamfi and Kirk Cooke*[52] the Court of Appeal dismissed a **5.57** conviction appeal based on entrapment. There had been nothing untoward in an undercover police operation in response to a high level of residential burglaries. A trading post shop was set up in which stolen property could be sold. The shop was operated by undercover officers and equipped with audio and visual surveillance. The operation was authorized by senior officers under the Regulation of Investigatory Powers Act 2000 (RIPA). Authorizations were renewed each month, the Crown Prosecution Service maintained operational oversight and officers were instructed not to act as provocateurs. The applicants, on entering the trading

---

[50] See also *Philip Hall* (CA, 23 February 2000 No.99/2823/Y4).
[51] [2006] EWCA Crim 928, [2006] 7 Archbold News 1.
[52] [2015] Crim LR 1 153, [2014] EWCA Crim 1681.

post, were individually told by undercover officers that they could sell items there. The applicants went on to sell passports, bank cards, laptops and other stolen goods. The Court of Appeal decided that there was nothing exceptional about the opportunity presented to the applicants, as per *Christou and Wright*.[53] The first instance Judge had found that the RIPA authorizations had been granted with good reason and that the undercover operation was necessary and proportionate. Residential burglary was prevalent in the area, conventional methods had not been working and the undercover operation had a legitimate aim of preventing and detecting serious offences which had considerable consequences to victims. The first instance judge rejected the applicant submissions that they were vulnerable or enticed by the officers. Having seen and heard the applicants on the surveillance tapes he formed the view that their only vulnerability was their greed.

5.58 Defence complaints of entrapment was also rejected by the Court of Appeal in *Mia Moore and Ben Peter Burrows*.[54] In dismissing the appeal, the Court of Appeal observed that the assessment to be applied, on the basis of *Looseley*, was a fact sensitive matter and an appellate court would not interfere with the first instance judge's assessment of the facts unless there were serious error.

5.59 In considering whether to stay proceedings because of alleged entrapment, the key question was whether the conduct of the police brought the administration of justice into disrepute. Lord Justice Rix identified[55] five factors of particular importance in considering the question:

- Was there reasonable suspicion of criminal activity, amounting to a legitimate trigger for the undercover operation?
- Was the operation properly authorized and supervised, so that there were legitimate proper control mechanisms in place?
- Were the means of subterfuge employed to police particular types of offence necessary and proportionate?
- Was there an 'unexceptional opportunity' to offend and causation of offending. Did the undercover officer cause crime or merely provide an opportunity to commit crime?
- Was there authentication of the evidence obtained?

5.60 In *Moore*, the Court of Appeal rejected the abuse of process grounds of appeal as the undercover officers had done no more than provide the appellant with an opportunity, which she seized immediately and resolutely, to volunteer herself as a participant to substantial offending.

State-generated crime

5.61 Contrast the post-*Looseley* decisions where the courts have found there to be state generated crime.

5.62 *Drug supply*. In the case of *Dianna Moon*,[56] the Court of Appeal quashed a conviction for possession with intent to supply a class 'A' drug (heroin), there having been state-generated drug supply. The trial judge should have stayed proceedings as an abuse. The appellant, a heroin addict as opposed to a drug supplier, was persuaded by an undercover police officer to supply a small amount of heroin. There was no evidence, save for the single act of supply, to

---

[53] [1992] 4 All ER 567, [1992] 95 Cr App R 320.

[54] [2013] EWCA Crim 85, [2014] Crim LR 364. See also judgment of Burnton LJ in *R v M* [2011] EWCA Crim 648.

[55] At para 52 of judgment, adopting the five factors identified by Professor Ormerod in 'Recent Developments in Entrapment' [2006] Covert Policing Review pp 65–86.

[56] [2004] EWCA Crim 2872. See also the case comment at 70(3) 2006 Journal Criminal Law, 194–97. *Moon* was distinguished in *James Jones* [2010] 2 Cr App R 10.

suggest that the appellant was prepared to supply any other would be purchaser. There was no predisposition to deal in drugs. The Crown accepted that there was no evidence that the appellant, either in the present case or any other occasion, had acted as a dealer—a fact which was supported by the appellant's antecedents as well as by the search of her home. It was not a case of 'mere opportunity' or of 'if not a deal with Jackie (the undercover police officer) then a deal with any other customer'.[57]

Financial Crime. Judicial aversion to state-generated financial crime lead to proceedings **5.63** being stayed in the case of *Finch and others.*[58] His Honour Judge Bathurst-Norman stayed proceedings as an abuse of process, based on state generated financial crime. The police illegality in *Finch* fell into two categories. First, the police committed offences under Section 50 of the Drug Trafficking Act 1994 by assisting in laundering £15 million back to the suspects in the case. Second, the police persuaded an accountant to compile false accounts for a business known as Ocean Park Investments Ltd, which were then filed at Companies House, the police having first given to that accountant's firm an assurance that they would not be prosecuted. The purpose of filing such accounts was to lend credibility to the business of Ocean Park Investments Ltd so that any enquirers, either for lawful or unlawful motives, would be re-assured by a company search. In filing such returns, the undercover officers were acting unlawfully with the approval of their superiors.

The police money laundering exercise was conceived as part of a major offensive against the **5.64** financial resources and profits available to major league drug traffickers through the setting up of a storefront style sting operation offering money laundering facilities. However no specific targets were identified.

Further, the police were aware of public and judicial disapproval of such operations. This can **5.65** be viewed in the context of, on the one hand, total support for the use of decoys to capture rapists, whilst, on the other hand, the almost universal disapproval in 1987 of the sting-type operation in the West End (Operation Temple Two). In the latter case, police parked two delivery vans in Oxford Street and Soho with the rear doors open showing boxes apparently containing videos and other valuable goods. Arrests followed, but the tactics were bitterly attacked by pressure groups as encouraging crime rather than preventing it. Most of those arrested were not persistent criminals but people who were unable to resist temptation.

The operation was then placed on hold, pending the decision of the Court of Appeal in **5.66** *Christou and Wright,*[59] the police being aware of the evidential difficulties surrounding undercover 'sting' operations. His Honour Judge Bathurst-Norman observed:

> I am satisfied that the police were so lulled into a sense of false security by the decision in Christou and Wright that their approach to obtaining advice was fatally flawed it was so casual ...[60]

> I am quite unable to accept that any advice was sought or given as to the criminality of police officers involved in this operation ...

> [T]he role played by the police in laundering about £15 million back to those suspected of money laundering ... (was) major and pivotal. No ordinary citizen could have transferred funds to the extent that they did and in the manner in which they did ...[61]

---

[57] [2004] EWCA Crim 2872 per Rix LJ at [50]. There was also a failure to comply with the Regulation of Investigatory Powers Act 2000 codes of practice, leading the Court of Appeal to doubt whether the police officer had stayed within the scope of authorization.

[58] *Christopher Finch, Plinio Bossino, Tony Harwood, William Hunt, Ian Howard, Peter Harwood, Anthony Zaitzeff, Michael Roper and Lee Doran* (Southwark Crown Court, 30 June 2003).

[59] (1992) 95 Cr App R 264.

[60] Ibid [12].

[61] Ibid [17].

In summary, therefore, I am satisfied that the undercover police officers played a (major) role … its illegality went far beyond the kind of role one usually encounters in such cases as where an undercover police officer solicits the supply of drugs to himself or where an undercover officer acts as a drugs courier in order to arrest those who are to receive the drugs, whilst making sure that he drugs themselves do not get into the hands of the recipient or get distributed on the streets.[62]

5.67 As per *Loosely*[63] His Honour Judge Bathhurst-Norman considered whether the conduct of the police was so improper as to bring the administration of justice into disrepute. Proper authorization was given by an appropriate officer, with appropriate directions given to the undercover officers not to actively engage in planning and committing crime and that they are intended to play a minor role. No abuse of process flowed from authorizations.

5.68 In terms of entrapment, the concept of the operation involved criminal conduct by the police and the building of their legend as dishonest money launderers involved further unlawful conduct by the police in that false accounts were filed with Companies House. At the time the police had no responsible grounds for suspecting that Finch had committed any offence within this jurisdiction. He was certainly not the subject of any investigation at that stage.

5.69 Furthermore, there was no contemporaneous record of the terms of the undercover officer's introduction to Finch over the telephone. There was no reliable evidence as to the exact terms of that important introductory meeting and no attempt was made to record the early conversations. The importance of the need for an independent record to show what was or was not said in this kind of situation, where undercover conversations are in dispute, was emphasized in *Bryce*.[64] The conversations could have been recorded without any real risk to the undercover officers.

5.70 His Honour Judge Bathurst-Norman concluded that what the police did amounted to state-created crime and that Finch was entrapped. The starting point was that, when the operation started, there was no target, there was no suspicion of Finch's involvement in drug trafficking. Further, the undercover officer was pushing Finch to introduce business to him and holding out sweeteners of other business.

5.71 What the police were offering in this case, initially via the banks, and secondly via means which would never be open to the ordinary money launderer or member of the public, was a wholly safe system for the transfer of funds without any questions being asked and with commission being paid to those who introduced business. This was a highly tempting package. The police were offering to Finch and others what was a wholly exceptional opportunity, which no ordinary citizen or money launderer could offer.

5.72 This was not a storefront operation such as might be the case with a bureau de change. The overall picture is one of state-created crime, within the test laid down in *Looseley* by Lord Nicholls.

5.73 In staying proceedings, His Honour Judge Bathurst-Norman observed:[65]

When this operation started, the police had no target, their operation could be described as state created crime, as the police carried out no independent investigation into these defendants, and yet by reward directly or indirectly lured two of them into committing more and more serious crime, offering to them a wholly exceptional opportunity to commit crime, and

---

[62] Ibid [19].
[63] [2001] UKHL 53, [2001] 4 All ER 897.
[64] [1992] 4 All ER 567, [1992] 95 Cr App R 320.
[65] (Southwark Crown Court, 2 July 2003) [12].

when I consider the fact that the police laundered about £15 million back to their suspects in the process of earning considerable commission, then I am bound to consider whether their actions have brought the criminal justice system into disrepute, especially as they played a leading role in the creation of this conspiracy and a major role throughout its course.

Interestingly, His Honour Judge Bathurst-Norman expressed[66] a number of thoughts for the future conduct of entrapment cases, which are worthy of consideration: **5.74**

In mounting an operation of this kind, the police need to take proper advice as to its legality, and to take that advice at the highest level, such as the level of the Director of Public Prosecutions or Treasury Counsel.

Secondly, directions as to the logging of recorded material should be followed meticulously. They were not in this case.

Thirdly, all material, whether it relates to evidence or to disclosure, needs to be carefully logged in a running log which should contain details of where such material is to be found to ensure that such material is preserved. Only if this is done can the prosecution properly fulfil its obligations as to disclosure.

Fourthly, the police need to distinguish between an intelligence gathering operation and an operation aimed at collecting evidence for the purposes of prosecution. In an ideal world, once intelligence is gathered, an independent operation should be mounted to collect evidence with a view to prosecution ...

Fifthly, to allow an operation to run and run and run for as many years as this did, and to launder money in such large quantities back to suspected criminals, will inevitably raise question marks in the mind of any right-thinking member of the public as to whether the police are in fact creating crime or at least encouraging it. When a operation continues for as many years as this did, the case spins out of control and becomes unmanageable, with the result that any court will have to spend much time on arguments as to abuse of process.

In terms of future legal developments in the area of entrapment, His Honour Judge Bathurst-Norman made a number of suggestions:[67] **5.75**

I consider that the time has come when either the Court of Appeal or Parliament should consider a complete overhaul of the law in this area. For instance, entrapment should be made a substantive defence, as it is in many States in the United States. It should be for a jury, looking at all the circumstances in the light of the judge's direction ...

Equally, whilst it is clearly right for a judge to rule upon the legality of police actions, the balancing act which a judge then performs would, in my view, be much better carried out by a jury, who could review all the evidence in the case at the same time. Indeed, similar considerations apply in relation to all questions of proportionality.

Private commercial entrapment

Crimes may also be incited and created by individuals other than state officials, constituting a form of private commercial entrapment.[68] The actions and activities of the private individuals, notably tabloid journalists, may be carried on outside state controlled perimeters, with no authorization, supervision or endorsement (at least at the time of the commission of the offence) by law enforcement agencies. **5.76**

---

[66] Ibid [15].
[67] Ibid [17].
[68] See K Hofmeyr, 'The Problem of Private Entrapment' [2006] Crim LR 319. For discussion of private commercial entrapment in a regulatory disciplinary context see the decision in *Council for the Regulation of Healthcare Professionals v General Medical Council (Re Saluja)* [2007] 1 WLR 3094 DC, with Goldring J leaving open the possibility of a successful application of a stay on the basis of entrapment by non-state agents.

Section 78 remedy

5.77 Section 78 of PACE is the appropriate means of dealing with private commercial entrapment.

5.78 In *R v Morley and Hutton*,[69] the Court of Appeal dismissed appeals based the conduct of the newspaper, *News of World*. A reporter from the paper set up and taped interviews, in which the reporter bought from the appellants counterfeit £50 notes. The police were informed and arrested the appellants at a subsequent meeting. Eight months prior to the appellant's trial, the newspaper ran an article entitled 'We smash £5 million fake notes racket', giving embellished and exaggerated information about the case.

5.79 On appeal, complaint was made that the reporter was an agent provocateur, the evidence of entrapment should have been excluded under section 78 of PACE and the contents of the newspaper article meant that a fair trial could not be had.

5.80 In dismissing the appeals, the Court of Appeal stated that there was no unfairness in admitting the evidence. The reality was that the offences would have been committed with or without the journalist. The appellants had access to and produced counterfeit currency. They were committing offences recorded on camera. The reporter did not incite, entice or provoke the appellants into committing the offences. The article was published eight months prior to trial, so even if any members of the jury had read the article, it was unlikely any detail would be remembered.

5.81 In *Hardwicke and Thwaites*,[70] the defendants applied to have counts of supplying cocaine stayed as an abuse of process, based on alleged journalistic entrapment. The trial judge refused the application and the decision was upheld on appeal. The Court of Appeal, in dismissing the appeals, held:

(1) That the trial judge had struck the correct balance between ensuring that serious offences were brought to trial and avoiding the impression that the end justifies the means.
(2) Having regard to the lapse of time between the prejudicial pre-trial publicity and the trial, the judge was entitled to find that a fair trial was possible.

European Court of Human Rights

5.82 In *Shannon*[71] and *Shannon v United Kingdom*[72] the trial judge, Court of Appeal and European Court of Human Rights (ECtHR) rejected arguments that there had been an unfair trial because of undercover journalistic entrapment.

5.83 The journalist, acting on information received, posing as a sheikh, arranged a meeting with the applicant, which was tape-recorded, and during which he asked for cocaine. The applicant willingly supplied cocaine. The journalist published a front page headline article based on the taped conversations. The applicant was arrested and tried on drugs charges. An application to exclude the taped conversations was refused. The applicant had volunteered to supply the drugs without being subject to pressure. The trial judge emphasized 'there was no suggestion of criticism of the part played by the police or CPS, the organs of the state responsible for gathering and presenting the evidence and instituting proceedings'.[73]

5.84 The defence application and arguments for disclosure of the identity of the informant were also refused and rejected (by all three courts), as non-disclosure did not affect the fairness of the trial.

---

[69] [1994] Crim LR 919.
[70] [2001] Crim LR 220.
[71] [2000] Crim LR 1001.
[72] [2005] Crim LR 133.
[73] *Shannon* [2001] 1 Cr App R 12 [21].

However, it is important to note that the ECtHR recognized that the issue of private com- **5.85** mercial entrapment is relevant to the right to a fair trial. The ECtHR stated that it 'does not exclude that the admission of evidence so obtained may in certain circumstances render the proceedings unfair for the purposes of article 6'.[74]

Informant entrapment

The third type of entrapment was recognized by the Court of Appeal in *Wilson*.[75] Appeals **5.86** against conviction based upon abuse of process arguments were dismissed, but the Court of Appeal recognized that there was a judicial discretion to stay proceedings where an offence was incited by an informer.

The discretion applies even to those who may be guilty of a crime; see Lord Lowry in *Bennett*: **5.87**

> It may be said that a guilty accused finding himself in the circumstances predicated is not deserving of much sympathy, but the principle involved goes beyond the scope of such a pragmatic observation and even beyond the rights of those victims who are or may be innocent. It affects the proper administration of justice according to the rule of law.[76]

When considering informant participation, the question will often turn on how active the **5.88** informant has been before the police or law enforcement agency become involved.

In *Paulssen v The Queen*,[77] the Court of Appeal held that where entrapment took place with- **5.89** out the knowledge of law enforcement agencies, an argument alleging an abuse of process could not apply to that aspect of the case in which the private individual informer was acting on his own (non-state authorized or supervised) initiative.

In *Ian Jones*[78] the informant did no more than reply to a message written by the appellant on **5.90** a public toilet door. The Court of Appeal rejected abuse of process arguments. The inform- ant, an adult female (journalist), whilst travelling on a public train, saw a message on a train door seeking girls aged 8 and 13 years old for sex, offering payment and asking the girls to telephone or text a mobile telephone number. The informant, pretending to be a child tele- phoned the number and received in reply sexually explicit messages and invitations to meet. The informant contacted the police who set up an undercover operation using a police officer pretending to be a 12-year-old girl. The appellant was arrested when he arrived at an agreed meeting place. He was charged with attempting intentionally to cause or incite a person under 13 to engage in sexual activity contrary to s 8 Sexual Offences Act 2003. In upholding the conviction, the Court of Appeal observed that the police did not create the offence—it was complete when the message was written by the appellant on the toilet door. To obtain evidence of the appellant's intention (as opposed to fantasy) to incite penetrative sex, it was necessary to mount the undercover operation. The undercover police officer was limited to giving the appellant an opportunity to attempt to commit a similar offence where no harm could come to a victim and which would provide the evidence necessary for conviction. Far from bringing the administration of justice into disrepute the undercover police officer's behaviour was necessary to apprehend the appellant before he incited an actual child. There was no abuse of process.

---

[74] At p 11 of the decision: ECHR section IV: Admissibility Decision, April 6, 2004; Application No 67537/01.
[75] (CA, 9 May 1996).
[76] At 76G.
[77] [2003] EWCA Crim 2855.
[78] [2007] 2 Cr App R 267; [2007] Crim LR 979.

C. Overseas Jurisprudence

5.91   The courts of Australia, Canada, New Zealand, and the United States of America, have developed both exclusionary rules and the doctrine of abuse of process to deal with entrapment. The rules aim to protect the individual citizen against the state's misuse of executive power, a purpose identified by Mr Justice Frankfurter in *Sherman v US*:[79]

> The power of Government is abused and directed to an end for which it was not constituted when employed to promote rather than to detect crime and to bring about the downfall of those who, left to themselves, might well have obeyed the law. Human nature is weak enough and sufficiently beset by temptations without government adding to them and generating crime.

5.92   Courts consider it unjust to expose an individual to the ordeal of trial and punishment for actions the like of which she would not have undertaken without calculated and persistent temptation and persuasion by Government agents.

New Zealand

5.93   The New Zealand Court of Appeal[80] adopts the same approach: where undercover police officers do more that give suspects an opportunity to commit crime, and instigate the commission of an offence, which would not have taken place without their encouragement, the judge should in his discretion exclude the evidence.

5.94   In *Pethig*,[81] Mr Justice Mahon emphasized that it is not sufficient for the prosecution to prove that the accused had a proclivity for this type of offence; 'The question is whether the accused without encouragement would have committed the specific offences charged in the indictment.'[82]

5.95   In *Wilson v The Queen*,[83] the New Zealand Supreme Court summarized the courts' balancing approach to undercover operation cases, identifying them as second category abuse cases, by citing the following extract from Professor Choo's book,[84] as cited by Lord Dyson in *Warren*:[85]

> The courts would appear to have left the matter at a general level, requiring a determination to be made in particular cases of whether the continuation of proceedings would compromise the moral integrity of the criminal justice system to an unacceptable degree. Implicitly at least, this determination involves performing a 'balancing' test that takes into account such factors as the seriousness of any violation of the defendant's (or even a third party's) rights; whether the police have acted in bad faith or maliciously, or with an improper motive; whether the misconduct was committed in circumstances of urgency, emergency or necessity; the availability pr otherwise of a direct sanction against the person(s) responsible for the misconduct; and the seriousness of the offence with which the defendant is charged.

---

[79]   (1958) 356 US 369 at 382.

[80]   See *Hartley* [1978] 2 NZLR 199(CA); *Lavelle* [1979] 1 NZLR 45 (CA); *Moevao v Department of Labour* [1980] 1 NZLR 464(CA).

[81]   (1977) 1 NZLR 448.

[82]   (1977) 1 NZLR 448 at p 453.

[83]   [2015] NZSC 189.

[84]   Andrew L-T Choo, *Abuse of Process and Judicial Stays of Criminal Proceedings* (2nd edn, Oxford University Press 2008) 24.

[85]   [2011] UKPC 10, [2012] 1 AC 22, [23].

Australia

In Australia, although there is no 'defence' to entrapment, a trial judge has a discretionary power to exclude evidence or to stay proceedings for abuse of process.[86] The Australian courts hold that entrapment occurs when (a) the authorities provide a person with the opportunity to commit an offence without acting on a reasonable suspicion that the person is already engaged in criminal activity; or (b) although having such reasonable suspicion, they go beyond providing an opportunity and induce the commission of an offence.[87]

5.96

The New South Wales Court of Appeal considers that the appropriate remedy for such entrapment is a permanent stay for abuse of process. Obtaining convictions 'at too high a price'[88] and 'avoiding the undesirable effect of curial approval, or even encouragement, being given to the unlawful conduct of those whose task it is to enforce the law.'[89] The objection to entrapment is that it uses seductive or dishonest tactics to induce a non-disposed person to commit the offence in a way that is 'inconsistent with the recognised purposes of the administration of justice'[90] and hence amounts to an abuse of process.

5.97

The High Court of Australia set out four factors to be considered when examining entrapment:[91]

5.98

(1) Whether conduct of the law enforcement authorities induced the offence.
(2) Whether, in proffering the inducement, the authorities had reasonable grounds for suspecting that the accused was likely to commit the particular offence or one that was similar to that offence or were acting in the course of a bona fide investigation of offences of a kind similar to that with which the accused has been charged.
(3) Whether, prior to the inducement, the accused had the intention of committing the offence or a similar offence if an opportunity arose.
(4) Whether the offence was induced as the result of persistent importunity, threats, deceit, offers of rewards or other inducements that would not ordinarily be associated with the commission of the offence or a similar offence.

Canada

The Canadian courts stay proceedings as an abuse of process that have an entrapment background. The abuse of process principle is relied upon, as the court:

5.99

> ... withholds its processes from the prosecution on the basis that such would bring the administration of justice into disrepute ... the issue is not the discipline of the prosecution but the avoidance of the improper invocation by the State of the judicial process and its powers in circumstances where the accused has been ensnared by the police force in order to bring about an offence for which he will be prosecuted.[92]

The societal interest in limiting the use of entrapment techniques by the state was described by the Canadian Supreme Court in these terms:

5.100

> One reason is that the State does not have unlimited power to intrude into our personal lives or to randomly test the virtue of individuals. Another is the concern that entrapment techniques may result in the commission of crimes by people who would not otherwise have

---

[86] *Romeo* (1987) 45 SASR 212; *Vuckov* (1986) 22 A Crim R 10.
[87] *Hsing* (1991) 57 A Crim R 88.
[88] *Ireland* (1970) 126 Crim LR 321 at 535.
[89] *Bunning v Cross* (1978) 141 Crim L R 54 at 741, per Stephen and Aitken JJ.
[90] *Ja go v District Court of NSW* (1989) 168 Crim L R 23 at 30, per Mason CJ.
[91] *Ridgeway v R* (1995) 184 CLR 19 at 92 of McHugh J dissenting judgment, which Lord Hutton approved in *Looseley.*
[92] *Amato v The Queen* (1982) 69 CCC 2d 31.

become involved in criminal conduct ... Ultimately we may be saying that there are inherent limits on the power of the State to manipulate people and events for the purpose of obtaining the specific objective of obtaining convictions.[93]

5.101 Two leading Canadian Supreme Court decisions on the subject are *Amato*[94] and *Mack*.[95] Like *Ameer*, Amato had no previous history of any drug trafficking. He was persuaded by a former girlfriend to obtain cocaine from her own sources. Mack, on the other hand, had previous convictions and addictions, but had been drug-free for some period of time before he was repeatedly approached and shown a large sum of cash as an inducement to re-offend. The Canadian court held that Mack was entitled to a stay of the criminal proceedings brought against him after he had yielded to temptation and returned to his old haunts and suppliers to fulfil the order. Both cases have fact situations similar to drug operations by police in Britain. All too typically, they concerned the prosecution of persons used as intermediaries, rather than of criminals centrally involved in importation, production, or distribution.[96]

5.102 Although the focus is upon the offensiveness of official conduct, this may detract from the particular vulnerability of the targets or the fact that human characteristics such as friendship have been exploited.

5.103 In deciding whether entrapment techniques are offensive, both the Canadian and Australian courts are inclined to envisage an ordinary person with the same characteristics and in the same position as the accused and to ask whether the nature of the persuasion offered by the police agent might induce such a person to commit the offence.

5.104 The Supreme Court of Canada has adopted, in line with the United Kingdom and New Zealand, a balancing approach in relation to second category abuse cases. In *Babos*,[97] Mr Justice Moldaver observed:

> [T]he question is whether the state has engaged in conduct that is offensive to societal notions of fair play and decency and whether proceeding with a trial in the face of that conduct would be harmful to the integrity of the justice system. To put it in simpler terms, there are limits on the type of conduct society will tolerate in the prosecution of offences. At times, state conduct will be so troublesome that having a trial – even a fair one – will leave the impression that the justice system condones conduct that offends society's sense of fair play and decency. This harms the integrity of the justice system.

Mr. Justice Moldaver went to state:[98]

> [W]hen the [second] category is invoked, the balancing stage takes on added importance. Where prejudice to the integrity of the justice system is alleged, the court is asked to decide which of two options better protects the integrity of the system: staying the proceedings, or having a trial despite the impugned conduct. This inquiry necessarily demands balancing. The court must consider such things as the nature and seriousness of the impugned conduct, whether the conduct is isolated or reflects a systemic and ongoing problem, the circumstances of the accused, the charges he or she faces, and the interests of society in having the charges disposed of on the merits. Clearly the more egregious the state conduct, the greater the need for the court to dissociate itself from it. When the conduct in question shocks the community's conscience and/or offends its sense of fair play and decency, it becomes less

---

[93] *Mack v The Queen* (1988) 44 CCC 3(d) 513 at 541.
[94] *Amato v The Queen* (1982) 69 CCC 2d 31, at 61 and 75.
[95] *Mack v The Queen* (1988) 44 CCC 3(d) 513 at 549, 560, and 568. Also see discussion of excluding evidence obtained by police misconduct in undercover operations in *The Queen v Nelson Lloyd Hart* [2014] 2 SCR 544.
[96] See also *Campbell* (1998) 2 SCR 903.
[97] 2014 SCC 16: [2014] 1 SCR 309 at para 39.
[98] 2014 SCC 16: [2014] 1 SCR 309 at para 41.

likely that society's interest in a full trial on the merits will prevail in the balancing process. But in [second] category cases, balance must always be considered.

United States

The United States of America judicial view is illustrated by Mr Justice Frankfurter, in *Sherman v US*:[99]   **5.105**

> No matter what the defendants' past record and present inclinations to criminality, or the depths to which he has sunk in the estimation of society, certain police conduct to ensnare him into future crime is not to be tolerated by an advanced society.

In applying this test the United States courts view the task as drawing a line between, 'the trap for the unwary innocent and the trap for the unwary criminal.'[100]   **5.106**

D. Summary

The present state of English law on entrapment can be summarized as follows: **5.107**

(1) There is no defence of entrapment.
(2) Cases should not be stayed, nor evidence excluded, for entrapment in 'test purchase' situations in which:
    (a) the law enforcement officers have reasonable grounds to suspect the targeted person of involvement in a particular kind of offence, or at least reasonable grounds to suspect people visiting a particular place, to be involved; or
    (b) the officers are duly authorized to carry out the test purchases in compliance with the relevant Codes of Practice; or
    (c) where the illegal activity is ongoing, the officers do no more than provide the suspect with an unexceptional opportunity to commit the offence, replicate ordinary customers' behaviour and impose no special trick, extra pressure nor added inducement.

(3) Although there is no single factor to determine the issue of entrapment, the overriding question is whether

> the officers did more than ... to afford the accused the opportunity to offend, of which he freely took advantage in circumstances where it appears that he would have behaved in a similar way if offered the opportunity by someone else or whether, on the other hand, by means of unworthy or shameful conduct, they may have persuaded him to commit an offence of a kind which otherwise he would not have committed.

> (*Attorney-General's Ref No. 3*).

Entrapment is 'conduct which causes the defendant to commit the offence as opposed to giving him an opportunity to do so.[101]

(4) Proceedings ought to be stayed for abuse of process if the law enforcement officer's conduct is an affront to the public conscience.
(5) It is necessary for law enforcement agencies to respect the ECHR but the law in relation to entrapment is that stated in *Looseley*;[102]
(6) In relation to private commercial entrapment by journalists, if the journalist is acting on information received, conversations are recorded and no pressure was brought to bear

---

[99] (1958) 356 US 369 at 383.
[100] See also *Sorrells v US* (1932) 287 US 435.
[101] *Attorney-General's Reference No 3* [2001] 4 All ER 897, Lord Hoffman at 70.
[102] See *Brett* (2005) EWCA Crim 893.

on the person targeted, proceedings are unlikely to be stayed. Concerns about private commercial entrapment can be dealt with under section 78 PACE.

(7) Exclusion of evidence under section 78 of PACE is to be determined by applying the *Smurthwaite* guidelines: who took the initiative is relevant to the exercise of the court's discretion.

(8) Entrapment may lead to mitigation of sentence per *Fletcher and Smith*:[103]

> entrapment is capable of being a significant mitigating factor with regard to sentence if the judge is satisfied that the crime would not have been committed but for the activities of the police.[104]

---

[103] (2005) EWCA Crim 2816.

[104] See also *Underhill* [1979] 1 Cr App R (S) 270; *Sang* [1980] AC 402, [1979] 69 Cr App R 282; *Beaumont* (1987) 9 Cr App R (S) 342; *Chapman and Denton* (1989) 11 Cr App R(S) 222; *Mackey and Shaw* (1993) 14 Cr App R(S) 53; *White and Harrison* (1994) 15 Cr App R(S) 714; *Tonnessen* [1998] 2 Cr App R(S) 328; *Springer* [1999] 1 Cr App R(S) 217; *Thornton and Hobbs* [2003] EWCA Crim 919; *Pittmann* [2003] EWCA Crim 460; *Stanley* [2005] EWCA Crim 1341; *Mann* [2005] EWCA Crim 2604; *MacDonald* [2005] EWCA Crim 1945.

6

DELAY

A. Historical Common Law

The common law provides that a fair hearing must be timely: see *Robins*[1] and *Connelly* **6.1**
v DPP.[2] The right to a speedy trial was recognized as far back as the thirteenth century.
Chapter 29 of Magna Carta 1215 (9 Hen.3) states '… we will not deny or defer to any man
either justice or right'.[3]

B. The European Convention on Human Rights (ECHR)

In more recent times, the right to a trial within a reasonable time has been enshrined, in **6.2**
broad terms, in Articles 5(3) and 6(1) of the European Convention of Human Rights.[4]
Article 5(3) provides:

> Everyone arrested or detained … shall be brought promptly before a judge or other officer
> authorised by law to exercise judicial power and shall be entitled to trial within a reasonable
> time or to release pending trial.

---

[1] (1884) 1 Cox CC 114.
[2] [1964] AC 1254.
[3] 4 Halsbury's Statutes (2nd) 263.
[4] For discussion of the relationship between the common law right to a speedy trial and Article 6(1)
see A Webster QC, 'Delay and Article 6(1): An End to the Requirement of Prejudice?' [2001] Crim LR
786–93; Emmerson and Ashworth, *Human Rights and Criminal Justice* (Sweet and Maxwell 2001), pp 353–
54; Jackson, Johnstone, and Shapland, 'Delay, Human Rights and the Need for Statutory Time Limits in
Youth Cases' [2003] Crim LR 510–24; Bajwa and Mendelle 'The Reasonable Time Provision in Article 6 (1)'
[2004] CBA Newsletter Issue 3 (September).

Article 6(1) states:

> In the determination of his civil rights and obligations or of any criminal charge against him, everyone is entitled to a fair and public hearing within a reasonable time by an independent and impartial tribunal.

The right to a trial within a reasonable time, stated in Article 6(1), is:

- undoubtedly of great importance for the proper administration of justice;[5]
- designed to protect all parties from excessive procedural delay, so as to prevent a person charged from remaining 'too long in a state of uncertainty about his fate'[6] and 'underlines the importance of rendering justice without delays which might jeopardise its effectiveness and credibility',[7] bearing in mind that delay may result in the loss of exculpatory evidence or in a deterioration in the quality of evidence generally;[8]
- a free standing protection, independent of the other Article 6(1) fair trial safeguards;[9]
- one which does not require a defendant to show prejudice by delay to establish a breach of the right;[10]
- emphasises the seriousness of any breach by the high threshold which must be crossed before a breach is established;[11] and
- measured from date of charge, which is defined as the 'official notification given to an individual by the competent authority of an allegation that he committed a criminal offence'[12] and not when the initial complaint is made or a preliminary investigation begun.[13]

6.3   The House of Lords in *Attorney General's Reference (No 2 of 2001)*,[14] considered, the Strasbourg *Eckle*[15] notification test, and upheld the Court of Appeal's observations that, 'an interrogation or an interview of a suspect by itself does not amount to a charging of that suspect for the purpose of the reasonable time requirement in Article 6(1)'.

6.4   Lord Bingham stated that, 'As a general rule, the relevant period will begin at the earliest time at which a person is officially alerted to the likelihood of criminal proceedings against him.'[16] Time will normally begin to run from the time of formal charge or service of a summons, and may start when an official indicates that a person will be reported with a view to a prosecution.[17] This is true regardless of the location of the charging decision. Accordingly, where a person could have been charged in England, but was later prosecuted in Scotland on the same facts, time runs from the time when a charge in England could have been laid.[18]

---

[5] See *Guincho v Portugal* (1984) 7 EHRR 223.

[6] *Stögmüller v Austria* (1979) 1 EHRR 155.

[7] *H v France* (1989) 12 EHRR 74, 90, para 58.

[8] *Mills v HM Advocate* [2002] 3 WLR 1597 per Lord Steyn.

[9] *Porter v Magil* [2002] 1 All ER 465.

[10] *Eckle v Federal Republic of Germany* (1983) 5 EHRR 1, 24, para 66. The House of Lords adopted the same approach for England and Wales in *Magill v Porter* [2001] UKHL 67. The same position is adopted in Scotland: *HM Advocate v Little* 1999 SCCR 625, 637A–638B; *McNab v HM Advocate* 2000 JC 80, 84A–B; *HM Advocate v McGlinchey* 2000 JC 564, 569A–E; and *Crummock (Scotland) Ltd v HM Advocate* 2000 SLT 677, 679A–B.

[11] See *R v Advocate General for Scotland* [2002] UKPC D3, [164] per Lord Walker.

[12] *Deweer v Belgium* (1984) 6 EHRR CD 406; *Eckle v Germany* (1983) 5 EHRR 1; *Foti v Italy* (1983) 5 EHRR 313; *Corigliano v Italy* (1983) 5 EHRR 334; *Reinhardt and Slimane –Kaid v France* (1999) 28 EHRR 59; *Ewing v United Kingdom* (1988) 10 EHRR CD141.

[13] Also *X v Austria* (1967) 24 CD 8; *United States v Patterson* (1893) 150 USR 65 p. 68; *Howarth v United Kingdom* (2001) 31 EHRR 37, and see commentary in [2005] Crim LR 3–23.

[14] [2004] 2 AC 72, [2004] 1 Cr App R 25.

[15] *Eckle v Germany* (1983) 5 EHRR 1.

[16] [2004] 1 Cr App R 25 [27].

[17] *Gibbons* [1997] 2 NZLR 585.

[18] *Burns v Her Majesty's Advocate* [2008] UKPC 63 [25]–[26] per Lord Rodger.

If the period of time that has elapsed gives ground for concern, and amounts to inordinate or **6.5** excessive delay (which is a high and difficult threshold to cross), the court has to consider the detailed facts and circumstance of the case. The burden is on the prosecution to explain and justify any excessive lapse of time.[19]

In determining whether there has been a trial within a reasonable time, the European **6.6** Court of Human Rights has been reluctant to apply rigid criteria under article 5(3) or 6(1). It has taken a case by case approach,[20] taking into account a range of diverse considerations, including: the actual time elapsed; the length of any pre-trial detention; the effect on and conduct of the accused; case complexity (including procedural complexity);[21] investigatory progress; and the efficiency of the administrative and judicial authorities.[22]

In *Stögmüller*,[23] dealing with the reasonable time requirement in Article 5(3), the ECtHR **6.7** pointed out that the guarantee could not be translated into a fixed number of days, weeks, months, or years.

In the event of a breach of the Article 6(1) reasonable time provision, a court is not compelled **6.8** to stay proceedings.[24] Lord Justice Steyn, in the Privy Council decision of *Mills v Advocate General for Scotland*,[25] cited with approval this passage of Lord Hutton's judgment in *Dyer v Watson*:[26]

> The judgments of the European Court, as I read them, suggest that where there has been unreasonable delay in breach of article 6(1) the court does not take the view that a conviction after such delay must automatically be quashed. In Bunkate v The Netherlands[27] the court found that there had been unreasonable delay in violation of article 6(1) and then stated:[28]

> The applicant's claims are based on the assumption that a finding by the Court that a criminal charge was not decided within a reasonable time automatically results in the extinction of the right to execute the sentence and that consequently, if the sentence has already been executed when the Court gives judgment, such execution becomes unlawful with retroactive effect.

> That assumption is, however, incorrect. And in X v Federal Republic of Germany the Commission stated[29] in respect of a claim to stay the proceedings:

> Insofar as the applicant claims a right to discontinuance of the criminal proceedings in view of the long delays which had occurred, the Commission considers that such a right, if it could at all be deduced from the terms of article 6(1) would only apply in very exceptional circumstances. Such circumstances did not exist in the applicant's case.

---

[19] *Dyer v Watson* [2002] UKPC D1, [2004] 1 AC 379.
[20] See *Martins Moreira v Portugal* (1988) 13 EHRR 517 at 530, para 54.
[21] *Howarth v United Kingdom* (2001) 31 EHRR 37.
[22] See *Neumeister v Austria* (No.1) (1979-80) 1 EHRR 91, *Konig v Germany* (No 1) (1979-80) 2 EHRR 170, *Eckle v Germany* 5 EHRR 1, 29, para 80; and Keir Starmer, *European Human Rights Law* (Legal Action Group, 1999).
[23] *Støgmüller v Austria* (1979–80) 1 EHRR 155, 191, para 4.
[24] See *Attorney-General's Reference (No 2 of 2001)*, [2004] 1 Cr App R 25, *HM Advocate v R* [2004] 1 AC 462 and *Spiers v Ruddy* [2007] UKPC D2; [2008] 1 AC 873.
[25] See *Mills v The Advocate General for Scotland* [2002] UKPC D2 [18].
[26] (2002) SLT 229 at 251, para 121.
[27] (1993) 19 EHRR 477.
[28] (1993) 19 EHRR 477 [25].
[29] (1980) 25 DR 144 [2].

6.9 The restrictive use that a defendant can make of a breach of the Article 6(1) reasonable time provisions, was highlighted again by Lord Steyn in *R v Advocate General for Scotland*[30] where he cited with approval the observations of Mr Justice Hardie Boys in *Martin v Tauranga District Court* that,[31] 'the right is to trial without undue delay: it is not a right not to be tried after undue delay'.

6.10 There is a body of Strasbourg case law[32] where there had been a breach of a party's right to trial within a reasonable time period, but the fairness of the trial had not been or would not be compromised. The cases make it clear that unreasonable delay did not mean that proceedings had to be discontinued. The breach of the right to trial within a reasonable time could be cured by expedition, reduction of sentence, or compensation, provided always that the breach, where it occurred, was publicly acknowledged and addressed. The European Court of Human Rights did not prescribe what remedy would be effective in every case, regarding that as a matter for the national court.[33]

Exceptional circumstances

6.11 Stays for abuse of process, where there has been delay in breach of Article 6(1), are confined to 'very exceptional' situations where it is no longer possible to have a fair hearing to try the accused.[34]

Alternative remedies

6.12 Ordinarily, a remedy for breach of the reasonable time requirement could and should be afforded by some other means—for example, a declaration, a reduction in sentence or compensation—falling short of a stay.[35]

6.13 The alternative remedies—mitigation of sentence,[36] declarations and monetary compensation (in the form of non-pecuniary damage, costs and expenses)[37]—have all been used by the ECtHR, following rulings that Article 6(1) reasonable time provisions have been breached.

---

[30] *HM Advocate v R* [2004] 1 AC 462.

[31] [1995] 2 NZLR 419 at 432.

[32] *Kudla v Poland* (2000) 35 EHRR 198; *Cocchiarella v Italy* (Application No 64886/01, 29 March 2006); *Scordino v Italy* (2006) 45 EHRR 207; *Zarb v Malta* (Application No 16631/04, 4 October 2006).

[33] *Spiers v Ruddy* [2007] UKPC D2; [2008] 1 AC 873.

[34] See Lord Bingham's comments in *Attorney-General's Reference (No 2 of 2001)* [2004] 1 Cr App R 25. The 'last resort' nature of the abuse of process jurisdiction was emphasized by the Privy Council in *Spiers v Ruddy* [2007] UKPC D2, [2008] 1 AC 873. For other general statements on the right to a trial within a reasonable time see *S v Geritis* (1966) (1) SA 753 (WLD); *Wemhoff v Federal Republic of Germany* (1979–80) 1 EHRR 55; *Stögmüller v Austria* (1979–80) 1 EHRR 155; *Zimmerman v Switzerland* (1984) 6 EHRR 17; *James Mills v R* (1986) 21 CRR 76 and 1 SCR 863; *Askov* (1990) 74 DLR (4th) 355, [1990] 2 SCR 1199; *Morin* (1992) 8 CRR (2d) 193, [1992] 1 SCR 771; *Doggett v US* (1992) 505 US 647; *S v Zuma* (1995) (2) SA 642; *Haig* [1996] 1 NZLR 184; Schriek [1997] 2 NZLR 147; *Sanderson v AG of the Eastern Cape* (1997) 3 BHRC 647 (SA Con Ct); *Zanner v DPP* [2006] SCA 56 [2006] Crim LR 673–74; *Ferrantelli and Santangelo v Italy* ((1997) 23 EHRR 288; *Zana v Turkey* (1999) 27 EHRR 667; *Reinhardt and Slimane –Kaid v France* (1999) 28 EHRR 59; *Garyfallou AEBE v Greece* (1999) 28 EHRR 344; *Darmalingum v Mauritius* [2000] 2 Cr App R 445; *Flowers v R* [2000] 1 WLR 2396 and *Kudla v Poland* (2002) 35 EHRR 11; *R v Ali* [2007] EWCA Crim 691; *R v P* [2010] NICA 44.

[35] *Attorney-General's Reference (No 2 of 2001)* [2004] 1 Cr App R 25 [320]. The 'last resort' nature of the abuse of process jurisdiction was again emphasized.

[36] *Beck v Norway* (Application No 26390/95), unreported, 26 June 2001 at [28] of the ECtHR judgment. See also *Marriner and Frain* [2002] EWCA Crim 2855 and [2004] EWHC 595 (Admin), for recognition that delay can mitigate sentence.

[37] *Yağci and Sargin v Turkey* (1995) 20 EHRR 505; *Mansur v Turkey* (1995) 20 EHRR 535; and *Massey v United Kingdom* (Application No14399/02), (2004) *Times* (24 November).

C. Common Law

At common law, there is no time limit for commencing criminal proceedings. In all cases where **6.14** time is not limited by statute, a prosecution may be commenced at point in time after the offence. However, delay in commencing or pursuing a prosecution may amount to an abuse of process, warranting a stay of proceedings.

Prejudice

The Privy Council in *Bell v DPP of Jamaica*[38] recognized that courts have an inherent power to **6.15** stay proceedings if there has been an unreasonable delay in bringing the matter to trial. Lord Templeman went further and rejected a submission that the accused would have to prove 'some specific prejudice' to come within the power. It is possible to infer prejudice from the passage of time.

However, delay per se is insufficient. It must be shown that the delay had produced genuine **6.16** prejudice and unfairness. In *Attorney General's Reference (No 1 of 1990)*,[39] Lord Chief Justice Lane observed:[40]

(1) that generally speaking a prosecutor has as much right as a defendant to demand a verdict of a jury on an outstanding indictment and, where either party demands a verdict, a judge has no jurisdiction to stand in the way of it and therefore the jurisdiction to stay proceedings is exceptional;

(2) a stay should never be imposed where the delay has been caused by the complexity of the proceedings;

(3) it would be rare for a stay to be imposed in the absence of fault on the part of the prosecutor or complainant;

(4) delay contributed to by the actions of the defendant should not found the basis of a stay;

(5) the defendant needs to show on a balance of probabilities that owing to the delay he will suffer serious prejudice to the extent that no fair trial can be held. In other words, the continuance of the proceedings amounts to an abuse of the process of the court. In assessing whether there is likely to be prejudice and if so whether it can properly be described as serious, the following matters should be borne in mind: first, the power of the judge at common law and under the Police and Criminal Evidence Act 1984, to regulate the admissibility of evidence; secondly, the trial process itself, which should ensure that all relevant factual issues arising from the delay will be placed before the jury as part of the evidence for their consideration, together with the powers of the judge to give appropriate directions[41] to the jury before they consider their verdict.

The *Attorney General's Reference (No 1 of 1990)* remains the leading authority on abuse of process **6.17** in relation to historical allegations, as confirmed by the Court of Appeal in *MacKreath*[42] and *F*.[43]

---

[38] [1985] 2 All ER 585.

[39] [1992] QB 630, [1992] 95 Cr App R 296.

[40] As followed in *Attorney-General's Reference No 2 of 2001* [2004] 1 Cr App R 25 and *J* [2002] 1 Cr App R 24.

[41] The Judicial Studies Board specimen direction suggests that the trial judge should inform the jury that, because the allegations relate to historical matters there may be a danger of real prejudice to the accused and this possibility should be taken into account when considering whether the prosecution have proved their case. The jury should be told that the longer the delay since the alleged events, the more difficult it may be for a defendant to answer the prosecution allegations.

[42] [2009] EWCA Crim 1849, [2010] Crim LR 226. In *Mackreth* the Court of Appeal analysed a number of historic allegation cases: *Turner* (CA, 27 March 2000); *O'Dell* (CA, 10 November 2000), (2007) 171 JPN 556 4–5; *B (Brian S)* [2003] EWCA Crim 319, [2003] 2 Cr App R 13 197; *Maybery* [2003] EWCA 783; *Sheikh* [2006] EWCA Crim 2625; and *Joynson* [2008] EWCA 3049.

[43] [2011] EWCA Crim 1844; [2012] QB 703; [2012] 2 WLR 1038; [2012] 1 All ER 565; [2011] 2 Cr App R 28; [2012] Crim LR 282.

Delay factors

6.18 The factors considered by the courts in deciding whether a defendant's right to a fair trial had been infringed by delay are set out in Lord Templeman's judgment in *Bell v DPP of Jamaica*.[44] He cited with approval the analysis contained in the United States Supreme Court decision in *Barker v Wingo*,[45] in which Mr Justice Powell identified four factors to which the court should have regard:

    a) the length of delay; dependent upon the peculiar circumstances of the case. To take but one example, the delay that can be tolerated for an ordinary street crime is considerably less than for a serious, complex conspiracy charge;

    b) the justification put forward by the prosecution; a deliberate attempt to delay the trial in order to hamper the defence should be weighed heavily against the government. A more neutral reason such as negligence or overcrowded courts should be weighed less heavily but nevertheless should be considered since the ultimate responsibility for such circumstances must rest with the government rather than the defendant. A valid reason, such as a missing witness, should serve to justify appropriate delay;

    c) the responsibility of the accused for asserting her/his rights; and,

    d) the prejudice to the accused. Prejudice, of course, should be assessed in light of the interests of the defendant, whom the right to a speedy trial was designed to protect. This court has identified three such interests:

        i) to prevent oppressive pre-trial incarceration;

        ii) to minimise anxiety and concern of the accused; and,

        iii) to limit the possibility that the defence will be impaired. If witnesses die or disappear during a delay, the prejudice is obvious. There is also prejudice if defence witnesses are unable to recall accurately events of the distant past. Loss of memory however, is not always reflected in the record because what has been forgotten can rarely be shown.

6.19 In another North American decision, *Dickey v Florida*,[46] Mr Justice Brennan observed that, 'it borders on the impossible to measure the cost of delay in terms of the dimmed memories of the parties and available witnesses.' This is a problem, as over time memories fade and 'recollection is replaced by reconstruction which in turn is transformed into recollection'.[47]

6.20 The essential elements of granting relief in delay cases are inordinate delay and prejudice, whether proved or inferred.[48]

6.21 Cases where relief can properly be granted in the absence of any fault on the prosecution will be rare. Delay attributable to the defendant or to the complexity of the case should not lead to a stay of proceedings.[49]

6.22 In *R v Bow Street Stipendiary Magistrates ex p DPP*,[50] Lord Justice Neill observed the court's need to consider the reasons for the delay. Factors include the responsibility of the prosecution and the defence for the delay and the trial issues.[51] The following example was cited:

---

[44] [1985] AC 937, 951–95.

[45] (1972) 407 US 514.

[46] (1970) 398 US 30 at 53J. See also *United States v Ewell* (1966) 383 US 116 at 120.

[47] Cooker v Purcell (1988) 14 NSWLR 51, 87 per Clarke SA.

[48] *R v Bow Street Stipendiary Magistrates ex p DPP* [1992] 95 Cr App R 9, [1992] Crim LR 790–92.

[49] *Attorney General's Reference (No 1 of 1990)* [1992] 3 All ER 169. See also *Wemhoff v Germany*, (1979–80) 1 EHRR 55; *Jago v District Court of NSW* [1989] 87 ALR 577 (High Court of Australia); *R v Cardiff Magistrates' Court ex p Hole* [1997] COD 84; IJL, GMR, *AKP v United Kingdom* (2001) 33 EHRR 11.

[50] [1992] 95 Cr App R 9, [1992] Crim LR 790–92.

[51] [1992] 95 Cr App R 9, 16.

... a case which depends largely on documentary evidence may be regarded very differently from one where witnesses will have to try and recollect some swiftly moving event which passed before their eyes years ago.

The nature of the case is a factor that must necessarily be considered by the courts in assessing the reasonableness of the delay. The Canadian Supreme Court observed in *James Mills v R*:[52] **6.23**

... the standard of reasonableness will be very flexible and will vary from case to case depending upon the circumstances of each individual case. Yet, it is important to stress that this criterion is wholly objective. It is not concerned with the adequacy of institutional resources; it is not concerned with the difficulties which a particular police force, Crown office or court may face in preparing or trying a case that result from institutional inadequacies such as lack of personnel, facilities ... It must determine the period which would normally be required, taking into account the number of charges, the number of accused, the complexity and volume and similar objective elements, for the preparation and completion of the case if fully adequate institutional resources and facilities were available ... the courts must, in assessing the delays which are required by the complexity of the case, seek the greatest degree of promptness which could objectively be met were institutional resources fully adequate to the task.

The overriding consideration for the trial judge is 'whether it is possible to hold a fair trial after a long delay'.[53] **6.24**

In *Tan v Cameron*,[54] Lord Mustill stated that the court must consider 'whether in all the circumstances, the situation created by the delay is such as to make it an unfair employment of the power of the court any longer to hold the defendant to account.' That question is 'to be considered in the round', taking all circumstances into account. **6.25**

The longer the delay in any particular case the less likely it is the accused can be afforded a fair trial.[55] **6.26**

Cases stayed or convictions quashed for delay

Specific examples of cases where delay has contributed to a stay of proceedings or a conviction being quashed on appeal include the following: **6.27**

- undue delay;[56]
- summary trials where there has been deliberate delay in prosecuting the matter;[57]
- inordinate or unconscionable delay due to the prosecution's inefficiency;[58]

---

[52] (1986) 1 SCR 863 [183]–[185] per Lamer J.
[53] *Wilkinson* [1996] 1 Cr App R 81 at 85C.
[54] [1992] 3 WLR 249 at 264.
[55] *Bell v DPP* [1985] 1 AC 937, 950H per Lord Templeman.
[56] *Watford Justices ex p Outrim* [1983] RTR 26 (22 months to issue a summons).
[57] *R v Brentford Justices ex p Wong* [1981] QB 445.
[58] *Oxford City Justices ex p Smith* [1982] 75 Cr App R 200; *R v West London Stipendiary Magistrate ex p Anderson* [1985] 80 Cr App R 143; *R v Gateshead Justices ex p Smith* [1985] 149 JP 681; and *R v Bow Street Stipendiary Magistrate ex p Cherry* [1990] 91 Cr App R 283. See also *R v Chief Constable of Merseyside Police ex p Merrill* [1989] 1 WLR 1077 where the Divisional Court quashed disciplinary proceedings against a detective constable where the Chief Constable had erroneously concluded that the service of a disciplinary complaint notice could be deferred until after the criminal proceedings had concluded. In relation to civil enforcement of confiscation proceedings, see Malik v Crown Prosecution Service [2014] EWHC 4591 (Admin).

- delay by the prosecution in naming a complainant thereby hampering the preparation of the defence;[59]
- delay in informing the defendant of the possibility of prosecution;[60]
- delay coupled with health reasons. In *Attorney General of Hong Kong v Cheung Wai-Bun*[61] the Privy Council upheld the trial judge's decision to stay proceedings because the long pre-trial delay had seriously affected the accused's health. The excessive delay in the case had not been caused by the accused.

Delay cases not stayed

6.28 On the other hand, there are numerous cases where delay has not led to a stay or a conviction being quashed.[62] Specific examples of the same are set out below.

Memory refreshing documents

6.29 In *Buzalek and Schiffer*[63] the defendants were charged with fraudulent trading. The trial judge held that a six-year delay did not prevent the defendants having a fair trial. The Court of Appeal dismissed the appeals against conviction because the case turned largely on documents and accordingly it was possible for witnesses to refresh their memories from documents. As stated by Lord Justice Neil in *R v Bow Street Stipendiary Magistrates ex p DPP*:[64]

> ... a case which depends largely on documentary evidence may be regarded very differently from one where witnesses will have to try and recollect some swiftly moving event which passed before their eyes years ago.

Published account

6.30 A published account of the criminality overcame a twenty-three-year delay in *R v Central Criminal Court ex p Randle*.[65] The applicants assisted in a prison escape in 1966. In 1989, they published their account of the escape and were charged with related offences. The applicants sought by way of judicial review to overturn a Crown Court decision refusing to stay proceedings.

6.31 The Divisional Court refused the application, for a number of reasons, despite the twenty-three-year delay. First, there was no evidence that the police had taken a policy decision in 1970 not to prosecute the applicants. Second, the prosecuting authorities had not been influenced by improper motives. Third, the applicants had not suffered prejudice by reason of the delay. It was accepted that delay itself could, in appropriate circumstances, be such as to render criminal proceedings an abuse of process. In this case however, the applicants had published a book in 1989, which had provided much of the material upon which the prosecution relied. In the light of its contents, the plea of failing memory could not be advanced. The Divisional Court refused to interfere with the trial judge's discretion.

---

[59] *Daventry District Council v Olins* (1990) 154 JP 478, [1990] Crim LR 414.

[60] *R v Bow Street Stipendiary Magistrates ex p DPP and Cherry* [1990] Crim LR 318, [1990] 91 Cr App R 283 and see *Chief Constable of Merseyside ex p Merrill* [1989] 1 WLR 1077.

[61] [1994] 1 AC 1, [1994] 98 Cr App R 17.

[62] See *R* [1994] Crim LR 948, CA (a 5–18 year delay in reporting sexual allegations was insufficient for stay purposes); *Christopher Hearn*, No 97/1233/Z4, 20 October 1997, CA (a 19–20 year delay did not warrant a stay); *JK* [1999] Crim LR 740, CA (a 9–23 year delay in reporting sexual allegations was insufficient for stay purposes—applying Lord Chief Justice Taylor's comments in *E (John)* [1996] 1 Cr App R 83 at 93A, CA); *Alan King* [2008] EWCA Crim 3301.

[63] [1991] Crim LR 115.

[64] [1992] 95 Cr App R 9, [1992] Crim LR 790–92.

[65] [1992] 1 All ER 370.

Credible forensic evidence

Credible forensic evidence linking a defendant to historical criminality may defeat any **6.32** delay arguments. In *Robert Rodgers*,[66] the appellant was convicted of murder in a public taxi (dating back to 1973), at a judge-only trial. He argued, in the Northern Ireland Court of Appeal, that the forty-year delay in the proceedings was the fault of the police. They had the appellant's fingerprints on file and relevant prints from the taxi in 1973. At no point during the period from 1973–1975 were the appellant's prints checked against the taxi prints. This was a failure by the investigating authorities to properly investigate for nearly forty years. In the intervening period, evidence had been lost, including the police file, which had a photo-fit prepared by one of those at the taxi depot, and key witnesses were deceased. The whole case against the appellant was based on his inability to provide an innocent explanation for his palm prints being found in the public taxi. The trial judge recognized that the loss of the police file was unsatisfactory but rejected the submission that this made a fair trial impossible. The trial judge rejected the submission that delay of itself provided an explanation as to why the appellant could not give evidence explaining why his prints were found in the taxi. In rejecting the appeal, Lord Chief Justice Morgan, stated:[67]

> This was a case in which there was credible evidence of a forensic nature linking the appellant to the vehicle involved in the murder which was unaffected by the passage of time. For the reasons given by the learned trial judge we consider that a fair trial was possible and he was correct to reject the application for a stay.

Complexity

The complexity of a case, both factual and legal, may lead to justifiable delay, not amounting **6.33** to an abuse. The Privy Council in *Mungroo v R*[68] dismissed an appeal based on unconscionable delay of four years between arrest and trial. The delay resulted from the complexity of the complainant authority body, which required investigation of twenty cases of suspected false claims, payments and forgeries, the factual and legal complexity of the case including the manner of proof.

No serious delay nor identifiable prejudice

In *R v Chief Constable of Devon and Cornwall Constabulary ex p Hay and PCA*,[69] the Divisional **6.34** Court quashed the decision of a police disciplinary tribunal not to proceed with charges against a police officer on the grounds that the proceedings would have been an abuse of process. There had been no serious or culpable delay, nor was there any evidence that the officer had suffered identifiable prejudice resulting from a nineteen-month delay between the commencement and amendment of charges.

In *Bennett v Secretary of State for War Pensions*,[70] the Administrative Court decided that there **6.35** had been no abuse of process. Although there had been an eleven-month delay in the investigation, (1) the prosecution under section 116(2) of the Social Security Administration Act 1992 (for failing to notify a change of circumstances affecting entitlement to state benefit) had been brought within the prescribed statutory time limit (2) there had been no serious failings on the part of the prosecution (as required per *Sadler*)[71] and (3) the appellant was not unfairly prejudicied by the passage of time caused by the slow proceedings.

---

[66] [2013] NICA 71.
[67] Ibid [38].
[68] [1991] 1 WLR 1351, [1992] 95 Cr App R 334.
[69] [1996] 2 All ER 711.
[70] [2012] EWHC 371 (Admin).
[71] [2002] EWCA Crim 1722.

D. Trial Process

6.36 The trial process itself is able, in many situations, to deal with the prejudice caused by long delays. Trial judges can use their discretion to exclude evidence, under section 78 PACE and/ or give an appropriate directions to the jury in the summing-up, to remedy any prejudice to the defence caused by delay, as an alternative to staying proceedings. Such alternative 'control mechanism' remedies were recognized by Lord Justice Latham in *Maybery*.[72] Trial judges should be made aware of their ability to regulate the admissibility of evidence and to warn the jury, in summing up, about the dangers the defendant might encounter in answering certain historic allegations.

Childhood sexual abuse cases

6.37 Childhood sexual abuse cases provide a good example of how the courts have showed a readiness to rely upon the trial process to ensure a fair trial, as opposed to staying proceedings.

6.38 Commentators[73] have recognized the rise in the number of reported cases of alleged childhood sexual cases, which are reported and prosecuted many years after the alleged abuse occurred. A number of factors may explain the delay in making such allegations: (a) the sense of betrayal felt by the complainant who has been abused by a person in a position of trust; (b) powerlessness felt by the complainant when faced by physical and moral threats from the abuser; (c) feelings of guilt; and (d) memory repression of the abuse. These factors result in a psychological inability to complain until many years after the abuse occurred.

6.39 Childhood sexual abuse cases present the courts with a number of inter-related issues, compounded in certain cases by the existence of multiple allegations, sometimes by a number of complainants.

6.40 In relation to the accused's right to a fair trial, the court may have to consider:

(a) whether severance of counts is appropriate where there are multiple allegations,[74] possibly with a number of different complainants;
(b) if counts are tried together, whether evidence has cross-admissibility;
(c) evidential problems with cogency and collusion; and
(d) any prejudice to the defence that may be associated with the delay between the alleged abuse and the trial.

6.41 These factors, which are common to many childhood sexual abuse cases, are issues to be considered when the defence applies for a stay of proceedings. Severance, judicial exclusion of evidence, and jury direction may suffice as alternative remedies to a defendant. The Court of Appeal also has a residual power to quash convictions that are unsafe.[75]

6.42 In relation to the granting of leave to prefer a voluntary bill of indictment under the Administration of Justice (Miscellaneous Provisions) Act 1933 s 2(2)(b), a previous magistrates' court decision (in 1998) to stay proceedings on the ground of delay was considered

---

[72] [2003] EWCA Crim 783.

[73] See P Lewis 'Similar Facts and Similar Allegations in Delayed Criminal Prosecutions of Childhood Sexual Abuse' [2004] Crim LR 39; P Lewis, *Delayed Prosecution for Childhood Sexual Abuse* (Oxford University Press 2006).

[74] There is no requirement for joinder for there to be a coincidence in time or place, if there are sufficient factual similarities between the allegations: *Paul Baird* [1993] 97 Cr App R 308.

[75] Under section 2(1) of the Criminal Appeal Act 1968, as amended by section 2(1) of the Criminal Appeal Act 1995, 'the Court of Appeal shall allow an appeal against conviction if they think that the conviction is unsafe'. See *Brian Selwyn Bell* [2003] 2 Cr App R 13.

in *Paul Gadd*.[76] Mr Justice Globe, sitting in the Queens Bench Division, granted leave to prefer the voluntary bill and acknowledged the exceptional nature of the decision. The court held that it was in the interests of justice to try ten counts of alleged historical sexual abuse (indecent assault and attempted rape between 1975 and 1980) and the defendant would not be denied a fair trial by reason of delay. The defendant had not identified any actual prejudice to his case caused by the passage of time.

Severance of counts

A defendant may apply[77] to have multiple counts severed from an indictment, as opposed to staying the whole indictment. A trial judge has a wide discretion when considering the question of severance. However, there must be 'some special feature of the case which would make a joint trial of the several counts prejudicial or embarrassing to the defendant and separate trials are required in the interests of justice'[78] before a trial judge should order severance. The trial judge must decide on joinder and severance based on fairness, considering whether directions to the jury will suffice to secure a fair trial if the counts are tried together.[79] **6.43**

If counts are tried together, the trial judge must then direct the jury in summing-up, on whether evidence on one count is admissible in relation to the issues raised by other counts on the indictment.[80] Historically, cross-admissibility applied if there was some significant connection or relationship in time and circumstances between the evidence on the two counts.[81] This may include similar sexual practices.[82] Regard has to be had to the Criminal Justice Act 2003. Evidence on one count will be admissible in relation to another count if it has substantial probative value in relation to a matter in issue which is of substantial importance. **6.44**

Further, if a count is stayed, the prosecution are still entitled to apply under the bad character provisions contained in sections 100–09 of the Criminal Justice Act 2003, to adduce evidence of the conduct alleged on the stayed count, in order to prove the remaining counts at trial. Evidence of allegations by complainants relating to stayed charges may be admissible to establish the defendant's propensity to commit other offences charged against him.[83] **6.45**

Witness collusion and contamination

Where there is the risk of collusion or contamination between witnesses and/or complainants, the courts are to assume that the allegations are true, and consider the admissibility of evidence by assessing whether its probative value outweighs its prejudicial effect.[84] Where the evidence is such that a jury could properly accept that the evidence was not contaminated, it is right for the judge to leave that evidence before the jury and for them to assess its weight: evidential credibility being a matter for the jury. If the trial judge finds cross-admissibility, the jury must be directed that the evidence cannot be relied upon on unless they are satisfied that is true, reliable, and not tainted by collusion. **6.46**

---

[76] [2014] EWHC 3307 (QB).

[77] An application to sever counts, resulting in separate trials, can be made under section 5(3) of the Indictments Act 1915.

[78] See *Ludlow v Commissioner for the Metropolitan Police* [1971] AC 29 at 41, [1970] 54 Cr App R 233.

[79] *Christou (George)* [1997] AC 117, [1996] 2 Cr App R 360.

[80] *D* [2004] 1 Cr App R 19 and commentary at [2005] Crim L R 163.

[81] *Mosquera*, 15 December 1998, CA.

[82] See *Massey* [2001] EWCA Crim 2850.

[83] *David Smith* (CA, 21 December 2005) per Scott Baker LJ, Gross, and Ramsey JJ.

[84] As set out by the House of Lords in *H* [1995] 2 AC 596, [1995] 2 Cr App R 437 using the test set out in *DPP v P* [1991] 2 AC 447, [1991] 93 Cr App R 267.

6.47 However, if the trial judge takes the view that, no reasonable jury could accept the evidence as free from collusion, the judge must direct the jury not to rely upon the evidence. Illustrative of the effect of witness collusion and contamination is the decision in *Jenkins*.[85] The Court of Appeal quashed convictions because of exceptional unexplained delay (of over thirty years) in the counts, evidential inconsistencies and instances of witnesses 'improved memory'.

6.48 The appellant in *Jenkins* was convicted in 1997 of four counts of indecent assault on a female, one count of attempted rape and one of attempted buggery. He was alleged to have committed specific offences against S and J between 1963 and 1967, and against C and M between 1981 and 1985. S, who was thirty-six at trial, said that her memory was poor for the first ten years of her life and she remembered the incidents only after receiving counseling in 1995. J, who was thirty-five at trial, said that she made no complaint until 1995. At first only J supported aspects of S's account, without making any allegations herself. The judge declined to order a stay.

6.49 In allowing the appeal against conviction, the Court of Appeal observed that the trial judge had a discretion in regulating proceedings and the court would not interfere with the exercise of it, even where members of the court would have exercised the discretion differently, unless the judge erred in principle or there was no material on which he could properly have arrived at his decision.[86] There were unexplained delays, inconsistencies and instances of 'improved memory', not as a result of 'false memory syndrome' flowing from counseling, but mysterious and dramatic improvement of S's memory as to matters of detail between her first visit to the police and the trial.

6.50 There was some evidence of contamination in relation to J's evidence, as J had accompanied S when S gave her account to the police. J made no complaint on her own behalf at that stage. Indeed there was some evidence from a police officer that at that time J had expressly denied that anything of the kind had ever been done to her. So concerned was the court about J that it ventured the opinion that her evidence was inadmissible under the exceptional basis identified in *H*[87] and that no reasonable jury could have considered it as anything other than contaminated.

6.51 Further, it was difficult for S and J (or the appellant) to recall precise details of events over thirty years ago and the delay accordingly caused prejudice to the appellant in putting his defence. Specific prejudices to the appellant included the inability to remember the identity of other young visitors who might have supported his account; or to recollect the kind of detail which, if innocent, might have enabled a skilful cross-examiner on his behalf to confound his accusers. The convictions involving S and J were not safe and because the other convictions were tainted, as evidence of the earlier incidents was led in support of them, those convictions too were quashed.

PACE sections 78 and 82: fairness safeguards

6.52 Sections 78 and 82 of PACE can be used to exclude the contaminated evidence from a number of witnesses.

6.53 Section 78 provides:

> 78(1) In any proceedings the court may refuse to allow evidence on which the prosecution proposes to rely to be given if it appears to the court that, having regard to all the circumstances, including the circumstances in which the evidence was obtained, the admission of

---

[85] [1998] Crim LR 411.

[86] *McCann (John Paul)* [1992] 92 Cr App R 239 at 251, per Beldam LJ.

[87] [1995] 2 AC 596, [1995] 2 Cr App R 437.

the evidence would have such an adverse effect on the fairness of the proceedings that the court ought not to admit it.

(2) Nothing in this section shall prejudice any rule of law requiring a court to exclude evidence.'

Section 82 (3) provides: **6.54**

82(3) Nothing in this part of the Act shall prejudice any power of a court to exclude evidence (whether by preventing questions from being put or otherwise) at its discretion.

However, there are situations involving witness contamination and collusion where the **6.55** PACE exclusionary safeguards are not competent to protect the defendant fully.[88]

One such situation, identified by commentators Summers and Winship, involves three **6.56** or more witnesses. Where witnesses A and B have been contaminated. The defendant can apply, under PACE, to exclude their evidence as being unfair and based on contamination. However, if a prosecutor seeks to proceed to trial on the evidence of a third uncontaminated witness, C alone, there is no unfairness under traditional interpretations of section 78. The defendant in that situation is deprived of the ability to undermine C's evidence by reference to inconsistencies with the (excluded) accounts of A and/or B. A fair trial in these circumstances may not be possible. Summers and Winship cogently argue that 'the abuse of process doctrine ought to be available to protect the defendant where PACE sections 78 and/or 82 cannot.'[89]

The abuse of process remedy, by contrast, 'focuses squarely upon the potential prejudice to **6.57** the defendant and the risk of an unfair trial'[90] and may afford a more just result.

Prejudice and judicial directions

Any risk of prejudice that the defendant may face, as a result of delay, may be offset by judi- **6.58** cial direction. This safeguard was recognized by Lord Chief Justice Lane's observations in *Attorney General's Reference (No 1 of 1990)*:[91]

... the defendant needs to show on a balance of probabilities that owing to the delay he will suffer serious prejudice to the extent that no fair trial can be held. In other words, the continuance of the proceedings amounts to an abuse of the process of the court. In assessing whether there is likely to be prejudice and if so whether it can properly be described as serious, the following matters should be borne in mind: first, the power of the judge at common law and under the Police and Criminal Evidence Act 1984, to regulate the admissibility of evidence; secondly, the trial process itself, which should ensure that all relevant factual issues arising from the delay will be placed before the jury as part of the evidence for their consideration, together with the powers of the judge to give appropriate directions to the jury before they consider their verdict.

In a similar vein, Lord Justice Hobhouse in *Bowley* stated:[92]   **6.59**

That it is incumbent upon the judge to give guidance to the jury on the issue of delay and its relevance. Appropriate assistance should be given to the jury on matters such as the difficulty of witnesses being able to give detailed evidence about incidents said to have occurred in the

---

[88] See Mark Summers and Julian Winship, 'Cross Contamination: Time to Extend the Abuse of Process Doctrine' [2003] Crim LR 446.

[89] Ibid. It would be interesting to argue that the non-contaminated witness (C in the Summers example) evidence should be excluded under section 78, because it would lead to unfairness at trial. In such a situation would it really be stretching the interpretation of section 78 unfairness beyond its intended use?

[90] At p 458.

[91] [1992] QB 630, [1992] 95 Cr App R 296.

[92] [1996] Crim LR 406.

distant past and the defendant's ability to check detail by reference to separate independent evidence.

6.60 The issue of judicial directions was also considered in *Hickson*.[93] Lord Justice Beldam said;

> ... that where specific aspects of disadvantage are raised by the defence it is incumbent on a Judge to remind the Jury of those aspects which have been raised, and to point out the particular difficulties of which the defence complained ... in a case where the offences can properly be regarded as of antiquity ... the Judge ought to refer generally to the difficulties faced by the defendant in meeting the charges and particularly if the defendant cannot be expected to remember or is unable to recall what he was doing at a particular time, but the nature of such a direction, and its extent and how far the Judge feels it necessary in a given case to direct a jury will depend on the circumstances of the case ... how old the offences are and on the issues which are raised.[94]

6.61 See also the comments of the Privy Council in *DPP v Tokai*[95] that, if proceedings were not stayed, the trial judge was under a duty to direct the jury as to any matter arising from the delay which was favourable to the defence.

Judicial intervention

6.62 The high watermark of judicial jury direction can be found in *Percival*.[96] Lord Justice Holland recognized:

> ... a developing concern with and, understanding of sexual abuse is reflected in a growing experience of cases featuring delays that at one time would have been regarded as intolerable. That experience of cases of unreported abuse has served to encourage experienced judges to be more liberal in their concept of what is possible by way of a fair trial in the face of delay, but, as we think there is a price, namely safeguarding the defendant from unacceptable resultant prejudice by a 'pro active' approach in terms of directions. Before a conviction following such a trial can appear to be safe, it is necessary to be satisfied that the judge has confronted the jury with the fact of delay and its potential impact on the formulation and conduct of the defence and on the Prosecution's fulfilment of the burden of proof ... (with) a conscientious concern for the burden and standard of proof (as approved by Lord Justice Buxton in *Whiffin*).[97]

6.63 The first instance judge erred in 'even handedly' drawing attention to the potential impact of the delay upon the prosecution's evidence. This was the wrong approach. Lord Justice Holland went on to state that;

> ... if long delayed cases are to go before juries, judges have to have a prominent role in ensuring that any convictions reflect a full appreciation of the problem, delay, and the solution, the burden and standard of proof.[98]

6.64 Although it is desirable to warn the jury of such problems, failure to do so will not automatically lead to a conviction being quashed.[99]

6.65 In *M*,[100] a prosecution for sexual offences was brought many years (14–26 years) after the offences complained of had been committed. The Court of Appeal stated that it was a matter for the trial judge whether or not any warning should be given to the jury as to potential

---

93 [1997] Crim LR 494.
94 (CA, 14 February 1997).
95 [1996] AC 856.
96 [1998] 7 *Archbold News* 2, *The Times* (London, 20 July 1998), CA.
97 CA, 13 May 1999, transcript no.98/5755/X4.
98 Ibid.
99 *J* [1997] Crim LR 297; *R v Lloyd* (30 November 1998, CA).
100 [2000] 1 Cr App R 49. See commentary in [1999] Crim LR 922.

prejudice to the accused. Lord Justice Rose said the appeal court had discouraged frequent attempts to rely on *Percival* as a blueprint for principle in the case of delay. Where there were many years of delay, a clear warning as to the impact on witnesses and difficulties for the defence should be left to the trial judge, who should look at all the circumstances.

In such cases it was necessary for the trial judge to direct the jury's attention to the burden **6.66** and standard of proof and on the particular difficulties experienced by a defendant in defending the case, caused by the delay in time.

Each case depended on its own facts and there was no universally applicable formula.[101] The **6.67** directions on delay should be tailored to the facts of the particular case and spelt out to the jury.[102]

Summing-up delay appeals

The Court of Appeal, when considering delay appeals based on summing-up 'prejudice' **6.68** warnings, does not require from the appellant, nor is helped by, an analysis of directions given in different cases. In *G(Y)*,[103] the Court of Appeal in dismissing an appeal against sexual convictions, held that the trial judge's summing-up drew to the jury's attention the potentially damaging consequences of the delay to the defendant. The trial judge had reminded the jury that they should bear in mind that the passage of time (twenty-three years) was bound to make it harder to answer the allegations and that it was for the prosecution to prove the allegations. Lord Justice Judge noted that a point-by-point analysis of different cases involving delay and different summing ups which had or had not been held to be sufficient on appeal was not appropriate. The precise formula used would depend on the nature of the case and the evidence before the jury.[104]

Insufficient judicial direction

A number of convictions have been quashed by the Court of Appeal because of insufficient **6.69** judicial warnings to the jury.

In *Dutton*,[105] the Court of Appeal quashed a conviction on the basis that the trial judge had **6.70** failed, in his summing-up, to warn the jury of the possible prejudice to the defence, caused by delay. There had been a substantial delay of almost twenty years between the first alleged incident of indecent assault and the date of first complaint to the police, and consequently witnesses who might have been able to give relevant evidence had disappeared or died. This was a case in which it was incumbent on the trial judge, to point out to the jury, that what was said by the defence about possible prejudice, as a result of the delay, was a matter to which the jury could and should properly have regard. The silence of the judge on the topic of delay, may have devalued the most important adversarial point that the defence could make.[106]

In *Freestone*,[107] the appellant was convicted of indecency with a child, attempted rape, bug- **6.71** gery, rape and indecent assault. There was a nineteen-year delay between the last alleged offence and the making of the complaint. The defence applied to have the trial stayed as an abuse of process as it was no longer possible to have a fair trial. The application was

---

[101] *G(M)* [1999] Crim LR 763.
[102] See for example Court of Appeal decision in *L (Graham)* [2009] EWCA Crim 1057.
[103] [1999] Crim LR 825.
[104] See also *G(M)* [1999] Crim LR 763 and *JK* [1999] Crim LR 740.
[105] [1994] Crim LR 910.
[106] *J A K* [1992] Crim LR 30.
[107] (CA, 1997), CA.

refused. Instead the trial judge directed the jury on the delays that had occurred between the alleged offences and trial. The Court of Appeal quashed the conviction (and ordered a re-trial) because the judge failed to direct the jury of the difficulties faced by the defence caused by the lapse of time. Such an omission was material rendering the convictions unsafe. The defendant could not properly prepare his defence and he was not in a position to bring evidence to show that a particular instance could not have taken place at a particular time or at a particular place. Further, the jury should have been directed that the lapse of time meant that the jury did not have the advantage of medical evidence which could have been available had an early complaint been made.

6.72 Lord Justice Roch in *Freestone* adopted the summarized principle in the case of *Richard Bowley*[108] given by Lord Justice Hobhouse that, '[e]ach case has to be considered on its own facts and circumstances, to which the judge's summing-up must be appropriate.'

6.73 In *King*[109] convictions for attempted buggery and indecency with a child were quashed. Although a stay was not appropriate, the appeal was allowed because the trial judge had failed to give the jury a sufficiently strong direction regarding the problems to the defendant, caused by a delay of twenty-five to thirty-one years.

Stay only remedy

6.74 There are some childhood sexual abuse cases, in which the prejudice to the defence, caused by delay, cannot be remedied by judicial direction.

6.75 In *Michael John T*,[110] the appellant was convicted of raping D on two occasions between 1975 and 1978, and raping C once in 1980 and on six occasions between 1984 and 1986. C complained to the police in 1985 and 1986. A single count of indecent assault was charged but no evidence was offered and the appellant was discharged. The police file, including witness statements, the police report, the record of interview and correspondence with the defence, had been destroyed as a matter of routine after three years. C's account in the instant trial was that she had told the police everything that had happened, including the rapes. The trial judge refused an application to stay proceedings. The defendant appealed.

6.76 The Court of Appeal allowed the appeal on two grounds. First, it was difficult to reconcile C's account at trial of what happened at the time of the earlier complaint, with what was known. Either C complained of rape at the time and the police did not believe her, or she did not complain, which would affect her credibility. The documents would have clarified what had happened, but the police had destroyed them. A potentially crucial plank in the appellant's defence would have been any discrepancy between what C said at trial and what was alleged about 12 years before. The destruction of the documents raised the possibility of serious prejudice to the defendant. It gave C the ability to say what she wished, confident that she could not be contradicted by the 1985–1986 documents. Second, the appellant was prevented from investigating, at trial, C and D's delay in making complaint, because the answers would have revealed the allegations by two other persons, who also withdrew complaints. The dilemma could not be avoided by the judge's direction to the jury not to speculate about the reasons for the delay in making complaint. The difficulty of avoiding speculation was illustrated by the judge's observation that it was difficult to see why D would wait seventeen years to make allegations she knew to be lies. The defence's dilemma was caused by the delay.

---

[108] [1996] Crim LR 406.
[109] [1997] Crim LR 298.
[110] [2000] Crim LR 832.

E. War Crimes

Cases charged under the War Crimes Act 1991 are illustrative of how trial process safeguards **6.77** can be used to ensure a fair trial, as opposed to staying proceedings.[111]

The trial process approach was confirmed by the Court of Appeal in *Sawoniuk*.[112] Anthony **6.78** Sawoniuk was convicted of two counts of murder, contrary to the War Crimes Act 1991, relating to two shootings in Belorussia in 1942. The prosecution case relied upon the eye witness evidence of two individuals—aged thirteen and twenty years old at the time of the offences. An application to stay proceedings was rejected by the trial judge, Mr Justice Potts. The appellant relied upon abuse of process arguments as his first ground of appeal. Reliance was placed upon a number of unusual features in the case, including (a) the passage of fifty-six years from the date of the alleged crime to the date of trial, (b) the fact that the sole, unsupported, witness was at the time of the incident a boy, who did not mention this incident to investigating authorities when interviewed after the war and who made no statement on the subject for over fifty years, (c) the inability of the defence, after this lapse of time, to identify or trace two policemen said to have been present at the time of the incident.

Mr Justice Potts directed himself in accordance with the principles laid down in *Attorney* **6.79** *General's Reference (No 1 of 1990)*[113] in finding that the prejudice which a defendant would have to show to justify a stay is that which could not be cured by an appropriate trial ruling, or by appropriate direction to the jury.

Mr Justice Potts concluded that the appellant had not discharged the burden of proving an **6.80** abuse. It was entirely speculative whether the unavailability of other witnesses represented a detriment to the appellant or a bonus. Mr Justice Potts was confident that the evidence of the single eye-witness could be properly and rigorously tested within the confines of the trial process, as in the event it was. For example, a view of the *locus* by the jury took place.[114]

In the Court of Appeal's judgment the conclusion reached by Mr Justice Potts, despite the **6.81** unprecedented passage of time since 1942, was correct. The appeal against conviction was refused.

The decision in *Sawoniuk*[115] is not surprising, as it must have been obvious to the legislature **6.82** that evidential difficulties would arise from prosecutions relating to the Second World War. It would be extremely surprising[116] if delay alone gave rise to a stay only eight years after enactment of the War Crime Act 1991. The delay involved is certainly longer than that in other reported cases, but that is inevitable in this sort of case where material has only recently come to light and there can be no suggestion of any fault on the part of the prosecution.

F. Grounds for a Stay

Applications to stay proceedings based on delay centre on arguments that an inordinate **6.83** amount of time has passed since the incident leading to serious prejudice to the defendant. The best evidence of specific prejudice relates to loss of documentary evidence and witnesses.

---

[111] See also *Serafinowitz* (Central Criminal Court, 17 January 1997).
[112] [2000] 2 Cr App R 220.
[113] [1992] QB 630, (1992) 95 Cr App R 296.
[114] See D Ormerod 'A Prejudicial View?' [2000] Crim LR 452.
[115] [2000] 2 Cr App R 220.
[116] See commentary to *Sawoniuk* decision at [2000] Crim LR 507.

The Court of Appeal retains a residual discretion to set aside convictions which if feels are unsafe.

Prejudice

6.84 Examples of possible prejudice to the defence include:

- difficulties in the tracing of witnesses who could support the defence case or contradict the complainant's account;
- changes to relevant locations such as the locus of the abuse;
- the non-availability of evidence through the destruction or loss of documentary evidence, such as medical reports, school records, social services files, care home records,[117] police files,[118] and employment records.[119]

6.85 The defence, because of the passage of time, may have lost the opportunity to gather evidence which positively supports the defence denial of the allegations and/or provides material upon which to cross-examine and test the complainants account.

6.86 In assessing prejudice, Lord Justice Sullivan, in *TBF*,[120] made the following important observations:

> In assessing what prejudice has been caused to the defendant on any particular count by reason of delay, the court should consider what evidence directly relevant to the defence case has been lost through passage of time. Vague speculation that lost documents or deceased witnesses might have assisted the defendant is not helpful. This court should also consider what evidence has survived the passage of time. The court should then examine critically how important the missing evidence is in the context of the case as a whole.

6.87 The Court of Appeal also considered the issue of prejudice and unfairness caused by lost records in *RD*.[121] Lord Justice Treacy stated:[122]

> In considering the question of prejudice ... it seems to us that it is necessary to distinguish between mere speculation about what missing documents or witnesses might show, and missing evidence which represents a significant and demonstrable chance of amounting to decisive or strongly supportive evidence emerging on a specific issue in the case. The court will need to consider what evidence directly relevant to the appellant's case has been lost by reason of the passage of time. The court will need to go on to consider the importance of the missing evidence in the context of the case as a whole and the issues before the jury. Having considered those matters, the court will have to identify what prejudice, if any, has been caused to the appellant by the delay and whether judicial directions would be sufficient to compensate for such prejudice as may have been caused or whether in truth a fair trial could not properly be afforded to a defendant.

No time period determinative

6.88 It is clear that each case has to be considered on its own facts. There is no period of time which is determinative on an application to stay a case on grounds of delay. Three cases illustrate this point.

---

[117] See the decision in *Maxwell Crosby Halahan* [2014] EWCA Crim 2079.

[118] Loss of material from an earlier police investigation, including tapes and transcripts of interviews conducted with the alleged victim, was considered in *H* [2015] EWCA Crim 782.

[119] Loss of work records formed one of the reasons for allowing an appeal in *F* [2011] EWCA Crim 726; [2011] 2 Cr App R 13.

[120] [2011] EWCA Crim 726 [37].

[121] [2013] EWCA Crim 159.

[122] Ibid [15].

First, in *Brian Selwyn Bell*,[123] the Court of Appeal quashed the conviction having regard to the lapse of time (in the order of thirty years) and the very limited evidence that was available.

6.89

Second, in *Derek Hooper*,[124] the Court of Appeal, in upholding forty convictions of a sexual nature, referred to the decision in *Brian Selwyn Bell* noting the judgment of the Vice-President Lord Justice Rose:

6.90

> It is to be noted that the delay in that case was of the order of 30 years. We find no statement of principle in the judgment given by that court that that period, or any other period, should be regarded as being determinative of a decision in relation to a stay on the grounds of abuse of process by reason of delay ... the length of delay is but one of the factors to be considered.

Third, in *E*,[125] the Court of Appeal, in upholding convictions for offences that occurred some thirty years earlier, said that there is no quantifiable cut-off point in terms of the number of years in cases of delay, since each case turns on its own facts.

6.91

Court of Appeal residual discretion

The Court of Appeal retains a residual discretion to set aside a conviction, where it feels that such a conviction is unsafe[126] or it would be unfair for it to stand. This is so even where the trial process itself cannot be faulted. It is a discretion which should only be exercised in limited circumstances and with caution: see *Brian Bell*,[127] over which Lord Chief Justice Woolf presided.

6.92

The defendant in *Brian Bell* was convicted of ten counts of indecent assault on a female under sixteen years old between September 1968 and September 1972. The defendant denied all the allegations. Before the start of the trial the defendant made an application for a stay for abuse of process based on the thirty-year delay between the alleged incidents and the complaint being made. The judge rejected the application but recognized that the delay could cause difficulties for the defendant in that it would be hard to gather witnesses or evidence so long after the incidents had happened. The judge considered that any possible unfairness to the defendant could be dealt with within the trial process. The defendant appealed on the ground that the conviction was unsafe as the evidence relied on was unreliable and unsupported by any independent evidence.

6.93

The Court of Appeal relied upon eight points in quashing the conviction:

6.94

(1) The appeal raised points of general interest regarding complainants of sexual offences alleged to have happened many years before trial. Unlike civil matters there was no statutory limitation in criminal cases and Parliament had removed the common law requirement of corroboration.

(2) No criticism could be made in the present case of the judge's summing up and directions given to the jury regarding the possible prejudice of delay.

(3) The passage of time has never been a reason to stop a prosecution. Who to believe was a matter for the jury, with the appropriate directions from the judge. The same was true in the way the court would not 'shut the door' on a case where new evidence was discovered many years after a trial, which showed a person was innocent.

---

[123] [2003] 2 Cr App R 13.

[124] [2003] EWCA Crim 2427, CA.

[125] [2008] EWCA Crim 604.

[126] Under section 2(1) of the Criminal Appeal Act 1968, as amended by section 2(1) of the Criminal Appeal Act 1995, 'the Court of Appeal shall allow an appeal against conviction if they think that the conviction is unsafe'.

[127] [2003] 2 Cr App R 13.

(4) The judge gave a clear summing up, however, he failed to deal with corroboration. Under section 33 of the Criminal Justice and Public Order Act 1994 corroboration was no longer needed for sexual offences. Parliament made the decision as to the balance between the prosecution and defence on the issue of corroboration and the court could not go behind that.

(5) The trial system was dependant on confidence in the jury system. The jury had seen the witnesses and heard the evidence. The judge clearly warned the jury on delay and the reason the jury convicted the defendant was that they believed the complainant was telling the truth and the defendant was not.

(6) The Court of Appeal had a residual power in cases where a conviction was unsafe. The court's power should only be exercised in limited circumstances. If the complainant was telling the truth then she had been treated in a despicable way and deserved justice. However, justice also had to be done for the defendant.

(7) It was most important that an injustice was not done to a defendant. That just result might mean some guilty go unpunished but that was better than an innocent person being punished. In the judgment of Lord Chief Justice Woolf, because of the delay that had occurred, the defendant was put in an impossible position in terms of his defence. He was not able to conduct any proper cross-examination of the complainant. There was no material he could put to the complainant to suggest that she had said something had happened on one occasion which could be established to be incorrect. There was no material in the form of notes that were given to the doctors which showed that she had changed her account. Given the effect of delay all he could do was to say he had not done anything. Saying that to a jury amounted to virtually no defence at all.

(8) In all the circumstances this was a residual case where, in the interests of justice, the court had to interfere and set aside the conviction. It was the court's duty to allow the appeal, having regard to the lapse of time and limited evidence that was available.

6.95 The decision in *Brian Bell* was distinguished in *E(T)*.[128] The appellant in *E(T)* complained that because of the lapse in time (13–24 years) since the commission of the alleged offences, the absence of any contemporaneous records which the appellant could use to challenge the complainant's evidence, and the supposed lack of supporting evidence for the complainant's allegations his convictions for buggery were unsafe. The Court of Appeal dismissed the appeal. The convictions for buggery were not unsafe. The appellant was not put in an impossible position to defend himself. Unlike in the case of *Brian Bell*, there was some, albeit not much, supporting evidence for the complainant's allegations. Moreover, unlike the case of *Brian Bell*, there was plenty of evidential material (such as inconsistencies in what the complainant told the police and his evidence in court) on which the complainant could be cross-examined to cast doubt his credibility and reliability as a witness.

G. Court of Appeal Guidance

Smolinski

6.96 Lord Chief Justice Woolf, in *Mark Smolinski*,[129] gave guidance on the correct procedures to be followed when an abuse of process application is based on delay.

6.97 The appellant was convicted of indecent assault, with the jury unable to reach a verdict on other counts relating to a second complainant. The two complainants were sisters, aged six

---

[128] [2004] 2 Cr App R 36 and see commentary [2005] Crim L R 75–76.
[129] [2004] 2 Cr App R 40.

and seven at the time of the alleged offences. The allegations were first reported to the police twenty years later. The appellant's case was that the allegations were untrue. At trial, an application was made on behalf of the appellant to stay the proceedings for abuse of process, arguing that the appellant could not receive a fair trial as a result of delay. He argued that he would be prejudiced by lack of memory because of the time that had elapsed. The trial judge rejected the submission.

The Court of Appeal recognized that, in the words of Lord Chief Justice Woolf,[130] 'the making of **6.98** applications to have cases stayed where there has been delay on the basis of abuse of process has become prevalent.' The court went on to question

> … whether it is helpful to make applications in relation to abuse of process before any evidence has been given by the complainants in a case of this nature. Clearly, having regard to the period of time which has elapsed, the court expects that careful consideration has been given by the prosecution as to whether it is right to bring the prosecution at all. If, having considered the evidence to be called, and the witnesses having been interviewed on behalf of the prosecution, a decision is reached that the case should proceed, then in the normal way we would suggest that it is better not to make an application based on abuse of process. It will take up the court's time unnecessarily. Unless the case is exceptional, the application will be unsuccessful.[131]

The timing of making an abuse application, based on delay was considered. In the view of **6.99** Lord Chief Justice Woolf:[132]

> If an application is to be made to a judge, the best time for doing so is after any evidence has been called.[133] That means that on the one hand the court has had an opportunity of seeing the witnesses, and, on the other hand the complainants have had to go through the ordeal of giving evidence. However, despite the latter point, which obviously is one of importance, it seems to us that on the whole it is preferable for the evidence to be called and for a judge then to make his decision as to whether the trial should proceed or whether the evidence is such that it would not be safe for a jury to convict. That is a particularly helpful course if there is a danger of inconsistencies between the witnesses.

In overturning the conviction, Lord Chief Justice Woolf emphasized the jury's differing ver- **6.100** dicts as between the complainants, and observed that:[134]

> We do not think it is right for this court to lay down the principle that because of the period which has elapsed (twenty years) when the complainant has given a reason for the delay, it is inevitably the case that the convictions will be unsafe. However, where there has been a long period of delay such as existed in this case, and where the complainants are young, as they were here (6 and 7 respectively at the time of the relevant matters), this court should scrutinize convictions with particular care. Likewise, we consider that trial judges should scrutinize the evidence with particular care and come to a conclusion whether or not it is safe for the matter to be left to the jury.

Although this was a case properly left to the jury, in light of their differing verdicts (con- **6.101** viction on a count relating to one of the two complainants, but not the other, despite their evidence that the appellant had behaved in the same way to each of them) the conviction was unsafe.

Following on from *Smolinski*, Mr Justice Aikens[135] stated in *P*:[136] **6.102**

---

130 [2004] 2 Cr App R 40, 663.
131 [2004] 2 Cr App R 40, 663.
132 [2004] 2 Cr App R 40, 664.
133 See also *Brian Selwyn Bell* [2003] 2 Cr App R 13.
134 per Lord Woolf CJ. [2004] 2 Cr App R 40, 664.
135 One of the Court of Appeal judges in *Smolinski*.
136 (Maidstone Crown Court, 28 October 2004).

If having scrutinised the evidence a judge comes to the conclusion that the defendant has discharged the burden on the balance of probabilities that he cannot have a fair trial because he has been seriously prejudiced by reason of delay, then the case is not safe to be left to the jury. That is because it cannot be safe to leave a case to the jury if the judge has concluded that a defendant cannot have a fair trial.

6.103   This reaffirms the established abuse of process test and sidesteps Lord Chief Justice Woolf's 'wait and see' approach.[137]

S

6.104   The correct approach for a judge, to whom an application for a stay of proceedings, based upon delay is made, was also considered by the Court of Appeal in *S*.[138]

6.105   Lord Justice Rose, having considered a number of authorities,[139] set out five principles which need to be considered:

1) Even where delay was unjustifiable, a permanent stay should be the exception rather than the rule.
2) Where there was no fault on the part of the complainant or the prosecution, it would be very rare for a stay to be granted.
3) No stay should be granted in the absence of serious prejudice to the defence so that no fair trial could be held.
4) When assessing possible serious prejudice, the judge should bear in mind his or her power to regulate the admissibility of evidence and that the trial process itself should ensure that all relevant factual issues arising from delay would be placed before the jury for their consideration in accordance with appropriate directions from the judge.
5) If, having considered all those factors, a judge's assessment is that a fair trial would be possible, a stay should not be granted.

6.106   Where an application was made to stay proceedings as an abuse of process because of delay, the judge's discretionary decision whether or not to grant the application was an exercise in judicial assessment, dependent on judgment rather than on any conclusion as to fact based on evidence. To apply to the exercise of that discretion the language of burden and standard of proof, which was more apt to an evidence-based fact-finding process, was therefore potentially misleading.

6.107   In *S*, the defence, at the close of the prosecution case had sought a stay of the proceedings on the grounds of delay. The judge refused the application. On the appeal (against conviction on counts of rape and indecent assault on a female, based on allegations dating back to the 1970s) counsel for the appellant relied upon the judgment in *EW*[140] to submit that once the issue of delay had been raised it was for the prosecution to satisfy the court that a fair trial was still possible.

6.108   In their Lordships' judgment, the discretionary decision whether to grant a stay as an abuse of process, because of delay, was an exercise in judicial assessment dependent on judgment

---

[137] See Elliott and Carter-Stephenson 'Abuse of Process in Historic Sexual Allegations' [2005] 1 Archbold News 5.

[138] [2006] EWCA Crim 756; [2006] 2 Cr App R 23; [2007] Crim LR 296. Cited with approval and followed by the Supreme Court of New Zealand in *CT v The Queen* [2014] NZSC 155 and *R* [2015] EWCA Crim 1941.

[139] *Attorney General's Reference (No 1 of 1990)* [1992] QB 630, 644; *EW* [2004] EWCA Crim 2901, [23]; *Attorney General's Reference (No 2 of 2001)* [2001] 1 WLR 1869 [16]; *Hooper* [2003] EWCA Crim 2427 [76]; *B* [2003] 2 Cr App R 197 [15]–[18]; *Smolinksi* [2004] 2 Cr App R 661 [7].

[140] [2004] EWCA Crim 2901 [23].

rather than on any conclusion as to fact-based evidence. It was, therefore, potentially mis-leading to apply to the exercise of that discretion the language of burden and standard of proof, which was more apt to an evidence-based fact-finding process. The Court of Appeal dismissed the appeal against conviction.

F

In *F*[141] the Court of Appeal, presided over by Lord Chief Justice Judge, comprehensively reviewed the abuse of process authorities concerning delay and distilled the principles to be applied. **6.109**

The Court of Appeal identified a number of important principles: **6.110**

(1) An application to stay for abuse of process on the ground of delay and a *Galbraith*[142] sub-mission of no case to answer were two distinct matters and had to be given separate consid-eration. An application to stay for abuse of process based upon delay had to be determined in accordance with the decision in *Attorney General's Reference (No 1 of 1990)*.[143] An abuse of process argument could not succeed unless a fair trial was no longer possible because the delay had caused prejudice to the defendant which could not be addressed in the normal trial process. While unjustified delay in the making of a complaint might make the judge more certain of prejudice, unjustified delay alone was insufficient reason for a stay.

(2) Although the timing of a ruling on a stay applications based on delay is a matter for the trial judge, in general, the question was best decided before evidence is called. If the ruling was deferred until after evidence was called there is a real danger the *Galbraith* principles would be conflated with the abuse of process issue.

(3) In abuse of process applications based upon delay, it is unnecessary, at first instance, to refer to any authorities other than *F*,[144] *Galbraith*,[145] *Attorney-General's Reference No.1 of 1990*,[146] and *S*.[147] These four authorities contain all the necessary discussion about the applicable principles relevant for first instance applications. In terms of appeal issues, with the separate question of the safety of a conviction only, the issues that may arise are illustrated by *Bell* and *Smolinski*. No further citation of authority is needed.

H. Re-trial

The question whether a defendant's retrial should be stayed on the ground of delay is pri-marily one for the trial judge, considering the public interest in trying serious allegations and fairness to the accused. The passage of time is, of itself, no impediment to the fairness of a retrial.[148] **6.111**

In *Charles v State of Trinidad and Tobago*[149] the Privy Council allowed an appeal against con-viction for murder and observed that although the Privy Council would not readily interfere **6.112**

---

[141] [2011] EWCA Crim 1844; [2012] QB 703; [2012] 2 WLR 1038; [2012] 1 All ER 565; [2011] 2 Cr App R 28; [2012] Crim LR 282. For case comment see Archbold Review 2011, 8, 1–2 and [2012] Crim LR, 282–286. F was applied in *Cornwell* [2013] EWCA Crim 2414 and followed by the Supreme Court of New Zealand in *CT v The Queen* [2014] NZSC 15.

[142] *Galbraith* [1981] 1 WLR 103.

[143] [1992] QB 630, [1992] 95 Cr App R 296.

[144] [2011] EWCA Crim 1844; [2012] Q.B.703; [2012] 2 W.L.R. 1038; [2012] 1 All ER 565; [2011] 2 Cr App R 28; [2012] Crim LR 282. Cited with approval in *R* [2015] EWCA Crim 1941.

[145] *Galbraith* [1981] 1 WLR 1039.

[146] [1992] QB 630, [1992] 95 Cr App R 296.

[147] [2006] EWCA Crim 756; [2006] 2 Cr App R 23; [2007] Crim LR 29.

[148] See *Dunlop* [2007] 1 Cr App R 8.

[149] [2000] 1 WLR 384.

with a trial judge's discretion, it was an abuse of the criminal process to allow the prosecution to proceed against the appellant on a murder allegation (a) more than nine years after the event and (b) to try him for a third time after an initial conviction had been quashed on appeal and a second trial had resulted in a hung jury.

6.113 The Privy Council noted that it was common practice, albeit not a rule of law, for the prosecution to offer no evidence where two juries have disagreed.[150]

6.114 Although a practice has developed not to proceed to a second re-retrial, the Court of Appeal in *James Bryne*[151] reiterated that there was no rule against a second re-trial. The Court of Appeal in *Bryne* rejected the appellant's submission that it was wrong in principle to permit a third trial. There is a convention that if a jury disagrees on the first trial and then a second jury also disagrees, the prosecution will then formally offer no evidence.[152] However, this is no more than a convention. There is no rule of law that forbids a prosecutor from seeking a second retrial after a jury has disagreed, as made clear by the Privy Council.[153]

6.115 Whether a second retrial should be permitted depended upon an assessment of the interests of justice, taking account of the defendant's interests and in particular whether the defence has been prejudiced by any delay.[154]

6.116 The ultimate question for the judge was whether the interests of justice, which require a fair trial in circumstances which are neither oppressive nor unjust, justified a second retrial. The broad public interest in the administration of criminal justice suggested that a second retrial should be confined to the very small number of cases in which the jury was being invited to address a crime of extreme gravity which had undoubtedly occurred and in which the evidence remained powerful, as discussed by Lord Chief Justice Judge in *Bell*.[155]

6.117 In *Norman Burton*,[156] Lord Justice Treacy applied the *Bell* test in allowing an appeal against conviction, based on a second retrial of a conspiracy to import class 'A' drugs (cocaine). The Crown had failed to demonstrate that the case was sufficiently exceptional to warrant a second retrial. The Court of Appeal went further and recognized that whilst the test in *Bell* would, in most cases, be sufficient to identify where the interests of justice lay, a wider consideration might be required in some cases. Where the case did not involve murder or serious violent crime, particularly strong justification would be needed to satisfy the test of extreme gravity. There had to be an informed, dispassionate, and searching examination of why a third trial was justified where there had been no irregularities in the first two. The CPS 'Guidance to Prosecutors' correctly identified the starting point presumption that a third trial should not be sought in the absence of exceptional circumstances (such as jury interference or additional evidence) justifying such a course. The number of cases in which a third trial was permitted should be strictly limited in order to maintain public confidence and achieve finality for defendants. Courts had therefore to proceed with caution.

---

[150] See also *Henworth* [2001] 2 Cr App R 4.

[151] [2002] 2 Cr App R 21.

[152] See Archbold Criminal Proceedings and Practice (2002) at 4–440.

[153] In *Forrester Bowe (Junior) v The Queen* (Privy Council Appeal No 48 of 2000) [2000] UK PC 19, see [37] per Lord Bingham of Cornhill, [2001] 6 Archbold News 3.

[154] See *Forrester Bowe (Junior) v The Queen* (Privy Council Appeal No 48 of 2000) [2001] UK PC 19, [2001] 6 Archbold News 3.

[155] [2010] EWCA Crim 3; [2010] 1 Cr App R 27.

[156] [2015] EWCA Crim 1307.

In relation to retrials generally, the decisions of *Stone*,[157] *Mercer*,[158] and *Bain v The Queen*[159] should be considered. **6.118**

Where a retrial is ordered following a conviction being quashed, the prosecution must act promptly in having a defendant re-arraigned. In *Horne*,[160] HM Customs and Excise failed, following an order for a retrial, to re-arraign the defendant within the two months time limit set by section 8 of the Criminal Appeal Act 1968. This was held by the Court of Appeal to be a failure to act with due expedition as required under the Act. The reason the prosecution did not act within the time limit was that the papers had gone astray. The court held that the prosecution could therefore not claim to have acted with due expedition. Therefore, there was a plain and simple dereliction of duty, which amounted to an abuse of process. **6.119**

I. Mitigation of Sentence

It should be noted that a long delay between offence and sentence can be powerful mitigation (see *R*,[161] *Marriner and Frain*,[162] and *R*[163]). However, in historic sexual abuse cases, the fact that the offences are of some age is not necessarily a sufficient reason for imposing a lesser sentence. The same starting point should apply, whilst the fact that the offences are stale can be taken into account, but only to a limited extent (see *Millberry*[164] and *Att-Gen's Ref Nos 91,119 and 120 of 2002*[165]). **6.120**

J. Summary

The following summary of principles can be derived from the delay case law: **6.121**

(1) A case should only be stayed as an abuse of process if the there has been inordinate delay in the proceedings, which has lead to prejudice and means a fair trial cannot be had: *Attorney General's Reference (No 1 of 1990)*;[166]
(2) Lord Justice Rose in *S*,[167] having considered a number of authorities,[168] set out five principles which need to be considered:
  (a) even where delay is unjustifiable, a permanent stay should be the exception rather than the rule;
  (b) where there was no fault on the part of the complainant or the prosecution, it would be very rare for a stay to be granted;
  (c) no stay should be granted in the absence of serious prejudice to the defence so that no fair trial could be held;

---

[157] [2001] Crim LR 465.
[158] [2001] EWCA Crim 638, [2001] 4 *Archbold News* 1.
[159] [2009] UKPC 4.
[160] (1992) *Times* 27 February.
[161] (1993) 14 Cr App R (S) 328. The Court of Appeal conviction ruling is reported as *R v R* [1994] Crim LR 948.
[162] [2002] EWCA Crim 2855.
[163] [2015] EWCA Crim 1941.
[164] (2003) 2 Cr App R (S) 142.
[165] (2003) 2 Cr App R (S) 338.
[166] [1992] QB 630, [1992] 95 Cr App R 296.
[167] [2006] EWCA Crim 756; [2006] 2 Cr App R 23;[2007] Crim LR 296.
[168] *Attorney General's Reference (No 1 of 1990)* [1992] QB 630, 644; *EW* [2004] EWCA Crim 2901, [23]; *Attorney General's Reference (No 2 of 2001)* [2001] 1 WLR 1869 [16]; *Hooper* [2003] EWCA Crim 2427, [76]; *B* [2003] 2 Cr App R 197 [15]–[18]; *Smolinksi* [2004] 2 Cr App R 661 [7].

(d) when assessing possible serious prejudice, the judge should bear in mind his or her power to regulate the admissibility of evidence and the fact that the trial process itself should ensure that all relevant factual issues arising from delay will be placed before the jury for their consideration in accordance with appropriate directions from the judge;

(e) if, having considered all those factors, a judge's assessment is that a fair trial would be possible, a stay should not be granted.

(3) The trial process itself, in terms of the judicial regulation of the admissibility of evidence and jury direction, will often be a suitable alternative remedy to a stay: *Attorney General's Reference (No 1 of 1990),*[169] *Bowley,*[170] *Hickson,*[171] *DPP v Tokai,*[172] *Percival,*[173] *Maybery.*[174]

(4) There is no period of time which is determinative on an application to stay a case on grounds of delay: *Brian Selwyn Bell,*[175] *Derek Hooper,*[176] *E,*[177]. In cases of delay, each cases turns on its own facts.

(5) In abuse of process applications based upon delay, it is unnecessary, at first instance, to refer to any authorities other than *F,*[178] *Galbraith,*[179] *Attorney-General's Reference No.1 of 1990,*[180] and *S.*[181] In terms of appeal issues, with the separate question of the safety of a conviction only, the issues that may arise are illustrated by *Bell*[182] and *Smolinski.*[183] No further citation of authority is needed.

(6) A breach of the Article 6 ECHR right to a trial within a reasonable time period may lead to a stay of proceedings but only in exceptional circumstances: *Attorney-General's Reference (No 2 of 2001),*[184] *and Spiers v Ruddy.*[185]

---

[169] [1992] QB 630, [1992] 95 Cr App R 296.
[170] [1996] Crim LR 406.
[171] [1997] Crim LR 494.
[172] [1996] AC 856.
[173] [1998] 7 *Archbold News* 2, (CA, 20 July 1998)A.
[174] [2003] EWCA Crim 783.
[175] [2003] 2 Cr App R 13.
[176] [2003] EWCA Crim 2427, CA.
[177] [2008] EWCA Crim 604.
[178] [2011] EWCA Crim 1844; [2012] QB 703; [2012] 2 WLR 1038; [2012] 1 All ER 565; [2011] 2 Cr App R 28; [2012] Crim LR 282.
[179] *Galbraith* [1981] 1 WLR 1039.
[180] [1992] QB 630, [1992] 95 Cr App R 296.
[181] [2006] EWCA Crim 756; [2006] 2 Cr App R 23; [2007] Crim LR 296.
[182] [2003] 2 Cr App R 13.
[183] [2004] 2 Cr App R 661.
[184] [2004] 1 Cr App R 25.
[185] [2007] UKPC D2, [2008] 1 AC 87.

7

NON-AVAILABILITY OF EVIDENCE

A. Introduction

Where evidence has been lost or destroyed and the defence has been deprived of a potential **7.1** opportunity to advance its case, the court has a discretion to stay proceedings.[1] The court, when considering an abuse application based on the non-availability of evidence, has to examine the relevance of the material, whether it should have been preserved, why it was destroyed (in terms of bad faith, serious fault or incompetence), and alternative trial remedies. All these issues are dealt with and guidance given in *R v Feltham*[2] and explored in the case law set out below.

B. Guidance

The leading case in this area is *R v Feltham Magistrates' Court ex p Ebrahim, Mouat v DPP*,[3] **7.2** in which the Divisional Court gave guidance as to the approach courts should adopt when faced with the non-availability of evidence at trial, with specific reference to video-tape evidence;

• First, the court should consider the duty, if any, of the investigator or prosecutor to obtain, retain, and preserve the evidence. Reference should be made to the Code of Practice

---

[1] See 'Lost and Destroyed Evidence: The Search for a Principled Approach to Abuse of Process'—S Martin (2005) 9 E&P 158; Victor Smith, 'Lost, Altered or Destroyed Evidence' (2007) 171 JPN 556. In relation to destruction of evidence by state agencies and any breach of Article 6, see *Sofri v Italy* [2004] Crim LR 846 (a murder trial in which the deceased's clothing and bullets from the deceased's body and the getaway car were all missing) and *Papageorgiou v Greece* (2004) 38 EHRR 30 (destruction of forged cheques).

[2] [2001] 1 All ER 831, [2001] 2 Cr App R 23.

[3] [2001] 1 All ER 831, [2001] 2 Cr App R 23. Ebrahim has been followed and cited as persuasive authority in other jurisdictions. See, for example, the Isle of Man decision in *AG v Tomlinson* [2010] Crim 59, Court of General Gaol Delivery judgment dated 20 April 2011 www.judgments.im/content/J1133.htm.

published pursuant to sections 23 and 25 of the Criminal Procedure and Investigations Act 1996[4] and the Attorney-General's disclosure guidelines.[5]

- Second, if there was no such duty before the defence first sought retention, there could be no question of a subsequent trial being unfair.

- Third, if the material had not been retained in accordance with the code or guidelines the following principles should be applied: (i) the ultimate objective was to ensure a fair trial to both the defence and prosecution; (ii) trial procedural safeguards can deal with the bulk of complaints; (iii) if there is sufficient credible evidence which, if believed, could sustain a safe conviction, the trial should proceed. A stay should not be granted unless the defence could show prejudice to the extent that a fair trial could not be had.

- Fourth, the proceedings could be stayed if the behaviour of the prosecution was so bad—in terms of bad faith or serious fault—that it would be unfair to try the defendant (as per the category 2 abuse cases).

7.3 The guidance set out in *R v Feltham* has been applied in a number of cases, with decisions set out below.

C. Bad Faith or Serious Fault

No bad faith or serious fault

7.4 Before a case is stayed for the loss of evidence there has to be evidence of bad faith or serious fault on the part of the investigative team.

7.5 In *Swingler*,[6] a rape case, the appellant applied at first instance for the proceedings to be stayed: video recordings of the locus were not available at trial as they had been destroyed. The trial judge refused a stay. The Court of Appeal dismissed a challenge to that decision. Video cameras were mounted at the locus of the rape, but the police officer in charge of the investigation was told by British Transport Police that the cameras were not switched on. In fact they were working, but the police did not ascertain that fact until a month later, by which time the video film had been destroyed. The Court of Appeal directed itself that before there could be any successful allegation of abuse of process based on the disappearance of evidence, there had to be either an element of bad faith or at the very least some serious fault on the part of the police or the prosecution authorities.[7] Since there was no bad faith and no serious fault on the part of the police it was possible to have a fair trial. The Court of Appeal suggested, obiter, that a lackadaisical failure on the part of the police to make proper investigation might in certain circumstances be held, in effect, to give rise to a stay as it would be unfair for the accused to be tried.

7.6 In *Dobson*[8] the Court of Appeal noted that where police fail to obtain CCTV footage, relating to a defendant's alibi, the following questions arise:

(a) what was the duty of the police;

(b) did the police fail in that duty by failing to obtain and retain the footage;

---

[4] See Paragraph 5.1 of the Code of Practice made under section 23 CPIA imposes a duty on the prosecutor to retain 'material obtained in a criminal investigation which may be relevant to the investigation'.

[5] Consider also: (1) section 19 PACE which gives police officers powers of seizure to prevent anything being concealed, lost, damaged, altered, or destroyed; and (2) section 56 Criminal Justice and Police Act 2001, which gives the police power to retain such property.

[6] 10 July 1998, CA.

[7] See also *Stallard,* 13 April 2000, CA.

[8] [2001] EWCA Crim 1606, [2001] All ER (D) 109.

(c) was there serious prejudice to the defence that meant a fair trial was impossible;

(d) was the failure motivated by bad faith or a result of serious fault so that a trial would not be fair.

On the facts of *Dobson*, although the police were under a duty to look at CCTV footage, their failure to do so did not amount to an abuse of process. The failure resulted from police oversight as opposed to malice or deliberate omission. The defendant did not suffer serious prejudice as it was unclear whether the footage would have assisted the defence and the defence could have sought other evidence to support the alibi advanced. The Court of Appeal upheld the conviction. **7.7**

In *DPP v S*[9] the defendant was arrested and interviewed by police in relation to kidnap and indecent assault charges. He denied any involvement and told police that supermarket CCTV cameras might show the complainant buying or drinking alcohol. Despite requests to keep the relevant CCTV images, the supermarket no longer had the footage. In arguing for a stay, the defence relied upon the absent footage as important, as it might support the defence's challenge to the complainant's credibility. In opposing the abuse application, the prosecution argued (a) that there had been no bad faith on the part of the police in failing to secure the supermarket tape, merely inadvertence and (b) the video footage would make no difference to the trial. **7.8**

The district judge stayed proceedings, as an abuse of process, on the basis that the prosecution were under a duty to preserve the CCTV recordings, the footage might have supported the defence case and without the potentially supporting evidence the defendant could not receive a fair trial. **7.9**

In quashing the order for a stay, the Divisional Court held that the district judge had applied the *Ebrahim* principles incorrectly. Although the video had not been retained in accordance with the CPIA issued code of practice,[10] a stay should not be imposed merely because there is some missing evidence. If there is sufficient, credible evidence to justify a safe conviction, then the trial should proceed, with the defence able to address the jury on the absence of the evidence. Whether the video footage was relevant depended on whether the complainant agreed that she was drinking alcohol. If she accepted such drinking, the video was irrelevant. Furthermore, the police had not acted in bad faith nor been at serious fault in failing to preserve the CCTV footage. **7.10**

Deliberate destruction

The misconduct of the Royal Ulster Constabulary (RUC) and Security Service in deliberately destroying and withholding audio tape recordings relating to a sensitive incident was considered by the Court of Appeal in Northern Ireland in *Martin McCauley*.[11] The appellant, by way of a Criminal Cases Review Commission (CCRC) reference, had his conviction for possessing firearms (three rifles) without a lawful object overturned and rendered unsafe. The CCRC had gained access to sensitive material revealing that an eavesdropping operation had been carried out at the scene of a RUC shooting at which the appellant was present, where a second man had been shot dead. The audio tape recordings showed that no warnings had been given by the police before they opened fire. The tape was destroyed, but an unauthorized copy came into the possession of the Security Service. The police initially misled the DPP **7.11**

---

[9] (2002) Lawtel Doc. No AC9500936; 167 JP 43.

[10] Paragraphs 2.1 and 3.4.

[11] [2014] NICA 60.

as to whether there had been a listening device. When the existence of the device was disclosed by the Security Service, the police failed to disclose that there had been an audio recording of the events and a transcription. Further, the Security Service failed to disclose the audio tape during an investigation into the incident by senior police officers from England.

7.12 The appellant successfully argued that his conviction was unsafe, as the prosecution and conviction constituted an abuse of process, based on two grounds. First, the police misconduct in destroying their copy of the eavesdropping tape and, second, that of the Security Service in not disclosing it's copy when it knew that the appellant was facing trial rendered his trial unfair. The eavesdropping tape may not have given much direct evidence of what the appellant did at the locus, but it seemed likely that the tape would have provided information as to what was said after the shooting. The appellant's account, rejected by the trial judge, was that he told police that he had found the guns at the scene. It was not possible now to determine what, if anything, was recorded of what was said by the appellant after the shooting, but the misconduct in deliberately destroying the source evidence deprived the appellant of the opportunity to examine the recording for the purpose of assisting his defence. Second, the tape, which was relevant evidence, was deliberately destroyed, arguably in the view of Lord Chief Justice Morgan, amounting to a perversion of the course of justice. In addition, the Security Service's failure to disclose their copy of the tape to the prosecution was reprehensible. The grave misconduct was such that it would be contrary to the public interest in the integrity of the criminal justice system to uphold the conviction.

7.13 Cases where the non-availability of evidence has led to a stay cover a number of different topics.

D. Destruction of Documents and Material

7.14 The Divisional Court in *Sunderland Magistrates' Court ex p Z*[12] granted a prohibition staying rape proceedings to prevent Justices continuing with committal proceedings. The defendant was charged with rape. It had initially been decided not to proffer charges because of insufficient evidence. However, the inquiry was reopened when a second complainant made a rape allegation against the defendant. The defence complained that the delay in proceedings, had caused prejudice in that relevant documents had been destroyed, as had clothing and vaginal swabs which might, scientifically have established the defendant's innocence. Further, an eight-year delay in initiating proceedings was deemed 'unconscionable' by the Divisional Court.

7.15 Likewise the destruction of documents in *Carosella v R*[13] led to a stay of proceedings being upheld by the Canadian Supreme Court. Charges of gross indecency were laid twenty-six to twenty-eight years after the alleged sexual offences. At trial, the appellant requested disclosure of records from a sexual crisis centre, where an interview with the complainant relating to the allegations had taken place. The trial judge stayed the proceedings because the notes of interview had been destroyed. The Canadian Supreme Court agreed with that decision. The

---

[12] [1989] Crim LR 56.
[13] [1997] 2 BHRC 23; (1997) 1 SCR 80; contrast the Supreme Court of Canada decision in *La* (1997) 2 SCR at 860 (as applied in *Glenn v North Antrim Magistrates Court* [2002] NIQB 61).

appellant had lost a realistic opportunity to garner evidence and to make decisions about the case, which impeded his right to a fair trial.

In *B (Prosecution Appeal)*[14] the loss of the original prosecution investigation case file lead to **7.16** proceedings for an attempted abduction of a child being stayed as an abuse of process. The issue in the case was identification. The material lost included (a) the complainant's original video evidence and transcript, (b) an e-fit said to resemble the accused at the time (the prosecution sought to call an officer to say there was a strong resemblance between the e-fit and the accused), and (c) the accused's original interviews.

In *Khalid Ali and Mohammed Altaf*,[15] the Court of Appeal quashed convictions for **7.17** false imprisonment and rape because of the cumulative effect of unjustified delay, missing evidence, and judicial directions given to the jury. It was agreed that, as a result of the delay in the proceedings, a number of documents were no longer available for use at trial. The missing documents included an application by one of the complainants to the Criminal Injuries Compensation Authority detailing the incident and a similar application by the co-complainant friend, in which she accepted that she had lied. Delay had removed any opportunity for the defence to investigate whether the complainant had adopted a similar (lying) approach to the CICA. Further, the delay lead to the destruction of a police officer's notebook which detailed the first account of the sexual complaint. In addition, there was no longer any video evidence to show what the female complainants looked like at the time of the allegations, which would have been of assistance to the defendants. The defence of consent was being advanced and, if the females looked older than their actual age of thirteen and a half years, that would have lent support to the assertion that the defendants had consensual sexual intercourse with the two females. Moreover, the complainant's friend, to whom an initial telephone call was made, once traced by the defence, could no longer assist the complainants.

The prejudice caused by the loss of the CICA application could only have been cured, in the **7.18** judgment of the Court of Appeal[16], by the trial judge directing the jury to assume that the complainant's application was as mendacious as that of her fellow complainant. But to so direct would have been to invite the jury to speculate as to its contents. It was the combination of the absence of the CICA application, and the way the jury were directed, that gave the Court of Appeal grave cause for concern as to the safety of the verdicts. There was no credible evidence which could be distinguished from the missing material. The complainant's credibility depended, in part, upon the reliability of her account to the CICA. Lord Justice Moses observed:[17]

> ... We have come to the conclusion that the loss of material evidence combined with unsatisfactory evidence as to how the complaints were first made, cause doubt as to the safety of the verdicts. We think that this is a rare case where the prejudice flowing from that loss of evidence was not cured by any direction given by the judge. Indeed the directions of the judge highlight the difficulties as to the fairness of the procedure caused by the loss of the evidence ... We wish to emphasise that this a rare case where prejudice following from the delay was not alleviated and probably could never have been cured during the course of the trial.

---

[14] [2008] EWCA Crim 1144; [2008] 6 Archbold News 1.
[15] [2007] EWCA Crim 691.
[16] Ibid: Lord Justice Moses judgment at para 38.
[17] Ibid at paras 45, 47.

E. Video Recording

Relevant video

7.19 In *Birmingham*,[18] an indictment charging seven defendants with violent disorder was stayed. The existence of a video recording of the nightclub where the incident took place, showing part of the incident itself, was not disclosed to the defence pre-trial. The police officer in charge of the case had viewed the videotape but by the time of the trial the video recording had been lost.

7.20 The court held that the prosecution had a duty to disclose the videotape, whether or not it had been requested, because the tape could have provided material evidence relevant to the defence. The deprivation of this material prejudiced the accused and made a fair trial impossible.

7.21 *Birmingham* was applied in *DPP v David Chipping*,[19] in which the Divisional Court refused to quash a stipendiary magistrate's decision to stay proceedings. Lord Justice Buxton[20] in giving judgment, referred to the fact that the video was likely to be the best evidence of any incident that it showed and that it was desirable that it should be shown to the defence. In the circumstances, it was appropriate to stay the proceedings.

Irrelevant video

7.22 Contrast the situation in which the video evidence lost is of no relevance. In *Reid*,[21] the appellant was convicted of robbery of a shop. A security video taken at the time was not disclosed because the investigating police officer took the view that it contained nothing of relevance and one of the cameras did not even cover the locus. At trial, the film was probably no longer on videotape. An application to stay the proceedings, on the basis of the films non-disclosure and absence, was rejected at first instance and on appeal. The Court of Appeal recognized the clear duty to preserve material which might be relevant. However, the investigating officer was entitled to make a judgment as to the relevance of the material. The trial judge was entitled to accept, on the evidence, that the video contained nothing of relevance.

7.23 The Court of Appeal came to the same decision in the case of *Medway*,[22] where the appellant was convicted of a street robbery. Closed circuit television cameras located in the street where the robbery took place might have captured something of the robbery. A police officer looked at the film. He was of the opinion that it showed nothing of value and he did not preserve the tape. The consequence was that the tape was used again and the police officer's opinion could no longer be confirmed or contradicted. The trial judge refused to stay proceedings on the basis of the absence of the video tape and the appellant, with the leave of the Single Judge, appealed his conviction.

7.24 The appeal was dismissed, Lord Justice Mantell, in giving the judgment[23] observed that:

> We recognised that in cases where evidence has been tampered with, lost or destroyed it may well be that the defendant will be disadvantaged. It does not necessarily follow that in such case the defendant cannot have a fair trial or that it would be unfair for him to be tried ... there would need to be something wholly exceptional about the circumstances of the case to

---

[18] [1992] Crim LR 117.
[19] 11 January 1999, DC – CO/2362/98.
[20] At page 11 of the transcript.
[21] [1997] CLY 1172.
[22] [2000] Crim LR 415.
[23] At p 9 of the transcript, No 98/7579/Y3.

justify a stay on the ground that evidence has been lost or destroyed. One such circumstance might be if the interference with the evidence was malicious.

Here it has never been suggested that the failure to preserve the tape stemmed from malice. The judge heard evidence from the officer that there was nothing on the tape to assist either side. There is not the slightest reason to suppose that the absence of the tape affected the fairness of the trial or rendered the conviction unsafe. In our judgment the trial judge was right to refuse an application for a stay.

7.25 In *Edmunds and Marsh*,[24] the two appellants were convicted of inflicting grievous bodily harm. A police constable had viewed CCTV footage, but saw nothing which he considered to be of any interest relating to the incident. Three days before the trial started, defence solicitors went to the locus and discovered that the CCTV system had been taken away. Before the trial started, the defence applied to stay the indictment arguing that the officer should have taken the video and preserved the footage, which might have contained vital evidence supporting the defence case. The defence accepted that the footage would not have shown the incident, but it might have shown the order in which the three men involved had entered the locus. This was important because on the complainant's account he entered first and the appellants followed, in contrast to the appellant's version. In dismissing this submission, the trial judge said that video footage was peripheral because it would not have shown the incident itself.[25]

7.26 In summing up, the trial judge said the jury might think it was unfair that the defence had not had the opportunity of seeing the video and how they could take into account the prejudice which this might have caused the appellants when they were considering whether the evidence of the complainant satisfied them that he had been assaulted. as opposed to the appellant's account of acting in self-defence.

7.27 In the Court of Appeal, dismissing the appeal, Lord Justice Tuckey stated that the appellants at trial

> ... had the benefit of being able to make a song and dance about the fact that they had not had the opportunity of seeing the tape on the basis that there had been a tape which the police officer could have taken and everyone could have seen ... [N]othing which happened prejudiced the appellants ... [T]his was a case in which the jury had, with or without videos, to decide whose account they could accept. They clearly accepted the complainant's evidence and rejected that of the appellants.[26]

7.28 In *Rasalingham Markandu*,[27] the Court of Appeal, in an appeal against conviction on two counts of wounding with intent, rejected the applicant's argument that the trial should have been stayed because video tapes of the inside of the night club, at which the incident took place, had been destroyed. Lord Justice Clarke, giving judgment, observed:

> Two different judges declined to stay these proceedings and rightly so. The videotapes, which were destroyed, did not depict the area in which the assault took place. All the evidence indicated that the assault took place in the spectator's gallery, and the camera covering that area is not working and has not done so for two years. There is simply no evidence that the camera which produced the destroyed tapes depicted those responsible for the assault.

The Court of Appeal allowed the appeal against the conviction on a separate, unrelated ground based on new evidence. The conviction was quashed and a re-trial was ordered.

---

[24] [2002] EWCA Crim 1801.
[25] See also *Jeremiahs* [2002] EWHC 2982; (2007) 171 JPN 556 at page 6.
[26] [2002] EWCA Crim 1801.
[27] [2003] EWCA Crim 1250.

7.29 Likewise in *Sahdev*,[28] in which the appellant had been convicted of an assault at a tube station. British Transport Police cameras monitored the area. The Court of Appeal considered the failure of the police to investigate evidence from shop cameras, unbeknown to the police at the time, which may have filmed the incident, not to have been unreasonable. The failure did not make the trial unfair.

F. Duty to Preserve Evidence

7.30 The court in considering a non-availability of evidence argument will consider the duty, if any, of the investigator or prosecutor to obtain, retain, and preserve the evidence.

Duty to preserve and retain evidence

7.31 The duty to preserve evidence was considered in *Parker*,[29] an arson case. The issue was whether a fire, which had as its source the defendant's bed, had been started deliberately or accidentally. The Court of Appeal dismissed the appeal. The trial judge, with reference to *Ebrahim*, had been correct in refusing an application for a stay made on the ground that the failure to preserve the bed and the bedding constituted an abuse. A fair trial was had despite the failure to preserve materials.

7.32 Although the fire officer conceded that photographs of the scene were inadequate for the purpose of allowing a defence assessment of the cause of fire and a literal reading of the CPIA code of practice might have imposed a duty to retain the material, a measure of flexibility had to be allowed as to the practicalities of retaining a large burnt-out item.

7.33 Further, there had been no bad faith on the part of the police and the failure had to be judged against (1) the likelihood of a challenge as to the cause of the fire, (2) the fact that no request for preservation had been made, and (3) the fact that defence expert said no more than that preservation might have assisted on the issue, but without giving any specifics.

7.34 The flexibility afforded to prosecuting authorities as to what articles are retained was endorsed by the Divisional Court in *Clay v South Cambridgeshire Justices*.[30] In rejecting an appeal by a driver, by way of case stated, challenging the Justice's refusal to stay proceedings because of the failure of police to preserve evidence (a car involved in the road traffic offence), Lord Justice Pitchford observed:[31]

> … paragraph 22 of the judgment in Parker is relevant because it acknowledges the need to apply common sense and proportionality to the question whether it is necessary to retain exhibits.

7.35 In coming to the same conclusion, Lord Justice Burton in *Clay*, observed:[32]

> The Justices were as my Lord has explained, entitled to conclude that injustice to the defendant could be avoided by judicious regulation of the trial

Namely, the Justices could make full allowance for the loss of the defendant's opportunity to inspect the destroyed evidence.

---

[28] [2002]EWCA Crim 1064.
[29] [2002] 2 Cr App R (S) 58; [2003] EWCA Crim 90; case comment at Archbold News 2003, 3, p 1.
[30] [2014] EWHC 321 (Admin); [2015] RTR 1.
[31] [2014] EWHC 321 (Admin) at para 53.
[32] [2014] EWHC 321 (Admin) at para 77.

Failure to preserve evidence

A failure to preserve relevant evidence may result in the stay of proceedings. One such **7.36** example is the Administrative Court decision in *Leatherland and Pritchard v Powys County Council*[33] in which the court considered whether the destruction of sheep carcases in proceedings alleging animal suffering and welfare offences amounted to an abuse of process. The appellants, who were convicted by magistrates,[34] appealed by way of case stated, arguing that the destruction of the animals deprived them of a proper opportunity to defend themselves.

In allowing the appeal, Justice Owen observed, in applying the *Feltham Magistrates'* guidance: **7.37**

(1) the prosecuting authority trading standards officers were under a duty to preserve the animal carcasses in accordance with the CPIA and Code of Practice;

(2) the officers failed to discharge the duty to retain relevant material. The separate statutory duty to dispose of animal carcasses did not override the prosecutor's duty to retain relevant material. A representative selection of the 69 carcasses could have been preserved for a sufficient period for the appellants to be informed that they were to be slaughtered, of the reason why and an opportunity given to them to have their own veterinary expert examine the carcasses. The appellants were not informed of what was happening. That failure was not remedied by making a photographic record because the photographs taken of the animals and presented to the Justices were inconclusive and of no evidential value;

(3) the appellants suffered serious prejudice to the extent that no fair trial could be held. As a result of the destruction of the carcasses the appellants were severely handicapped in mounting a challenge either to the factual or opinion evidence of the respondent's expert veterinary surgeon inspector witness. The appellants were not in a position to comment on the respondent expert's specific findings and their own expert could only give general evidence of the methodology adopted by the respondent expert. Since the sole issue in the case was the condition of the sheep when delivered to market and the prosecution case was reliant solely on the veterinary inspector, basic considerations of fairness required that the appellants be given the opportunity to inspect a representative selection of the sheep or their carcasses. No such inspection was available. Accordingly, the appellant's convictions were quashed.

Preservation of sample

In *Boyd*,[35] the appellant was convicted of causing the death (of her ten-year-old daughter) **7.38** by careless driving (the appellant's car collided with a lorry), while under the influence of drugs. The prosecution alleged that the appellant had taken heroin on the afternoon of the road accident and a blood sample taken shortly after the accident gave a positive result for morphine and opiate drugs. A second blood test had not been possible and the sample that the prosecution had taken had not been refrigerated, with the result that there had been no sample fit to be tested by the defence. The trial judge decided to exclude from the jury evidence of the blood sample.

On appeal, the appellant argued that the trial judge ought to have excluded the evidence **7.39** and then stayed the proceedings as an abuse of process, given the incompetence of the prosecution in relation to the preservation of the sample and fact that the defence was therefore prevented from presenting its own expert evidence, which might have shown the appellant had not been under the influence of heroin.

---

[33] [2007] EWHC 148 (Admin).
[34] Under s 1 Protection of Animals act 1911 and s 72 Animal Health Act 1981, relating to 69 sheep.
[35] [2002] EWCA Crim 2836, [2004] RTR 2.

7.40 The Court of Appeal allowed the appeal and quashed the conviction. The fairness of the trial required the proceedings to be stayed and the trial judge had erred in not doing so. The prosecution's interpretation of the test results was open to challenge. The defence had been deprived of the opportunity of establishing a complete defence to the charge and accordingly her conviction was quashed.

G. Investigative Failures

7.41 Investigative failures which lead to the loss of evidence or loss of opportunity to gather evidence may amount to an abuse of process.

Loss of opportunity

7.42 In *Gajree*,[36] initial police failure and delay in forensically examining a carpet for semen led to a conviction being quashed by the Court of Appeal. If the matter had been pursued properly and expeditiously, the question of seminal staining of the carpet would have been capable of forensic resolution one way or the other. Mr Justice Sachs stated:

> We are satisfied that because of the passage of time, and the inertia of the police officers, this appellant was deprived of evidence that might have otherwise been available to him, and in our view, renders the verdict in the case unsafe and unsatisfactory.

7.43 Contrast *Gajree* with the US Supreme Court decision in *Arizona v Youngblood*[37] in which the prosecution's negligent failure to test or preserve semen samples was deemed not to render the trial fundamentally unfair.

Cumulative failures

7.44 In *Northard*,[38] the Court of Appeal quashed the defendant's conviction for robbery because of police investigative failures. The failure to carry out proper enquiries had prejudiced the preparation of the defendant's case and precluded a fair trial. One example cited by the Court of Appeal was that the police did not disclose to the defence the existence of relevant video film footage (of shop CCTV cameras, which could have supported the defendant's alibi) nor was it available at trial (as the shopping centre video tape was re-used after twenty-eight days).

Considerable ineptitude

7.45 Contrast the decision in *Clayton Sadler*,[39] in which the Court of Appeal dismissed abuse of process arguments based, inter alia, upon investigative failures. The appellant was convicted of wounding with intent to do grievous bodily harm, arising out of an incident at a nightclub. During the trial there was an application by the defence for a stay on the basis that there had been delay by the prosecution in disclosing various matters and the destruction of certain exhibits. The delays in disclosure related, inter alia, to four video tapes from CCTV cameras inside the club. The videos did not show either the dance floor or the area near the stairs where the attack took place. The defence argued that the lateness of the delivery of the videos delayed the trial, which must have affected the memories of witnesses or potential witnesses to the prejudice of the appellant. The appellant also relied upon the destruction of certain exhibits by the police. The exhibits in question were a

---

[36] 20 September 1994, No 94/3269/Y2.
[37] (1988) 488 US 51, 102 L Ed 2d 281, 109 S Ct 333.
[38] 19 February 1996, CA, 95/1475/Z3—see Archbold Criminal Appeal Office Index 1997, no 3, para T-4. See Chapter 8.
[39] [2002] EWCA Crim 1722, 166 JP 481.

broken bottleneck found at the club after the incident, the defendant's shoes and socks and the complainant's clothing. The evidence was that the broken bottleneck was examined forensically. No blood or fingerprints were found on it, but it was not examined by the prosecution for traces of DNA. It was submitted that the destruction of this broken bottleneck prejudiced the appellant.

7.46 The trial judge rejected an allegation that the police had been acting in bad faith, although the judge criticized them for inept and sloppy work. Certainly the negligent failings of the police, thoroughly reprehensible though they were, fell far short, in the view of the Court of Appeal, of making it unfair to try the appellant.

7.47 So far as the videos were concerned, there was late disclosure, and there was a breach of at least one if not more court orders. However, the videos did not show the dance floor or bar area. They were always, therefore, likely to be of very limited value. The appellant's advisers did have these videos some three months before the trial began and yet there was no evidence that it was possible to see anything or anyone on them that would have assisted the appellant or weakened the prosecution case. The destruction of some of the exhibits clearly should not have taken place. Again, however, the Court of Appeal was of the opinion that there was no material prejudice suffered by the appellant. The broken bottleneck was found to have no blood on it, casting doubt on whether it was the attack weapon. The history of the late delivery and disclosure of certain items and the destruction of exhibits was one of considerable ineptitude, but in the judgment of the Court of Appeal, the trial judge was right to conclude that there was no abuse of process.

7.48 Cases where the non-availability of evidence did not lead to a stay likewise cover a number of different factual situations and issues, notably reliance upon sources of evidence other than those which had been destroyed or were no longer available.

H. Reliance on Other Evidence

Photographic

7.49 In *R v Uxbridge Justices ex p Sofaer*,[40] the defendants were accused of attempting to export aircraft parts contrary to the Export of Goods (Control) Order 1981. The defendants judicially reviewed the decision to commit the case for trial on the basis that Customs officers had disposed of the aircraft parts, causing prejudice to the defence case that the material was scrap. The defence expert had been unable to carry out a proper examination to see whether they were serviceable aircraft parts or just scrap. Further, the defence argued that the prosecution were under an overriding duty to preserve evidence. Thus there had been a breach of the rules of natural justice. The application was refused, as there was a set of photographs giving full detail of the parts, sufficient for the jury to decide whether the parts were usable or merely scrap. Reliance on secondary evidence sufficed.

7.50 Although it was desirable that prosecuting authorities should preserve evidence, that was not always possible. Evidential exhibits sometimes went astray, and sometimes it was only by destruction that the evidence could be obtained in the first place. Thus where customs authorities disposed of aircraft parts, which they alleged were serviceable and the applicants maintained were scrap, but produced photographs of those parts, that did not prejudice the applicants' defence.

---

[40] (1987) 85 Cr App R 367.

7.51 Likewise in *Hilliers Ltd v Sefton Metropolitan Borough Council*,[41] the availability of photographic evidence was sufficient to cure the loss of evidence. The defendant company had been convicted of a section 14 Food Safety Act 1990 offence relating to the sale of a steak and kidney pie containing a metal bolt. It was argued on appeal that the trial was an abuse of process as the prosecution had lost the pie and its wrapping. The date of manufacture of the pie was unknown and this prevented the defendant company from carrying out a proper investigation into the manufacture of the pie. Without the date on the wrapper the defence had been denied the opportunity to rely upon on the statutory defence of due diligence. Lord Justice Schiemann dismissed the appeal. Although the loss of the wrapper caused the defence difficulties in carrying out an audit trail based on the date of manufacture, the bolt had been retained and photographs of the pie were available.

7.52 Photographic evidence of two lost exhibits and an earlier examination of the same (a blood-stained jacket worn by the appellant and the murder weapon) sufficed in *Derek Barron*[42] to preserve the safety of a murder conviction in the Court of Appeal. An application to stay proceedings as an abuse, at first instance, at the retrial were rejected. The lost exhibits had been photographed and examined during the first trial, meaning that the raw data, which would form the basis for any expert opinion, had been preserved. Although defence experts at the second trial could not examine the jacket or take DNA samples from the knife, the defence experts had access to full and detailed notes of the earlier findings.

Police witnesses

7.53 In *Roberts v DPP*,[43] a CCTV tape of a police station area had been requested by the defence, which arguably would have shown the custody area where a statutory warning under section 7(7) Road Traffic Act 1988 should have been given for an offence of driving with excess alcohol. However, prior to proceedings in the magistrates' court, it was discovered that CCTV of the custody area was no longer available. The Divisional Court upheld the magistrates' court decision not to stay proceedings as an abuse of process, since the appellant had signed a form, which contains the questions to be asked by a police officer when dealing with an excess alcohol offence. The officer asserted that this procedure had been conducted in the custody area, but even if that material was not on the CCTV tape, it would not have established that the procedure had not been conducted properly, merely that it was not conducted in the place where it was believed to have been conducted.[44]

7.54 *Roberts* was cited with approval in *Jamie Morris v DPP*[45] where the Divisional Court decided that there was no abuse of process where police station custody suite CCTV footage, which potentially recorded the administering of the statutory warning under section 7(7) of the Road Traffic Act 1988 (for an offence of driving with excess alcohol), had not been retained by the police. The defence had not asked for the footage and it had been destroyed three months after the incident. There was independent evidence of the statutory warning being given.

7.55 The Divisional Court in *DPP v Petrie* again considered the availability of police station CCTV footage in a situation of driving with excess alcohol.[46] At the magistrates' court, the CPS sought to adjourn proceedings because the police station CCTV footage required for trial had not been formatted correctly and could not be played on any equipment in court.

---

41 CO/2165/96, (2007) 171 JPN 556 at page 4.
42 [2010] EWCA Crim 2950.
43 [2008] EWHC 643.
44 [2008] EWHC 643 at para 9 judgment of Lord Justice Leveson.
45 [2008] EWHC 2788 (Admin).
46 [2015] EWHC 48 (Admin).

An adjournment was refused and the accused successfully applied for a stay of proceedings as an abuse of process on the basis that it would be unfair to proceed without the footage.

The Divisional Court, on a case stated, allowed the prosecution appeal, finding that the **7.56** Justices were wrong to have stayed the proceedings. However regrettable the prosecution failure to provide the CCTV footage in a playable format, that failure fell well short of justifying a stay.

In coming to that conclusion, Lord Justice Gross relied upon three reasons. First, the deci- **7.57** sion was speculative. The facts in the case did not disclose that anyone had ever watched the CCTV footage. It is not known, whether the recording covered the relevant part of the statutory warning procedure or, if it did, whether it captured the precise details of what was said by the police and/or the accused. Second, the trial could have proceeded on the available evidence. The prosecution could have called the police officer who had administered the procedure and the defence could, if they so chose, have called the accused. The defence could have made much of the fact that the CCTV footage which they had requested was unavailable through no fault of their own. Third, and assuming that at the conclusion of the live evidence the Justices were driven to the view that the interests of justice did require the viewing of the CCTV footage, they could at that stage have revisited the question of the adjournment.

Compliance with the statutory requirements of sections 7 and 8 of the Road Traffic Act 1988 **7.58** was also considered in *DPP v Spalluto*.[47] In applying *Petrie*,[48] the Divisional Court, by way of case stated, decided that the magistrates' court had not been justified in staying the prosecution of an Italian speaking national for failing to give a breath specimen in the absence of CCTV audio footage of the police custody suite booking-in procedure. Although the served CCTV footage lacked a sound recording it was impossible to say the accused could not have received a fair trial. The issue could have been dealt with by evidence given by the police officers who had administered the procedure. The accused could cross-examine the officers, he could give evidence and the issue of the accused's difficulty with the English language could have been explored in evidence. The accused had not raised a positive defence, rather he could not recall the procedure.

Investigating officers

In *Aylesbury Vale District Council v Basharat Khan*,[49] the Administrative Court allowed an **7.59** appeal by the prosecuting local authority, by way of case stated, against the decision of Thames Valley Justices to stay a set of informations as being an abuse of process. Charges were brought at the magistrates court against a number of cab drivers, who held private hire vehicle licences, for plying for hire when they had no licence to do so. The evidence against them had been obtained by council officers who approached the cabs in the street. The intended corroborative evidence, in the form of a closed circuit television film of the approaches made by the officers, had been wiped because of the negligent failure of the relevant council official to require it to be preserved.

It was the defendant's case that the film might well do more, or perhaps less, than corroborate **7.60** the council's case. It might, it was argued, support a defendant's case that he was waiting to pick up a booked fare and thought that the council official was the passenger. The Justices, according to the stated case, concluded that 'the CCTV evidence was crucial as to whether the drivers had been aware or not that the fares had not been pre booked …' and that 'the

---

[47] [2015] EWHC 2211 (Admin).
[48] [2015] EWHC 48 (Admin).
[49] [2005] EWHC 841 (Admin), No CO/6696/2004.

investigation procedure was fundamentally flawed in its failure to gather the appropriate evidence.' They accordingly stayed the proceedings for abuse of process.

7.61 In allowing the council's appeal, Lord Justice Sedley observed[50] that:

> The council was in a perfectly good position to proceed on the evidence of the investigating officers and other material documentary evidence. They did not require the CCTV film in order to prove their case. If the film had been kept it would, of course, have been the council's duty to disclose it. If it had been deliberately wiped to conceal evidence inconsistent with the council's case that would be a clear instance of abuse, but nothing of the kind was suggested here.

> This apart, they were, as it seems to me, under no independent obligation to furnish a CCTV film of their operation as part of their case. How they presented their case was a matter for them, and whether it would stand up was, in due course, to be a matter for the justices. The loss of film undoubtedly was a serious blunder from the council's own point of view, but I am unable to accept that it was, in any sense going to abuse of process, a fundamental flaw in the case presented to the court.

7.62 In considering *R v Feltham Magistrates' Court ex p Ebrahim*, Lord Justice Sedley stated[51] that:

> Here there cannot be said to have been any breach of the rules or guidelines governing the gathering of evidence. It follows, as the court said in Ebrahim, that absent some duty to obtain or retain the CCTV film there can have been no suggestion of the subsequent trial being unfair on this ground.

Lord Justice Sedley went on to state:[52]

> The absence of the CCTV film was, in my judgment, not a legitimate foundation for the finding of abuse made by the justices. Either the evidence of the council officials would make the case against each defendant or it would not. In the absence of any suggestion that the film had been deliberately suppressed, the defendants had no special entitlement to rely on it.

Eye witnesses

7.63 The *Aylesbury* decision was cited in argument in *R.(Environmental Agency) v Drake*[53] highlighting the discretion that prosecutors enjoy as to how they present their case in court. In *Drake*, the Environment Agency brought a prosecution for polluting a river contrary to sections 85 and 90 of the Water Resources Act 1981. The District Judge stayed two charges because, although the prosecuting agency had taken water samples of the river, it had destroyed them after they had been considered by scientists, prior to trial. The prosecution therefore decided on the day of trial to rely instead not on the scientific evidence of water samples, but instead on DVD footage, photographs, and eye witnesses of the river pollution. The Administrative Court allowed the Environment Agency's appeal, by way of case stated, as the prosecution's late decision not to rely upon scientific evidence did not prejudice the defendant as the case against him had never been put on that basis alone. It was not necessary for the prosecution to prove the actual polluting matter which was poisonous or noxious but that the defendant had polluted the waterway river. There was ample evidence of pollution by way of DVD footage, photographs and eye witness testimony of agency officers. The samples that had been destroyed were merely corroborative of other pollutant evidence.

---

[50] [2005] EWHC 841 (Admin) at para 6 of the judgment, No CO/6696/2004.
[51] [2005] EWHC 841 (Admin) at para 10 of the judgment, No CO/6696/2004.
[52] [2005] EWHC 841 (Admin) at para 17 of the judgment, No CO/6696/2004.
[53] [2009] EWHC 1344 (Admin); [2010] Env LR 3.

Eye witness evidence was also preferred to blood sample evidence in *Jason Bolger*.[54] The Court **7.64** of Appeal upholding the safety of a murder conviction outside a public house, witnessed by a number of people. An examination by a police surgeon of the applicant did not reveal that the applicant was under the influence of alcohol. The applicant had drunk lager and whiskey. The deceased had given the applicant some pills. A toxicologist gave evidence that a sample taken from the applicant revealed there was no trace of alcohol in his blood, but low traces of Benzodiazpine and that the delay in supplying the applicant's blood meant that it was not possible to comment as to whether or not he might have been intoxicated through the use of alcohol or drugs when the killing occurred.

The applicant gave evidence that he had suffered a complete loss of memory in relation to the **7.65** activities which gave rise to the deceased's death. The applicant sought leave to appeal the conviction, inter alia, on the basis that the trial judge should have stayed proceedings as an abuse of process. The twelve-hour delay in taking a blood sample from the applicant had prejudiced his defence. There was inertia, amounting to negligence on the part of the investigative team. The Court of Appeal refused leave to appeal the conviction. The trial judge's ruling on the abuse application included a reference to the eye witness evidence. The weight which was to be attributed to the eye witness evidence was preeminently a matter for the learned judge in the exercise of his discretion. The learned judge did not misdirect himself.

Expert examination

The loss of the opportunity to examine evidence by an expert may give rise to an abuse of pro- **7.66** cess application. In *Beckford*,[55] the Court of Appeal dismissed an appeal against conviction for causing death by careless driving. Police officers at the scene of the crash gave instructions for the removal of the appellant's motor vehicle. The car was inspected by two police specialist investigators and scrapped before a defence expert was able to examine it. An abuse of process application was made on the ground that examination of the car might have provided vital evidence for the defence. This submission was rejected by the trial judge. His ruling was upheld by the Court of Appeal on the particular facts of the case. The absence of the car did not affect the fairness of the trial.[56]

In *Howell and Howell*,[57] the appellants were convicted of causing death by dangerous driving **7.67** and attempting to pervert the course of justice. At trial both appellants stated that the person who died in the car crash had been driving. Scientific evidence called by the prosecution pointed to one of the appellant's being the driver, leading to the perverting count. A defence expert carried out an accident reconstruction, prior to the car being scrapped. The prosecution disclosed their expert's working notes to the defence. The day before the trial the defence expert realized the possible evidential significance of the fibres on the front passenger door and an immediate request was made to examine the car. At trial the prosecution expert gave evidence that the fibres evidence pointed to one of the appellant's being the driver, not the deceased. The defence applied to stay proceedings as an abuse of process on the basis that the destruction of the vehicle constituted a breach of Code B under CPIA1996, Pt 2. The defence argued they were prevented from (a) examining the front passenger door in order to determine who the driver was at the time of the accident and (b) from exploring the deficiencies in the prosecution's evidence. The trial judge rejected the submission observing

---

[54] 11 February 2000, No 99/1522/Y2.
[55] [1996] 1 Cr App R 94.
[56] *Beckford* was followed in *Thind*, 27 July 1999, CA, No 98/7242/Y2 and *Amjad Ahmed Khan*, 14 March 2000, CA, No 99/4824/Z2, 99/4825/Z2; (2007) 171 JPN 556 at page 5, where samples of a chicken donor kebab had decayed prior to trial on a Food Safety Act 1990 matter.
[57] [2001] EWCA Crim 3009.

that although a thorough examination of the car would have been useful, the absence of the vehicle was not significant and that on a balance of probabilities the defendants would have a fair trial.

7.68 In dismissing the appeal, the Court of Appeal held that if there had been any prejudice from the destruction of the vehicle it did not prevent a fair trial. There was substantial expert evidence called and the judge had directed the jury carefully on the matter. If the prosecution was at fault for not preserving the car, such fault was minimal. Considering the other evidence, which pointed to the identity of the driver, the Court of Appeal was satisfied that the safety of the convictions could not be questioned.

7.69 In *DPP v Martin Cooper*,[58] Magistrates stayed proceedings charging possession of diamorphine where the video of the Prosecution forensic drugs expert carrying out examination of banknotes had been destroyed prior to trial. The examination process (by spraying a chemical on the banknotes) meant that the Defence were unable to carry out their own independent forensic testing. The CPS succeeded in appealing the Magistrates' Court decision by way of case stated. The Administrative Court accepted that the loss of the expert examination video and the spraying of the banknotes hindered the defence case. However, the defence still had adequate means to challenge the prosecution case by cross-examination of the prosecution expert witness. In addition, the Magistrates would have been able to make adequate allowance for the fact that the defendant had not been able to see a video of the forensic testing of the banknotes or to carry out a defence examination of the banknotes. Further, if the matter had been before a jury, the trial judge could have explained to the jury that the defendant had been deprived of the opportunity of carrying out the tests and seeing how the prosecution expert had in fact carried out their tests. The trial judge would have directed the jury to bear this in mind as an important factor in the defendant's favour when considering his guilt. Such a direction would have compensated the defendant adequately for the fact that the video was no longer available and tests could not be carried out on the banknotes.[59]

Non-original evidence

7.70 In *McNamara*,[60] the defendant was charged with possession with intent to supply cannabis. As a result of poor exhibit management, the police lost Book 101, a pro forma search record of the premises. The Court of Appeal dismissed the appeal and held that the said loss did not amount to an abuse of process. It ruled that the book 101 was not original evidence and its loss was only detrimental to the prosecution.

I. Judicial Inquiry

7.71 Judicial inquiry into the loss and destruction of evidence is difficult. This was recognized by the US Supreme Court in *California v Trombetta*, which observed:[61]

> The absence of doctrinal development in this area reflects, in part, the difficulty of developing rules to deal with evidence destroyed through prosecutorial neglect or oversight. Whenever potentially exculpatory evidence is permanently lost, courts face the treacherous

---

58 [2008] EWHC 507 (Admin).
59 [2008] EWHC 507 (Admin) at para 9 Justice Silber judgment.
60 [1998] Crim LR 278.
61 467 US 479 at 486; 81 L Ed 2d 413; 104 S Ct 2528 (1984).

task of divining the import of materials whose contents are unknown and, very often, disputed.

7.72 This difficulty has also been recognized by Professor Spencer, in the commentary to *Medway*[62] when he states;

> When the evidence has gone missing, there is no means of knowing what difference it would have made. Even if the police officer who viewed the tape acted in perfect good faith, he may have been mistaken. He may have missed something which would have weakened the prosecution's case—just as he may have missed something that would have strengthened it. Presumably, the court has to assess how likely it is that the particular evidence would have made a difference. Since there must always, or almost always, be a possibility, a stay will be refused where that possibility is remote.

7.73 However, such judicial inquiry must be made to ensure the right to a fair trial.

J. Summary

7.74 The following summary of principles can be derived from case law on the non-availability of evidence:

(1) the leading authority in the area is *R v Feltham Magistrates' Court ex p Ebrahim, Mouat v DPP*.[63] Proceedings are stayed if the behaviour of the prosecution is so bad—in terms of bad faith or serious fault—that it would be unfair to try the defendant.

(2) Before a case is stayed for loss of evidence there has to be evidence of bad faith or serious fault on the part of the investigative team: *Swingler*.[64]

(3) Investigative failures which lead to the loss of evidence or loss of opportunity to gather evidence may amount to an abuse of process: *Gajree*.[65]

(4) Courts afford prosecuting authorities a great deal of discretion and flexibility as to what physical articles they have to retain: *Parker*[66]; *Clay v South Cambridgeshire Justices*.[67]

(5) Courts allow the prosecution to replace the loss of primary evidence with alternative means of proving a case: photographs (*R v Uxbridge Justices ex p Sofaer*,[68] *Hilliers Ltd v Sefton Metropolitan Borough Council*,[69] *Derek Barron*[70]); police witnesses (*Roberts v DPP*,[71] *Jamie Morris v DPP*,[72] *DPP v Petrie*,[73] *DPP v Spalluto*[74]); investigating officers (*Aylesbury Vale District Council v Basharat Khan*[75]); and non-original evidence (*McNamara*[76]).

---

[62] [2000] Crim LR 415.

[63] [2001] 1 All ER 831, [2001] 2 Cr App R 23. Ebrahim has been followed and cited as persuasive authority in other jurisdictions see for example the Isle of Man decision in *AG v Tomlinson* [2010] Crim 59, Court of General Gaol Delivery judgment date 20th April 2011 www.judgments.im/content/J1133.htm.

[64] 10 July 1998, CA.

[65] 20 September 1994, No 94/3269/Y2.

[66] [2002] 2 Cr App R (S) 58; [2003] EWCA Crim 90; case comment at Archbold News 2003, 3, p 1.

[67] [2014] EWHC 321 (Admin); [2015] RTR 1.

[68] (1987) 85 Cr App R 367.

[69] CO/2165/96, (2007) 171 JPN 556 at p 4.

[70] [2010] EWCA Crim 2950.

[71] [2008] EWHC 643.

[72] [2008] EWHC 2788 (Admin).

[73] [2015] EWHC 48 (Admin).

[74] [2015] EWHC 2211 (Admin).

[75] [2005] EWHC 841 (Admin), No CO/6696/2004.

[76] [1998] Crim LR 278.

8

UNFAIR CONDUCT AND ABUSE
OF EXECUTIVE POWER

A. Introduction

8.1 It is clear that the power to ensure that there is a fair trial according to law (category one abuse) does not exhaust the abuse of process jurisdiction. The courts also have a duty to protect and promote the dignity and integrity of the criminal justice process and judicial system (category two abuse).[1] Such cases run the risk of tarnishing the court's process. In this second category of case, the court is concerned to protect the integrity of the criminal justice system.[2]

The leading case in this area is *R v Horseferry Road Magistrates' Court, ex p Bennett*.[3] Lord Lowry observed: **8.2**

> I consider that a court has a discretion to stay any criminal proceedings on the grounds that to try those proceedings will amount to an abuse of its own process either (1) because it will be impossible (usually by reason of delay) to give the accused a fair trial or (2) because it offends the court's sense of justice and propriety to be asked to try the accused in the circumstances of a particular case.[4]

Lord Griffiths[5] made it clear that, in the circumstances of that case, there was no suggestion that the appellant could not have had a fair trial. Further, it was not suggested that it would have been unfair to try him if he had been returned to the country through the proper extradition procedures. **8.3**

Lord Griffiths stated: **8.4**

> If the court is to have the power to interfere with the prosecution in the present circumstances, it must be because the judiciary accept the responsibility for the maintenance of the rule of law that embraces a willingness to oversee executive action and to refuse to countenance behaviour that threatens either basic human rights or the rule of law. I have no doubt that the judiciary should accept this responsibility in the field of criminal law.

Lord Griffiths further observed: **8.5**

> The courts have no power to apply direct discipline to the police or the prosecuting authorities, but they can refuse to allow them to take advantage of abuse of power by regarding their behaviour as an abuse of process and thus preventing a prosecution.[6]

The House of Lords decision in *Bennett* confirms the fundamental importance to be attached to the protection and promotion of the dignity and integrity of the judicial system. Lord Bridge[7] cited with approval the decision of the South African Court of Appeal in *S v Ebrahim*,[8] allowing an appeal on the grounds that the appellant had been abducted from outside the jurisdiction. **8.6**

The decision resulted from the application of 'fundamental legal principles ... human rights ... the sound administration of justice ... the fairness of the legal process guaranteed and the abuse thereof to be prevented so as to protect and promote the dignity and integrity of the judicial system. The State was bound by these rules and had to come to court with clean hands.'[9] **8.7**

---

[1] The two categories of abuse classification have also been adopted in other jurisdictions: see Canadian decisions in *O'Connor* [1995] 4 SCR 411 at [73], *Olga Nixon* [2011] 2 SCR 566, *Antal Babos* [2014] 1 RSC 309, and *Nur* 2015 SCC 15; and New Zealand decisions in *Fox v Attorney-General* [2002] NZCA 158, [2002] 3 NZLR 62 (CA), *Max John Beckham v The Queen* [2015] NZSC 98, *McGurk v R* [2015] NZCA 148, and *Trevor John Wilson v The Queen* [2015] NZSC 189.

[2] As highlighted by Lord Kerr's observations at [84] of the *Warren* judgment [2011] UKPC 10, [2012] 1 A.C. 22: 'second category cases (are) based on the primary consideration of whether the stay is necessary to protect the integrity of the criminal justice system'.

[3] [1994] AC 42, [1994] 98 Cr App R 114.

[4] [1994] AC 42 [72G].

[5] [1994] AC 62 [61].

[6] [1994] AC 62 [62].

[7] [1994] AC 62 [65C].

[8] 1991 (2) SA 553.

[9] See also *United States v Toscanino* (1974) 500 F 2ed 267 and *Hartley* [1978] 2 NZLR 199—Australian police, at the request of the New Zealand police, had illegally arrested an accused wanted in New Zealand for murder and placed him on an aircraft returning to New Zealand.

8.8 The approach of the courts to category two cases is usefully summarized by Professor Andrew Choo in *Abuse of Process and Judicial Stays of Criminal Proceedings*[10] as follows:

> The courts would appear to have left the matter at a general level, requiring a determination to be made in particular cases of whether the continuation of the proceedings would compromise the moral integrity of the criminal justice system to an unacceptable degree. Implicitly at least, this determination involves performing a 'balancing' test that takes into account such factors as the seriousness of any violation of the defendant's (or even a third party's) rights; whether the police have acted in bad faith or maliciously, or with an improper motive; whether the misconduct was committed in circumstances of urgency, emergency or necessity; the availability or otherwise of a direct sanction against the person(s) responsible for the misconduct; and the seriousness of the offence with which the defendant is charged.

8.9 The overarching question for the court in category two cases will be whether a stay is necessary to maintain public confidence in the integrity of the criminal justice system.

8.10 An infinite variety of cases can arise and the way in which the discretion to stay proceedings should be exercised will depend on the particular circumstances of the case.[11]

8.11 Courts have repeatedly made clear that the power to stay is 'not available for disciplinary purposes.'[12]

8.12 The court's supervisory jurisdiction where misconduct by a prosecutor threatens the integrity of the criminal process was considered in *Curtis Francis Warren and others v Her Majesty's Attorney General for the Bailiwick of Jersey*[13] by the Privy Council.

8.13 *Warren* involved serious prosecutorial misconduct on the part of the police.[14] State authorities were in Jersey and three other jurisdictions. The police falsely claimed the audio devices they fitted were mere tracking devices, as the French and Dutch authorities had refused permission for audio monitoring. Without the product of the unlawful activity of the police there would have been no trial, as the evidence obtained by the audio devices was crucial to the prosecution's case.

8.14 The Privy Council stressed, in the judgment of Lord Dyson, that:

> ... the balance must always be struck between the public interest in ensuring that those who are accused of serious crimes should be tried and the competing public interest in ensuring that executive misconduct does not undermine public confidence in the criminal justice system and bring it into disrepute.[15]

---

[10] Andrew Choo, *Abuse of Process and Judicial Stays of Criminal Proceedings* (Oxford: OUP, 2008), 132. This summary was cited and approved by Lord Dyson in *Warren* at [24] and [25].

[11] A point highlighted by Lord Dyson in *Warren* [2011] UKPC 10, [2012] 1 AC 22 at [26].

[12] See for example *Fox v Attorney-General* [2002] 3 NZLR 62(CA); *Antonievic* [2013] NZCA 483; *Trevor John Wilson v The Queen* [2015] NZSC 189.

[13] [2011] UKPC 10, [2012] 1 AC 22; case comment at Archbold Review 2011, 6, [6]–[9]. See also Hong Kong Court of Appeal decision in *Hong Kong v Ng Chun To Raymond* [2013] HKCA 380 and Canadian Supreme Court decision in *Nixon* [2011] 2 SCR 566, SCC 34 (as discussed in Journal of Commonwealth Criminal Law 2011, 2, 333–44).

[14] As Lord Dyson stated at [45] 'The police were unquestionably guilty of grave prosecutorial misconduct in this case. They acted in the knowledge that the Attorney General and the Chief of Jersey police had not given authority to install the audio device without the consent of the relevant foreign authorities and would not do so; and that the foreign authorities had refused their consent.' Lord Hope described the law-breaking by the police at paragraph 63 of the judgment as 'sustained, deliberate and cynical'.

[15] [2011] UKPC 10 [26] (Lord Dyson).

This passage of Lord Dyson's judgment was cited with approval by Mr. Justice O'Regan in the **8.15** Supreme Court of New Zealand's decision in *Max John Beckham v The Queen*.[16] The *Warren* approach was approved by Mr. Justice O'Regan as being appropriately nuanced, 'taking into account a number of factors such as seriousness of the violation of the defendant's rights, the presence or absence of bad faith, whether there was any emergency or necessity for the conduct, other available sanctions, the seriousness of the charges and the causal link between the conduct and the trial or proposed trial'.[17]

The last of those factors, i.e. a causal link, did not in the opinion of Lord Dyson in *Warren*,[18] always **8.16** or even in most cases necessarily determine whether a stay would be granted on the grounds of abuse of process. Further, the existence of such a causal link is not a pre-condition for a stay.[19]

In dismissing the appeal in *Warren,* the Privy Council considered the following factors: **8.17**

- The seriousness of the charge faced (conspiracy to import 180 kilos of cannabis valued in excess of £1 million) and Mr Warren being a professional drug dealer were factors which entitled a stay to be refused.
- Advice which was obtained from a senior member of the Law Officers' Department in Jersey that, despite the refusal of the foreign authorities to allow audio monitoring, he did not believe that a Jersey court would exclude the evidence.
- There was no attempt to mislead or deceive the Jersey court.
- The police were faced with a fast moving situation which required real urgency.

The Privy Council in *Warren* did say that it would have been open to the Commissioner to **8.18** stay the proceedings as an abuse. However, the decision not to grant a stay was not perverse, nor one which no reasonable judge could have reached.

Finally, the Privy Council went on to stress its condemnation of the police misconduct which **8.19** had taken place in this case and described it as 'a sustained and deliberate act of law breaking' and further future repetition of such behaviour may well tip the balance in favour of a Court granting a stay.

A rigid categorization of the factors to consider when deciding whether to grant a stay **8.20** is undesirable.[20] As stated in *Beckham*,[21] a fact-senstive balancing exercise is to be taken. The factors identified by the Privy Council in *Warren*[22] will often be relevant, but are not exhaustive or necessarily determinative. Each case will turn on the balance of its own circumstances.

Category two cases

It is possible to identify a number of different legal and factual situations within the category **8.21** two type of abuse case (i.e. unfair conduct, abuse of executive power, protecting the integrity of the court).

---

[16] [2015] NZSC 98 [142].
[17] [2015] NZSC 98 [142].
[18] [2011] UKPC 10 [30] (Lord Dyson). Lord Dyson, went on at [36], to make clear that the Court of Appeal's decision in *Grant* was wrong as it had placed too much weight on the gravity of the police misconduct and insufficient weight on the linkage between the misconduct and the trial. Lord Dyson noted, at [36], that the 'but for' factor had no part to play in *Grant* and the misconduct had not influenced the proceedings at all.
[19] As recognized in *Antonievic* by Mr. Justice O'Regan at para 96.
[20] See *Antonievic* [2013] NZCA 483 judgment of Mr. Justice O'Regan at para 57.
[21] *Beckham v R* [2012] NZCA 603 at [60]–[71].
[22] *Warren v Attorney-General for Jersey* [2011] UKPC 10, [2012] 1 AC 22.

B. Rule of Law

State kidnapping

8.22 The House of Lords in *Bennett*[23] recognized the importance of upholding the rule of law, as highlighted by the judgment of Lord Griffiths:[24]

> ... the judiciary accept the responsibility for the maintenance of the rule of law that embraces a willingness to oversee executive action and to refuse to countenance behaviour that threatens either basic human rights or the rule of law to protect and promote the dignity and integrity of the judicial court system.

8.23 In *Bennett* the House of Lords was dealing with a spectacular situation. It held that the Divisional Court had wrongly decided it had no power to inquire into the circumstances under which an accused had been brought into the jurisdiction. A New Zealand citizen, who had allegedly committed offences in England, was forcibly returned to England from the Republic of South Africa by English police, in disregard of an available extradition process and in breach of international law. The House of Lords held that in the exercise of the High Court's supervisory jurisdiction it should inquire into the circumstances of the accused's return and if appropriate stay the prosecution as an abuse of process.

Torture

8.24 This adherence to the rule of law also extends to the admissibility of evidence. In *A and Others v Secretary of State for the Home Department*,[25] the House of Lords accepted arguments that obtaining evidence by torture was such a serious breach of international standards. The admission of the evidence would, regardless of its reliability, degrade the administration of justice. In such circumstances, the House of Lords agreed that it would be appropriate for a court to exercise its discretion to exclude the evidence as its admission would constitute an abuse of the process of the court. Lord Hoffmann observed:[26]

> ... the courts will not shut their eyes to the way the accused was brought before the court or the evidence of his guilt was obtained. Those methods may be such that it would compromise the integrity of the judicial process, dishonour the administration of justice, if the proceedings were to be entertained or the evidence admitted. In such a case the proceedings may be stayed or the evidence rejected on the ground that there would otherwise be an abuse of the processes of the court.

Rule of law observed

8.25 Where the rule of law is observed proceedings will not be stayed as a category two abuse.

8.26 In *R v Staines Magistrates' Court ex p Westfallen*[27] proceedings were not stayed for an abuse of process as the state had not procured, influenced, or colluded in either the decision of a foreign state or a third country via this country. Further, there had been no illegality, abuse, or violation of international law, nor of the domestic law of the foreign country concerned upon which a stay application could be founded.

---

[23] [1994] AC 42.
[24] [1994] AC 42 [61].
[25] [2005] UKHL 71, [2006] 2 AC 221. See also *Rangzieb Ahmed* [2011] EWCA Crim 184; [2011] Crim LR 734; Archbold Review [2011] 3, 4–5 in which a prosecution for membership of a proscribed organization was deemed by the Court of Appeal not to be an abuse of process as the British authorities had not been complicit in the appellant's torture in Pakistan, nor had the torture produced any evidential trial material.
[26] [2005] UKHL 71 [87].
[27] [1998] 1 WLR 652, DC.

In *R v Swindon Magistrates' Court ex p Nangle*[28] the defendant complained that he had been **8.27** brought into the UK by improper state-disguised extradition. On the facts of *Nangle* there was no abuse. The British authorities had not influenced the Canadian government to deport the applicant nor the choice of route, through Glasgow airport en-route to Ireland. There was neither illegality nor violation of international or domestic law. Proceedings were not stayed.

Lord Chief Justice Bingham, considered the test to be followed by the court as follows:

> The question in each of these cases is whether it appears that the police or the prosecuting authorities have acted illegally or procured or connived at unlawful procedures or violated international law or the domestic law of foreign states or abused their powers in a way that should lead this court to stay the proceedings against the applicant.[29]

Unlawful deportation

Contrast the situation in *Nicholas Mullen*.[30] The Court of Appeal quashed a conviction for **8.28** conspiracy to cause explosions as unsafe because of pre-trial abuse. The grounds of appeal relied solely upon the circumstances of Mullen's deportation from Zimbabwe to England prior to his trial. No complaint was made about the conduct of the actual trial. No trial should have taken place. The behaviour of the British security services and police in procuring the deportation of the appellant by unlawful means was, in view of the court, a blatant and extremely serious failure to adhere to the rule of law with regard to the production of a defendant in the English courts. But for the unlawful manner of his deportation, Mullen would not have been in this country to be prosecuted.

In the exercise of their Lordships' discretion, great weight had to be attached to the nature **8.29** of the offence alleged, as against the misconduct of the British authorities and the encouragement of voluntary pre-trial disclosure of material and information by the prosecution relevant to the defence. The trial was preceded by an abuse of process which, had it come to light at the time, as it would have done had the prosecution made the appropriate voluntary disclosure, would properly have justified the proceedings then being stayed. In each case, it was a matter of discretionary balance with particular regard to the specific state misconduct complained of and the actual offence charged.

Ignorance of the Law

Courts will uphold the rule of law and, as a general rule, reject abuse of process arguments **8.30** based on 'ignorance of the law'. In *Christian*,[31] six men charged with sex crimes, under the Sexual Offences Act 1956, in the British Overseas Territory of Pitcairn Island, had argued that the sex involved was consensual, against a cultural background according to which girls as young as twelve years old could expect to be engaging in sex with older boys and men. Under-age sex was common on Pitcairn Island. Convictions followed.

The appellants argued at the Privy Council that proceedings should have been stayed as an **8.31** abuse of process because the men were unaware and ignorant of the Sexual Offences Act 1956. The Pitcairn islanders argued that the earlier administrative failures, specifically the

---

[28] [1998] 4 All ER 210.

[29] [1998] 4 All ER 210 [222].

[30] [2000] QB 520. For a similar result, see High Court of Australia decision in *Julian Roland Moti v R* [2011] HCA 50.

[31] [2006] UKPC 47, [2007] 2 A.C.400; see also H Power 'Pitcairn Island: Sexual Offending, Cultural Differences and Ignorance of the Law' [2007] Crim LR 609 and F Wright 'Legality and Reality: Some Lessons from the Pitcairn Islands' [2009] JoCL (69).

failure to publicize the law and the colonial neglect of the islands (with no English police presence) meant it was an abuse of process to prosecute them now for breaches of colonial law.

8.32   The Privy Council accepted that 'the fact that a law had not been published and could not reasonably have been known to exist may be a ground for staying a prosecution for contravention of that law as an abuse of process'.[32]

8.33   The 'ignorance of the law' abuse submission was rejected by the Privy Council on the facts of the appeal.

8.34   It was accepted that English law was never published on Pitcairn and implicitly accepted that the islanders had no knowledge of the minutiate of sexual offences law. Nevertheless, the appeal court concluded that:[33]

> At all relevant times Pitcairn was a developed society in which rape and various sexual offending were known to be criminal ... Pitcairn was left in no doubt that if there was any matter not covered by the law of Pitcairn, the law of England could be invoked.

8.35   Further, all Pitcairn Islanders had access to the law, through the legal advice available at the governor's office. Lord Woolf regarded this fact as being of the greatest significance:

> The criminal law can only operate on Pitcairn, as elsewhere, if the onus is firmly placed on a person, who is or ought to be on notice that conduct he is intending to embark on may contravene the law, to take the action that is open to find out what are the provisions of the law.[34]

8.36   Accordingly the Privy Council decided that the appellants were aware that their conduct was contrary to the criminal law. That being so the prosecution did not prejudice the appellants in any way. The Pitcairn courts were right not to stay proceedings as an abuse of process.

Disregard for international law

8.37   Disregard of international law by domestic agencies may lead to a stay in proceedings. In *Carrington*,[35] His Honour Judge Foley, stayed drug trafficking proceedings involving the interception of a boat containing cannabis in international waters. HM Customs had made false representations as to the location of the boat to obtain the consent of the Maltese Attorney General to board the boat. Maltese witnesses had confirmed that they would not have given consent had they known of the true location.

8.38   HHJ Foley held that the behaviour of HM Customs was shameful:

> ... this case has revealed a culture, a climate, of carelessness and recklessness for disregard for the rules of procedures, convention of Maltese law, British law and International law ... this court cannot abdicate its judicial responsibility. It gives me no pleasure, the case for a stay is overwhelming, there was mala fides here'.

Abuse of executive authority

8.39   In *Doran*,[36] the retrial judge, Mr Justice Turner stayed an indictment as the conduct of HM Customs officers had struck at the rule of law. Customs had deliberately misled the judge at the first trial and the defence on two factual issues: the failure of Customs to obtain the consent of hotel management when bugging hotel rooms and their failure to follow internal

---

[32] [2006] UKPC 47 [24] (Lord Hoffman). See also Lord Woolf at [44].
[33] [2006] UKPC 47 [108].
[34] [2006] UKPC 47 [41].
[35] (February 1999).
[36] (6 July 1999) [43].

surveillance authorization procedures. To conceal these facts the officers had allegedly created a trail of false paperwork. This meant that the defence was:

> ... deprived of a point which they were entitled to make as part of a broad attack on the character of the conduct of the investigation.

Mr Justice Turner continued: **8.40**

> By abuse of executive authority, the prosecution, viewed as a single entity, have, by means which are at least arguably unlawful, deprived the defence of its strategic ability to mount the challenge to the integrity of the prosecution case ... What has happened has had a significant impact on the ability of the defendants to defend themselves, and to that extent, and as a matter of probability, they have been seriously prejudiced in the conduct of their defence.[37]

C. Investigative Failures

Once a suspect is apprehended, the manner of the investigation may give rise to an abuse of **8.41** process, in terms of the interview process, the collection and investigation of evidence, and consideration of lines of enquiry which point towards and away from the suspect.

No interview

In *Trustham*,[38] money laundering proceedings were stayed, as the defendant after arrest, was **8.42** charged but not interviewed. This prejudiced the defendant in two ways. First, a defendant who does not give evidence having answered questions in interview is nevertheless entitled to have the interview explanation considered by the jury. Second, to deprive the suspect of the right to give an explanation at the earliest opportunity, despite having been cautioned, is a breach of a person's human rights.

Cumulative investigative failures

In *Northard*,[39] the Court of Appeal quashed the defendant's conviction for robbery. The **8.43** unsatisfactory features of the police investigation had prejudiced the preparation of the defendant's case in that:

(a) His alibi had not been investigated.
(b) No identification parade had been held, despite the defendant initially agreeing to stand on one. After the defendant withdrew his consent the police did not attempt any other method of identification, such as the showing of photographs or a group identification or confrontation.
(c) The police failed to investigate the defendant's assertion that the car he had borrowed from a friend (and used in the robbery) had been stolen at the time of the offence (albeit reported as stolen to the police post-offence). The police did not have the car inspected by an expert, which may have thrown light on whether the car had been stolen; and
(d) The existence of relevant video film footage (of shop CCTV cameras, which could have supported the defendant's alibi) had not been disclosed to the defence nor was it available at trial (as the shopping centre video tape was re-used after twenty-eight days).

---

[37] See also the related case report at *Togher, Doran and Parsons* [2000] Crim LR 783.
[38] (Southwark Crown Court, 27 November 1997).
[39] (CA, 19 February 1996). See *Archbold* Criminal Appeal Office, 1997, [T–4].

8.44 Cumulatively, the failures precluded a fair trial. In the words of Lord Justice Auld:[40]

> ... the result of it all is, we believe, an accumulation of lost opportunities to the defence to vouch for the alibi, if a true one. Whilst we are satisfied that there was no bad faith on the part of the police officers concerned, we are left in real doubt, as a result of these deficiencies, about the safety of the verdict. In our view, the judge should have stayed the prosecution as an abuse of process, or, failing that, he should have withdrawn the matter from the jury when the same evidence going to the deficiencies was called before them. Accordingly, for those reasons, we allow this appeal.

8.45 A re-trial was not ordered as the Court of Appeal were of the view that the defective investigation would also plague a re-trial.

D. Discretion to Prosecute

8.46 The delivery of basic justice relies on prosecutors and other state agencies exercising their discretion sensibly. This covers the discretion to prosecute, as discussed in the CPS Code for Crown Prosecutors. Courts have recognized that prosecutors have a wide discretion to prosecute, with which courts are reluctant to interfere.[41]

8.47 Courts will not interfere with the decision to prosecute a case unless it can be shown that there was insufficient evidence upon which a person prosecuted could properly have been convicted and/or prosecution policies were not adhered to.[42]

Alternative disposals

8.48 In relation to general application and policy, it is not in the public interest to pursue criminal proceedings if the Crown Prosecution Service and a suspect are prepared to dispose of a case by way of an alternative disposal. The issue of prosecuting or cautioning will now be examined.

Prosecute or caution

8.49 The prosecution has an ongoing duty to keep a case under review in accordance with their public interest criteria, which may involve defence lawyers making representations to the police and CPS that a caution is the suitable means of disposal. In terms of autrefois convict or acquit, a caution is not a conviction. Where, however, criminal conduct has been the subject of an agreed caution, Lord Justice Stanley Burnton, in *DPP v Alexander*,[43] observed:

> ... in the absence of good reason for it to be the subject of a subsequent prosecution, such a prosecution will generally constitute an abuse of the process of the court. Information or evidence[44] obtained subsequent to a caution, such as details of injury to a victim significantly exceeding what had previously been known would generally constitute a good reason.

---

[40] *Northard* (CA, 19 Feburary 1996) [12D].

[41] See *R v DPP Ex p. Kebelene* [2000] 2 AC 326; *R (on the application of Pepushi) v CPS* [2004] EWHC 798 (Admin); *Sharma v Brown-Antoine* [2006] UKPC 57; *A* [2012] EWCA Crim 434, [2012] 2 Cr App R. 8; *Moss & Sons Ltd v CPS* [2012] EWHC 3658. (Admin) and *R.(on the application of Barons Pub Company Limited) v Staines Magistrates' Court* [2013] EWHC 898 (Admin).

[42] See *Ideal Waste Paper Co. Ltd* [2011] EWCA Crim 3237 in which the Court of Appeal refused to interfere with a first instance preparatory ruling that despite the extreme difficulty in setting out a precise the definition of household waste for Waste Regulations prosecutions, the prosecution did not amount to an abuse of process. The trial judge being able to give sufficient directions to the jury as to whether a particular consignment is properly described as household waste, upon which they can decide as a question of fact.

[43] [2011] 1 WLR 653.

[44] See *G* [2013] EWCA Crim 1492 in which subsequently obtained medical evidence led to a prosecution for a more serious offence than the one for which a caution had initially been agreed.

Private prosecution

In *Hayter v L*,[45] the defendants, having received legal advice, admitted their involvement in **8.50** offences and signed a form indicating that a caution did not preclude the bringing of proceedings against them by an aggrieved party. The substantive matter raised in the Divisional Court was whether in the circumstances it was an abuse of the process for a private prosecution to be launched subsequent to the caution by someone with an interest in what had happened. It was not an abuse. The Divisional Court were not prepared to limit a private individual's right to pursue a private prosecution.

In *Jones v Whalley*,[46] the Divisional Court decided that a private prosecution, subsequent **8.51** to an offender's admission of guilt in exchange for a police caution, was not necessarily an abuse of process. The caution form signed by the offender should have contained a proviso that the caution did not prevent the bringing of a private prosecution by the aggrieved party. The absence of such a proviso was not sufficient to render the right of a private prosecution an abuse of process.

Victim consultation

Likewise the Divisional Court in *R (on the application of Omar) v Chief Constable of* **8.52** *Bedfordshire Police*[47] considered whether the prosecution of a person for an offence for which they had been cautioned was an abuse of process.

In *Omar*, the suspect was formally cautioned by the police, without consulting the vic- **8.53** tim about the case disposal. The victim judicially reviewed the caution decision. The Administrative Court quashed the decision to caution, as the police had failed (a) to consult the victim without sufficient good cause and (b) to carry out a sufficiently comprehensive investigation.

Conditional caution

The Divisional Court, in *Guest v DPP*,[48] quashed a decision by the CPS to rely upon a con- **8.54** ditional caution (with £200 compensation payable to the victim) rather than prosecute for assault. The decision not to prosecute was fundamentally flawed in the view of Lord Justice Goldring for a number of reasons:[49]

(1) The assault passed both the evidential and public interest limbs of the Code for Crown Prosecutors. The evidence against the suspect was strong, including admissions. was a serious assault, late at night at a person's home address, involving kicking the victim in the presence of his partner.
(3) Annex A of the DPP's guidance on conditional cautioning did not permit the administration of a conditional caution in such circumstances. It did not permit conditional cautioning for an offence of assault.
(4) Conditional cautioning was not an appropriate and proportionate response to the offending behaviour as required by the guidance.
(5) The victim was not involved in the decision. He did not agree with the decision (although this is not necessarily decisive). Paragraph 5 of Annex B of the Secretary of State's Code contemplates the victim's involvement. Paragraph 11 of the Director's guidance requires

---

[45] [1998] 1 WLR 854.
[46] [2005] EWHC 931, (2005) 169 JP 466 DC; see commentary at Crim LR [2006] 67–69.
[47] [2002] EWHC 3060 Admin, *The Independent* (24 February 2003).
[48] [2009] EWHC 594, [2009] Crim LR 730. See also L Leigh 'Judicial Review and Prosecutorial Discretion' [2009] 5 Archbold News 5. See also *DPP v Alexander* [2010] EWHC 2266 (Admin), [2011] 1 WLR 653 (DC), [2010] 9 Archbold Review 2010 4.
[49] See [42]–[47].

it wherever possible. It also requires consultation where possible on the condition to be imposed as part of the caution.

(6) In light of the injuries suffered by the victim there was only limited consideration of the appropriateness of £200 as compensation. In the circumstances, the decision not to prosecute and to administer a conditional caution was quashed. A further prosecution would not necessarily amount to an affront to public justice.

Sensible prosecuting

8.55 When applying the evidential and policy tests, prosecutors must act sensibly. One area in which the need to exercise sensible prosecuting is paramount involves prosecution decisions relating to victims of human trafficking. The reasoning is not always spelled out. The culpability of any victim of trafficking may be significantly diminished, and in some cases effectively extinguished, not merely because of age factors but because no realistic alternative was available to the exploited victim but to comply with the dominant force of another individual.

Human Trafficking victim cases

8.56 The Court of Appeal have considered the issue of sensible prosecuting in a number of human trafficking victim appeals.

8.57 In *LM, BM and GD*,[50] the Court of Appeal considered the public policy and evidential basis for a prosecution in the context of human trafficking. The Council of Europe Convention on Action against Trafficking Human Beings[51] was identified as imposing specific and positive obligations upon the United Kingdom to combat trafficking and as providing measures to assist victims. Article 26, specifically, provides for the possibility of not imposing penalties on those who have been trafficked victims who are subsequently compelled to engage in unlawful activity, such as offences connected with prostitution and unlawful cannabis factories. Article 26 is implemented in England and Wales, in the words of Lord Justice Hughes:

> [7] … through three mechanisms. First, English law recognises the common law defences of duress and necessity ('duress of circumstances'). Second, specific rules have been made for the guidance of prosecutors in considering whether charges should be brought against those who are or may have been victims of trafficking. Thirdly, in the event that the duty laid on the prosecutor to exercise judgment is not properly discharged, the ultimate sanction is the power of the court to stay the prosecution for what is conveniently, if not very accurately, termed 'abuse of process'.

8.58 CPS guidance requires prosecutors to consider the public interest in prosecuting a 'credible trafficking victim' and not to prosecute where there is credible evidence of duress. This is set out clearly in the guidance:

> Victims of human trafficking may commit offences whilst they are being coerced by another. When reviewing such a case it may come to the notice of the prosecutor that the suspect is a 'credible' trafficked victim. For these purposes 'credible' means that the investigating officers have reason to believe that the person has been trafficked. In these circumstances prosecutors must consider whether the public interest is best served in continuing the prosecution in respect of the offence. Where there is evidence that a suspect is a credible trafficked victim, prosecutors should consider the public interest in proceeding. Where there is clear evidence that the defendant has a credible defence of duress, the case should be discontinued on evidential grounds.

---

[50] [2010] EWCA Crim 2327, [2011] 1 Cr.App.R.12, [2011] Crim LR 425.
[51] Council of Europe, Council of Europe Convention on Action against Trafficking in Human Beings and its Explanatory Report (2005).

Lord Justice Hughes considered the CPS guidance and concluded that: **8.59**

> [10] The effect of that is to require of prosecutors a three-stage exercise of judgment. The first is: (1) is there a reason to believe that the person has been trafficked? If so, then (2) if there is clear evidence of a credible common law defence the case will be discontinued in the ordinary way on evidential grounds, but, importantly, (3) even where there is not, but the offence may have been committed as a result of compulsion arising from the trafficking, prosecutors should consider whether the public interest lies in proceeding to prosecute or not.

Article 26 works at the level of public policy, it does not create a defence or blanket immunity **8.60** from prosecution. It does not say that no trafficked victim should be prosecuted, whatever offence has been committed. Article 26 requires prosecuting authorities to carefully consider whether public policy calls for a prosecution and punishment. Accordingly, the application of Article 26 is fact-sensitive in every case.

Proceedings may be stayed as an abuse of process if the CPS failed properly to exercise their **8.61** discretion (on evidential and policy grounds) or a decision had been reached which no reasonable prosecutor could make.

Lord Justice Hughes helpfully sets this out: **8.62**

> ... the convention obligation is that a prosecuting authority must apply its mind conscientiously to the question of public policy and reach an informed decision ... If, however, this exercise of judgment has not properly been carried out and would or might well have resulted in a decision not to prosecute, then there will be a breach of the convention and hence grounds for a stay. Likewise, if a decision has been reached at which no reasonable prosecutor could arrive, there will be grounds for a stay.

In *NR and Le*,[52] the Lord Chief Justice, Lord Judge, adopted and applied the approach in **8.63** *LM*, summarizing the essential principles:

> [21] ... the implementation of the United Kingdom's Convention obligation is normally achieved by the proper exercise of the long established prosecution discretion which enables the Crown Prosecution Service, however strong the evidence may be, to decide that it would be inappropriate to proceed or to continue with the prosecution of a defendant who is unable to advance duress as a defence but who falls within the protective ambit of Article 26. This requires a judgment to be made by the CPS in the individual case in the light of all the available evidence. The responsibility is vested not in the court but in the prosecuting authority. The court may intervene in an individual case if its process is abused by using the 'ultimate sanction' of a stay of the proceedings. The burden of showing that the process is being or has been abused on the basis of the improper exercise of the prosecutorial discretion rests on the defendant. The limitations on this jurisdiction are clearly underlined in *LM* ... Apart from the specific jurisdiction to stay proceedings where the person is abused, the court may also, if it thinks appropriate in the exercise of its sentencing responsibilities implement the Article 26 obligation in the language of the article itself, by dealing with the defendant in a way which does not constitute punishment by ordering an absolute or a conditional discharge.

The Court of Appeal in *L, T, THN and HVN*[53] gave guidance to courts on the approach to **8.64** be taken towards those who were, or might be, victims of people trafficking, after criminal proceedings against them had begun. The Court considered the decisions in *LM* and *NR* in

---

[52] [2012] EWCA Crim 189, [2012] 1 Cr App R 35, [2013] QB 379; case comment in Crim LR (2012), 958–64; Archbold Review (2012) 3, 3.
[53] [2013] EWCA Crim 991, [2014] 1 All ER 113, [2013] 2 Crr App R 23, [2014] Crim LR 150, discussed in Cambridge Law Journal 2014, 73(1), [11]–[14].

light of the EU Directive 2011/36/EU on Preventing and Combatting Trafficking in Human Beings and Protecting its Victims which came into effect on 6 April 2013. Article 8 makes provision for the non-prosecution or the non-application of penalties to victims echoing Article 26 of the Council of Europe Convention On Action Against Trafficking Human Beings, 2005.

8.65 The Lord Chief Justice made a number of important remarks in giving guidance:

[13] … when there is evidence that victims of trafficking have been involved in criminal activities, the investigation and the decision whether there should be a prosecution, and, if so, any subsequent proceedings require to be approached with the greatest sensitivity. The reasoning is not always spelled out, and perhaps we should do so now. The criminality, or putting it another way, the culpability, of any victim of trafficking may be significantly diminished, and in some cases effectively extinguished, not merely because of age (always a relevant factor in the case of a child defendant) but because no realistic alternative was available to the exploited victim but to comply with the dominant force of another individual, or group of individuals.

[14] In the context of a prosecution of a defendant aged under 18 years of age, the best interests of the victim are not and cannot be the only relevant consideration, but they represent a primary consideration. These defendants are not safeguarded from prosecution or punishment for offences which were unconnected with the fact that they were being or have been trafficked, although we do not overlook that the fact that they have been trafficked may sometimes provide substantial mitigation. What, however, is required in the context of the prosecutorial decision to proceed is a level of protection from prosecution or punishment for trafficked victims who have been compelled to commit criminal offences. These arrangements should follow the 'basic principles' of our legal system. In this jurisdiction that protection is provided by the exercise by the 'abuse of process' jurisdiction.

[17] … In the context of an abuse of process argument on behalf of an alleged victim of trafficking, the court will reach its own decision on the basis of the material advanced in support of and against the continuation of the prosecution. Where a court considers issues relevant to age, trafficking and exploitation, the prosecution will be stayed if the court disagrees with the decision to prosecute …

[19] The question whether a potential defendant has indeed been a victim of trafficking, and the extent to which his ability to resist involvement in criminal activities has been undermined is fact specific. Usually, but not always, the starting point is the moment of arrest. When a young person is arrested the police must consider his age, and in the overwhelming majority of cases it is known or can readily be discovered. Arrangements are then made for attendance at a police station by an appropriate adult. After charge the child is brought before the Youth Court or before an Adult Court if no Youth Court is sitting. Difficulties relating to age are most likely to arise where a young person has entered the United Kingdom illegally, and has no genuine passport or similar identifying documents. When a young person without parents comes to the attention of a local authority (often via the United Kingdom Border Agency (UKBA) as an illegal entrant), the Children Act 1989 imposes a duty on the local authority to determine whether he is a child in need. If so, he is entitled to number of services, including the provision of accommodation. However the first step is to establish the person's age. Since 2003 local authorities have assessed age by a process which complies with the principles set out in *R(B) v London Borough of Merton*[54] …

[20] When the defendant may be a child victim of trafficking, two linked questions must be addressed. First, the defendant's age must be ascertained, and second, the evidence which suggests that he has been trafficked must be assessed. In the vast majority of cases the questions will be investigated by and in the same processes. Assuming that the factual conclusion is that the defendant was a child victim of trafficking, a quite distinct question for

---

[54] [23] EWHC 1689 (Admin).

consideration is the extent to which the crime alleged against him was consequent on and integral to the exploitation of which he was the victim. That question also arises in the case of an adult victim. In some cases (as in these appeals) the answer to both questions will be that the criminal offence is here, or at least, a manifestation of the exploitation.

[...]

[22] ... when an age issue arises, the court must be provided with all the relevant evidence which bears on it. Although the court may adjourn proceedings for further investigations to be conducted, these have to be undertaken by one or other or both sides, or by the relevant social services. The court is not vested with any jurisdiction, and is not provided with the resources to conduct its own investigations into the age of a potential defendant until after the investigation has completed its course, and the individual in question is brought before the court.

[23] ... this approach was underlined in *R v O*[55] where the court emphasised that:

(W)here there is doubt about the age of a defendant who is a possible victim of trafficking, proper enquiries must be made, indeed statute so required.

[24] ... Article 10(3) of the Anti-Trafficking Convention provides:

When the age of the victim is uncertain and there are reasons to believe that the victim is a child, he or she shall be presumed to be a child and shall be accorded special protection measures pending verification of his/her age'.

[25] ... In our judgment Article 10(3) addresses evidential issues. Where there are reasons to believe that the defendant is a child, then he should be treated as a child. In other words it is not possible for the court to brush aside evidence which suggest that the defendant may be a child. The issue must be addressed head on. If at the end of an examination of the available evidence, the question remains in doubt, the presumption applies and the defendant must be treated as a child ...

[26] The National Referral Mechanism (NRM) was set up on 1 April 2009 to give effect in the United Kingdom to Article 10 of the Council of Europe Anti-Trafficking Convention. Enough is now known about people who are trafficked into and within the United Kingdom for all those involved in the criminal justice process to recognise the need to consider at an early stage whether the defendant (child or adult) is in fact a victim of trafficking. The NRM establishes a three stage process for this purpose:

i. An initial referral of a potential victim of trafficking by a first responder to a competent authority. At present there are two competent authorities. They are UKBA and the United Kingdom Human Trafficking Centre (UKHTC), a multi disciplinary organisation led by SOCA (The Serious and Organised Crime Agency). In the present appeals we are concerned only with UKBA because the potentially trafficked individuals were subject to immigration control. We note that where the potential victim of trafficking is a child his consent is not necessary before the referral is made, but where he is an adult consent is required.

ii. An UKBA official decides whether the person referred might have been a victim of trafficking. This is known as a 'reasonable grounds' decision, for which UKBA have a target of five days. We are told that the average time is nine days. If and when a favourable reasonable grounds decision has been made the first responder is notified, and, in effect that decision allows for a period of forty-five days during which the final stage of the NRM process continues, leading to

iii. consideration by UKBA whether the evidence is sufficient to confirm conclusively that the individual has been trafficked.[...]

[29] In the final analysis all the relevant evidence bearing on the issue of age, trafficking, exploitation and culpability must be addressed. The Crown is under an obligation to disclose all the material bearing on this issue which is available to it. The defendant is not so obliged,

---

[55] [2008] EWCA Crim 2835.

but if any such material exists, it would be remarkably foolish for the investigating authority to be deprived of it. Without any obligation to refer the case to any of the different organisations or experts specialising in this field for their assessments or observations, the court may adjourn as appropriate, for further information on the subject, and indeed may require the assistance of various authorities, such as UKBA, which deal in these issues. However that may be, the ultimate responsibility cannot be abdicated by the court.

[…]

[31] We suggest that where any issue arises, it should be addressed head on at the first appearance before the court, and that the documentation accompanying the defendant to court should record his date of birth, whether as asserted by him, or as best known to the prosecution, or indeed both. Alternatively, the issues should be raised at the plea and case management hearing and appropriate adaptations should be made to the relevant forms to ensure that potential problems on this question are not overlooked.

8.66   Regard should also be had to the defence available in section 45 of the Modern Slavery Act 2015.[56]

E. Choice of Charge

Wide discretion

8.67   If the evidential and public policy tests have been satisfied and it is ensible to prosecute, the Crown Prosecution Service has a wide discretion as to the choice of appropriate charge upon which to prosecute. In *R v Sutton Youth Justices, ex p 'LJI' and 'DSI'*,[57] no promise, representation or assurance was given by the arresting police officers to the defendants to lead them to believe or expect to be prosecuted for less serious charges than those for which they were arrested. Accordingly, no abuse of process arose when the CPS chose to prosecute the defendants, on charges (of assault) that were more serious than the offences for which they were originally arrested (disorderly conduct)

Removal of potential defence

8.68   Likewise CPS charging policy was considered in *Asfaw*,[58] the appeal court deciding there was no scope for a legitimate expectation argument to found an abuse of process stay. Asfaw, an Ethopian en route to the United States of America, where she was to seek asylum, arrived at Heathrow airport and passed through immigration on a forged passport. She purchased a flight ticket, using false documents, to Washington. At trial she was acquitted by a jury of count 1, using a false instrument with intent, relying upon a defence under section 31 Immigration and Asylum Act 1999 to the border offence. The section 31 defence did not extend to count 2, attempting to obtain air services by deception. She pleaded guilty to count 2, the trial judge having ruled that Article 31 of the Refugee Convention[59] and Protocols relating to the Status of Refugees 1951 did not afford her protection.

---

[56] See Part 5, including the section 45—defence for slavery or trafficking victims who commit an offence. Brought into force 31 July 2015.

[57] DC—CO/2664/97.

[58] [2006] EWCA Crim 707, [2006] Crim LR 906, [2008] 1 AC 1061. *R v Uxbridge Magistrates' Court Ex.p. Adimi* [2001] QB 667 and *R (on the application of Pepushi) v CPS* [2004] EWHC 798 considered.

[59] Article 31 of the *Convention and Protocols Relating To The Status of Refugees* 1951 contains a protection which applied to those apprehended en route to their intended country of refuge, so that prosecutions should not be brought unless 'the offence itself appears manifestly unrelated to a genuine quest for asylum'. Since the enactment of section 31 Immigration and Asylum Act 1999 the courts have preferred to treat section 31 as the exhaustive source of protection for genuine asylum seekers.

The Court of Appeal dismissed the appeal against conviction on count 2. The protection **8.69** afforded by section 31 did not extend as far as that provided for by Article 31. Asylum seekers were not afforded protection if they stopped en route in this country to another country in which they could reasonably have expected to be granted asylum. The effect of section 31 was that there was no scope for a legitimate expectation that Article 31 would be respected outside the scope of section 31.

The Court of Appeal expressed concern with the CPS practice of combining the two counts. **8.70** If it were the case that count 2 was added for purposes of immigration control, in order to prevent the asylum seeker from invoking the section 31 defence, there would be strong grounds for arguing that the practice constituted an abuse of process. In the circumstances of the case, the conviction appeal was rejected but the sentence of nine months' imprisonment quashed and replaced with an absolute discharge.

On appeal to the House of Lords,[60] it was held that if count 2 was included to prevent Asfaw **8.71** from relying on the section 31 defence, there would be strong grounds for staying the proceedings as an abuse.

Fixed penalty notices

In *Gore and Mather*,[61] the Court of Appeal decided that the imposition of a fixed penalty **8.72** notice issued at the time of the offence did not prevent a subsequent prosecution for a more serious (non-penalty notice) offence for the same incident. Police officers who issued the fixed penalty notices (for section 5 POA 1986 disorderly conduct and section 91 CJA 1967 drunk and disorderly) were unaware at the time of issue that the victim of a street attack had suffered a fractured elbow. The police officers at the scene were acting on the basis of reports to them of an incident, rather than the evidence actually provided by CCTV footage. Prior to the issue of the fixed penalty notice, no complaint of assault was made to them and there was no reason that they should have appreciated the extent of the injury suffered by the victim. If the police had known at the time of the injuries then a fixed penalty notice would have been wholly inappropriate. The notice received by each appellant did not suggest the he had committed a serious offence of violence or that by paying the penalty, his liability to be convicted of an offence of violence would be discharged. The notice to one of the appellants involved an assertion of anti-social behavior not assault. There is nothing in the Criminal Justice and Police Act 2001, which suggests that the issue of a penalty notice asserting one offence, and the payment of the penalty, relieves the recipient of any possible further proceedings if and when it becomes apparent that a more serious, and in particular a non-penalty offence (section 18 inflicting GBH in this case), has in fact been committed. What is abundantly clear is that the CJPA 2001 only precludes a prosecution for an offence in relation to which a notice was issued.[62]

Likewise, in *R (Michael and Connor Gavigan) v Enfield Magistrates' Court*,[63] it was not an **8.73** abuse of process to prosecute an accused for section 4 Public Order Act 1986 threatening behaviour, arising out of an incident for which the police had issued a penalty notice[64] for the lesser offence of section 5 Public Order Act 1986 disorderly conduct and which the accused chose to contest. In rejecting the accused claimant's application for judicial review of a district judge's refusal to stay the proceedings as an abuse of process, the Divisional Court

---

60 [2008] UKHL 31.
61 [2009] EWCA Crim 1424, [2009] 1 WLR 2454, [2009] Crim LR 879, [2009] 7 Archbold News 1.
62 [2009] EWCA Crim 1424 [14] (Lord Judge LCJ).
63 [2013] EWHC 2805 (Admin), (2013) 177 JP 609.
64 Issued under section 2 Criminal Justice and Police Act 2001.

held that there was no principle or policy which required that a person who had rejected a penalty notice should not be prosecuted for another offence arising from the same set of circumstances. As Mr Justice Mitting observed:[65]

> ... payment of a penalty only discharges liability for the offence identified in the notice and not for any other, still less any other more serious offence ... If, on the facts of the case, the claimants had paid the £80 penalty and not exercised their right to have the case determined by the court, then it may be that by analogy with *Beedie* it might have been unfair subsequently to prosecute them for a more serious offence.

Misconceived charges corrected

8.74   In *Jordan Antoine*,[66] an offender had been convicted of two firearms offences, and nineteen days afterwards prosecuted for further, more serious firearms offences arising from the same facts. The Court of Appeal dismissed the appeal against conviction for the later offences as there were special circumstances, as per *Connelly*,[67] that made the subsequent trial just and convenient. This was not an escalation from minor charges to more serious charges, contrary to the general rule in *Elrington*,[68] but a move from misconceived charges to correct charges.[69] The court's sense of justice and propriety was not offended. Public confidence in the criminal justice system was not undermined; on the contrary, a stay would have brought it into disrepute: *Warren*[70] applied. Serious mistakes were made but there was no bad faith and the mistakes were quickly rectified by the Crown Prosecution Service. There had been no abuse of process. The decisions in *Beedie*[71] and *Howard Dwyer*[72] were considered and distinguished.

Circumvention of statutory time limit

8.75   Although the CPS have extensive powers in the exercise of their discretion to prosecute cases, the CPS are not permitted to take decisions to evade statutory provisions. The circumvention of a statutory time limit for a prosecution is unlawful. Procedural safeguards should not be avoided by the actions of the prosecution.

8.76   In *J*,[73] the defendant was indicted on three counts of indecent assault under section 14(1) of the Sexual Offences Act 1956. He made a pre-trial application for those counts to be stayed as an abuse of process on the ground that the alleged conduct amounted to unlawful sexual intercourse with a girl under the age of sixteen, contrary to section 6(1) of the SOA 1956, which was subject to a twelve month time limit for prosecution.[74] The defence argued that it was an abuse of process for the prosecution to circumvent the time limit by bringing the charges of indecent assault. The trial judge refused the application, the defendant was convicted, and the Court of Appeal dismissed his appeal.

8.77   The House of Lords allowed the defendant's appeal. Parliament's intention where the twelve month limit is concerned was clear, as was the prosecution's intention in charging indecent

---

[65] [2013] EWHC 2805 (Admin) see [11] and [15].

[66] [2014] EWCA Crim 1971, [2015] 1 Cr App R 8.

[67] The phrase 'special circumstances' originates in the judgment of Lord Devlin in Connelly v DPP [1964] AC 1254, 1359–60.

[68] 121 ER 870; (1861) 1 B & S, 688.

[69] [2014] EWCA Crim 1971, [2015] 1 Cr App R 8, see the judgment of Thirwell J at [31]. See Archbold Review 2012, 2, pp 1–2.

[70] [2011] UKPC 10, [2012] 1 AC 22, [2011] 3 WLR. 464, [2011] 2 All ER 513, [2011] 2 Cr App R 29.

[71] [1998] QB 356.

[72] [2013] EWCA Crim 10.

[73] [2005] 1 AC 562, [2005] 1 Cr App R 19.

[74] Parliament abolished the time limit with effect from 1 May 2004 by the Sexual Offences Act 2003.

assault to get around the statutory time limit. If Parliament has provided a protection for a defendant it is not for any court to sanction a device by which such protection is denied.

Lord Steyn makes this clear in the judgment:

> In the present case the intent to avoid the statutory time limit is freely acknowledged and, in any event manifest. In these circumstances the conclusion is inescapable: as a matter of construction of the Act the time limit cannot be circumvented by the manipulation of the indictment to charge conduct falling squarely within section 6(1) as an offence under section 14 solely in order to avoid the time limit under the former provision.[75]

These sentiments were echoed by Lord Bingham: **8.78**

> It is the duty of the court to give full effect to the meaning of a statute ... If a statutory provision is clear and unambiguous, the court may not decline to give effect to it.[76]

In addressing whether it was permissible for the Crown to prosecute a charge of indecent   **8.79**
assault under section 14 SOA, in respect of which no prosecution might be commenced under section 6(1) SOA (by virtue of the statutory time limit), Lord Bingham observed that the prosecution of J should have been stayed or the counts dismissed.

Lord Steyn, agreed in allowing the appeal, and observed:[77]   **8.80**

> ... In our system of government Parliament has the primary responsibility for the bulk of the criminal law which is statute based ... The CPS as an independent law enforcement agency carry out duties of a public character. It must act fairly and within the law. It must observe statute law as Parliament framed it ... It is plain as a pikestaff that the CPS policy under challenge in the present appeal was intended to circumvent the intent of Parliament in creating a time limit for prosecutions under section 6(1). It is, of course, true that the CPS has acted in good faith and in what it considered the public interest. But the particular policy it adopted unquestionably fell beyond its powers. It was ultra vires ... [T]he decision of the CPS to charge the defendant under section 14 in order to avoid the time limit under section 6(1) was unlawful.

Parity of treatment

Parity between accused

In *Forsyth*[78] the Court of Appeal held that even though the principal defendant had fled the   **8.81**
jurisdiction, it was not an abuse of process for the Serious Fraud Office to proceed against a defendant who had played a minor part in the overall criminal conduct. Proceedings against another accused, who had been more centrally involved, were abandoned on the grounds that he could not have a fair trial in the absence of the principal defendant. The decision to continue proceedings against Forsyth was within the prerogative of the Serious Fraud Office.

In *Thomas Petch and George Coleman*,[79] the prosecution's acceptance of a plea of guilty to   **8.82**
manslaughter by principal offenders at a subsequent trial to the appellants did not amount to an abuse of process. The disparity of treatment did not render the appellant's convictions for murder unsafe. Before the appellant's trial had begun, two alleged principal offenders, against whom there were allegations arising out of the same events, had fled the jurisdiction.

The two appellants, Thomas Petch and George Coleman, were convicted of murder, receiving   **8.83**
life imprisonment.

---

[75] [2005] 1 AC 562, 577E.
[76] [2005] 1 AC 562, 571.
[77] [2005] 1 AC 562, 577H—578A.
[78] [1997] 2 Cr App R 299.
[79] [2006] Crim LR 273.

8.84 Subsequently, the two alleged principal offenders were extradited to the United Kingdom and at their subsequent trials the prosecution had accepted pleas to manslaughter and other offences, for which they had each been sentenced to nine years' imprisonment.

8.85 The appellants appealed against the convictions by leave of the full court on the ground that, since the prosecution had subsequently accepted a plea of guilty to manslaughter arising out of the same events from a co-accused, the disparity of sentencing treatment amounted to an abuse of process.

8.86 On appeal, the appellants, who had been secondary parties in the events, argued that the prosecution decision to accept the pleas had been perverse, leading to a large and unfair disparity in sentencing, and that, relying on *Hui Chi-ming v The Queen*,[80] the prosecution was required to act consistently.

8.87 The Court of Appeal dismissed the appeals. The disparity of sentences imposed at the subsequent trials did not affect the safety of the convictions of the defendants. Further, the prosecution's alleged lack of consistency, resulting from the pragmatic consideration that it was not confident that a jury in the later trials would reach a verdict of guilty of murder, did not cast doubt upon the guilty verdicts.

8.88 That conclusion was plainly supported by the approach taken in *Hui Chi-Ming*, although Lord Justice Pill observed that subsequent developments in the law might encourage a review of how prosecutions in second trials based upon the same events as earlier trials were to be conducted.

Parity by different prosecuting agencies

8.89 In *W*,[81] the Court of Appeal dismissed the appellant's challenge to the CPS decision to prosecute a time-share fraud after the Inland Revenue agreed to accept a monetary settlement in relation to the company's tax liability. Lord Justice Rose held that the Crown was divisible as the CPS and Inland Revenue were pursuing separate policies.

8.90 However, Lord Justice Rose, remarked, *obiter*:

> … Crown indivisibility may well be pertinent to a claim for abuse of process if, for example, the CPS were to prosecute when the Revenue, in accepting settlement from a taxpayer, had told him with the concurrence of the CPS, that he would not be prosecuted by anyone.

F. Local Authority Prosecutions

Prosecution policy

8.91 Prosecution policy must be adhered to with care when a local authority prosecution is undertaken. In *Adaway*,[82] the Court of Appeal emphasized that if the local authority failed to give proper consideration to its policy or it reached a conclusion which was wholly unsupported by material, the courts will have little sympathy in any attempts to justify such a prosecution given the the other demands on time at Crown Court and Appellate level. In *Adaway*, the decision to prosecute (false trade descriptions contrary to section 1 Trade Descriptions Act 1968) strict liability offences did not satisfy the criteria for prosecution. The Court of Appeal

---

[80] [1992] 1 AC 34.
[81] (1998) STC 550, No 98/559/52, 12 March 1998, CA.
[82] [2004] EWCA Crim 2831, November 3 2004, (2004) 168 JP 645, *The Times* (22 November 2004), [2005] 1 Archbold News 1.

assessed the local authority decision to prosecute on public law grounds, and called it an abuse of process.[83]

In *R. (on application of Mondelly) v Commissioner of Police for the Metropolis*[84] Lord Justice   **8.92**
Moses confirmed the proposition that whilst courts are reluctant to intervene regarding decisions to prosecute, they may do so where there has been a breach of a prosecuting authority's clear and settled policy, as cited by Mr. Justice Charles in *Craig Jones v DPP*.[85]

Reasoned departure

In *R (on the application of Barons Pub Company Limted) v Staines Magistrates' Court*,[86] owners   **8.93**
of a pub food business were prosecuted by Runnymede Borough Council for breaches of the Food Hygiene (England) Regulations 2006 that raised health hazards. The company failed during the magistrates' court proceedings to have the proceedings stayed as an abuse. On appeal, the Divisonal Court refused the company's appeal. It was open to the local authority to decided to prosecute in circumstances which were outside their enforcement policy, but only if the council addressed the issue and was able to provide a reasoned decision to go outside the enforcement policy. The council relied upon the company's blatant disregard of the law and failure to heed advice to close the premise kitchens as an alternative means of resolving the health hazard concerns. The Divisonal Court rejected the arguments that the proceedings were oppressive. Dismissing the appeal the court emphasized that save in an exceptional case, decisions to prosecute were for the prosecutor, as made clear in *A(RJ)*.[87] The criminal court was, save in an exceptional case, to determine whether the prosecution had been proved on the merits.

Independent exercise

In *Moss & Son Ltd v CPS*,[88] a diary farming business appealed, by way of case stated, against   **8.94**
the dismissal of its application to stay a prosecution against it, initiated by the Gangmasters Licensing Authority but taken over by the Crown Prosecution Service. The Divisonal Court held that the GLA had not breached its 'Dairy Policy' on prosecuting. The court observed that there should be clear arrangements which ensured that decisions on prosecution policy and the decision to prosecute were made by persons who could exercise their judgment independently of the Government or an executive agency.

Non-prosecution alternatives

The underlying principle remains that it is for prosecutors to decide when to prosecute. The   **8.95**
local authority is not required to go through each of the non-prosecution courses of enforcement action in order to justify the lawfulness of the prosecution. In *Wandsworth LBC v Rashid*,[89] the Divisional Court, in allowing a prosecution appeal by way of case stated, noted that magistrates erred in staying a local authority prosecution of a shop keeper for leaving refuse bags under section 34 Environmental Protection Act 1990. Although the local authority had not considered all of its waste management enforcement policy, which detailed alternative measures including education, and the issue of warnings and cautions, that failure did not warrant proceedings being

---

[83] Contrast the situation in *North Yorkshire Trading v Coleman*, [2001] EWHC Admin 818, (2002) 166 JP 76.
[84] [2006] EWHC 2370.
[85] [2011] EWHC 50 (Admin), [2011] Archbold Review 2, 1.
[86] [2013] EWHC 898 (Admin).
[87] [2012] EWCA Crim 434, [2012] 2 Cr App R 8.
[88] [2012] EWHC 3658 (Admin), (2013) 177 JP 221; case comment at Cambridge Law Journal 2013, 72(2), 247–50.
[89] [2009] EWHC 1844 (Admin), (2009) 173 JP 547; [2009] 8 Archbold News 1.

stayed as an abuse of process. The magistrates' finding that it would have been reasonable for the local authority to take another course of action did not necessarily mean that proceedings should be stayed.

Jurisdiction

8.96 In *Jonathon Clayton and Paul Dockerty*,[90] the appellants were prosecuted for failing to comply with an enforcement notice contrary to section 179 of the Town and Country Planning Act 1990 by letting flats as long-term residencies rather than short lets. At the Crown Court hearing, the appellants submitted that the proceedings should be stayed as an abuse of process on two grounds. First, in bringing the prosecution, the local authority had known that the enforcement notice was invalid because at the time it was issued the council knew that the property had been used as permanent residencies for more than four years. Second, the council had deliberately concealed its knowledge. The local authority was relying on its own unlawful acts. The Crown Court judge rejected the stay application. The judge held that by virtue of section 285 (1) of the Town and Country Planning Act 1990 (an enforcement notice should not be questioned in any proceedings, except by way of appeal) the Crown court did not have jurisdiction to hear the stay application. The Court of Appeal agreed with the first instance judge. The enforcement notice cannot be challenged in the criminal proceedings. The issue on appeal would be for the Adminstrative Court. Further, the fact that a local authority officer had concealed information would not render it in any way abusive for the council to prosecute for breach of an enforcement order properly made. The wrongdoing of the officer solicitor was independent of the effect on the enforcement order.

Care proceedings

8.97 In *L*,[91] findings in local authority care proceedings under the Children Act 1989 did not preclude a subsequent prosecution, on the same facts, for the death of the baby which had provided the background of the family proceedings. In *L*, the judge in the care proceedings held that the cause of the baby's death had not been established. At the subsequent trial for murder, the defence argued that the family judge's decision and findings were conclusive of the criminal proceedings and that the indictment should be stayed as an abuse of process. That submission was rejected and the appellant was convicted of manslaughter of the baby. The appellant appealed on the ground that it was an affront to justice that he been convicted of manslaughter when another competent court, considering the same evidence, was not satisfied that the baby's death was murder. The Court of Appeal dismissed the appeal. The purpose of the care proceedings was to establish where, and with whom, another child should reside and his future welfare arrangements. The proceedings brought and conducted by the local authority were not concerned with whether the appellant had killed the baby and the family court had no jurisdiction to convict or acquit the appellant of a criminal offence.It was not competent to decide criminal proceedings.[92] The decision in the care proceedings was not a final determination of the criminal proceedings. Moreover, no question of *autrefois acquit*, issue estoppel, or double jeopardy could arise.

---

[90] [2014] EWCA Crim 1030, [2014] 2 Cr App 20.

[91] [2007] 1 Cr App R 1, [2007] Crim LR 472, case comment at Archbold News 2006, 8 p 5. See also *Re W(Children) (Concurrent criminal and care proceedings)* [2009] 2 Cr App R 23 (each set of proceedings should be fully informed of the other); *Re L (Care proceedings: risk assessment)* [2010] 1 FLR. 790 (an example of where criminal proceedings should have been held first).

[92] See decision in *Imperial Tobacco v Attorney-General* [1981] AC 718 in which it was stated 'a declaration as to lawfulness by the civil court is not in itself a bar to a criminal prosecution, even when the parties are the same in both proceedings.'

G. Double Jeopardy

It is an important principle of criminal justice that a person should not be prosecuted and **8.98** punished twice for the same offence. This principle is referred to as the 'rule against double jeopardy'.

Raising the issue

Where it is argued that a defendant has, on a previous occasion, been acquitted or convicted **8.99** of an offence alleged in a charge in an indictment, the defendant can seek the protection of the double jeopardy rule by raising a plea of 'autrefois acquit' or 'autrefois convict'. If success-fully raised before a judge only,[93] the plea is a bar to further proceedings.

Rationale

The rationale for the double jeopardy principle is explained in *Green v US*[94] by Mr **8.100** Justice Black:

> The underlying idea, one that is deeply ingrained in at least the Anglo-American system of jurisprudence, is that the State with all its resources and power should not be allowed to make repeated attempts to convict an individual for an alleged offence, thereby subjecting him to embarrassment, expense and ordeal and compelling him to live in a continuing state of anxiety and insecurity, as well as enhancing the possibility that even though innocent he may be found guilty.[95]

The risk of litigation is highlighted by the commentator Professor Andrew Choo[96] when he **8.101** states, 'The accused may, as a result of having revealed his complete defence at the first trial, be at a greater disadvantage at the second trial and thus less able to defend him or herself effectively.'

The Law Commission[97] identifies four rationales for the double jeopardy rule: **8.102**

(1) risk of wrongful conviction;
(2) distress of the trial process;
(3) need for finality;
(4) need to encourage efficient investigation.

Autrefois acquit and *convict*

The House of Lords in *Connelly v DPP*[98] considered double jeopardy examining the pleas **8.103** in bar of *autrefois acquit* and *autrefois convict* as devices to stay proceedings. It decided that the abuse of process principle was the principal remedy to prevent unfairness from double jeopardy outside of three situations.

In summary their Lordships in *Connelly* made the following points: **8.104**

(1) The coincidence of factual evidence during the two proceedings is not the basis of a suc-cessful plea in bar (see *Connelly*—in which the defendant's acquittal on a murder count,

---

[93] See section 122 Criminal Justice Act 1988.
[94] 355 US 184.
[95] A passage expressly cited with approval by Sir John Thomas P at [7] in *JFJ* [2013] EWCA Crim 569, [2014] 2 WLR 701, [2013] 2 Cr App R 10, [2013] Crim LR 988.
[96] [1995] Crim LR 864 at 866.
[97] Law Commission, 'Double Jeopardy', Consultation Paper No 156, 1999.
[98] (1964) AC 1254, [1964] 48 Cr App R 183. Generally, see also *Humphries* [1997] ACT 1, HL; *Beedie* [1997] 2 Cr App R 167; *Z* [2000] 2 AC 483; as applied in *Cheong* [2006] Crim LR 1088.

during the course of a robbery, did not prevent a subsequent trial on a count of robbery (no robbery count was initially indicted as the practice in 1967 was to try murder counts alone)—and *Thomas*[99] (in which it was stated that a conviction for violence did not preclude a later prosecution for murder should the victim later die of his injuries).

(2) A defendant cannot be tried for an allegation:

- identical in law and based on the same facts for which the defendant has previously been acquitted or convicted (as per *autrefois acquit* and *autrefois convict*);

- for which the defendant could on a previous indictment have been convicted of a lesser offence (e.g. an acquittal on a murder count allows a defendant to raise *autrefois acquit* on any subsequent manslaughter indictment);

- proof of which would, as a matter of law, prove a charge of which the defendant has already been acquitted (e.g. an acquittal on a manslaughter count allows a defendant to raise *autrefois acquit* on a subsequent murder charge, as proof of manslaughter is a necessary step to proving murder).

(3) Outside the three situations noted above in (2), Lord Devlin stated that the trial judge should use his discretionary power to halt the prosecution[100] if letting it continue would be unfair or oppressive to the defendant in light of the earlier proceedings.

An example of where proceedings were halted is *Moxon-Tritsch*.[101] The defendant was fined and disqualified for careless driving involving the death of car passengers. A subsequent private prosecution for causing death by reckless driving was deemed oppressive by the trial judge, and the count left to lie on the file marked not to be proceeded with.

(4) The principles of *autrefois acquit* and *autrefois convict* apply to summary trials, with the defendant entering a not guilty plea to raise the issue.

Similar offences

8.105 What matters is not similar facts but whether similar offences are alleged. In *Velasquez*,[102] a not guilty verdict on a count of attempted rape did not, in the view of the Court of Appeal, amount to a successful plea of *autrefois acquit* on the substantive count of rape, upon which a guilty verdict was returned. They were logical alternative charges. There was no necessary inconsistency in the verdicts. A point highlighted by the comment of Lord Grant in the Scottish case of *HM Advocate v Cairns*,[103] 'identity of the charges and not of the evidence is the crucial factor'. See also the Court of Appeal decision in *Sherry and El Yamani*.[104]

Health and safety

8.106 Double jeopardy arguments can arise in health and safety situations. In *Beedie*,[105] the appellant was the landlord of premises in which a woman died of carbon monoxide poisoning caused by a defective gas fire. He pleaded guilty in the magistrates' court to a charge, brought by the Health and Safety Executive, under the Health and Safety at Work Act 1974, and was

---

[99] (1949) 33 Cr App R 200, (1950) 1 KB 26.

[100] Where the narrow application of the *autrefois* principle would result in unfairness or injustice to the defendant amounting to oppression, the remedy lies in the power of the court to stay proceedings; as recognized in *JFJ* [2013] EWCA Crim 569 [29] (Sir John Thomas P).

[101] [1988] Crim LR 46.

[102] (1996) 1 Cr App R 155.

[103] (1968) JC 37.

[104] (1993) Crim L R 536.

[105] [1997] 2 Cr App R 167. This decision prompted the relevant prosecution authorities to produce the '*Work-related Deaths—a Protocol for Liaison*' in 1998, which aims for greater co-ordination of such prosecutions.

fined. The local authority also obtained convictions against the appellant for offences relating to dangerous gas fires.

Following the two sets of prosecutions and an inquest, the appellant was subsequently **8.107** charged with manslaughter. At trial, after the judge refused the appellant's application to stay the indictment on the grounds of *autrefois convict*, he pleaded guilty. The Court of Appeal quashed the conviction for two reasons.

First, although the trial judge had correctly analysed the case as falling outside the *autrefois* **8.108** principle, (which Lord Justice Rose confined to the situation where the second indictment charges the same offence as the first, so the subsequent manslaughter charges were outside *autrefois acquit*) the trial judge still had a discretion to stay the proceedings where the second offence arose out of the same or substantially the same set of facts as the first. That discretion should be exercised in favour of an accused unless the prosecution establishes that there are special circumstances for not doing so.[106]

The appellant relied upon: **8.109**

(1) *Connelly v DPP*,[107] where Lord Devlin stated that the prosecution must 'as a general rule join in the same indictment' charges founded on the same facts; and
(2) the almost invariable rule that 'where a person is tried on a lesser offence, he is not to be tried again on the same facts for a more serious offence' (as stated by Lord Justice Neill in *Forest of Dean Justices ex p Farley*,[108] in which the Divisional Court held that it would be an abuse of process to prosecute the applicant for causing death by reckless driving where the excess alcohol charge to which the accused had earlier pleaded guilty in summary proceedings was, as Mr Justice Garland put it ' ... the very foundation of the recklessness'[109]).[110]

Secondly, the Court of Appeal in *Beedie* decided that the trial judge had failed to consider **8.110** whether there were special circumstances for departing from the general rule. There were no such special circumstances and the indictment should have been stayed.[111]

The decision in *Beedie* was distinguished by the New Zealand High Court in *Spencer v* **8.111** *Wellington District Council*,[112] in which an employee died at work. The employer company was convicted and fined, as it was in breach of its duty of care under health and safety legislation. Subsequently, an information alleging manslaughter was laid against the company director, Mr Spencer. He applied to have the proceedings stayed on the basis that if he was personally punished it would amount to double punishment. The High Court rejected such an argument. There could only be double punishment so as to justify a stay when the same legal person was punished. The prosecutions had not been successive proceedings against the same accused nor prosecutions escalating on the scale of gravity as the charge of manslaughter could not have been brought against the company. The health and safety charge against the company required only proof of negligence, whilst manslaughter required proof of gross negligence by Mr Spencer personally. *Beedie* was distinguished on the basis that in *Beedie* it was the same defendant who was charged, first with the statutory safety offences, and after being

---

[106] See for example, *R v South East Hampshire Magistrates ex p CPS* [1998] AC 695, [1998] Crim LR 422, DC and *Phipps*[2005] EWCA Crim 33.
[107] [1964] AC 1254, 1347.
[108] [1990] RTR 228, 239.
[109] [1990] RTR 228, 236.
[110] See also *Moxon-Tritsch* (1988) Crim LR 46.
[111] *Martello* April 4 2000, CA, No 99/7052/X4, [2000] Archbold News 8, October 26.
[112] [2000] 3 NZLR 102.

dealt with on those charges, with a manslaughter charge some months later. The argument in *Spencer* was whether there were two separate and distinct and legal persons, the director and the company, so that each can be charged and face the jeopardy of separate punishment.

Different conduct

8.112 The rule that 'where a person is tried on a lesser offence, he is not to be tried again on the same facts for a more serious offence' as noted in *Farley*,[113] was distinguished by the Court of Appeal in *Harnett*.[114]

8.113 In *Harnett*, a police officer constable saw the appellant driving his motor car in an erratic way. The appellant produced a positive breath test for excess alcohol. He was initially charged with the summary offence of driving a motor vehicle while the proportion of alcohol in his breath exceeded the proscribed limit.[115] At the magistrates' court the CPS added a second charge of dangerous driving, which was an either way offence. The defendant pleaded guilty to the summary alcohol charge, and was committed for trial to the Crown Court on the driving charge and for sentence on the alcohol matter. At the Crown Court, the sentencing judge rejected the appellant's submission that for him to be tried on the driving charge, after he had pleaded guilty to the excess alcohol, was either an abuse of process or involved double jeopardy.

8.114 The Court of Appeal dismissed his appeal for a number of reasons:

- First, the fact of driving whilst intoxicated was not the sole basis of the evidence of dangerous driving. A special constable witnessed the erratic driving complained of. So the general principle requiring prosecution of offences in decreasing order of magnitude, as per *Elrington*,[116] was not breached. There is no real double jeopardy issue because the two charges relate to separate, different conduct—having excess alcohol/being intoxicated and driving dangerously.[117]
- Second, the prosecution had not manipulated the courts procedures. The CPS had not used any stratagem or tactical ploys to obtain evidence in the course of the excess alcohol proceedings for use in the subsequent trial of the driving offence. The appellant had entered a guilty plea to the alcohol charge.
- Furthermore, evidence of the appellant having consumed excess alcohol could have been excluded under section 78 PACE, if it was felt that it was unfair to rely upon it. The appellant could also have applied to have had the excess alcohol matter dealt with after the driving matter.

Incontrovertible acquittal

8.115 The need for decisions of the courts, unless set aside or quashed, to be accepted as incontrovertibly correct is a principle which requires that it is the verdict of acquittal that should be regarded as incontrovertible. This principle is founded in the finality of judicial proceedings. If the prosecution seeks to go behind a verdict of acquittal, then a court's jurisdiction to prevent an abuse of process comes into play (see powerful speeches by Lord Hailsham, Lord Salmon, and Lord Edmund-Davies in *DPP v Humphrys*[118]).

---

[113] As stated by Lord Justice Neill in *Forest of Dean Justices ex p Farley* [1990] RTR 228, [1990] Crim LR 568.

[114] [2003] EWCA Crim 345, [2003] Crim LR 719. *Farley* and *Hartnett* were considered in *Arnold* [2008] 2 Cr App R 37.

[115] Contrary to section 5(1) of the Road Traffic Act 1988.

[116] (1861) 1 B & S 688.

[117] See commentary to *Hartnett* [2003] Crim LR 719.

[118] [1977] AC 1.

An Australian example of the inconvertible acquittal principle can be found in *Carroll*.[119] The **8.116**
High Court of Australia decided that, where the defendant had given evidence at his trial for
murder denying the killing and his conviction had been quashed on appeal, his subsequent
prosecution for perjury at his murder trial (the false evidence alleged being his denial of the
killing) should have been stayed as an abuse because the prosecution inevitably sought to
controvert the earlier acquittal. There was manifest inconsistency between the charge of perjury and the acquittal of murder, the inconsistency arising because the prosecution based the
perjury charge solely upon the defendant's sworn denial of guilt.

The laying of the charge of perjury solely on the basis of the defendant's sworn denial of guilt **8.117**
for the evident purpose of establishing his guilt of murder was an abuse of process regardless
of the cogency and weight of any new evidence that the prosecution had available.

The position would be different if the charge of perjury related not to an ultimate issue in **8.118**
contest in a previous trial, but to evidence given at such a trial by the defendant which, if
subsequently proved to be false, would not directly impeach the prior acquittal.

Reserve charges

An indictment charging wounding with intent, after defendants were acquitted of murder **8.119**
and manslaughter, based on the same facts, was stayed in *Turipa v R*.[120] The second prosecution of the accused represented an abuse of process. It was offensive to propriety for the
prosecution to keep a lesser charge of wounding with intent, in reserve, up its sleeve, during
a homicide trial, as a backstop if its preferred charges of murder and manslaughter should
fail. The prosecution had sought to rely upon the same evidence to secure a conviction on a
lesser charge. In the judgment of Mr Justice Priestley, 'the criminal justice system does not
contemplate nor will the courts countenance, any process of prosecution by attrition'.[121]

Not in jeopardy

There are a vast array of situations outside of the double jeopardy principle. **8.120**

- A defendant is not in peril if a charge is dismissed as a simple reorganization of the prosecution case to reflect a more serious charge in a manner to which the defendant did not
  object: see *JFJ*.[122]
- Where a court has acted *ultra vires*, an accused can not be legally convicted and is not in
  jeopardy. The prosecution can appeal to the Divisional Court to state a case on the basis
  that a summary acquittal was wrong in law, pursuant to section 111 of the Magistrates
  Court Act; section 28 of the Supreme (Senior) Court Act 1981. For example, in *West*,[123]
  magistrates purported to acquit a defendant of an indictment only offence. As the summary proceedings were a nullity, the defendant was never in peril of being convicted legally,
  and could not, therefore, rely upon *autrefois acquit*. See also *R v Dorking Justices ex p
  Harrington*[124] and *Dabhade*;[125]

---

[119] [2002] HCA 55, (2002) 194 ALR 1.
[120] [2004] 2 NZLR 706.
[121] [2004] 2 NZLR 706, 719.
[122] [2013] EWCA Crim 569, [2013] EWCA Crim 569 which considers the decisions in *Dabhade* [1993]
QB 329, (1993) 96 Cr App R 146; *DPP v Riches* [1993] COD 457; *Brookes* [1995] Crim LR 630; *DPP v
Khan* [1997] RTR 82. See also *Daill Arran Fawcett* [2013] EWCA Crim 1399 in which it was not an abuse of
process to convict an offender of burglary and vacate prior charges of handling stolen goods arising from the
same set of facts. The handling indictment had gone forward because of a prosecution mistake.
[123] [1964] 1 QB 15.
[124] (1978) Crim LR 377.
[125] (1993) 96 Cr App R 146.

- Where the information is so faulty that the accused could never have been in jeopardy upon it (see *DPP v Porterhouse*[126]).
- Where proceedings are terminated by the prosecution serving a notice of discontinuance under section 23 of the Prosecution of Offences Act 1985. The prosecution can later restart proceedings against the same defendant.
- The withdrawal of a summons without the justices examining the merits. Contrast the situation where a person pleads not guilty, the prosecution offer no evidence, justices dismiss the summons, the defendant is acquitted and there can be no further proceedings (see *Grays Justices ex p Low*[127]).
- The defendant needs to have been sentenced: without such punishment there is no *autrefois convict* (see *Richards*[128]).
- the taking into consideration of an offence when passing sentence for other convicted offences.[129]
- An indictment marked 'not to be proceeded with without leave of this Court or Court of Appeal' is not a bar per se. Provided leave is obtained proceedings can follow.
- A defendant may be retried for an offence (committed on or after 15 April 1997) for which an acquittal resulted if that acquittal is judged to be tainted (for example, in cases of 'jury nobbling' or witness intimidation), pursuant to sections 54–6 of the Criminal Procedure and Investigations Act 1996. This is a major exception to the availability of *autrefois acquit*. In circumstances where jurors or witnesses have been intimidated or interfered with, and there is a real possibility that, but for the interference or intimidation, the acquitted person would not have been acquitted, an application may be made to the High Court for an order quashing the acquittal.
- A major exception to the rule against double jeopardy is contained in sections 75–97 of the Criminal Justice Act 2003. A prosecutor can apply to the Court of Appeal to quash an acquittal for a qualifying offence[130] if there is new (not adduced at the original trial) and compelling (reliable, substantial and highly probative) evidence in the case and it is in the interests of justice to do so (taking into account whether a fair trial can be had, the delay involved, and whether the prosecution have acted with due diligence and expedition with regard the new evidence).[131]
- Following a conviction being quashed on appeal, the Court of Appeal can exercise its discretionary power to order a retrial in the interests of justice (see section Criminal Appeal Act 1968 as amended by CJA 1988 and CJA 2003). The Court of Appeal has indicated that the period which elapsed since the original trial, whether or not the appellant had been in custody for that period, and the apparent strength of the case against the appellant, were

---

[126] (1988) 89 Cr App R 21.

[127] [1990] 1 QB 54.

[128] [1993] AC 217.

[129] *James Nicholson* (1947) 32 Cr App R 98. See *Batchelor* (1952) 36 Cr App R 64 for recognition by Goddard LJ of the practice of taking offences into consideration as a convention. In practice, the police are unlikely to institute proceedings for an offence which has been 'taken into consideration' for two reasons. First, for the policy reason that the 'tic' system increases the 'clear-up' rate of crimes reported to the police by reducing the list of unsolved crimes. Second, for the practical reason that in many cases, in the absence of an admission by a defendant, there is usually no evidence upon which to identify the offender or to prosecute the defendant.

[130] Including murder, manslaughter, rape, supplying/importing class A drugs, arson endangering life, causing an explosion likely to endanger life or property, war crimes and terrorism.

[131] See *Dunlop* [2006] EWCA Crim LR 1354, [2007] Crim LR 390 and D Harmer 'The Expectation of Incorrect Acquittals and the New and Compelling Evidence Exception to Double Jeopardy' [2009] Crim LR 63. In *Dunlop*, the Crown was permitted to have a third trial (following two hung jury trials, resulting in a directed acquittal) under Part 10 of the Criminal Justice Act 2003, the defendant having subsequent to the first two trials, confessed to the alleged murder.

factors to be taken into account in deciding whether the interests of justice required a re-trial (see *Flower*[132] and *Saunders*[133]).

- Allegations of criminal behaviour not pursued in a separate prosecution but relied upon in confiscation proceedings for another offence, do not amount to double jeopardy since confiscation proceedings do not amount to the bringing of a criminal charge. The fact that the prosecution has adduced evidence of criminality in confiscation proceedings but not charged that crime does not offend the double jeopardy principle: see *Darren Bagnall*,[134] in which the appellant was convicted of money laundering (being in possession of £99,200 in cash). However, evidence of an uncharged VAT fraud was adduced during confiscation proceedings to allow a judicial finding under section 10 POCA for purposes of the amount of the confiscation order to be made in relation to the money laundering conviction. The appellant was never at risk of conviction on the fraud, hence the double jeopardy principle did not apply.

- Issue estoppel, where the prosecution are estopped from re-opening a particular issue of fact which had clearly been decided in the defendants favour at an earlier trial acquittal. The House of Lords in *DPP v Humphrys* decided that the doctrine of issue estoppel had no place in criminal proceedings. Neither the prosecution nor defence can rely upon issue estoppel.[135]

- Civil contempt proceedings do not constitute a conviction. In *Bryan Green*,[136] the defend-ant in county court contempt proceedings was punished for breaching a non-molestation injunction. A plea of *autrefois convict* at the subsequent Crown Court trial for assault (based on the same assault allegation) was rejected. The civil contempt proceedings were not criminal in nature. Although there was a criminal background, arising from the same set of factual circumstances, the contempt proceedings flowed from an inherent County Court jurisdiction to enforce its own orders.[137]

- Disciplinary findings of guilt by non-prosecuting authorities. In *Hogan and Tompkins*,[138] prisoners who were punished under the Prison Rules for trying to escape, could not rely upon the prison adjudication as *autrefois convict* at a subsequent criminal trial for escaping prison.[139]

- Proceedings before the Special Immigration Appeals Commission relating to certifi-cation under section 21 CJA 2003, depriving a person of their liberty, do not consti-tute criminal proceedings. SIAC proceedings are not and do not determine criminal proceedings.[140]

- Although an acquittal or conviction in a foreign court or a court martial could form the basis of a successful *autrefois* application,[141] where an accused was convicted and sentenced in his absence by a foreign court, with there being no realistic possibility of the defendant ever returning to that jurisdiction to serve the punishment, *autrefois convict* will not apply if the defendant is prosecuted in this country.[142]

---

[132] (1966) 50 Cr App R 22.
[133] (1974) 58 Cr App R 248.
[134] [2012] EWCA Crim 677.
[135] [1977] AC 1.
[136] [1993] Crim L R 46.
[137] See *Szczepanski v Szczepanski* [1985] Fam Law 120.
[138] (1960) 2 QB 513.
[139] See also *Secretary of State for Trade and Industry v Baker* (6 July 1998), Securities and Futures Authority regulatory investigation.
[140] See *IK, AB and KA* [2007] EWCA Crim 971, [2007] Crim LR 882.
[141] *Aughet* (1919) 13 Cr App R, 101.
[142] *Thomas* [1985] QB 604.

H. Collateral Motive

Political motive

8.121 A prosection which satisfies the evidential and public policy tests must be independently and objectively prosecuted. A politically motivated prosecution may amount to an abuse of process. For a stay application to succeed, the sole or dominant motive for the prosecution must be overtly political. In *R v Bow Street Metropolitan Stipendiary Magistrates ex p South Coast Shipping*,[143] the defendant complained, inter alia, that the proceedings should be stayed as the private prosecution had a collateral purpose of drawing attention to the Marchioness boat disaster to highlight the need for a public inquiry. The Divisional Court rejected the application. Even if the political motive attributed to the private prosecution was true, the prosecution would not be an abuse unless that motive was the sole or dominant motive. The mere presence of an indirect or improper motive in launching a prosecution did not necessarily vitiate it.

The Divisional Court is slow to halt a prosecution in the case of mixed motives unless the conduct was truly oppressive.[144]

8.122 Likewise, the Privy Council in *Antoine v Sharma*[145] recognized that a decision to prosecute that was arrived at under political pressure rather than by an objective review of proper prosecutorial considerations could amount to an abuse of process. Although a decision to prosecute was susceptible to judicial review on the ground of interference with a prosecutor's independent judgment, such relief would in practice be granted extremely rarely.[146] In considering whether to grant leave for judicial review, the court had to be satisfied not only that the claim had a realistic prospect of success but also that the complaint could not adequately be resolved within the criminal process itself, either at the trial or by way of an application to stay a an abuse of process. The court's power to stay proceedings for abuse of process should be interpreted widely enough to cover an application challenging a decision to prosecute that was politically motivated.

Prosecution objectivity and independence

8.123 Independent and objective consideration needs to be given to a prosecution. In *R v Milton Keynes Magistrates' Court ex p Roberts*,[147] the Divisional Court recognized (a) that the jurisdiction to restrain a prosecution is to be sparingly exercised, and only if the misconduct undermines the rule of law or is an affront to justice, and (b) 'if a prosecutor makes himself the creature of a private interest in exercising his powers, then the conduct would at least be prima facie abusive.' A stay was not granted as the trading standards prosecutor had given independent consideration to the evidence, collected by a trade source, as to the importation of counterfeit spare parts.

---

[143] [1993] QB 645, [1993] 96 Cr App R 405, [1993] Crim LR 221.

[144] *R (on application of Dacre) v Westminister Magistrates' Court* [2009] 1 Cr App R 6, [27] (Latham LJ).

[145] [2006] UKPC 57, [2007] 1 WLR 780.

[146] See similar judicial comments in *R v DPP ex.p. C* [1995] 1 Cr App R 136; *R v DPP ex.p. Manning* [2001] QB 330 QBD (Admin) [23]; *R. (on the application of Bermingham) v Director of the Serious Fraud Office* [2006] EWHC 200, [2007] QB 727 at [63]-[64]; *Mohit v DPP of Mauritius* [2006] UKPC 20, [2006] 1 WLR 3343 at [17], [21]; *R. (on the application of Corner House Research) v Director of the Serious Fraud Office* [2008] UKHL 60, [2009] Crim LR 47.

[147] [1995] Crim LR 224.

In *R v Leominster Magistrates' Court ex p Aston Manor Brewery Co*[148] the Divisional Court **8.124** decided that proceedings were an abuse of process where the plaintiff (claimant) in civil proceedings controls criminal proceedings against the same defendant to the extent that the prosecution are unable to exercise their prosecutorial duties independently (contrast the decision in *R v Gloucester Crown Court ex p Jackman*[149]).

Funding

In *Hounsham, Mayes, Blake*,[150] the Court of Appeal considered whether financial contri- **8.125** butions by victim insurance companies to fund police prosecutions amounted to an abuse of process. Three car dealers were convicted of conspiracy to defraud. The prosecution case was that road traffic accidents were 'staged' as part of a scheme to make fraudulent claims against various insurance companies. The three defendants participated in a dishonest scheme involving the acquisition of vehicles which were used in 'staged' collisions. Insurance companies were deceived into paying out third-party claims for the total loss, at an inflated value of the cars.

Towards the end of the prosecution's case, it was disclosed to the defence that three of the **8.126** insurance companies which had paid out on claims made by one or other of the defendants, had at the request of the police, paid sums to the police, to assist in funding the arrest stage of the investigation.

Arising out of this disclosure, the appellants applied for the proceedings to be stayed as an abuse of the process of the court.

The trial judge refused to stay the proceedings as an abuse of process on a number of funding **8.127** and disclosure grounds:

(1) The payments were not prima facie illegal (a point deemed wrong by the Court of Appeal, as the Police Authority for the area were the statutory body responsible for securing the maintenance of a police force and establishing the police fund to receive all receipts and fund all expenditure of the police force[151]).
(2) The transactions did not involve an intention to corrupt. The police acted in good faith and were not acting corruptly.
(3) The 'modest payments' (totalling £4,500) did not demand a stay of the indictment on that ground alone.
(4) Letters sent by the police to the insurance companies seeking financial contributions were relevant and should have been disclosed by the prosecution.
(5) Those documents and the financial contributions from the insurance companies were capable of undermining the prosecution case or assisting the defence and should have been disclosed as such.
(6) The police had not removed these documents from the unused and non-relevant unused material available to be inspected by defence solicitors: the defence solicitors must have overlooked these documents.
(7) None of the defendants had suffered prejudice or been handicapped in their defence by the absence of any other material which might have been available to them if disclosure of the documents had been made at an earlier stage.

---

[148] *The Times* (8 January 1997).
[149] [1993] COD 100.
[150] [2005] Crim LR 991; case comment at Archbold News 2005, 1, 5–6. Cited in *Zinga* [2014] EWCA Crim 52, [2014] 1 Cr App R 27. See also *Smallman* [2010] EWCA Crim 548.
[151] See sections 3, 6 and 14 of the Police Act 1996.

In the summing-up, the trial judge gave the jury a clear direction, which was favourable to the appellants, as to how to deal with the funding issue.

8.128 The Court of Appeal dismissed the defendants' appeals. The integrity of the prosecution had not been compromised as the police, in seeking and obtaining funding from the interested insurers, had acted in good faith. No corruption was involved.

Further, the defendants had not demonstrated any prejudice from the acceptance of the money from the insurance companies.[152]

8.129 However, the Court of Appeal noted[153] that soliciting by the police of funds from potential victims of crime, quite apart from being unlawful, was a practice which was fraught with danger. It might compromise the essential independence and objectivity of the police when carrying out a criminal investigation. It might lead to police officers being selective as to which crimes to investigate and which not to investigate, and to victims persuading a police investigating team to act partially. It might also lead to investigating officers carrying out a more thorough preparation of the evidence in a case of a 'paying' victim; or a less careful preparation of the evidence in the case of a non-contributing victim. It could lead to a loss of confidence in a police force's ability to investigate crime objectively and impartially, leading to the public questioning the objectivity of police investigations.

8.130 In the view of the Court of Appeal, the absence of bad faith and the surrounding circumstances of the case rendered the trial judge's decision not to stay proceedings wholly justifiable.

I. Legitimate Expectation

8.131 There have been a series of cases in which abuse of process arguments have centred upon representations and promises made by state officials, investigating officers and prosecution authorities which have led a defendant to believe that no prosecution would follow. Abuse of process arguments based on a legitimate expectation that no prosecution would follow occur in a number of different ways set out below, covering reneging on a promise by state officials and a change in stance by the prosecution authorities.

Reneging on a promise

8.132 The prosecution of a person who has received a promise, undertaking, or representation from the police that he would not be prosecuted is capable of being an abuse of process.[154]

8.133 The nature, circumstances, and reasons for the representation will always be important for courts to consider but may differ enormously from case to case.

8.134 In addition to considering objectively the form and content, there is the more basic question of whether it is reasonable for the accused to have relied on the representation in the circumstances in which it was made. Only in the strongest cases will courts stay proceedings as an abuse, where such promises have been breached.

---

[152] Likewise appeal points surrounding non-disclosure complaints were dismissed by the Court of Appeal.
[153] [2005] Crim LR 991 [31] (Gage LJ). The potential dangers of police receiving funds from potential victims was also recognized in *Zinga* [2014] EWCA Crim 52.
[154] *R v Croydon Justices ex p Dean* [1994] 98 Cr App R 76 [77] (Staughton LJ).

Witness

In *R v Croydon Justices ex p Dean*,[155] the prosecution reneged on its promise that a seventeen-year-old boy would not be prosecuted if he assisted the police. Proceedings were instigated despite implied representations by the police that he was viewed solely as a witness. In view of the quite exceptional circumstances of the case and having regard to the applicant's age at the time and the assistance he gave to the police for over five weeks, it was clearly an abuse of process for him to be prosecuted subsequently. Accordingly, the committal was quashed. **8.135**

Other commonwealth cases[156] were cited by Lord Justice Staughton, with particular reference to *Chu Piu-Wing v Attorney-General*.[157] **8.136**

The Hong Kong Court of Appeal, in *Chu Piu-Wing* set aside a subpoena of a witness as an abuse of process along with the consequent conviction of the witness for contempt of court. The witness had been assured by the Independent Commission Against Corruption that he would not be required to give evidence, although the subpoena was in the event obtained by the police. Both were held to be 'arms of the Executive in its investigative function.' **8.137**

Authority and motive

It is not essential in order for a stay of proceedings to be given for the state official making the promise to (a) have had sufficient authority (to make such a promise) or (b) to have made the promise in bad faith. In the words of Lord Justice Staughton:[158] **8.138**

> In my judgment the prosecution of a person who has received a promise, undertaking or representation from the police that he will not be prosecuted is capable of being an abuse of process ... provided (i) that the promisor had power to decide, and (ii) that the case was one of bad faith or something akin to that. I do not accept that either of those requirements is essential.

Public interest

In *Chu Piu-Wing v Attorney General*,[159] Vice President McMullin stated;[160] **8.139**

> ... there is a clear public interest to be observed in holding officials of the state to promises made by them in full understanding of what is entailed by the bargain.[161]

Public confidence and reliance

It is important that citizens are able to rely upon the statements of public officials. In *Postermobile PLC v Brent LBC*[162] the Divisional Court quashed convictions for displaying advertisements contrary to planning regulations. The appellants had been told by local authority officers that planning consents were not required. Although there was no promise not to prosecute, Lord Justice Schiemann considered the appellants were correct in relying **8.140**

---

[155] [1993] 3 All ER 129, [1994] 98 Cr App R 76. See also *H v Guildford Youth Court* [2008] EWHC 506 (Admin), [2008] 4 Archbold News 1. Contrast the decision in *Sherif, Ali, Mohamed, Abdurahman, Fardosa* [2008] EWCA Crim 2653.

[156] *Milnes and Green* (1983) 33 SASR 211, *Georgiadis* [1984] VR 1030, *Betesh* (1975) 30 CCC (2d) 233 and *Crneck, Bradley and Shelley* (1980) 116 DLR (3d) 675.

[157] [1984] HKLR 411.

[158] *R v Croydon Justices ex p Dean* [1994] 98 Cr App R 76, 83.

[159] (1984) HKLR 411.

[160] (1984) HKLR 411, 417–18.

[161] Cited with approval by Lord Griffiths in *Bennett* [1994] AC, 61E. See also Australian State Supreme Court decision in *Milnes and Green* (1983) 33 SASAR 498.

[162] *The Times* (8 December 1997). See also another local authority prosecution, *East Northamptonshire Council v Monks and Gamlin*, (Northampton Crown Crown, 25–28 July 2003).

on the advice of the officers, as the expression of opinion clearly informed the appellants that they could proceed without planning consents.

8.141 *Postermobile* was applied in *Salloum and Sharifh*.[163] Mr Justice Mitting stayed a money laundering count against a background of customs dealings with the proprietor and staff of two bureaux de change as it would be unfair to try the defendants.

8.142 Customs policy[164] up to the end of 2000 in the handling of intelligence from bureaux de change was (a) to attempt to ensure the bureaux complied with the Money Laundering Regulations 1993 (in terms of record keeping, obtaining the identity of customers, forestalling and preventing money laundering) and (b) to use bureaux de change as a source of intelligence about money laundering. Only in blatant cases was investigation and prosecution of operators of bureaux de change for statutory offences considered. This policy, in Mr Justice Mitting's view, was both lawful and reasonable. It certainly involved no abuse of state power. Provided that the operators made accurate disclosure of suspect transactions within a reasonable time, bureaux de change operators committed no crime.

8.143 The bureaux de change had made on average over one hundred money laundering disclosures a year to customs, over a ten-year period. The proprietor of the two offices had been providing information to customs as a 'trade source', being registered as an informant up until 2000. The activities at the two bureaux were not 'state-sponsored crime', but 'trade source' information providers.

8.144 From July 2001 onwards, there was a change in customs' approach to bureaux de change, shifting away from gathering intelligence about money laundering to preventing it.

8.145 In January 2003, Ammar Salloum became manager of the bureau. He reported a number of transactions to customs and followed their advice, making timely and accurate disclosures of suspect transactions, with faxed reports to NCIS and customs.

8.146 In February 2003, Part 7 of the Proceeds of Crime Act came into force. The changes in the law, in particular the new requirement to obtain the consent of NCIS before doing any prohibited act in relation to criminal property, were not explained to Ammar Salloum. The only advice given to Ammar Salloum related to a specific transaction and was misleading.

8.147 Mr Justice Mitting found that the cumulative effect of the advice given to Salloum, by two customs officers, both before and after POCA came into force, was to misstate to Salloum the true position under POCA.

8.148 In staying proceedings, Mr Justice Mitting cited the principle of public law, recognized in *Postermobile*,[165] that 'the citizen should be able to rely upon assurances given by public officials'. By close analogy, Mr Justice Mitting was of the view that it would 'undoubtedly be an abuse of process for a prosecuting authority, charged with the statutory function of receiving disclosures about and giving consent to suspect transactions, to advise a person to act in a particular way and then prosecute him for doing so'.[166]

8.149 The prosecution case against the two staff members was that they did two acts prohibited under POCA, by arranging for the deposit of cash and accepting cash, which the law required them to disclose to the authorities before they did them. However, customs officers told them, via Ammar Salloum, that they did not have to make prior disclosure. They were in the

---

163 (Southwark Crown Court, 5 November 2004).
164 See Homan Report, October 2000.
165 11 November 1997. See Lord Justice Schiemann's remarks at page 6. *The Times* (8 December 1997).
166 At p 49 of the transcript.

words of Justice Mitting 'being prosecuted for what they were told they could do by the law enforcement authority which prosecutes them'.[167] On the facts alleged by the prosecution, the defendants had been 'deprived of the opportunity of acting lawfully by customs' incorrect advice. That is sufficient to make it an abuse to prosecute them for doing those acts'.[168]

State engendered legitimate expectation

If an expectation is created in a defendant's mind, an abuse of process may result. In *Att.-Gen. of Trinidad and Tobago v Phillip*,[169] the Privy Council decided that the re-prosecution of offenders, after a pardon had been granted and an order of *habeas corpus* made, was an abuse of process and stayed proceedings, even though the initial pardon may have been invalid. It was the expectation aroused in the offender by the pardon that lead to the unfairness.

8.150

Turning a blind eye

If state agencies 'turn a blind eye' to conduct, a legitimate expectation may be created that such conduct will not be prosecuted. In *John Barrett and others*,[170] counts of living off the earnings of prostitution and immigration conspiracies were stayed as an abuse of process. Over many years, the police in Sheffield, at senior levels, were aware (through public press advertisements and internet references) of saunas that were making money as brothels. The police adopted a laissez faire policy towards the saunas. As part of their crime management system and with resources needing to be directed towards more serious crime, they turned a blind eye to what was going on, either explicitly or by implication through the action of officers. The message was that, providing they were free of underage girls, abuse generally, drugs, alcohol, and serious crime (rape, kidnap and assaults) they would not be targeted. On the other hand, street prostitution and addresses in residential areas were targeted with a zero tolerance police policy and a crackdown. This policy ended up in writing, adding to the impression in the minds of those who ran the saunas that they would not be prosecuted provided they kept to the rules. There were many visits to saunas by the police over a number of years to ensure that things were in order. One officer who visited the saunas agreed at the time that he was permitting them to operate if they stuck to the rules. The saunas were given an implied permission to operate.

8.151

The defence successfully argued that the police policy created in the minds of those involved in the saunas, the clearest impression that, provided they stayed within certain ground rules, their unlawful activities would be tolerated. Conversely, if they did not stay within the bounds of the ground rules, they would be targeted. The management of the saunas cooperated with the police.

8.152

Further, the involvement of the local autrhority suggesting a licensing system or register, combined with media reporting of the police attitudes which went unchallenged, reinforced the policy and the impression created in the minds of those managing the saunas.

8.153

In staying the proceedings, His Honour Judge Lawler QC emphasized[171] that his decsision did not lay down any precedent in relation to saunas and their operation. The decision stands on its own unusual and exceptional facts. He went on to observe:[172]

8.154

> … the way the policy was carried out in very difficult circumstances from senior officers to their subordinates on the front line was a recipe for confusion. It lacked clarity about

---

[167] At pages 51–52 of the transcript.
[168] At page 53 of the transcript.
[169] [1995] 1 All ER 93.
[170] (Sheffield Crown Court, 23 Feburary 2007).
[171] At p 83 paras C–F of the transcript judgment.
[172] At p 109 paras A–D of the transcript judgment.

all that happened or did not happen. It must, at the very least, have created in the minds of the sauna operators over several years a reasonable and legitimate expectation that their activities were at best tolerated and they would not be prosecuted, provided they abided by the rules. It seems to me that in all the circumstances I have outlined, to turn round and prosecute several years later on the evidence remaining, which is no more nor less that that which to the knowledge of the police had been happening for years and apparently continues, and when the gravamen of the enquiry was not evidenced, is unfair.

Reliance to detriment

8.155 Before a case is stayed for legitimate expectation a defendant needs to rely upon the representation and act to his detriment. If there is no detriment there is no abuse.

8.156 In *Robert Thomas*,[173] the defendant was charged with affray, wounding with intent, and assault. The Crown Prosecution Service, by letter, stated that a plea to a lesser wounding count was acceptable. The defendant pleaded guilty to the lesser count, but prosecution counsel told the court that the plea was not acceptable and sought to continue proceedings for the more serious count. The trial was stayed on the basis that state officials were bound by promises they had made. The defendant had made a damaging admission in reliance on the representation that he would not be prosecuted for the more serious offence.[174]

8.157 In *Townsend, Dearsley and Bretscher*,[175] the Court of Appeal stated that it was manifestly unfair to prosecute a defendant after he had been initially treated as a prosecution witness, interviewed without caution and having provided a witness statement to police. The material forming the basis of the prosecution case only emerged as a consequence of his co-operation.

Prejudice to defendant

8.158 In *D*[176] the appellant was convicted of sexual offences, originating from a complaint in 1986. He was initially written to by a chief inspector, to the effect that 'no further police action will be taken'. Proceedings were resurrected after a second complainant made an allegation, and a conviction resulted. The Court of Appeal held, in quashing the conviction, that proceedings should have been stayed as an abuse of process. The letter indicated a final decision not to prosecute, which the prosecution went back on, and various materials which might have been of use to the defence had, as a result of the earlier decision not to proceed, been disposed of, including the terms of the earlier complaint. The consequence was the appellant was substantially prejudiced.[177]

No promise or undertaking

8.159 Where there has been no bargain struck, a stay will not be granted. In *Abbas Kassimali Gokal*,[178] the Court of Appeal dismissed an appeal against convictions for conspiracy to account falsely and conspiracy to defraud, involving the BCCI bank. The appellant was arrested in Frankfurt on his way from Pakistan to New York to be interviewed by American authorities. He claimed that he had gone there on the assurance by the American authorities that he would not be arrested by the Serious Fraud Office.

---

173 [1995] Crim LR 938.
174 Contrast *Hobbs*, 27 April 1998, CA, No 97/6508/Y2.
175 [1997] 2 Cr App R 540, [1998] Crim LR 126.
176 [2000] 1 *Archbold News* 1, CA.
177 As applied and approved in *T (Michael John)* [2000] Crim LR 832.
178 (CA, 11 March 1999).

The appellant argued on appeal, inter alia, that the proceedings should have been stayed as **8.160** an abuse of process, as he had been tricked into travelling to New York. In rejecting that submission, the Court of Appeal observed that there had been no abuse of power by the SFO. The appellant had left Pakistan voluntarily and, although an undertaking could be a bargain, no bargain had been relied on by the appellant. There was no evidence that the appellant had left Pakistan because of the assurance.

The assurance to the appellant that he would not be arrested was not a promise, nor an **8.161** undertaking of non-arrest; it only referred to the current plans by the authorities.

Whilst recognizing the doctrine of expectation, the Court of Appeal decided that there was **8.162** no evidence of any clear and specific statement to which an expectation (of no arrest or prosecution) could have been founded. In fact, the appellant had been aware of the SFO intention to prosecute him.

Discontinuance

No promise or prejudice

In *Davies*,[179] the Crown Prosecution Service had initially issued a notice of discontinuance of **8.163** proceedings[180] in relation to two charges of rape. Two years subsequently, the complainants laid informations instigating a private prosecution. The appellant was convicted, inter alia, of rape. It was submitted that because of the discontinuance of proceedings and delay, the proceedings should have been stayed as an abuse of process. The Court of Appeal dismissed the appeal against conviction. The court held that the exceptional circumstances needed to justify a stay did not exist. Discontinuance under section 23(3) of the Prosecution of Offences Act 1985 was no bar to further proceedings under section 23(9). Further, there had been no prejudice to the appellant from the delay and no promise to the court that he would not be prosecuted.

Not free from jeopardy

In *R v DPP ex p Burke*,[181] the defendant was informed by means of a standard letter that **8.164** the Crown Prosecution Service intended to discontinue proceedings, save 'exceptionally, if further significant evidence [were] to become available'. That decision was revoked and proceedings instigated even though no further evidence had come to light. Lord Justice Phillips, sitting in the Divisional Court, held that the terms of the letter were not calculated to let the defendant believe he was free from jeopardy.

Change of prosecution stance

In *Hyatt*,[182] prosecution counsel promised the defence that if a scientific test which was **8.165** awaited favoured the defence then the prosecution would offer no evidence. In fact though the test did favour the defence, the prosecution added a further count to the indictment and continued to prosecute. The defendant pleaded guilty after the judge refused to stay the proceedings. The Court of Appeal quashed the conviction as something so unfair had occurred that the proceedings were an abuse of process.

Failure to give reason

A prosecution failure to give a reason for going back on a promise may amount to an **8.166** abuse.

---

[179] (CA, 27 June 1996), *Archbold Criminal Appeal Office Index* (1997) 3, [T–2].
[180] Under section 23(3) of the Prosecution of Offences Act 1985.
[181] [1997] COD 169, DC.
[182] (1997) 3 Archbold News 2.

8.167 In *Bloomfield*,[183] prosecution counsel at a plea and directions hearing indicated to defence counsel that the prosecution wished to offer no evidence because the prosecution accepted that the defendant had been 'set-up'. The case was adjourned to allow the prosecution to offer no evidence at a subsequent pre-trial hearing. The CPS then informed the defence solicitors that they intended to continue the prosecution. At trial, an application to stay the proceedings as an abuse of process failed and the defendant pleaded guilty.

8.168 The Court of Appeal quashed the conviction, irrespective of whether the appellant had suffered prejudice, on two grounds:

(a) the decision by the prosecution to continue proceedings would bring the administration of justice into disrepute, as no reason was given for their change of stance; and

(b) neither the court nor the defendant could be expected to inquire whether prosecuting counsel had authority to conduct a case in court in any particular way and they were therefore entitled to assume in ordinary circumstances that counsel did have such authority.[184]

Post-Bloomfield

8.169 Subsequent to *Bloomfield*, courts are increasingly reluctant to adopt the broad interpretation of 'promise' abuse. Courts are increasingly distinguishing *Dean* and *Bloomfield*, and emphasizing that in this area there are no strong precedents.[185] What is certain is that there is no requirement that the defendant has suffered any prejudice over and above that of facing a trial/charges that he did not anticipate. Beyond that, each case turns on its merits.

8.170 In *Graham Murphy*,[186] the Court of Appeal distinguished *Bloomfield*. The appellant was originally charged with two offences of indecent assault against two complainants. At the magistrates' court a decision was taken not to proceed with one of the two charges. At the Crown Court the prosecution restored the second count. On appeal against conviction, it was argued that it was an abuse of process to have put the appellant on trial on the second count. The Court of Appeal dismissed the appeal. It held that it was clear from *Bloomfield* that in principle a defendant did not have to show prejudice in order to succeed in an argument on abuse. However, cases relying on a promise had to be looked at very carefully on their own particular facts. There could not be a rule to the effect that an early decision in the magistrates' court not to proceed on one charge, absent further evidence, could never be re-visited by counsel prosecuting in the Crown Court, even though there was no fresh evidence in the case.

8.171 *Graham Murphy* was not a case where it was proposed to offer no evidence, but rather one where a charge was sought to be withdrawn in the magistrates' court. The withdrawal of a summons or a charge was no bar to the issue of a further summons in the same matter. The fact that the two decisions were taken in different courts at significantly different stages in the process was of some importance.

---

[183] [1997] 1 Cr App R 135.

[184] *R v Croydon ex p Dean* applied. See also *R v Horseferry Road Magistrates Court ex P DPP* [1999] Archbold News 7, QBD; *(S)C*, (CA, 7 June 2001) (Wright J).

[185] See commentary to *Patricia Ann Gripton* [2010] EWCA Crim 2260; at [2010] Crim LR 388 stating *Bloomfield* does not lay down any firm rules.

[186] [2003] Crim LR 47.

Judicial view

The decision in *Bloomfield* was also distinguished by the Court of Appeal in *Yacub Ebrahim* **8.172**
Mulla.[187] The prosecution indicated to the intended trial judge that on an indictment charging causing death by dangerous driving they had decided to accept a plea of guilty to careless driving. The judge invited prosecution counsel to reconsider the decision, and having done so, the prosecution, decided by the afternoon of the same day that they would proceed with the original charge. The Court of Appeal decided that the subsequent prosecution of that charge did not constitute an abuse of process. The appellant had been aware from the outset, having heard the exchange between counsel and judge, that the judge was not happy with the decision not to proceed. Thereafter, it was only a short time before the change of view and there had been no prejudice to the appellant.[188]

No unequivocal representation

The 'legitimate expectation' line of authorities was considered by the Court of Appeal in *Abu* **8.173**
Hamza, observing:[189]... that it is not likely to constitute an abuse of process to proceed with a prosecution unless (i) there has been an unequivocal representation by those with the conduct of the investigation or prosecution of a case that the defendant will not be prosecuted and (ii) that the defendant has acted on that representation to his detriment. Even then, if facts come to light which were not known when the representation was made, these may justify proceeding with the prosecution despite the representation.[190]

In *Abu Hamza*, the police had seized and examined, in 1999, an encyclopaedia and recordings **8.174**
of the appellant's public speeches. The police returned the material to the appellant after nine months, informing him that no further action would be taken against him. During those nine months, cassettes that recorded sermons that were subsequently to be the subject of trial counts received close examination. The appellant argued that the actions of the police in returning the material after scrutiny naturally and reasonably created in the appellant the clear impression that the contents of the material were not criminal. He had a legitimate expectation that he would not be prosecuted for possession of the material. In those circumstances the appellant argued it was an abuse of process to prosecute him five years later for their possession.

The Court of Appeal rejected these arguments. It would have been open to the police to initiate a **8.175**
prosecution when the items were first seized. The fact that they did not do so could not, however, be taken as an assurance, let alone an unequivocal assurance, that they would not do so in the future. The materials were seized, not in the course of some general investigation, but in an investigation aimed specifically at the possibility that the appellant was implicated in a terrorist incident in 1998 in Yemen. The appellant was aware of this. By 2004, the police and Crown Prosecution Service in 2004 attached greater significance to the speeches, cassettes and encyclopaedia.

The Court of Appeal, in rejecting the legitimate expectation argument, held that:[191] **8.176**

There is no reason to conclude that the appellant placed any reliance on the reaction, or lack of reaction, of the police to the cassettes and the encyclopaedia when deciding to retain them

---

[187] [2004] 1 Cr App R 6. Commentary [2004] Crim LR 144.
[188] See also *DPP v B* [2008] EWHC 201 (Admin), [2009] Crim LR 707 in relation to the laying of 17 additional counts by the prosecution at the invitation of the judge, who felt that a single count of sexual assault failed to reflect the criminality alleged. The laying of 17 additional counts did not amount to an abuse of process.
[189] [2007] Cr App R 27 at para 54 of Lord Phillip's judgment; [2007] Crim LR 320.
[190] A passage cited with approval by the Northern Ireland Court of Appeal in *R v McGeough* [2013] NICA 22.
[191] [2007] Cr App R 27 at para 57 of Lord Phillip's judgment.

in his possession. He was simply continuing a course of conduct that had commenced before the police had intervened.

8.177 Likewise in *Killick*,[192] the Court of Appeal dimissed an appeal against conviction (for buggery and sexual assault) as there had been no unequivocal representation that there would be no prosecution. Further, appellant solicitors were aware of the complainants' right (under the Crown Prosecution Service Code of Practice for Victims of Crime) to seek a review of any decision not to prosecute. The fact that, in reviewing a decision not to prosecute, the Crown Prosecution Service was responding to the complainant's right of review was a relevant factor when considering whether proceedings, brought as a result of a third tier review (by the DPP), were an abuse of process.

Acceptable disposal

8.178 Agreements between the prosecution and defence in relation to acceptable pleas, basis of plea, and alternative disposals are jealously guarded by the courts, as an essential means of allowing the criminal justice to work with certainty, efficiently, and with integrity.

Pleas

8.179 The Divisional Court, in *DPP v Deborah Edgar*,[193] decided that it was within the magistrates' discretion to decide that for the prosecution to go back on an agreement regarding acceptable pleas was an abuse of process. The prosecutor's appeal against the magistrates' decision to stay proceedings was dismissed.

8.180 Deborah Edgar was charged with three offences: driving over the limit prescribed in relation to alcohol; failing to stop and give her name after an accident; and failing to report an accident as soon as reasonably possible. She entered a plea of guilty to the second and third of these offences and the prosecutor asked to withdraw the first charge. Subsequently, the prosecutor attempted to reinstate the alcohol charge. The justices refused and indicated that they thought this would be an abuse of process.

8.181 In dismissing the appeal, Lord Justice Schiemann, observed:

> … compromises of this kind between prosecution and defence, where the defence agrees to plead to some charges in return for the prosecution dropping others, are a commonplace of our criminal proceedings and they occur in magistrates' courts and crown courts. It is important in principle that such compromises should generally be stuck to and the integrity of the criminal process requires that they should be.

Basis of Plea

8.182 Once the prosecution accepts a basis of plea[194] from a defendant, it can be an abuse of process, at any subsequent trial, for it to prosecute on a basis strikingly in conflict with the basis on which the guilty plea had been accepted and sentenced passed.

8.183 In *Mattu*,[195] a defendant pleaded guilty to a conspiracy to supply a Class 'A' drug on an agreed basis of plea and was sentenced accordingly. At a subsequent trial money laundering counts

---

[192] [2011] EWCA Crim 1608; [2012] 1 Cr App R 10. See also *R(S) v CPS: R(S) v Oxford Magistrates' Court* [2015] EWHC 2868 (Admin). For other examples where there had not been an unequivocal representation see *Ryan Thom* [2011] EWCA Crim 3146 and *Munim Abdul v DPP* [2011] EWHC 247 (Admin).

[193] (2000) 164 JP 471.

[194] See also (1) section 73 SOCA 2005 signed plea agreements: *Dougall* [2010] EWCA Crim 1048; [2010] 6 Archbold News 3; (2) sentencing remarks of Thomas LJ in *Innospec*, (CA, 26 March 2010). See also discussion in [2010] 4 Archbold News 4.

[195] [2009] EWCA Crim 1483, [2010] Crim LR 229, case comment [2009] 7 Archbold News 1 and Crim LR 2010, 3, 229–30. Contrast the decision in *Dowty* [2011] EWCA Crim 3138.

were quashed as an abuse of process because the counts went against the earlier basis of plea. The prosecution appealed under section 58 of the Criminal Justice Act 2003 arguing that the basis of plea accepted in one case did not bind the prosecution in other cases, involving separate offences. The Court of Appeal rejected the prosecution arguments and dismissed the appeal. Although there are cases, where, for example, fresh evidence emerge and circumstances change, in which a previously agreed basis of plea could be circumvented, this was not such a case. The prosecution in subsequently charging money laundering offences on a basis strikingly in conflict with the previous accepted plea, meant the proceedings were fundamentally unfair to the defendant.

In *Mattu*, there had been a carefully prepared and detailed basis of guilty plea. The basis had **8.184** been agreed between the parties and approved by the court for the purposes of a *Goodyear*[196] sentencing indication and for deciding the actual sentence. To allow a subsequent trial, on the same facts, would have undermined the rationale behind the sentencing indication. The basis of plea had achieved a status which rendered the subsequent prosecution attempt (through a different regional Crown Prosecution Service office) to go behind the plea, an abuse of process.

Restraining order

In *Robert Smith v CPS*,[197] the claimant was prosecuted for harassment contrary to section 2 of **8.185** the Protection from Harrassment Act 1997. An agreement was reached between the prosecutor and the claimant's lawyers, expressed in open court, with no reservations set out by either party, that no evidence would be offered and that the claimant would, by agreement, be the subject of a restaining order. An adjournment occurred to allow the claimant to attend court for the agreed disposal; not for the prosecutor to consider its position. A different prosecutor appeared on the adjourned later date and did not agree with the earlier agreed disposal on the ground that there had been no discussion with the complainant or supporting agencies. The claimant argued that it would be an affront to justice to try him since in reality an agreement was struck at the earlier hearing. The judicial review application was allowed. The decision of the Crown Prosecution Service to proceed was quashed by the Administrative Court. It would be unfair as an abuse of process to try the claimant. If the granting of adjournments to enable someone to attend for the working out of an agreement put the whole agreement at risk, there would be much greater need for defendants to attend, considerably adding to the cost and burden of summary cases.

Indication not to call a witness

It is not an abuse of process for the prosecution to call a witness, contrary to a previous indi-**8.186** cation. The Court of Appeal in *Drury, Clark and others*[198] were not prepared to extend the abuse doctrine to cover a broader range of prosecution representations (in that case relating to the calling of witnesses) and to apply it in the absence of detrimental reliance by the accused on the representation.

In dismissing the appeals, the Court of Appeal observed that whether an abuse of process **8.187** had occurred depended on the nature and circumstances of the indication, the reason for the indication, the explanation for the change in the original decision, and whether any detriment to the defendants had resulted. As to the indication itself, the prosecution's statement of intention not to call the witness (initially a co-accused, who pleaded guilty and gave

---

[196] [2005] EWCA Crim 888, [2005] 1 WLR 2532.
[197] [2010] EWHC 3593 (Admin); see case comment Journal of Criminal Law 2011, 75(4), 256–59.
[198] [2001] Crim LR 847.

evidence on behalf of the prosecution) at the time when the first jury was discharged was not an undertaking (*Bloomfield*[199] distinguished, *Latif*[200] considered).

8.188 The Court of Appeal observed that it was in the interests of justice that a witness who was available and willing to give relevant evidence should be called unless there was good reason to the contrary. There was an important difference between calling a witness in support of a count and proceeding on the count at all where there had been an indication that there would be no such proceeding (as per *Bloomfield*). Although the prosecution had indicated that the witness would not be called in future proceedings there was no indication that it would be wrong to proceed even if the witness were a willing witness.

8.189 The defendants had not suffered any real detriment since there was no evidence of pressure on the witness by the police to change her position. Further no 'legitimate expectation' on the part of the defendants had been frustrated.[201]

Representations in appeal cases

8.190 Prosecution representations do not override the Court of Appeal's control of appeal cases.

8.191 In *R*,[202] on an appeal against conviction for conspiracy to rob, the Crown Prosecution Service in a written response to the appellant, expressed the view that the conviction was unsafe. The case was listed at the Court of Appeal on the basis that the CPS did not oppose the appeal against conviction. Shortly before the hearing, the CPS withdrew the concession that the conviction was unsafe, counsel having so advised. On an application for leave to appeal, the appellant argued that the withdrawal of the concession amounted to an abuse of process, and the court should refuse to allow the CPS to change its stance and submit on a new basis.

8.192 The Court of Appeal rejected the appellant's arguments, and, distinguishing *Bloomfield, Hyatt,* and *Dean*, held that the case was concerned not with control of the CPS' power to pursue a criminal prosecution, but the Court of Appeal's own duty to determine leave applications and, where granted, the safety or otherwise of convictions. The Court of Appeal was not bound by the stance taken by the CPS. Nevertheless the circumstances were regrettable. The CPS should have recognized that the Court of Appeal would require assistance from counsel, and they should have obtained counsel's advice before communicating any definite view to the appellant.

Change of stance factors

8.193 The following issues[203] are to be taken into account in determining whether an abuse of process has arisen, as a result of a change of prosecution stance:

(1) Whether the prosecution had indicated an unequivocal commitment not to prosecute, as opposed to something less (such as acceptance of a plea to lesser charges or a failure to disabuse the defendant of a mistaken belief that proceedings have terminated); and in what form: whether it is to offer no evidence or to withdraw the charge.

(2) Whether the undertaking not to proceed is delivered in open court by the prosecution.

(3) Whether the judge had expressed a view.

(4) Whether there had been a significant time between the prosecution's change of view.

---

[199] [1997] 1 Cr App R 135.
[200] [1996] 1 WLR 104 at 112, [1996] 2 Cr App R 92.
[201] *R v East and North Devon Health Authority ex p Coughlan* [2000] 3 All ER 850 considered.
[202] [2000] 4 Archbold News 1, CA, No 94/6631/Y4.
[203] See commentary to *R v Mulla* at [2004] Crim LR 144–45.

(5) Whether the defendant's hopes had been inappropriately raised and then dashed.

(6) Whether the defendant relies to his detriment and suffers prejudice relying on the undertaking.

J. Proceedings Misconduct

The category two type of abuse case extends to the actual court proceedings, with state **8.194** enforcement agencies subject to court orders, rules, and procedures. The integrity and protection of the criminal justice process and judicial system requires all parties to comply with court orders, rules, procedures, and ethical practices: see Criminal Procedures Rules 2015 and Leveson Review of Efficiency in Criminal Proceedings 2015. Prosecution failures to comply with court orders and effective case management can amount to an abuse of process.

Obedience of court orders

The importance of judges efficiently managing the work of the court by effective case man- **8.195** agement and parties adhering to court orders is illustrated by Sir Brian Leveson's observations in *Boardman*:[204]

> The [Leveson] Review goes on to deal with the critical importance of the Criminal Procedure Rules (CPR) and the role of judges in effectively managing the work of the court. It emphasizes (at para 199):
>
> Whatever we do, we must encourage a reduced tolerance for failure to comply with court directions along with a recognition of the role and responsibilities of the Judge in matters of case management. It cannot be right that a 'culture of failure' has developed in courts, fed by an expectation that deadlines will not be met. If a deadline is not met, there must be good reason for it and there must be an expectation that the party that failed to comply can provide that reason. A failure to tackle this culture leads to a general indifference to rule compliance ...

In *LR*,[205] a prosecution relating to the making of indecent photographs of children was stayed **8.196** as an abuse of process as court orders were not complied with. The trial judge decided that prosecution proposals for the defence to view the (240) images of the children, on a laptop in a glass walled interview room under police observation, were not acceptable, and ordered that the defence be provided with copies of all the images, subject to undertakings as to their safe custody and control. Consideration of the material was crucial to the defence case that some, if not most, of the images were of adults. The prosecution declined to comply with the court order, the trial judge stayed proceedings, and the prosecution appealed under section 58 CJA 2003.

The Court of Appeal dismissed the prosecution appeal. The starting point was that court **8.197** orders must be obeyed. Failure to comply with court orders made in the interests of a fair trial will lead either to the relevant evidence being excluded, or, where the case, as it did here, depended on the evidence, a stay of proceedings. The trial judge had given careful thought to all the issues. The defendant was entitled to private and confidential discussions with his legal advisers, unsupervised and unobserved by police officers or representatives of the Crown Prosecution Service. The prosecution had failed to propose any sensible means of ensuring that the defendant and his legal team were provided with a proper opportunity to consider

---

[204] [2015] EWCA Crim 715; [2015] 1 Cr.App.R.33, [2]. See also *Jisl* [2004] EWCA Crim 464 and other CrimPRs at Chapter 3 Forum paragraph 3.24.
[205] [2010] EWCA Crim 924; 174 J.P. 271 CA; (2010) 6 Archbold News 1; [2010] 4 Blackstone's Criminal Practice Bulletin 7.

the images in a confidential setting. It will be rare for the Crown to refuse to comply with a court order and then successfully challenge the consequent stay on appeal.

Pre-trial coaching of witnesses

8.198 In *Momodou*,[206] the Court of Appeal examined the important issue of pre-trial coaching of witnesses. The prosecution arose from a Violent Disorder at Yarl's Wood Immigration Detention Centre in Bedfordshire in 2002. The centre was run by detention custody officers (DCO) employed by Group 4. The DCO witnesses received trauma de-briefings (run by the Independent Counselling and Advisory Service (ICAS)) as they had witnessed the disorder and received advice from commercial solicitors who represented Group 4 in a linked civil claim by the police against Group 4. Witness training was arranged by Group 4 for the DCO's, the inference being that Group 4 was concerned to protect its position in the civil proceedings.

8.199 Once prosecution counsel became aware of the training proposals, he advised that it was wrong in criminal proceedings and might constitute a contempt of court both by Group 4 and the training company. The training programme was stopped immediately. However sixteen potential witness for the prosecution had received training. The names of the trained witnesses were provided to the defence. Group 4 responded to the concerns about witness training, asserting that the programme did not involve witness coaching nor evidence rehearsal: the course was simply intended to familiarize witnesses with court process and procedures 'so that giving evidence is not so intimidating'.

8.200 It was an agreed fact between the prosecution and defence at trial that the training offered was 'wholly inappropriate and improper'. The trial judge expressly agreed and directed the jury that 'there is no place for witness training in our country, we do not do it. It is unlawful'. In the case of one defendant against whom the evidence largely consisted of witnesses who had been trained, he withdrew the case from the jury.

8.201 The Court of Appeal also considered the danger of witness contamination, as some DCO witnesses received cognitive therapy in group de-briefing sessions, as part of a counselling programme. The prosecution expressed great concern about the de-briefing as discussions between witnesses before a trial could give rise to a number of difficulties. For example a witness may adopt the experiences of others taking part in the therapy. The prosecution sought assurances that full records of 'everything to do with the therapy' would be kept and made available in good time for the trial.

8.202 The Court of Appeal in upholding the convictions stated that the trial judge's decision to proceed with the case was correct. The trial process was capable of dealing with the defence difficulties. The conduct of Group 4 in relation to DCO witnesses and the potential difficulties created by it was capable of full explanation before and analysis by the jury. All areas of defence complaint were fully ventilated and put into their proper evidential context before the jury. Further, in summing-up, the trial judge went to great lengths to give unequivocal and robust support to the prosecution and defence criticisms of Group 4's conduct.

8.203 In relation to the ICAS trauma de-brief sessions adopted by Group 4, Lord Justice Judge observed:[207]

> [57] The ICAS arrangements were not improperly motivated. As employers, Group 4 provided this facility for members of staff who wished to have it, or thought they needed it. Two

---

[206] [2005] EWCA Crim 177.
[207] [2005] EWCA Crim 177 at para 57–58.

potential dangers were identified. First, discussions between those who had grouped together during specific parts of the incident might influence individual recollections, and second, there was no means of checking whether this had happened.

[58] We understand the submission, but we are unimpressed with it as a matter of complaint. It was not unreasonable for employers to do everything they could to alleviate the pressures and stresses endured by those members of their staff who were involved in or witnessed this incident. In its immediate aftermath, we can well understand why little, if any, thought was given to the position of potential witnesses who might become involved in any subsequent prosecutions of any detainees. At that time there was no process to be abused. Litigation, civil or criminal, would have been far from the mind of any of these potential witnesses. Many of them had endured a ghastly experience. Provided that no attempt was made to conceal what had happened from the jury (and none was), it was not abused. Each relevant witness for the prosecution was cross-examined about his or her involvement in the ICAS arrangements, and the jury was properly informed of the relevant facts.

In relation to the later cognitive therapy, the Court of Appeal recognized the potential conflict between necessary pre-trial treatment for a witness or victim of crime and the possible contamination of that evidence by out-of-court reiteration or treatment which consciously or unconsciously involved the prodding of memory. Without treatment, some victims and witnesses may suffer serious continuing psychological ill-health. On the other hand, treatment which involves discussion and analysis of the incident may affect the clarity and accuracy of the witnesses' memory. The court should be properly informed of any witness who has received pre-trial treatment, to enable its possible impact on the evidence to be investigated at trial. In *Momodou*, the jury had been fully informed of precisely which prosecution witnesses had attended the cognitive therapy, when it happened and who received the treatment at the same time. Accordingly, the jury could properly evaluate the evidence. **8.204**

In relation to witness training and coaching Lord Justice Judge made the following observations: **8.205**

[61] There is a dramatic distinction between witness training or coaching and witness familiarisation. Training or coaching for witnesses in criminal proceedings (whether for prosecution or defence) is not permitted ... The witness should give his or her own evidence, so far as practicable uninfluenced by what anyone else has said, whether in formal discussions or informal conversations. The rule reduces, indeed hopefully avoids any possibility, that one witness may tailor his evidence in the light of what anyone else said, and equally, avoids any unfounded perception that he may have done so. These risks are inherent in witness training. Even if the training takes place one-to-one with someone completely remote from the facts of the case itself, the witness may come, even unconsciously, to appreciate which aspects of his evidence are perhaps not quite consistent with what others are saying, or indeed not quite what is required of him. A honest witness may alter the emphasis of his evidence to accommodate what he thinks may be a different, more accurate, or simply better remembered perception of events. A dishonest witness will very rapidly calculate how his testimony may be 'improved'. These dangers are present in one-to-one witness training. Where however the witness is jointly trained with other witnesses to the same events, the dangers dramatically increase. Recollections change. Memories are contaminated. Witnesses may bring their respective accounts into what they believe to be better alignment with others. They may be encouraged to do so, consciously or unconsciously. They may collude deliberately. They may be inadvertently contaminated. Whether deliberately or inadvertently, the evidence may no longer be their own. Although none of this is inevitable, the risk that training or coaching may adversely affect the accuracy of the evidence of the individual witness is constant. So we repeat, witness training for criminal trials is prohibited.

[62] This principle does not preclude pre-trial arrangements to familiarise witnesses with the lay-out of the court, the likely sequence of events when the witness is giving evidence, and

a balanced appraisal of the different responsibilities of the various participants. Indeed such arrangements, usually in the form of a pre-trial visit to the court, are generally to be welcomed ... Such experience can also be provided by out of court familiarisation techniques ...

[63] In the context of an anticipated criminal trial, if arrangements are made for witness familiarisation by outside agencies, not, for example, that routinely performed by or through the Witness Service, the following broad guidance should be followed. In relation to prosecution witness, the Crown Prosecution Service should be invited to comment in advance on the proposals. If relevant information comes to the police, the police should inform the Crown Prosecution Service. The proposals for the intended familiarization programme should be reduced into writing, rather than left to informal conversations. If, having examined them, the Crown Prosecution Service suggests that the programme may be breaching the permitted limits, it should amended. If the defence engages in the process, it would be extremely wise for counsel's advice to be sought, again in advance, and again with written information about the nature and extent of the training. In any event, it is in our judgment a matter of professional duty on counsel and solicitors to ensure that the trial judge is informed of any familiarisation process organized by the defence using outside agencies, and it follows that the Crown Prosecution Service will be aware of what has happened.

[64] This familiarisation process should normally be supervised or conducted by a solicitor or barrister, or someone who is responsible to a solicitor or barrister with experience of the criminal justice process, and preferably by an organisation accredited for the purpose by the Bar Council and Law Society. None of those involved should have any personal knowledge of the matters in issue. Records should be maintained of all those present and the identity of those responsible for the familiarisation process, whenever it takes place. The programme should be retained, together with all the written material (or appropriate copies) used during the familiarisation sessions. None of the material should bear any similarity whatever to the issues in the criminal proceedings to be attended by the witness, and nothing in it should play on or trigger the witness's recollection of events. As already indicated, the (case study) document quoted in paragraph 41, would have been utterly flawed. If discussion of the instant criminal proceedings begins, as it almost inevitably will, it must be stopped. And advice given about precisely why it is impermissible, with a warning against the danger of evidence contamination and the risk that the course of justice may be perverted. Note should be made if and when any such warning is given.

[65] All documents in the process should be retained, and if relevant to prosecution witness, handed to the Crown Prosecution Service as a matter of course, and in relation to defence witnesses, produced to the court. None should be destroyed. It should be a matter of professional obligation for barristers and solicitors involved in these processes, or indeed the trial itself, to see that this guidance is followed.

Indictment amendments

8.206 In *Piggott and Litwin*,[208] it was found that a submission of no case to answer would have been successful, but the prosecution were allowed to amend the indictment after the close of its case. In the circumstances, a retrial should not have been ordered where evidence on the amended indictment was deemed inadmissible because it had already been heard by the jury. To do so was an abuse of process.

8.207 The accused was entitled to know the case he had to meet. The prosecution was not entitled to chop and change the way in which the case was submitted and then hope that leave to amend would be given if it had got it wrong. Section 5(5) of the Indictments Act 1915 contemplated amendments only at the very early stage at which a decision may be taken to

---

[208] [1999] 2 Cr App R 320. Contrast the situation in *TJC* [2015]EWCA Crim 1276 where a decision to stay proceedings as an abuse of process becaused of a poorly particularized indictment was reversed by the Court of Appeal on a section 58 CJA 2003 prosecutor's appeal.

order a separate trial or to postpone the trial. To allow amendment after a trial lasting ten days and by ordering a re-trial which would traverse the same ground as the first trial and on nine counts which the appellant was entitled to think had been withdrawn, caused injustice. The judge at the re-trial had a separate jurisdiction to consider whether the second trial was an abuse of process (also see *Jackson*[209]).

Defendant right to conduct defence

In *Schlesinger*,[210] the Court of Appeal quashed convictions because of the behaviour of state officials in relation to potential defence witnesses. The defence wished to call witnesses, live in court, from two embassies, as to specific facts relevant to the defence. Subsequently, senior officers from the Foreign and Commonwealth Office, at the behest of Customs, visited the embassies and successfully urged the witnesses to claim diplomatic immunity, so as to avoid giving evidence. The defendants were thereby deprived of the witnesses whom they wished to call. Their non-availability was the operative factor in the defendants' pleading guilty to exporting arms to Iraq. **8.208**

The Court of Appeal ruled that such conduct would have been likely to have caused the trial judge to stay the proceedings had he been aware of the situation. The convictions were quashed. The defendants had not had a fair trial as they were effectively precluded from calling witnesses whom they believed were necessary for their defence. It was for the jury, not customs, to decide whether the defence account was credible. It was for the defence to decide how to conduct their defence, without interference from the prosecution. **8.209**

Inadvertent disclosure

In *Martin Tobias-Gibbins*,[211] Mr Justice Field[212] stayed proceedings, as an abuse of process, following inadvertent disclosure by the prosecution. **8.210**

The Serious Fraud Office prosecuted five defendants, as part of an investigation which commenced in 2000, following an extensive prior investigation by the Law Society and City of London Fraud Squad into three of the accused who were practicing solicitors. When the five defendants were eventually charged in early 2002, the SFO alleged that they had all conspired to commit over seventy advance fee fraud transactions against hundreds of mainly foreign investors netting over £50m. When the trial of the five eventually started in May 2004, it was estimated to last one year, with the SFO prosecution papers filling 25 CD-Roms. **8.211**

The collapse of the prosecution against Martin Tobias-Gibbins was caused, in the words of Mr Justice Field, by the SFO's 'gross negligence' in mistakenly disclosing on the first day of the trial to some of the defendant's lawyers an SFO report about the case to the Attorney General which contained top secret information. **8.212**

The SFO attempted to obtain court orders against the defence lawyers 'in the know' prohibiting them from disclosing the information to their clients but on 27 May 2004, in *G and B*, the Court of Appeal rejected this attempt to gag the lawyers. **8.213**

The SFO dropped their case against the solicitors and the fourth defendant on 21 June 2004 and asked Mr Justice Field to acquit them. **8.214**

---

[209] [1999] 1 All ER 572, [1998] Crim LR 835.
[210] [1995] Crim LR 137.
[211] *The Times* (28 July 2004).
[212] (Southwark Crown Court, 27 July 2004), following the earlier acquittal of four accused: Michael Wilson-Smith, Peter Barnett, Minesh Ruperalia, and Imdad Ullah.

8.215 The SFO elected to continue its case against the one remaining defendant, Martin Tobias-Gibbins, but on 27 July 2004 Mr Justice Field ruled that by doing so the SFO was guilty of abuse of process, as it wished to assert in the forthcoming trial of the remaining defendant that the three solicitors were nonetheless guilty of the frauds for which the SFO had previously sought their acquittal.

Court martial

8.216 The appellant in *Alan Martin*[213] was a seventeen-year-old civilian, charged with the murder of a young woman in Germany. His father, an army corporal, was serving with the British Forces in Germany. The German Government waived its right to exercise its jurisdiction. By virtue of Section 71A of the Army Act 1955 as amended by the Armed Forces Act 1976, the appellant was tried by Court Martial and convicted of murder. The House of Lords upheld his conviction and held that the trial of the appellant by Court Martial could not in itself have been an abuse of process when that form of trial had been approved by Parliament for juveniles charged with murder. It further held that his trial by Court Martial was not contrary to the rule of law nor did it deprive the appellant of any basic human right.

Technical mistake

8.217 In *Dean and Bolden*,[214] a technical mistake by the prosecution, made in good faith, of proceeding under the wrong enforcement procedure (article 17(4) of the Vienna Convention against Illicit Traffic in Narcotics Drugs and Psychotropic Substances) did not constitute an abuse of process as such action was justified under another provision (article 17(2) of the same convention). Technical mistakes, made in error, did not challenge the integrity of the court process.

Privileged documents

8.218 In *Mohan Singh Kula*,[215] legally privileged documents belonging to the appellant had been seized by police prior to trial. The appellant was convicted of murder (of his wife by strangulation) and sentenced to life imprisonment. Leave to appeal conviction was granted as it was arguable that the trial judge should have ordered the proceedings to be stayed.

8.219 At trial, counsel on behalf of the appellant applied to have proceedings stayed on the following basis:

(1) Documents belonging to the appellant were unlawfully seized during two searches of his prison cell whilst on remand. A huge amount of material protected by legal professional privilege was seized and read when it should not have been. It constituted a significant factor in the prosecution of the appellant. The significance of the seizure was so great that of itself, and without the need to demonstrate prejudice, there was such an abuse of process of the court, that the judge should have stayed the proceedings.

(2) the jury's verdict should be regarded as unsafe because the appellant did not give evidence before the jury, no doubt because the contents of the papers being known to the prosecution was preying on the appellant's mind.

8.220 The Court of Appeal dismissed the appeal. Despite the seizure of legally privileged documents, the trial judge was entitled to reach the conclusion he did. Bad faith on the part of the prosecuting authorities was not alleged, either against the police officers who carried out

---

[213] [1998] 2 WLR 1.
[214] [1998] 2 Cr App R 1.
[215] (CA, 18 April 2000).

the searches or against the prosecuting legal representatives. There was no proper basis for staying the proceedings.

Whatever reasons may have prompted the decision of the defendant not to give evidence, **8.221** the Court of Appeal found that it could not realistically be suggested that the appellant had a legitimate fear that material might be used improperly and adversely against him. Not only had the trial judge already ruled that there was no basis for a genuine fear of that kind, but, during the course of the prosecution case, there is no suggestion that there had been any improper use made of material available to the prosecution by reason of these searches.

There was an overwhelming body of evidence against the appellant. The conviction was not **8.222** unsafe.

Prosecution misconduct and retrials

In *Maxwell*,[216] the defendant had been convicted principally on evidence given by an informer. **8.223** Following trial, whilst serving his sentence, the defendant admitted his involvement in the offences to various persons. A subsequent independent police investigation found that the West Yorkshire police had concealed (from the Crown Prosecution Service, prosecuting counsel, and the defence) and lied about a variety of rewards and benefits receieved by the informer principal witness. On a section 19 Criminal Appeal Act 1995 reference by the Criminal Cases Review Commission, the Court of Appeal quashed the defendant's conviction on the ground that it had been obtained by prosecutorial misconduct. The Court of Appeal ordered a retrial as the admissions made by the defendant amounted to clear and compelling evidence of guilt, notwithstanding that the admissions would not have been made but for the conviction which had been obtained by police misconduct.

The Supreme Court in *Maxwell* dismissed the defendant's appeal against the decision to order **8.224** a re-trial. It was in the interest of justice to order a re-trial. The question of whether the interests of justice required a retrial was broader than the considerations involved in an application for a stay. A decision to order a retrial should only be upset if it was plainly wrong in the sense that it was one which no reasonable court could have made or the court had taken into account immaterial factors or failed to take into account material factors. The fact that the defendant's admissions would not have been made but for the police misconduct was a relevant factor, but not determinative of the issue. The Court had been entitled to conclude that the interests of justice required a retrial because of the gravity of the offences and the existence of new and compelling evidence untainted by police misconduct. Lord Mance highlighted the importance of the voluntary element of the admissions as 'it breaks the directness of the chain of causation and it relegates the police misconduct to the status of background.'[217]

K. Summary

In relation to category two cases a stay may be granted where there is state misconduct that **8.225** will undermine public confidence in the integrity of the judicial process if a trial is permitted to proceed. The analysis is not backward-looking, but rather forward-looking, in that it relates to the impact of the misconduct on the integrity of the justice process if the trial proceeds.

---

[216] [2010] UKSC 48, [2011] 2 Cr App R 31.
[217] [2010] UKSC 48, [57].

8.226 The court's supervisory jurisdiction in cases where prosecution misconduct threatens the integrity of the criminal process is summarized in *Warren*[218] as a balancing exercise. Lord Dyson stated that:

> ... the balance must always be struck between the public interest in ensuring that those who are accused of serious crimes should be tried and the competing public interest in ensuring that executive misconduct does not undermine public confidence in the criminal justice system and bring it into disrepute.[219]

8.227 The *Warren* approach takes into account a number of factors, such as

(1) seriousness of the violation of the defendant's (or even a third party's) rights,
(2) the presence or absence of bad faith by the police and/or prosecution,
(3) whether there was any emergency or necessity for the misconduct,
(4) the availability or otherwise of sanctions against the person(s) responsible for the misconduct.
(5) the seriousness of the charges, and
(6) the causal link between the conduct and the trial or proposed trial.[220]

---

[218] [2011] UKPC 10, [2012] 1 A.C. 22; case comment at Archbold Review 2011, 6, 6–9. See also Hong Kong Court of Appeal decision in *Hong Kong v Ng Chun To Raymond* [2013] HKCA 380 and Canadian Supreme Court decision in *Nixon* [2011] 2 SCR 566, SCC 34 (as discussed in Journal of Commonwealth Criminal Law 2011, 2, 333–44).
[219] [2011] UKPC 10, [2012] 1 AC 22, [26].
[220] As cited with approval in *Max John Beckham v The Queen* [2015] NZSC 98 at para 142 of judgment.

9

ADVERSE PUBLICITY

A. Introduction

Media-generated notoriety can prejudice an accused and this may lead to a jury being discharged, an indictment being stayed, or a conviction being quashed because of adverse publicity. Such adverse media coverage may also give rise to a breach of the right to a fair trial under Article 6(1) of the European Convention of Human Rights and lead to contempt of court proceedings against the offending publisher. **9.1**

Judicial concern over prejudicial pre-trial publicity dates back to the nineteenth century,[1] with the state initiating contempt of court proceedings against offending sectors of the media.[2] **9.2**

Such concern has also been expressed in Strasbourg. Although the European Court on Human Rights has recognized that media reporting of court proceedings plays an important part in the public administration of justice by imparting information which the public has a right to receive,[3] the limits of permissible media comment may not, however, extend to statements that are likely to prejudice a fair trial or undermine the confidence of the public in the fair administration of justice.[4] Media reporting which creates an atmosphere of animosity towards an accused can prejudice a fair trial.[5] **9.3**

The ECtHR has held that whilst Article 6(2) cannot prevent the authorities from informing the press and the public about criminal investigations in progress, it nevertheless requires that **9.4**

---

[1] *Fisher* (1811) 2 Camp 563, *Attorney-General v Parnell* (1880) 14 Cox CC 474, and *Tibbits* (1902) 1 KB 77.

[2] *Attorney-General v Times Newspapers Ltd* (1974) AC 273.

[3] *Pretto v Italy* (1984) 6 EHRR 182, *Axen v Germany* (1984) 6 EHRR 195, *Natsvlishvili v Georgia* (2014) 37 BHRC 593.

[4] *Worm v Austria* (1997) 25 EHRR 454.

[5] *Berns and Ewart v Luxembourg* (1991) 68 DR 137.

they do so 'with all discretion and circumspection necessary if the presumption of innocence is to be respected'.[6]

9.5 Media freedom of expression can be restricted under Article 10(2) to protect the rights of others (which includes those on trial) and to maintain the authority and impartiality of the judiciary (which includes jurors).

9.6 In *Crociani v Italy*,[7] the ECtHR recognized that media freedom of expression 'may be limited by the state's obligation to ensure that every person charged with a criminal offence has a fair trial and not what is sometimes referred to as a "press trial"'.

9.7 Likewise, in *Hodgson, Woolf Productions and the NUJ v UK*,[8] the ECtHR made it clear that jurors should be protected from exposure to prejudicial influences. Media freedom of expression can be restricted to protect the 'pressing social need' to ensure a defendant receives a fair trial.

9.8 The ECtHR has also considered and assessed whether the effect of prejudicial media coverage has been appropriately dealt with by judicial directions to a jury to ignore the same and decide the case on the evidence alone.[9]

B. Test

Real risk of prejudice

9.9 In considering an application to stay proceedings based on adverse publicity, the court considers whether there is a real risk of prejudice to the defendant. In *McCann, Cullen and Shanahan*,[10] the principle was enunciated that if the media coverage at trial had created a real risk of prejudice against the defendants, any subsequent convictions should be regarded as unsafe and unsatisfactory. Lord Justice Beldam[11] stated that in some circumstances public discussion and debate may be so pointed and so prejudicial that it would be necessary to discharge a jury to avoid the risk of injustice to an accused.

9.10 In *McCann,* the Court of Appeal held that proceedings should have been stayed as an abuse of process. During closing speeches, when the defendants had exercised their right to silence, the Secretary of State for Northern Ireland and Lord Denning took part in radio or television broadcasts, which might have been heard by the jury, in which they equated the exercise of the right of silence with guilt.

9.11 In *T and V*,[12] a child murder case, which attracted high levels of media interest, Mr Justice Morland, in dealing with an application for a stay on the grounds of adverse publicity, formulated the following test:

> No stay should be imposed unless the defendant shows on the balance of probabilities that owing to the extent and nature of the pre-trial publicity he will suffer serious prejudice to the extent that no fair trial can be held.

---

[6] As per *Allenet de Ribemont v France* (1995) 20 EHRR 557, see also *X v Austria*, (1963) 11DR 31, *Hodgson v UK* (1988) 10 EHRR 503.

[7] (1980) 22 DR 147.

[8] (1988) 10 EHRR 503.

[9] See *X v UK* (1978) App No 7542/76 and Noye v UK (2003) 36 EHRRCD 231.

[10] [1991] 92 Cr App R 239.

[11] [1991] 92 Cr App R 239 at 251.

[12] 1 November 1993 at Preston Crown Court. See also *T and V v UK* (2000) 30 EHRR 121, [2000] Crim LR 187, in which the ECtHR found there to be violations of Article 6(1).

In *Maxwell and others*,[13] Mr Justice Phillips stated that: **9.12**

> the effect of pre-trial publicity alone can constitute a valid ground for ordering a stay of proceedings … the court will only be justified in staying a trial on the ground of adverse pre-trial publicity if the effect of the pre-trial publicity will be such as to render the verdict unsafe and unsatisfactory.

Further:

> The fact that a juror may have read or heard prejudicial matter about a defendant, and even formed an adverse opinion of him on the basis of it, does not of itself disqualify the juror on grounds of bias.

Serious prejudice

The meaning of the term 'serious prejudice' has been considered in a number of cases. In   **9.13**
Attorney General v Hat Trick Productions Ltd,[14] Lord Justice Auld stated 'serious prejudice is not capable of useful paraphrase save possibly as something which puts the course of justice at risk, as, in a criminal trial, by affecting its outcome or necessitating the discharge of the jury'. Also see comments of Lord Justice Simon Brown in *Attorney General v Birmingham Post and Mail*[15] and the differing views of Lord Justice Sedley and Mr Justice Collins in *Attorney-General v Guardian Newspapers Ltd*.[16]

Where the prejudice is 'unremitting, extensive, sensational, inaccurate and misleading'[17] and   **9.14**
the risk of prejudice is both national and ongoing, if a jury is discharged or a conviction quashed, the relevant court is unlikely to order a re-trial.

Substantial risk

When deciding whether publications created a substantial risk[18] that the course of justice   **9.15**
would be seriously impeded or prejudiced, each should be regarded separately. Further, the date, time and circulation of each publication, the likelihood of it having been read by a potential juror, its likely impact on an ordinary reader at the time of the publication, and its residual impact on a notional juror at the time of trial should all be considered.[19]

Generalized publicity

Generalized publicity, which does not refer to specific defendants, may not pose a serious risk   **9.16**
of prejudice.[20]

Historical reporting

Where the media coverage complained of is historical, the passage of time between the   **9.17**
reporting and the trial may mitigate against any potential prejudice.

In *R v Bow Street Stipendiary Magistrate ex p DPP*,[21] the Divisional Court quashed the   **9.18**
Stipendiary Magistrate's decision to stay committal proceedings based, in part, on prejudice caused by adverse publicity. The defendants were charged with conspiracy to pervert the

---

[13] Unreported, 6 March 1995, Central Criminal Court.
[14] (1997) EMLR 76.
[15] (1999) 1 WLR 361.
[16] (1999) EMLR 904.
[17] Lord Justice McGowan in *Taylor and Taylor* (1994) 98 Cr App R 361 at 368.
[18] See Lord Denning's remarks in *R v Horsham Justice, ex p Farquharson* [1982] QB 762.
[19] *Attorney-General v MGN Limited* [1997] 1 All ER 456.
[20] See Mr Justice Turner's comments in *Alcindor* (unreported) 11 June 1990 concerning media coverage of the *Herald of Free Enterprise*.
[21] (1992) 95 Cr App R 9, DC.

course of justice, arising from the Guildford Four (Patrick Armstrong, Carole Richardson, Paul Hill, and Gerard Conlon) miscarriage of justice cases.

9.19 In the Guildford Four case, the Court of Appeal judgment of the Lord Chief Justice stated that the defendants 'must have lied'. The freeing of the Guildford Four and the comments made by the Court of Appeal attracted immediate and very widespread publicity in the press and television. Much of the publicity was sensational, critical, and hostile to the police. The comment that the respondents were liars provided headline news.

9.20 The three defendants, in *ex p DPP*, made a preliminary application for a stay on the ground that the continuance of the prosecution would amount to an abuse of process. The Stipendiary Magistrate granted a stay for a number of reasons, including the adverse media comment being of a highly prejudicial nature.

9.21 The Divisional Court in quashing the stay decision held that the publicity surrounding the release of the Guildford Four could not affect a fair trial three years later, which was the earliest the defendants could be brought to trial. An order to proceed with the committal proceedings was granted. In the judgment of Lord Justice Neill:[22]

> ... a clear distinction can be drawn between the publicity in the period immediately after the release of the Guildford Four and the reports and broadcasts after December 1989.[23] The earlier material could have been prejudicial to a trial in, say, the first part of 1990... [I]n relation to the earlier material, however, I am quite satisfied that none of the publicity which I have seen could affect a fair trial in, at the earliest, the autumn of 1992. A jury would be perfectly capable of deciding the case on the evidence without regard to what they might have seen or read three years or so before.

9.22 Lord Justice Neill's observation is illustrative of the judiciary's reliance on the trial process (directions to the jury) and a 'fade' factor (of the passage of time) to mitigate and cure any prejudicial effects of adverse publicity.[24]

C. Trial Process

Prejudice and judicial direction

9.23 The trial process offers an alternative remedy than staying proceedings. Judicial direction to the jury is the preferred judicial option in dealing with the prejudicial affect of adverse publicity. In *R v Central Criminal Court ex p The Telegraph PLC*, Lord Chief Justice Taylor stated:[25]

> In determining whether publication of matter would cause a substantial risk of prejudice to a future trial, a court should credit the jury with the will and ability to abide by the judge's direction to decide the case only on the evidence before them.

Jury discharge

9.24 Where judicial direction is insufficient to cure the prejudicial affect of the adverse publicity, the jury may be discharged and a re-trial ordered. In *McCann, Cullen and Shanahan*,[26]

---

[22] (1992) 95 Cr App R 9 at p 18.

[23] The time of arrests of the police officer defendants.

[24] See the unreported case of *R v Southend-on-Sea Magistrates Court ex p Paskin*, Queen's Bench Division, High Court, Lord Justice Watkins and Justice Evans, 11 July 1991, for an example of the trial process and fade factor being considered and applied as an alternative remedy to staying proceedings.

[25] (1994) 98 Cr App R 91 at 98.

[26] (1991) 92 Cr App R 239.

the Court of Appeal quashed convictions, as the court, in the words of Lord Justice Beldam:[27]

> ... was left with the definite impression that the impact which the statements in the television interviews may well have had on the fairness of the trial could not be overcome by any direction to the jury, and that the only way in which justice could be done and be obviously seen to be done was by discharging the jury and ordering a re-trial.

D. Cases Stayed for Adverse Publicity

Cases where adverse publicity had led to a stay cover a number and range of factual situations, the decisions being factually sensitive and specific. It is difficult to discern any common factual matrix save that the media reporting has been factually inaccurate, widespread, unremitting, sensational, misleading, and highly prejudicial.   **9.25**

Nationwide publicity and continuing prejudice

In *Reade, Morris and Woodwiss*,[28] Mr Justice Garland, in staying the proceedings against three West Midlands police officers, took into account the adverse publicity and the delay of eighteen years between the offences and trial date. Mr Justice Garland recognized that applications were frequently made to change venues because of adverse local publicity. Such local prejudice may be temporary and may have an element of 'fade factor'. However, where prejudice becomes nationwide and does not abate, a stay may be appropriate. Proceedings were stayed in this case because: **9.26**

a) 'The Birmingham Six' has become a synonym for 'forced confessions'; and
b) 'The publicity attending the 1991 appeal gave the impression that the court was finding the defendants (i.e. the police officers) guilty of perjury and conspiracy'.

In *Hassan and Caldon*,[29] trial proceedings, originating from a News of the World 'sting' operation, were stayed, on the basis of a grossly prejudicial pre-trial newspaper article, which described the defendants as 'veteran villains' with 'long criminal records'. Subsequently the Divisional Court fined the *News of the World* £50,000 for contempt.[30]   **9.27**

In *Taylor and Taylor*,[31] the Court of Appeal quashed the appellants' convictions for murder on two grounds. First, the failure by the prosecution to disclose to the defence important matters regarding identification evidence and a claim for reward money. Secondly, the press coverage of the trial was, in the words of Lord Justice McCowan, 'unremitting, extensive, sensational, inaccurate and misleading'.[32] Although the trial judge gave the jury several warnings that they ought to decide the case on the evidence before them, it was impossible to say that the jury had not been influenced in its decision by newspaper articles. The press coverage of the trial had created a real risk of prejudice against the appellants. The Court of Appeal refused to order a re-trial since the risk of prejudice was deemed to be both national and ongoing.   **9.28**

In *Wood*,[33] the Court of Appeal quashed the appellant's conviction for having an explosive substance with intent to endanger life on the basis that, inter alia, highly prejudicial matters   **9.29**

---

[27] (1991) 92 Cr App R 239 at 253.
[28] At the Central Criminal Court, 15 October 1993 (referred to in *The Independent* (19 October 1993)).
[29] His Honour Judge Colgan at Isleworth Crown Court, July 1995, unreported.
[30] *Attorney-General v News Group Newspapers, The Independent* (17 July 1997).
[31] (1994) 98 Cr App R 361.
[32] (1994) 98 Cr App R 361 at 368.
[33] [1996] 1 Cr App R 207.

were reported in the press during the week of the trial. Lord Justice Staughton, stated that 'fairness demands that pressure shall not be put on jurors in a particular case by the press or anyone else'.[34]

9.30   In *Attorney General v MGN Limited*,[35] proceedings at Harrow Crown Court were stayed as a result of prejudicial media reporting. The trial judge held that 'the reporting was unlawful, misleading and scandalous ... the massive media publicity in this case was unfair, outrageous and oppressive'. The media had impugned the defendant's character by making reference to his previous convictions. Consequently, it was held that the pre-trial press coverage made it impossible for the defendant to have a fair trial.

9.31   Thereafter, the Attorney General applied to the High Court for orders against MGN Limited, Express Newspapers Plc, News Group Newspapers Limited, News (United Kingdom) Limited, and Associated Newspapers Limited for contempt of court. In assessing the residual impact which media coverage would have had on the mind of a notional juror, at the time of the trial the court will have to consider amongst other matters:

(a)   the length of time between the publication and the likely date of trial;
(b)   the focusing effect of listening over a prolonged period to evidence in a case; and
(c)   the likely effect of the judge's directions to the jury.[36]

E. Non-Stay Cases

9.32   In general, however, the criminal courts have not been prepared to accede to submissions that publicity before a trial has made a fair trial impossible. Rather they have decided that judicial directions coupled with the trial process itself will result in the jury disregarding such publicity.[37]

Judicial direction

9.33   In *Rosemary West*,[38] an application for a stay based on hostile publicity was rejected by the trial judge. The applicant applied for leave to appeal against conviction on ten counts of murder on the grounds that, inter alia, the pre-trial media publicity was so extensive and hostile that it precluded a fair trial.

9.34   The Court of Appeal, in refusing the appeal application, held that although press coverage in advance of the trial had been adverse to the applicant, it would be absurd if allegations of murder of a horrific nature caused such shock to the nation that an accused could not be tried. Lord Chief Justice Taylor stated that 'providing the judge effectively warns the jury to act only on the evidence given in court, there is no reason to suppose they would do otherwise',[39] and by extension, no reason to suppose that the trial would be unfair.

9.35   Support for judicial direction being used to cure potential prejudice caused by publicity can be found in a number of similar remarks in other cases:

---

[34]   [1996] 1 Cr App R 207 at 214.
[35]   [1997] 1 All ER 456.
[36]   Ibid Lord Justice Schiemann's judgment at 461.
[37]   See Lord Phillips observations in *Abu Hamza* [2007] Cr App R 27 at para 89; *Barry George* [2002] EWCA Crim 1923; and *Jeffrey Archer* [2003] 1 Cr App R (S) 86.
[38]   [1996] 2 Cr App R 374.
[39]   [1996] 2 Cr App R 374 at 386A.

- *Kray*: 'I have enough confidence in my fellow-countryman to think that they have got newspapers sized up ... and they are capable in normal circumstances of looking at a matter fairly and without prejudice even though they have to disregard what they may have read in a newspaper';[40]
- *Coughlan*:[41] 'juries are capable of disregarding that which is not properly before them. They are expected to disregard what one accused says about another in his absence. If they can do that, which is far from easy, they can disregard what is said in the newspapers';
- *Ex p B*:[42] 'jurors are well able to put out of their minds extraneous material and try the case on the evidence they hear in court';
- *Irvin v Dowd* (a US Supreme Court decision):[43] 'it is sufficient if the juror can lay aside his impression or opinion and render a verdict based on the evidence presented in court'.

The use of judicial direction as a remedy against adverse publicity was endorsed by the Court **9.36** of Appeal in *Abu Hamza*.[44] Lord Phillips[45] endorsed the following statement made by the President of the Queen's Bench Division (Sir Igor Judge) in *Re Barot*:[46]

> There is a feature of our trial system which is sometimes overlooked or taken for granted. The collective experience of ... the present constitution of the court, both when we were in practice at the Bar and judicially, has demonstrated to us time and time again, that juries up and down the country have a passionate and profound belief in, and a commitment to, the right of a defendant to be given a fair trial. They know that it is integral to their responsibility. It is, when all is said and done, their birthright; it is shared by each one of them with the defendant. They guard it faithfully. The integrity of the jury is an essential feature of our trial process. Juries follow the directions which the judge will give them to focus exclusively on the evidence and to ignore anything they may have heard or read out of court.

Lord Phillips went on to adopt the following from *Montgomery v HM Advocate*:[47]

> [T]here is the discipline to which the jury will be subjected of listening to and thinking about the evidence. The actions of seeing and hearing the witness may be expected to have far greater impact on their minds than such residual recollections as may exist about reports about the case in the media. This impact can be expected to be reinforced on the other hand by such warnings and directions as the trial judge may think it appropriate to give them as the trial proceeds, in particular when he delivers his charge before they retire to consider their verdicts.

The Court of Appeal rejected the appellant's arguments in relation to adverse publicity. It was **9.37** accepted that there had been a sustained hostile media campaign against Abu Hamza, over a two-year period, treating him as an ogre. However, the trial judge had postponed the trial date until (about a year) after the most intense publicity had subsided. Further, he described steps which would need to be taken in order to counter the effects of the adverse publicity including an explanation to the jury of the difference between their task in sifting and evaluation of evidence and indiscriminate hostile labeling of a suspect by public commentators. The trial judge concluded that with a proper direction a jury would be able to bring impartial

---

[40] [1969] 53 Cr App R 412 at pages 414–15 by Justice Lawton.

[41] [1977] 64 Cr App R 11 by Lord Justice Lawton.

[42] [1994] AC 42 by Justice Scott Baker.

[43] 366 US 717, 6 L Ed 2d 751, 81 S Ct 1639 at 756.

[44] [2007] Cr App R 27: citing New Zealand Law Commission research into the impact of pre-trial publicity and of prejudicial media coverage during the trial as minimal (Young, Cameron, and Tinsley, *Juries in Criminal Trials*, Part two, Vol 1, Ch 9 para 287 (NZLC November 1999).

[45] [2007] Cr App R 27 at para 90 of Lord Phillips judgment.

[46] *In re Barot* [2006] EWCA Crim 2692 at para 32.

[47] At para 91 of the judgment, Lord Phillips cites Lord Hope's remarks in *Montgomery v HM Advocate* [2003] 1 AC 641.

judgment to the case and to decide whether, despite being labelled by some as a public enemy, the defendant really did commit the offences with which he was charged. The Court of Appeal agreed with that view and rejected the adverse publicity appeal ground.[48]

9.38 The judicial remedy approach adopted in *Abu Hamza* was followed and applied by the Court of Appeal in *Abdulla Ahmed Ali*.[49] The Court of Appeal acknowledged Minister of Justice research material from February 2010, which showed that more jurors said they saw information on the internet than admitted looking for it on the internet. In the study, jurors admitted to doing something they should have been told by the trial judge not to do. Lord Justice Thomas dealt with the point by observing:[50]

> To the extent that there remains the risk that, despite what jurors are told by a judge, an individual juror might look up matters on the internet, any attempt by an individual juror to use what was found to influence the views of the other jurors is, in our judgment, bound to fail. For what was found on the internet to have any influence on the verdict of a jury, it would require other members of the jury to disobey their oath. In our judgment, the observations in *Barot* and *Abu Hamza* hold good and the trial process in this trial was capable of coping with the adverse publicity.

F. Re-Trial Publicity

Re-trial following conviction being quashed

9.39 The judicial direction approach also applies to publicity surrounding a retrial as illustrated by the Court of Appeal decision in *Stone*.[51] The Court of Appeal allowed Michael Stone's appeal against his conviction on two counts of murder because a witness, who gave crucial evidence at trial of an alleged confession by the appellant, had retracted his evidence the day after the jury returned their verdicts. The witness told journalists that he had given false evidence at the trial.

9.40 In addressing the Court of Appeal, it was contended on behalf of Michael Stone that so much publicity had been generated by the trial, coupled with the shocking nature of both the crime and allegations, that the appellant could not receive a fair trial in the future and therefore a retrial should not be ordered.

9.41 The publicity complained of by Michael Stone took place in the months after the jury verdict in October 1998, when matters were revealed which had not been disclosed to the jury. Immediately prior to and during the appeal further publicity occurred. The appellant contended that even if the retrial was delayed until September 2001, some of the new jury would recall matters which should not have be placed (by the media) in the public domain.

9.42 In ordering a retrial, the Court of Appeal stated that the *Stone* case was one where but for the publicity a retrial would certainly be ordered. In such instances, a retrial should take place unless the Court were satisfied, on a balance of probabilities, that if, at the retrial, the jury returned one or more verdicts of guilty, the effect of the publicity to which reference had been made would be such as to render that verdict or verdicts unsafe. Lord Justice Kennedy, in

---

[48] See para 103 of Lord Phillips judgment. See similar comments in other jurisdictions:(Canada*) Corbett* [1988] 1 SCR 670 at 692; (Australia*) Glennon* (1992) 173 CLR 592 at 603; (Ireland) *Z v DPP* [1994] 2 IR 476 at 496.

[49] [2011] EWCA Crim 1260; [2011] 3 All ER 1071; [2011] 2 Cr App R 22; [2012] Crim LR 378. In particular see Lord Justice Thomas judgment at para 89 citing from *In re Barot*.

[50] [2011] EWCA Crim 1260, para 92 of judgment.

[51] (2001) Crim LR 465. See also *Dunlop* [2007] 1 Cr App R 8.

giving judgment, stated that in justice to the victim's family and the wider community there should be a retrial.

The Court of Appeal accepted that the early publicity was sensational, possibly in parts inaccurate, extended far beyond what a jury in 2001 might normally be told, but the accurate reporting was legitimately in the public interest. Aside from recognizing the right of the media to report criminal proceedings, the Court of Appeal noted that the retrial would not start until nearly three years after the October 1998 publicity, which was the appellant's main complaint. The fade factor of three years mitigated against any residual prejudice. **9.43**

The Court further observed that a change of trial locality, away from the Kent or London area, would reduce prejudice, as the impact of the crimes was at its greatest locally. The retrial was to take place in Birmingham. In addition the Court of Appeal also suggested that it might be that a few careful jury panel questions might act as a further safeguard to a fair trial. **9.44**

Re-trial following acquittal

In *R v D (acquitted person: retrial)*[52] the Court of Appeal considered the first application under s 76(1) Criminal Justice Act 2003 for the quashing of an acquittal and the ordering of a retrial. In a preliminary hearing, the court considered an application for reporting restrictions to be imposed on the substantive application, and gave general guidance on sections 82(1) and 82(3) of the CJA 2003. **9.45**

The applicant, supported by the acquitted person, applied for an order restricting publication under s 82 CJA 2003 of the substantive application to quash the acquittal and of the judgment of the court if the application were successful. The media made representations opposing the application for reporting restrictions. **9.46**

The Court of Appeal held:

(1) It was in the interests of justice to order reporting restrictions on the substantive application in the instant case. Sections 82(1) and 82(3) of the CJA 2003 addressed wider considerations than s.4 of the Contempt of Court Act 1981, and acknowledged the detailed process required before a retrial could take place. For an acquittal to be quashed and a retrial ordered, new and compelling evidence had to be adduced. Such evidence would, in open court, be analysed and addressed by both sides and the court would comment on it, all of which would take place in the context of the evidence given in the earlier trial, which had not been sufficient to convict the acquitted person;

(2) Such cases were likely to generate a great deal of publicity either nationally or locally. Sections 82(1) and 82(3) CJA 2003 were intended, so far as practicable, to ensure the same fairness of process to any retrial following the quashing of an acquittal as was afforded to a defendant in a normal trial. Without some restriction, publicity would be given to all the evidence considered by the Court of Appeal on an application to quash the acquittal, which posed a substantial risk to the administration of justice at a retrial;

(3) The court had to examine each application and only make an order imposing reporting restrictions if satisfied it was in the interests of justice to do so. The court had to examine the responsibility of the media for the reporting of the criminal process and principles of open justice. Juries should be treated as robust, open-minded and able to distinguish evidence before them from pre-trial gossip;

(4) In the instant case it was understandable that the DPP thought it appropriate to issue a press release, as it was the first example of a new procedure that had arisen under a new statutory scheme that disturbed the centuries-old common law principle against double jeopardy. However, in future cases it was doubtful whether any form of press release

---

[52] (2006) CA (Civ Div) (Sir Igor Judge (President QB), David Steel J, Hedley J) 27/2/2006, Lawtel LTL 27/02/2006.

would be appropriate. At the very least it would suggest that the DPP had personally concluded that there was compelling new evidence sufficient to expose the acquitted person to the risk of double jeopardy. Further, in a case where the original trial had attracted significant public interest, the press release itself would create publicity;

(5) The DPP was entitled to make an application to prohibit publication only after the investigation was restored following the acquittal. Whilst neither the media nor the acquitted person could set the process in motion, if the DPP made no application where one should have been made, the court could act of its own motion. The DPP should make an application to restrict potentially prejudicial material as soon as that material becomes apparent;

(6) The acquitted person should be notified of the intention to make an application under section 82 of the Criminal Justice Act 2003 and the court should be fully informed of his attitude to the publicity. The media should be informed, at least 14 days before the application is heard, and be permitted to make submissions and attend the hearing. Representatives of the media should notify the court and the DPP not later than 48 hours before the hearing of their intention to attend and make submissions. Where the media expressed no intentions, and the DPP and acquitted person agreed, the court could proceed on a consideration on the papers.

9.47 Any order under s 82 CJA 2003 would be made in open court and would not act as a permanent restriction on publication.

G. Judicial Remedies

9.48 Judicial discretionary remedies to mitigate the effects of adverse publicity include, inter alia:

(a) Where prejudice is local to a particular geographical location, alter the trial venue (as in *Irvin v Dowd*[53] and *Stone*[54]).

(b) Where there is pre-trial publicity, postpone the trial to allow a 'fade factor' to operate (as in *Attorney-General v News Group Newspapers*[55] and he US Supreme Court decision in *Patton v Yount*[56]).

(c) Where there is adverse publicity during the trial, direct the jury to ignore publicity (relying on the good sense and ability of jurors to consider the case on the evidence inside court, as opposed to media coverage outside of court).

(d) Where a judicial direction would not suffice, discharge the jury and order a re-trial, with a date sufficiently far enough in the future to allow a 'fade factor' to operate;

(e) consider a jury questionnaire (as in the *Maxwell*[57] case, where the jury panel was asked to answer a forty-item questionnaire, and as was suggested in *Stone*[58] for the re-trial). However, the questioning process may (i) fail to identify prejudiced jurors (as it is unlikely that prejudiced jurors will recognize their own personal prejudice, or knowing it, admit to it as identified in *Murphy v R*[59]) and (ii) cause the very problem it was designed to solve, by bringing, for the first time, to the potential jurors attention, the adverse publicity. Also note, in *Tracey Andrews*,[60] the trial judge rejected the defence

---

[53] 366 US 717, 6 L Ed 2d 751, 81 S Ct 1639.
[54] (2001) Crim LR 465.
[55] (1987) 1 QB 1.
[56] 467 US 1025, 81 L Ed 2d 847, 104 S Ct 2885.
[57] Unreported, 6 March 1995, Central Criminal Court.
[58] (2001) Crim L R 465.
[59] (1989) 167 CLR 94 by Chief Justice Mason.
[60] (1999) Crim LR 156.

submission that a juror questionnaire be used to mitigate the affects of adverse pre-trial publicity. The Court of Appeal, in rejecting the appeal, noted that the principle of random jury selection meant that there was in general no jury vetting or questioning. Only if there was a real danger of bias would the court intervene.[61]

The appropriate remedy depends on the circumstances of the case, each case turning on its own facts. **9.49**

H. North American Media Coverage Cases

The United States Supreme Court has considered, on a number of occasions, the inter-related right to a fair trial, right to freedom of expression, and media coverage of criminal proceedings. **9.50**

In short, the Sixth Amendment guarantees 'trial, by an impartial jury ...'[62] **9.51**

In essence, the right to jury trial guarantees to the criminally accused a fair trial by a panel of impartial, 'indifferent' jurors. A fair trial in a fair tribunal is a basic requirement of due process.

In the overwhelming majority of criminal trials in the United States, pre-trial publicity presents few unmanageable threats to the accused's right to a fair trial. But when the case is a 'sensational' tensions develop between the right of the accused to trial by an impartial jury and the rights to freedom of expression, guaranteed by the First Amendment to the US Constitution. **9.52**

The relevant decisions of the US Supreme Court, even if not directly applicable, are instructive by way of background, and may point towards future developments. **9.53**

Change of venue

In *Irvin v Dowd*, the defendant was convicted of murder following intensive and hostile news coverage. The trial judge had granted a defence motion for a change of venue, but only to an adjacent county, which had been exposed to essentially the same news coverage. At trial, 430 persons were called for jury service; 268 were excused because they had fixed opinions as to guilt. Eight of the twelve who served as jurors thought the defendant was guilty, but said they could nevertheless render an impartial verdict. On review, the Court vacated the conviction and death sentence and remanded to allow a new trial: '[w]ith his life at stake, it is not requiring too much that petitioner be tried in an atmosphere undisturbed by so huge a wave of public passion.'[63] **9.54**

Filming

Similarly, in *Rideau v Louisiana*,[64] the Court reversed the conviction of a defendant whose staged, highly emotional confession had been filmed with the co-operation of local police and later broadcast on television for three days while he was awaiting trial, saying '(a)ny subsequent court proceedings in a community so pervasively exposed to such a spectacle could be but a hollow formality.'[65] **9.55**

---

[61] *Gough* (1993) AC 646, (1993) 97 Cr App R 188.
[62] See *Duncan v Louisiana*, 391 US 145 at 149, 88 S Ct 1444 at 1447, 20 L Ed 2d 491 (1968).
[63] 366 US at 728, 81 S Ct at 1645.
[64] 373 US at 723, 83 S Ct 1417, 10 L Ed 2d 663 (1963).
[65] 373 US at 726, 83 S Ct at 1419.

9.56 Further in *Estes v Texas*,[66] the Court held that the defendant had not been afforded due process where the volume of trial publicity, the judge's failure to control the proceedings, and the telecast of a hearing and of the trial itself 'inherently prevented a sober search for the truth.'[67]

Re-trial

9.57 In *Sheppard v Maxwell*,[68] the Supreme Court focused sharply on the impact of pre-trial publicity and a trial court's duty to protect the defendant's constitutional right to a fair trial. The Supreme Court ordered a new trial for the petitioner, even though the first trial had occurred twelve years before.

9.58 Beyond doubt, the press had shown no responsible concern for the constitutional guarantee of a fair trial; the community from which the jury was drawn had been inundated by publicity hostile to the defendant.

9.59 The Supreme Court noted that 'unfair and prejudicial news comment on pending trials has become increasingly prevalent,'[69] and issued a strong warning:

> Due process requires that the accused receive a trial by an impartial jury free from outside influences. Given the pervasiveness of modern communications and the difficulty of effacing prejudicial publicity from the minds of the jurors the trial courts must take strong measures to ensure that the balance is never weighed against the accused ... Of course, there is nothing that proscribes the press from reporting events that transpire in the courtroom. But where there is a reasonable likelihood that prejudicial news prior to trial will prevent a fair trial, the judge should continue (adjourn) the case until the threat abates, or transfer it to another county not so permeated with publicity. If publicity during the proceedings threatens the fairness of the trial, a new trial should be ordered. But we must remember that reversals are but palliatives; the cure lies in those remedial measures that will prevent the prejudice at its inception. The courts must take such steps by rule and regulation that will protect their processes from prejudicial outside interferences. Neither prosecutors, counsel for defense, the accused, witnesses, court staff nor enforcement officers coming under the jurisdiction of the court should be permitted to frustrate its function. Collaboration between counsel and the press as to information affecting the fairness of a criminal trial is not only subject to regulation, but is highly censurable and worthy of disciplinary measures.[70]

9.60 Because the trial court had failed to use even minimal efforts to insulate the trial and the jurors from the 'deluge of publicity',[71] the Court vacated the judgment of conviction and a new trial followed, in which the accused was acquitted.

Fair trial

9.61 The US Supreme Court has held in other cases that trials have been fair in spite of widespread adverse pre-trial publicity.

9.62 In *Stroble v California*,[72] for example, the Court affirmed a conviction and death sentence that was challenged on the ground that pre-trial news accounts, including the prosecutor's release of the defendant's recorded confession, were allegedly so inflammatory as to amount to a denial of due process. The Court disapproved of the prosecutor's conduct, but noted that

---

[66] 381 US at 532, 85 S Ct 1628, 14 L Ed 2d 543 (1965).
[67] 381 US at 551, 85 S Ct at 1637. See also *Marshall v United States* 360 US at 310, 79 S Ct 1171, 3 L Ed 2d 1250 (1959).
[68] 384 US at 333, 86 S Ct 1507, 16 L Ed 2d 600 (1966).
[69] 384 US at 362, 86 S Ct at 1522.
[70] 384 US 333 at 362–363, 86 S Ct at 1522.
[71] 384 US 333 at 357, 86 S Ct at 1519.
[72] 343 US 181, 72 S Ct 599, 96 L Ed 872 (1952).

the publicity had receded some six weeks before trial, that the defendant had not moved for a change of venue, and that the confession had been found voluntary and was admitted in evidence at trial. See also *Murphy v Florida,*[73] *Beck v Washington,*[74] *and Reynolds v United States.*[75]

The capacity of the jury to decide the case fairly is influenced by the tone and extent of the publicity, which is in part, and often in large part, shaped by what lawyers, police, and other officials do to precipitate news coverage. The trial judge has a major responsibility to mitigate the effects of pre-trial publicity.   **9.63**

The costs of failure to afford a fair trial are high. In the most extreme cases, the risk of injustice was avoided when the convictions were reversed. But a reversal means that justice has been delayed for both the defendant and the state. In some cases, because of lapse of time, a retrial is impossible or further prosecution is gravely handicapped.   **9.64**

I. Summary

In *Abu Hamza,*[76] the Court of Appeal recognized that, in general: **9.65**

> ... the courts have not been prepared to accede to submissions that publicity before a trial has made a fair trial impossible. Rather they have held that directions from the judge coupled with the effect of the trial process itself will result in the jury disregarding such publicity.

---

[73] 421 US 794, 95 S Ct 2031, 44 L Ed 2d 589 (1975).
[74] 369 US 541, 82 S Ct 955, 8 L Ed 2d 98 (1962).
[75] 98 US 145, 155–56, 25 L Ed 244 (1879).
[76] [2007] 1 Cr App R 27 at para 89 of the judgment.

10

ABILITY TO PARTICIPATE IN CRIMINAL PROCEEDINGS

10.1 This chapter, which is split into two parts, examines a defendant's ability to participate effectively in criminal proceedings, both in terms of the defendant's mental capacity and legal representation.

A. Ability to Participate—Mental Incapacity or Disorder and Vulnerability

Introduction

10.2 The first part of this chapter[1] traces the development of the stay jurisdiction where a defendant lacks the ability to effectively participate in criminal proceedings for reasons linked to mental incapacity, or disorder, or vulnerability.

10.3 The principle has been established, through case law, that the right to a fair trial under Article 6 of the European Convention on Human Rights (ECHR) involves the defendant being able to participate effectively in the court process. Judicial endorsements of procedural modifications to assist defendant participation in the trial have also followed, acting as an alternative to staying proceedings as an abuse of process. Further, encouragement is also given to summary courts to use procedures that do not result in a criminal conviction, but an adjudication that the actus reus was committed by the defendant, without making a determination as to mens rea.

10.4 People with mental disorders may appear in the criminal justice system as victims, witnesses, and defendants. In the latter role, they appear to be overrepresented: a 1998 survey demonstrated that over 90 per cent of prisoners had a recognizable psychiatric condition.[2]

---

[1] Kris Gledhill, Barrister, Associate Professor, AUT Law School, Auckland, New Zealand.

[2] Singleton et al., Psychiatric Morbidity Among Prisoners in England and Wales, HMSO 1998; a summary is available at <http://www.ons.gov.uk/ons/rel/psychiatric-morbidity/psychiatric-morbidity-among-prisoners/index.html> (as of 14 November 2015). At p 23 of the summary, the authors comment on the

The substantive law accommodates issues of mental disorder. For example, the special verdict **10.5** of not guilty by reason of insanity operates as a defence to criminal liability[3] and there is the partial defence to murder of diminished responsibility. Mental disorder may also have an impact on the procedures to be followed at trial. One aspect of this is the fitness to stand trial process;[4] the substantive test, at least in so far as trials on indictment are concerned, is whether the accused can comprehend proceedings so as to make a proper defence.[5] The abuse of process jurisdiction may also be relevant, since case law has revealed situations in which a defendant is not unfit to stand trial but cannot participate adequately in the process to ensure a fair trial.[6]

The right to participate as an element of a fair trial: Article 6 ECHR

The fundamental right to a fair trial in relation to any criminal trial is set out in Article **10.6** 6(1) of the ECHR with a number of specific rights set out in Article 6(3), including the right to defend oneself in person (Article 6(3)(c)) and to examine witnesses (Article 6(3)(d)). There is also a right to an interpreter (in Article 6(3)(e)), which applies if the person cannot 'understand or speak' the language of the court: this only makes sense if there is a right to participate in the process. The express language indicates that a right to participate is implicit in Article 6.

The question of defendants' participation in the trial process was considered by the European **10.7** Court of Human Rights (ECtHR)in *Stanford v UK*.[7] The complaint was from a man convicted of serious sexual offences who alleged that he could not hear the evidence of the victim clearly. This was the result of the design of the court, and the arrangements made to allow the victim to give evidence, because of her soft voice. While she could be heard by the judge, jury and lawyers, it was difficult for Mr Stanford to hear her from the dock. His trial solicitor

---

fact that many prisoners had several disorders, noting that '[o]nly one in ten or fewer showed no evidence of any of the five disorders considered in the survey (personality disorder, psychosis, neurosis, alcohol misuse and drug dependence) and no more than two out of ten in any sample group had only one disorder.' See also Seena Fazel and John Danesh, 'Serious Mental Disorder in 23,000 Prisoners: A Systematic Review of 62 Surveys', The Lancet Vol 359, pp 545–50 (16 February 2002), who concluded, '[o]ur results suggest that typically about one in seven prisoners in Western countries have psychotic illnesses or major depression (disorders that might be risk factors for suicide), and about one in two male prisoners and about one in five female prisoners have antisocial personality disorders'.

[3] In the magistrates' court, where the special verdict under s 2 of the Trial of Lunatics Act 1883 is not applicable, insanity leads to a verdict of not guilty: *R (Singh) v Stratford Magistrates Court* [2007] EWHC 1582 (Admin), [2007] Mental Health Law Reports 274. The Administrative Court noted that it might be possible to use the process under s 37(3) of the Mental Health Act 1983 of a finding that the actus reus was committed and imposing an order on that basis (which is discussed in this chapter).

[4] In the Crown Court, this arises under sections 4, 4A, and 5 of the Criminal Procedure (Insanity) Act 1964, as amended (in particular by the Criminal Procedure (Insanity and Unfitness to Plead Act) 1991). The magistrates court may achieve a similar process by way of section 11(1) of the Power of Criminal Courts (Sentencing) Act 2000 and section 37(3) of the Mental Health Act 1983: see *R (P) v Barking Youth Court* [2002] EWHC 734 (Admin), [2002] Mental Health Law Reports 304, [2002] 2 Cr App R 19 (discussed below).

[5] *Pritchard* (1836) 7 C&P 303; *Robertson* 52 Cr App R 690. For a detailed discussion of these matters, see Ronald Mackay's chapters on criminal matters in Larry Gostin et al., *Principles of Mental Health Law and Policy* (Oxford University Press 2010); and Kris Gledhill, *Defending Mentally Disordered Persons* (Legal Action Group 2012).

[6] In addition, the High Court has jurisdiction to control decisions as to prosecution through judicial review, but the ability to make an abuse of process application to a court will usually mean that there is an alternative remedy such that judicial review—a discretionary remedy—will be refused. For an example of this, see *C v Sevenoaks Youth Court* [2009] EWHC 3088 (Admin), [2009] Mental Health Law Reports 329.

[7] Application 16757/90, judgment adopted on 24 January 1994; (1994) Series A/282-A, p 11.

confirmed in a statement made to the Solicitors' Complaints Bureau that it was known that Mr Stanford had hearing difficulties, but also noted that he had provided full instructions on the victim's statement and stated that the view was taken by his legal team that he did not need to hear her give evidence; there was also a tactical decision taken that it would appear intimidating to place Mr Stanford in proximity to the victim.

10.8   Mr Stanford's application for leave to appeal to the Court of Appeal was dismissed despite the Court accepting evidence that he had had difficulties hearing the key evidence against him. The ECtHR noted that English law, as to the need for defendants to attend trial, was to ensure that they could hear the evidence and be able to answer it.[8] It also recorded that the parties had not disputed that

> Article 6, read as a whole, guarantees the right of an accused to participate effectively in a criminal trial. In general this includes, inter alia, not only his right to be present, but also to hear and follow the proceedings. Such rights are implicit in the very notion of an adversarial procedure and can also be derived from the guarantees contained in sub-paragraphs (c), (d) and (e) of paragraph 3 of Article 6: 'to defend himself in person', 'to examine or have examined witnesses', and 'to have the free assistance of an interpreter if he cannot understand or speak the language used in court'.[9]

10.9   However, the ECtHR found there was no breach of Article 6 on the facts because

(1) the lack of a complaint in the course of the trial meant that there was no decision by a state official that the trial should proceed without him being able to hear; and

(2) Mr Stanford had not disagreed with the tactical decision taken by competent counsel not to position him so that he could hear.

10.10   The necessity to secure defendant participation has been examined in cases subsequent to *Stanford*.

Participation and vulnerability

10.11   The right to the effective participation of vulnerable defendants in criminal proceedings was considered by the Grand Chamber of the ECtHR in *T and V v United Kingdom*.[10] This involved two ten-year-old boys who were charged with murder and stood trial in the Crown Court[11] when they were aged eleven. Despite their age, the only change made to the normal trial procedure was an early end to the court day (to match the end of the school day) and a 10-minute break every hour. T and V were convicted of murder and sentenced to an indeterminate sentence of detention during Her Majesty's Pleasure.

10.12   It was argued in the ECtHR that Article 6(1) fair trial rights had been breached because of the defendants' inability to participate, based on their age and their respective mental states.

---

[8] Citing *Lee Kun* [1916] 1 KB 337, at 341, where Lord Reading CJ stated: 'There must be very exceptional circumstances to justify proceeding with the trial in the absence of the accused. The reason why the accused should be present at the trial is that he may hear the case made against him and have the opportunity … of answering it. The presence of the accused means not only that he must be physically in attendance, but also that he must be capable of understanding the nature of the proceedings.' The Court also noted that it had been held in *Smellie* (1919) 14 Cr App R 128 that a trial judge could remove a defendant from the dock but not out of the hearing of a witness who might be intimidated by the presence of the defendant.

[9] Para 26. See also *Ekbatani v Sweden* (1988) 13 EHRR 504, in which the failure of the Swedish Court of Appeal to hold an oral hearing on a review of a conviction, when it had power to review the facts and the law, breached the 'right to be heard in person' (para 33). For a case relying on the provision of an interpreter, see *Cuscani v UK* (2003) 36 EHRR 2.

[10] (2000) 30 EHRR 121, [1999] Prison Law Reports 189.

[11] Section 24 of the Magistrates' Courts Act 1980 required a trial on indictment when a child was charged with homicide. There was a discretion to commit to the Crown Court if the offence was sufficiently serious that it might require a sentence beyond the powers of the summary courts.

There was expert evidence that V was immature and showed post-traumatic effects, extreme distress and guilt, and had fears of the terrible retribution he expected as a result of the trial, as a result of which he had difficulty in thinking or talking about the events in question and so had not revealed a full account.[12] Expert evidence demonstrated that T was of average intelligence, had signs of post-traumatic stress disorder, and was affected by a high level of anxiety and poor eating and sleeping patterns. These features limited his ability to instruct his lawyers, testify adequately in his defence and understand the procedures fully (though not to the extent that he was unfit to stand trial for the purposes of the Criminal Procedure (Insanity) Act 1964, as amended).[13] There was also evidence to demonstrate that the boys knew the difference between right and wrong.[14]

The defendants made an application to stay the criminal trial, but only on the basis that **10.13** adverse publicity made a fair trial impossible. The application was rejected.[15] There was no application to stay proceedings based on the children's inability to participate. This was despite a Privy Council decision confirming the common law rule that a person had to be able to participate: see *Kunnath v the State*.[16]

In addition to the material concerning the pre-trial assessments of the defendants, outlined **10.14** above, there was evidence before the ECtHR as to the impact of the proceedings on the defendants. V[17] had not been able to pay attention to the proceedings and T's [18] evidence to the ECtHR had been that he had shut out the trial process as he felt intimidated.

The ECtHR held that, although it was not impermissible to try such young children,[19] **10.15** account had to be taken of:

- their vulnerability in terms of their level of maturity and intellectual and emotional capacities;
- arrangements that had be made to promote their ability to participate;
- arrangements that had be made to reduce the level of intimidation arising from the intense media and public interest in the case, and;
- the available expert evidence as to mental health matters that showed that V was unlikely to have been able to give informed instructions and T had a limited ability.

The ECtHR decided that the steps taken in the domestic proceedings had been inadequate, **10.16** such that Article 6 had been breached.[20] It was noted that whilst the applicants had received explanations of the trial process, had seen the courtroom in advance, hearing times had been

---

[12] *T v UK*, para 11. There was also prosecution expert evidence that, although he knew the difference between right and wrong, he had wept inconsolably and shown signs of distress whenever he was asked about the events in question and 'was not able to talk about the events in issue in any useful way': para 12.

[13] Paragraph 11 in *T v UK*.

[14] Paragraph 12 in *V v UK*, para 11 in *T v UK*. At the time, it was presumed that children aged less than fourteen did not know that a crime was wrong and so this had to be proved by the prosecution: this—the doli incapax rule—was abolished by section 34 of the Crime and Disorder Act 1998 (as interpreted by the House of Lords in *JTB* [2010] UKHL 20).

[15] *V v UK*, para 10.

[16] [1993] 1 WLR 1315. This related to the absence of an interpreter. The Privy Council noted that the presence of the defendant at a trial was required '... not simply that there should be corporeal presence but that the defendant, by reason of his presence, should be able to understand the proceedings and decide what witnesses he wishes to call, whether or not to give evidence and if so, upon what matters relevant to the case against him.'

[17] *V v UK*, paras 17–19.

[18] *T v UK*, paras 16–17.

[19] Section 50 of the Children and Young Persons Act 1933 as amended by section 16(1) of the Children and Young Persons Act 1963 sets the age of criminal responsibility in England and Wales at ten years.

[20] A minority opinion was that the process amounted to a breach of Art 3 ECHR as well.

shortened, one particular modification—a raised dock that had been used to allow them to see proceedings—had in fact left them exposed to a heightened level of scrutiny and discomfort.

10.17   The ECtHR specifically distinguished *Stanford* on the basis that Mr Stanford could consult with his lawyers during the proceedings and during breaks, whereas the problems faced by V and T were such that they would not be able to cooperate with or provide instructions to their lawyers.[21]

10.18   Lord Reed, in the ECtHR, accepted that where a child's level of maturity was such that criminal responsibility could be ascribed to them, they could be put on trial, but the procedure does not have to mirror the process applied to adults. He then noted that, whilst it was recorded on the face of Article 6(1) that the normal rules as to public trials could be modified when juveniles were involved,

> [t]here is on the other hand nothing in Article 6 to indicate that there can be any derogation, in cases involving children, from the principle that the trial process should provide for the effective participation of the accused, who must be able to follow the proceedings and to give instructions where necessary to his lawyer.

To secure this required modifications of the process that took into account the maturity and intellectual and emotional capacity of the child. He agreed that not enough had been done on the facts.

10.19   *V and T v UK* identified a gap between the formal test for fitness to stand trial in English law and the need to ensure effective participation. The evidence that T and V required therapy to overcome the enormity of what they had done suggested that a criminal trial was not an appropriate course of action, at least not at the time when it occurred. What is implicit in the decision is that attributing criminal guilt has to be secondary to the central aim of securing justice, of which a fair trial process is a component part; if that cannot be done, the trial should not proceed.

Effective participation

10.20   The ECtHR again considered the need for defendant participation in the case of *SC v UK*.[22] The defendant, aged eleven, and an older boy were involved in an attempted bag-snatch robbery of an elderly lady, who fell and fractured her arm. The case was committed to the Crown Court for trial on the basis that it might be appropriate to impose a sentence beyond the powers of the Youth Court. The expert evidence was that SC had learning difficulties that put his powers of reasoning and communication at the level of a younger child, although the experts could not say confidently that he met the test for being unfit to stand trial. An application to stay the proceedings was rejected by the trial judge who, having described SC as 'streetwise', noted that wigs and gowns would not be worn, SC would not be in the dock, and frequent breaks would be taken.[23] SC was convicted, and sentenced to two and a half years' detention; leave to appeal was refused.[24] He then applied to the ECtHR.

10.21   The ECtHR gave a detailed account of what was meant by effective participation, stating that it:

---

[21]   *V v UK* para 90.

[22]   (2005) 40 EHRR 10, appn 60958/00, judgment of 15 June 2004.

[23]   It should be noted that these were consistent with the Practice Direction issued in response to the case of *V and T*, and discussed below, even though the trial took place before it had been issued: this made it clear that more could have been done in V and T's trial.

[24]   (2005) 40 EHRR 10, para 31: the ECtHR records that the Court of Appeal felt that the judge had borne in mind the decision in *T and V v UK*.

presupposes that the accused has a broad understanding of the nature of the trial process and of what is at stake for him or her, including the significance of any penalty which may be imposed. It means that he or she, if necessary with the assistance of, for example, an interpreter, lawyer, social worker or friend, should be able to understand the general thrust of what is said in court. The defendant should be able to follow what is said by the prosecution witnesses and, if represented, to explain to his own lawyers his version of events, point out any statements with which he disagrees and make them aware of any facts which should be put forward in his defence …[25]

The ECtHR held that this test was not met in light of the evidence of SC's limited intellectual ability and the view of the social worker who sat with him.[26] **10.22**

The ECtHR stated that the involvement of a defendant whose ability to participate was restricted meant that a specialist tribunal should be involved that could take into account his difficulties and adapt its procedures accordingly.[27] In relation to a young defendant, the obvious choice of specialist venue is the Youth Court. For adults with mental disorder, there is not that option—though it is common-place in some other common law jurisdictions to have special mental health courts designed to deal with persons with mental disorder who are somehow engaged in the criminal justice system.[28] There may, however, be methods by which advocates can seek to avoid a trial, meaning that an alternative approach has to be adopted. The abuse of process jurisdiction is central to this. **10.23**

Other relevant international standards

Lord Reed in *V and T* also suggested that ECtHR's conclusion as to the requirements under the ECHR was consonant with other standards in international law, in particular the Convention on the Rights of the Child (CRC)[29] and the International Covenant on Civil and Political Rights (ICCPR).[30] The latter is in many respects a worldwide version of the ECHR. Both indicate in their preambles that they seek to give effect to the Universal Declaration of Human Rights,[31] and they set out a similar list of rights. However, in a number of respects, **10.24**

---

[25] (2005) 40 EHRR 10, para 29.

[26] (2005) 40 EHRR 10, para 31.

[27] (2005) 40 EHRR 10, para 35.

[28] For basic information, see the Bradley Report: Lord Bradley's Review of People with Mental Health Problems or Learning Disabilities in the Criminal Justice System, Department of Health, April 2009 (available at <http://webarchive.nationalarchives.gov.uk/20130107105354/http:/www.dh.gov.uk/en/Publicationsandstatistics/Publications/PublicationsPolicyAndGuidance/DH_098694>, last accessed 14 November 2015), p 70. The Bradley Commission has been formed by the Centre for Mental Health to review progress on implementing the recommendations of the report: see Durcan et al, The Bradley Report Five Years On, 2014, Centre for Mental Health (available at <http://www.centreformentalhealth.org.uk/the-bradley-report-five-years-on>, last accessed 14 November 2015). One matter trialled was mental health courts in Brighton and Stratford: the pilot was apparently successful (see Winstone and Pakes, Process Evaluation of the Mental Health Court Pilot, Ministry of Justice 2010, available at <https://www.justice.gov.uk/downloads/publications/research-and-analysis/moj-research/mhc-process-evaluation.pdf>, last accessed 14 November 2015), but has not been taken further.

[29] Adopted by the General Assembly of the United Nations in November 1989, resolution 44/25 of 20 November 1989; text available at <http://www.ohchr.org/EN/ProfessionalInterest/Pages/CoreInstruments.aspx> (last accessed 14 November 2015). The UK signed it on 19 April 1990 and ratified it on 16 December 1990.

[30] Adopted and opened for signature, ratification, and accession by General Assembly resolution 2200A (XXI) of 16 December 1966; text is available at <http://www.ohchr.org/EN/ProfessionalInterest/Pages/CoreInstruments.aspx> (last accessed 14 November 2015). The UK signed it on 16 September 1968 and ratified it on 20 May 1976: it has neither signed nor ratified the First Optional Protocol to the ICCPR, which allows individual complaints to be taken to the UN Human Rights Committee. The rationale for this is that the ECtHR provides an appropriate forum, but (i) various other signatories to the ECHR allow access to the UN Human Rights Committee and (ii) some of the rights set out in the ICCPR are not set out in the ECHR.

[31] UN General Assembly Resolution 217(III) of 10 December 1948; the text is available at <http://www.un.org/en/universal-declaration-human-rights/index.html> (last accessed 14 November 2015).

the ICCPR contains supplemental language, and in relation to the right to a fair trial, Article 14(4) it provides that:

> In the case of juvenile persons, the procedure shall be such as will take account of their age and the desirability of promoting their rehabilitation.

10.25 The CRC seeks to apply the rights set out in other conventions relating to children. Article 40 sets out the rights of children in criminal proceedings, including the need for special procedures (Article 40(2)(vii) refers to a right to privacy, Article 40(3) encourages the use of diversion, and Article 40(4) sets out the need to have additional rehabilitative options for disposal). This approach is consistent with a theme running through human rights jurisprudence to the effect that ensuring equality of respect may require that more be done to assist people who have specific disadvantages: see *Megyeri v Germany*[32] which found that in a review of mental health detention, there should be legal representation in the absence of special circumstances. The underlying principle is that the vulnerabilities of a participant have to be taken into account, as per *V and T v UK*.

10.26 A further core document of international human rights law to be considered is the UN Convention on the Rights of Persons with Disabilities 2006 (CRPD).[33] This follows the model of the CRC in providing that all groups in society have human rights and that supplemental or modified rights that take account of the special circumstances of a particular group might be required. The CRPD sets a general obligation in Article 4 that governments should 'ensure and promote the full realisation of all human rights and fundamental freedoms for all persons with disabilities without discrimination of any kind on the basis of disability'.

10.27 To understand the import of this, it is necessary to understand what amounts to 'discrimination on the basis of disability'. This is defined in Article 2 of the CRPD:

> Discrimination on the basis of disability' means any distinction, exclusion or restriction on the basis of disability which has the purpose *or effect* of impairing or nullifying the recognition, enjoyment or exercise, on an equal basis with others, of all human rights and fundamental freedoms in the political, economic, social, cultural, civil or any other field. It includes all forms of discrimination, including denial of reasonable accommodation (emphasis added).

10.28 'Reasonable accommodation' is defined in Article 2 as 'necessary and appropriate modification, and adjustments not imposing a disproportionate or undue burden, where needed in a particular case, to ensure to persons with disabilities the enjoyment or exercise on an equal basis with others of all human rights and fundamental freedoms'.

10.29 The need to ensure equality of treatment means that appropriate adjustments have to be made to procedures to overcome the impact of any disability by modification of existing laws and practices to overcome to discrimination (Article 4)[34] so as to guarantee the 'equal protection and equal benefit of the law' (Article 5).

10.30 In the context of the right to a fair trial, Article 13 of the CRPD notes the need to ensure effective access to justice on the same terms for persons with disabilities. This requires, inter alia, 'the provision of procedural and age-appropriate accommodations, in order to facilitate their effective role as direct and indirect participants, including as witnesses, in all legal proceedings'.

---

[32] (1993) 15 EHRR 584.

[33] Adopted by the UN General Assembly on 13 December 2006, during the 61st session of the UN; General Assembly resolution A/RES/61/106. It was opened for signature on 30 March 2007, in accordance with Art 42: the UK signed it on that date and ratified it on 8 June 2009. It entered into force on the 20th ratification, which occurred as of 3 May 2008. The text can be found at <http://www.ohchr.org/EN/ProfessionalInterest/Pages/CoreInstruments.aspx> (last accessed 14 November 2015).

[34] Part of this is the obligation of awareness-raising under Article 8.

The response to *V and T v UK*—practice directions and procedural rules

The immediate response to the decision in *V and T v UK* was the issuance of a Practice **10.31**
Direction to cover trials of young persons in the Crown Court: Practice Direction (Crown
Court: Young Defendants) of 16 February 2000.[35] It required that account be taken of the
'age, maturity and development (intellectual and emotional) of the young defendant on trial
and all other circumstances of the case',[36] with a view to adapting the trial process to avoid
intimidation, humiliation or distress' and ensure that '[a]ll possible steps ... be taken to assist
the young defendant to understand and participate in the proceedings'.[37]

Specifically, it provided that attempts should be made to: **10.32**

- have all participants at the same level in the courtroom;
- that the defendant should normally be able to sit with family or those providing support;
- that procedures should be explained;
- that the trial timetable should reflect the difficulties of concentration for long periods (and
  so have regular and frequent breaks);
- that wigs and gowns should not be worn unless there was good reason;
- that police and uniformed security staff should not be present; and
- that a proper balance should be drawn in relation to those who might want to attend the
  trial in the public or press galleries (in addition to the practice of making reporting restrictions in relation to the identification of young defendants).[38]

This became paragraph IV.39 of the Consolidated Practice Direction of 8 July 2002.[39] **10.33**
Eventually, by the 15th Amendment to the Consolidated Practice Direction, the need to
consider defendants who were vulnerable by reason of mental disorder was added.

Special measures

A parallel statutory development has been the creation of the regime of 'special measures' **10.34**
designed to protect vulnerable witnesses from the rigours of adversarial cross-examination,
and added by the Youth Justice and Criminal Evidence Act 1999 in relation to witnesses.
This regime has been amended, by making clear that the special measures of giving live link
evidence can apply to defendants (see section 47 of the Police and Justice Act 2006, which
added section 33A to the 1999 Act). A particular special measure worth noting is that set
out in section 29 of the 1999 Act, namely the use of intermediaries. An intermediary is an
'interpreter or other person approved by the court' (section 29(1)) and their function is to
explain questions to the witness and their answers to the court.[40] In *Cox*,[41] the Court of
Appeal welcomed the role of intermediaries, and recorded that the normal practice was that

---

[35] [2000] 1 WLR 659. At para 17, it was noted that regard should be had to its terms in relation to appeal
hearings and committals for sentence involved young defendants. This did not deal with the process for
defendants whose vulnerability was not just on account of their age (which had not been the sole concern
raised in relation to T and V).

[36] Para 2.

[37] Para 3. It was also noted at para 4 that a young person indicted with an adult defendant should ordinarily be tried on his own unless 'a joint trial would be in the interests of justice and would not be unduly
prejudicial to the welfare of the young defendant'.

[38] Paras 9–15. Also suggested was the step that had been taken in *T and V* of ensuring that the defendants
visited the courtroom in advance (para 6). In relation to high profile trials, the need for the police to provide
appropriate security to avoid harassment was noted (para 7).

[39] Practice Direction (Criminal Proceedings: Consolidation) [2002] 1 WLR 2870.

[40] Note also section 30, which allows the use of aids to communication if the witness has any disorder or
impairment.

[41] [2012] EWCA Crim 549, [2012] 2 Cr App R 6, (summarized at Criminal Law Review (2012) 8, pp
621–23).

questions were put directly to the witness, but that intermediaries would intervene when miscommunication appeared likely.[42]

Criminal Procedure Rules

10.35 As the Practice Direction has developed and has been supplemented by the more formal Criminal Procedure Rules, the detail of the provision for vulnerable defendants and witnesses has been extended. The 2015 version of the Criminal Procedure Rules and Practice Direction (CrimPR and CPD) contain a number of elements dealing with vulnerable defendants.

10.36 First, there is the overriding objective of dealing with cases justly: Crim PR 1.1(1). Although the CrimPR does not mention stays of proceedings for abuse in the examples of what 'dealing with cases justly' includes, it does refer to fair treatment of defendants and compliance with Article 6 ECHR. The Criminal Practice Directions that supplement the general matters parts of the Rules include the Practice Direction that relates to stays of proceedings and several relating to matters of vulnerable participants in the criminal process, including defendants.

10.37 Second, Crim PR 3.9 relates to case progression and states that directions have to be given to allow a case to be concluded as soon as possible. This includes the court taking steps to 'facilitate the participation of any person, including the defendant' (Crim PR 3.9(3)(b)) and the potential need for interpreters (in Crim PR 3.9(4)).

10.38 Third, Crim PR 3.9(6) notes the need for giving directions as to the 'appropriate treatment and questioning' of a witness or defendant, which is noted to be particularly prominent as an obligation on the court where use is made of an intermediary (and CrimPR 3.9(7) gives further details of this). Note also CrimPR 3.11(c), which includes the power of courts to require the parties to facilitate the giving of evidence by a witness or defendant.

Criminal Practice Direction

10.39 These latter provisions make more sense when considered together with the practice directions that exist in relation to general matters, particularly CPD I 3D, Vulnerable People in the Courts. This includes the indication at para 3D.1 that the term 'vulnerable' includes those under 18 'and people with a mental disorder or learning disability'. Although this is referred to in the context of the eligibility of witnesses for special measures under the Youth Justice and Criminal Evidence Act 1999 as amended by the Coroners and Justice Act 2009, CPD I 3D and those associated with it then refer to defendants and witnesses interchangeably. The definition goes on to make clear both that there is wider coverage, with reference made also to those with a 'physical disorder or disability' and also to those who might be affected by reason of either 'their own circumstances or those relating to the case'; and also that being within this definition is not the key question, because as para 3D.2 indicates, 'many other people giving evidence ... whether as a witness or defendant, may require assistance.' It then cross-refers to CrimPR 3.9. The concept of participation 'includes enabling a witness or defendant to give their best evidence, and enabling a defendant to comprehend the proceedings and engage fully with his or her defence'; this in turn leads to the requirement that 'The pre-trial and trial process should, so far as necessary, be adapted to meet those ends.'

---

[42] [2012] EWCA Crim 549, [2012] 2 Cr App R 6, [28]–[29]. Significant material has developed in relation to the role of intermediaries: see, for example, the Registered Intermediary Procedural Guidance Manual, Ministry of Justice 2012 (available at <http://www.cps.gov.uk/publications/docs/RI_ ProceduralGuidanceManual_2012.pdf>); and various links from the Advocate's Gateway, <http://www. theadvocatesgateway.org/intermediaries> (both last accessed 14 November 2015). Information relating to the use of intermediaries is recorded in evidence given in *R (OP) v Secretary of State for Justice* [2014] EWHC 1944 (Admin), [2015] Mental Health Law Reports 421; importantly, the Court in this case deprecated the development of the situation in which regulated and trained Registered Intermediaries were available only to prosecution witnesses, leading defendants only able to use non-regulated intermediaries.

Mental disorder and learning disability

There is no specific indication in the text of the Criminal Procedure Rules or Criminal **10.40** Practice Directions as to what is meant by 'mental disorder or learning disability' such as to include someone within the definition of vulnerable (which in turn will mean that the provisions of CrimPR 3.9 apply). Section 1 of the Mental Health Act 1983 (as amended by the Mental Health Act 2007) defines mental disorder for its purposes as 'any disorder or disability of the mind'; and learning disability as 'a state of arrested or incomplete development of the mind which includes significant impairment or intelligence and social functioning'. Since various provisions of the 1983 Act also feature in other parts of the CrimPR and PDs, it is likely that the definitions in the 1983 Act are intended to apply in this context.

Advocacy Training Council toolkits

The recommendations of the Advocacy Training Council's 2011 report 'Raising the Bar: the **10.41** Handling of Vulnerable Witnesses, Victims and Defendants in Court' and the toolkits it has produced are specifically noted: CPD 3D.5–3D.7. These were endorsed in *Wills*,[43] at least in relation to vulnerable witnesses in sex trials. The report deals with vulnerability on account of age, learning disabilities or mental health. Note that there is also a toolkit provided by the charity Mind and aimed at prosecutors, the theme being best practice for dealing with victims and witnesses with mental health conditions.[44]

One of the aspects of the advice as to questioning vulnerable people in 'Raising the Bar' is **10.42** that there has to be accommodation for their needs: this is consistent with the idea of 'reasonable accommodation' set out in the Convention on the Rights of Persons with Disabilities.

Ground Rules hearing

CPD 3E deals specifically with this by requiring that ground rules be set for the trial **10.43** to assist the questioning of a vulnerable witness or defendant who has 'communication needs' as a result. The aim of this is noted in CPD 3E.4: '[a]ll witnesses, including the defendant and defence witnesses, should be enabled to give the best evidence they can', which, it is suggested, might require a radical change to the traditional conception of cross-examination and putting the defence case. The court must include the parties in the discussion of ground rules. There may be directions about relieving a party of putting their case, the manner of questioning, the duration of questioning, the topics that may or may not be covered, allocations of questions amongst co-defendants, and the use of communications aids (CPR 3.9(7)). The Court of Appeal in *Lubemba*[45] endorsed the ground rules approach:

> We would expect a ground rules hearing in every case involving vulnerable witness, save in very exceptional circumstances … The ground rules hearing should cover amongst other matters, the general care of the witness, if, when and where the witness is to be shown their video interview, when, where and how the parties (and the judge if identified) intend to introduce themselves to the witness, the length of questioning and frequency of breaks and the nature of the questions to be asked. So as to avoid any unfortunate misunderstanding at trial, it would be an entirely reasonable step for a judge at the ground rules hearing to invite defence advocates to reduce their questions to writing in advance.

---

[43] [2011] EWCA Crim 1938, [2012] 1 Cr App R 2, [22].
[44] It can be found on the CPS website at <http://www.cps.gov.uk/publications/docs/mind_toolkit_for_prosecutors_and_advocates.pdf> (last accessed 14 November 2015).
[45] [2014] EWCA Crim 2064 at para 43. The Court of Appeal adopted the ground rules approach in *FA* [2015] EWCA Crim 209.

Intermediary

10.44 There may be an intermediary appointed for a vulnerable witness as one of the special measures applied under the Youth Justice and Criminal Evidence Act 1999. If one has been appointed, they must be involved in setting the ground rules for the questioning; CPD 3E.2. CPD 3F gives further guidance on intermediaries, including noting the common-law power to make use of them in any event (namely, not relying on the 1999 Act, which is important because it does not apply to defendants, except in relation to live link evidence).[46]

10.45 Specific provisions relating to vulnerable defendants are contained in CPD 3G, relating to pre-hearing matters and steps to be taken at the hearing.

Pre-hearing matters

10.46 In relation to pre-hearing matters, it is suggested in CPD 3G.2–4 that there be familiarization visits (accompanied by any intermediary) and a practice session with any live link being used (if that has been directed, in accordance with CPR 18.14–17). The court is also reminded of the need to consider the need for separate trials of a vulnerable co-defendant charged with one who is not, though there is the reminder that this should only happen if a fair trial is not possible with a joint trial (which remains the default option): CPD 3G.1. Naturally, various directions will have to be made as to the steps to be taken at the substantive hearings.

Court hearing modifications

10.47 As for modifications at the hearing (whether trial, sentence or appeal), it is suggested that:

- A court room should be used in which all participants are at the same level in the courtroom and that the defendant should normally be able to sit with family or those providing support, both of which are subject to security arrangements: CPD 3G.7–8.
- Procedures be explained to the defendant on an ongoing basis.
- The trial timetable reflect the difficulties of concentration for long periods, by having regular and frequent breaks.
- Ground rules as to questioning are followed and any relevant toolkits used.
- Consideration be given as to whether wigs and gowns be worn in Crown Court proceedings.
- Police and uniformed security staff should not generally be present: CPD 3G.9–12.
- Any high profile matter that involves a vulnerable defendant may require police engagement to ensure that relevant restrictions on abuse and photography are enforced.
- Reporting restriction be made (if a young person is involved): CPD 3G.5.
- Arrangements reflect a proper balance between those who might want to attend the trial in the public or press galleries and the interests of the defendant CPD 3G.13–14. It is noted that arrangements can be made to relay proceedings to another courtroom.

10.48 There is a statutory regime relating to special measures for witnesses, which has been extended to defendants in relation to the use of a live link: as per Crim PR 18 and CPD 18.[47] See also

---

[46] Section 33BA, which allows for intermediaries for defendants whilst they are giving evidence, is inserted into the 1999 Act by section 104 of the Coroners and Justice Act 2009 but has not yet been brought into force. Given that a wider common-law power has been identified, it might be thought unnecessary to bring into force a limited statutory power. For a full discussion of the role of intermediaries, see Joyce Plotnikoff and Richard Woolfson, 'Intermediairies in the Criminal Justice System' (Policy Press 2015).

[47] Another statutory regime that may feature when questions of participation arise is the admission of hearsay statements when a medical reason means that a defendant cannot participate, which might include a proof of evidence given before an intervening cause for unfitness: see section 116(2) of the Criminal Justice Act 2003, and note its discussion in *R (Hamberger) v Crown Prosecution Service* [2014] EWHC 2814 as a reason for not finding a decision to prosecute arguably irrational. The Divisional Court did note that an application to stay proceedings was available if various other steps did not ensure the participation of a man with both heart problems and psychiatric concerns. (See also *Jagnieszko* [2008] EWCA Crim 3065 as to

Chapter 6 of the Crown Court Benchbook 2010, which sets out directions that should be given to the jury when orders for special measures have been made.

Abuse of process and participation under the current procedural regime

The Practice Direction provisions originally emphasized the importance of modifying pro- **10.49** cedures so that the criminal process was more 'user-friendly' for vulnerable defendants. The core requirement remains that the defendant be able to participate to a proper extent; as reflected in CrimPR and CPDs development and case law decisions.

The starting point for confirming that a stay for abuse of process is an available option when **10.50** a defendant cannot participate is *R (TP) v West London Youth Court*.[48] It was argued on the basis of *SC v UK* that the low intellectual capacity of a defendant in the Youth Court facing charges of robbery and attempted robbery meant that the trial should not proceed. TP was aged fifteen, and the expert evidence was that his mental age was that of an eight-year-old and that he would need assistance and simple language in order to follow proceedings, but might struggle to generate questions and so provide full instructions. However, TP was aware that his solicitor was there to assist him, and would be able to point out things in evidence he did not agree with. The District Judge refused the application to stay, stating that he was not satisfied on the balance of probabilities that TP, appearing in a Youth Court as opposed to a Crown Court, and assisted by specialist and experienced Youth Court representatives, would be unable to participate to the extent required for a fair trial. He also noted that TP had been before the Youth Court before.

The District Judge's refusal of a stay was upheld by the Divisional Court. The central ques- **10.51** tion was, 'Should the District Judge have asked whether there was a real risk that TP could not participate in the proceedings?' Lord Justice Scott Baker noted that there was no reason to apply a different standard of proof to that applicable in other abuse of process applications simply because Article 6 was involved. The balance of probabilities was the required standard in considering whether the inability to participate amounted to unfitness to stand trial.[49]

The Divisional Court in *TP* confirmed that staying proceedings was an available remedy, **10.52** though only exceptionally and only if other steps had been taken but found wanting. Lord Justice Scott Baker noted:[50]

> ... there is a fundamental public interest in cases and defendants being tried. The CPS decide, according to well known criteria, which cases should proceed and it is only in exceptional circumstances that the court should descend into the arena and prevent a case from being heard. The first port of call is not to prevent the court from hearing the case but to grapple with the difficulties. A trial should not be abandoned before all practical steps to overcome the difficulties have been exhausted. It is also, we think, an important point that the judge who is hearing the trial has a continuing jurisdiction to stay proceedings for abuse of process. Thus, if it becomes apparent during the course of the hearing that the claimant is unable effectively to participate, the judge can stay the proceedings at that point. This is surely a better course than staying a prosecution at the outset when events would have shown it could fairly have proceeded.

---

the existence for the power to admit a proof of evidence in the formal unfitness to stand trial process in the Crown Court.)

[48] [2005] EWHC 2583 (Admin), [2006] Mental Health Law Reports 40.

[49] [2005] EWHC 2583 (Admin), [2006] Mental Health Law Reports 40, para 13ff. The 'real possibility' test was one that came from other areas of law, such as the apparent bias test in *Porter v Magill* [2002] 2 AC 357.

[50] [2005] EWHC 2583 (Admin), [2006] Mental Health Law Reports 40, para 18.

10.53 Although a stay is a last resort remedy, consideration of it should be revisited if the efforts made to modify the process do not achieve their aim of allowing participation. The importance of expert evidence in this regard should be noted: it was central in both *V and T* and *SC* (involving a medical professional in the former and social worker in the latter).[51]

10.54 The Divisional Court in *TP* provided useful guidance as to the elements of a fair trial that should be examined in determining whether a trial can continue or be stayed. Lord Justice Scott Baker noted[52] that:

> The judge had earlier correctly directed himself that the minimum requirements for a fair trial for the claimant were:
> i) he had to understand what he is said to have done wrong;
> ii) the court had to be satisfied that the claimant when he had done wrong by act or omission had the means of knowing that was wrong;
> iii) he had to understand what, if any, defences were available to him;
> iv) he had to have a reasonable opportunity to make relevant representations if he wished;
> v) he had to have the opportunity to consider what representations he wished to make once he had understood the issues involved.
>
> He had therefore to be able to give proper instructions and to participate by way of providing answers to questions and suggesting questions to his lawyers in the circumstances of the trial as they arose.

10.55 Accordingly, the assessment of ability to participate should be based on the defendant's ability to provide instructions on both the pre-trial prosecution disclosure and any evidential developments during the trial.

10.56 The Divisional Court in *TP* also examined what special steps can be taken to meet the requirements of a fair trial. On the facts, the trial was to take place in a specialized court, in front of judges who had appropriate training and with the case argued by advocates with expertise and experience in the issues presented by vulnerable defendants.[53] In addition to these systematic points, there were also various specific steps that could be taken. Lord Justice Scott Baker LJ commented[54]

> It is apparent from the judge's judgment and Dr Marriott's evidence that there are indeed a number of steps that can be taken during the trial. These include:
> i) keeping the claimant's level of cognitive functioning in mind;
> ii) using concise and simple language;
> iii) having regular breaks;
> iv) taking additional time to explain court proceedings;
> v) being proactive in ensuring the claimant has access to support;
> vi) explaining and ensuring the claimant understands the ingredients of the charge;
> vii) explaining the possible outcomes and sentences;
> viii) ensuring that cross-examination is carefully controlled so that questions are short and clear and frustration is minimised.

---

[51] Note the importance of the expert dealing with the issue of the ability of the defendant to participate rather than on the propriety of having a trial in light of the condition of the defendant: see *G v DPP* [2012] EWHC 3174 (Admin), [2013] Mental Health Law Reports 143, where Mr Justice Pitchford noted at [23] that evidence from a defence expert 'contains a mix of opinion relating to the morality of the proceedings in a criminal court, to the level of the Appellant's comprehension that what he did was wrong and as to his cognitive ability' whereas 'The sole question for the District Judge at the conclusion of the evidence was whether the Appellant was fit to take part in the trial'.

[52] [2005] EWHC 2583 (Admin), [2006] Mental Health Law Reports 40, para 7.

[53] [2005] EWHC 2583 (Admin), [2006] Mental Health Law Reports 40, para 25.

[54] [2005] EWHC 2583 (Admin), [2006] Mental Health Law Reports 40, para 26.

The conclusion on the facts in *TP* was that there was no need to prevent the trial occurring.[55]   **10.57**

The steps to secure participation—intermediaries

A significant range of steps can be taken to secure participation. Aside from the various mod-   **10.58**
ifications to the process that are outlined above, one of the features mentioned in *TP* was the
need for a court to be 'proactive in ensuring the claimant has access to support',[56] in relation
to which there have been significant developments after the need for participation has been
recognized.

Intermediaries in the Youth court

In *C v Sevenoaks Youth Court*,[57] it was held that access to support extends to ensuring that a   **10.59**
defendant has an intermediary to assist both at trial and prior to trial. *C* involved a twelve-
year-old boy who was due to stand trial in the Youth Court on charges of assault with intent
to rob and theft. His complex mental health issues included hyperactivity (which was not
adequately controlled by medication), low comprehension suggestive of a learning disability, a personality disorder, and possibly Asperger's Syndrome. A clinical psychologist who
assessed him concluded that he did understand what he was charged with and the nature of
his plea, could give an account of events, but that he could not concentrate during a trial, nor
listen to the evidence, nor instruct his solicitor about which parts of the evidence he did or
did not accept. *C* was fit to stand trial, but only if an intermediary was appointed to explain
the evidence to *C* during the trial and interpret questions for him and his answers. A neuro-
psychiatrist, confirmed that *C*'s problems limited his ability to assimilate information or form
coherent conclusions in a way that was required in court. The use of intermediaries would
assist *C*.

The Magistrates Court appointed an intermediary but then decided that it had no power to   **10.60**
do so as the special measures regime applicable to vulnerable witnesses under the Youth and
Criminal Evidence Act 1999, which includes under section 29 the power to allow a witness
to give evidence through an intermediary, could not apply to defendants: section 16(1) of the
Act excluded it. This decision was challenged.

The High Court determined that the lack of a statutory power to appoint an intermedi-   **10.61**
ary was not problematic. There was an inherent power to allow a defendant to participate.
Indeed, it was a duty in light of the overriding objective under the Criminal Procedure Rules
of dealing with criminal cases justly, which included recognizing the rights of a defendant
under Article 6 ECHR. The High Court made it plain that this duty extended not just to the
conduct of the trial but also covered the preparation for the trial.[58] The intermediary had to
be someone with whom the defendant would be able to develop a suitable rapport.[59]

The corollary of the power to take steps such as appointing an intermediary was that it would   **10.62**
be a highly unusual case that could be stayed as an abuse of the process. Such a challenge was
taken on the facts. It was dismissed as the Crown Prosecution Service had reached a rational
conclusion in deciding that it was in the public interest to proceed. The CPS had complied

---

[55] A case that confirms the jurisdiction to stay proceedings, and also upheld a decision to allow a trial to
proceed, is *G v DPP* [2012] EWHC 3174 (Admin), [2013] Mental Health Law Reports 143.

[56] [2005] EWHC 2583 (Admin), [2006] Mental Health Law Reports 40, para 26.

[57] [2009] EWHC 3088 (Admin), [2009] Mental Health Law Reports 329.

[58] [2009] EWHC 3088 (Admin), [2009] Mental Health Law Reports 329, para 17.

[59] Also raised was the question of the payment of the intermediary: at the time, it was done on a voluntary
basis by the Ministry of Justice, but the Court noted that in the absence of such payments, it might be proper
for the Legal Services Commission to make payments under s14(2)(g) Access to Justice Act 1999 (i.e. its
catch-all power 'to do anything else which it considers appropriate for funding representation').

with the Code for Crown Prosecutors.[60] However, it was noted that the CPS and the trial court had to keep the situation under review and could switch to the process of determining whether the actus reus had been committed.[61]

Intermediaries in the Adult Courts

10.63 The inherent power of the Court to appoint an intermediary applies equally to adult proceedings in the Magistrates' Court (see *R (OP) v Secretary of State for Justice)*[62] and Crown Court (see Anthony Cox).[63]

10.64 On the facts of *Cox*, the appointment of an intermediary had been directed but it had not been possible to find one. Instead, the trial judge directed that the matter proceed with various modifications to protect the interests of the defendant. The Court of Appeal determined that the steps taken by the trial judge had been sufficient, commenting that the desirability of having an intermediary did not mean that a trial without one was necessarily unfair: rather, the lack of success in finding an intermediary should not lead to a stay, since it would be 'a most unusual case for a defendant who is fit to plead to be found to be so disadvantaged by his condition that a properly brought prosecution would have to be stayed'.[64] The Court of Appeal was concerned that the interests of the victim had to be secured, since a stay would be a 'gross unfairness to the complainant' (this case concerned an allegation of rape).

10.65 *Cox* is a troublesome decision for three reasons. First, the whole point of the intermediary regime is that someone with the relevant training and expertise can assist a vulnerable person; the judge is at best a competent amateur in this regard. Second, the alternative course of action was not necessarily a stay but an adjournment to allow the organs of the state to make good on the obligation to ensure that the defendant could participate through an intermediary. Third, it seems to minimize the fact that the case law from the European Court of Human Rights makes clear that there is a requirement as to ability to participate that goes beyond the restricted fitness to plead test.

10.66 The nature of the state's obligation is made clear in the *OP*[65] case, which involved a successful judicial review of the refusal of the Ministry of Justice to provide a registered intermediary to a defendant, where they had applied a new policy of making them available only for witnesses (ie where there was a statutory power of appointment) and not defendants (i.e. where the power was through the court's inherent power).

10.67 The Divisional Court in *OP* quashed the decision, noting that the distinction between the registered intermediary—who is trained, regulated, and subject to professional codes—and the unregulated non-registered intermediary meant that the policy created the impression of an inequality of arms in relation to a defendant. This supports the critique of *Cox*, where part of the problem was that a registered intermediary had not been made available and a point taken against Mr Cox was that his solicitors were responsible for locating a non-registered intermediary. *OP* clarifies that this is not an appropriate approach.

10.68 At the same time, it must be noted that part of the reasoning in *OP* is also problematic. It was central to the Divisional Court's reasoning that the Ministry of Justice had erred by

---

[60] The Code requires that there be a realistic prospect of a conviction (an evidential sufficiency test) and also that the public interest be in favour of prosecution: the 2013 edition of the Code is available at <http://www.cps.gov.uk/publications/code_for_crown_prosecutors/index.html> (last accessed 14 November 2015).

[61] Paras 29–31.

[62] [2014] EWHC 1944 (Admin), [2015] Mental Health Law Reports 421.

[63] [2012] EWCA Crim 549, [2012] 2 Cr App R 6.

[64] [2012] EWCA Crim 549, [2012] 2 Cr App R 6, [30].

[65] [2014] EWHC 1944 (Admin), [2015] Mental Health Law Reports 421.

concluding that the appointment of registered intermediaries to defendants had significant resource implications because they were mainly appointed for the whole trial. The Court suggested that a defendant could have sensible adult support at most points of the trial, and would only need the supplemental support of a trained registered intermediary when giving evidence. The problem with this is two-fold. First, it is necessary for any intermediary to have a rapport with the defendant, whereas the introduction of a different person as the intermediary, at what might be the most stressful time for the defendant, namely the giving of evidence, may cause more problems than it solves. Second, the aim of the intermediary is to secure participation in the entire process, so that the defendant can provide instructions on matters as they arise and recognize what might be necessary for them to give evidence on. It might well be necessary for fairness to have Registered Intermediaries for the entire trial.

Criminal Practice Directions 2015

On 23rd March 2016 the Lord Chief Justice handed down amendments to the Criminal Practice Directions 2015 which include a replacement practice direction (CPD I General matters 3F: Intermediaries) which makes various changes[66] to the guidance regarding intermediaries. It provides that: **10.69**

- In light of the scarcity of intermediaries, the appropriateness of assessment must be decided with care to ensure their availability for those witnesses and defendants who are most in need.
- There is no presumption that witnesses and defendants under 18 (including those under 11) will be assessed by an intermediary.
- Use of the court's inherent powers to direct the appointment of intermediaries for defendants will be rare.
- Where such directions are ineffective (e.g. non-availability of an intermediary for the purpose directed), it remains the court's responsibility to adapt the trial process to address defendants' communication needs, as was the case prior to the existence of intermediaries.
- It is preferable that trials involving intermediaries are fixed rather than placed in warned lists.

Trial of the facts under Mental Health Act

In relation to adult defendants who are vulnerable on account of mental disorder, the first remedy identified in *TP* is not available as there is no specialist mental health court. However, alternative approaches are available. One possibility is that of dealing with a defendant in the adult magistrates court through a process that can only lead to a non-conviction disposal under section 37 of the Mental Health Act 1983, subsection (3) of which provides that: **10.70**

> Where a person is charged before a magistrates court with any act or omission as an offence, and the court would have power on convicting him of that offence to make an order under subsection (1) above in his case, then if the court is satisfied that the accused did the act or made the omission charged, the court may if it thinks fit, make such an order without convicting him.[67] (The orders under section 37(1) are the hospital order or the guardianship order.)

Section 37 MHA applies to both the adult and youth jurisdiction. It is to be read in conjunction with section 11 of the Powers of Criminal Courts (Sentencing) Act 2000, which provides that:

> (1) If on the trial at a magistrates court of an offence punishable on summary conviction punishable with imprisonment, the court
>   (a) is satisfied the accused did the act or made the omission charged, but

---

[66] Operative as of 4 April 2016.
[67] Before this section was amended by the Mental Health Act 2007, the power could only be exercised in relation to those whose mental disorder was 'mental illness or severe mental impairment'.

(b) is of the opinion that an enquiry ought to be made into his physical or mental condition, before the method of dealing with him is determined, the court shall adjourn the case to enable a medical examination and report to be made, and shall remand him.

10.71 The use of the two statutory provisions provides a mechanism that provides a proxy for the fitness to stand trial process in the magistrates court (in which the Criminal Procedure (Insanity) Act 1964 and the Criminal Procedure (Insanity and Unfitness to Plead) Act 1991 do not apply). This was established in *R (P) v Barking Magistrates Court*,[68] in which the magistrates had purported to follow a process analogous to that applicable in the Crown Court (on the application of the defence and without objection from the prosecution or the court clerk) and had found the defendant, who had a low IQ, fit to stand trial. The High Court in a judicial review challenge held that the lower court erred in law by failing to recognize that section 11(1) of the 2000 Act and section 37(3) of the 1983 Act 'provide[s] a complete statutory framework for a determination by the magistrates' court of all the issues that arise in cases of defendants who are or may be mentally ill or suffering from severe mental impairment in the context of offences that are triable summarily only'.[69] It was also noted that the powers given to the summary courts 'are considerably less strict and more flexible than the common law rules governing the issue of fitness to plead in the Crown Court'.[70]

10.72 At the time of the *P* judgment, the provisions of section 37(3) MHA applied only to mental illness or severe mental impairment. Other forms of mental disorder, such as psychopathic personality disorder, which might provide difficulties to a defendant in following a trial or providing instructions, were not covered. However, section 37(3) had since been amended by the Mental Health Act 2007 to cover all instances of mental disorder.

10.73 The availability of the amended section 37 MHA and the abuse of process jurisdiction provided a remedy for all mental disorder situations. [71]

10.74 There does remain the problem that a hospital order or a guardianship order may not be an appropriate disposal. In particular, the power arises only in relation to imprisonable offences, and relatively strict criteria have to be met, as set out in section 37(2) MHA:

(a) the court is satisfied, on the written or oral evidence of two registered medical practitioners, that the offender is suffering from mental disorder and that either-
   (i) the mental disorder from which the offender is suffering is of a nature or degree which makes it appropriate for him to be detained in a hospital for medical treatment and
   (ii) in the case of an offender who has attained the age of 16 years, the mental disorder is of a nature or degree which warrants his reception into guardianship under this Act; and
(b) the court is of the opinion, having regard to all the circumstances including the nature of the offence and the character and antecedents of the offender, and to the other available methods of dealing with him, that the most suitable method of disposing of the case is by means of an order under this section.

---

[68] [2002] EWHC 734 (Admin), [2002] Mental Health Law Reports 304. It has also been adopted as a possible solution if a defendant in a summary trial might be acquitted on the ground of insanity at the time of the offence: see *R (Singh) v Stratford Magistrates Court* [2007] EWHC 1582 (Admin), [2007] Mental Health Law Reports 274.

[69] [2002] EWHC 734 (Admin), [2002] Mental Health Law Reports 304, per Mr Justice Wright at para 10.

[70] [2002] EWHC 734 (Admin), [2002] Mental Health Law Reports 304, per Mr Justice Wright at para 10.

[71] In *G v DPP* [2012] EWHC 3174 (Admin), [2013] Mental Health Law Reports 143 Lord Justice Pitchford noted at para 30 that there was no fitness to plead process in the Youth Court, with there being 'two tools in the box available to the youth court. The first was the application for stay and the second was, in an appropriate case, to proceed to a finding of fact rather than a conviction'.

Accordingly, if the defendant has a mental disorder but it is not such as to require detention **10.75** in hospital, then a hospital order cannot be made. A hospital order also requires supporting medical evidence and evidence that a bed is available.[72]

A guardianship order can only be made in relation to those aged 16 or over; it provides the **10.76** right to control where a person lives and can require their attendance for matters such as medical treatment and education or training.[73] Further a guardianship order is invariably made to a local authority and requires the local authority to form a view that it is appropriate (in relation to which the local authority does not have to follow the view of the court).[74]

In *DPP v P*[75] the High Court considered the proper approach to the court's assessment **10.77** in cases in which the mental capacity of the defendant might by relevant to the question of stay, of *doli incapax* and of the application of section 11 of the Powers of Criminal Courts (Sentencing) Act 2000 and section 37(3) of the Mental Health Act 1983.

The Youth Court in *DPP v P* rejected an application for a Mental Health Act finding, **10.78** but stayed the proceedings against P, a thirteen-year-old defendant who had a low IQ and attention deficit hyperactivity disorder. P had been found unfit to stand trial in the Crown Court. The experts agreed that his poor ability to concentrate meant that following evidence to give instructions, giving evidence, and taking advice from his lawyers was beyond his abilities, such that he was not fit to stand trial.[76] One report, from a child and adolescent psychiatrist, included the view that a hospital order under the Mental Health Act 1983 was not warranted. On the basis of the same reports and a supplemental one commissioned for the Youth Court proceedings, which confirmed that there was no improvement in P's situation, the District Judge stayed the Youth Court trial. P was unable to participate effectively in the trial, even with appropriate assistance.[77]

The timing of when an application to stay proceedings should be made, whether at the outset **10.79** of the trial or at a later stage, was considered in *P*. The District Judge concluded that such an application should be determined at the outset but did not give reasons.[78] A case stated appeal was taken, raising, inter alia, when the question of fitness to stand trial or ability to participate was to be determined and whether it had been proper to stay the proceedings on the facts.

The prosecution position on the appeal was that, as a hospital order could only be made if it **10.80** was determined that the actus reus had been committed, the trial should, save for exceptional cases, proceed that far.[79] That would require three steps:

(1) consideration of the medical evidence as to fitness to participate;
(2) hearing the prosecution case and considering whether there was a case to answer; and if there was a case to answer

---

[72] Section 37(4) of the Mental Health Act 1983.

[73] Section 8 of the Mental Health Act 1983.

[74] See *R (Buckowicki) v Northamptonshire County Council* [2007] EWHC 310 (Admin), [2007] Mental Health Law Reports 121.

[75] [2007] EWHC 946 (Admin), [2007] Mental Health Law Reports 262, [2008] 1 WLR 1005.

[76] The Crown Court judge had apparently stayed the proceedings rather than swearing a jury to determine whether P had committed the actus reus of the offences charged (in accordance with sections 4, 4A, and 5 of the Criminal Procedure (Insanity) Act 1964).

[77] The District Judge referred to *R (P) v Barking Youth Court* (as to the existence of the fitness to stand trial process in the summary court) and also the *SC* and *TP* cases (as to participation in a trial, and the jurisdiction to stay proceedings in the absence of an ability to participate).

[78] [2007] EWHC 946 (Admin), [2007] Mental Health Law Reports 262, [2008] 1 WLR 1005, para 18.

[79] [2007] EWHC 946 (Admin), [2007] Mental Health Law Reports 262, [2008] 1 WLR 1005, paras 27–29.

(3) determining whether there was effective participation, the answer to which would lead to the continuation of the matter as a trial or as a finding of whether the defendant committed the actus reus.

10.81 P's position is recorded as accepting this proposal, though seeking to emphasize the prosecution's concession that there might be cases in which that was not the appropriate course, and arguing that the facts revealed such a case because the evidence of inability to participate was very clear.[80]

10.82 The High Court confirmed that a trial could be stayed as an abuse of the process if the defendant did not have the capacity to participate. However, this should rarely be determined before evidence on the charge had been called. Also, a finding of inability to participate should invariably be followed by the making of factual findings. Lady Justice Smith, giving the leading judgment, gave several rationales for the proposition that it would rarely be proper to stay proceedings before evidence had been heard:

- Firstly, the medical evidence available at the outset could only be part of the material relevant to the decision. The real evidence obtained by the court in the form of its assessment of the ability of the defendant to participate might result in it forming an opinion different to that of the medical professionals.[81]
- Secondly, the assessment had to be made in light of the impact of any special arrangements put in place.
- Thirdly, the court might want to consider whether there might be no case to answer and so an acquittal should follow.[82] As the District Judge had not followed this approach, the decision was declared to be wrong in law.[83]

10.83 The suggestion that the magistrates might proceed to the stage of determining whether there is a case to answer is no doubt pragmatic. However, whilst a court could find that it was

---

[80] [2007] EWHC 946 (Admin), [2007] Mental Health Law Reports 262, [2008] 1 WLR 1005, paras 30 and 58. Lady Justice Smith did accept at para. 58 that 'if the child is so severely impaired that he clearly cannot participate in the trial and if it is clear that there would be no point in finding the facts with a view to making an order under the MHA 1983, there would seem to be little purpose in proceeding.'

[81] [2007] EWHC 946 (Admin), [2007] Mental Health Law Reports 262, [2008] 1 WLR 1005, paras 51–55. See *Ghulam* [2009] EWCA Crim 2285, [2009] Mental Health Law Reports 325: the Court of Appeal held that a judge who decided that a defendant was fit to stand trial had been able to rely on his own observations of the defendant during the course of the trial and so reject a medical report to the effect that the defendant was not fit to stand trial. To the extent that this amounts to a reminder that the decision remains one for the court and so cannot be devolved to experts, it is unproblematic. However, there is a risk that a court will overstate its own abilities to assess the cognitive abilities of an individual, which may well require more than 'common sense' but instead turn on matters that do require expert evidence.

[82] Lady Justice Smith also felt that it was necessary for the court to consider whether the child knew the difference between right and wrong, as her tentative (and obiter) view was that the doli incapax rule had not been abolished by section 34 of the Crime and Disorder Act 1998, but rather changed from a presumption to a matter that had to be raised by the defence (i.e. an evidential burden, which would then require the prosecution to prove to the usual criminal standard that the child knew that the conduct was wrong): see [2007] EWHC 946 (Admin), [2007] Mental Health Law Reports 262, [2008] 1 WLR 1005, paras 37–47. The relevance of this was the prospect that proceedings should continue despite the inability of the child to participate because of a possible acquittal on the grounds of doli incapax, which might often be demonstrated by the same reports as were relevant to the issue of the ability of the child to participate: see [2007] EWHC 946 (Admin), [2007] Mental Health Law Reports 262, [2008] 1 WLR 1005, para 58. Mr. Justice Gross, the other judge in the court, accepted that the issue needed to be resolved, but did not think it right to express an obiter view: see [2007] EWHC 946 (Admin), [2007] Mental Health Law Reports 262, [2008] 1 WLR 1005, para 64. The House of Lords subsequently confirmed that the defence has been abolished: see *JTB* [2009] UKHL 20. That leaves, however, the question of the court determining whether there is a case to answer.

[83] [2007] EWHC 946 (Admin), [2007] Mental Health Law Reports 262, [2008] 1 WLR 1005, para 59. It was not set aside on the facts, given the passage of time.

appropriate to review the question of the ability of the defendant to participate at the end of the prosecution case and make all relevant rulings at that stage, a court cannot engage in a sham. The evidence in the trial, it should be remembered, is not the witness statements given in advance but the evidence heard at the trial. If a defendant cannot participate by following the evidence and providing ongoing instructions, then the decision as to whether a stay is necessary may have to be made earlier.

The High Court held that consideration should be given in most cases to determining **10.84** whether the defendant had committed the actus reus if the criminal trial was stayed. As Lady Justice Smith noted, section 11(1) of the 2000 Act and section 37(3) of the 1983 Act 'do not provide the solution to all the problems which may confront a youth court before which a young person of doubtful capacity appears'.[84] The High Court accepted that the discretion to carry out this process should usually be followed if there was a possibility of a hospital order.[85]

However, it was noted that the fact-finding process might have other benefits, principally **10.85** alerting the authorities to the possible need for care proceedings, and perhaps simplifying such proceedings, even though findings made by the Youth Court would not be binding in that context. Lady Justice Smith's conclusion was that,

> proceedings should be stayed as an abuse of process before fact-finding only if no useful purpose at all could be served by finding the facts.[86]

This is a radical suggestion, namely that a trial court has the jurisdiction to make fac- **10.86** tual findings not in order to determine the propriety of a disposal within its express powers, but to assist a more general process of securing the welfare of the defendant. The reasoning of the court rests on the purpose of the youth justice system, as set out in the Crime and Disorder Act 1998, namely the prevention of offending by children and young people.[87] Lady Justice Smith suggested that the framework was designed to provide for the taking of steps short of criminal proceedings if possible (such that they would occur only when it had been decided that alternative steps were not appropriate). This in turn meant that the obligation imposed on anyone who laid an information to commence criminal proceedings against a child to inform the local authority, as set out in section 5 of the Children and Young Persons Act 1969,[88] provided the opportunity to consider diversion from the criminal justice system for children who had problems that might be dealt with by way of a care or supervision order under the Children Act 1989.[89] The facts relevant to the issue of diversion included the capacity of the defendant to participate in the trial.

---

[84] [2007] EWHC 946 (Admin), [2007] Mental Health Law Reports 262, [2008] 1 WLR 1005, para 16. Lady Justice Smith did not consider whether they provide a complete framework for all situations when mental disorder is in issue, merely repeating the view expressed in *TP* that the provisions are the code for when mental illness or severe mental impairment are the forms of disorder in question.

[85] [2007] EWHC 946 (Admin), [2007] Mental Health Law Reports 262, [2008] 1 WLR 1005, paras 56–57.

[86] [2007] EWHC 946 (Admin), [2007] Mental Health Law Reports 262, [2008] 1 WLR 1005, para 56.

[87] [2007] EWHC 946 (Admin), [2007] Mental Health Law Reports 262, [2008] 1 WLR 1005, paras 31 and 32, citing sections 37–39 of the Crime and Disorder Act 1998 (which put duties on local authorities to secure that aim, including by setting up youth-offending teams).

[88] [2007] EWHC 946 (Admin), [2007] Mental Health Law Reports 262, [2008] 1 WLR 1005, para 34.

[89] [2007] EWHC 946 (Admin), [2007] Mental Health Law Reports 262, [2008] 1 WLR 1005, para 35. The most obvious purpose of the notification is to allow the local authority to carry out its duty under section 9 of the 1969 Act of providing pre-sentence and other reports to the court.

10.87 Further, the context identified by Lady Justice Smith of the desirability of diversion from the criminal justice system is equally applicable to those who are mentally disordered. This can be found in Home Office Circular 66/90 on the diversion of mentally disordered offenders from custody.

10.88 In addition, the Code for Crown Prosecutors accepts that evidential sufficiency that an offence has been committed does mean that there should be a prosecution if there are public interest factors against a prosecution. Public interest factors include whether

> the suspect is, or was at the time of the offence, suffering from significant mental or physical ill health, as in some circumstances this may mean that it is less likely that a prosecution is required.[90]

Fairness in the Fact-Finding Process

10.89 If the court examines as part of a fact finding process whether the actus reus is made out, it is not conducting a criminal trial. There is no risk of punishment. The requirements of Article 6 do not apply to the fact-finding process. This proposition follows from the House of Lords' decision in *H*.[91] This case was concerned with the formal fitness to stand trial process in the Crown Court, involving as it does a process of finding whether the defendant was responsible for the acts or omissions of the offence charged.

10.90 The House of Lords emphasized that a fair procedure had to be followed,[92] which might require a process equivalent to that applicable under Article 6. Moreover, the question of whether there was a determination of civil rights and obligations such that Article 6 applied was not considered by the House of Lords. The case proceeded on the basis that if the civil aspect of Article 6 applied, it was satisfied.[93] It is clear from European Court case law that the right to liberty is a civil right, and so if it is lost, as it may be if a hospital disposal is made, then Article 6 does apply.[94]

10.91 Moreover, there must be effective participation in any such process. In *Shtukaturov v Russia*,[95] the European Court of Human Rights gave guidance.

10.92 First, whilst the ECtHR has invariably dealt with questions of the detention of psychiatric patients under Article 5 rather than Article 6:

> the Court has consistently held that the 'procedural' guarantees under Article 5 are broadly similar to those under Article 6 of the Convention ...[96]

10.93 Second, whilst the requirements of Article 6 could be modified:

> in order to secure the good administration of justice, protection of the health of the person concerned, etc, the margin of appreciation allowed to the member states in this regard was

---

[90] Code for Crown Prosecutors 2013, para 4.12(b).
[91] [2003] UKHL 1, [2003] Mental Health Law Reports 209. See also *Antoine v UK*, [2003] Mental Health Law Reports 292, in which the domestic conclusion was upheld by the European Court of Human Rights.
[92] [2003] UKHL 1, [2003] Mental Health Law Reports 209, per Lord Bingham at para 20.
[93] [2003] UKHL 1, [2003] Mental Health Law Reports 209, para 13: the argument of the prosecution was that any loss of liberty was justified by reason of Article 5(1)(e) of the ECHR. The appellant's case was limited to the criminal aspects of Article 6.
[94] See *Aerts v Belgium* (1998) 29 EHRR 50, para 59; in *R (PD) v West Midlands and North Mental Health Review Tribunal* [2003] EWHC 2469 (Admin), [2004] Mental Health Law Reports 25, [2004] EWCA Civ 311, [2004] Mental Health Law Reports 174, the question arising was whether the medical member of the Tribunal appeared biased, and the Administrative Court and then the Court of Appeal discussed this in the context of Article 6 applying to the detention of a patient.
[95] [2008] Mental Health Law Reports 238.
[96] [2008] Mental Health Law Reports 238 para 66.

limited by the overarching principle that 'such measures should not affect the very essence of the applicant's right to a fair trial as guaranteed by Article 6'.[97]

On the facts, a breach of Article 6 was found because Mr Shtukaturov had not been able to **10.94** participate in the court proceedings as to the loss of his capacity, in which he was both an interested party and the subject of the proceedings:

> His participation was therefore necessary not only to enable him to present his own case, but also to allow the judge to form his personal opinion about the applicant's mental capacity ... The Court concludes that the decision of the judge to decide the case on the basis of documentary evidence, without seeing or hearing the applicant, was unreasonable and in breach of the principle of adversarial proceedings enshrined in Article 6 ...[98]

In cases relating to the loss of liberty, it had been found that 'a person of unsound mind **10.95** must be allowed to be heard either in person or, where necessary, through some form of representation'. The conclusion from the ECtHR is that the loss of personal autonomy arising from a declaration as to the lack of capacity is just as important.[99] This language replicates Article 6(3)(c) on which, together with the right to challenge witnesses and the right to an interpreter, the *Stanford* decision as to the right to participate was based.

Accordingly, when the court in domestic proceedings is engaged in the finding of facts, it **10.96** cannot be said that Article 6 is not engaged. The inability of the defendant to participate in this process may make the process fundamentally unfair and/or in breach of Article 6. So, whilst it has been decided that questions of mens rea are not relevant to the question of whether the actus reus was committed (see *Antoine*,[100] in which it was held that a defendant could not argue that his responsibility was diminished and so should not be found responsible for the actus reus of murder) there may be instances where the lawfulness of the actus reus depends on what was in the mind of the defendant.

In *Antoine*, the House of Lords accepted that: **10.97**

> If there is objective evidence which raises the issue of mistake or accident or self-defence, then the jury should not find that the defendant did the 'act' unless it is satisfied beyond reasonable doubt on all the evidence that the prosecution has negatived that defence ... [T]he same approach is to be taken if defence counsel wishes to advance the defence that the defendant, in law, did not do the 'act' because his action was involuntary, as when a man kicks out and strikes another in the course of an uncontrollable fit brought about by a medical condition. In such a case there would have to be evidence that the defendant suffered from the condition.[101]

This limited concession does not cover all the situations in which it cannot be fair to find facts **10.98** if a defendant cannot participate. For example, if the issue is one of whether the defendant or one witness is telling the truth (or even more than one witness if there are real issues of the quality of the evidence or dangers of collaboration), such that the credibility of the defendant is central, the inability of the defendant to participate in the fact-finding process may render it improper.[102]

---

[97] [2008] Mental Health Law Reports 238 para 68.
[98] [2008] Mental Health Law Reports 238 paras 72–73.
[99] [2008] Mental Health Law Reports 238 para 71.
[100] [2001] 1 AC 340, [2000] Mental Health Law Reports 28.
[101] [2001] 1 AC 340 per Lord Hutton at paras 57–58. What is meant by the 'act' and whether it includes any mental element, and what is meant by 'objective evidence' remain difficult to discern. The Court of Appeal has attempted to give some guidance: see *Wells and Others* [2015] EWCA Crim 2, [2015] 1 WLR 2797.
[102] See also the discussion at para 10.113 below of the importance of a defendant being present.

Fact finding in the Crown Court

10.99 Aside from the formal fitness to stand trial process in the Crown Court, there is a much more restrictive version of the power of the magistrates under section 37(3) of the Mental Health Act 1983. Section 51(5) MHA applies only if a defendant has been remanded in custody by a court, transferred to hospital by the Secretary of State under section 48 MHA, and it is 'impractical or inappropriate' to bring the detainee before the court. Section 51(5) and (6) together allow the court to make a hospital order under section 37 and a restriction order under section 41 (if the risk posed by the defendant requires it) if it is 'proper to make such an order' in light of the committal documentation.

10.100 In *R (Kenneally) v Snaresbrook Crown Court*,[103] the Divisional Court held that, whilst the orders made were not punitive, the power to deprive someone of his or her liberty had to be construed restrictively, and so it could only be 'inappropriate' to bring someone before a court at all if a high degree of disability was present.[104] If the defendant can be brought to court (or if the preconditions of section 51(5) are not met), the question of fitness to stand trial or ability to participate may have to be answered.

Practical steps

10.101 The important practical points to take from the jurisprudence are the following:

- a defendant's ability to participate is distinct from the formal fitness to stand trial, though both rest on the need for a fair trial;
- reliance on expert evidence is important;
- the issues of mental disorder and vulnerability require constant review;
- courts have taken into account other matters, such as the reactions of the vulnerable person to police questioning on arrest and interview, when questioned by the court, the adequacy of their instructions for the purposes of cross-examination, and their ability to follow proceedings on an ongoing basis, not just to provide instructions on the witness statements;
- consider the use of trained intermediaries.

Miscellaneous matters

10.102 In *R (Varma) v Redbridge Magistrates Court*,[105] a summary conviction was quashed when magistrates decided to proceed to a trial when a matter had been set down for a finding of the facts because of evidence that the defendant was not fit to stand trial. Further evidence had been adduced to the contrary effect, but no effective notice had been given that an application would be made to proceed at a trial, nor was there a process to determine which medical view should be followed.

10.103 It is worth noting that in relation to the formal fitness to stand trial process in the Crown Court, once a determination has been made that the defendant is unfit to stand trial, the question of whether the actus reus was committed involves consideration of the evidence already heard and any further evidence, including evidence 'adduced by the person appointed by the court under this section to put the case for the defence'. In other words, the court has to make an order to appoint someone to represent the defendant. In *Norman*,[106] the Court of Appeal noted that:

> The duty under section 4A(2) is a duty personal to the court which must consider afresh the person who is to be appointed; it should not necessarily be the same person who has

---

[103] [2001] EWHC Admin 968, [2002] Mental Health Law Reports 53.
[104] Para 32.
[105] [2009] EWHC 836 (Admin), [2009] Mental Health Law Reports 173.
[106] [2008] EWCA Crim 1810, [2008] Mental Health Law Reports 206.

represented the defendant to date, as it is the responsibility of the court to be satisfied that the person appointed is the right person for this difficult task. As is evident from Professor MacKay's paper to which we have referred,[107] there are relatively few cases where the trial of the issue as to whether the defendant did the act are contested and are therefore outside the experience of most. The responsibility placed on the person so appointed is quite different to the responsibility placed on an advocate where he or she can take instructions from a client. The special position of the person so appointed is underlined by the fact that the person is remunerated not through the Criminal Defence Service, but out of central funds. Given the responsibility that the Act places on the court, it would not be unusual if the judge needed a little time to consider who was the best person to be so appointed.[108]

There is no obvious reason why this approach should not be followed in situations where **10.104** the process of fact-finding arises in the magistrates court or in circumstances where it is not a question of unfitness to stand trial but inability to participate. The purpose of fact-finding is not criminal but involves a different purpose and may entail a different set of skills from the advocate.

Another question that may arise is whether matters should proceed if a defendant is not able **10.105** to attend as a result of mental health issues. Given the account above of the duty to secure participation, reflecting standards arising under Article 6 of the ECHR, it is no surprise that the ECtHR has found problematic situations in which criminal trials have proceeded with a defendant being excluded because of mental disorder. In *Proshkin v Russia*,[109] the defendant was convicted but found not criminally responsible and made subject to a hospital disposal (essentially similar to a finding of not guilty by reason of insanity in English procedure). But, he had not been present in light of a medical report that it would be unhelpful. Deprecating this and finding a breach of Article 6, the ECtHR set out a reminder of the principles (citations omitted):

> 101. The Court reiterates that the object and purpose of Art 6§§1 and 3(c) presuppose the accused's presence ... It is of capital importance that a defendant appear, both because of his right to a hearing and because of the need to verify the accuracy of his statements and compare them with those of witnesses ... The Court reiterates further that the trial court may exceptionally continue hearings where the accused is absent on account of illness, provided that his or her interests are sufficiently protected ... However, where proceedings involve an assessment of the personality and character of the accused and his state of mind at the time of the offence and where their outcome could be of major detriment to him, it is essential to the fairness of the proceedings that he be present at the hearing and afforded the opportunity to participate in it together with his counsel ...

The view that continuing proceedings when a defendant is absent may be possible in excep- **10.106** tional circumstances is to be noted but the Court then qualified this by providing a reminder of the corollary of the reasonable accommodation principles which have been noted above, and which have been placed into the Convention on the Rights of Persons with Disabilities. This is expressed in the following (with emphasis added):

> [102] ... The Court ... believes that, although not having an absolute character, the right of being heard enjoys such a prominent place in a democratic society and has such a fundamental value for the protection of an individual against arbitrariness on the part of public authorities, that the mere fact of the individual suffering from a mental illness, as well as his being declared legally incapacitated, cannot automatically lead to the exclusion of the exercise of that right

---

[107] Professor McKay 'Continued Upturn in Unfitness to Plead—More Disability in Relation to the Trial under the 1991 Act' published at [2007] Crim LR 530.

[108] [2008] EWCA Crim 1810, [2008] Mental Health Law Reports 206, para 34 (iii).

[109] App no 28869/03, [2015] Mental Health Law Reports 402.

altogether. *It is the very weakness of a mentally ill defendant which should enhance the need for supporting his rights.* In this context, authorities must show requisite diligence in ensuring the accused's right to be present in an effective manner and must act particularly carefully when infringing upon that right, so as not to place the mentally ill at a disadvantage when compared with other defendants who do enjoy such a right ...

10.107 Note, in contrast, the position adopted by the Court of Appeal in *R v Ali*.[110] An objection that confiscation proceedings had continued in the absence of a defendant who had been admitted to a psychiatric hospital under the Mental Capacity Act 2005 as lacking capacity to decide to be there voluntarily was dismissed on the basis that he had been represented. The proceedings had turned on whether criminal lifestyle assumptions should apply, and resulted in a significant confiscation order (reduced on appeal but still sufficient to carry a default term of imprisonment of five years). This clearly involves a major detriment, and it is suggested that the principles in favour of offering support to allow participation have been lost sight of in the judgment of the Court of Appeal.

B. Ability to Participate—Legal Representation

10.108 This second part of the chapter examines the defendant's ability to participate in criminal proceedings by way of legal representation.

Importance of legal representation

10.109 The importance of legal representation in protecting and advancing a defendant's right to a fair trial has long been recognized and is illustrated by judicial remarks set out in *P*[111] and *Crawley*.[112]

Inadequate state funding

Confiscation proceedings

10.110 Confiscation proceedings have been stayed as an abuse of process because inadequate state funding has lead to defendants being deprived of sufficiently experienced counsel.

The media headline, 'Drugs Offender Keeps £4.5 m after 30 Barristers Refuse to Take Case',[113] highlighted the difficulties with publicly funded representation that offenders have faced when contesting complex and draconian confiscation proceedings.

10.111 The headline related to HHJ Mole QC's decision in *P*,[114] at Harrow Crown Court, to stay Proceeds of Crime Act 2002 (POCA) confiscation proceedings as an abuse of process, because the offender, P, could not be adequately represented as (a) a statutory provision (section 41(4) POCA) prevented him paying for his representation himself and (b) publicly funded Legal Aid did not provide sufficient state funding to pay for the necessary representation.

10.112 P had pleaded guilty to two counts. A restraint order was made against P and he was sentenced to imprisonment when confiscation proceedings were initiated. At the earlier stage of proceedings, P was paying his lawyers privately. Subsequently, he was awarded state funding to defend the confiscation proceedings.

---

[110] [2014] EWCA Crim 1658, [2015] 1 WLR 841, [2015] Mental Health Law Reports 446.
[111] On 18 March 2008, reported on BAILII and cited in *Re M (Restraint Order)* [2010] 1 WLR 650 at 655.
[112] *Crawley, Walker, Forsyth, Petrou and Daley* [2014] EWCA Crim 1028.
[113] *The Times* (6 May 2008).
[114] On 18 March 2008, reported on BAILII and cited in *Re M (Restraint Order)* [2010] 1 WLR 650 at 655.

An application was made on P's behalf to release money from the restrained funds on the **10.113** basis that since the Crown was alleging that the appellant had a criminal lifestyle, the appellant was, effectively, having to justify the movement of all money through his bank accounts which involved, some 4,548 individual transactions. The size and complexion of the confiscation hearing had become such that experienced senior counsel would be necessary in order to be able to put the proceedings into a manageable form. The estimated length of the confiscation hearing was said to be six weeks.

The justification for the request for the variation which, prima facie, was precluded by section **10.114** 41(4) of POCA, was that the state representation order had been granted at a time when the funding regime had changed, so that the provision of fees for counsel was governed by the graduated fee regime. This restricted payment to counsel to £178.25 per day or £99.50 per half day, unless counsel were able to persuade those determining his claim after the event that the case required 'special preparation', payment for which could not be guaranteed on taxation. The consequence was that no barrister of remotely appropriate experience and ability had been prepared to take on the case from any of the chambers that the appellant's solicitors had contacted.

HHJ Mole QC, sitting at Harrow Crown Court, heard the application to vary the restraint **10.115** order, accepting that the proceedings were unusually complex and justified the employment of counsel of substantial experience to allow P to have proper representation and to enable the Court to deal with the matter in a reasonable period of time.

HHJ Mole QC found as a matter of fact that: **10.116**

> Putting it bluntly, if he must rely on public funding, he would not be adequately represented; that is, not adequately represented unless he is able to pay for his own representation because P, I am told, is happy, indeed, anxious to pay his own legal fees and, hence, the application that I amend the restraint order to permit him to do so. The answer to the application is, indeed, that I cannot do so. That is because of section 41.

HHJ Mole QC considered that he was bound by the decision of *S (In Re S Restraint Order,* **10.117** *Release of Assets)*[115] which held that the prohibition applied fairly and squarely to restraint proceedings and that there was no escape from the prohibition.

P appealed to the Court of Appeal, who refused to vary the restraint order and thereafter, to **10.118** the House of Lords. The prosecution argued in the House of Lords that:

> The remedy for the petitioner's complaint lies not in a declaration of incompatibility, but instead in the Crown Courts' inherent power to ensure its proceedings are fair and not an abuse of process ... It is open to the petitioner to argue before the learned judge that, by reason of the inadequacy of his representation, he cannot have a fair hearing and that the proceedings should, therefore, be stayed as an abuse of process.

P took up the prosecution's suggested remedy and applied to Harrow Crown Court to stay **10.119** the POCA confiscation proceedings as an abuse of process. P represented himself, with the assistance of a solicitor, making submissions and giving evidence on oath. P argued that he could not receive a fair confiscation hearing, as he did not have sufficient advocate representation. Eighteen sets of barristers' chambers were contacted on P's behalf, to see whether or not there was a possibility of instructing barristers for this case at a daily rate of £178.25. No chambers were able to put forward counsel of sufficient experience, in accordance with paragraph 603 of part VI of the Bar Code of Conduct.

---

[115] [2005] 1 WLR 1338.

10.120   Having heard P, on oath, HHJ Mole QC, accepted at the stay hearing:

1. P was anxious to have his own representation if he could and would be able to find the cost from funds that had been restrained by the prosecution;
2. There was no serious prospect that the cost of a five to six week confiscation hearing would be found by friends and family, who had been prepared to fund P;
3. If P had to rely upon the legal aid fund, there is no prospect of him getting properly qualified counsel.

10.121   The significance of legal representation, HHJ Mole QC observed,

has to be judged in the context of the particular proceeding. It has been recognised by the courts that confiscation proceedings, employing as they do harsh or draconian assumptions for a justifiable and proper purpose, are a considerable, if necessary, imposition upon the person who faces them.

The burden will be upon P to displace the assumptions throughout and to prove both that assets do not represent benefit and to prove whether or not they are truly realisable or not.

10.122   The Australian High Court case of *Dietrich v The Queen*[116] was considered on the issue of whether or not representation by counsel is essential to a fair trial and whether, in the absence of it, the Court should stay proceedings. HHJ Mole QC cited a passage in the joint judgment of Chief Justice Mason and Justice McHugh in *Dietrich* in which they expressed the importance of representation by counsel:

The advantages of representation by counsel are even more clear today than they were in the nineteenth century. It is in the best interests not only of the accused but also of the administration of justice that an accused be so represented, particularly when the offence charged is serious. Lord Devlin stressed the importance of representation by counsel when he wrote, 'Indeed, where there is no legal representation, and save in the exceptional case of the skilled litigant, the adversary system, whether or not it remains in theory, in practice breaks down.'[117]

An unrepresented accused is disadvantaged, not merely because almost always he or she has insufficient legal knowledge and skills, but also because an accused in such a position is unable dispassionately to assess and present his or her case in the same manner as counsel for the Crown.

The hallowed response that in cases where the accused is unrepresented the judge becomes counsel for him or her, extending a 'helping hand' to guide the accused throughout the trial so as to ensure that any defence is effectively presented to the jury, is inadequate for the same reason that self-representation is generally inadequate: a trial judge and a defence counsel have such different functions that any attempt by the judge to fulfil the role of the latter is bound to cause problems.

10.123   The Australian judges in *Dietrich* then make the point that the right to retain counsel and the right to have counsel provided at the expense of the state are two different things. As a matter of fact HHJ Mole QC, found that P will have neither and went on to comment:

I would simply add to what Sutherland J said about the judge's ability to help out my comment that how much more difficult, indeed impossible, is it for the judge to take on the role of defence counsel when it is the judge and not the jury who has to determine the facts, as in confiscation proceedings? It would be particularly difficult in such circumstances for the judge to extend any real 'helping hand' to the accused.

---

[116]   [1992] 177 CLR p 292.
[117]   *The Judge*, (1979), p 67.

HHJ Mole QC stayed the confiscation proceedings stating that: **10.124**

> I fully appreciate the statutory purpose behind the confiscation legislation and I fully under-
> stand the public interest in it. I know perfectly well from my years in the Crown Court that
> to those who make a living from their crimes the loss of some of the material property and
> the comfort that their criminal profits have brought them may be a much greater punish-
> ment and a much greater deterrent to them than the, perhaps not very long prison sentences
> they serve. In other words, the principle underlying confiscation is a just one so long as the
> confiscation is carried out justly. The over-riding principle is, in my judgment, that for these
> serious matters, the defendant must be able to have a fair trial and in this case I am confident
> that he cannot, unrepresented by counsel. I, therefore, stay these proceedings as an abuse of
> the process of the Court.

Similar funding problems were encountered in *Susan Campbell*.[118] HHJ Heath sitting at   **10.125**
Lincoln Crown Court, stayed as an abuse of process proceedings brought against the offender,
Susan Campbell, following her convictions for money-laundering offences. Despite having a
state-funded representation order, she was unable to find suitably qualified counsel to repre-
sent her at the rate of remuneration applicable under the graduated fee structure. The Legal
Services Commission refused to make an exception to provide adequate funding for counsel.
Therefore, she could not have a fair trial without representation.

The Crown Prosecution Service appealed to the Court of Appeal against HHJ Heath's deci-   **10.126**
sion to stay proceedings as an abuse of process and make no confiscation order. However,
prior to the full leave hearing the CPS abandoned their application.

As a result of cases such as *P, Susan Campbell*, and *Graeme Carlton*,[119] the Ministry of Justice,   **10.127**
amended the Criminal Defence Service (CDS) Funding Order 2007,[120] to allow for enhanced
representation fees in confiscation proceedings.

Very High Cost Cases (VHCC)

In *Crawley*,[121] the Court of Appeal recognized and examined the applicability of the abuse of   **10.128**
process stay remedy when issues of lack of legal representation arose.

His Honour Judge Leonard QC, sitting in the Crown Court at Southwark, stayed as an abuse   **10.129**
of process a prosecution initiated by the Financial Conduct Authority (FCA) for offences of
conspiracy to defraud (land banking fraud), possessing criminal property, and offences contrary to sections 19, 23 and 177(4) of the Financial Services Act 2000. The evidence was complex and substantial, totaling 46,030 pages and 194 Excel spreadsheets with 864,200 entries.

The defendants had the benefit of state-funded Legal Aid Authority (LAA) representation   **10.130**
orders under the Very High Cost Case (VHCC) scheme. The Ministry of Justice had imposed
a 30 per cent cut in the fees to be paid to counsel in VHCC cases. The Bar Standards Board
made it clear that VHCC cases were no longer covered by 'deeming' provision so that individual barristers were free to make their own judgment as to whether the VHCC fees offered were
proper fees. At the same time, the Public Defender Service (PDS), a department of the LAA
providing criminal defence services, began actively recruiting a pool of employed advocates.

---

[118] As reported in *In re M (Restraint Order)* [2009] EWCA Crim 997, [2010] 1 WLR 650, at 652–54.
[119] As reported in *In re M (Restraint Order)* [2009] EWCA Crim 997, [2010] 1 WLR 650, at 652 and
660–62.
[120] By the Criminal Defence Service (Funding) (Amendment No.2) Order 2009, which came into force
on 21 August 2009. The amendment introduced enhanced remuneration in graduated fee cases where the
page count in confiscation proceedings exceeds 50 pages and for a system to allow additional hours properly
and reasonably spent in preparing such cases to be claimed by application to the National Taxing Team.
[121] *Crawley, Walker, Forsyth, Petrou and Daley* [2014] EWCA Crim 1028.

10.131 In argument before HHJ Leonard QC, it was accepted by the defence and the FCA that:

- In the circumstances of the case, it would be unfair to try the defendants if they wished to be represented and, through no fault of their own, they were not represented. To try the defendants in those circumstances would be a breach of their common law rights and contrary to Article 6(3) of the ECHR.
- At the time the trial was due to start the defendants would not be represented by advocates who had had sufficient time to prepare the case.
- The reason for the absence of advocates was the collective refusal of the self-employed Bar to accept the reduction in fees payable to advocates under the VHCC, regime leading to advocates returning their instructions or not accepting instructions.
- If a competent advocate were available, the defendant could not refuse to instruct him and claim he was involuntarily unrepresented.
- There was no fault on the part of the FCA.

10.132 HHJ Leonard QC stayed the proceedings as an abuse, as no suitably qualified advocates were available for the intended trial date and an adjournment would not remedy the situation. The judge found that the PDS pool of available advocates was insufficient to cover all the VHCC cases due to be tried and that the defendants were entitled to delay instructing an advocate in order to choose the best available advocate for the case.

10.133 The FCA appealed the stay decision to the Court of Appeal, pursuant to section 58 of the Criminal Justice Act 2003. The Court of Appeal allowed the appeal.

10.134 Sir Brian Leveson P gave the lead judgment, identifying that the appeal turned on the prospective availability of suitably qualified advocates to conduct the defence and commenting:[122]

[45] The agreed test to be applied was 'Is there a realistic prospect of competent advocates with sufficient time to prepare being available in the foreseeable future?' At the date of the hearing before the judge, on our analysis, there was a sufficient prospect of a sufficient number of PDS advocates who were then available who would enable a trial to proceed.

[46] … It had been made plain by the PDS that its available advocates would be assigned on a 'first come first served' basis …

[47] In those circumstances, the finding of the judge that there was no realistic prospect of competent advocates with sufficient time to prepare being available in the future cannot be sustained: neither was it reasonable for him to reach it.

[55] In our judgment, there is no question of a present breach of Article 6 of the ECHR and, should that state of affairs arise in the future, there would, in any event, be remedies short of a stay that could be deployed. We are not saying that there could not come a time when it may be appropriate to order that this indictment be stayed: that time, however, remains very much in the future and problems about representation will have to have developed considerably before such an exceptional order be justified. It would be a matter for the judge to assess on the basis of how matters stand at that point in time.

10.135 The importance of high quality representation was recognized in the judgment

[57]The criminal justice system in this country requires the highest quality advocates both to prosecute and to defend those accused of crime: in addition, they are the potential judges of the future. The better the advocates, the easier it is to concentrate on the real issues in the case, the more expeditious the hearing and the better the prospect of true verdicts according to the evidence. Poor quality advocates fail to take points of potential significance, or take them badly, leading to confusion and, in turn, appeals and, even more serious, leading to potential miscarriages of justice. We have no doubt that it is critical that there remains a

---

[122] [2014] EWCA Crim 1028.

thriving cadre of advocates capable of undertaking all types of publicly funded work, developing their skills from the straightforward work until they are able to undertake the most complex.

C. Summary

The ability of a defendant facing criminal charges to effectively participate in the criminal justice process is a fundamental part of the right to a fair trial under common law and Article 6 ECHR. The ability to participate includes not only a mental capacity to participate but also having adequate legal representation. **10.136**

Procedural modifications to the trial process such as special measures have developed over time to assist defendant participation, as a preferred alternative to staying proceedings as an abuse of process. The use of trained intermediaries with appropriate questioning (in terms of manner, duration, and topics to be covered) and trial modifications, as determined at Ground Rules hearings have developed in the recent past to assist the defendant's ability to participate. **10.137**

In terms of mental capacity the following points are worthy of summary: **10.138**

- The ability to participate is considered by the courts, by taking account of the defendant's calender age, mental capacity, level of maturity, intellectual and emotional capacity, ability to instruct lawyers, ability to testify and comprehend evidence, ability to challenge the prosecution allegations and raise defence points, and understand court procedures both in terms of pre-trial disclosure and any evidential developments during the trial. Ideally this court assessment is considered with expert medical evidence.
- There is a gap between a defendant's traditional fitness to stand trial and the need for effective participation.
- the amended section 37 MHA and the abuse of process jurisdiction provide a remedy for all mental disorder situations.
- legal representation is vital

The importance that courts, at first instance and appellate level attach to a defendant's right to participate is illustrated by the recent decision of the Court of Appeal in *Siddiqua Akhtar*.[123] The defendant was charged with racially aggravated intentional harassment (section 4A Public Order Act 1986, section 31 Crime and Disorder Act 1998) involving a street argument between two people of the same ethnicity about cycling on the pavement. The defendant had a history of mental illness in the form of generalized anxiety disorder, panic disorder, and recurrent depressive disorder, fully evidenced by expert reports. The Crown Court ordered that special measures were appropriate, with an intermediary being appointed by the court to assist the defendant in giving evidence, which was to be via live link in a separate room from the main court room. On the day of the trial, the appropriate camera technology was not available to enable the defendant to participate throughout the entire trial. Suitable arrangements could not be made to allow the defendant to meaningfully participate in the trial process in any sensible way. In staying proceedings as an abuse of process the trial judge HHJ Gledhill QC said: **10.139**

> But today this court, in my judgment, is not in a position to be able to put in place those procedures and measures that are needed in order for her to have a fair trial. So the prosecution application was adjourn it and then we will find in some other way an opportunity to

---

[123] [2016] EWCA Crim 390, Archbold Review Issue 4, 24 May 2016.

have a fair trial. I am not going to allow an adjournment in this case. This case has gone on for far too long … I am ruling now that this defendant cannot have a fair trial and in those circumstances I stay the proceedings.

10.140 The prosecution appealed the stay decision under the section 58 CJA 2003 terminatory ruling process. In refusing the prosecutor's appeal, the Court of Appeal, in the judgment of Lord Justice Davis, found that what the trial judge was concerned about were the complete technological failures that had occurred at court which meant that the case could not properly be tried that day. The trial judge was entitled to find as fact that there could be no fair trial on that day. Further, all the indications are that an adjournment, as sought by the prosecution, would have served no purpose. The case would have to be put off again. In deciding whether to adjourn further, the trial judge was entitled to have regard to the fact that (a) this was by no means an important matter of its type and (b) the mental health position of the defendant with the anxieties the whole court process was placing on her. It was not fair for there to be an adjournment to some date in the future with all the attendant pressures on the mentally vulnerable defendant.

11

EXTRADITION

A. Introduction

There is a fundamental difference between general criminal proceedings and extradition proceedings. Where domestic criminal proceedings look to try accused persons and result in the punishment of those found guilty, extradition proceedings involve neither a trial per se, nor punishment. Extradition procedure, unlike criminal procedure is founded on concepts of reciprocity, comity, and respect for differences in other jurisdictions. **11.01**

As a result of this difference, the doctrine of abuse of process was, for many years, held not to apply to extradition proceedings. The enactment of the Human Rights Act 1998 opened the door to the possibility that extradition proceedings could be stayed on the grounds of abuse of process, although only in very limited circumstances. **11.02**

After briefly sketching the statutory bars to extradition and the background to the court's reluctance to permit the use of abuse of process in extradition cases, this chapter will examine the way in which the abuse of process jurisdiction has developed following the case of *R (Bermingham & Ors) v Director of the Serious Fraud Office*[1] which conclusively put the availability of abuse of process as a bar to extradition beyond question. **11.03**

Bars to extradition

The grounds on which a person can resist a request for extradition made by a state, with whom extradition arrangements are in place, are circumscribed by statute. The Extradition Act 2003 ('the Act') was enacted to give effect to the Framework Decision 2002 ('the FD'), which aimed to simplify and accelerate extradition between member states of the European Union.[2] The arrangements applying to European countries are dealt with in Part 1 of the Act. Under Part 1, EU member states need not issue an extradition request; they need only issue a European Arrest Warrant ('EAW') which will, in principle, be recognized as the basis for the surrender of the requested person without the need for protracted extradition proceedings. **11.04**

---

[1] [2007] QB 727 (hereafter *Bermingham v SFO* [2007]).
[2] Note, however, that the Act did not simply transpose the Framework Decision into UK law: there are differences between the provisions of the FD and the Act.

The FD, and the Act itself, are based on the principle of mutual recognition, that is, the idea that legal and judicial systems in other member states are inherently worthy of trust and confidence. The Act also introduced changes to extradition arrangements with countries outside the EU. Whilst the EAW scheme does not apply to countries outside the EU, similar concepts are used in relation to the statutory bars to extradition, with some sections mirroring verbatim those found in Part 1.

11.05 In summary, the grounds for resisting extradition, as set out by the Act, are as follows:[3]

- Section 12/80—the rule against double jeopardy;
- Section 12A—absence of prosecution decision;
- Section 13/81—extraneous considerations;
- Section 14/82—unjust or oppressive by reason of the passage of time;
- Section 15—the person's age;
- Section 18,19 and 19A/96 and 96A—earlier extradition from territory or by the ICC;
- Section 19B /83A—forum;
- Section 20/86—conviction in absence;
- Section 21/87—human rights;
- Section 21A—proportionality;
- Section 21B—request for temporary transfer; and
- Section 25/91—unjust or oppressive by reason of mental or physical condition;
- Section 83—hostage-taking considerations;
- Section 94—death penalty.

11.06 There is no bar preventing the extradition of those who are demonstrably innocent:[4] the guilt or innocence of the requested person is not relevant to extradition proceedings, nor, in relation to EU member states and a number of non-EU countries, is any evidence of guilt required. It will also be apparent that abuse of process is not explicitly included in the limited statutory grounds for refusing extradition. The statutory regime does however contain some protections against states that seek to extradite persons in circumstances that would amount to an abuse of process in this jurisdiction. Most obviously, protection is offered by sections 21 and 87 of the Act which prevents extradition where it would be incompatible with a requested person's human rights. Article 6 of the European Convention on Human Rights (ECHR) provides that everyone has the right to a fair trial. Double jeopardy, extraneous considerations, passage of time, specialty, forum, conviction in absence and mental or physical condition are all bars to extradition and offer some form of remedy where those types of abuse identified in this book might occur. Given the fact that abuse of process arguments rarely succeed in domestic criminal cases, it is not an exaggeration to say that requested persons have, in some respects, better protection against abusive requests that fall into these categories than defendants in general criminal proceedings. Nonetheless, it is clear that there are some heads of abuse which the statutory bars to extradition, as set out in the Act, do not cover. This chapter will go on to look at this residual jurisdiction.

---

[3] The Part 1 bars are set out first, and are at sections 12–25. The number following the slash indicates the Part 2 equivalents, which are at sections 80–94.

[4] See for example the case of *Italy v Edmond Arapi* EWHC (Admin) 15 June 2010 (unreported) where, despite evidence that the requested person, Mr. Arapi, could not have committed the offence for which his extradition was sought, the UK courts had no power to go behind the extradition request.

B. Recognition of Jurisdiction

The rationale for the reluctance of the courts to recognize an abuse of process jurisdiction **11.07** prior to the Human Rights Act 1998 came primarily from the fact that an alternative means of remedying abusive requests existed. Under the 1989 Extradition Act, the court was required to discharge a defendant 'if it appeared that the accusation against him is not made in good faith in the interests of justice'.[5] In addition, in relation to those persons requested under the old Extradition Acts,[6] the Secretary of State for the Home Department had the discretionary power to refuse to surrender a person whenever 'in his view, it would be wrong, unjust or oppressive',[7] and the courts reasoned that that offered sufficient protection from extradition requests made in other circumstances which might amount to an abuse of the court's process. This changed with the incorporation of the ECHR into domestic law by the Human Rights Act 1998. It was held in *R (Kashamu) v Governor of Brixton Prison (No 2)*[8] that Article 5 ECHR, which requires the lawfulness of detention to be determined by a court, applies to extradition proceedings and is not satisfied by the lawfulness of detention being determined by the exercise of the discretion of the Home Secretary.

Kashamu[9] was a case under the Extradition Act 1989. The Act severely curtailed the **11.08** Home Secretary's discretion to refuse to surrender a person. Following the introduction of the Act, the case of *Bermingham v Director of the Serious Fraud Office*[10] determined that the judge conducting an extradition hearing under the Act had the power to hold that the prosecutor is abusing the process of the court. In that case, Lord Justice Laws stated that:

> Now, it is plain that the judge's functions under the 2003 Act, and those of the magistrate under the predecessor legislation, are and were wholly statutory. He therefore possesses no inherent powers. But that is not to say that he may not enjoy an *implied* power. The implication arises from the express provisions of the statutory regime which it is his responsibility to administer. It is justified by the imperative that the regime's integrity must not be usurped.[11]

It has been suggested that because *Bermingham*[12] was a case under Part 2 of the Act, the **11.09** jurisdiction is only applicable in Part 2 cases. The Divisional Court has, however, repeatedly recognized abuse of process as applying to Part 1 cases as well. Whilst this point has never been fully argued, given the large number of cases which have been decided on the basis that the jurisdiction applies equally to Part 1 cases, it appears unlikely that this trend would be reversed by full argument on the matter.[13]

For an analysis of the applicability of abuse of process in Scottish extradition cases, see *Lord* **11.10** *Advocate (for the Government of the United States of America) v Johar Mirza.*[14]

---

[5] Section 11(3)(c).
[6] See section 12(2) Extradition Act 1989 or section 10 Extradition Act 1870.
[7] See paragraph 232G of *Atkinson v USA*, [1971] AC 197.
[8] [2002] QB 887, hereafter *Kashamu (No 2)* [2002].
[9] *Kashamu (No 2)* [2002] (n 8).
[10] *Bermingham v SFO* [2007] (n1).
[11] *Bermingham v SFO* [2007] (n 1), para 97.
[12] *Bermingham v SFO* [2007] (n 1).
[13] See, in particular, the comments of the Divisional Court in the case of *Sofia City Court Bulgaria v Atanasova-Kalaidzhieva* [2011] EWHC 2335 (Admin) paras 29–30.
[14] [2015] SCED 132.

C. Procedure

11.11 Although the decision in *Bermingham*[15] confirmed the availability of abuse of process as a ground upon which extradition proceedings could be stayed, it was the case of *R (Government of the United States of America) v Bow Street Magistrates' Court (Tollman & Tollman)*[16] which articulated the procedure which should be followed. Lord Chief Justice Phillips stated that the judge 'has a duty to decide whether the process is being abused if put on enquiry as to the possibility of this'.[17] He directed a procedure in which the allegation of abuse is identified and then evaluated by the judge to assess whether it is capable of amounting to an abuse. If it is found to be capable of amounting to an abuse, the court should call for an explanation from the requesting state in order to determine whether an abuse has occurred. The issue should normally be considered within the extradition hearing.[18]

11.12 The procedure is set out as follows:

> No steps should be taken to investigate an alleged abuse of process unless the judge is satisfied that there is reason to believe that an abuse may have taken place. Where an allegation of abuse of process is made, the first step must be to insist on the conduct alleged to constitute the abuse being identified with particularity. The judge must then consider whether the conduct, if established, is capable of amounting to an abuse of process. If it is, he must next consider whether there are reasonable grounds for believing that such conduct may have occurred. If there are, then the judge should not accede to the request for extradition unless he has satisfied himself that such abuse has not occurred.[19]
>
> [...]
>
> The appropriate course for the judge to take if he has reason to believe that an abuse of process may have occurred is to call upon the judicial authority that has issued the arrest warrant, or the State seeking extradition in a Part 2 case, for whatever information or evidence the judge requires in order to determine whether an abuse of process has occurred or not.[20]

11.13 Following this course, a requested person seeking to stay proceedings on the grounds of abuse of process should:

1. Identify with specificity what is alleged to constitute the abuse
2. Satisfy the court that the matter complained of is capable of amounting to an abuse
3. Satisfy the court that there are reasonable grounds for believing that such conduct has occurred.[21]

11.14 Only after these three steps have been taken will the court move to the next stage of requiring an explanation from the requesting state.[22] Whilst the court cannot compel the provision of information from a requesting state, if no satisfactory explanation is provided, the conclusion that the judge has come to (i.e. that there are reasonable grounds for believing that abusive conduct may have occurred) may remain unchallenged.

---

[15] *Bermingham v SFO* [2007] (n 1).

[16] [2006] EWHC 2256 (Admin) (hereafter *R (USA) v Bow Street Magistrates' Court (Tollman & Tollman)* [2006]).

[17] *R (USA) v Bow Street Magistrates' Court (Tollman & Tollman)* [2006] (n 16), para 83.

[18] *R (USA) v Bow Street Magistrates' Court (Tollman & Tollman)* [2006] (n 16), para 80.

[19] *R (USA) v Bow Street Magistrates' Court (Tollman & Tollman)* [2006] (n 16), para 84.

[20] *R (USA) v Bow Street Magistrates' Court (Tollman & Tollman)* [2006] (n 16), para 89.

[21] The procedure was re-iterated by Richards LJ in *Haynes v Malta* [2009] EWHC 880, para 6 (hereafter *Haynes v Malta* [2009]).

[22] See *Haynes v Malta* [2009] (n 21): if the matter gets that far, the court should require the judicial authority to provide an explanation. The court should not order extradition unless satisfied that no such abuse has taken place (para 6).

Where the judge has reasonable grounds for believing that the conduct is capable of amount- **11.15** ing to an abuse, the final question for the judge to decide is whether such abuse has occurred. If the judge is unable to decide that an abuse has occurred, the requested person must be discharged.

D. Ambit of the Jurisdiction

The overlap between many of the bars to extradition and the abuse of process jurisdiction has **11.16** been noted in paragraph 11.06, however it is worth emphasizing that the court has repeatedly stated that it is a *residual* jurisdiction, that is, that it applies 'only when the issues raised can- not be addressed by the statutory protection'.[23] As such, the judge should deal with the issue after having considered all of the statutory bars to extradition.[24]

It should also be noted that the jurisdiction is limited to allowing a court to hold *that the* **11.17** *prosecuting authorities of the requesting state* are abusing the process of the court. In the case of *Symeou*,[25] the Divisional Court said this of the abuse of process jurisdiction of the court:

> The focus of this implied jurisdiction is the abuse of the requested state's duty to extradite those who are properly requested, and who are unable to raise any of the statutory bars to extradition. The residual abuse jurisdiction identified in *Bermingham* and *Tollman* concerns abuse of the extradition process by the prosecuting authority. We emphasise those latter two words. That is the language of those cases. It is the good faith of the requesting authorities which is at issue because it is their request, coupled with their perverted intent and purpose, which constitutes the abuse. If the authorities of the requesting state seek the extradition of someone for a collateral purpose, or when they know that the trial cannot succeed, they abuse the extradition processes of the requested state.
>
> The abuse jurisdiction of the requested state does not extend to considering misconduct or bad faith by the police of the requesting state in the investigation of the case or the prepara- tion of evidence for trial.

The reason for the distinction lies in the respective functions of the courts of the requested **11.18** and requesting state within the EAW framework. The former are entitled to ensure that their duties and the functions under the Act Part 1 are not being abused. It is the exclusive function of the latter to try the issues relevant to the guilt or otherwise of the individual. This necessarily includes deciding what evidence is admissible, and what weight should be given to particular pieces of evidence having regard to the way in which an investigation was car- ried out. It is for the trial court in the requesting state to find the facts about how statements were obtained, which may go to admissibility or weight, both of which are matters for the court conducting the trial. It is the function of that court to decide whether evidence was improperly obtained and if so what the consequences for the trial are. It is for the trial court to decide whether its own procedures have been breached.

It is not therefore open to the court in the requested state to hold that the actions of the police **11.19** in the requesting state could found a stay on the grounds of abuse of process. Should there be a suggestion of police misconduct which would, in equivalent circumstances in this country, provide such grounds, this will be an issue for trial in the requesting state.

---

[23] *Mehtab Khan v Government of the United States of America* [2010] EWHC 1127 (Admin), para 11.
[24] *Branko Loncar v County Court in Vukovar (Croatia)* [2015] EWHC 548 (hereafter *Loncar v Croatia* [2015]).
[25] *Andrew Symeou v Public Prosecutor's Office at the Court of Appeals, Patras, Greece* [2009] EWHC 897 (Admin) (hereafter *Symeou v Public Prosecutor's Office* [2009]).

11.20   In the case of *Douglas Belbin v The Regional Court of Lille, France*,[26] the Divisional Court concluded that the implied jurisdiction required the court to consider whether there had been an abuse of process by the requesting judicial authority under Part 1 of the Act,[27] noting (following *Swedish Prosecution Authority v Assange*[28]) 'that the acts of a prosecutor, in contradistinction of those of a judge, must be subjected to "rigorous scrutiny" because a prosecutor is (unlike a judge) a party to the criminal proceedings in the requesting state.'[29]

11.21   Taking up a phrase used by the court in *Bermingham*,[30] Lord Justice Aikens' analysis of the jurisdiction in *Belbin*[31] put a further gloss on the type of behaviour that could amount to an abuse of process. He stated that it could only amount to an abuse of the extradition process if the court is satisfied on cogent evidence[32] that 'the statutory regime in the [Act] is being "usurped" and, further, that as a result of such "usurpation" of the statutory regime, the requested person will be unfairly prejudiced in his subsequent challenge to extradition in this country or unfairly prejudiced in the proceedings in the requesting country if surrendered there.'[33]

Bad faith

11.22   The question of whether an element of bad faith is essential to a successful application to stay the proceedings on the grounds of abuse of process is moot. There is case law which expressly states that abuse of process is not confined to bad faith on the part of the requesting state.[34] Nevertheless, a lack of bad faith is frequently cited as a basis for a refusal of an abuse applications made by requested persons.[35] It is the author's view that bad faith on the part of the requesting state is not essential to the success of any abuse argument put forward by the requested person given that there are categories of abuse which clearly do not envisage a requirement that the requesting state has acted in bad faith (see *Dytlow*[36]—in such cases, the requesting state will be almost bound not to know that the requested person has been granted asylum and therefore cannot be extradited—or paragraph 11.42 *Zakrzewski*[37]).

11.23   Nonetheless, most complaints of abuse of process will arise in the context of bad faith. The passage from *Symeou*[38] (see para 11.17) illustrates that there is a presumption of good faith on the part of the requesting state.[39] This will be the starting point in considering any application that proceedings be stayed on the grounds of abuse of process.[40] The more established the relationship between the UK and the requesting state, the more difficult it will be to rebut this presumption.[41]

---

[26]   [2015] EWHC 149 (hereafter *Belbin v France* [2015]).
[27]   *Belbin v France* [2015] (n 26), para 43.
[28]   [2011] EWHC 2849.
[29]   *Belbin v France* [2015] (n 26).
[30]   *Bermingham v SFO* [2007] (n 1).
[31]   *Belbin v France* [2015]) (n 26).
[32]   *Belbin v France* [2015]) (n 26), para 59.
[33]   *Belbin v France* [2015] (n 26), para 44.
[34]   See, for example, *Janovic v Prosecutor General's Office Lithuania* [2011] EWHC 710 (Admin).
[35]   See, for example, *Mehtab Khan v Government of the United States of America* [2010] EWHC 1127 (Admin), paragraph 33.
[36]   *District Court in Ostroleka, Second Criminal Division (A Polish Judicial Authority) v Dytlow & Dytlow* [2009] EWHC 1009 (Admin) hereafter *Poland v Dytlow* [2009] EWHC 1009 (Admin).
[37]   *Zakrzewski v Regional Court of Lodz, Poland* [2013] UKSC 2 (hereafter *Zakrzewski v Poland* [2013]).
[38]   *Symeou v Public Prosecutor's Office* [2009]) (n 25).
[39]   See also paragraph 101 *R(Ahmad) v Secretary of State* [2006] EWHC 2927 (Admin) (hereafter *Ahmad v Secretary of State* [2006])—there is a fundamental presumption that a requesting state is acting in good faith.
[40]   *Patel v Government of India and SSHD* [2013] EWHC 819 (Admin), paras 13–14.
[41]   *Ahmad v Secretary of State* [2006] (n 39 para 101.

E. Heads of Abuse

The heads of abuse that apply in extradition proceedings are more limited than those available **11.24** in domestic criminal proceedings given that the courts will only look at abuse arising from prosecutorial conduct and not from abuse on the part of the investigating authorities. In addition, the residual nature of the jurisdiction means that where, for example, in a domestic case a defendant might make an application to stay the proceedings on the grounds that they cannot receive a fair trial because of delay, in extradition proceedings the requested person would raise the passage of time bar under section 14 or section 82 of the Act. Nevertheless, there are few cases in which abuse of process is raised as a stand-alone ground for resisting extradition, and it is frequently raised alongside a complementary statutory provision.

This chapter will now examine the case law relevant to the following specific heads of **11.25** abuse: re-issue of request; collateral motive; disclosure; incorrect particulars; forum issues and asylum cases. Note that, given the nature of the jurisdiction, these categories are not exhaustive.

Re-issue of request

Given that the extradition courts will not determine guilt or innocence, there is no legal **11.26** principle that prevents an extradition request or EAW being re-issued following a discharge. In reality, the reason for the discharge will often determine whether a second request is made. If, for example, the person is discharged because the warrant does not comply with the requirements of s 2 of the Act (for example, it omits a detail such as the place or time of the conduct), it is likely that the requesting state will be advised that the warrant or request should be withdrawn, re-drafted properly and the requested person re-arrested. The subsequent proceedings will not be abusive.[42]

If the discharge is under one of the bars to extradition (i.e. sections 12–20/80–86) it is hard **11.27** to envisage circumstances in which a renewed request for extradition would not amount to an abuse of the court's process. The case of *Office of the Prosecutor-General of Turin v Franco Barone*[43] turns on its own particular facts, but it does provide a useful illustration of the stance that the courts will take in the face of a court in another jurisdiction disregarding a UK court's rulings. The requested person, Mr Barone, had been discharged in 1997 under provisions of the 1989 Extradition Act, equivalent to section 20 of the 2003 Act. Mr Barone had been convicted in his absence and it was held that it would not be in the interests of justice to return him on the ground of that conviction. In 1997, the Divisional Court looked at the strength of the evidence in the case and based its decision on the unfairness of the Italian Code of 1930, which applied in that case. The new request was issued following the implementation of the Act, which does not require the requesting state to adduce evidence to show a case to answer. Upon the issue of the new request, the judicial authority did not attempt to refute the findings made by the Divisional Court in 1997, but relied instead upon these changes in extradition procedure. Of this, the court said:

> It is true that the new regime depends upon trust in the integrity and fairness 'of each other's judicial institutions'. But not even the expert Italian witnesses, in their uncontradicted evidence, seem to have placed any trust in the Italian criminal procedure introduced in 1930.

---

[42] See *Wilson-Campbell v Court of Instruction No 4, Orhuela, Spain* [2010] EWHC 3316 (Admin), paragraph 11. See also *USA v Wood* [2013] EWHC 1971 (Admin) in which an unexcused delay of three and a half years prior to the issue of a second request did not 'get anywhere near establishing an abuse of process' (para 50).

[43] [2010] EWHC 3004 (Admin) (hereafter *Prosecutor-General of Turin v Barone* [2010]).

The Deputy Prosecutor has not sought to advance any fresh evidence under the new regime as to why the courts in the United Kingdom should do so now. Moreover, the Framework Decision depends upon *mutual* respect and the stance adopted by the Italian judicial authority pays no respect, indeed, seeks to ignore the decision of the Divisional Court and of the Judicial Committee of the House of Lords, solely on the basis that under the 2003 Act courts would now not be able to adopt the approach to the evidence which the Divisional court previously adopted ...[44]

I conclude that the response to the ruling of the Divisional Court, which amounts to an attempt to ignore it merely on the basis of the Framework Decision, does amount to an abuse of process and I uphold the decision of the District Judge on that basis.[45]

11.28 See also *Sofia City Court, Bulgaria v Atanasova-Kalaidzhieva*[46] in which the Bulgarian court's failure to recognize the concerns of the Divisional Court in the UK in relation to an earlier request led to a discharge on the grounds of abuse of process.

11.29 In *Loncar*,[47] the Divisional Court explicitly left open the question of 'whether a second extradition request by a state made long after its first extradition request on a technically valid extradition request was rejected by the English court (and not appealed) would constitute an abuse of the English court's process, in circumstances where, as here ... there are no material changes.'[48]

Collateral motive

11.30 There is a long and unfortunate history of misuse of the extradition machinery by governments for reasons other than the prosecution or punishment of offenders, associated typically (although not exclusively) with the former Soviet states.[49] Given the inherent potential in extradition for this kind of abuse, there is a well-established principle in extradition law that prevents a person from being extradited for a political offence. It is notable that this exception is not contained per se in the Act. The extraneous considerations bar (sections 13 and 81of the Act) does prevent extradition where it appears that extradition is sought for the purpose of prosecuting or punishing the requested person on account of her race, religion, nationality, gender, sexual orientation or political opinions, or where it appears that if extradited she might be prejudiced at trial or punished, detained, or restricted in her personal liberty by reason of her race, religion, nationality, gender, sexual orientation or political opinions. Nevertheless, there remain some cases where a person's extradition is sought for some collateral motive but where the facts do not fall squarely into the categories covered by the extraneous considerations bar, or alternatively, where the facts give rise to an argument that extradition should be refused by reason both of the extraneous considerations bar and on the grounds of abuse of process.

11.31 The question of a collateral motive was raised in the case of *Bermingham*,[50] in which the requested persons submitted that their extradition was sought in order to obtain evidence against others involved in a conspiracy to defraud Enron. Ultimately, the Court did not find

---

[44] *Prosecutor-General of Turin v Barone* [2010] (n 42) para 34.

[45] *Prosecutor-General of Turin v Barone* [2010] (n 42) para 39.

[46] [2011] EWHC 2335 (Admin).

[47] *Loncar v Croatia* [2015] (n 24).

[48] *Loncar v Croatia* [2015] (n 24), para 32.

[49] See, for example, the comments of lawyer Martin Richmond published in *the New York Times*, relating to the 1947 request from the USSR to the US for the return of Kirill Alexeiev, who had defected to the US. According to the *New York Times* '[he asserted] that the embassy action followed a "well-worn Soviet pattern" of first minimising the importance of an individual, "then, when word comes from Moscow, accuse him of whatever crime is handiest" '. The Times Record, Troy[(New York, 6 January 1947).

[50] *Bermingham v SFO* [2007] (n 1).

such a motive, but Lord Justice Laws did say, 'the prosecutor must act in good faith. Thus if he knew he had no real case, but was pressing the extradition request for some collateral motive and accordingly tailored the choice of documents accompanying the request, there might be a good submission of abuse of process.'[51]

One example of a case in which both abuse of process and the extraneous considerations bar   **11.32**
led to discharge is that of *Republic of Serbia v Ejup Ganic*.[52] The requested person had been sought for war crimes said to have been committed in Bosnia in May 1992 and the Senior District Judge heard (and accepted) evidence that 'during the course of these extradition proceedings attempts were made to use the proceedings as a lever to try to secure the Bosnian Governments [*sic*] approval to the Srebrenica Declaration.' The Judge went on to say: 'If indeed the Government was prepared not to pursue these extradition proceedings in return for Bosnian co-operation that in itself must be capable of amounting to an abuse of this process of this court.'[53] The Judge also found that information in the request contained 'significant misrepresentations' and that '[t]he combination of the two leads me to believe that these proceedings are brought and are being used for political purposes and as such amount to an abuse of the process of this court.' The requested person was also discharged on the basis that his extradition was barred by s.81 (a) and (b) on the grounds that his extradition was being sought for political reasons, and on the grounds that he would be prejudiced at trial for the same reasons.

Disclosure

The issue of disclosure does raise important questions about the role of the Crown Prosecution   **11.33**
Service in extradition proceedings. The statutory regime under the Criminal Procedure and Investigations Act 1996 does not apply to extradition proceedings. Nevertheless, where the CPS is acting as the prosecutor in extradition proceedings (as it will in almost all cases[54]), it will remain bound by section 6 of the Human Rights Act 1998 as a public body. By virtue of this section, it is unlawful for any public authority to act in a way which is incompatible with a Convention right. In addition, the prosecution also owes its primary duty to the UK court.[55] This means that the CPS, which acts as the solicitor of the foreign state,[56] do have a duty of disclosure in extradition proceedings, albeit a more circumscribed one than in domestic criminal proceedings.

The cases of *Bermingham*[57] and *Tollman*[58] both touched on issues of disclosure. In   **11.34**
Bermingham,[59] the Divisional Court rejected the defence submission that the prosecutor's refusal to disclose anything beyond that set out in the request could justify a finding of abuse.[60] In the case of the Tollmans, and that of the case heard with it,[61] orders for disclosure of documents were made by the District Judge in the Magistrates' Court. The Divisional Court recognized that there could only be one effective sanction for a failure to

---

[51] *Bermingham v SFO* [2007] (n 1), para 100.
[52] [2010] EW Misc 11 (EWMC) (27 July 2010).
[53] [2010] EW Misc 11 (EWMC) (27 July 2010) (hereafter *Serbia v Ganic* [2010]), para 39.
[54] At the time of writing, there has only been one case since the implementation of the Extradition Act 2003 where the requesting state has instructed a private prosecutor.
[55] *R (on the application of Lotfi Raissi) v Secretary of State for the Home Department*, EWCA [2008] Civ 72 (hereafter *Raissi v Secretary of State* [2008]) para 138.
[56] *Raissi v Secretary of State* [2008] (n 55) para 139 and 140.
[57] *Bermingham v SFO* [2007] (n 1).
[58] *R (USA) v Bow Street Magistrates' Court (Tollman & Tollman)* [2006] (n 16).
[59] *Bermingham v SFO* [2007] (n 1).
[60] *Bermingham v SFO* [2007] (n 1) para 98.
[61] *R (USA) v Bow Street Magistrates' Court (Tollman & Tollman)* [2006] (n 16).

comply with an order for disclosure, that is, that the court must order the discharge of the requested person. This is the basis on which the Court set out the procedure requiring the Court to seek an explanation from the requesting state only when it is satisfied that there are reasonable grounds for believing that conduct amounting to an abuse has occurred (see para 11.12).

11.35 The case of *Raissi*[62] looked at the question again in relation to an application for compensation under the Home Office *ex gratia* payment scheme for a man who had been arrested under the 1989 Extradition Act on 'holding charges', which were, the CPS said, to be amended to charge serious terrorist offences. He was remanded in custody for four and a half months, and during this time bail had been repeatedly refused, it having been said by the CPS that the requested person was under investigation for involvement in the 9/11 attacks. The charges were not amended, and Mr Raissi was discharged on the extradition request for the 'holding charges', as the District Judge was not satisfied as to dual criminality.[63] The court found that, 'on the papers before us, it appears that the proceedings were brought for an ulterior motive and that the opposition to bail, based on unsubstantiated assertions, was also an abuse.' In examining whether there had been 'serious default' by the CPS, the court looked at the duty of the CPS and the requesting state in extradition proceedings. The court stated that the duty of the CPS to the court includes a duty to ensure that the requesting state complies with its duty of disclosure. It approved the judgment in *Knowles*,[64] which said of the requesting state that:

> [i]t does, however, owe the court of the requested state a duty of candour and good faith. While it is for the requesting state to decide what evidence it will rely on to seek a committal, it must in pursuance of that duty disclose evidence which destroys or very severely undermines the evidence on which it relies.

From this duty of the requesting state, it follows that 'the CPS has a duty to disclose evidence about which it knows and which destroys or severely undermines the evidence on which the requesting state relies.'[65]

11.36 In *Government of Ukraine v Kononko*,[66] a case not prosecuted by the CPS, lack of disclosure was one of the complaints made by the requested person. In fact, the requested person had submitted material on his own behalf, which came from those instructing the prosecution, in the form of email traffic between the Ukrainian firm instructing the private UK lawyers and the prosecutor at the General Prosecutor's Office (GPO) of Ukraine. The defence submitted that this material showed that not only had there been a failure to disclose material information, but it was clear that the material upon which the request was based was orchestrated by Ilyashev [the Ukrainian firm] and the two individuals named who were particularly concerned with this and who put to Mr Melnik [the prosecutor at the GPO] various statements and documents. All he was required to do was simply, where necessary, append his signature so that they appeared to be his investigation, whereas, in fact, they were nothing of the sort. They were what he was put up to requesting by the two involved with Ilyashev.[67]

---

[62] *Raissi v Secretary of State* [2008] (n 55).

[63] Although the requested person had argued that the extradition proceedings should be stayed as an abuse of process, because the judge was not satisfied as to dual criminality, he did not go on to consider the abuse.

[64] *Knowles v Government of the United States* [2006] UKPC 38.

[65] Paragraph 140 *Raissi v Secretary of State* [2008] (n 55).

[66] *Government of Ukraine v Kononko* [2014] EWHC 1420 (Admin) (hereafter *Ukraine v Kononko* [2014]) para 11.

[67] *Government of Ukraine v Kononko* [2014] (n 66).

On the basis of this, Mr Justice Collins stated, from 'the material that I have seen that the abuse of process in relation to this extradition request is fully made out.'[68] Whilst the discharge of the requested person in this case was upheld, it is notable that the material which led to the finding of an abuse had not been disclosed by the private prosecutor. **11.37**

Incorrect particulars

Pursuant to sections 2 and 78 of the Act (for Part 1 and Part 2 requests respectively), the document requesting a person's extradition must contain the information specified by those sections, known as the 'particulars'.[69] **11.38**

Where the particulars are lacking, this may give rise to a direct challenge to the validity of the EAW or request under the statutory scheme. See, for example, the case of *Von Der Pahlen v Austria*,[70] in which a challenge was made to the sufficiency of the description of the conduct, or *Crean v Government of Ireland*,[71] in which the defence argued that the time of the conduct was insufficiently particularized. This will not be considered to be an abuse of process. **11.39**

What, then, is the position when the warrant or request contains sufficient but incorrect particulars? The Administrative Court has held that the contents of a warrant must be 'proper, accurate and fair'.[72] In the case of *Murua*,[73] an EAW gave particulars which, taken in isolation, complied with the requirements of s 2 of the Act. Documents obtained from the Spanish proceedings in relation to seven co-defendants, however, showed that the prosecutor there had positively asserted that the charges as set out in the EAW were not made out. Sir Antony May, the President of the Queen's Bench Division, held that: '[t]he 2010 warrant does not, therefore, give particulars of conduct capable of constituting a viable extradition offence, so that it does not contain a description of the conduct alleged which is proper, fair and accurate.' In addition to the argument as to the validity of the warrant, the UK prosecutor argued that the requested person's case should have been advanced as an abuse of process, rather than as a challenge under s 2. The judge rejected this argument on the grounds that the invalidity argument stood on its own, without reliance on abuse. **11.40**

In the Supreme Court case of *Zakrzewski v Regional Court of Lodz, Poland*,[74] the requested person had been arrested on a conviction warrant specifying four separate sentences. During the course of the extradition proceedings, *Zakrzewski* had successfully applied to the court in Poland to aggregate those four sentences, resulting in a total sentence of 22 months rather than the 45 months stated in the warrant. The defence argued that because, following aggregation, the particulars of sentence as set out in the warrant were now incorrect, it failed to comply with s 2 of the Act. **11.41**

---

[68] *Ukraine v Kononko* [2014] (n 66) para 21.

[69] Note that although the particulars required by s 2(4)(c) are wider than those set out in s 78(4)(c), Lord Justice Thomas stated that: 'it would be an odd result if Parliament had intended that the request of persons to be extradited to countries in the European Union required particulars of the offence that were more onerous than the requirements of those to be extradited to other countries. Accordingly, the provision in s 78(4)(c) should be interpreted to the same effect as that in s 2(4)(c) using solely, as Dyson LJ suggested, the plain and ordinary meaning of that section without any gloss.' *Dudko v Government of the Russian Federation* [2010] EWHC 1125 (Admin), paragraph 16.

[70] [2006] EWHC 1672 (Admin).

[71] [2007] EWHC 814 (Admin).

[72] See *Castillo v Spain & Anor* [2004] EWHC (Admin) 1672, paragraph 25 and *The Criminal Court at the National High Court, 1st Division (A Spanish Judicial Authority) v Murua* [2010] EWHC 2609 (hereafter *Murua* [2010]), paragraph 64.

[73] *Murua* [2010] (n 72).

[74] [2013] UKSC 2.

11.42 In his judgment, Lord Sumption examined the decision in *Murua*.[75] He stated that, in that case, the UK prosecutor had been correct in submitting that the case should have been addressed as an abuse of process, rather than as a question of the validity of the warrant. He stated that:

> In my view, Ms Cumberland was right to submit to Sir Anthony May in *Murua* that the sole juridical basis for the inquiry into the accuracy of the particulars in the warrant is abuse of process. I do not think that it goes to the validity of the warrant. This is because in considering whether to refuse extradition on the ground of abuse of process, the materiality of the error in the warrant will be of critical importance, whereas if the error goes to the validity of the warrant, no question of materiality can arise.[76]

11.43 In seeking to re-orientate the question of incorrect particulars away from the question of validity and towards the abuse of process jurisdiction, the Supreme Court went some way to restoring judicial discretion to 'technical' arguments raised regarding the content of a request.[77]

11.44 Lord Sumption also made the following statements regarding incorrect particulars, framed as observations on the relevant paragraphs of *Murua*:[78]

1. The jurisdiction is exceptional. The statements in the warrant must comprise particulars which are wrong or incomplete in some respect which is misleading (though not necessarily intentionally);
2. The true facts required to correct the error or omission must be clear and beyond legitimate dispute;
3. The error or omission must be material to the operation of statutory scheme.[79]

11.45 It is noteworthy that the first of these observations suggests that the Supreme Court accepts that bad faith is not an essential element to establish abuse of process, particularly when seen in light of the fact that, in *Murua*, Sir Antony May stated that he did not find that 'abuse or bad faith on the part of the appellant, who has been quite open with the District Judge and with this court, was capable of being established.'[80]

Forum issues

11.46 'Forum' in extradition proceedings is generally understood to refer to the jurisdiction in which the trial will take place. Across the world, with both criminals and investigators having easy access to international networks, criminal courts are increasingly seeing proceedings which involve several different jurisdictions. The United States of America has shown a particular appetite for prosecuting offences where the large part (or all) of the alleged conduct has taken place elsewhere, using what is known as their 'exorbitant jurisdiction'.

11.47 The implementation of the forum bar at section 19B and section 83A if the Act bars extradition if by reason of forum it would not be in the interests of justice to extradite the requested person. Prior to the implementation of this bar, there had been a number of cases which attempted to raise a forum argument as an abuse of process. See, for example, the case of

---

[75] *Murua* [2010] (n 72).

[76] *Zakrzewski v Poland* [2013] (n 37) para 13.

[77] *Zakrzewski v Poland* [2013] (n 37) see Lord Sumption's description of the defence argument at paragraph 4: 'The argument advanced on Mr Zakrzewski's behalf is therefore hardly overburdened with merit. It is about as technical as it could possibly be.'

[78] *Murua* [2010] (n 729), paras 58–59.

[79] *Zakrzewski v Poland* [2013] (n 37) para 13.

[80] *Zakrzewski v Poland* [2013] (n 37) para 69.

Kulibaba and Konovalenko v Government of the United States of America[81] in which a failure to follow the Attorney General's Guidance on handling criminal cases affecting the United Kingdom and the USA was held not to amount to an abuse of process.

The new forum bar contains a means by which a prosecutor can effectively veto a forum **11.48** argument raised by the defence by issuing 'a prosecutor's certificate'. The complex provisions of sections 19B–19F are prescriptive as to the grounds on which such a certificate may be issued and seek to limit the means of recourse where questions are raised about the issuing of certificates. Nonetheless this unusual provision vests a significant amount of control over proceedings in the prosecution who, in most cases, will be the CPS acting both for the requesting state and as the prosecutor in domestic proceedings.

The extent to which prosecutor's certificate will be used is as yet unknown, however, in light **11.49** of these provisions, it appears that the implementation of the forum bar is unlikely to mean the end of abuse of process arguments in relation to forum issues.

Asylum cases

Under section 39 of the Act, a person who makes a claim for asylum after an EAW has been **11.50** certified cannot be extradited until her claim has been determined. Similar provisions apply to Part 2 requests—see section 121 of the Act.

For Part 2 requests, section 70 of the Act states that the Secretary of State may refuse to certify **11.51** a request where the person whose extradition is requested has been recorded by the Secretary of State as a refugee within the meaning of the Refugee Convention. There is, however, no express provision within the Act which deals with the situation where an EAW has been issued in respect of someone who has refugee status because of a well-founded fear of persecution in the issuing state. The Divisional Court looked at this problem in the case of two brothers, *District Court in Ostroleka, Second Criminal Division (A Polish Judicial Authority) v Dytlow and Dytlow*.[82] It found that a decision by an extradition court would effectively amount to a decision on the requested person's refugee status, which had already been determined by the Secretary of State (and then, in many instances, the Asylum and Immigration Tribunal). In such a case, the District Judge is, it was held 'the wrong forum to revisit the decision on the grant of asylum'. In the absence of any specific mechanism as set out in the statutory scheme, Lord Justice Keene stated that '[t]o order the extradition of a person or persons enjoying the status of refugees in this country would, for the reasons I have set out earlier, amount to an abuse of process.'[83]

---

[81] [2014] EWHC 176 (Admin).
[82] *Poland v Dytlow* [2009] (n 36).
[83] *Poland v Dytlow* [2009] (n 36), para 30.

12

CONFISCATION PROCEEDINGS
AND CIVIL RECOVERY

12.1 This chapter examines abuse of process arguments that have featured in both confiscation and civil recovery proceedings.

A. Confiscation Proceedings

Introduction

12.2 Confiscation proceedings as a form of restitution were first established in English law in 1987 with the introduction of the Drug Trafficking Offences Act 1986.[1] A number of stautes followed (Criminal Justice Act 1988, Criminal Justice (International Co-operation) Act 1990, Drug Trafficking Act 1994) culminating in the Proceeds of Crime Act 2002.[2]

12.3 Whilst confiscation proceedings usually follow a criminal conviction, the procedure adopted is a criminal and civil hybrid: both the prosecution and defence discharge the burden of proof on the civil balance of probabilities and any contested hearing is determined by a judge alone. The objective and effect of confiscation proceedings is draconian in nature. However since a confiscation order is not a penalty, but a civil debt, the safeguards surrounding the criminal trial process do not apply.

12.4 The Crown Court must proceed with a POCA confiscation hearing if a defendant is convicted of an acquisitive crime, and either the prosecutor has asked for the court to proceed[3] or the court believes it is appropriate to do so.[4]

---

[1] Operative from 10 January 1987.
[2] Operative from 24 March 2003. All offences committed prior to that date are covered by the CJA 1988 and DTA 1994.
[3] The prosecutor has a discretion to instigate proceedings. Guidance on the exercise of the discretion was issued to the Crown Prosecution Service in May 2009.
[4] Section 6(1) POCA.

Proportionality in making a confiscation order

12.5 The Supreme Court in *Waya*,[5] ruled that 'there was no need to invoke the concept of abuse of process'[6] in the making of confiscation orders. The better approach, it was said, was to make findings in appropriate cases if the position was that an order was 'wholly disproportionate' or there had been a breach of Article 1 of the First Protocol to the European Convention on Human Rights and Fundamental Freedoms (A1P1). Thus whilst not doubting the correctness of the decisions in previous Court of Appeal cases, such as *Mahmood and Shahin*,[7] which recognized that in exceptional cases confiscation proceedings, at the time of the making of the order, were subject to the abuse of process doctrine,[8] the reasoning is now no longer necessary.

12.6 That however needs to be qualified where, for example, the abuse of process sought to be raised does not directly have to do with the application of the terms of the confiscation legislation. For example, in *Ali*,[9] the Court of Appeal considered the question of the defendants' absence and whether or not a fair hearing on that basis could be held. Whilst concluding that the judge had not exercised his discretion improperly to conclude that no unfairness would occur, the Court of Appeal again emphasized the need to proceed with caution in relation to the abuse of process jurisdiction. In *Gavin and Tasie*,[10] the Court of Appeal held that, if the state has caused the absence, then a court's discretion should never be exercised to continue with confiscation. Such an approach would be an abuse of process.

12.7 In *Mahmood and Shahin*, the only ground on which an abuse of process argument could have been advanced was that when the prosecution entered into an arrangement with the thief, this was done on the basis of an agreement or common understanding or representation that the contributions made by the appellants would either be the limit of their contributions or brought into account. Such an approach would now fall to be considered with reference to 'proportionality'.

12.8 If the loser institutes or is about to institute civil proceedings against the defendant, the mandatory element in the confiscation proceedings disappears and the court is given complete discretion whether to make a confiscation order at all, or to determine the amount of the confiscation. If, in *Mahmood*, the Royal Mail had instituted civil proceedings against the defendants (not against the brother who had stolen the money in the first place) the court would have been empowered to make a confiscation order against them in such amount as it considered fit.

12.9 The decision in *Waya* has been given statutory force by an amendment to section 6 of the Proceeds of Crime Act 2002 which now requires any order to be 'proportionate'. What is 'proportionate' will need to be considered on a case by case basis, but some situations are considered further.

---

[5] [2012] UKSC 51; [2013] 2 Cr App R.(S) 20; [2013] 1 AC 294. *Waya* has been applied in *Axeworthy* [2012] EWCA Crim 2889, *Hursthouse* [2013] EWCA Crim 517 and *Javad* [2013] EWCA Crim 644. See also *Warwick* [2013] NICA 13 and *Harvey* [2013] EWCA Crim 1104 for discussion of pre-*Waya* cases.

[6] [2012] UKSC 51 at para 18.

[7] [2006] Cr App R(S) 96; [2006] Crim LR 75.

[8] See also *Gokal v Serious Fraud Office* [2001] EWCA Civ 368; *James McKinsley v CPS* [2006] EWCH 1092 Civ; *Hockey* [2007] EWCA Crim 1577, [2008] 1 Cr App R(S) 50; *Nield* [2007] EWCA Crim 993; *Farquhar* [2008] EWCA Crim 806, [2008] Crim LR 645; *Morgan and Bygrave* [2008] EWCA Crim 1323; *Neuberg* [2007] EWCA Crim 1994; *Shabir* [2008] EWCA Crim 1809, [2008] Crim LR 991; *R(Minshall) v Marylebone Magistrates' Court* [2008] EWHC 2800 (Admin), [2010] 1 WLR 590.

[9] [2015] 1 WLR 841.

[10] [2010] EWCA Crim 2727; [2011] 1 Cr App R (S) 126;[2011] Lloyd's Rep F C 122; [2011] Crim LR 239.

Oppressive confiscation

12.10 In *Morgan and Bygrave*,[11] (again a case in which the result was upheld by the Supreme Court in *Waya* as correct; but now not the analysis by reference to abuse) the Court of Appeal set out the circumstances where confiscation proceedings might be oppressive as:

> … where demonstrably (i) the defendant's crimes are limited to offences causing loss to one or more identifiable loser(s), (ii) his benefit is limited to those crimes, (iii) the loser has neither brought nor intends any civil proceedings to recover the loss, but (iv) the defendant either has repaid the loser, or stands ready willing and able immediately to repay him, the full amount of the loss.

12.11 That approach will now fall to be considered by reference to *Waya* principles and proportionality as opposed to oppression. In *Waya*,[12] the Supreme Court expressly held that such an order would be disproportionate.

12.12 Another (and extreme) example, which lead to an confiscation order being overturned on appeal, is *Shabir*.[13] The offender pharmacist had fraudulently overclaimed £464 of prescription fees. His benefit figure was correctly calculated to include all the fees he had received (£179,731), the vast majority of which were legitimate, and the indictment was drawn so as to engage the criminal lifestyle provisions. The result was a confiscation claim of over £400,000 and an order for £212,464.17.

12.13 In *Waya*, the Supreme Court endorsed the result that the Court of Appeal had arrived at in *Shabir* and concluded that such a set of facts would also make for a 'disproportionate' order.

12.14 *Shabir* is a rare case where the use of the POCA 'lifestyle' assumptions provisions of POCA, was considered to be abusive (now disproportionate). Ordinarily, as was said in *Waya*, the application of the assumptions will mean any order is a proportionate one. In *Beazley*,[14] in an infringement of trademarks case, the Court of Appeal indicated there was nothing inappropriate in making an order based upon the entirety of the proceeds of a business that was founded entirely on illegality.

12.15 A distinction between that situation and one where a defendant would have been entitled to the monies notwithstanding the commission of an offence (e.g. the failure to obtain a permit) needs to be drawn. In *Sumal and Sons*,[15] the Court of Appeal held that where a landlord would have a complete right to obtain rental payments that would be due to it, those sums were not obtained for the purposes of the confiscation legislation if there was a failure to obtain a licence to rent the property out. Although not strictly an application of proportionality, the distinction is important.

Benefit

12.16 Having determined that a confiscation order is required, the court will next proceed to calculating the benefit obtained by a defendant either by way of their criminal conduct, or as a result of a criminal lifestyle. There are a number of considerations that the court must bear in mind when arriving at such a figure.

---

[11] [2008] EWCA Crim 1323 at para 29.
[12] [2012] UKSC 51 at para 28 of the judgment.
[13] [2008] EWCA Crim 1809, [2008] Crim LR 991; where confiscation proceedings are disproportionate and thus a breach of Article 1 of the First Protocol to the ECHR (the peaceful enjoyment of possessions), a stay may result. *Shabir* was considered in *Del Basso and Goodwin* [2010] EWCA Crim 1119; [2011] 1 Cr App R (S) 41.
[14] [2013] 1 WLR 3331.
[15] [2013] 1 WLR 2078.

Joint benefit

When considering the value of the benefit figure in confiscation proceedings the Supreme **12.17**
Court, in *Ahmed and Fields*,[16] decided that where there was a joint obtaining of benefit
(which was still the correct approach in appropriate cases), it would be disproportionate to
make an order against two or more persons the result of which would be at least the 'double'
recovery of the benefit obtained.

Entire contract value

In *Sale*,[17] the Court of Appeal held that in a case where contracts were obtained by a corrupt **12.18**
process, the legislation was apt to include the entire value of the contracts as the benefit.
However, it went on to conclude that a proportionate order would be limited to the profits
obtained and the advantage gained by obtaining a market share, excluding competitors and
saving on the costs of preparing proper tenders.

No allowance

It appears it is not disproportionate to make no allowance for any expenses incurred in rela- **12.19**
tion to the criminal activity when it comes to making a confiscation order.[18]

Just order

In relation to a prosecutor's request to increase the value of a confiscation order on the basis **12.20**
of after-acquired assets, section 22 of the Proceeds of Crime Act 2002 specifically requires the
court to make a 'just' order. Provided that occurs, an order will be proportionate.[19]

DPP guidance

As a result of the Court of Appeal decisions in *Nelson, Pathak, and Paulet*,[20] the DPP has issued **12.21**
a document entitled 'Guidance for Prosecutors on the Discretion to Instigate Confiscation
Proceedings' in an attempt to secure consistency of approach by prosecutors. In *Paulet,* the
defendant had obtained a pecuniary advantage (paid employment) by falsely representing that
he could work in this country. After paying income tax and national insurance, the benefit figure
for confiscation amounted to £50,000, with realisable assets of £21,949 and a confiscation order
made in the sum of the realisable assets. The Court of Appeal upheld the confiscation order as the
wages paid to the defendant were obtained as a result of and in connection with the deception over
his employment status. The deception being ongoing throughout the period of the paid work.
It was a continuing dishonest representation attaching the whole of the sums received as wages.

However, the decision in *Paulet* pre-dated *Waya*. Indeed in *Paulet v United Kingdom*,[21] the **12.22**
European Court of Human Rights concluded that an order based upon such circumstances
would be disproportionate.

The DPP guidance applies to all prosecutors, state and private. The Court of Appeal have **12.23**
made it clear that private prosecutors, whether individuals, commercial companies,or trade
organizations, can initiate confiscation proceedings under section 6 POCA as part of a private prosecution, and it is not an abuse of process to do so: see *Zinga*.[22]

---

[16] [2014] 2 Cr App R (S) 75.
[17] [2014] 1 Cr App R (S) 60.
[18] *McDowell* [2015] 2 Cr App R (S) 14.
[19] *Padda* [2014] 2 Cr App R (S) 22.
[20] [2009] EWCA Crim 1573; [2009] Crim LR 811.
[21] (2015) 61 EHRR 39; *The Times* (19 May 2014) (ECHR).
[22] [2014] EWCA Crim 52; [2014] 1 Cr App R 27. The right to bring a private prosecution is long established: its history is summarized in the judgments of Lord Wilson and Lord Mance in *R.(Gujra) v Crown
Prosecution Service* [2012] UKSC 52; [2013] 1 Cr App R 12. See also *Rollins* [2010] UKSC 39: 1 Cr App R

Double jeopardy

12.24   Allegations of criminal behaviour not pursued in a separate prosecution but relied upon in confiscation proceedings for another offence, do not amount to double jeopardy as confiscation proceedings do not amount to the bringing of a criminal charge. The fact that the prosecution has adduced evidence of criminality in confiscation proceedings but not charged that crime does not offend the double jeopardy principle: see *Darren Bagnall*, [23] in which the appellant was convicted of money laundering (being in possession of £99,200 in cash). However, evidence of an uncharged VAT fraud was adduced during confiscation proceedings to allow a judicial finding under section 10 POCA for the amount of the Confiscation Order to be made in relation to the money laundering conviction. The appellant was never at risk of conviction on the fraud, hence the double jeopardy principle did not apply.

Confiscation order enforcement

12.25   Once a confiscation order is made, unless paid, it stands to be enforced. If an enforcement receiver is appointed, it appears that the court's process is capable of being abused although this will, as ever, be rare and difficult to demonstrate. In *Re. Danher*,[24] the applicant applied for his family home to be removed from the list of assets available to the receiver in order to satisfy the confiscation order, due to the alleged delay in the receiver realization. The High Court held that, in contrast to the position with enforcing in the magistrates' court by way of a warrant of commitment to prison or other financial enforcement there, an applicant can approach the court responsible for the superintendence of the receiver directly. He cannot apply to enforce against himself in the magistrates' court. If he does not apply directly to the court superintending the receivership due to a perceived delay or other problem with the receivership, he cannot complain about any unconscionable delay thereafter.

12.26   In relation to enforcement in the magistrates' court, either by warrant of commitment to prison, or by one or more of the civil remedies available to secure payment of a confiscation order, the abuse of process doctrine, by reference to the breach of the reasonable time guarantee within Article 6 of the European Convention on Human Rights, is an applicable one in the right circumstances. Each case must be judged on its own merits.

12.27   In *R (Lloyd) v Bow Street Magistrates' Court*,[25] the defendant was committed to custody for non-payment of a confiscation order some five years after his release from custody. The Divisional Court ruled that:

   (i)   a defendant enjoyed the full protection of Article 6 (1) including in relation to any application to commit the defendant to prison for non payment of a confiscation order

   (ii)   that the continuing non payment by a defendant of a confiscation order cannot affect the question of whether he is entitled to the protection of the reasonable time guarantee

   (iii)   the threshold for proving a breach is high and all the circumstances of the case must be taken into account

   (iv)   in deciding what amounts to a reasonable time attention should be given as to what other efforts have been made by the state to extract payment and the behavior of the defendant. Any evasion or avoidance of diligent attempts to extract the money will result in the defendant being unable to rely upon any resultant delay

   (v)   if unreasonable delay is established the remedy must be proportionate.

---

4. In relation to the statutory powers vested in a private prosecutor, see Divisional Court decision in *Lamont-Perkins v Royal Society for the Prevention of Cruelty to Animals* [2012] EWHC 1002 (Admin).

   [23] [2012] EWCA Crim 677.
   [24] [2010] EWHC 3397 (Admin).
   [25] [2004] 1 Cr App R 11.

Commitment to custody is only one weapon in the available armoury. The effect upon the defendant of a return to custody, especially if there is a family life and a long gap between release from custody and enforcement, will also be an important feature.

However *Lloyd* must be read in conjunction with *R (Marsden) v Leicester Magistrates' Court*.[26] **12.28**
In that case the defendants were committed to custody for a term of six years some six and a half years after being released from their sentence. The Divisional Court held, in considering what was a reasonable time, that regard had to be had to:

(i) all the circumstances of the case including the complexity of it, the defendant's conduct, the conduct of the state authorities and the importance of what is at stake for the defendant

(ii) whether or not the defendant was aware that the prosecution's intention was to enforce against them by way of commitment to prison in the absence of payment of the order

(iii) that the non payment of the confiscation order is not relevant to whether or not the state must act within a reasonable time but is relevant to what will be considered a reasonable time or not and raises the bar of proving the same.

Delay in enforcement of a confiscation order can lead to such proceedings being stayed. In **12.29**
Malik v Crown Prosecution Service, Lord Justice Fulford[27] quoted Lord Justice Dyson's observation in *Lloyd*:

[25] Convicted criminals who are subject of confiscation orders do not attract sympathy, and are not entitled to favoured treatment. But there is nothing surprising about a requirement that, if the prosecuting authorities/magistrates court seek to enforce a confiscation order, they should do so within a reasonable time. It is potentially very unfair on a defendant that he should be liable to be committed to prison for non-payment of sums due under a confiscation order many years after the time for payment has expired, and long after he has been released from custody and resumed work and family life.

In *Malik*, the appellant pleaded guilty, in 2004, to conspiracy to defraud the Department of **12.30**
Works and Pensions (DWP) by processing fake Giro cheques. The appellant was sentenced, at Snaresbrook Crown Court, to two and a half years imprisonment, with confiscation proceedings being adjourned. In 2005, a confiscation order was imposed. During 2005 and 2006 the appellant contacted the DWP on numerous occasions with a view to lifting the restraint order, so that assets could be sold. The DWP failed to respond. There was then silence for four years and four months. The prosecution authorities comprehensively failed to respond substantively to any attempts by the appellant to communicate with the prosecution to enable him properly to address his liability under the confiscation order. In 2011, a letter from Her Majesty Court Service London Regional Confiscation Unit reminded the appellant of his obligation to pay the confiscation order. The DWP could provide no real explanation for its wholesale failure to take active enforcement steps during the four year four months period.

In 2012, the matter was listed for an enforcement order in the Westminster Magistrates' **12.31**
Court. The appellant contended that there had been 'undue inexcusable and culpable delay in the instigation of the enforcement proceedings', and that the enforcement proceedings should be stayed as an abuse of the process. The prosecution accepted that it would not be appropriate to seek the committal of the appellant to prison but it was suggested the delay should not otherwise act as a bar to recovery of the outstanding confiscation monies. District Judge Purdy ruled that 'civil enforcement must follow'; that whilst a term of imprisonment

---

[26] [2013] EWHC 919 (Admin).
[27] [2014] EWHC 4591 (Admin).

was unconscionable, it was otherwise appropriate not to impose a stay on the enforcement process.

12.32 District Judge Purdy provided the following question, on the issue of delay, for consideration by the High Court by way of Case Stated: 'Is 6 years and 5 months delay, despite full co-operation with the authorities such a period that all forms of enforcement including civil should be stayed as an abuse of process of the court per Article 6 ECHR?'.

12.33 Lord Justice Fulford in considering the case stated identified[28] two principal questions to be answered on the facts of *Malik*:

(1) Whether the reinstatement of the enforcement proceedings after such a long period of time was oppressive ... given the delay caused by the prosecuting authorities.

(2) Whether the delay for which the prosecution is responsible is so extensive and so culpable or unexplained that a stay is appropriate. In reaching a decision as to whether to impose a stay the court must ensure that the order it makes is not disproportionate.

12.34 Lord Justice Fulford, found on the facts of *Malik*, that the learned judge was wrong to decide that the civil enforcement proceedings should continue:

[36] ... Although the threshold for finding a breach of the reasonable time requirement is a high one (see *Lloyd* [26]) the delay here was not only extensive (six and half years) but it is also culpable and it is essentially unexplained ... Moreover, of real additional significance is the fact that the appellant and his solicitors repeatedly sought the co-operation of the prosecution to enable him to discharge his obligations responsibly ...

Concluding that 'all forms of enforcement are to be stayed as an abuse of the process of the court'.

B. Civil Recovery: Part 5 POCA Cases

12.35 In addition to criminal confiscation proceedings, state enforcement authorities[29] can apply under Part 5 Proceeds of Crime Act 2002[30] to the High Court for civil recovery of the proceeds of crime. This power is independent of any criminal proceedings and can be used where a defendant has been acquitted of criminal charges.[31] In civil recovery proceedings the court need only find on a balance of probabilities that any matters alleged to constitute unlawful conduct have occurred, or that any person intended to use any cash in unlawful conduct.[32]

12.36 Whether a claim for civil recovery amounts to an abuse of process has been considered in a number of cases, leading to some settled principles:

• A claim for civil recovery is not an abuse where it is based on unlawful conduct (keeping a brothel) nothwithstanding the fact that the unlawful conduct appeared to have been tolerated by senior police officers, leading to a stay of the related criminal proceedings: see *The Queen (Director of Assets Recovery Agency) v E and B*.[33]

---

[28] [2014] EWHC 4591 (Admin) at para 35 of the judgment.

[29] The relevant agencies are specified at section 2A POCA as the Serious Organised Crime Agency, the Director of Public Prosecutions and the Director of the Serious Fraud Office.

[30] Section 240(2) POCA.

[31] On 5 November 2009 the Attorney-General issued guidance on the use of asset recovery powers under POCA in cases where there has been no conviction.

[32] Section 241(3) POCA.

[33] [2007] EWHC 3245 (Admin).

- Bad faith leading to a stay in criminal proceedings does not preclude a civil recovery claim under Part 5 POCA: see *The Queen (Director of Assets Recovery Agency) v T and others*,[34] in which Mr Justice Collins said:[35]

  > ... even if it were established, that there had been bad faith in the manner in which the prosecution had conducted the criminal proceedings, [it] would not enable the defendants successfully to argue that it was an abuse of process to bring proceedings under Part V. The reason is simply this: these proceedings are civil proceedings instituted by the Director who is an independent person.

- A confiscation order quashed on appeal does not preclude the subsequent making of a civil recovery order: see *Director of Assets Recovery Agency v Singh*[36] in which Lord Justice Latham identified[37] the purpose behind the enactment of Part 5 POCA:

  > The clear intention of parliament was to ensure that, so far as possible, criminals should be deprived of the possibility of benefiting from crimes ... in the present case the meaning of the words and the purpose of the legislature are both abundantly clear and march had in hand. To permit the technicality which resulted in the confiscation order being quashed to preclude recovery by the civil recovery route would be to perpetuate a mischief which the 2002 Act was clearly designed to prevent.

- Compromised settled cash forfeiture proceedings do not preclude a Part 5 SOCA civil recovery order being made: see *Serious Organised Crime Agency v Christopher Agidi and Angela Agidi*.[38] SOCA was entitled under Part 5 POCA to recover property worth £1.2 million (the subject of a Property Freezing Order) from the respondents who had benefited from corrupt relationships with companies in obtaining multi-million $US dollar contracts from Nigeria. The fact that the Metropolitan Police had settled cash forfeiture proceedings (under section 298 POCA) against the respondents, in the sum of £171,367.53, did not preclude SOCA from subsequently applying and obtaining a Part 5 POCA Recovery Order made under section 266. SOCA had brought Part 5 proceedings within the relevant limitation period, the respondents held recoverable property, SOCA had acted in good faith and the circumstances in which the proceedings were brought were not in conflict with Part 5. The onus was on the respondents to establish abuse and they had, in the judgment of Mr Justice Sweeney, failed to do so.

---

[34] [2004] EWHC 3340 (Admin).
[35] [2004] EWHC 3340 (Admin) at para 20 of the judgment.
[36] [2005] 1 WLR 3747. See also *Olupitan and Makinde v The Director of the Assets Recovery Agency* [2008] EWCA Civ 104.
[37] [2005] 1 WLR 3747 at para 19 of the judgment.
[38] [2011] EWHC 175(QB);[2011] Lloyd's Rep F C 276.

13

TACTICAL AND PROCEDURAL CONSIDERATIONS

A. Advising upon the Merits of a Stay Application

Sparingly exercised

13.1 When considering and advising upon the merits of an abuse of process application, it is important to remember that the discretionary power to stay an indictment for abuse of process is sparingly exercised for two reasons.

13.2 First, abuse of process applications should not be viewed as usurping the Crown's prosecutorial prerogative nor an acceptance of the pre-eminence of the interests of the accused, but rather as judicial control of the trial process to ensure fair play and maintain public confidence in the criminal justice system. Account has to be taken of the public interest in the testing of allegations at a public trial.

13.3 Second, there are alternative remedies available as part of the trial process. Options other than staying proceedings are available to avoid or minimize prejudice at trial. These include, inter alia, granting the accused bail, expediting the trial, imposing reporting restrictions, transferring venue, postponing the trial, discharging a jury, exclusion of evidence, use of special measures, and judicial direction in the summing-up; all these can offset any prejudice the accused might suffer as a result of loss of evidence, delay, media attention, and mental incapacity.

Warranted grounds

13.4 The judicial view that abuse of process arguments should not be advanced in criminal cases unless they are really warranted is highlighted by the comments of the Lord Chief Justice in *Childs*:[1]

---

[1] *The Times* (30 November 2002), CA.

Practitioners should not advance arguments of abuse of process unless they were warranted. If they were not warranted, courts should make it clear that that was inappropriate conduct and would take appropriate steps where, as sometimes happened, a huge amount of court time was wasted in consequence. The trial process was complicated enough. It was not desirable to add to that complexity by putting forward unnecessary allegations.

Defence authorization

If so advised and an abuse of process application is made, it is essential that the defendant's **13.5** express authorization is obtained as the application may reveal part of the defence case.

Reviewable power

The power to stay an indictment is ongoing during a trial and reviewable throughout.[2] **13.6**

Particular counts

The power to stay need not be used to stay the whole of an indictment. It can be used to **13.7** stay individual counts. The partial stay of an indictment is within the power of a trial judge.[3]

If a conviction is quashed on one count because it should have been stayed as an abuse of **13.8** process at trial, it does not automatically follow that other, closely linked but distinct counts, should be stayed nor the conviction quashed on appeal.[4]

B. Adherence to Procedural Matters

Practice directions and rules

When preparing the application, it is important to adhere to the Criminal Practice Direction **13.9** (General matters) 3C:[5]

ABUSE OF PROCESS STAY APPLICATIONS
3C.1 In all cases where a defendant in the Crown Court proposes to make an application to stay an indictment on the ground of abuse of process, written notice of such application must be given to the prosecuting authority and to any co-defendant as soon as practicable after the defendant becomes aware of the grounds for doing so and not later than 14 days before the date fixed or warned for trial ('the relevant date'). Such notice must (a) give the name of the case and the indictment number; (b) state the fixed date or the warned date as appropriate; (c) specify the nature of the application; (d) set out in numbered sub-paragraphs the grounds on which the application is to be made; (e) be copied to the chief listing officer at the court centre where the case is due to be heard.

3C.2 Any co-defendant who wishes to make a like application must give a like notice not later than seven days before the relevant date, setting out any additional grounds relied upon.

3C.3 In relation to such applications, the following automatic directions shall apply: (a) the advocate for the applicant(s) must lodge with the court and serve on all other parties a skeleton argument in support of the application, at least five clear working days before the relevant date; if reference is to be made to any document not in the existing trial documents, a paginated and indexed bundle of such documents is to be provided with the skeleton argument; (b) the advocate for the prosecution must lodge with the court and serve on all other parties a responsive

---

2 *Birmingham* [1992] Crim LR 117.
3 *Munro*, 97 Cr App R 183.
4 *Alfrey* [2005] EWCA Crim 3232, [2006] 2 Archbold News 1.
5 [2013] 1 WLR 3164.

skeleton argument at least two clear working days before the relevant date, together with a supplementary bundle if appropriate.

3C.4 All skeleton arguments must specify any propositions of law to be advanced (together with the authorities relied on in support, with paragraph references to passages relied upon), and, where appropriate, include a chronology of events and a list of dramatis personae. In all instances where reference is made to a document, the reference in the trial documents or supplementary bundle is to be given.

3C.5 The above time limits are minimum time limits. In appropriate cases the court will order longer lead times. To this end in all cases where defence advocates are, at the time of the preliminary hearing or as soon as practicable after the case has been sent, considering the possibility of an abuse of process application, this must be raised with the judge dealing with the matter, who will order a different timetable if appropriate, and may wish, in any event, to give additional directions about the conduct of the application. If the trial judge has not been identified, the matter should be raised with the resident judge.

13.10 Further, it is important to adhere to the Criminal Procedure Rules 2015 which provide as follows:

Application to stay case for abuse of process
3.20–(1) This rules applies where a defendant wants the Crown Court to stay the case on the grounds that the proceedings are an abuse of the court, or otherwise unfair.
(2) Such a defendant must –
   (a) apply in writing –
      (i) as soon as practicable after becoming aware of the grounds for doing so,
      (ii) at a pre-trial hearing, unless the grounds for the application do not arise until trial, and
      (iii) in any event, before the defendant pleads guilty or the jury (if there is one) retires to consider its verdict at trial:
   (b) serve the application on –
      (i) the court officer, and
      (ii) each other party; and
   (c) in the application –
      (i) Explain the grounds on which it is made,
      (ii) Include, attach or identify all supporting material,
      (iii) Specify relevant events, dates and propositions of law, and
      (iv) Identify any witness the applicant wants to call to give evidence in person.
(3) a person who wants to make representations in response to the application must serve the representations on –
   (a) the court officer; and
   (b) each other party,
Not more than 14 days after service of the application.

13.11 In relation to abuse of process in heavy fraud and complex criminal cases, the following should also be noted:

- arguments on both sides must be reduced to writing. Oral evidence is seldom relevant.[6]
- The judge should direct full written submissions (rather than 'skeleton arguments') on any abuse application in accordance with a timetable set by him; these should identify any element of prejudice the defendant is alleged to have suffered.[7]

---

[6] As per 5 (iii) of the 'Control and Management of Heavy Fraud and other Complex Criminal Cases' protocol, issued by the Lord Chief Justice, 22 March 2005.
[7] As per 5 (iv) of the 'Control and Management of Heavy Fraud and other Complex Criminal Cases' protocol.

- The judge should normally aim to conclude the hearing within an absolute maximum limit of one day, if necessary in accordance with a timetable. The parties should therefore prepare their papers on this basis and not expect the judge to allow the oral hearing to be anything more than an occasion to highlight concisely their arguments and answer any questions the court may have of them; applications will not be allowed to drag on.[8]

Disclosure

The prosecution must give proper disclosure of unused material that is relevant to an abuse **13.12** of process application.[9]

C. Abuse of Process Hearing

Representations and evidence

Both the prosecution and defence are entitled to be heard and present evidence, and magis- **13.13** trates should hear from both parties.[10]

It is good practice to attach to the skeleton argument in adverse publicity cases the press cut- **13.14** tings, radio transcripts and television footage complained of. In the case of double jeopardy cases a copy, should be included, of court records (including indictment) which establish whether a person has previously been prosecuted for an offence, and if so, the result of the prosecution.

The abuse of process principle is not applicable to proceedings, evidentially, in a number **13.15** of ways. First, it does not operate in relation to rulings as to evidential admissibility.[11] Second, it cannot be used to exclude evidence under section 78 of PACE.[12] Third, in relation to bad character, there is no reason in principle why evidence relating to stayed allegations should not be admissible in any subsequent trial.[13] Fourth, information supplied by a person/company (under statutory compulsion) to one government agenc, can be used to form the basis of a subsequent prosecution by another law enforcement agency.[14]

Citation of case law

Avoid citing too many cases in skeleton arguments and/or oral submissions. Courts are **13.16** discouraging such an approach as each case is to be decided on the merits of its own facts.[15] The Divisional Court in *R v Newham Justices ex p C*[16] held that 'it was a mistake to seek to compare one case with another because the factors in each case were often substantially different'.

---

[8] As per 5 (v) of the 'Control and Management of Heavy Fraud and other Complex Criminal Cases' protocol.

[9] *R v DPP ex p Lee* [1999] 2 All ER 737, [1999] 2 Cr App R 304, DC, *R v Early* [2003] 1 Cr App R 19, CA and *R v Gell*, [2003] EWCA Crim 123, CA.

[10] *R v Clerkenwell Stipendiary Magistrate ex p Bell* (1991) 155 JP 669, DC, *Crawley Justices ex p DPP* (1991) *Times* (5 April) and *R v Manchester Crown Court ex p Cunningham* [1992] COD 23, No CO/372/91.

[11] *Mauire and Heffenan* [2009] EWCA Crim 462.

[12] *Aujla* [1998] 2 Cr App R 16.

[13] *Edwards, Rowland, McLean, Smith, Enright and Gray* [2006] 2 Cr App R 62.

[14] *Brady* [2005] 1 Cr.App.R. 78; [2005] Crim LR 224.

[15] *Sheffield Stipendiary Magistrate ex p Stephens* (1992) 156 JP 555.

[16] [1993] Crim LR 130.

13.17 The following cases should be cited in argument, as the leading authorities in their respective areas: *Beckford,*[17] *Bennett*[18] *and Warren*[19] (jurisdiction); *F,*[20] *Attorney-General's Reference No.1 of 1990*[21] (delay at first instance) and *S*[22]*, Bell,*[23] and *Smolinski*[24] (delay at appellate level); *R*[25](disclosure); *Boardman*[26] (case management); Feltham Magistrates'[27] (non-availability of evidence); *Bennett*[28] (unfair conduct); *Looseley*[29] (entrapment); *Connelly*[30](double jeopardy); and *R v Central Criminal Court ex p The Telegraph PLC*[31] *and Abu Hamza*[32](adverse publicity).

Burden and standard of proof

13.18 The burden of proving that a prosecution is an abuse of process is on the accused in delay cases. The standard of proof in these circumstances is on the balance of probabilities.[33] In *AG's Reference (No.1 of 1990)*[34] Lord Lane Chief Justice observed[35] that, 'no stay was to be imposed unless the defendant established on the balance of probabilities that, owing to the delay, he would suffer serious prejudice to the extent that no fair trial could be held.'

13.19 In terms of the burden and standard of proof in abuse of process applications, the commentary[36] to the *MacKreth* case makes the interesting point that, 'Though the rule is that he who asserts the abuse of process must prove it, the Court of Appeal in *S(SP)*[37] found the language of burden and standard of proof to be potentially misleading given that the decision is "a matter of assessment dependent on judgment [rather] than a conclusion of fact based on evidence". It is rather more accurate to state that the burden of persuasion rests on the defendant.'

Open court

13.20 Abuse of Process applications should not be held in camera unless the procedure laid down in rule 16.10 Criminal Procedure Rules 2010 (SI 2010 No 60) has been complied with.[38]

---

[17] [1996] 1 Cr App R 94.
[18] [1994] AC 42, [1994] 98 Cr App R 114.
[19] [2012] 1 AC 22.
[20] [2011] EWCA Crim 1844; [2012] QB 703; [2012] 2 WLR 1038; [2012] 1 All ER 565; [2011] 2 Cr App R 28; [2012] Crim LR282.
[21] [1992] QB 630, [1992] 95 Cr App R 296.
[22] [2006] EWCA Crim 756; [2006] 2 Cr App R 23; [2007] Crim LR 296.
[23] [2003] 2 Cr App R 13.
[24] [2004] 2 Cr App R 661.
[25] [2015] EWCA Crim 1941.
[26] [2015] EWCA Crim 175.
[27] [2001] 1 All ER 831.
[28] [1994] AC 42.
[29] [2002] 1 Cr App R 29.
[30] [1964] AC 1254.
[31] (1994) 98 Cr App R 91.
[32] [2007] 1 Cr App R 27.
[33] See *R v Telford Justices ex p Badhan* [1991] 93 Cr App R 171, *R v Crown Court at Norwich ex p Belsham,* [1992] 94 Cr App R 382 DC and *R v Great Yarmouth Magistrates' ex. P. Thomas David and Darlington* (1992) Crim LR 116 DC.
[34] (1992) QB 630.
[35] (1992) QB 630 at 631.
[36] [2010] Crim LR 228.
[37] [2006] 2 Cr App R 23 at p 341; [2007] Crim LR 296; [2006] 4 Archbold News 1.
[38] *Ex p Guardian Newspaper Ltd,* (30 September 1998), CA, No 98/5678/S1.

Content ruling

When giving judgment on an abuse application, judges should cite the relevant law and a **13.21** summary of the reasons for granting or rejecting the application.[39]

Successful applications to stay proceedings as an abuse of process should attract a Defendant's **13.22** Cost Order being made in favour of the successful applicant, unless there are positive reasons for not doing so, such as the defendant's own conduct in bringing suspicion on himself and by misleading the prosecution into thinking that the case against him was stronger than it was.[40]

D. Custody Time Limits

A retrial may be stayed as an abuse of process to cure any unfairness suffered as a result of the **13.23** loss of the protection offered by custody time limits.[41]

In relation to custody time limits, generally, the abuse of process principle can be used to **13.24** enforce the protections offered by the CTL, without a stay of the proceedings being made.[42]

E. Civil Law and Regulatory Proceedings

A defendant's remedies at civil law and/or in disciplinary/criminal proceedings do not cure **13.25** an abuse of process. As Lord Bridge observed in *Bennett*, 'Having then taken cognisance of the lawlessness it would again appear to me to be wholly inadequate response for the court to hold that the only remedy lies in civil proceedings at the suit of the defendant or in disciplinary or criminal proceedings against the individual officers of the law enforcement agency … Since the prosecution could never have been brought if the defendant had not been illegally abducted, the whole proceeding is tainted.'[43]

In relation to civil proceedings consider the rule in *Hunter v Chief Constable of West Midlands*,[44] **13.26** as to a collateral attack in civil proceedings, on earlier criminal court proceedings (as applied in *Re Barings PLC (No2) v Baker*[45] and *Daar v Chief Constable of Merseyside Police*[46]).

Abuse of process in relation to police disciplinary proceedings has been considered in a num- **13.27** ber of cases.[47] The issue of double jeopardy being considered in *R (Redgrave) v Commissioner of Police of the Metropolis*[48] in which disciplinary proceedings followed on from criminal proceedings. The authorities establishing that, even assuming an acquittal by a criminal court,

---

[39] *R v Manchester Crown Court ex p Cunningham* [1992] COD 23, DC (CO/037/91) and *R v Dutton* [1994] Crim LR 910, CA.

[40] *Re Williams & Sons (Wholesale) Limited v Hereford Magistrates' Court* [2008] EWHC 2585 (Admin), section 16 Prosecution of Offences Act 1985 and Practice Direction on Costs: [2004] 1 WLR 2657.

[41] *R v Leeds Crown Court, ex p Whitehead* 17 June 1999, QBD, CO/795/99, *Times* (5 July 1999).

[42] *R v Bradford Crown Court ex p Crossling* [2000] 1 Cr App R 463 DC.

[43] [1994] 1 AC 42 at 67H.

[44] [1982] AC 529.

[45] [1999] 1 All ER 311. See also *Secretary of State for Trade and Industry v Bairstow* [2004] Ch 1.

[46] [2005] EWCA Civ 1774.

[47] *R v Chief Constable of Merseyside Police ex p Merrill* [1989] 1 WLR 1077; *R (Redgrave) v Commissioner of Police of the Metropolis* [2002] EWHC 1074 Admin; [2003] 1 WLR 1136; *R (on the application of the Independent Police Complaints Commission) v The Chief Constable of West Mercia* [2007] EWHC 1035 (Admin).

[48] [2002] EWHC 1074 Admin; [2003] 1 WLR 1136.

the double jeopardy rule has no application save to courts of competent jurisdiction, and is therefore no bar to the bringing of disciplinary proceedings in respect of the same charge.

13.28 The double jeopardy rule was considered by the Divisional Court, Sir Brian Leveson P presiding, in *Ashraf v General Dental Council*.[49] The *Redgrave* approach was considered and followed by the Divisional Court. The fact of an acquittal of a dentist in criminal proceedings for fraud and theft from the National Health Service did not, of itself, make it inherently abusive for the same matters to be heard by a disciplinary panel of the General Dental Council. The GDC professional committee held that the public interest in hearing the allegations, which if true would be likely to affect the acquitted dentist's fitness to practise, outweighed the hardship caused to him facing the allegations for a second time. The disciplinary hearing found the allegations proved and the dentist was erased from the register. The dentist's appeal against the GDC decision was dismissed by the Divisional Court which followed the approach in *Redgrave*. It was essential that regulators were confident in exercising their discretion in disciplinary matters. The focus on regulators was to maintain the standards and integrity of the profession to ensure that public confidence was and could be maintained. It would not be in the public interest for a form of regulatory arbitrage to take place if there was an either/or approach to whether proceedings should be pursued through the criminal courts or by the regulator. The appropriate test was whether, viewing the case through the lens of the obligations placed on the regulator, it was in the public interest to pursue disciplinary proceedings.

13.29 The need for care in bringing appropriately framed disciplinary proceedings was at the forefront on the Supreme Court's consideration of abuse of process and autrefois acquit in *R.(Coke-Wallis) v Institute of Chartered Accountants in England and Wales*.[50] The wrong charge had been brought within accountancy disciplinary proceedings but, after an acquittal, they tried again on the same facts. Having convinced the Court of Appeal that this was no abuse given the public interest in professional regulation and the confidence it provided, the second attempt was, albeit in a very technical and somewhat reluctant judgement, set aside.

13.30 Abuse of process within inquest proceedings is examined in *R v Derby and South Derbyshire Coroner ex p Hart*.[51]

13.31 For discussion of abuse of power within an administrative law context see *R v Department for Education and Employment ex p Begbie*,[52] *R v North and East Devon Health Authority ex p Coughlan*,[53] *R (Zeqiri) v Secretary of State for the Home Department*,[54] and *R (Harpers Leisure International Ltd) v Guildford Borough Council*.[55] However, some commentators question as 'debatable whether this developing public law doctrine transposes easily into the criminal setting where distinctions between 'procedural' and 'substantive' expectations may be difficult to apply.[56]

---

[49] [2014] EWHC 2618 (Admin).
[50] [2009] EWCA Civ 730.
[51] (2000) 164 JP 429. See discussion at 'Inquests', L Thomas QC, A Straw, D Machover and D Friedman QC 3rd edition (2014) Legal Action Group at p 212 n 21.
[52] [2000] WLR 1115 CA.
[53] [2000] 3 All ER 850.
[54] [2002] UKHL 3.
[55] Times Law Report 14 August 2009.
[56] Commentary to *Drury, Clark and others* [2001] Crim L R 85.

APPENDICES

APPENDIX 1

Skeleton Argument: Delay

In the Youth/Magistrates/Crown Court
Regina
-V-
Defendant

APPLICATION TO STAY CRIMINAL PROCEEDINGS AS AN ABUSE OF PROCESS:
DELAY

Introduction

1. Application is made to stay the criminal proceedings against Defendant as an abuse of process on grounds of delay.
2. Defendant faces criminal allegations in relation to

Factual and Procedural Background

3.

Abuse of Process—The law

4. All criminal courts have a general and inherent power to stay proceedings in order to protect their process from abuse and to secure fair treatment for those accused of crime.
5. This common law power was recognized in *Connelly v DPP*,[1] where Lord Reid stated the court had 'a residual discretion to prevent anything which savours of abuse of process',[2] and Lord Devlin stated the courts have 'an inescapable duty to secure fair treatment for those who come or are brought before them'.[3] Sentiments echoed in *Mills v Cooper*[4] where Lord Chief Justice Parker stated that 'every court has undoubtedly a right in its discretion to decline to hear proceedings on the ground that they are oppressive and abuse of process of the court'.[5] Lord Justice Diplock expressed his agreement with this view[6] and was cited with approval by Lord Edmund-Davies in *DPP v Humphreys*.[7]
6. The most often cited definition of the abuse of process principle can be found in *R v Derby Crown Court ex p Brooks*.[8] Lord Chief Justice Roger Ormrod stated:

    The power to stop a prosecution arises only when it is an abuse of the process of the court. It may be an abuse of process if either (a) the prosecution have manipulated or misused the process of the court so as to deprive the defendant of a protection provided by law or to take unfair advantage of a technicality, or (b) on the balance of probability the defendant has been, or will be, prejudiced in the preparation or conduct of his defence by delay on the part of the prosecution which is unjustifiable ...

7. The ultimate objective of this discretionary power is to ensure that there should be a fair trial according to law, which involves fairness both to the defendant and the prosecution.[9]

---

[1] [1964] AC 1254.
[2] [1964] AC 1254 at 1296.
[3] [1964] AC 1254 at 1354.
[4] [1967] 2 QB 459.
[5] [1967] 2 QB 459 at 467.
[6] [1967] 2 QB 459 at 470.
[7] [1977] AC 1 at pp 52–53.
[8] [1985] 80 Cr App R 164.
[9] [1985] 80 Cr App R 164 at 168.

8. In *R v Martin (Alan)*,[10] Lord Clyde stated: 'No single formulation will readily cover all cases, but there must be something so gravely wrong as to make it unconscionable that a trial should go forward, such as some fundamental disregard for basic human rights or some gross neglect of the elementary principles of fairness.'

9. In line with the above observations, proceedings are only stayed, in the words of Viscount Dilhorne in *DPP v Humphrys*,[11] in 'exceptional circumstances.'[12]

10. The exceptional nature of the power was also recognized by Lord Chief Justice Lane in *Attorney General's Reference No 1 of 1990.*[13]

11. Similarly in *R v Haringey Justices ex p DPP*,[14] Lord Justice Stuart-Smith, in recognizing that justices had a power to stay proceedings as an abuse of process, observed that 'it is a power that should only be exercised sparingly.'

The Test

12. When a court considers the exercise of its discretionary power to stay proceedings for an abuse, the test to be applied is that of fairness. Lord Justice Neill, in *R v Beckford*,[15] observed that:

The jurisdiction to stay can be exercised in many different circumstances. Nevertheless two main strands can be detected in the authorities:
a) Cases where the court concludes that the defendant cannot receive a fair trial;
b) Cases where the court concludes that it would be unfair for the defendant to be tried.[16]

Delay

13. At common law, there is no time limit for commencing criminal proceedings. In all cases where time is not limited by statute, a prosecution may be commenced at any length of time after the offence. However, delay in commencing or pursuing a prosecution may amount to an abuse of process, warranting a stay of proceedings.

14. However, delay per se is insufficient. It must be shown that the delay had produced *genuine prejudice and unfairness*.

15. In *Attorney-General's Reference (No 1 of 1990)*,[17] Lord Chief Justice Lane observed:[18]
   (1) that generally speaking a prosecutor has as much right as a defendant to demand a verdict of a jury on an outstanding indictment and, where either demands a verdict, a judge has no jurisdiction to stand in the way of it and therefore the jurisdiction to stay proceedings is exceptional;
   (2) a stay should never be imposed where the delay has been caused by the complexity of the proceedings
   (3) it would be rare for a stay to be imposed in the absence of fault on the part of the prosecutor or complainant;
   (4) delay contributed to by the actions of the defendant should not found the basis of a stay;
   (5) the defendant needs to show on a balance of probabilities that owing to the delay he will suffer serious prejudice to the extent that no fair trial can be held. In other words, the continuance of the proceedings amounts to an abuse of the process of the court. In assessing whether there is likely to be prejudice and if so whether it can properly be described as serious, the following matters should be borne in mind: first, the power of the judge at common law and under the Police and Criminal Evidence Act 1984, to regulate the admissibility of evidence; secondly, the trial process itself, which should ensure that all relevant factual issues arising from the delay

---

[10] [1998] AC 917.
[11] [1977] AC 1.
[12] [1977] AC 1 at 26.
[13] [1992] QB 630.
[14] [1996] QB 351.
[15] [1996] 1 Cr App R 94.
[16] [1996] 1 Cr App R 94 at 100G.
[17] [1992] QB 630, [1992] 95 Cr App R 296.
[18] As followed in *Attorney-General's Reference No 2 of 2001* [2004] 1 Cr App R 25 and *R v J* [2002] 1 Cr App R 24.

will be placed before the jury as part of the evidence for their consideration, together with the powers of the judge to give appropriate directions to the jury before they consider their verdict.

Delay Factors

16. The factors considered by the courts in deciding whether a defendant's right to a fair trial had been infringed by delay are set out in Lord Templeman's judgment in *Bell v DPP of Jamaica*.[19] He cited with approval the analysis contained in the United States Supreme Court decision in *Barker v Wingo*,[20] in which Mr Justice Powell identified four factors to which the court should have regard:

    a) the length of delay; dependent upon the peculiar circumstances of the case. To take but one example, the delay that can be tolerated for an ordinary street crime is considerably less than for a serious, complex conspiracy charge;

    b) the justification put forward by the prosecution; a deliberate attempt to delay the trial in order to hamper the defence should be weighed heavily against the government. A more neutral reason such as negligence or overcrowded courts should be weighed less heavily but nevertheless should be considered since the ultimate responsibility for such circumstances must rest with the government rather than the defendant. Finally, a valid reason, such as a missing witness, should serve to justify appropriate delay;

    c) the responsibility of the accused for asserting her/his rights; and,

    d) the prejudice to the accused. Prejudice, of course, should be assessed in the light of the interests of the defendants which the speedy trial right was designed to protect. This court has identified three such interests:

        i) to prevent oppressive pre-trial incarceration;

        ii) to minimise anxiety and concern of the accused; and,

        iii) to limit the possibility that the defence will be impaired ... If witnesses die or disappear during a delay, the prejudice is obvious. There is also prejudice if defence witnesses are unable to recall accurately events of the distant past. Loss of memory however, is not always reflected in the record because what has been forgotten can rarely be shown.

17. In exercising the 'balancing' test, the weight to be afforded to the factors noted in *Barker*, depends upon the circumstances of the case. A balancing test necessarily compels courts to approach cases on an ad hoc basis.

18. The essential elements of granting relief in delay cases are inordinate delay and prejudice, whether proved or inferred.[21]

19. Cases where relief can properly be granted in the absence of any fault by the prosecution will be rare. Delay attributable to the defendant or to the complexity of the case should not lead to a stay of proceedings.[22]

20. The correct approach for a judge to whom an application for a stay of proceedings based upon delay is made was considered by the Court of Appeal in *R v S*.[23] Lord Justice Rose, having considered a number of authorities,[24] set out five principles which need to be considered:

    1) even where delay was unjustifiable, a permanent stay should be the exception rather than the rule;

    2) where there was no fault on the part of the complainant or the prosecution, it would be very rare for a stay to be granted;

    3) no stay should be granted in the absence of serious prejudice to the defence so that no fair trial could be held;

---

[19] [1985] AC 937 at 951–952D–F.

[20] (1972) 407 US 514.

[21] *R v Bow Street Stipendiary Magistrates ex p DPP* [1992] 95 Cr App R 9, [1992] Crim LR 790–92.

[22] *Attorney General's Reference (No 1 of 1990)* [1992] 3 All ER 169 see also *Wemhoff v Germany*, (1979-80) 1 EHRR 55, *Jago v District Court of NSW* [1989] 87 ALR 577 (High Court of Australia), *R v Cardiff Magistrates' Court ex p Hole* [1997] COD 84, IJL, GMR, *AKP v United Kingdom* (2001) 33 EHRR 11.

[23] Court of Appeal Criminal Division: Rose LJ, Stanley Burnton and Hedley JJ: 6 March 2006.

[24] *Attorney General's Reference (No 1 of 1990)* [1992] QB 630 at 644; *R v EW* [2004] EWCA Crim 2901, para 23; *Attorney General's Reference (No 2 of 2001)* [2001] 1 WLR 1869, para 16; *Hooper* [2003] EWCA Crim 2427, para 76; *B* [2003] 2 Cr App R 197, paras 15–18; *Smolinksi* [2004] 2 Cr App R 661, para 7.

4) when assessing possible serious prejudice, the judge should bear in mind his or her power to regulate the admissibility of evidence and that the trial process itself should ensure that all relevant factual issues arising from delay would be placed before the jury for their consideration in accordance with appropriate directions from the judge;

5) if, having considered all those factors, a judge's assessment was that a fair trial would be possible, a stay should not be granted.

Circumstances of Present Case

21. The delay in the present proceedings amounts to an abuse of process warranting a stay of proceedings, for a number of reasons.

22. Firstly, there has been an inordinate delay in investigating the matter. A chronology of events is set out below:

23. Secondly, the prosecution have failed to explain or justify the delay in the proceedings. The CPS have given no reason for the delay.

24. The case itself is not complicated. This is a straightforward allegation of [ ].

25. Thirdly, the Defendant has not been responsible for any of the delay.

26. Fourthly, the Defendant has asserted his right to a speedy trial, as per the complaint letter of.

27. Fifthly, Defendant has suffered genuine specific prejudice as follows:

28. For all of the above reasons the proceedings should be stayed as an abuse of process, on the grounds of delay.

Advocate
Dated:

APPENDIX 2

Skeleton Argument: Inability to Participate and Unfit to Plead

In the Youth/Magistrates/Crown court

Between

REGINA

-V-

DEFENDANT

APPLICATION TO STAY PROCEEDINGS: INABILITY
TO PARTICIPATE AND UNFIT TO PLEAD

Introduction Submission

1. Application is made on behalf of defendant to stay proceedings as an abuse of process because of his inability to effectively participate in the trial process, as evidenced by his unfitness to plead. He is unable to have a fair trial, as per his common law and Article 6 ECHR fair trial rights, as he lacks capacity to give instructions and is unable to understand and effectively take part in the proceedings in terms of mental capacity, social functioning, maturity, intellect, and emotional capacity.

Prosecution Case

2. Summarize

Procedural Background

3. Summarize

Medical Evidence of Inability to Participate

4. Summarize medical evidence of inability to participate [and fitness to plead]. Including ability to participate with his legal team in the preparation of his defence including giving instructions and participating in the court process, including giving evidence and being cross-examined.
5. In relation to the defendant's fitness to plead, consultant psychiatrist is of the opinion that (at para [ ] of the report):

   In terms of the Pritchard test, as operationalized in R v M (John) [2003] EWCA Crim 3452 CA, I am concerned that her/his mental disorder compromises her/his capacity to decided rationally whether to plead guilty or not guilty. In my opinion, a combination of his mental state and the exhaustion that this appears to cause, results in her/his becoming quickly distracted and unable to concentrate to a degree which would prevent him being able to instruct solicitors and counsel so as to prepare and make a proper defence, and also prevent him from being able to follow the course of the proceedings in court. I think it is unlikely that s(he) would be able intelligibly to give evidence in her/his own defence. In brief, s/he is unfit to plead and stand trial.

Evidence

6. The defence, in making this abuse of process application, rely upon:
   (a) The medical reports of Dr. and Dr. [passages cited]
   (b) A witness statement from defence solicitor outlining the difficulties in taking instructions.

Law

7. The legal principle has been established, through case law that the right to a fair trial under common law and Article 6 of the European Convention on Human Rights involves the defendant being able to effectively participate in the court process. A defendant who lacks capacity to give instructions and is unable to understand and effectively take part in the proceedings—in terms of mental capacity, social functioning, maturity, intellect and emotional capacity (see *Stanford v UK* Application 16757/90 (1994) Series A/282 A at p11, *T and V v United Kingdom* [2000] Crim LR 187; *SC v United Kingdom* (2005) 40 EHRR 10; *Subramaniam v The Queen* [2004] HCA 51)—is not able to participate effectively in the trial process. In such circumstances proceedings can be stayed as an abuse of process.

8. Judicial endorsements of procedural modifications to assist defendant participation in the trial have also followed, acting as an alternative remedy to staying proceedings as an abuse of process. The use of special measures, modified court procedures, would not in this case cure the problems faced by the defendant.

Fitness to Plead Issue

9. If the primary application to stay proceedings is unsuccessful, the court is invited to consider the above evidence in relation to fitness to plead. The Defence submit that the Defendant is unfit to plead in accordance with *R v Pritchard* (1836) 7 C.&P.303 and *R v M (John)* [2003] EWCA Crim 3452 CA.

10. The onus of proof is on the defence to prove on a balance of probabilities.

11. The question of disability is determined by the court (no longer a jury) as per sections 4 and 4(A) Criminal Procedure (Insanity) Act 1964.

12. Section 4(6) CP(I)A is satisfied as there are two written reports from approved medical practitioners.

13. If the defendant is deemed unfit by the court, a jury should be empanelled to determine on evidence whether the accused did the act or omissions charged against him.

14. The defence are not in any position to challenge the prosecution evidence.

Advocate:
Dated:

APPENDIX 3

Skeleton Argument: Loss of Evidence and Investigative Failure

In the Youth/Magistrates/Crown Court

Regina-v-Defendant

APPLICATION TO STAY PROCEEDINGS AS AN ABUSE OF PROCESS:
LOSS OF EVIDENCE AND INVESTIGATIVE FAILURE

1. Application is made on behalf of [defendant], to stay proceedings as an Abuse of Process at [insert] Court, on one charge alleging [insert].
2. The short point is that CCTV video footage of the alleged criminality has not been disclosed to the defence, nor is the footage, through passage of time, now available, being destroyed as an investigative failure.

Abuse of Process Principle

3. All criminal courts have a general and inherent power to stay proceedings in order to protect their process from being abused and to secure fair treatment for those accused of crime. This is a common law discretionary power.

The Test

4. When a court considers the exercise of its discretionary power to stay proceedings for an abuse, the test to be applied is that of fairness. Lord Justice Neill in *R v Beckford*,[1] observed that;

   The jurisdiction to stay can be exercised in many different circumstances. Nevertheless two main strands can be detected in the authorities:

   Cases where the court concludes that the defendant cannot receive a fair trial;

   Cases where the court concludes that it would be unfair for the defendant to be tried.[2]

Factors to be Considered

5. When an application is made for proceedings to be stayed, consideration should be given to the process by which the defendant was brought to court, including, inter alia, the disclosure and availability of evidence.

Disclosure and Non-availability of Evidence

6. Where evidence has been lost or destroyed, and the defence has been deprived of a potential opportunity to advance its case, the court has discretion to stay proceedings.
7. The leading case in this area is the Divisional Court decision in *R v Feltham Magistrates' Court ex p Ebrahim, Mouat v DPP*.[3] The Divisional Court gave guidance as to the approach courts should adopt when faced with the non-availability of evidence at trial—with specific reference to video-tape evidence;

   - First, the court should consider the duty, if any, of the investigator or prosecutor to obtain, retain, and preserve the evidence. Reference is made to the Code of Practice published pursuant to sections 23 and 25 of the Criminal Procedure and Investigations Act 1996 and the Attorney-General's disclosure guidelines.[4]

---

[1] [1996] 1 Cr App R 94.
[2] [1996] 1 Cr App R 94 at 100G.
[3] [2001] 1 All ER 831, [2001] 2 Cr App R 23.
[4] Published on 29 November 2000, with an updated version operative from 4 April 2005.

- Second, if there was no such duty before the defence first sought retention, there could be no question of a subsequent trial being unfair.
- Third, if the material has not been retained in accordance with the code or guidelines, the following principles should be applied: (i) the ultimate objective is to ensure a fair trial to both the defence and prosecution; (ii) trial procedural safeguards can deal with the bulk of complaints; (iii) if there is sufficient credible evidence which, if believed, could sustain a safe conviction, the trial should proceed. A stay should not be granted unless the defence can show prejudice to the extent that a fair trial cannot be had.
- Fourth, the proceedings can be stayed if the behaviour of the prosecution is so bad—in terms of bad faith or serious fault—that it is not fair to try the defendant (as per the second limb in *Beckford*).

Loss of Video Recording

8. In *Birmingham*[5] an indictment charging seven defendants with violent disorder was stayed. The existence of a video recording of the nightclub involved and part of the incident itself was not disclosed to the defence pre-trial. The police officer in charge of the case had viewed the video tape. However, by the time of the trial the video recording had been lost.

9. The court held that the prosecution had a duty to disclose the video tape, whether or not it had been requested, because the tape could have provided material evidence relevant to the defence. The deprivation of this material prejudiced the accused and made a fair trial impossible.

10. Birmingham was applied in *DPP v David Chipping*,[6] in which the Divisional Court refused to quash a stipendiary magistrates' decision to stay proceedings. Lord Justice Buxton[7] in giving judgment, referred to the fact that the video was likely to be the best evidence of any incident that it showed and that it was desirable that it should be shown to the defence. He continued;

> That conclusion might be offset if it could be shown that such evidence would have no effect on the trial at all and, therefore, that the learned Magistrate was simply mistaken in thinking that she should dismiss the proceedings on the basis of a process. As I have sought to demonstrate, that cannot be shown in this case. In the circumstances I am of the view that it was well within the limits of the judgment of the magistrate to take the course that she did, namely stay the proceedings ...

Investigative Failures

11. Initial police failure and delay in forensically examining a carpet for semen led, in *Gajree*[8] to the conviction being quashed by the Court of Appeal. If the matter had been pursued properly and expeditiously, the question of seminal staining of the carpet would have been capable of forensic resolution one way or the other.

Mr Justice Sachs stated:

> We are satisfied that because of the passage of time, and the inertia of the police officers, this appellant was deprived of evidence that might have otherwise been available to him, and in our view, renders the verdict in the case unsafe and unsatisfactory.

12. In *Northard*,[9] the Court of Appeal quashed the defendant's conviction for robbery because of police investigative failures. The failure to carry out proper enquiries had prejudiced the preparation of the defendant's case and precluded a fair trial. One example cited by the Court of Appeal was that the police did not disclose to the defence the existence of relevant video film footage (of shop CCTV cameras), which could have supported the defendant's alibi, nor was it available at trial (as the shopping centre video tape was re-used after 28 days).

---

5 [1992] Crim LR 117.
6 11 January 1999, DC–CO/2362/98.
7 At page 11 of the transcript.
8 20 September 1994, No 94/3269/Y2.
9 19 February 1996, CA, 95/1475/Z3—see Archbold Criminal Appeal Office Index 1997, no 3, para T-4.

Present Case

13. [Factual submissions]
14. The defence submit that the CCTV video footage would have shown the alleged criminality.
15. Defence solicitors have written on a number of occasions requesting the footage.
16. The police failed to obtain the footage, preserve the same, or obtain a copy prior to the footage being destroyed.
17. The defence are prejudiced as they have lost an opportunity to advance a positive case by being deprived of exculpatory evidence.
18. For all of the above reasons, the proceedings should be stayed as abuse of process.

Advocate:
Dated.

APPENDIX 4

Skeleton Argument: Human Trafficking

Regina-v-Defendant

-v-

APPLICATION TO STAY PROCEEDINGS AS AN ABUSE OF PROCESS:
HUMAN TRAFFICKING

1. Application is made on behalf of [defendant] to stay proceedings against him, as an abuse of process at Youth/ Magistrates/Crown Court, on a charge alleging [ ]

2. The defendant is a victim of human trafficking and committed the offence as a consequence of being trafficked. The defendant relies upon the non-punishment provisions in (a) Article 26 of the Council of Europe Convention on Action against Trafficking Human Beings (2005) (Anti-Trafficking convention) and (b) Article 8 of the EU Directive 2011/36/EU on Preventing and Combating Trafficking in Human Beings and Protecting its Victims.

Abuse of Process Principle

3. All criminal courts have a general and inherent power to stay proceedings in order to protect their process from being abused and to secure fair treatment for those accused of crime. This is a common law discretionary power.

The Test

4. When a court considers the exercise of its discretionary power to stay proceedings for an abuse, the test to be applied is that of fairness. Lord Justice Neill in *R v Beckford*,[1] observed that:

   The jurisdiction to stay can be exercised in many different circumstances. Nevertheless two main strands can be detected in the authorities:

   Cases where the court concludes that the defendant cannot receive a fair trial;

   Cases where the court concludes that it would be unfair for the defendant to be tried.[2]

Human Trafficking: Legal Background

5. The court's attention is drawn to the following matters which provide the legal background to human trafficking cases.

6. Article 26 of the Council of Europe Convention on Action against Trafficking Human Beings (2005) (Anti-Trafficking convention), which the United Kingdom ratified on 17 December 2008, provides:

   Each Party shall, in accordance with the basic principles of its legal system, provide for the possibility of not imposing penalties on victims for their involvement in unlawful activities, to the extent that they have been compelled to do so.

7. The non-punishment provision is echoed by Article 8 of the EU Directive 2011/36/EU on Preventing and Combating Trafficking in Human Beings and Protecting its Victims, (the EU Directive) which came into effect in the United Kingdom on 6 April 2013. It provides:

   Member States shall, in accordance with the basic principles of their legal systems, take the necessary measures to ensure that competent national authorities are entitled not to prosecute or impose penalties on victims of trafficking human beings for their involvement in criminal

---

[1] [1996] 1 Cr App R 94.
[2] [1996] 1 Cr App R 94 at 100G.

activities which they have been compelled to commit as a direct consequence of being subjected to (trafficking).

English Case Law on Human Trafficking

8. The Court of Appeal Criminal Division examined the question of human trafficking and the discretion to prosecute in *LM and others* [2010] EWCA Crim 2327.

9. Lord Justice Hughes gave the lead judgment in *LM* identifying three ways in which the Article 26 non-punishment provisions are recognized in English law:

> [7] ... through three mechanisms.
>
> First, English law recognises the common law defences of duress and necessity ('duress of circumstances').[3]
>
> Second, specific rules have been made for the guidance of prosecutors in considering whether charges should be brought against those who are or may have been victims of trafficking.
>
> Thirdly, in the event that the duty laid on the prosecutor to exercise judgment is not properly discharged, the ultimate sanction is the power of the court to stay the prosecution for what is conveniently, if not very accurately, termed 'abuse of process'.

10. Lord Justice Hughes went on to consider the CPS guidance which requires prosecutors to consider the public interest in prosecuting a 'credible trafficking victim' and not to prosecute where there is credible evidence of duress. This is clearly set out in the CPS guidance:

> Victims of human trafficking may commit offences whilst they are being coerced by another.
>
> When reviewing such a case it may come to the notice of the prosecutor that the suspect is a 'credible' trafficked victim. For these purposes 'credible' means that the investigating officers have reason to believe that the person has been trafficked.
>
> In these circumstances prosecutors must consider whether the public interest is best served in continuing the prosecution in respect of the offence. Where there is evidence that a suspect is a credible trafficked victim, prosecutors should consider the public interest in proceeding. Where there is clear evidence that the defendant has a credible defence of duress, the case should be discontinued on evidential grounds.

11. Lord Justice Hughes considered the CPS guidance and concluded that:

> [10] The effect of that is to require of prosecutors a three-stage exercise of judgment.
> The first is: (1) is there a reason to believe that the person has been trafficked? If so, then (2) if there is clear evidence of a credible common law defence the case will be discontinued in the ordinary way on evidential grounds, but, importantly, (3) even where there is not, but the offence may have been committed as a result of compulsion arising from the trafficking, prosecutors should consider whether the public interest lies in proceeding to prosecute or not.

12. The leading Court of Appeal Criminal Division decision is now *L, HVN, TH, T v R, The Children's Commissioner for England, Equality, and Human Rights Commission* [2013] EWCA Crim 991 which gives important guidance in relation to human trafficking and the criminal justice process.

13. The Lord Chief Justice of England and Wales, in giving the lead judgment, makes a number of important points in relation to human trafficking cases:

> 2. This vile trade in people has different manifestations. Women and children, usually girls, are trafficked into prostitution: others, usually teenage boys, but sometimes young adults, are trafficked into cannabis farming: yet others are trafficked to commit a wide range of further offences. Sometimes they are trafficked into this country from the other side of the world: sometimes they enter into this country unlawfully, and are trafficked after their arrival: sometimes they are trafficked within the towns or cities in this country where they live.

---

[3] The defences of duress and/or necessity ('duress of circumstances') may be in question where an offence has been committed by a trafficked victim whose case is that she was coerced into committing it. See *Z* [2005] 2 AC 467. Also consider the defence contained in section 45 Modern Slavery Act 2015.

Whether trafficked from home or overseas, they are all victims of crime. That is how they must be treated and, in the vast majority of cases they are: but not always.

... 12. We need not further expound the principles. They can be readily found in *Siliadin v France* (Application No 73316/01, 26 October 2004); *Rantsev v Cyprus and Russia* (Application No 25965/05, 10 January 2010); and *K(S) [2013] QB 82* and *R v Connors* [2013] EWCA Crim. 324 where, in effect repeating what had just been said in *N and L* [2013] QB 379 at paras [2][6], the court observed:

> Every vulnerable victim of exploitation will be protected by the criminal law ... there is no victim, so vulnerable to exploitation, that he or she somehow becomes invisible or unknown to or somehow beyond the protection of the law. Exploitation of fellow human beings ... represents deliberate degrading of a fellow human being or human beings.

13 ... It has not, however, and could not have been argued that if and when victims of trafficking participate or become involved in criminal activities, a trafficked individual should be given some kind of immunity from prosecution, just because he or she was or has been trafficked, nor for that reason alone, that a substantive defence to a criminal charge is available to a victim of trafficking. What, however, is clearly established, and numerous different papers, reports and decided cases have demonstrated, is that when there is evidence that victims of trafficking have been involved in criminal activities, the investigation and the decision whether there should be a prosecution, and, if so, any subsequent proceedings require to be approached with the greatest sensitivity. The reasoning is not always spelled out, and perhaps we should do so now. The criminality, or putting it another way, the culpability, of any victim of trafficking may be significantly diminished, and in some cases effectively extinguished, not merely because of age (always a relevant factor in the case of a child defendant) but because no realistic alternative was available to the exploited victim but to comply with the dominant force of another individual, or group of individuals.

14. In the context of a prosecution of a defendant aged under 18 years of age, the best interests of the victim are not and cannot be the only relevant consideration, but they represent a primary consideration. These defendants are not safeguarded from prosecution or punishment for offences which were unconnected with the fact that they were being or have been trafficked, although we do not overlook that the fact that they have been trafficked may sometimes provide substantial mitigation. What, however, is required in the context of the prosecutorial decision to proceed is a level of protection from prosecution or punishment for trafficked victims who have been compelled to commit criminal offences. These arrangements should follow the 'basic principles' of our legal system. In this jurisdiction that protection is provided by the exercise by the 'abuse of process' jurisdiction.

[...]

17 ... In the context of an abuse of process argument on behalf of an alleged victim of trafficking, the court will reach its own decision on the basis of the material advanced in support of and against the continuation of the prosecution. Where a court considers issues relevant to age, trafficking and exploitation, the prosecution will be stayed if the court disagrees with the decision to prosecute ...

18. If issues relating to the age of the victim arise, and questions whether the defendant is or was a victim of trafficking, or whether the alleged offences were an aspect of the victim's exploitation, have reached the Crown Court, or a magistrates court, they must be resolved by the exercise of the jurisdiction to stay a prosecution ...

19. The question whether a potential defendant has indeed been a victim of trafficking, and the extent to which his ability to resist involvement in criminal activities has been undermined is fact specific. Usually, but not always, the starting point is the moment of arrest. When a young person is arrested the police must consider his age, and in the overwhelming majority of cases it is known or can readily be discovered. Arrangements are then made for attendance at a police station by an appropriate adult. After charge the child is brought before the Youth Court or before an Adult Court if no Youth Court is sitting. Difficulties relating to age are most likely to arise where a young person has entered the United Kingdom illegally, and has no genuine passport or similar identifying documents. When a young person without parents comes to the attention of a local authority (often via the United Kingdom Border Agency

(UKBA) as an illegal entrant), the Children Act 1989 imposes a duty on the local authority to determine whether he is a child in need. If so, he is entitled to number of services, including the provision of accommodation. However the first step is to establish the person's age. Since 2003 local authorities have assessed age by a process which complies with the principles set out in *R(B) v London Borough of Merton* [2003] EWHC 1689 (Admin).

[...]

20. When the defendant may be a child victim of trafficking, two linked questions must be addressed. First, the defendant's age must be ascertained, and second, the evidence which suggests that he has been trafficked must be assessed. In the vast majority of cases the questions will be investigated by and in the same processes. Assuming that the factual conclusion is that the defendant was a child victim of trafficking, a quite distinct question for consideration is the extent to which the crime alleged against him was consequent on and integral to the exploitation of which he was the victim. That question also arises in the case of an adult victim. In some cases (as in these appeals) the answer to both questions will be that the criminal offence is here, or at least, a manifestation of the exploitation.

[...]

22 When the issue arises, we agree that compliance with these provisions in contemporary society requires much more than superficial observation of the defendant in court or in the dock to enable the judge to make an appropriate age assessment. The facial features of the defendant may provide a clue or two, but experience has shown that this is very soft evidence indeed and liable to mislead. What we do know is that young people mature at different ages, and that their early life experiences can sometimes leave them with a misleading appearance. We also appreciate that young people from an ethnic group with which the court is unfamiliar may seem older, or indeed younger, than those from ethnic groups with which the court has greater experience. Therefore when an age issue arises, the court must be provided with all the relevant evidence which bears on it.

[...]

23. In this context we repeat the observations of this court in Steed [1990] 12 Cr. App. R(S) 230, where the question of the appellant's age was significant to the different methods of the disposal of the case on sentence, and therefore went to the legality of the sentence,

> It may often be right, indeed might usually be right, for the matter to be adjourned, if there is any real doubt about it, so that it may be more satisfactorily determined.

More recently, this approach was underlined in *O [2008] EWCA Crim. 2835* where the court emphasised that:

> (W)here there is doubt about the age of a defendant who is a possible victim of trafficking, proper enquiries must be made, indeed statute so required.

[...]

25. The explanatory report to the Anti-Trafficking Convention also refers to a requirement that the parties should 'presume that a victim is a child if there are reasons for believing that to be so and if there is uncertainty about their age.' In our judgment Article 10(3) addresses evidential issues. Where there are reasons to believe that the defendant is a child, then he should be treated as a child. In other words it is not possible for the court to brush aside evidence which suggest that the defendant may be a child. The issue must be addressed head on. If at the end of an examination of the available evidence, the question remains in doubt, the presumption applies and the defendant must be treated as a child...

26 The National Referral Mechanism (NRM) was set up on 1 April 2009 to give effect in the United Kingdom to Article 10 of the Council of Europe Anti-Trafficking Convention. Enough is now known about people who are trafficked into and within the United Kingdom for all those involved in the criminal justice process to recognise the need to consider at an early stage whether the defendant (child or adult) is in fact a victim of trafficking. The NRM establishes a three stage process for this purpose:

> i) An initial referral of a potential victim of trafficking by a first responder to a competent authority. At present there are two competent authorities. They are UKBA and the United

Kingdom Human Trafficking Centre (UKHTC), a multi disciplinary organisation led by SOCA (The Serious and Organised Crime Agency)…

ii) An UKBA official decides whether the person referred might have been a victim of trafficking. This is known as a 'reasonable grounds' decision, for which UKBA have a target of five days … If and when a favourable reasonable grounds decision has been made the first responder is notified, and, in effect that decision allows for a period of forty five days during which the final stage of the NRM process continues, leading to

iii) consideration by UKBA whether the evidence is sufficient to confirm conclusively that the individual has been trafficked.

[…]

28. Whether the concluded decision of the competent authority is favourable or adverse to the individual it will have been made by an authority vested with the responsibility for investigating these issues, and although the court is not bound by the decision, unless there is evidence to contradict it, or significant evidence that was not considered, it is likely that the criminal courts will abide by it.

29. In the final analysis all the relevant evidence bearing on the issue of age, trafficking, exploitation and culpability must be addressed …

[…]

33 As we have already explained the distinct question for decision once it is found that the defendant is a victim of trafficking is the extent to which the offences with which he is charged, or of which he has been found guilty are integral to or consequent on the exploitation of which he was the victim. We cannot be prescriptive. In some cases the facts will indeed show that he was under levels of compulsion which mean that in reality culpability was extinguished. If so when such cases are prosecuted, an abuse of process submission is likely to succeed. That is the test we have applied in these appeals. In other cases, more likely in the case of a defendant who is no longer a child, culpability may be diminished but nevertheless be significant. For these individuals prosecution may well be appropriate, with due allowance to be made in the sentencing decision for their diminished culpability. In yet other cases, the fact that the defendant was a victim of trafficking will provide no more than a colourable excuse for criminality which is unconnected to and does not arise from their victimisation. In such cases an abuse of process submission would fail.

Present Case

14. The Defendant was brought into England by force, being forced to work, against her/his will. S(he) feared for her/his own safety as s(he) was regularly threatened. See the Defence Statement which highlights the human trafficking background.

15. The defendant's date of birth is [ ] making him sixteen years of age.

16. The CPS have referred the case to local City Council for an age assessment to be carried out. The police referred the defendant to the United Kingdom Border Agency who produced a negative decision at the 'reasonable grounds' stage.

17. The defendant's solicitors have written to the CPS inviting them not to prosecute the defendant on the basis that to do so would contravene the CPS Guidance relating to the Prosecution of Victims of Trafficking.

18. The defence attach the following:
   • Defendants date of birth certificate, copy of passport …
   • Report confirming the operation of debt bondage within Vietnam
   • Defence Statement
   • Defence Prepared Statement
   • Local City Council Social Services age assessment report (Merton compliant)

19. For all of the above reasons the proceedings should be stayed as abuse of process.

Advocate:
Dated.

INDEX